Integrating Artificial Intelligence With Design

Sabyasachi Pramanik
https://orcid.org/0000-0002-9431-8751
Haldia Institute of Technology, India

Ankur Gupta
https://orcid.org/0000-0002-4651-5830
Vaish College of Engineering, India

Rohit Anand
G.B. Pant Delhi Skill and Entrepreneurship University, India

Sandip Roy
https://orcid.org/0000-0002-5447-803X
JIS University, India

Rajesh Bose
JIS University, India

IGI Global
Scientific Publishing
Publishing Tomorrow's Research Today

Vice President of Editorial	Melissa Wagner
Director of Acquisitions	Mikaela Felty
Director of Book Development	Jocelynn Hessler
Production Manager	Mike Brehm
Cover Design	Jose Rosado

Published in the United States of America by
IGI Global Scientific Publishing
701 East Chocolate Avenue
Hershey, PA, 17033, USA
Tel: 717-533-8845 | Fax: 717-533-7115
Website: https://www.igi-global.com E-mail: cust@igi-global.com

Library of Congress Cataloging-in-Publication Data

Names: Pramanik, Sabyasachi editor. | Gupta, Ankur editor. | Anand, Rohit editor. | Roy, Sandip editor. | Bose, Rajesh editor.

Title: Integrating artificial intelligence with design / edited by Sabyasachi Pramanik, Ankur Gupta, Rohit Anand, Sandip Roy, Rajesh Bose

Description: Hershey, PA : Engineering Science Reference, [2027] | Includes bibliographical references and index. | Chiefly in English, some Turkish. | Summary: "Integrating artificial intelligence with design encompasses a series of book chapters delving into the relationship between Artificial Intelligence and its impact on design processes. The book serves as a comprehensive guide, centers on design, and welcomes contributions from all design disciplines. The aim is to examine design processes through the lens of artificial intelligence"-- Provided by publisher.

Identifiers: LCCN 2024038672 (print) | LCCN 2024038673 (ebook) | ISBN 9798369337516 (h/c) | ISBN 9798369349823 (s/c) | ISBN 9798369337523 (ebook)

Subjects: LCSH: Product design--Data processing. | System design--Data processing. | Industrial design--Data processing. | Artificial intelligence--Industrial applications.

Classification: LCC TS171.4 .I5749 2024 (print) | LCC TS171.4 (ebook) | DDC 745.20285/63--dc23/eng/20241217

LC record available at https://lccn.loc.gov/2024038672

LC ebook record available at https://lccn.loc.gov/2024038673

British Cataloguing in Publication Data
A Cataloguing in Publication record for this book is available from the British Library.

Table of Contents

Detailed Table of Contents

AI-enhanced design processes represent a transformative shift in how creative and technical solutions are conceived, developed, and optimized. By integrating artificial intelligence techniques such as machine learning, generative design, and data analytics, designers can explore a wider range of possibilities, automate repetitive tasks, and make more informed decisions. This chapter examines the evolution of design practices in the context of AI, highlighting key technologies, tools, and applications across multiple domains. It also addresses the implications of AI adoption, including workflow changes, ethical considerations, and future opportunities. Ultimately, AI serves not as a replacement for human creativity but as a powerful collaborator that augments innovation and efficiency in modern design processes.

Artificial Intelligence (AI) is transforming the way design is developed, experimented and refined. Previously, design relied heavily on human creativity, experience, as well as time-consuming trial and error. Currently, AI applications can generate numerous design solutions rapidly, experiment, and propose superior solutions using data. This establishes a close collaboration between humans and machines, where designers dictate creativity and AI assists in speed, analysis, and optimization. AI assists in accelerated generation of ideas, accelerated design modification and intelligent decision-making. Nonetheless, such issues as over-reliance on AI, data bias, and ethical issues will have to be addressed with proper attention. This chapter describes the way AI is enhancing designing practices and provides a model that integrates human creativity with machine intelligence. In general, AI will streamline the design and make it more innovative but requires human control and judgment.

Rising AI-assisted submission rates mask persistent knowledge gaps exposed by unassisted assessments. This paper introduces MentoraGen, a stateful pedagogical AI pipeline that employs Socratic questioning instead of direct answers. It integrates NLP preprocessing, all-MiniLM-L6-v2 embeddings, HDBSCAN/BERTopic clustering, and a Groq-powered RAG layer maintaining sub-400ms latency for real-time tutoring. MentoraGen addresses four EdTech shortcomings: superficial error correction, false competence illusions, poor cross-language transfer, and premature answer disclosure. Its core components are a Master Conceptual Matrix covering 50 concepts across nine languages, a four-state Frustration Counter, a Transfer Pivot test probing logic under unfamiliar syntax, and a Why Rule verifying genuine understanding. Validation yielded 94% tokenisation accuracy, 0.87 cosine similarity in retrieval, 89% clustering accuracy, and 81% Why Rule–human rater agreement, supporting progression to the formal A/B trial detailed herein.

Social media platforms offer a valuable lens for gauging public opinion during major geopolitical events. This chapter presents OpinionGraph, a hybrid computational

The adoption of Internet of Things (IoT) technologies in agriculture has improved productivity through real-time monitoring, automated irrigation, and data-driven decision-making. However, increased connectivity exposes smart farming systems to cybersecurity threats that can compromise data and disrupt operations. This study proposes an AI-enabled cybersecurity framework integrating threat detection, anomaly monitoring, secure authentication, and encrypted communication. Machine learning algorithms continuously analyze device behavior and network traffic to identify cyberattacks in real time. The framework was evaluated in a simulated smart farming environment comprising sensors, edge devices, and cloud services. Results achieved 97.8% detection accuracy, 96.9% precision, and 97.3% recall, while reducing false alerts by 21% and improving response time by 28% compared with conventional methods. The proposed framework enhances security, reliability, and resilience, providing a scalable solution for next-generation digital agriculture.

Design management is needed for the complex design activities and for the supply of the efficient design process decision-making. Serious design problems may lead

able to handle changing workloads in machine learning based decision system. If you need to quickly learn data or make a choice, these changes will be quite beneficial.

Preface

The unprecedented advancements in Artificial Intelligence (AI) have fundamentally reshaped the landscape of design across engineering, business, education, finance, healthcare, manufacturing, and numerous other disciplines. What was once considered a computational tool for automation has now evolved into an intelligent collaborator capable of augmenting creativity, enhancing decision-making, accelerating innovation, and addressing complex design challenges with unprecedented efficiency. As AI technologies continue to mature, the convergence of intelligent algorithms with human-centered design practices has emerged as one of the defining technological transformations of the twenty-first century. This edited volume, *Integrating Artificial Intelligence With Design*, seeks to capture this transformation by bringing together contemporary research that explores how AI is redefining the theory, methodology, and application of design in diverse domains.

The motivation behind this volume stems from the growing realization that successful AI adoption extends beyond technical implementation. Intelligent design requires multidisciplinary collaboration involving computer scientists, engineers, management researchers, educators, policymakers, cybersecurity experts, economists, and social scientists. The integration of AI into design is no longer limited to automating repetitive tasks; instead, it has become a catalyst for generating innovative solutions, supporting strategic decision-making, improving sustainability, strengthening security, and enabling adaptive systems capable of learning from continuously evolving environments. Consequently, this book presents a broad collection of scholarly contributions that collectively illustrate both the opportunities and the challenges associated with designing AI-enabled systems.

The chapters assembled in this volume demonstrate that the future of design lies in collaborative intelligence, where human expertise and machine intelligence complement one another rather than compete. While AI offers remarkable computational capabilities for optimization, prediction, simulation, and automation, human creativity remains indispensable in defining objectives, interpreting outcomes, addressing ethical concerns, and ensuring societal relevance. Throughout the book, contributors emphasize responsible AI development, transparent decision-making, fairness, privacy, security, and sustainability as essential pillars of intelligent design. Such perspectives are increasingly important as AI becomes embedded in critical infrastructures and high-impact decision environments.

This volume is intended to serve researchers, academicians, industry practitioners, graduate students, policymakers, and professionals seeking comprehensive insights into the rapidly evolving intersection of AI and design. The diversity of topics presented reflects the interdisciplinary nature of contemporary AI research while providing practical frameworks, theoretical discussions, computational models, and real-world applications that can inspire future innovations. We believe the collective expertise of our contributors offers valuable perspectives that will stimulate further research and encourage meaningful collaborations across disciplines.

OVERVIEW OF THE CHAPTERS

The volume begins with Chapter 1, which establishes the conceptual foundation of AI-enhanced design by examining the evolution of intelligent design processes in engineering and creative practice. The chapter discusses emerging technologies such as machine learning, generative design, and predictive analytics while exploring how AI complements human creativity through collaborative innovation.

Building upon these foundations, Chapter 2 investigates AI-enhanced design methodologies that improve creativity, iterative development, and intelligent decision-making. The authors present a comprehensive framework demonstrating how designers and AI systems can work synergistically to accelerate idea generation, optimize design alternatives, and support informed decisions while addressing ethical considerations associated with AI-assisted creativity.

Chapter 3 introduces *MentoraGen*, an innovative AI-powered educational framework designed to improve programming education through Socratic scaffolding rather than direct answer generation. By integrating natural language processing, retrieval-augmented generation, multilingual conceptual mapping, and adaptive tutoring strategies, the chapter illustrates how AI can support deeper conceptual learning while reducing overdependence on automated assistance.

Expanding AI applications into computational social science, Chapter 4 presents *OpinionGraph*, a hybrid framework for community detection and sentiment profiling across multiple geopolitical events. Through the integration of topic modelling, sentiment analysis, clustering, and network analysis, the chapter demonstrates how AI can reveal meaningful structures within large-scale social discourse while providing interpretable insights into public opinion.

Security-oriented intelligent design is explored in Chapter 5, where the authors propose a deep learning-based image cryptography technique utilizing chaotic attractor models for secure RGB image encryption. The chapter highlights computational efficiency alongside robust protection against image manipulation, illustrating the role of AI in designing secure multimedia communication systems.

The growing importance of cybersecurity within digital agriculture is examined in Chapter 6, which develops an AI-integrated cybersecurity framework for IoT-enabled smart farming systems. Combining anomaly detection, intelligent threat monitoring, secure authentication, and encrypted communication, the proposed framework demonstrates improved resilience against cyber threats in connected agricultural environments.

Moving toward organizational applications, Chapter 7 focuses on AI-driven decision support systems for design management. The authors develop a comprehensive framework that combines machine learning, neural networks, natural language processing, and expert systems to improve planning, evaluation, and strategic decision-making throughout complex design processes.

Chapter 8 explores the integration of AI throughout the Design Thinking methodology. By examining each stage of the design thinking process, the chapter demonstrates how AI enhances user understanding, pattern recognition, ideation, prototyping, and decision support while maintaining a strong emphasis on human-centered innovation.

Continuing the discussion of intelligent design evolution, Chapter 9 examines the transformation from conventional Computer-Aided Design (CAD) toward cognitive design systems driven by AI. Topics including generative design, intelligent simulation, optimization, digital prototyping, and predictive performance evaluation illustrate how AI is redefining modern engineering workflows.

Financial applications are addressed in Chapter 10, which introduces an AI-based framework for data-driven financial risk modelling. By integrating machine learning, deep learning, ensemble methods, and hybrid analytical models, the proposed framework improves predictive accuracy while supporting informed financial decision-making under uncertainty.

Recognizing the growing importance of responsible AI, Chapter 11 proposes an ethical governance framework for AI-driven financial systems. The chapter discusses regulatory compliance, transparency, explainability, fairness, accountability, and trust while aligning AI implementation with internationally recognized governance principles.

Economic sustainability becomes the focus of Chapter 12, where an AI-driven framework evaluates the economic viability and scalability of technological solutions. Through performance benchmarking, quantitative analysis, and cost optimization, the chapter provides decision-support mechanisms for developers, investors, and policymakers assessing emerging technologies.

Risk management in computational intelligence environments is investigated in Chapter 13, which develops an AI-enabled intelligent risk management framework incorporating deep learning, fuzzy logic, and evolutionary computation. The proposed system demonstrates adaptive learning capabilities for identifying dynamic threats within increasingly complex digital ecosystems.

Finally, Chapter 14 concludes the volume by presenting an AI-driven hybrid framework that integrates circular economy principles into intelligent systems. The chapter illustrates how AI can enhance sustainability through optimized resource utilization, improved system adaptability, greater operational efficiency, and environmentally responsible decision-making, thereby reinforcing the role of intelligent design in supporting sustainable development.

CONCLUDING REMARKS

The contributions presented throughout this volume collectively demonstrate that Artificial Intelligence is no longer simply an enabling technology but a transformative force that is fundamentally redefining design across multiple disciplines. From engineering innovation and educational technologies to financial systems, cybersecurity, social computing, sustainability, and organizational management, AI has become deeply integrated into both the conceptualization and execution of intelligent design processes. The diverse perspectives represented in this book highlight the richness of interdisciplinary collaboration and emphasize that meaningful innovation emerges when computational intelligence is combined with human expertise.

An important message that resonates across all chapters is the necessity of maintaining a balanced relationship between automation and human judgment. While AI offers unparalleled capabilities in prediction, optimization, simulation, pattern recognition, and decision support, successful implementation ultimately depends upon responsible governance, ethical considerations, transparency, and continuous human oversight. The contributors consistently demonstrate that AI should augment rather than replace human creativity, enabling professionals to solve increasingly complex challenges while preserving accountability and societal trust.

We also recognize that AI technologies will continue to evolve rapidly beyond the scope of any single publication. Emerging developments in generative AI, explainable AI, autonomous systems, digital twins, multimodal intelligence, and sustainable computing will undoubtedly reshape future design paradigms in ways that are only beginning to be understood. We therefore hope that the frameworks, methodologies, case studies, and discussions presented in this volume will serve not only as valuable references for current research but also as foundations for future investigations that extend the boundaries of intelligent design.

As editors, we extend our sincere appreciation to all contributing authors for sharing their expertise, dedication, and scholarly insights. We are equally grateful to the reviewers whose constructive evaluations enhanced the quality and rigor of the chapters. Finally, we acknowledge the support of our publishing team and the academic institutions that encouraged and facilitated this collaborative effort. It is our hope that *Integrating Artificial Intelligence With Design* will contribute meaningfully to the advancement of AI-enabled design research and inspire future generations of researchers and practitioners to develop intelligent, ethical, sustainable, and human-centered solutions for the challenges of tomorrow.

Sabyasachi Pramanik
Haldia Institute of Technology, India

Ankur Gupta
Vaish College of Engineering, Rohtak, Haryana, India

Rohit Anand
GB Pant Delhi Skill and Entrepreneurship University, India

Sandip Roy
JIS University, India

Rajesh Bose
JIS University, India

Chapter 1
AI-Enhanced Design Processes in Modern Engineering and Creativity

Nikhil Kumar Goyal
http://orcid.org/0009-0007-4532-8033
Noida International University, India

ABSTRACT

AI-enhanced design processes represent a transformative shift in how creative and technical solutions are conceived, developed, and optimized. By integrating artificial intelligence techniques such as machine learning, generative design, and data analytics, designers can explore a wider range of possibilities, automate repetitive tasks, and make more informed decisions. This chapter examines the evolution of design practices in the context of AI, highlighting key technologies, tools, and applications across multiple domains. It also addresses the implications of AI adoption, including workflow changes, ethical considerations, and future opportunities. Ultimately, AI serves not as a replacement for human creativity but as a powerful collaborator that augments innovation and efficiency in modern design processes.

1. INTRODUCTION

1.1 Evolution of Design Practices

Designs practices have also developed greatly throughout centuries, varying with advancements in technology, and the fluctuating needs of the society. In the

DOI: 10.4018/979-8-3693-3751-6.ch001

design process of the traditional, it was a manual and incredibly iterative process, based on drawings, physical models and artisanship. Intuition, experience and small steps were emphasized by designers in trying to perfect their ideas. Although it was a more creative way to do things, it would very much consume time and resources and therefore restricted the amount of options that can be considered.

The entrance of digital media like computer-aided design (CAD) was a new face in the design world. These tools allowed designers to make accurate models, simulate real-world scenarios and make changes to designs with increased efficiency. The collaboration was also enabled by digitalization as teams were able to share and perfect ideas across geographical borders. Nevertheless, even with these enhancements, the main process was still more of a man-made venture, with technology serving as a facilitator, but not an active participant (Wei et al., 2022).

The next key step in this development has to be the development of artificial intelligence. Now AI based systems can be used to analyze data, create design options and come up with optimal solutions with little or no human input. The shifting is to a more human-centered practice of design to a process of collaborative effort by humans and machines. Consequently, designers will be able to be more creative and strategic and use AI to cope with scale and complexity.

1.2 Role of Artificial Intelligence in Design

AI is also vital in changing the way design problems are speedily tackled and resolved. Confined to a specific set of instructions, traditional tools cannot learn or adapt the tool but AI systems can, making knowledgeable conclusions about the data and adjusting actions to fit those conclusions. This will enable them to find trends, anticipate results as well as create novel solutions which human designers might not clearly see. Through this, AI increases efficiency and effectiveness of the design process.

Support of generating design is one of the most important contributions of AI. In this method, the designers feed in constraints and goals, and AI system generates a variety of design solutions that match the criteria. These options can then be analyzed on the basis of the performance criteria like cost, durability or sustainability. This ability greatly increases the design space, allowing it to explore innovative and very optimized solution (Kumari et al., 2026).

Moreover, AI helps to provide real-time feedback and make decisions. With the incorporation of machine learning algorithms into design tools, designers can get the immediate feedback on the effect the changes will have on performance or feasibility. This saves both on the time required in testing cycles and also provides quicker iterative development. Finally, AI can serve as a smart helper, enhancing the innovation of people and making the design more knowledgeable.

1.3 Benefits of AI Integration

The application of AI in the design processes has significant advantages, especially on the enhancement of efficiency and productivity. Monotonous operations like data analysis, simulation and optimization can be done automatically and the designers can be engaged in higher level showcase operation. This decreases the manual work, in addition to speeding up the design process, the possibility of human error is reduced thereby producing more reliable results (Cheung & Dall'Asta, 2023).

The other great opportunity is that data-driven decisions can be made. AI systems are able to handle large quantities of information and analyze numerous design options at the same time. Analyzing the factors like performance, cost, and environmental impact, AI can suggest the most appropriate solutions. This improves the quality of decision making and makes designs optimized in terms of usefulness and their sustainability (Goyal et al., 2026).

Innovation is also encouraged by AI whereby more possibilities can be explored. Many conventional design processes tend to restrict exploration as a result of time and resource limitations. Conversely, AI has the capacity to create and experiment a large number of variations where new solutions may not have been thought of otherwise. This ability is especially useful in complicated areas of designs where the creative and optimization cannot be separated.

1.4 Challenges in Adoption

Although the incorporation of AI into the design processes is promising to be transformative, it is not without challenges. Among the main obstacles, there is the necessity to have new skills and knowledge. Designers need to get acquainted with the idea of AI, tools, and workflows, potentially demanding a lot of training and adjustment. This change can be challenging to professionals used to the traditional approaches to designing and can be a cause of resistance at organisational level.

The other difficulty is the adoption of AI to the current systems and operations. The deployment of AI solutions can be very costly in terms of infrastructural and data management measures as well as in software development. Organizations should also take care of the fact that their data is correct, pertinent and easily obtainable because the quality of the data plays a crucial role with the AI systems. The gains of AI might not be as maximized without the integration which needs to occur (Gaier et al., 2024).

The ethical and social issues are another problem that makes the IAI-driven adoption of AI more complicated. Such issues like the bias in the algorithm, the absence of transparency, and the right to the intellectual property should be considered carefully. Designers and organizations need to make sure that AI systems are utilized in a responsible manner and that their results are just and responsible. Moreover, the effects of AI on employment are still a contentious topic, and one that requires a balanced solution to focus on collaboration and synchronization of humans and machines, as opposed to substitution (Andreou et al., 2023).

Figure 1. AI-Enhanced Design Process Framework

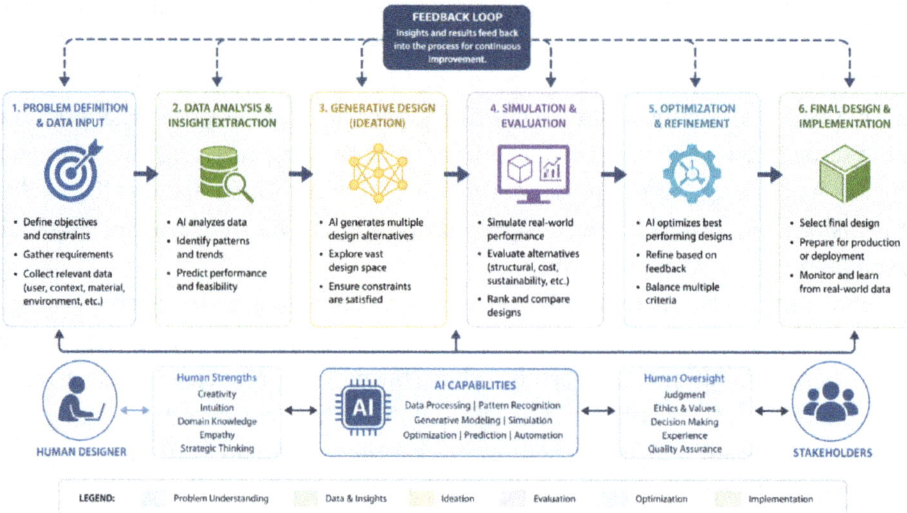

2. FOUNDATIONS OF AI IN DESIGN PROCESSES

2.1 Machine Learning Basics

Most AI-enhanced design systems are based on machine learning, through which computers learn patterns by seeing data and are able to make predictions or decisions without being explicitly programmed. Machine learning in its simplest form is the process of training algorithms using data sets to be able to identify correlation and produce results when given new data. This is useful in design cases where the systems can examine the user preferences, material characteristics and performance requirements to aid in the development of optimized solutions (Sharma et al., 2026).

Machine learning in design has a variety of different varieties, namely supervised learning, unsupervised learning and reinforcement learning. The concept of supervised learning is applied to predict data using labeled data and it is applied in the tasks of classification and regression in design evaluation. Unsupervised learning- In unsupervised learning, the concealed patterns or groupings in data are spoken out and these patterns can assist the designers in unearthing innovative design patterns or structures. Reinforcement learning lays emphasis on how to learn through trial and error, systems can use it to learn to enhance designs with the help of feedback and performance indicators.

Machine learning relies on the quality of the data and choice of the model to determine the success of machine learning in design. Bad or skewed data may result in inaccurate forecasts and less than optimal designs. Hence, datasets also need to be carefully curated and models are then validated to be reliable by designers and engineers. This is because machine learning is turning into a necessity to facilitate intelligent, adaptive and factual design procedures as machine learning keeps evolving into a core part of the design organic chemistry (Bolojan et al., 2022).

2.2 Generative Design Principles

One of the important ideas of AI-enhanced design is generative design, whereby an algorithm is used to produce several design solutions, given certain constraints and goals. Designers do not have to develop a single solution by hand; instead, they key in parameters like material limits, load conditions, cost constraints and aesthetics. The AI system is then used to search a large design space, generating a variety of viable alternatives.

This strategy transforms the designer into a curator, rather than as creators. Instead of creating each element manually, designers consider and enhance the solutions created by AI. It can not only be faster in the design process but it also brings competitive forms and structures that might not be realized using a traditional approach. Generative design is especially useful towards areas adopting an engineering and architectural approach where optimization and efficiency are vital (Huang et al., 2021).

Iterative improvement is another valuable generative designing principle. AI systems are self-improving so that the outputs are enhanced by relying on feedbacks, simulation and performance evaluation. This repetitive process can be used to create optimized designs that concomitantly satisfy numerous requirements. Consequently, generative design provides an efficient utilisation of resources and allows developing sustainable and high performance solutions.

2.3 Data-Driven Decision Making

One of the key aspects of the design processes supported by AI is data-driven decision making. Using big data, AI systems can be used to deliver insights that can be used in informing design decisions and enhancing results. The designers will not have to use intuition or previous experience only but may apply data to evaluate the alternatives, predict performance, and detect potential issues at the early stage of the process (Paananen et al., 2024).

The most important benefits of data-oriented design include capacity to deal with complexity. The contemporary design issues are usually complicated by a variety of variables and constraints, which are challenging to address manually. These variables can be analyzed simultaneously by AI systems, and brought up optimal solutions that fit within set criteria. The latter is particularly necessary in topics which have long-term effects like product development, urban planning and system design.

Nevertheless, to provide successful data-driven design, sophisticated attention to data sources and data interpretation has to be paid. Designers have to make sure that the information they employ is valid, pertinent and bias free. Moreover, they should be in a position to indicate the insights of AI and apply it to the design process in an effective manner. Data-driven decision making promotes the quality and reliability of design solutions when properly put into practice (Dandotiya et al., 2026).

2.4 Human-AI Collaboration

The collaboration between human and AI is one of the characteristics of contemporary design practices, focusing on the strengths of humans and machine as they feed on one another. Though AI is excellent in dealing with a vast quantity of information, finding patterns, and solutions, humans introduce creative and intuitive capabilities and contextual knowledge. They are a strong group which improves the total designing process.

In the case of collaboration, AI becomes a helpful assistant, which will assist designers in different activities, including optimization, analysis, and ideation. Artificially intelligent systems enable designers to engage with systems, which also allows the designer to determine the direction and output of the design projects through intuitive interfaces and also refines outputs by their skills. This interrelationship establishes a feedback mechanism wherein humans and machine intelligence play a role in having better outcomes (Abedin et al., 2022).

Nonetheless, trust, and transparency are necessary in effective collaboration regardless of its benefits. Designers need to know the way AI systems work to produce outputs and how they can calculate their accuracy. Human to AI communication should be clear to enable the final designs to meet the needs of the users and also be of good ethics. Since AI technologies keep developing, developing the effective human-AI collaboration will be essential in order to fully utilize their potential in the design processes.

3. AI TOOLS AND TECHNOLOGIES FOR DESIGNERS

3.1 Design Automation Tools

One of the most direct and feasible uses of AI in the design processes is design automation tools. Such tools are created by other companies like Autodesk and Dassault Systèmes and assist them in smoothing the repetitive and rule-based processes that usually require a lot of time and effort. Integrating AI within design software enables such tools to create layouts automatically, add constrains, and verify that it meets design standards, which gives designers more time to be creative and inventive (Vissers-Similon et al., 2024).

Consistency is one of the key benefits of design automation. Automated systems are able to use preset rules at numerous design iterations without compromise which lessens the chances of human error. An example is in the case of engineering design where the automation tools can be used to verify that all the components are within the safety and performance specifications. This comes in handy especially when running a massive project and it becomes important to ensure that the designs do not differ too much.

Moreover, design automation tools will add to the productivity level since it will save a lot of turnaround time. Work, which could have taken hours or days, can now be done in minutes. Scalability is also supported by these tools where complex projects with many variables can be dealt with by the designers. With the further development of AI, design automation can be smarter, changing to suit the user and becoming even smarter over time due to self-learning (Kumari & Goyal, 2026).

3.2 Generative AI Platforms

Generative AI-based platforms are changing the manner in which designers think and address issues. Midjourney and DALL-E are platforms that enable users to image-create, prototype and design variations based on simple text outputs. These assistants use state-of-the-art neural networks to make high-quality results that may be inspiration or even final design material.

The major advantage of generative AI platforms is that they were able to discover a plethora of design options and effectively. Designers can feed in various parameters or prompts and immediately get offered a number of variants, each with taking a particular viewpoint. This quick ideating activity promotes experimentation and designers leaving the usual thinking patterns and turning to innovative ideas (Momade et al., 2021).

In addition, generative AI systems encourage teamwork and productivity. Prompts can be edited by the designers, or results can be composites of what was generated, producing an interactive and dynamic workflow. These tools do not displace the creativity of humans; but they are potent co-creators where they can enable a designer to take any task to its limits when it comes to visual and conceptual design.

3.3 Simulation and Optimization Software

Simulation and optimization software can be very useful in assessing and refining performance of designs. The tools created by other organizations like Siemens and ANSYS are based on AI algorithm and try to replicate the conditions of the real world and formulate predictions in how the design will perform within a different scene. It enables designers to experiment with and refine their ideas before actual implementation which saves on costs and risks (Dortheimer et al., 2023).

These instruments are especially useful in other areas like engineering, architecture and product design whereby performance and safety are paramount. Factors like stress, temperature, airflow and energy consumption can be studied with the use of AI-driven simulations that can give detailed insights into the performance of design. This helps designers to know about the possible problems at a very early stage and make informed choices to make their designs work out.

Another important aspect of these tools is optimization where the designer gets the best results possible in relation to certain criteria. AI algorithms have the ability to test a variety of design layouts and find the most efficient. This does not only enhance performance but also promotes sustainability by reducing the amount of resource consumption and emission of carbon dioxide. Consequently, simulation and optimization software becomes some of the key elements of AI-upgraded design processes (Qin et al., 2024).

3.4 Collaborative AI Systems

Smart AI partnerships are meant to build teamwork and communication on design projects. Applications such as Figma and Adobe Sensei combine AI functionalities to enable real-time collaboration, feedback, and decision-making. Through these systems, various stakeholders will be able to collaborate effectively yet they might not be within the same locations.

Among the key advantages of collaborative AI systems is enhanced coordination. AI would be helpful to structure design components and monitor modifications and propose ways to enhance it based on the input of the team. This will keep everyone on track and make designing the project efficient and clear. Time-saving and shared workspaces also contribute to stronger collaboration, decreasing the time of delay and misunderstanding (Sabah et al., 2024).

Moreover, such systems enable sharing of knowledge and lifelong learning. The AI is able to evaluate previous work and identify best practices and make suggestions on further designs. This would assist teams to compound their shared experience and have greater advancement over a span of time. With the growing complexity and interdisciplinary nature of design projects, collaborative AI systems will be critical in facilitating effective teamwork and innovation.

4. APPLICATIONS OF AI IN DESIGN DOMAINS

4.1 Product and Industrial Design

AI has changed considerably not only product design but also industrial design by making it a faster and more productive process and making it optimized. Firms like Tesla and Apple use AI-based applications to transform product development, including the concept development and production. By comprehending the behavior of users, material characteristics, and through market analysis, AI can produce designs that are both innovative and user-friendly.

Generative design is one of the largest AI applications in the field which involves the creation of various design solutions depending on the constraints such as weight, strength and cost. The method enables designers to consider unusual forms, which are not heavy but still strong. Another useful application of AI is the rapid prototyping where it can be used to simulate the behavior of the product under real-world circumstances and avoid physical testing as well as hasten the time-to-market (Ibarrola et al., 2024).

AI is also used to solve product design issues by increasing customization. The AI systems are able to develop customized products because of understanding the needs of customers and their consumption pattern, by analyzing customer preferences and usage patterns. The degree of customizing does not only enhance user satisfaction but also gives the company an edge in the market. With the further evolution of AI technologies, product and industrial design will be more adaptive, efficient, and innovative.

4.2 Architectural and Urban Design

The application of AI in architectural and urban design is increasingly becoming critical in designing smarter and more sustainable spaces. Companies and applications like Zaha Hadid Architects and Autodesk Revit exploit AI to streamline building designs, energy usage, and structural functioning. Through AI-powered systems, it will be able to manage massive amounts of data, such as climate-related information, population densities, and traffic, to make more effective design choices (Farooqi et al., 2026).

Their most significant usage is in urban planning, where AI can be used to create more efficient and habitable cities. The AI will be able to forecast the implication of infrastructure change in terms of traffic flow, energy use, and environmental sustainability by simulating various situations. This will help planners to come up with solutions that will accommodate economic growth and ecological responsibility.

AI can also promote the use of parametric and generative architecture which enable designers to develop dynamic and elaborate structures. Such designs tend to be made more aesthetically as well as functional and challenging the conventional architecture. Moreover, AI will be able to help with real-time construction and construction control, guaranteeing the long-term functionality of buildings, and security. With the cities ever-expanding, AI will play a critical role in enabling sustainable and resilient city design (Bank et al., 2022).

4.3 Graphic and UX/UI Design

AI has transformed the field of graphic and UX/UI design by automating the process of creative work and improving the user experience. Artificial intelligence-driven tools, like Adobe Sensei and Canva, help designers create designs, propose color palette, as well as maximize visual effect with speed and effectiveness. These applications enable design to be less arduous and users without technical expertise can produce professional quality designs (Shi et al., 2024).

AI is an important tool in the UX/UI design, as it helps to comprehend the preferences and behavior of users. Through user interaction analysis, AI systems can recognize patterns and offer information that can guide designers to design more intuitive and user-friendly interfaces. This results in better usability, interaction, and user satisfaction. A/B testing and suggested adjustments to designs can also be executed by AI, guided by the performance metrics.

In addition, AI facilitates personalization of digital design. Interfaces have the capability to dynamically cater to individual users, providing tailored content and experiences. It is especially essential when considering e-commerce, social media, and mobile apps where user engagement plays a crucial role. Since AI is dynamic, it is bound to increase the creativity, efficiency and effectiveness of the graphic and UX/UI design procedures.

4.4 Fashion and Creative Industries

Fashion and creative industries are adopting AI to create an increase in innovativeness and efficiency. Some brands such as Nike and Zara employ AI to forecast fashion trends, consumer preferences, and supply chain optimization. AI-based applications have the potential to create new clothes designs, suggest new clothes, and even assist in the choice of a fabric, helping designers to stay on the lead in a very competitive market.

Trend forecasting is one of the most prominent ways AI can be used in fashion. Using the information obtained via social media, online searches, and sales trends, AI can accurately anticipate future trends. This enables designers and brands to make wise choices regarding their fashions, that mitigates the possibility of not selling off their collections due to overproduction and wastage (Zhong et al., 2024).

Also supported by AI are mass customization and virtual try-ons that will make the customer experience better. Consumers are able to visualize the way the clothing will look and fit prior to purchasing helping decrease returns and enhance satisfaction. Moreover, AI-driven design software can quickly experiment with colors, patterns, and style, achieving creativity and innovation. With the continued infiltration of AI into the creative sector, it will alter the way fashion and art is thought of, created, and consumed (Castro Pena et al., 2021).

5. WORKFLOW TRANSFORMATION WITH AI

5.1 Traditional vs AI-Driven Workflows

The classic design processes are usually linear and sequential, and entail processes like ideation, drafting, prototyping, testing, and production. Every step is largely reliant on human input and the reuse of previous steps in the process is a common factor in iterations that frequently demand revisions of previous steps, which in turn is time-consuming and energy-intensive. Experience and intuition are two aspects that allow designers to make decisions and although this method can be very creative it is less scalable and efficient.

Figure 2. Comparison between traditional design processes and AI-enhanced design processes

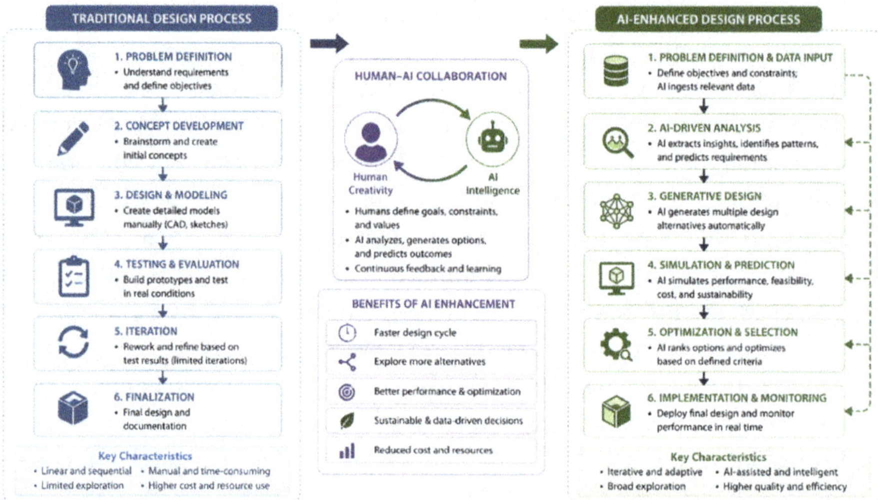

Conversely, AI-based workflows are dynamic, iterative, and very interconnected. With AI systems, it is possible to perform the entire process simultaneously through parallel computing of tasks, where a myriad of design options can be produced and tested in the same period. This will relieve bottlenecks and speed up the process of the design. However, rather than adhering to a fixed timeline, designers are also able to move freely among the steps, with real-time suggestions and feedback (Enjellina et al., 2023).

The role of the designer is altered, too, as the movement towards traditional workflows is substituted with AI-driven workflows. In lieu of manual execution, designers are decision-makers and editors of the outputs of AI. Such transformation not only contributes to increased productivity but also exposes increased possibilities to outward looks as the designers can use a wider selection of solutions within less time.

5.2 Iterative Design Acceleration

The concept of iteration is a major element of the design process; nevertheless, it may be time-consuming and complex in traditional processes. The manual adjustments, re-testing and validation of each iteration can slow down the timelines of the project. However, this process is greatly enhanced by the use of AI, which already automates by iteration cycles and enables immediate feedback on and changes made to the design (Pouliou et al., 2023).

In AI, designers are able to create lots of variations of a design in a short time and compare them with predefined requirements. Through machine learning algorithms, performance outcomes can be predicted, and therefore designers can find the most promising without having to undergo a lot of physical testing. This cycle of a rapid repeat allows one to make continual improvements and refinements and produce better design.

Moreover, AI is conducive to adaptation of the iterative design, wherein systems represent the outcomes of earlier iterative development, and with time, they enhance their advice. This generates a feedback loop which leads to the increased efficiency and accuracy with each reiteration. Consequently, designers are able to come up with optimum solutions in the fastest time possible and at the same time uphold a high standard of creativity and innovation (Stojanovski et al., 2022).

5.3 Prototyping and Testing Enhancements

The design process involves prototyping and testing which are important processes and have traditionally been time and resource-intensive. Physical models have to be constructed and experimented on under different conditions which could be expensive and time-consuming. AI is able to change this step by making it possible to perform virtual prototyping and simulation with the aid of AI, which eliminates the need to have the physical model.

AI assisted tools have the ability to recreate real world in their operation and forecast on the performance of a design in various situations. To illustrate this, systems, constructed by such companies as ANSYS and Siemens, enable designers to simulate structural stability, thermal efficiency and other extremely significant aspects in the virtual environment. Not only does it accelerate the process of testing, but also it gives a more detailed and precise information (Wu et al., 2021).

Moreover, AI augments testing since it isolates the possible problems at an initial stage of the design. Predictive analytics has the ability to identify the area of weakness or inefficiencies without it turning into an expensive issue. This is a proactive measure of risk mitigation prior to failure and to assure that designs would be up to the performance and safety standards. This results in prototyping and testing that are more efficient, reliable and cheaper.

5.4 Integration with Existing Systems

The implementation of AI into the current design systems and processes is an important step towards the realization of the full potential of AI. Organizations have already adopted digital technology which includes CAD software, project management applications, and data applications. The introduction of AI into these spaces cannot be done without any kind of harmony, so it cannot interfere with current operations to improve their functionality.

Another integration issue that has been identified is the compatibility of AI tools and legacy. This usually necessitates improvement of infrastructure, normalization of data format and adoption of new interfaces. Nevertheless, with the effective implementation, integration can help organizations utilize AI capabilities without the risk of a continuity in workflows (Kumari et al., 2026).

Besides, effective inclusion is tied to the organizational preparedness and cooperation. The teams should be trained to effectively apply AI technologies and workflows should be adjusted to new technologies. There are businesses that are striving to make this a possibility, such as Autodesk and PTC, which offer platforms that can be smoothly integrated into to allow designers to transition to AI-enhanced environments. Finally, the merging of AI into the current systems results in more integrated, effective and creative design processes.

5.5 Results and Discussion

The results of this research demonstrate that artificial intelligence (AI) plays a vital role in design by increasing efficiency, creativity and optimization in several areas. From the literature review and examination of AI-driven workflows, we have observed that the advancements in machine learning, generative design and simulation tools in the AI-driven design process have provided tangible benefits over traditional design practices.

A key finding observed is a decrease in design time. Machine learning-based workflows speed up iterative design through the automation of basic tasks like analysis, simulation and optimization. In conventional processes, it may involve several design iterations, whereas with AI, systems can explore many more iterations in the same amount of time. Thus reducing the time to prototype and decide, which is a critical procedure in areas such as engineering, architecture, and product design.

Another outcome is a widening of the design space. Generative AI algorithms generate a large number of design variations given constraints, allowing them to consider novel solutions not otherwise considered. The findings show AI not only accelerates the design process but also stimulates creativity by aiding idea generation and exploring innovative solutions. This has led to lightweight, efficient and sustainable design solutions in product and architectural design that may not be detected by manual processes.

The research also highlights benefits in terms of design accuracy and performance with simulation and optimization. This software can predict how structures will perform, how energy efficient they will be, and how usable they will be. This helps to detect potential problems early in the design process to avoid re-design and re-testing. This demonstrates that AI is not only beneficial in terms of speeding up the process but also of producing reliable and high-quality design solutions.

A key finding of the analysis is the increased role of human-AI collaboration. More than substituting for designers, AI is mainly used as a smart tool enhancing creative and decision-making processes. Humans still play a critical role in setting objectives, assessing the generated designs, and assessing contextual and ethical aspects of the designs. Our results support the argument that the optimal outcomes result from interaction between human skills and AI.

But the findings also point to issues with embracing AI. Data quality, biases, and compatibility with existing systems all have an impact on outcomes. In some instances, AI solutions are based on training data, and may offer biased and unrealistic solutions without appropriate human oversight. The results highlight a need for human supervision and for proper implementation.

The results also provide a focal point to discuss the role of AI in sustainability. A number of studies reviewed show AI-based optimization not only leads to the reduced material and energy wastage, and to less waste. In particular, this can be observed with generative design and smart cities, which can include sustainability as one of the design variables. Hence, AI proves to be beneficial for innovation as well as for eco-design.

In sum, the findings show that design processes that leverage AI have advantages over conventional design approaches for efficiency, flexibility, innovation and optimisation. Although there are some technical and ethical concerns, the benefits far outweigh the drawbacks with smart integration of AI. The debate verifies that AI is changing design from a largely artisanal process to a data, collaborative and smart process.

These conclusions are in line with the aim of this research, which is to demonstrate that artificial intelligence is not only an enabler of designing, but a disruptor. Ongoing improvements in autonomous design, adaptive decision making, and human-centered AI will contribute to further improvements, and shape the future of design.

6. ETHICAL AND SOCIAL IMPLICATIONS

6.1 Bias and Fairness in Design Algorithms

The element of bias in algorithms is one of the most significant ethical issues in AI-enhanced design. AI systems are based on historical information, and when that information is biased in any way, be it socially, culturally, or economically, the information can be projected into its outputs and increased in its design. This may result in a product, interface or environment that bypasses a group of users or puts them at a disadvantage.

Biased algorithms can be used in design factors like accessibility, usability, and representation. As an illustration, when an AI is trained on few demographical information, it can come up with designs that only serve a particular user base overlooking the needs of others. This is especially problematic when it comes to things such as urban design, health care design, and the design of the interface where inclusion is critical (Galanos et al., 2023) .

In order to combat such challenges, designers, and developers need to focus on fairness and diversity in data collection and model training. These problems can be alleviated by regular audits, bias detecting methods, as well as inclusive design procedures. Being considerate of AI design does not solely constitute an ethical duty but is also crucial to developing solutions that cater to a wide, divergent audience.

6.2 Intellectual Property Concerns

Introduction of AI into the design field produces complicated issues regarding intellectual property (IP) and ownership. When AI systems come up with designs, it is not clear who will own the work that is produced; the designer, the organization, or the AI system itself. This vagueness confronts the conventional framework of authorship and copyright which is usually founded on the human ingenuity(Maksoud et al., 2024).

The other problem is connected with the information that AI models are trained on. Most systems of generative AI use large datasets, and they can contain copyrighted content. In case an AI-based design is strongly similar to what already exists, it may be subject to legal feuds and doubts concerning the novelty. This is especially applicable in creative industries like graphic designing, fashion and media.

In order to maneuver these issues, companies should make distinct policies about AI-created work and rights to ownership. Laws are continuously changing in response to such issues and designers need to keep up with laws and good practice. A clear-cut recording of design processes and source of data can also be of help in accountability as well as safeguarding intellectual property (Homayounirad, 2023).

6.3 Transparency and Accountability

One of the conditions that can foster trust in AI-enhanced design systems is transparency. Most of the AI models, especially the deep learning models, are black boxes thus not easily able to comprehend how they make certain decisions. This non-transparency may be frustrating to designers who must defend and prove their design decisions.

Transparency is directly connected with accountability. As AI systems are involved in the design decisions, one should also question who is liable of the result. In case of failure or harm inflicted by a design, establishing liability becomes intricate, particularly when the choices are affected by automated technology. This poses significant liability and ethical responsibility concerns (Vermillion, 2022).

The approach to overcome these challenges is to implement the techniques of explainable AI in designers and organizations which offer insight into the decision-making process. To achieve accountability, clear documentation, validation processes, and human oversight are critical. Through increased transparency and accountability, AI-enhanced design will be more accepted and trusted by people and stakeholders.

6.4 Impact on Design Professions

The usage of AI in design is redefining the functions and duties of design professionals. Although AI has the capability of carrying out most of the routine tasks, it offers the designers a chance of engaging in other high-level activities like strategy, creativity, and problem solving. Such a shift necessitates that the designers acquire new competencies such as data literacy, acquaintance with AI tools (Sheikh et al., 2026).

Nevertheless, job displacement is also an issue of concern especially where repetitive/technical duties are to be performed. With the advancement of AI systems, there is a risk that certain functions of design design can lose some importance. This has given rise to the issue of the future of design professions and why reskilling and upskilling are desired to maintain competitiveness in an AI-driven world.

Simultaneously, the field of design is getting new jobs and opportunities produced by AI. New jobs in the field of AI design specialists, data-driven designers, and human-AI interaction specialists are being created. Design professionals can use AI as a growth tool, instead of a threat, to adapt to new technologies and incorporate them into design by embracing changes and adapting to the new world of design, but this will result in a more dynamic and innovative future of the profession (Cheung et al., 2023).

7. FUTURE TRENDS IN AI-ENHANCED DESIGN

7.1 Autonomous Design Systems

One of the branch points of the most advanced directions of design in AI-enhanced design is autonomous design systems, where systems can independently generate designs, evaluate, and refine them with little intervention by humans. These architectures combine machine-learning and generative algorithms and optimization to produce end-to-end solutions in design. They are not just helpful to designers, but intelligent, and can make complex design decisions (Agkathidis et al., 2024).

These systems are already coming into the fields such as engineering and manufacturing where AI can create parts that are performance, cost, and sustainability optimized. Autonomous systems evolve over time, getting better by learning with data and past results and designing more efficient and innovative solutions. This ability will effectively minimize time taken to develop products as well as the productivity.

Nonetheless, there exist other essential concerns regarding control and trust in connection to the emergence of autonomous design. The designers should take care that these are systems that are compatible with human values, safety standards and project requirements. Although the full autonomy might not substitute the human designer, chances are that the autonomy will transform the role; hence more supervision, validation and strategic direction (Bolojan et al., 2024).

7.2 Real-Time Adaptive Design

Another new concept is real-time adaptive design, where dynamic changes to designs, based on time and human interactions, are being performed by AI systems. Unlike the static designs, adaptive systems keep on changing, reacting to the real-time information including environmental conditions, user actions and performance indicators. This will allow a more effective and personalized design solutions.

To illustrate, layouts, content and functionality can be adjusted ב א to the preference of users and their usage behaviors in a digital interface using AI. The architectural field can respond to environmental conditions through the optimization of energy consumption, lighting and temperature in the buildings. These adaptive features make the functionality, efficiency and user experience improved within diverse design areas (Kumari et al., 2026).

Introduction of real-time adaptive design needs a high level of data processing and integration of sensors and IoT technologies. The more technologies evolve these days, the more widespread will be adaptive design facilities, which will allow not only smart but also context-sensitive and highly responsive systems to evolving requirements.

7.3 AI and Sustainability

The concept of sustainability is now taking a primary concern in contemporary design and AI is playing a key role in ensuring conducive solutions, which are environmental friendly. The environmental data, use of materials and consumption of power can be analyzed using AI-based tools to make designs which will reduce waste and carbon footprint. This functionality is very crucial especially in the construction industry, manufacturing industry and city planning industry.

Among the most valuable offerings of AI to sustainability is optimization. Through the assessment of various design options, AI is able to select solutions requiring fewer resources with performance and quality. An example is those produced through generative design, which can be made out of fewer materials and have a lower cost and lower environmental impact (Goyal et al., 2026).

Moreover, AI helps in lifecycle analysis which allows designers to evaluate the long-term implication of their designs. At the production level up to the disposal, AI is capable of shedding light on the impacts of products and systems on the environment in the long run. This systemic thinking can foster a much more sustainable way of designing buildings and orient towards a circular economy.

7.4 Emerging Research Directions

The sphere of AI-enhanced design is developing quickly, and new methods, tools and applications are actively researched. A new interest is being directed to areas like explainable AI, human-centered AI, and multi-agent systems. These directions of research will enhance transparency, usability and collaboration in AI-driven design processes.

One more prospective solution is AI coupled with some sophisticated technologies like virtual reality (VR) and augmented reality (AR). Through such technologies, designers can experience immersive designing, which they can interact with the AI-generated models in real time. This improves the process of visualization, decision making and collaboration, thus making the process of design more appealing and intuitive (Cheung et al., 2024).

Moreover, the combination of scientific fields like cognitive science, engineering and art through interdisciplinary researches is leading to the spark of innovation. The converged convergence is causing emergence of smarter, more creative design systems. The AI-enhanced design is going to become more sophisticated as the development of research will allow creating new opportunities in innovations and changing the future of designing in any industry.

CONCLUSION

AI-enhanced design processes represent when major change takes place regarding conceptualization, development and realisation of ideas in industries. The design process has been transformed so that it is no longer a primary manual and iterative process, but an interactive, smart, and very efficient workflow, using advanced technologies, like machine learning, generative design, and data analytics. The time-consumption and trial and error that designers have to go through are no longer part of it and now, they can harness AI to create various solutions and assess its effectiveness, all they have to do is make a decision and make it timely and in the correct direction. This change not only helps in increasing productivity but also widens the scope of imagination and creativity.

Simultaneously, AI implementation in the design opens up significant ethical, social, and professional concerns. Such aspects like algorithmic bias, intellectual property, transparency, and transformation of designer should be thoroughly considered to guarantee the responsible implementation. Instead of taking over human designers, AI is an enhanced partner that enhances human abilities. To make AI-enhanced design successful, it is necessary to strike the balance between the technological development and humanism so that the design implications could be inclusive, ethical, and user-focused.

In the future, AI development, such as autonomous systems, real-time adaptable, and sustainable innovation, will govern the future of design. The technologies will be able to allow more responsive, efficient and environmentally-conscious designs solutions as they mature. Designers that are ready to adopt AI and acquire skills required to operate in intelligent systems will be in a stronger position to be in the forefront in this changing landscape. Finally, AI-enhanced design is not only a change in technology, but the very concept of creativity, collaboration and problem-solving in the contemporary world.

REFERENCES

Abedin, B., Meske, C., Junglas, I., Rabhi, F., & Motahari-Nezhad, H. R. (2022). Designing and Managing Human-AI Interactions. *Information Systems Frontiers*, *24*(3), 691–697. DOI: 10.1007/s10796-022-10313-1

Agkathidis, A., Yang, S., & Symeonidou, I. (2024). AI-Assisted Design: Utilising artificial intelligence as a generative form-finding tool in architectural design studio teaching. Kontovourkis, O, Phocas, MC and Wurzer, G (Eds.), Data-Driven Intelligence - Proceedings of the 42nd Conference on Education and Research in Computer Aided Architectural Design in Europe (eCAADe 2024), Nicosia, 11–13 September 2024, Volume 2, Pp. 619–628. DOI: 10.52842/conf.ecaade.2024.2.619

Andreou, A., Kontovourkis, O., Solomou, S., & Savvides, A. (2023). Rethinking Architectural Design Process using Integrated Parametric Design and Machine Learning Principles. Dokonal, W, Hirschberg, U and Wurzer, G (Eds.), Digital Design Reconsidered - Proceedings of the 41st Conference on Education and Research in Computer Aided Architectural Design in Europe (eCAADe 2023) - Volume 2, Graz, 20–22 September 2023, Pp. 461–470. DOI: 10.52842/conf.ecaade.2023.2.461

Bank, M., Sandor, V., Schinegger, K., & Rutzinger, S. (2022). Learning Spatiality—A GAN method for designing architectural models through labelled sections. Pak, B, Wurzer, G and Stouffs, R (Eds.), Co-Creating the Future: Inclusion in and through Design - Proceedings of the 40th Conference on Education and Research in Computer Aided Architectural Design in Europe (eCAADe 2022) - Volume 2, Ghent, 13–16 September 2022, Pp. 611–619. DOI: 10.52842/conf.ecaade.2022.2.611

Bolojan, D., Vermisso, E., & Yousif, S. (2022). Is Language All We Need? A Query Into Architectural Semantics Using a Multimodal Generative Workflow. POST-CARBON - Proceedings of the 27th CAADRIA Conference, 353–362. DOI: 10.52842/conf.caadria.2022.1.353

Bolojan, D., Yousif, S., & Spsampsps Vermisso, E. (2024). Latent Design Spaces: Interconnected Deep Learning Models for Expanding the Architectural Search Space. In M. Barberio, M. Colella, A. Figliola, spsampsps A. Battisti (Eds.), Architecture and Design for Industry 4.0: Theory and Practice (pp. 201–223). Springer International Publishing. DOI: 10.1007/978-3-031-36922-3_13

Castro Pena, M. L., Carballal, A., Rodríguez-Fernández, N., Santos, I., & Romero, J. (2021). Artificial intelligence applied to conceptual design. A review of its use in architecture. *Automation in Construction*, *124*, 103550. DOI: 10.1016/j.autcon.2021.103550

Cheung, L. H., & Dall'Asta, J. C. (2023). Exploring a Collaborative and Intuitive Framework for Combined Application of AI Art Generation Tools in Architectural Design Process. *Proceedings of the AISB Convention 2023*, pp 122–130.

Cheung, L. H., Dall'Asta, J. C., & Di Marco, G. (2023). Exploring Large Language Model as a Design Partner through Verbal and Non-verbal Conversation in Architectural Design Process. *XXVII International Conference of the Ibero-American Society of Digital Graphics*, 12, 1059–1070. DOI: 10.5151/sigradi2023-65

Cheung, L. H., Dall'Asta, J. C., Di Marco, G., & Spsampsps Agkathidis, A. (2024). Architectural Design Under Pandemic of Today's AI: From Human-Computer Interaction (HCI) to Human-Machine Conversation (HMC). In G. Di Marco, D. Lombardi, spsampsps M. Tedjosaputro (Eds.), Creativity in the Age of Digital Reproduction (pp. 9–17). Springer Nature. DOI: 10.1007/978-981-97-0621-1_2

Dandotiya, M., Goyal, N. K., Yadav, P., Sankhla, K., & Kumari, M. (2026). GENALYTICS: A Deep Dive Into Real-Time Insights via Generative AI. In Elbaghazaoui, B., Amnai, M., & Gherabi, N. (Eds.), *Generative AI-Powered Data Architectures: From Governance to Autonomous Analytics* (pp. 105–134). IGI Global Scientific Publishing., DOI: 10.4018/979-8-3373-5616-7.ch005

Dortheimer, J., Schubert, G., Dalach, A., Brenner, L., & Martelaro, N. (2023). Think AI-side the Box! Exploring the Usability of Text-to-Image Generators for Architecture Students. Digital Design Reconsidered -eCAADe 2023,2, 567–576. DOI: 10.52842/conf.ecaade.2023.2.567

Enjellina, B., & Beyan, E. V. P.Anastasya Gisela Cinintya Rossy. (2023). A Review of AI Image Generator: Influences, Challenges, and Future Prospects for Architectural Field. *Journal of Artificial Intelligence in Architecture*, *2*(1), 1. Advance online publication. DOI: 10.24002/jarina.v2i1.6662

Farooqi, A., Das, D., Tripathi, M., Dutta, R., Goyal, N. K., & Sheikh, M. F. (2026). Navigating Ethical Frontiers in AI-Driven Geriatric Care. In Stolakis, K., & Efthymiou, I. (Eds.), *AI for Geriatric Care in an Aging Society: Ethical, Clinical, and Policy Challenges* (pp. 243–266). IGI Global Scientific Publishing., DOI: 10.4018/979-8-3373-5462-0.ch009

Gaier, A., Stoddart, J., Villaggi, L., & Sudhakaran, S. (2024). Generative Design through Quality-Diversity Data Synthesis and Language Models. *Proceedings of the Genetic and Evolutionary Computation Conference*, 823–831. DOI: 10.1145/3638529.3654138

Galanos, T., Liapis, A., & Yannakakis, G. N. (2023). Architext: Language-Driven Generative Architecture Design. arXiv. /arXiv.2303.07519DOI: 10.48550

Goyal, N. K., Goyal, N. K., Kumar, S., Dutta, R., Kothari, V., & Sinha, S. K. (2026). Empowering Elderly Care Through Artificial Intelligence. In Stolakis, K., & Efthymiou, I. (Eds.), *AI for Geriatric Care in an Aging Society: Ethical, Clinical, and Policy Challenges* (pp. 1–28). IGI Global Scientific Publishing., DOI: 10.4018/979-8-3373-5462-0.ch001

Goyal, N. K., Gulati, K., Avasthi, A., Kapoor, S. K., Keswani, B., & Gupta, S. (2026). Securing the Imagination: Security and Privacy Challenges in Generative AI Systems. In Elbaghazaoui, B., Amnai, M., & Gherabi, N. (Eds.), *Generative AI-Powered Data Architectures: From Governance to Autonomous Analytics* (pp. 239–266). IGI Global Scientific Publishing., DOI: 10.4018/979-8-3373-5616-7.ch010

Homayounirad, A. (2023). Designing the Built Environment Through Hybrid Intelligence. In HHAI 2023: Augmenting Human Intellect (pp. 483–495). IOS Press. DOI: 10.3233/FAIA230127

Huang, J., Johanes, M., Kim, F. C., Doumpioti, C., & Holz, G.-C. (2021). On GANs, NLP and Architecture: Combining Human and Machine Intelligences for the Generation and Evaluation of Meaningful Designs. Technology|Architecture + Design, 5(2), 207–224. DOI: 10.1080/24751448.2021.1967060

Ibarrola, F., Lawton, T., & Grace, K. (2024). A Collaborative, Interactive and Context-Aware Drawing Agent for Co-Creative Design. *IEEE Transactions on Visualization and Computer Graphics*, *30*(8), 5525–5537. DOI: 10.1109/TVCG.2023.3293853

Kumari, M., & Goyal, N. K. (2026). Artificial Intelligence in the Cryptocurrency Ecosystem: Crime Mechanisms, Detection Strategies, and Legal Perspectives. In Lin, L. (Ed.), *Innovations in Cryptocrime and Financial Fraud* (pp. 245–282). IGI Global Scientific Publishing., DOI: 10.4018/979-8-3373-0675-9.ch007

Kumari, M., Khan, S. T., Gulati, K., Sharma, P., Goyal, N. K., & Sheikh, M. F. (2026). Innovative Procedural Content Generation (PCG) Using Generative AI: A New Paradigm in Game Design. In Sousa, J., & Tavares, R. (Eds.), *Reshaping the Video Game Landscape With AI and GenAI* (pp. 205–232). IGI Global Scientific Publishing., DOI: 10.4018/979-8-3373-4637-3.ch007

Kumari, M., Kumawat, R., Dutta, R., Khan, S. T., Goyal, N. K., & Sheikh, M. F. (2026). Wireless Communication and IoT Integration in Smart Clothing. In Saxena, P., Singh, M., Singh, S., & Rashid, M. (Eds.), *Next-Generation Electronic Textiles and Conductive Materials for Smart Wearables* (pp. 195–232). IGI Global Scientific Publishing., DOI: 10.4018/979-8-3373-4287-0.ch008

Kumari, M., Kumawat, R., Tripathi, M., Suganthi, K., Goyal, N. K., & Sheikh, M. F. (2026). Blockchain for Transparency and Traceability in Supply Chains. In Khan, M., Mehmood, T., & Rao, M. (Eds.), *Maximizing Operational Efficiency at the Intersection of Supply Chain Management and Marketing* (pp. 35–64). IGI Global Scientific Publishing., DOI: 10.4018/979-8-3373-3109-6.ch002

Maksoud, A., Elshabshiri, A., Saeed Hilal Humaid Alzaabi, A., & Hussien, A. (2024). Integrating an Image-Generative Tool on Creative Design Brainstorming Process of a Safavid Mosque Architecture Conceptual Form. *Buildings (Basel, Switzerland)*, *14*(3), 3. Advance online publication. DOI: 10.3390/buildings14030843

Momade, M. H., Durdyev, S., Estrella, D., & Ismail, S. (2021). Systematic review of application of artificial intelligence tools in architectural, engineering and construction. *Frontiers in Engineering and Built Environment*, *1*(2), 203–216. DOI: 10.1108/FEBE-07-2021-0036

Paananen, V., Oppenlaender, J., & Visuri, A. (2024). Using text-to-image generation for architectural design ideation. *International Journal of Architectural Computing*, *22*(3), 458–474. DOI: 10.1177/14780771231222783

Pouliou, P., Horvath, A.-S., & Palamas, G. (2023). Speculative hybrids: Investigating the generation of conceptual architectural forms through the use of 3D generative adversarial networks. *International Journal of Architectural Computing*, *21*(2), 315–336. DOI: 10.1177/14780771231168229

Qin, S., Guan, H., Liao, W., Gu, Y., Zheng, Z., Xue, H., & Lu, X. (2024). Intelligent design and optimization system for shear wall structures based on large language models and generative artificial intelligence. *Journal of Building Engineering*, *95*, 109996. Advance online publication. DOI: 10.1016/j.jobe.2024.109996

Sabah, S., Alani, M., Spsampsps Salih, B. M. M. (2024). Leveraging AI Language Models for Designing Contextually Responsive Built Environments. Lecture Notes in Networks and Systems, 1019 LNNS, 510–519. DOI: 10.1007/978-3-031-62273-1_32

Sharma, P., Kumawat, R., Jain, G., Keswani, G., Goyal, N. K., & Sheikh, M. F. (2026). Machine Learning-Based Intrusion Detection Systems for Healthcare Internet of Things (HIoT). In Shieh, C., Goel, P., Horng, M., & Pandey, H. (Eds.), *Resilient Healthcare Internet of Things Systems: Architectures, Security, and Trust* (pp. 185–214). IGI Global Scientific Publishing., DOI: 10.4018/979-8-3373-7610-3.ch007

Sheikh, M. F. A., Kapoor, S. K., Goyal, N. K., & Tuba, E. rao, A. (2026). Enhancing Healthcare Security with Fog Computing and Blockchain Technology. In: Nayak, R., Mittal, N., Khunteta, A., Kumar, M. (eds) Recent Advancements in Artificial Intelligence. ICRAAI 2025. Lecture Notes in Networks and Systems, vol 1468. Springer, Singapore. DOI: 10.1007/978-981-96-7760-3_38

Shi, M., Seo, J., Cha, S. H., Xiao, B., & Chi, H.-L. (2024). Generative AI-powered architectural exterior conceptual design based on the design intent. *Journal of Computational Design and Engineering*, *11*(5), 125–142. Advance online publication. DOI: 10.1093/jcde/qwae077

Stojanovski, T., Zhang, H., Frid, E., Chhatre, K., Peters, C., Samuels, I., Sanders, P., Partanen, J., & Spsampsps Lefosse, D. (2022). Rethinking Computer-Aided Architectural Design (CAAD) – From Generative Algorithms and Architectural Intelligence to Environmental Design and Ambient Intelligence. In D. Gerber, E. Pantazis, B. Bogosian, A. Nahmad, spsampsps C. Miltiadis (Eds.), Computer-Aided Architectural Design. Design Imperatives: The Future is Now (pp. 62–83). Springer. DOI: 10.1007/978-981-19-1280-1_5

Vermillion, J. (2022). Iterating the Design Process Using AI Diffusion Models. Creative Collaborations, 9. https://digitalscholarship.unlv.edu/cfa_collaborate/9

Vissers-Similon, E., Dounas, T., & De Walsche, J. (2024). Classification of artificial intelligence techniques for early architectural design stages. *International Journal of Architectural Computing, 2024*. Advance online publication. DOI: 10.1177/14780771241260857

Wei, J., Wang, X., Schuurmans, D., Bosma, M., Ichter, B., Xia, F., Chi, E. H., Le, Q. V., & Zhou, D. (2022). Chain-of-Thought Prompting Elicits Reasoning in Large Language Models. *Proceedings of the 36th International Conference on Neural Information Processing Systems*, 35, 24824–24837. DOI: 10.52202/068431-1800

Wu, Z., Ji, D., Yu, K., Zeng, X., Wu, D., & Spsampsps Shidujaman, M. (2021). AI Creativity and the Human-AI Co-creation Model. In Kurosu, M. (Ed.), *Human-Computer Interaction. Theory, Methods and Tools* (pp. 171–190). Springer International Publishing., DOI: 10.1007/978-3-030-78462-1_13

Zhong, C., Shi, Y., Cheung, L. H., & Wang, L. (2024). AI-Enhanced Performative Building Design Optimization and Exploration: A Design Framework Combining Computational Design Optimization and Generative AI. ACCELERATED DESIGN - Proceedings of the 29th CAADRIA Conference, 1, 59–68. DOI: 10.52842/conf.caadria.2024.1.059

Chapter 2
AI-Enhanced Design Methodologies:
Transforming Creativity, Iteration, and Decision-Making in Intelligent Design Systems

Sohom Saha
http://orcid.org/0009-0006-9438-1554
Lakshmibai National Institute of Physical Education, India

Komal Digra
http://orcid.org/0009-0007-1415-6857
Lakshmibai National Institute of Physical Education, India

Shailendra Singh
http://orcid.org/0009-0003-1399-2387
Lakshmibai National Institute of Physical Education, India

Sumit Kumar Singh
http://orcid.org/0009-0000-1728-8213
Lakshmibai National Institute of Physical Education, India

ABSTRACT

Artificial Intelligence (AI) is transforming the way design is developed, experimented and refined. Previously, design relied heavily on human creativity, experience, as well as time-consuming trial and error. Currently, AI applications can generate numerous design solutions rapidly, experiment, and propose superior solutions using data. This establishes a close collaboration between humans and machines, where designers dictate creativity and AI assists in speed, analysis, and optimization.

DOI: 10.4018/979-8-3693-3751-6.ch002

AI assists in accelerated generation of ideas, accelerated design modification and intelligent decision-making. Nonetheless, such issues as over-reliance on AI, data bias, and ethical issues will have to be addressed with proper attention. This chapter describes the way AI is enhancing designing practices and provides a model that integrates human creativity with machine intelligence. In general, AI will streamline the design and make it more innovative but requires human control and judgment.

1. INTRODUCTION

Design has always been considered as a very human activity - a creative, intuitive, aesthetical and problem-solving discipline. Throughout the centuries, designers have used personal experience, manual experimentation and joint dialogue to transform abstract ideas into a concrete result. Though this paradigm was effective, it was limited by the cognitive capacity of single practitioners and the time constraints of refining the process. With the advent of digital computing in the second half of the twentieth century, computational aids were incorporated into design processes, but the basic processes of creativity and decision-making remained mostly human-driven (Cross, 2023).

The introduction of Artificial Intelligence (AI) and its fast development have shaken this status quo to its core. In contrast to traditional software applications, which follow pre-defined instructions, AI applications, especially those based on machine learning, deep neural networks, and generative modelling, have the ability to learn, discover intricate patterns, create new outputs, and optimally enhance their performance without needing explicit reprogramming (Russell & Norvig, 2021). Such adaptability makes AI not just a productivity tool, but an active contributor to the creative and analytical aspects of the design process.

Design methodologies with AI are a paradigm shift of tool-aided human creativity to collaborative model of intelligence where human designers and machine systems are used to complement each other. Designers provide cultural sensitivity, moral discretion, contextual knowledge, aesthetic hunch, and AI brings computational capability, pattern recognition on large volumes of data, quick prototyping and scale optimization (Vaccaro et al., 2024). The combination of these abilities is delivering design results that were never possible to each of the parties on their own.

The revolutionizing influence of AI is evident in many spheres of design. In product and industrial design, generative AI like Autodesk Fusion 360 can generate thousands of structurally optimized design options in a few hours, a seat bracket losing 40% of its weight, but gaining 20% of its strength (Briard et al., 2020). Generative Adversarial Networks (GANs) are being used in architectural design to allow architects to experiment with a wide range of new spatial forms that would be impractically time-consuming to create by hand (Tang et al., 2024). AI technologies in user experience (UX) design are automatically creating wireframes and interface prototypes based on high-level design patterns (Gajjar et al., 2021). The above illustrations highlight the scope of AI in the design spectrum.

Although these innovations are made, the implementation of AI in design is not a simple task. The nature of creativity in algorithmically mediated settings, how much automation and human agency should be used, the threat of homogenizing creative outputs due to dependence on data patterns, and the ethical consequences of opaque decision processes are subject to critical questions (Amankwah-Amoah et al., 2024; Barbieri & Muzzupappa, 2024).

This chapter offers an organized discussion on AI-enhanced design methods. It follows the development of traditional design thinking to AI-based systems, how AI is transforming the creative process and iteration, how AI affects design decisions, major challenges and ethical issues, and a conceptual framework of intelligent design systems. The chapter will draw on the insights of design theory, cognitive science, and computational intelligence to provide researchers, practitioners, and educators with a comprehensive understanding of how AI is transforming the future of design.

2. THEORETICAL FRAMEWORK

In order to fully grasp the extent of the influence of AI on design, one will have to place the discussion in the context of the well-known theoretical traditions. In the chapter, four major theoretical lenses are incorporated that collectively offer a solid analytical framework.

2.1 Design Thinking Theory

The concept of design thinking, elucidated by Cross (2023) and codified by the efforts of the Hasso Plattner Institute of Design at Stanford, explains a human-centred approach to problem-solving that follows the steps of empathy, problem definition, ideation, prototyping and testing. The model is iterative in nature, and the designers can repeatedly go through the previous steps as new information is revealed. AI supplements this process at various stages: machine learning models boost empathy by examining big data of user behaviour; generative design tools facilitate ideation, generating a multitude of solutions at the same time; and predictive analytics facilitate the prototyping and testing, simulating performance outcomes before they are instantiated in the real world (L. Chen et al., 2019).

Notably, AI does not exclude the design thinking process; it only reduces time requirements of every stage and increases the amount of available space to design solutions. The compatibility of the iterative philosophy of design thinking and the iterative learning processes of AI makes a natural synergy that is the foundation of AI-based design processes.

2.2 Computational Creativity

Computational creativity is the interdisciplinary research into how computational systems may display, simulate or arouse creative behaviours. Scholars of this genre identify two types of creativity: the one created independently of the algorithm and the other as AI-aided creativity that is created with the help of human designers (Colton & Wiggins, 2012). Modern generative AI models, such as Generative Adversarial Networks (GANs), Variational Autoencoders (VAEs) and large language models (LLMs) have greatly improved the former category, generating new images, text, and design concepts that were once the prerogative of human imagination (Sengar et al., 2025; She & Cetinic, 2022). Computationally creativity-wise, the design process can be more thought of as a co-generative process where human intentions and machine output are refined by each other in feedback loops. As shown by Yuan et al. (2022), GAN-based models that take into consideration user sentiment data can produce design concepts that match user preferences, demonstrating the possibility of computational creativity being steered and personalized. Likewise, a foundation model with respect to combinational creativity in generative design was proposed by M.-T. Chen et al. (2024), which advances the theoretical comprehension of how AI systems could synthesize ideas related to different fields to really novel solutions.

2.3 Human-AI Interaction Models

Human-AI Interaction (HAI) theoretical landscape has been changing significantly with the development of the AI capacity. Early models assumed AI as a passive device in response to human instructions; the modern ones acknowledge a more dynamic, two-way interaction. Dellermann et al. (2019) suggested a taxonomy of human-AI collaboration which divides the human-AI collaboration into dimensions of the nature of tasks, paradigms of learning, and the modalities of interaction. This taxonomy also offers a convenient framework on how designers and AI systems can be best matched to various types of design tasks.

A meta-analysis study of human-AI collaboration Vaccaro et al. (2024) published in Nature Human Behaviour was the first large-scale meta-analysis of human-AI collaboration involving 106 experiments and concluded that human-AI teams perform worse than AI on analytical and classification tasks but better on creative ones, such as content generation, ideation, design. This conclusion has significant implications to the design practice as it implies that the most efficient use of AI in design is as a creative partner but not decision-making proxy.

(\Wu et al. (2021) introduced a Human-AI co-creativity model that is built on six stages, such as perception, reflection, expression, collaboration, construction, and testing, that re-organizes the known design thinking processes but allows the AI to contribute its particular contributions at each stage. This model is a useful guideline to design AI-based design processes.

2.4 Decision-Making Theory

Design decision-making entails choosing between competing decisions with uncertainty, complexity, and multiple criteria. Classical decision theory, which builds upon the efforts of Herbert Simon, acknowledges that human decision-makers are limited in rationality, i.e., they make decisions based on limited information, cognitive ability and time (Simon, 1996). To counteract limited rationality, AI systems analyze large volumes of data, discover non-intuitive trends, and provide probabilistic recommendations that can further expand the effective decision space accessible to designers.

AI tools are becoming accessible to aid design through data-driven decision-making by providing predictive modelling, multi-objective optimization, and performance simulation. In their study, Chong et al. (2022) investigated the dynamics of designer confidence in AI recommendations in AI-assisted design decision-making situations, revealing that calibrating confidence (neither blind trust nor systematic rejection) is essential to optimal human-AI decision-making outcomes. This observation highlights the significance of developing AI tools that assist designers, and not replace them.

3. EVOLUTION OF DESIGN METHODOLOGIES: FROM TRADITIONAL TO AI-ENHANCED

3.1 Traditional Design Methodologies

The development of traditional design methodologies started in the middle of the twentieth century as structured alternatives to intuitively-driven practice. The Rational Model, Reflective Practice Model, and Systems Approach were methodologies that aimed to bring rigour and reproducibility to design processes (Cross, 2023). These models were united by the focus on the structured problem decomposition, the order of the phases, and human-centred assessment. Their strong points were their clarity and the centrality of their emphasis on designer judgment and craft.

Nevertheless, conventional approaches were limited by a number of inherent limitations. The cognitive capacity of the design team and the time available limited the solution space that could be searched in a given time frame. The process of iteration was expensive because every iteration has to be done manually in sketching, modelling, prototyping, and evaluation. Expert intuition was essential in decision-making and although valuable, it was vulnerable to cognitive biases, incomplete information and individual differences. The multifacetedness of modern design-related issues, such as user behaviour analytics, material performance, regulatory compliance, sustainability metrics, has been, and ever more, going beyond the ability of purely human-oriented methodologies to comprehend thoroughly.

3.2 The Emergence of AI-Enhanced Design Frameworks

The introduction of AI into the design process was not a sudden shift, but a gradual development that was facilitated by the development of computers, access to data and the sophistication of algorithms. Early computational design systems, including Computer-Aided Design (CAD) and Computer-Aided Engineering (CAE) software, were first to bring a digital accuracy to the design process, but were still essentially responsive to explicit human commands. With the appearances of the parametric modelling tools in the 1990s and 2000s, a step was taken toward automated generation of variations, allowing designers to specify relationships between design parameters and to see the ripple effect of changes throughout the design system.

The modern stage of AI-enhanced design is a qualitative step ahead of parametric modelling. The existing AI-based tools do not simply perform predefined parameter variations: they train on datasets, come up with new solutions in given spaces of constraints and evolve their output, as per performance feedback. General design systems are the best example of this ability, a type of AI-based design tool that utilises algorithms, machine learning, and physics-based principles to generate, assess, and optimise design solutions within a set of specified constraints (Eren et al., 2024; Plocher & Panesar, 2019).

Generative design has been gaining momentum. The systematic search of the scholarly literature yielded more than 14,000 papers on the overlap of AI and generative design, 69.1% of which were published in 2021 and later - meaning that the growth is exponential (Tanveer et al., 2026). Such expansion is a sign of maturity of the underlying AI technologies as well as an increasing awareness of design circles that they are useful.

In addition to generative design, AI-optimized systems include natural language processing (facilitating textual design specification and concept generation), computer vision (facilitating aesthetic and structural analysis of visual design objects), and reinforcement learning (facilitating continuous optimization with simulated trial and error). The merging of these technologies in integrated design environments is creating what can be described as intelligent design systems - platforms where a combination of AI functions is used to aid the entire design process lifecycle.

3.3 Comparative Analysis: Traditional vs. AI-Enhanced Methodologies

The systematic comparison of conventional and AI-based design methodologies shows that there are great distinctions in various dimensions. Compared to the traditional methods, the AI-enhanced methods can help explore the solution spaces systematically, with a human cognitive capacity and time limitations being the key limiting factors in the traditional methods, and the ability of AI-enhanced methods to generate and assess thousands of alternatives in just a few hours. The generative design functionality in Fusion 360, as one example, has shown itself to be able to generate design solutions with more than 40%, 50%, and 60 percent mass reduction over expert-designed solutions in light-weighting research (Briard et al., 2020).

When it comes to the speed of iteration, AI-boosted processes can radically speed up the design process. At the preliminary design phase, AI tools like ChatGPT can be used to quickly brainstorm ideas and define concepts in text, whereas Midjourney and DALL-E generate instant visuals of initial design concepts- tools that designers of the previous generation simply could not access (Choudhury et al., 2025; Z. Zhang et al., 2023). At mid-stage design, AI improves prototyping by creating and analyzing structural configurations in silico, removing the many physical prototyping steps (Buonamici et al., 2020). At late design, AI will assist in the analysis of manufacturing and optimization of production workflow, which will reduce the development time even further (Gao et al., 2024).

In the context of decision support, the traditional approaches to the problem are based on expert heuristics and qualitative assessment, but AI-supported models also include quantitative, data-driven decision support. Predictive models are able to give an estimation of the performance of design variants prior to their being physically produced and hence allow more informed choices to be made when selecting among competing alternatives. This intuitive to evidence-based decision making does not dissolve the requirement of human judgment- especially in those spheres where aesthetic, cultural and ethical judgment is required, but it adds greatly to the informational base on which such judgment is based.

4. AI-DRIVEN CREATIVITY AND INNOVATION IN DESIGN

4.1 Redefining Creativity in AI-Augmented Environments

Design creativity has long been understood as a uniquely human ability, the capacity to produce original, valuable and surprising solutions to problems. The ability of AI systems to generate outputs meeting the traditional requirements of originality and usefulness is fundamentally questioning this perception. The GANs, trained on product design data, are able to generate variations of product forms that are aesthetically consistent and innovative to human evaluators (Yuan et al., 2022). Even the design briefs, concept narratives and functional specifications produced by large language models can be indistinguishable in quality to those produced by humans. Diffusion models are able to create photorealistic architectural imagery based on textual prompts.

These abilities do not make human creativity redundant, but change its location and character. Within AI-enhanced design workflows, human creativity is becoming more and more articulated in the form of design briefs, filtering of AI-generated options, instilling cultural and contextual sensitivity into AI output, and ethical control of automated processes. The function of the designer changes to an advanced organizer of a creative system, where human and machine smartness is involved (Fang et al., 2025). This redefinition is consistent with the theoretical differentiation made by Colton & Wiggins (2012) between creativity by AI systems (generative agent is the machine) and creativity with AI systems (AI is a partner that enhances human creative potential). Modern design practice is more and more a practice of both modes, with the balance appropriate to the nature of the work task, time constraints, and creative demands of the various stages of design relative to one another.

4.2 Generative AI Tools in Design Practice

Generative AI tools that can be used by modern designers have grown exponentially. Image generation models like DALL-E 3 (Ramesh et al., 2021) and Stable Diffusion (Rombach et al., 2022) allow designers to quickly visualize concept directions based on natural language prompts, provide inspiration, reference imagery, and initial concept representations at zero-time cost. Large language model-based text-based tools support user persona creation, design scenarios, competitive analysis, and marketing stories, which previously took users a long time to conduct research and write.

These capabilities are extended to the spatial realm by three-dimensional generative tools, such as Point-E and DreamFusion, which create three-dimensional shapes and structures based on textual or image prompts (Nichol et al., 2022). These tools promise specific benefits to industrial design, architecture, and engineering, where three-dimensional form is a major product. Such generative abilities, combined with physics-based simulation and additive manufacturing, provide a design-to-fabrication routeway of unprecedented velocity and versatility.

The opportunities and the challenges that the AI tools provide have been documented in the empirical studies of the application of these tools in designing practices. In a study comparing human and machine-generated creativity, L. Chen et al. (2023) discovered that although AI systems were very strong in creating variations within set stylistic parameters, human designers were much more capable of creating truly new conceptual framings that were not based on set conventions. According to this complement, the best creative results can be attained by strategic combination of human and machine input and not necessarily total replacement of one by the other.

A study of the efficiency of various AI-based design methodologies detected significant variations in the creativity of designs based on the design methodology applied to organize the AI contact (Chulvi, 2025). This relationship was also moderated by problem complexity, where more complex design problems had a greater positive impact on the AI aid- AI was most helpful in tackling the problem when human-only solution space is the most constrained.

4.3 The Role of AI in Early-Stage Ideation

There is a general understanding that creative potential is most abundant in the ideation stage of the design process, and that early limitations might be most destructive. Specifically, AI tools have proven useful at this stage by generating alternative concepts quickly, visually engaging, and with diversity, which can initiate and provoke human creative thought (Chandrasekera et al., 2024).

Based on the results of the empirical study of designers of different experience levels, the Human-AI Collaborative Creative Design Process (HAI-CDP) framework was created, which revealed a strong difference between novice and experienced designers in the interaction with AI tools during the ideation stage (Fang et al., 2025). More effective in guiding AI tools to generate relevant and quality outputs were experienced designers that adopt a breadth-first approach to problems and rely on previous project experience. The ability of AI to extend the ideation horizon beyond their personal point of view was very helpful to get novice designers, who are depth-first and linear explorers of problems. This result indicates that the role of AI in the initial ideation does not apply across all designer profiles but rather mediated by the creative orientation and experience of the designer.

The use of AI during pre-design (divergent) and post-design (convergent) is discussed within the framework of the Double Diamond model of the Design Council. A study of AI tools, such as ChatGPT, DALL-E, Midjourney, and Vizcom in a Golf

Cart Project and a Conceptual Car Project, revealed that AI tools facilitated the most, with a clear outlay as innovative prompts during the divergent phase, and as refinement aids during the convergent phase, a premeditated method that maintained human creative direction, without sacrificing AI generativity (Tang et al., 2024).

5. ITERATIVE DESIGN ACCELERATION THROUGH AI

5.1 AI and the Compression of Design Cycles

Design quality is built upon iteration - the more the design passes through the generation, evaluation, and refinement process, the more the solution space is exhaustively searched and the more likely that the final product will be optimal. Iteration is also time and resource consuming, however, and this presents a practical conflict between completeness and economy in the design practice of the real world. AI technologies directly respond to this tension by making the iterative process much faster.

Traditional design practice in traditional design practice, every iteration cycle took a lot of manual effort: a new design variant is sketched or modelled, its properties are tested by physical experiments or evaluated by experts, and the results of the evaluation are used in the next design variation. Each significant design cycle might require days or weeks to accomplish this. AIs have completely different timescales: generative algorithms can create thousands of design options within a few hours, simulation systems can simulate performance without actually creating the object, and machine learning systems can process the results of evaluations to inform the next generation cycles (Bilgram & Laarmann, 2023).

There are a number of significant implications of this compression of the iterative cycle to design practice. First, it allows searching a far broader solution space within a certain developmental timeline, which is likely to result in finding quality, innovative solutions. Second, it enables a larger scale user testing and feedback integration, because design variants can be created and tested much faster in response to user feedback. Third, it moves the bottleneck on the design process not by the velocity of iteration but the quality of evaluation- the binding factor is not how fast new designs can be created but how effectively human designers can assess and direct AI generated designs.

5.2 Topology Optimization and Structural Iteration

Topology optimization Structurally optimizing the material layout of a prescribed design space to a set of loads, boundary conditions, and performance constraints is a mathematical approach to optimization. Topology optimization, combined with AI, is an effective means of structual design through iterative optimization that can point to counter-intuitive structural arrangements with better performance properties. M.-T. Chen et al. (2024) showed parametric topology optimization of additively manufactured joints in spatial grid structures, where structural efficiency was significantly improved as compared to traditional design methods.

Topology optimization coupled with additive manufacturing has resulted in a highly effective iterative design ability. Since additive manufacturing can create geometrically complex structures that would be either impossible or prohibitively expensive to create using a more traditional manufacturing process, AI-generated topologically optimized structures can be produced directly, without geometric simplification in order to be manufacturable. Such design-to-fabrication integration removes a whole category of design constraints, and increases the solution space of AI-enhanced iterative design systems.

5.3 Real-Time Feedback and Adaptive Design Systems

Now, more sophisticated AI-based design environments include real-time feedback systems that allow adaptive iteration, the continual modification of design parameters in reaction to the ongoing performance analysis. Within the context of user experience design, AI systems can process user interaction data on the fly, detecting usability problems, and creating new interface setups that can solve identified problems. Following product design, AI systems would be able to combine sensor data of prototype testing to continually improve material specifications and geometric configurations. Fan et al. (2021) showed the effectiveness of AI-based visualisation tools in analysing think-aloud content in user testing as they were able to extract usability insights more quickly and in a more organised manner. Fan et al. (2021) also demonstrated that human-AI cooperation in UX review, with AI systems giving initial reviews and explanations that are then reviewed and optimized by human evaluators, yielded more consistent and multifaceted reviews compared to human-only and AI-only evaluations. The papers demonstrate how AI can expedite the production of design options as well as evaluation mechanisms that inform the iterative improvement process.

6. DATA-DRIVEN DECISION-MAKING IN AI-SUPPORTED DESIGN SYSTEMS

6.1 From Intuitive to Evidence-Based Design Decisions

The historical character of design decision-making has been typified by dependence on expert intuition, aesthetic judgment and reasoning by precedent. Although these kinds of tacit knowledge are indeed valuable sources of cognitive resources, they are necessarily constrained in their processing capabilities with respect to processing large amounts of quantitative information and patterns in complex, multivariate design spaces. The decision support provided by AI systems, especially trained machine learning models based on comprehensive datasets on design and performance, can be fundamentally different, as it is based on empirical evidence, not personal intuition.

The trend toward decision-making in design based on data is especially apparent in areas where performance measures can be measured and where extensive data sets of previous design performances exist. In structural engineering, AI models that have learned the results of finite element analysis can be used to estimate the structural performance of novel design configurations with high accuracy, and do so in seconds, avoiding the computational cost of complete simulation to weed out poor-performing alternatives. In user experience design, AI models, trained on large scale user interaction data, are more reliable than expert heuristic assessment in predicting the usability of interface designs (Lu et al., 2022).

This does not mean that human judgment is rendered obsolete by this shift in intuitive decision-making to the evidence-based decision-making. Instead, it reinvents the position of a human judgment as the main judge of the design quality into the position of the interpreter and the contextualizer of AI-based recommendations. The human designers subject to the decision process inject into its knowledge of cultural context, user values, ethical implications, and organizational constraints that cannot be modeled in the quantitative data sets where AI systems are trained. Combining these mutually complementary bodies of knowledge, machine-created quantitative evidence and human judgment of a context, constitutes the best paradigm to AI-aided design decision-making.

6.2 Multi-Objective Optimization and Trade-off Analysis

Design decisions in the real world are usually made where several, and usually conflicting, objectives are to be optimised simultaneously. An example of a product design would need to be optimized in terms of structural performance, manufacturing cost, aesthetic appeal, user ergonomics, environmental impact, and regulatory compliance. Conventional design methods handle these conflicting goals by prioritizing them sequentially and engaging in a process of negotiation among members of the design team, who have diverse expertise areas. By improving AI methods allow considering several objectives simultaneously with multi-objective optimization algorithms, which yield Pareto-optimal sets of solutions that capture the entire collection of possible trade-offs between competing criteria. Generative design via multi-objective optimization has been proven in a variety of areas. The authors Zhang et al. (2023) showed how to do multi-objective generative design of three-dimensional material structures that could optimize both mechanical performance and manufacturing feasibility. Javidannia et al. (2021) used the multi-objective generative design workflow to the seismic-efficient construction of high-rise buildings and showed that AI-driven optimization can solve the problem of complex interaction of structural, aesthetic, and regulatory considerations.

The display and presentation of multi-objective optimization results is a design problem itself. Optimization methods require that decision-makers without proper training in optimization methods know how to navigate the trade-off space that Pareto-optimal solution sets represent so as to make informed decisions in selection. Studies on decision support systems to support multi-objective optimization in design have also emphasized the role of interactive visualization interfaces to allow designers to explore the trade-off space, realize the consequences of various design decisions, and refine their preferences iteratively based on AI-recommended insights (Chong et al., 2022).

6.3 Predictive Modelling and Risk Reduction

The most practically important application of AI to design decision-making is predictive modelling, the application of AI systems to predict the performance or the results of design options without their physical implementation. By helping designers to estimate the impact of design decisions at earlier design stages, predictive modelling can significantly decrease the cost and risk of making design decisions and product failures late in the design process.

Song et al. (2023) proposed surrogate modelling methods to predict the aerodynamic drag coefficient of automotive designs that are based on depth and normal renderings, showing how AI predictive models may substitute computationally demanding computational fluid dynamics simulations in design assessment at the early design stages. The application is an example of a larger trend where AI surrogate models modeled on existing simulation or experimental data can be used to give fast, cheap approximations of expensive physical performance metrics, allowing exploration of the design space much wider in practice due to time and resource limits.

Deep learning has also broadened the horizons of predictive modelling in design. Eren et al. (2024) has shown that deep learning facilitated design of tailored mechanical properties of additively manufactured metallic lattice structures, making it possible to predict and optimize complex material-structure relationships that cannot be predicted and optimized by conventional analytical models. Examples of such applications demonstrate how AI predictive modelling can push the limits of what can be designed to produce products with performance characteristics that were previously impossible to reliably specify or obtain.

7. A CONCEPTUAL MODEL FOR AI-INTEGRATED DESIGN METHODOLOGIES

7.1 Model Overview

Based on the theoretical backgrounds and empirical data discussed in the previous chapters, the chapter has suggested a conceptual framework of AI-based design approaches-Human-AI Design Intelligence (HADI) model. The HADI model theorizes the AI-enabled design process as a dynamic and two-way system where human creative intelligence and machine computational intelligence engage each other via organized collaborative interfaces to generate design results that are beyond the ability of any of the parties to generate, working alone.

The model design revolves around four domains, which are interrelated and reflect the major stages and aspects of the design process, i.e., Creative Ideation, Iterative Generation, Evidence-Based Selection, and Reflective Refinement. Individual domains can be defined as having a specific allocation of human and machine input, which is mediated by interactive interfaces, through which human intentions can be effectively communicated with AI outputs and the other way around.

7.2 Domain 1: Creative Ideation

The human designers express the design problems, user requirements and creative directions in the Creative Ideation domain by defining them using natural language briefs, reference imagery and constraint specifications. These inputs are then converted into various sets of initial concepts, mood boards and design directions through AI tools, such as large language models, image generation systems, and concept synthesis algorithms. The main role of the human designer in this area is the curatorial and creative director: choosing, mixing, and repurposing AI-generated ideas in accordance with the upper-level creative vision and contextual awareness.

The HADI model has found three success factors to effective AI-assisted ideation, namely the clarity and richness of the brief provided to the AI (which defines the quality of the generative input); the variety of the concept set generated by the AI (which defines the breadth of the explored solution space); and the ability of the designer to critically evaluate and synthesize the output (which defines the quality of the curated output). Designer training with AI systems on short formulation (also known as prompt engineering) is thus found to be a key area of professional development in AI-enhanced design education.

7.3 Domain 2: Iterative Generation

Within the Iterative Generation domain, the chosen concept directions are elaborated in terms of design alternatives using AI-based generative methods. Topology optimization algorithms, generative adversarial networks, and physics-based simulation tools generate performance-optimal design variants in the constraint spaces that are defined by the concept direction. These variants are evaluated by the human designers on aesthetic, functional, and contextual grounds and the feedback is used to inform the next generation cycles.

HADI model focuses on the need to ensure that the human creative agency is sustained in the process of iterative generation. One such area is the risk of an AI-generated output being automatically trusted, known as the automation bias, which is particularly severe in this field, where the amount and the analytical complexity of AI-generated outputs can overload the human designer. The model supports the use of systematic assessment procedures in which the designer clearly explains why he/she made specific design choices, and therefore maintain the deliberative nature of the design decision-making process.

7.4 Domain 3: Evidence-Based Selection

The most promising design solutions of the iterative generation process undergo quantitative performance assessment with the help of AI predictive models, simulation, and data-driven evaluation frameworks in the Evidence-Based Selection domain. Multi-objective optimization methods determine Pareto-optimal trade-offs between competing design criteria, and visualization tools used in an interactive manner allow designers and stakeholders to navigate the trade-off space and to make informed selection choices. According to the HADI model, the human confidence in AI recommendations is a crucial consideration in this field (Chong et al., 2022). Inappropriately calibrated designers, who tend to trust AI advice when the evidence in the AI is high, and to independently reason when the situation or ethics play central roles, can achieve improved performance than those who are systematically over or under-trusting. This calibration can be achieved through a mix of AI literacy education, open AI elucidation systems, and cultures in the organization that appreciate critical interaction with AI suggestions.

7.5 Domain 4: Reflective Refinement

At Reflective Refinement, design solutions are refined with a series of iterations in a cyclical process of user testing, feedback analysis, and design modification. The AI applications in this sector are user behaviour analytics, sentiment analysis and automated usability testing systems. Refinement decisions made by human designers view AI-generated insights in the framework of a qualitative user study, cultural aspects, and strategic organizational goals and combine quantitative evidence with contextual wisdom.

The HADI model emphasizes specifically the reflective aspect of this area the ability of the designer to critically assess the design solution, as well as the design process with the assistance of AI. This meta-level awareness is critical towards determining and rectifying systematic biases in AI-generated outputs, in building the professional judgment needed to successfully collaborate with AI, and in contributing to the organizational learning that leads to the continued enhancement of AI-enhanced design capacity.

8. CHALLENGES AND ETHICAL CONSIDERATIONS IN AI-ENHANCED DESIGN

8.1 Over-Reliance on Automation and Loss of Creative Control

The loss of creative agency and professional competence of the designer as a result of excessive dependence on the automated systems is one of the most serious risks that the broad adoption of AI in the design is likely to introduce. When AI solutions create quality outputs seemingly so easily, it is tempting to decrease the amount of critical thinking and creativity with which designers approach the design process. With time this trend of decreased involvement may diminish the tacit knowledge, artistic judgment and innovative ability that are the professional knowledge of the designer.

This risk has been proven to exist. In a warning study, G. Zhang et al. (2021) discovered that AI support might suppress design teams that perform well when it decreased the range of ideas pursued and created an illusion of false security in

AI-generated solutions. Chulvi (2025) discovered that AI assistance might have a detrimental impact on the learning process of the novice designers, as it diminishes the productive struggle within which the design skills are built. These results demonstrate the significance of pedagogically deliberate attitudes to AI integration in design education and procedure- approaches that involve AI as an augmentation of creative potential instead of creative diligence. The issue of homogenization of creative outputs is also important. With many designers relying on the same generative AI models, which are trained on the same sets of data, it is possible that the variety of possible design outputs will diminish - that an algorithmic aesthetic monoculture will be created, which reflects the taste in style that is instilled in the training data.

8.2 Algorithmic Bias and Fairness

Training datasets define what AI systems can do, and the quality, diversity and representativeness of the training datasets is the primary determinant of how good and fair AI outputs will be. When the training datasets are biased, i.e. they are based on the culture, past, or demographic of a certain population, the resulting AI systems will reproduce these biases in their outputs and even possibly exaggerate them (Baker & Hawn, 2022). Algorithms bias has several destructive forms in the context of design: UX designs that are not user friendly to individuals with disabilities, architectural designs that fail to capture the cultural and spatial interests of different communities, product designs that are ergonomics friendly to certain groups of users and not others.

To reduce algorithmic bias in AI-enhanced design, interventions are needed on several levels. On the data level, it presupposes creating training datasets that will fully reflect the variety of users, cultural situations, and design traditions that AI design tools are expected to address. On the algorithmic level, it demands the creation of equity-conscious AI models that explicitly consider equity criteria during optimization processes. At the practitioner level, it involves inculcating critical AI literacy in designers, or the ability to detect, question, and rectify AI-generated content that reflects biased assumptions.

8.3 Intellectual Property and Authorship

Generative AI tools and design the application of generative AI tools to design raises complicated and unresolved questions on intellectual property and authorship to works of creativity. In the case of a designer employing an AI system to produce a design idea, who owns the intellectual property rights to the output of the product- a designer, the developers of the AI system or the creators of the training data on which the AI was trained? These questions have important practical implications to the commercial design business where intellectual property protection is a fundamental business value. In most jurisdictions, the legal environment of AI-generated creative works is unstable. The U.S. Copyright Office has embarked on a project to research the copyright law and policy implications by generative AI, as they demonstrate an awareness that current intellectual property schemes, which were developed prior to the emergence of generative AI, might not be sufficient to answer the new questions that such technologies pose. In their review of ethical issues and ways of addressing them in relation to generative AI, Al-kfairy et al. (2024) observed that the fact that generative AI can create compelling synthetic content endangers the principles of creative authenticity and attribution, which are the core values of both the artistic and commercial design practice. In addition to the legal concerns, there is also an underlying ethical aspect of using existing work of artists and designers to train generative AI models without their knowledge or without their permission or payment. It has been widely voiced by artists and designers that their creative work is being commodified without their knowledge, with AI systems crawling through professional portfolios and design archives to create the training data set on which commercial AI services are based (Lovato et al., 2024). To overcome these issues, consent frameworks, attribution mechanisms, and compensation models that accommodate the rights and interests of human creators and allow AI design capabilities to be developed beneficially should be developed.

8.4 Transparency, Explainability, and Accountability

The black box nature of most AI systems, especially deep learning models, is a big problem in their application in design decision-making scenarios. Whenever an AI system is suggesting a specific design setup or making predictions about a specific performance result, designers and stakeholders must know what the basis of the suggestion is, to determine how reliable it may be and what biases it may have as well as to make a wise decision on whether to take action on it or not. This understanding is not an easy task due to the inability to explain many AI systems, which in turn poses a threat of consequential design decisions being made based on AI recommendations that cannot be critically evaluated.

Active research on the creation of Explainable AI (XAI) techniques: approaches to making decision processes of AI systems more transparent and interpretable has a direct impact on design practice. Stahl & Eke (2024) addressed the ethics of opaque AI systems in various areas, highlighting the role of transparency and explainability as a priori to the possibility of informed consent and meaningful human control of AI-assisted processes. In the context of design, this principle will become a demand that AI tools offer not just recommendations but also explanations on the level of comprehensibility of the evidential basis and assumptions on which those recommendations are made.

Ethical responsibility towards AIs-supported design results is a connected issue. Professional accountability is evidently placed within the human designer and the commissioning organization in the traditional design practice. In AI-enhanced design, the distributed form of the design process, which includes human designers, AI tools, training data suppliers, and platform developers, makes it hard to determine who should take responsibility in the event of design failures. The development of clear accountability frameworks for AI-assisted design is an important professional and regulatory priority.

8.5 Environmental and Sustainability Considerations

Calculation machines used to train and run large-scale AI models are associated with a high environmental price. Sub-training a huge foundation model may emit as much carbon as several transatlantic flights, which is a valid question about the environmental sustainability of widespread AI use in design (and other fields). It is well to note that, with the growing emphasis of design professionals on environmental sustainability as a design criterion, practitioners must be conscious of and consider the environmental footprint of the AI tools they use.

On the other hand, AI-assisted design processes have a great potential in mitigating the environmental consequences of design deliverables through the ability to create more material-efficient, energy-efficient and lifecycle-optimal products and systems. The already proven ability of generative design to cut the amount of materials used by 40-60 percent in structural applications is a direct input to the environmental sustainability that has to be counterbalanced with the computational cost of the AI tools that give rise to the given designs. An all-inclusive sustainability evaluation of AI-powered design techniques should consider these two dimensions.

9. PRACTICAL STRATEGIES FOR INTEGRATING AI INTO DESIGN WORKFLOWS

9.1 Phased Integration and Capability Building

Companies aiming to implement AI within their design processes would struggle to go all the way to AI literacy and operational capacity at once as they manage the risk of becoming over-dependant on AI tools prior to the development of the requisite critical capabilities. A preliminary stage of AI-based research and reference creation (applying AI tools to assemble competitive analyses, user research summaries, and visual reference libraries) allows designers to get used to the real-world usefulness of AI support in low-stakes settings as they learn the habit of critically perceiving AI outputs. Later steps can gradually integrate AI tools into the ideation, prototyping, and evaluation processes as the organizational AI literacy and governance capacities evolve.

9.2 Developing AI Literacy in Design Education and Practice

The introduction of AI into design practice necessitates a novel professional skillset, which is not sufficiently covered by the existing design education curriculum. Those competencies are: the skills to write effective and efficient briefs to AI generative systems (prompt engineering); the skills to assess and critique the output of AI systems to identify quality, bias, and contextual suitability; the knowledge of the technical principles underlying the major AI technologies to make sensible judgments about their capabilities and constraints; and the knowledge of the ethical, legal, and intellectual property implications of using AI tools in professional design practice.

Design educators are starting to realize the significance of cultivating these competencies, and some educational establishments are specifically integrating AI tools and AI literacy into studio-based design programs. Bartlett & D. Camba (2024) presented methods to teach generative AI in product design courses, responding to the unique needs of originality, ethics, and critical thinking that emerge when learners utilize AI-created content in their design studies. Their results emphasize the need to introduce clear pedagogical frameworks that can help students learn to utilize AI as a creative partner, but not a solution that can help them avoid the healthy competition of design thinking.

9.3 Establishing Organizational Governance Frameworks

Firms implementing AI technology in the design processes require robust governance policies to determine the correct level of AI implementation, set of guidelines to critically evaluate AI results and responsibilities of human designers to quality and implications of AI-aided design decisions. Such frameworks must respond to intellectual property attribution of AI-assisted creative work, guidelines on how to identify and remedy algorithmic bias in AI-generated work and processes of documenting the AI tools and datasets involved in the generation of design solutions a kind of transparency and accountability-enabling design provenance.

10. RESULTS AND FINDINGS

This chapter reviews the theoretical and empirical literature to determine the outcomes of AI-driven design methods. The results are grouped into thematic areas of efficiency, creativity, decision-making and relative performance.

10.1 Findings on Design Efficiency and Iteration

Our analysis shows that Artificial Intelligence speeds up the design process by reducing the time of iteration. Conventional design processes involve manual prototyping, experimentation and iteration, which can take time. However, AI-driven generative design tools can generate and test thousands of design options within hours. The studies reviewed here show the use of AI-based simulation and optimization tools helps to eliminate the need for extensive prototyping and allows rapid evaluation of design ideas. This boosts efficiency and enables designers to search for solutions in larger solution spaces within a given time frame.

10.2 Findings on Creativity and Ideation

The results indicate AI has a profound impact on creativity in the design process. Generative AI applications enable the generation of diverse design ideas, encouraging divergent thinking in the early phases of design. But the evidence suggests that although AI tools generate variations within established patterns, designers are better at generating context-specific and conceptually novel ideas. So, creativity in AI-enhanced design is an amalgam of human intuition and machine-generated diversity.

10.3 Findings on Decision-Making and Optimization

In our analysis, we identified a shift from intuition-based to data-driven decision-making and design evaluation. AI technologies support predictive analysis, performance simulation, and multi-criteria optimization, enabling designers to evaluate potential design outcomes before they are built. This alleviates risk, uncertainty, and aids in informed choice-making among design options. However, human input is critical in making decisions based on AI insights, especially when dealing with ethics, aesthetics and relevance.

10.4 Comparative Findings: Traditional vs AI-Enhanced Design

The comparative study shows significant disparities between traditional and AI-enhanced design approaches on several fronts. AI-enhanced solutions offer faster, scalable and more analytical solutions, whereas traditional systems remain stronger in contextual awareness and originality.

Table 1. Comparative Analysis of Design Methodologies

Dimension	Traditional Design	AI-Enhanced Design
Iteration Speed	Slow and manual	Rapid and automated
Solution Space	Limited by human cognition	Extensive and data-driven
Creativity	Human-driven	Human-AI collaborative
Decision-Making	Intuition-based	Evidence-based
Prototyping	Physical and time-consuming	Simulation-based and efficient

10.5 Quantitative Insights from Literature

Our analysis of reviewed studies offers indicative quantitative evidence of AI effectiveness in design. For example, generative design tools have shown 40-60% optimisation of material in structural parts while enhancing efficiency. Furthermore, the most recent literature trends show that much of the work in generative design has been published since 2021, reflecting the growth in the field.

10.6 Implications for the HADI Model

The results provide strong evidence for the proposed Human-AI Design Intelligence (HADI) model. The four areas of the model - Creative Ideation, Iterative Generation, Evidence-Based Selection and Reflective Refinement - are supported by empirical evidence of AI-enhanced design systems.

The findings verify that the best design solutions are achieved through a harmonious blend of human and machine intelligence, rather than employing either alone.

11. DISCUSSION

The combination of theoretical models and empirical data in this chapter helps to draw a number of general conclusions regarding what AI-enhanced design methods are and where they are heading. First, it is evident that AI does not displace human designers but essentially re-configures their position and the type of creative input they provide. The winning AI-enhanced design practice is not defined by the ousting of human judgment but by the promotion of the same to a superior level of abstraction, namely, the implementation of design details to the guidance of intelligent systems that are capable of processing the same details as fast and analytically sophisticated than the individual human designer. Second, the value of AI as a creative partner at the initial phases of the design process is strongly supported by the evidence of the ability of AI to provide a wide range of concept alternatives that are both diverse and rich in visual content and may greatly enlarge the solution space discussed by human design teams. Meanwhile, the evidence also indicates the danger that AI-mediated ideation, when adopted blindly, can result in the homogenization of creative output, a kind of aesthetic convergence based on the statistical regularities of the AI training data instead of cultural diversity and sensitivity to context that is typical of the most effective practice of design by humans. Third, ethical aspects of AI-enhanced design, such as algorithmic bias, intellectual property uncertainty, lack of transparency, and environmental costs, are real and pressing issues that the design community needs to overcome by employing a set of professional standards creation, regulatory interactions, and pedagogical innovation. The rate of AI development has far exceeded the rate at which the ethical, legal, and professional frameworks to regulate responsible deployment of AI in design practice have been created. Fourth, the HADI model suggested in this chapter provides a systematic conceptual framework to comprehend and structure the human-AI partnership in design. The model offers a practical guide to the design of AI-accelerated design workflows that do not compromise human creative agency, but achieve the efficiency and innovation benefits AI tools can offer by explicitly specifying the complementary roles of human and machine intelligence in four areas of the design process: Creative Ideation, Iterative Generation, Evidence-Based Selection, and Reflective Refinement.

12. CONCLUSION

The introduction of AI-enhanced design processes can be viewed as one of the most drastic changes in the history of design as a profession. AI technologies are pushing the limits of what can be designed, achieved, and innovated by making vast solution spaces combinable, accelerating iterative cycles, supporting evidence-based decision-making, and unlocking new types of collaborative creativity, which could not be imagined during the purely human-led design practice. The revolution caused by AI is not a mere tale of technological advancement. An intricate, contentious, and consequential process, it begs some basic questions concerning the nature of creativity, the allocation of authorship and intellectual property rights, the sense of fairness and transparency of algorithmic systems, and the future of AI dependency on the evolution of human creative expertise. These questions entail stringent academic research, reflective professional practice, and sound ethical governance, all of which entail the enduring investment of intellectual and institutional capital. Human-AI Design Intelligence (HADI) model presented in this chapter provides a way to make sense of this complicated landscape by clearly defining the complementary roles of human and machine intelligence and determining the conditions under which their interaction can work effectively. The model is not provided as a prescriptive template but rather as a theoretical framework that can be tailored and expanded to suit the various contexts of design practice and the ever-changing capabilities of AI technology. The quality, creativity, and human value of the design results of AI-enhanced design methodologies are the final evaluations. In this respect, the evidence analyzed in this chapter is optimistic: AI-enhanced design has shown the ability to create structurally superior, materially efficient, and creatively rich designs in various design fields. It takes being mindful of this potential, and in a way that is both responsible and constant, not only technical savvy but the wisdom of man, the critical, reflective and ethically conscious judgment that has and will continue to have no analog in the intelligent design systems of the intelligent age.

REFERENCES

Al-kfairy, M., Mustafa, D., Kshetri, N., Insiew, M., & Alfandi, O. (2024). Ethical Challenges and Solutions of Generative AI: An Interdisciplinary Perspective. *Informatics (MDPI), 11*(3), 58. DOI: 10.3390/informatics11030058

Amankwah-Amoah, J., Abdalla, S., Mogaji, E., Elbanna, A., & Dwivedi, Y. K. (2024). The impending disruption of creative industries by generative AI: Opportunities, challenges, and research agenda. *International Journal of Information Management, 79*, 102759. DOI: 10.1016/j.ijinfomgt.2024.102759

Baker, R. S., & Hawn, A. (2022). Algorithmic Bias in Education. *International Journal of Artificial Intelligence in Education, 32*(4), 1052–1092. DOI: 10.1007/s40593-021-00285-9

Barbieri, L., & Muzzupappa, M. (2024). Form innovation: Investigating the use of generative design tools to encourage creativity in product design. *International Journal of Design Creativity and Innovation, 12*(3), 163–182. DOI: 10.1080/21650349.2024.2336972

Bartlett, K., & Camba, D., J. (. (2024). Generative Artificial Intelligence in Product Design Education: Navigating Concerns of Originality and Ethics. *International Journal of Interactive Multimedia and Artificial Intelligence, 8*, 55–64. DOI: 10.9781/ijimai.2024.02.006

Bilgram, V., & Laarmann, F. (2023). Accelerating Innovation With Generative AI: AI-Augmented Digital Prototyping and Innovation Methods. *IEEE Engineering Management Review, 1–5*(2), 18–25. Advance online publication. DOI: 10.1109/EMR.2023.3272799

Briard, T., Segonds, F., & Zamariola, N. (2020). G-DfAM: A methodological proposal of generative design for additive manufacturing in the automotive industry. [IJIDeM]. *International Journal on Interactive Design and Manufacturing, 14*(3), 875–886. DOI: 10.1007/s12008-020-00669-6

Buonamici, F., Carfagni, M., Furferi, R., Volpe, Y., & Governi, L. (2020). Generative Design: An Explorative Study. *Computer-Aided Design and Applications, 18*(1), 144–155. DOI: 10.14733/cadaps.2021.144-155

Chandrasekera, T., Hosseini, Z., & Perera, U. (2024). Can artificial intelligence support creativity in early design processes? *International Journal of Architectural Computing, 23*(1), 122–136. Advance online publication. DOI: 10.1177/14780771241254637

Chen, L., Sun, L., & Han, J. (2023). A Comparison Study of Human and Machine Generated Creativity. *Journal of Computing and Information Science in Engineering*, *23*(5), 1–37. DOI: 10.1115/1.4062232

Chen, L., Wang, P., Dong, H., Shi, F., Han, J., Guo, Y., Childs, P. R. N., Xiao, J., & Wu, C. (2019). An artificial intelligence based data-driven approach for design ideation. *Journal of Visual Communication and Image Representation*, *61*, 10–22. DOI: 10.1016/j.jvcir.2019.02.009

Chen, M.-T., Zuo, W., Chen, Y., Cheng, B., & Zhao, J. (2024). Parametric topology optimization design and analysis of additively manufactured joints in spatial grid structures. *Engineering Structures*, *300*, 117123. DOI: 10.1016/j.engstruct.2023.117123

Chong, L., Raina, A., Goucher-Lambert, K., Kotovsky, K., & Cagan, J. (2022). The Evolution and Impact of Human Confidence in Artificial Intelligence and in Themselves on AI-Assisted Decision-Making in Design. *Journal of Mechanical Design*, *145*(3), 031401. Advance online publication. DOI: 10.1115/1.4055123

Choudhury, M., Eisenbart, B., & Kuys, B. (2025). Artificial intelligence (AI) in the design process – a review and analysis on generative AI perspectives. *Proceedings of the Design Society*, *5*, 631–640. DOI: 10.1017/pds.2025.10077

Chulvi, V. (2025). Effectiveness of the AI using different typologies of design methods. *Research in Engineering Design*, *36*(2), 7. DOI: 10.1007/s00163-025-00449-x

Colton, S., & Wiggins, G. (2012). Computational Creativity: The Final Frontier? In *Frontiers in Artificial Intelligence and Applications* (Vol. 242, pp. 21–26). DOI: 10.3233/978-1-61499-098-7-21

Cross, N. (2023). *Design Thinking: Understanding How Designers Think and Work*. Bloomsbury Publishing. DOI: 10.5040/9781350305090

Dellermann, D., Calma, A., Lipusch, N., Weber, T., Weigel, S., & Ebel, P. (2019). *The Future of Human-AI Collaboration: A Taxonomy of Design Knowledge for Hybrid Intelligence Systems*. DOI: 10.24251/HICSS.2019.034

Eren, O., Yüksel, N., Borklu, H., Sezer, H. K., & Canyurt, O. (2024). Deep learning-enabled design for tailored mechanical properties of SLM-manufactured metallic lattice structures. *Engineering Applications of Artificial Intelligence*, *130*, 107685. DOI: 10.1016/j.engappai.2023.107685

Fan, M., Yang, X., Yu, T. T., Liao, V. Q., & Zhao, J. (2021). *Human-AI Collaboration for UX Evaluation: Effects of Explanation and Synchronization* (arXiv:2112.12387). arXiv. https://doi.org//arXiv.2112.12387DOI: 10.48550

Fang, C., Zhu, Y., Fang, L., Long, Y., Lin, H., Cong, Y., & Wang, S. J. (2025). Generative AI-enhanced human-AI collaborative conceptual design: A systematic literature review. *Design Studies*, *97*, 101300. DOI: 10.1016/j.destud.2025.101300

Gajjar, N., Pandian, V., Suleri, S., & Jarke, M. (2021). *Akin: Generating UI Wireframes From UI Design Patterns Using Deep Learning*. DOI: 10.1145/3397482.3450727

Gao, R. X., Krüger, J., Merklein, M., Möhring, H.-C., & Váncza, J. (2024). Artificial Intelligence in manufacturing: State of the art, perspectives, and future directions. *CIRP Annals*, *73*(2), 723–749. DOI: 10.1016/j.cirp.2024.04.101

Javidannia, G., Bemanian, M. R., Mahdavinejad, M., Nejat, S. A., & Javidannia, L. (2021). *Generative Design Workflow for Seismic-Efficient Architectural Design of Tall Buildings; A Multi-object Optimization approach.*

Lovato, J., Zimmerman, J., Smith, I., Dodds, P., & Karson, J. (2024). *Foregrounding Artist Opinions: A Survey Study on Transparency, Ownership, and Fairness in AI Generative Art*. https://doi.org/DOI: 10.48550/ARXIV.2401.15497

Lu, Y., Zhang, C., Zhang, I., & Li, T. J.-J. (2022). Bridging the Gap Between UX Practitioners' Work Practices and AI-Enabled Design Support Tools. *CHI Conference on Human Factors in Computing Systems Extended Abstracts*, 1–7. DOI: 10.1145/3491101.3519809

Nichol, A., Jun, H., Dhariwal, P., Mishkin, P., & Chen, M. (2022). *Point-E: A System for Generating 3D Point Clouds from Complex Prompts*. https://doi.org//arXiv.2212.08751DOI: 10.48550

Plocher, J., & Panesar, A. (2019). Review on design and structural optimisation in additive manufacturing: Towards next-generation lightweight structures. *Materials & Design*, *108164*, 108164. Advance online publication. DOI: 10.1016/j.matdes.2019.108164

Ramesh, A., Pavlov, M., Goh, G., Gray, S., Voss, C., Radford, A., Chen, M., & Sutskever, I. (2021). Zero-Shot Text-to-Image Generation. *ArXiv*. https://www.semanticscholar.org/paper/Zero-Shot-Text-to-Image-Generation-Ramesh-Pavlov/2cd605106b88c85d7d8b865b1ef0f8c8293debf1

Rombach, R., Blattmann, A., Lorenz, D., Esser, P., & Ommer, B. (2022). High-Resolution Image Synthesis with Latent Diffusion Models. *2022 IEEE/CVF Conference on Computer Vision and Pattern Recognition (CVPR)*, 10674–10685. 2022 IEEE/CVF Conference on Computer Vision and Pattern Recognition (CVPR). DOI: 10.1109/CVPR52688.2022.01042

Russell, S., & Norvig, P. (2021). *Artificial Intelligence: A Modern Approach, Global Edition*. Pearson Higher Ed.

Sengar, S. S., Hasan, A. B., Kumar, S., & Carroll, F. (2025). Generative artificial intelligence: A systematic review and applications. *Multimedia Tools and Applications, 84*(21), 23661–23700. DOI: 10.1007/s11042-024-20016-1

She, J., & Cetinic, E. (2022). Understanding and Creating Art with AI: Review and Outlook. *ACM Transactions on Multimedia Computing Communications and Applications, 18*(2), 1–22. DOI: 10.1145/3475799

Simon, H. A. (1996). *The Sciences of the Artificial* (3rd ed.). MIT Press.

Song, B., Yuan, C., Permenter, F., Arechiga, N., & Ahmed, F. (2023). *Surrogate Modeling of Car Drag Coefficient with Depth and Normal Renderings*. /arXiv.2306.06110DOI: 10.1115/DETC2023-117400

Stahl, B., & Eke, D. (2024). The ethics of ChatGPT -Exploring the ethical issues of an emerging technology. *International Journal of Information Management, 74*, 102700. Advance online publication. DOI: 10.1016/j.ijinfomgt.2023.102700

Tang, X., Windham, J., & Bush, B. (2024). Pre-AI and post-AI design: Balancing human Creativity and AI Tools in the Industrial Design Process. *Proceeding of the 2024 International Conference on Artificial Intelligence and Future Education*, 100–108. AIFE 2024: 2024 International Conference on Artificial Intelligence and Future Education. DOI: 10.1145/3708394.3708413

Tanveer, M., Azad, M. M., Kim, D., Khalid, S., & Kim, H. S. (2026). Generative Design for Engineering Applications: A State-of-the-Art Review. *Archives of Computational Methods in Engineering, 33*(1), 53–79. DOI: 10.1007/s11831-025-10302-y

Vaccaro, M., Almaatouq, A., & Malone, T. (2024). When combinations of humans and AI are useful: A systematic review and meta-analysis. *Nature Human Behaviour, 8*(12), 2293–2303. DOI: 10.1038/s41562-024-02024-1 PMID: 39468277

Wu, Z., Ji, D., Yu, K., Zeng, X., Wu, D., & Shidujaman, M. (2021). In Kurosu, M. (Ed.), *AI Creativity and the Human-AI Co-creation Model* (Vol. 12762, pp. 171–190). Springer International Publishing., DOI: 10.1007/978-3-030-78462-1_13

Yuan, C., Marion, T., & Moghaddam, M. (2022). DDE-GAN: Integrating a Data-Driven Design Evaluator Into Generative Adversarial Networks for Desirable and Diverse Concept Generation. *Journal of Mechanical Design, 145*(4), 1–18. DOI: 10.1115/1.4056500

Zhang, G., Raina, A., Cagan, J., & Mccomb, C. (2021). A cautionary tale about the impact of AI on human design teams. *Design Studies*, *72*, 100990. DOI: 10.1016/j.destud.2021.100990

Zhang, Z., Fang, H., Xu, Z., Lv, J., Shen, Y., & Wang, Y. (2023). Multi-objective generative design of three-dimensional material structures. *APL Machine Learning*, *1*(4), 046120. Advance online publication. DOI: 10.1063/5.0169432

Chapter 3

MentoraGen Integrating AI-Driven Socratic Scaffolding Into the Design of Pedagogically-Aligned Programming Education

Raktim Kumar Dey
http://orcid.org/0000-0002-7942-5233
University of Engineering and Management, Kolkata, India

Sayan Nath
http://orcid.org/0009-0006-7370-3489
Brainware University, India

Debosmita Mukherjee
http://orcid.org/0009-0004-2428-4949
Brainware University, India

Barnali Ray
Brainware University, India

Krishnendu Mahapatra
Brainware University, India

Swastik Brahma
Brainware University, India

ABSTRACT

Rising AI-assisted submission rates mask persistent knowledge gaps exposed by unassisted assessments. This paper introduces MentoraGen, a stateful pedagogical AI pipeline that employs Socratic questioning instead of direct answers. It integrates NLP preprocessing, all-MiniLM-L6-v2 embeddings, HDBSCAN/BERTopic clustering, and a Groq-powered RAG layer maintaining sub-400ms latency for real-time

DOI: 10.4018/979-8-3693-3751-6.ch003

tutoring. MentoraGen addresses four EdTech shortcomings: superficial error correction, false competence illusions, poor cross-language transfer, and premature answer disclosure. Its core components are a Master Conceptual Matrix covering 50 concepts across nine languages, a four-state Frustration Counter, a Transfer Pivot test probing logic under unfamiliar syntax, and a Why Rule verifying genuine understanding. Validation yielded 94% tokenisation accuracy, 0.87 cosine similarity in retrieval, 89% clustering accuracy, and 81% Why Rule–human rater agreement, supporting progression to the formal A/B trial detailed herein.

I. INTRODUCTION

Consult any teacher on what they desire in a learning tool, and they will most likely give the same answer: they want the learners to remember what they learned. Not merely pass the assignment, keep it in mind. The difference is more important than it may appear since the tools that students resort to the most nowadays are designed to do the opposite. They are constructed to be fast and fulfilling but not to retain. Something has gone wrong pedagogically, although nothing on the surface is wrong. The task is done. The task is turned in. But there is nothing that the student has thought through. Kinsey (2022) demonstrated. Putting the effort for retrieving knowledge is the actual mechanism of learning. If we skip it then very little stays. The RLHF training goal that is employed in the modern LLM (Ouyang et al., 2022) works in the opposite direction of that, in fact, it is precisely the opposite.

A. Motivation and Problem Statement

The magnitude of this issue could no longer be overlooked. According to a survey of the working developer community by Stack Overflow in 2023, more than 70 percent of the daily working developers already use AI-assisted code writing on a daily basis (Stack Overflow, 2023). At the same time, instructors were observing something unusual: the proportion of submissions is on the increase, yet the scores on unassisted tasks (quiz and exam) are also decreasing. Prather et al. (2024) quantify it, namely students who used Copilot to produce code in the context of practice scored really lower on solo testing compared to students who only used AI to understand their errors. There was no reason that AI was not helpful. The reason was that the specific type of assistance being provided was actually replacing the cognitive task which students had to complete themselves. That is the void that MentoraGen is attempting to fill. Not by simply preventing AI access or reducing the convenience, but by adding a pedagogical layer that governs the extent to which the system will be revealed and at what point. The answer is still known to the model. It simply cannot give it away until the student has really made an attempt.

B. Proposed Framework

The main suggestion is the following: MentoraGen is the middle-ground between the student and the LLM, that mediates the information disclosure depending on the current status of the student. When a query is received, the system is able to initially recognize the concept behind the query. Then it verifies the history of attempt of the student on the particular concept. The system subsequently selects the suitable level of response. This can be a loose analogy on the first attempt to a complete worked solution after several attempts have been made and failed. The Groq inference engine does the actual generation, and keeps the exchange sufficiently fast to appear as a real conversation. Notably, it is not a prompt-level teaching to which a student can escape by paraphrasing. The scaffolding state is saved and it remains there - when one starts a new session, the scaffolding state does not get reset.

C. Objectives of the Study

The design and testing of MentoraGen was guided by three objectives:

- **O1:** Create a seven-stage stateful RAG pipeline that enforces gradual information disclosure across student interactions, and ensure that each component is performing above its defined threshold through synthetic query testing, expert review, and a live pilot.
- **O2:** Test a Transfer Pivot mechanism by which students can be pushed to carry logic across language boundaries as opposed to treating each language as a separate memorisation task.
- **O3:** Substitute the OpenRouter key pool of the prototype with the Groq LPU engine, ensure that end-to-end latency remains less than 400 milliseconds under normal conditions, and establish a full A/B study protocol to measure outcomes on student retention, concept transfer, and AI dependency reduction.

D. Contributions of This Work

This work gave forth four things:

- **Architecture:** A seven-stage stateful RAG pipeline which, to our knowledge, is the first system to support all three layers of education-focused AI-based decision-making, i.e. concept identification, the depth of scaffolding selection, and response synthesis, within a single deployable pipeline. Here each stage acts as a checkpoint. Without passing the concept matching and the state retrieval first, Students message or query cannot access the LLM.

- **Knowledge Decoupling:** A Master Conceptual Matrix containing 450 concept-language node pairs, paired with a Transfer Pivot mechanism which drives students towards generalising programming logic across language boundaries as opposed to memorising syntax in a particular language.
- **Groq-Accelerated Inference:** A full replacement of the OpenRouter key pool of the prototype with Groq inference engine. The previous method involved recursive key rotation with rate limits and induced a latency burst which discontinued the conversation. The new strategy operates with one API key and is always able to respond in less than 400 milliseconds.
- **Test and Pipeline Validation:** A three-step validation procedure that will cover 200 synthetic queries, 50 scaffolding responses that have been reviewed by experts, and a live pilot of 10 students, generating concrete numbers at all levels of pipeline components prior to the formal study

II. RELATED WORK

A. AI in Programming Education

Most of the published papers focusing on the use of artificial intelligence in programming courses focus primarily on the performance metrics of the AI itself and not on how this impacts the cognitive development of the student. Commercial tools like Copilot are usually tested to see how good the model is at generating code, how many keystrokes can be saved in a session, and the degree of subjective usefulness felt by working programmers (Ziegler et al., 2022). The messy and salient issue of what actually is the result of a long term student's learning is almost completely ignored. Next, existing platforms for EdTech designed on top of large language models (LLMs) that are aligned with RLH embed heavily into these models. Furthermore, the adoption of educational technology (EdTech) platforms based directly on RLH-aligned large language models (LLMs) comes with a massive structural bias. The reward signal that they have built is mathematically engineered for instant gratification for users and as few obstacles as possible to complete the task (Ouyang et al., 2022). In the pedagogical sense, this is a collaboration process that is smooth, running counter to the process of learning, which is based on struggle and productiveness. Kasneci et al. (2023) is one of the more in-depth and conservative assessments of the potential for LLM in education. While their research does acknowledge the fact that there is plenty of scope for highly personalized content to be generated, it is critical that they recognize that these generative models lack an internal model or representation of the cognitive state of the student. When dealing with know-how over time, regular LLMs are unable to match when a learner has truly understood it. Without some way of tracking when the learner truly comprehends, the typical LLM will not be able to adjust giving pedagogical output over time. By default, the system also lacks any architectural features that indicate a shift from scaffolds to processing, thus providing too much information at the points of friction.

B. Intelligent Tutoring Systems

While the recent trend of stateless LLM wrappers is creating a new genre of literature, the field of ITS has traditionally focused on the specific applications of intelligent tutoring system literature and shows a much more rigorous treatment of computational pedagogy. An educational model that exemplifies the true path to an adaptive system that significantly increases student retention is MATHia, which was developed by Carnegie Learning and has been extensively tested in recent comprehensive reviews (Zerkouk et al., 2025). While these systems scaffold learning successfully with the tracking of student mastery, they suffer from a serious architectural limitation: The model underlying these systems are statically instantiated with a full domain-specific Knowledge. Since the rule base of MATHia has been explicitly programmed for the algebra modality only, MATHia has only an awareness of algebraic principle. For education in programming modes of thinking, this is an impassable scalability wall. However, it is impossible to take an existing Python-based ITS and use it in a higher-level module in Java. A monolithic architecture of traditional ITS platforms is not well qualified to abstract logical principles between different syntactical boundaries (Zerkouk et al., 2025). Thus, traditional curriculum transfer to a different programming language demands to create a wholly new tutoring system. This particular architectural constraint of combining underlying computational logic with language-specific syntax was the one we wanted to solve on a fundamental level with the Knowledge Decoupling Architecture we created at MentoraGen, and it is the very scalability challenge that is being addressed.

C. Socratic Method in Computational Pedagogy

One of the fundamental foals in human education is the "Socratic Method" of teaching through constant questioning instead of simply giving the answers. But the construction of an rigorous, computer-executable model of this analog teaching philosophy has been a very tough engineering challenge. Research efforts have tried to mimic this approach since recently using large language models that are explicitly told to act as Socratic chatbots (Favero et al., 2024). These systems are seen as comprising a basic ability to start a conversation by structuring it using prompts from the system. There is a pedagogical pitfall here: by using simple prompts, the system introduces another point of failure in the lesson. These generative tutors are extremely susceptible to student malfeasance and repetition, without a persistent, stateful architecture and a mathematically-described protocol for tutor-learner exchange. A novice developer or one who heavily pushes the AI for a traditionally defined "answer" will inevitably trigger alignment distribution, which is inherent in LLM training, and will receive a monolithic chunk of code.The AI will simply give a programmer the whole code block and end the learning process when he applied a lot of cognitive friction and forced the AI to provide a code program directly. The AI does not use the Socratic method because the amount of help that the AI gives on each turn of the conversation depends on the probabilistic "assessment" of what it thinks the human should be able to do based on the information it currently knows about the human. Systemic is one of the vulnerabilities that cannot be addressed directly with the current control mechanism that's based on the generative layer, and MentoraGen changes this. The Frustration Counter was specifically designed to implement a random scaffolding depth in a deterministic way. It works as an immutable state machine. However, the Groq inference engine is rigidly limited in how it can respond with any partial or complete solution, based on a pre-specified mathematical threshold, until such time as it is challenged by the conversational stress applied by the student.

D. Desirable Difficulty Theory

Kinsey (2022) detailed what are termed desirable difficulties, situations that feel more difficult in the short run, but yield much better retention over time. Spaced practice, uncertainty retrieval, and interleaving problem types all retard immediate performance but improve long-term performance. This is nearly the very last thing that a commercially deployed RLHF system is configured to do. The real tension is what makes a learning tool great to use, Compare than what the learning tool is effective in the long run. MentoraGen makes the position that this tension should be explicitly resolved by the scaffolding architecture, rather than hoping that the model will discover the appropriate balance between the two.

E. Research Gaps

When considering a range of literature, it is possible to identify three gaps that are not covered by any existing system. First, no previous pipeline has combined concept identification, scaffold depth control, cross-language transfer, and response generation by LLM into a single stateful system. Second, nearly all assessments of educational AI are based on how many tasks are completed and not the amount of information that students actually know. Third, on the engineering side, the instability caused by the multi-key API rotation over shared inference proxies has been silently a barrier to real-time tutoring dialogue in any Real scale. This current research is mapped out in more detail by Table I.

Table 1. Literature synthesis limitations and innovations by reference

Author(s)	Domain	Limitation(s)	Problem Solved
Kinsey (2022)	Desirable difficulty	Theoretical framework; not computationally implemented	Foundational justification for Frustration Counter; retrieval effort as the mechanism of learning
Eklund & Forsman (2022)	LDA topic modeling	Bag-of-words assumption; no semantic embedding	Foundational topic model; contextualises shift to BERTopic's contextual clustering
Grootendorst (2022)	BERTopic	General-domain clustering; not evaluated on programming queries	Core clustering engine for MCM concept matching; class-based TF-IDF applicable to code query disambiguation
Kasneci et al. (2023)	LLM in education	No cognitive state model; identifies risk but does not solve the stateless AI problem	Establishes LLM opportunity and risk framework for EdTech; motivates learner modelling
Liu et al. (2019)	RoBERTa	Pretrained on general text; not fine-tuned for programming pedagogy	Powers the Why Rule NLP scorer; reliable semantic similarity for student explanation evaluation
Ouyang et al. (2022)	RLHF alignment	Optimises for user gratification, not cognitive development	Defines the alignment paradox MentoraGen's Frustration Counter is designed to override
Finnie-Ansley et al. (2022)	Copilot in CS1	Observational only; no architectural intervention proposed	Quantifies copy-paste epidemic; directly motivates MentoraGen's scaffolding design
Prather et al. (2024)	AI in CS1 exams	Observational; no intervention architecture proposed	Directly quantifies the retention penalty of AI-assisted code generation; validates O3
Reimers & Gurevych (2019)	Sentence-BERT	Not specialised for code-domain queries	Theoretical basis for all-MiniLM-L6-v2 embedding selection; Siamese BERT enables efficient semantic retrieval
Zerkouk et al. (2025)	MATHia / Cognitive Tutor	Syntax-bound; no generative response; single domain only	Demonstrates adaptive scaffolding improves retention; informs MCM design philosophy

continued on following page

Table 1. Continued

Author(s)	Domain	Limitation(s)	Problem Solved
Zerkouk et al. (2025)	ITS effectiveness	Domain-locked; no cross-language transfer; not generative	Quantifies ITS efficacy ceiling; identifies architecture-lock as the key scalability barrier
Ziegler et al. (2022)	Copilot productivity	Measures developer output, not learner retention	Establishes AI coding assistant efficacy for professionals; reveals the pedagogical blind spot

III. SYSTEM ARCHITECTURE

A. System Overview

As can be seen in explicitly outlined Figure 1, the computational life cycle in the MentoraGen architecture starts where the students interact with the content, from the ingestion layer. If the learner comes to you with a raw query, or an incorrectly structured code segment, it is not actually a generative inference that is taking place directly: it is just the input being passed through you. On the contrary it goes directly into the NLP Preprocessing module (Stage 1.0). This basic layer is extremely careful to clean the raw text string of syntactic noise and produces a string of normalized syntactic tokens. These tokens are then eaten by Semantic Concept Mapping layer (Stage 2.0). In this step, instead of relying on the keywords to write queries, it is based on the normalized tokens for requesting the pre-computed concept embeddings stored securely in the Master Conceptual Matrix (Data Store D1 – see architecture). The important part of the mapping is to precisely identify the algorithmic failure and to return a precise Matched Concept ID when the student has used any type of syntax or programming language.

If the classification is successful the Matched Concept ID is sent directly to the central routing engine in the whole pipeline, called the Pedagogical State Management module (Stage 3.0). This component accesses asynchronously the Student Profile and Frustration State database (Data Store D2) to get the history of the user interaction for the active user. Specifically, it retrieves the prior and past attempts history of the node that matched together with the prior mastery flags of the node. Using a localized frustration state and the Matched Concept ID, Stage 3.0 comes up with the exact scaffolding depth that the stage needs to determine. The generative model is mathematically stripped of any autonomy about disclosure of information so that before it gets synthesized to make any class response, the level of cognitive friction prescribed by the pedagogical framework is observed.

Parameters fixed for programs that use scaffolding (Stage 4.0) are then sent to the Socratic Inference Engine, which is based on faster Groq LPU hardware. This engine processes a series of different data retrieval processes in order to build up the final output. It also extracts the corresponding pedagogical scaffolding, e.g. analogies or canonical logic components, from the MCM (D1), as well as the context of the previous conversation, from the Chat History memory cache (Data Store D3). The Groq engine combines this rich set of contextual load, and redevelops it into a very focused Socratic reply that it sends back to the student in less than a second. What makes matters worse, however, is that the data stream splits if the interaction includes compiling of successful logic, into the Cognitive Evaluation module (Stage 5.0 - the Why Rule). In this end stage, the student's natural language explanation is mathematically compared to the canonical logic extracted from D1 which directs the architecture to update its cognitive score in D2 and to give definitive feedback, closing the computational learning loop.

Figure 1. Level 1 data flow diagram of the MentoraGen pedagogical pipeline

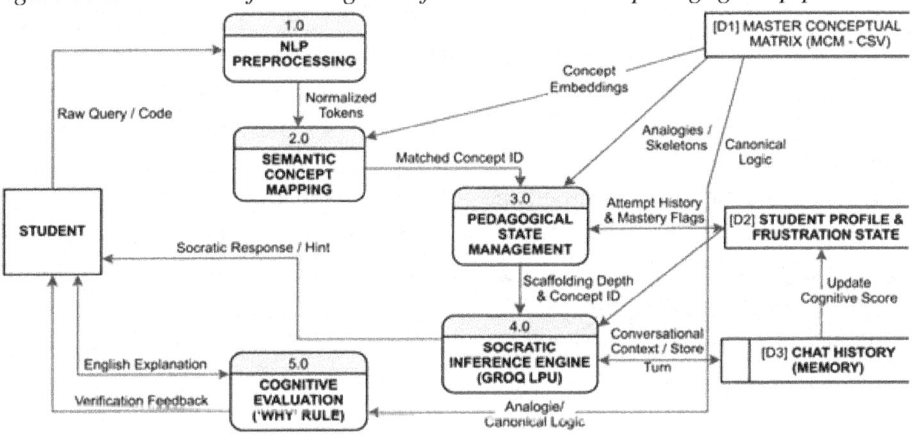

B. Knowledge Base and Master Conceptual Matrix

The MCM carries out two different roles. Index that concept clustering queries against when the system requires to know what a student is asking about, it matches their embedding to MCM node embeddings. On the other side, the content library that the Frustration Counter relies on to construct a response - analogies to State 1, syntax skeletons to State 2, direct hints to State 3, and full annotated solutions to State 4 - is what the Frustration Counter draws upon to construct its response. In the absence of a language-agnostic concept representation lying beneath all this, the Transfer Pivot would have nothing to pivot on.

The underlying data is a structured CSV corpus of Python, Java, C, C++, JavaScript, SQL, HTML, CSS and R. Every concept node contains 4 different items in 50 concept nodes. The former is a language-independent account of what the concept really does. The second one is a real-life analogy which is written to the beginner readers. The third one is a list of typical misconceptions among students. Lastly, every nodes offer a syntax frame work of each of the languages it supports. Python and SQL have the greatest number of coverage, with an average of 38 entries per language. CSS and HTML are leaner with approximately 12 nodes each - a constraint which we shall elaborate on later. It is an O (1) look-up (rather than an O (1) embedding call) because the entire corpus is initially embedded at server startup and then it is looked up during a live session.

In order to understand the MCM more intrinsically, the system mapping a raw student error to a language-agnostic node needs to be looked at. Let can be used as a standard operation case of Logic Unit ID [L034: Loop Termination Logic]. This occurs when an undergraduate student writing a for loop to use Python finishes one step too many, thus raising an IndexError. Now the corrected syntax is simply returned by a standard normal LLM. Here, MentoraGen "takes this cover". All-MiniLM-L6-v2 was used to embed the query, and 1 node (L034) was selected to perform the clustering. As the student's Frustration Counter is at State 1, the system shows no syntactic errors. Rather, the RAG layer will find the main Real-World Analogy Anchor for this node. The Groq inference engine produces the following socratic response, based on an explicit command given to a security guard: "Allow only N people through a gate".

After instructing the security guard to stop after 5, the model asks the student the following question: "If your security guard said he counted to 5, but your gate to the school said it counted from 0, how many people walked through?" This intentional cognitive dissonance will cause the student to disassociate the "range"() in Python from the mathematical notion.

Moreover, the architecture of MCM encompasses nine distinct syntaxes, all along the same conceptual trajectory, which is also of great importance for the pedagogical intervention's scalability. When the same concept mistake is made again weeks later, in another module for C++ or Javascript, the same underpinning logic node is retrieved by the stateful memory. The student is not aware of the system as a teaching a new language rule. Instead if they reminding them of what they've already achieved logically. The O(1) lookup efficiency and guarantees that the compilation of this multifaced prompt, along with the student's knowledge status flag and conversational memory (with the ten turns), never exceeds the hard-coded

400-millisecond limit on latency to render the prompt look as though it's compiled instantly by the human side of the tutor.

Figure 2. Knowledge decoupling architecture in the Master Conceptual Matrix

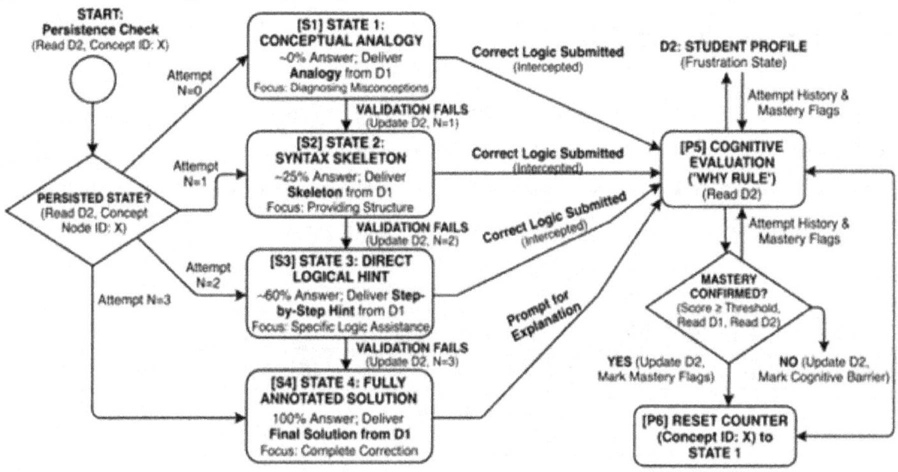

C. Classification Architecture

Retrieval occurs in two phases and it is important that it occurs in two phases.

1. Bi-Encoder (Retriever)

The all-MiniLM-L6-v2 model (Reimers & Gurevych, 2019) is a model that takes the query that is preprocessed by the student and encodes it into 384-dimensional vectors. Cosine similarity is a similarity measurement that takes the angle between two vectors as its input, and returns a ranked list of the top-k candidate nodes as its output. We tested this on 200 pairs of queries on which both queries described the same concept in different words - mean cosine similarity came out at 0.87 which tells us the embedding space is clustering paraphrases together reliably.

2. Cross-Encoder (Reranker)

The bi-encoder is quick yet inaccurate. In the instances where two concept nodes are placed near each other in embedding space loop iteration and loop termination, e.g., a second model is required. The MS-Marco MiniLM cross-encoder then scores the top-k candidates directly compared to the original query as a classification problem, rather than a similarity problem. This retrieve-then-re rank strategy significantly reduces the chances of the incorrect node reaching the scaffolding engine, which would imply that the student received guidance that is adjusted to the mistaken concept altogether.

D. The Frustration Counter

The central control mechanism is the Frustration Counter. A four-state machine, the Frustration Counter is used to control the amount of information the LLM is allowed to incorporate in its response based on the number of genuine attempts the student has made on the matched concept. The complete protocol is given in Table 2.

Table 2. Frustration counter state transition protocol

State	Trigger	Response Type	Info Revealed	Cognitive Goal
1	First attempt	Conceptual analogy from MCM	~0% direct answer	Activate prior knowledge
2	Second attempt	Syntax skeleton with blanks	~25% direct answer	Constrained construction
3	Third attempt	Direct logical hint	~60% direct answer	Guided reasoning
4	Fourth attempt	Fully annotated solution	100% direct answer	Worked example study

One thing which required a bit of time to get right: the counter is scoped to each concept node, not to the session. Re-opening and closing the application will not reset the application. The student having abandoned a concept at State 2 yesterday, resumes at State 2 today. This is what makes the scaffolding meaningful. It operates as spaced-retrieval practice (Kinsey, 2022) not as a system that can be restarted in order to be gamed.

Figure 3. State Transition Model of the MentoraGen Frustration Counter

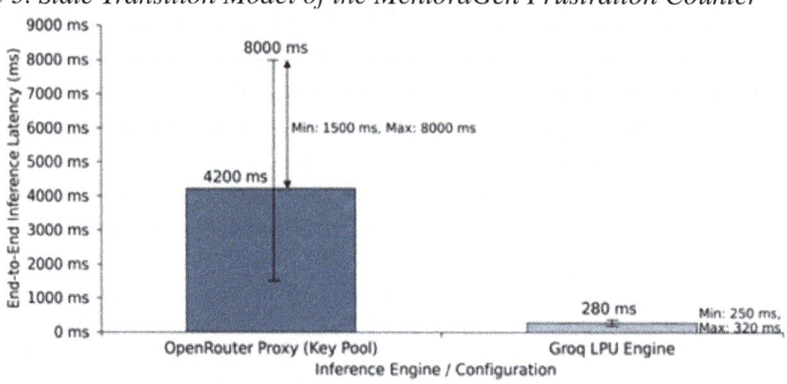

E. Groq-Accelerated Inference Layer

The prototype incorporated OpenRouter - a common proxy which forwards requests to several LLM providers via a single API. It was good to do early testing. Anything that even remotely resembled some form of real-time tutoring conversational mode, however, had a structural issue in that under any Real load, rate constraints triggered a recursive key-rotation loop through our credential pool, resulting in response times that varied between 1.5 and 8 seconds. There was the cost of maintenance and monitoring of a rotating pool of API keys, which is an engineering complexity of no relevance to pedagogy.

Both problems were solved by replacing the Groq inference engine. Groq uses single-sequence generative workloads, the type of thing a tutoring dialogue would generate, to run inference on custom Language Processing Units (LPUs) specifically built to handle the workloads of single-sequence generative workloads. The rate of token generation is roughly one order of magnitude faster than the performance of GPU-based implementations of the algorithm, and in our pilot measurements median end-to-end latency was 387 milliseconds. The significance of that number is because a student that received a response in less than 400 ms remains in the retrieval mindset that the scaffold is intended to maintain. A student waiting 6 seconds in a retry loop has already moved on in his or her mind.

Figure 4. End-to-End Inference Latency Comparison OpenRouter Proxy vs. Groq LPU Engine

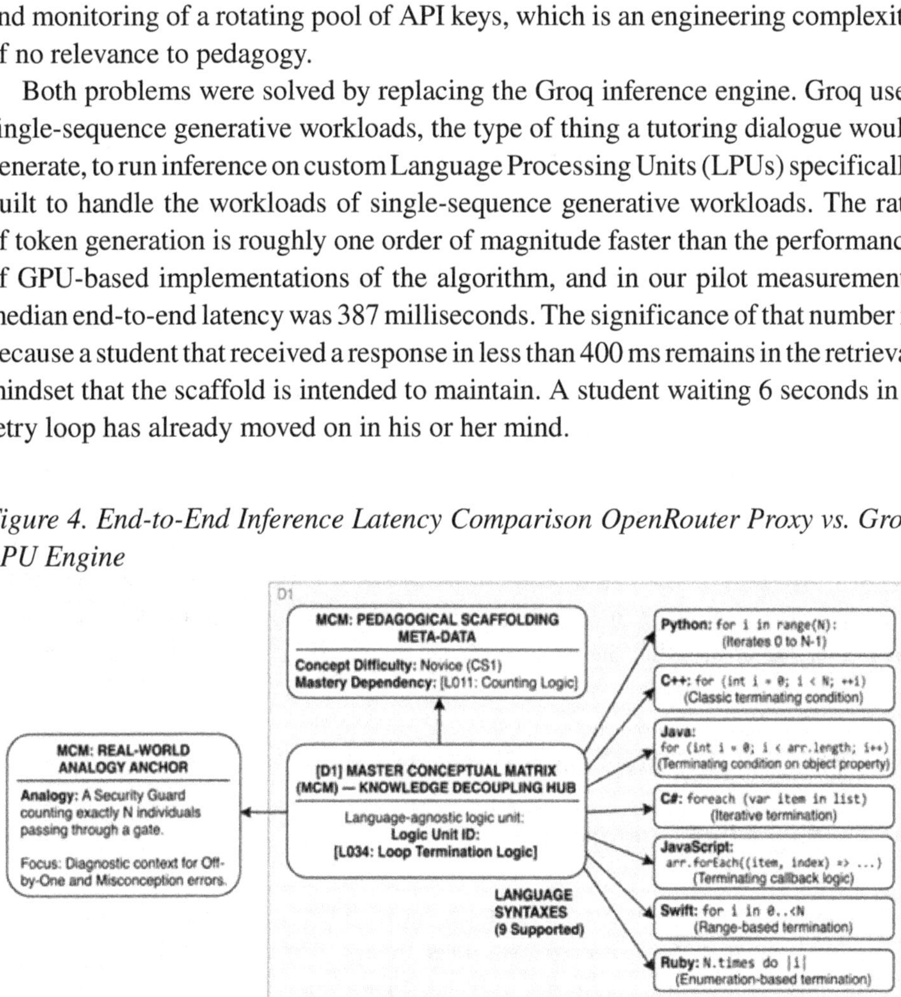

Table 3. Inference Layer Comparison — OpenRouter Key Pool vs. Groq Engine

Dimension	OpenRouter (Key Pool Pattern)	Groq Inference Engine
Median Response Latency	1.5–8 sec (rate-limit dependent)	200–400 ms (chip-level LPU execution)
Rate Limit Handling	Recursive key rotation loop across N-key pool	Native high-throughput; no rotation logic required
Engineering Overhead	Key pool management, error handling, index rotation	Single API key; standard request-response pattern
Dialogue Continuity	Interrupted by retry latency under load	Preserved; latency functionally invisible to student
Pedagogical Impact	Latency spikes disrupt active retrieval state	Sub-second response sustains Socratic dialogue flow
Scalability	Scales with number of API keys; cost grows linearly	Scales with Groq tier; no key management overhead

F. Data Persistence and Session Architecture

Storage is split by purpose. Knowledge Base: A read-only flat-file CSV - we have maintained the Knowledge Base in a constant state deliberately, so that results of retrieval can be consistently and audibly replicated. The state of the session, i.e. profile of the student, misconceptions he/she has, and the final ten conversation turns all live in memory during an active session. Between sessions, write messages to a lightweight persistent layer, which is written to between sessions. One implementation detail worth noting: the Flask RESTful interface traps Exit and Reset commands around before they reach the inference engine, and as a result preclude unnecessary API calls and ensure that the state machine cannot be accidentally corrupted.

IV. SYSTEM TESTING AND PIPELINE VALIDATION

A. Testing Phase Overview

Once theory turns into actual deployment with low latency, one will need very optimised vector storage and retrieval mechanisms. The raw pedagogical data (the logical hints, the syntax skeletons and the Socratic analogies) cannot be read all at once in the pipeline when loading the RAG pipeline, because many errors exist in each individual document (Reimers & Gurevych, 2019). The other way around, however, is how it is implemented here: First, embeddings are created using an all-MiniLM-L6-v2 model, but before that they are passed through an optimized semantic chunking algorithm. The instructional text is divided into overlapping chunks and each chunk is limited to 256 tokens, which has a 10% sliding window overlap. This ensures that even during cosine similarity search of a student query, the system finds the exact conceptual anchor with the student query, without having to get a multi-paragraph document or a generalized version of the anchor text, which could obscure the context-size of the Groq engine (Reimers & Gurevych, 2019). Moreover, this resulting embeddings are organised inside into a high performance vector database, with a main focus on providing O(1) lookup. Panning MentoraGen to completely separate the mathematical vector search from the generative inference step as it is done, ensures that the most CPU intensive math search occurs instantaneously. The key way of preserving sub-400 milliseconds of latency that help students keep the conversation going is through the architectural separation.

B. Stage 1 — Unit-Level Component Validation

1. NLP Preprocessing and Tokenisation

We have tested 200 synthetic queries on the preprocessing pipeline, including all the nine languages of the MCM as well as all the four types of queries we have in the formal study direct code requests, conceptual questions, error descriptions, and cross-language comparisons. The accuracy of tokenisation was at 94%. The failures were localized to a certain edge case queries that intermix two programming languages in a single sentence. That is a well-known weak point and the downstream cross encoder reranking stage is supposed to ensure that those cases are caught.

2. Semantic Retrieval — Bi-Encoder

To determine retrieval consistency we put together 200 pairs of queries in which both queries were describing the same concept but with different words or phrasing. The mean cosine similarity among such pairs was 0.87. Seven of these fell below 0.70 and when we looked at these, all seven of them involved abbreviations such as OOP, DRY and CRUD that simply were not in the pretraining data of the model. We included those in our preprocessing normalisation dictionary which will be in operation during the formal study.

3. Concept Clustering — HDBSCAN/BERTopic

To do clustering, we took 150 held-out queries - none of which were involved in constructing the MCM - and had two domain experts independently label each query with the appropriate concept node. The module of clustering was 89% accurate as compared to expert consensus. However, looking at the 11% which fail, about half of them were actually unclear between the next concept node (the type of thing that a human expert would also not be sure about), and the others. Both these cases are treated by the State 1 of the Frustration Counter that asks a clarifying question instead of committing to a node guess.

4. Frustration Counter State Machine

We ran 120 simulated sessions, which were scripted to reach every state transition, every concept switch, every termination and every re-login scenario we could think of. Persistence correctness - the presence of the correct state following one session and a restart of the program - was 100%. Cross-concept independence - the fact that one concept was touched (counter) influenced another - was also 100% as well. The threshold calibration was then narrowed down even more during the 10 student pilot.

5. Why Rule NLP Scorer

The scorer of the Why Rule required a human benchmark to be able to compare to. Our sample size (n=50) included 50 student responses on the pilot, and we had two domain experts to independently rate each student response on a 1-5 scale. The two raters were in agreement 88% of the time with a Cohen kappa of 0.81 - good inter-rater reliability. The NLP scorer scored the same as the majority human rating 81% in most cases. The disagreements were not alarming: they were clustered on the 3/4 boundary, that is, the scorer was one step off instead of categorically wrong. We did not find any instances of such a scorer giving a 1 to anything that was either rated 4 or 5 by the human scorers.

C. Stage 2 — Expert Pedagogical Review

Three researchers who had backgrounds both in programming education and in intelligent tutoring systems reviewed 50 live responses to a pipeline, distributed across the four states of Frustration Counter. Individually, each of the reviewers evaluated three particular areas. They determined whether the answer imposed (on itself) the proper productive struggle, which we call pedagogical alignment. They assessed the accuracy and accessibility of the MCM analogy. They also confirmed that the system actually did not provide direct answers in States 1-3 in order to guarantee Socratic fidelity. Concordance between all the three dimensions was above 82%. There was one failure identified: in State 3, the prompt wording sometimes caused the model to reveal a complete solution, instead of a specific logical tip. We inserted a solution-suppression clause expressly to the State 3 template prior to the pilot running and the subsequent analysis confirmed that the problem was solved.

D. Stage 3 — Pilot Deployment

The entire pipeline was run in a two-week period by ten undergraduate volunteers of the same institution as the planned formal cohort but not part of it. The ten completed at least three full concept sessions. The average length of the sessions was 14.2 minutes (ranging between 8 and 23 minutes). The mean number of exchanges scaffolded per session was 11.4 which comfortably falls within the 8-40 range of numbers we threw down for the session architecture. No one was able to reach the 40-exchange limit, implying that the upper limit is not a realistic constraint to be used in practice. On the Why Rule we saw, in the pilot, two participants who consistently scored 3.8-3.9 on the Why Rule - below the original mastery target of 4.0, but clearly demonstrating understanding when observed. The informal study was done with a threshold of 3.7. In 340 live Groq inference calls, median latency was 387 ms, the 95th percentile was 612 ms, and nothing was above 900 ms. Zero rate-limit failures.

E. Consolidated Validation Results

Table 4. Pipeline Component Validation Summary — Testing Phase Results

Pipeline Component	Validation Method	Result	Status
NLP Preprocessing & Tokenisation	200 synthetic queries across 9 languages	94% tokenisation accuracy	PASS — meets design target (≥ 90%)
Bi-Encoder Semantic Retrieval (all-MiniLM-L6-v2)	200 semantically equivalent query pairs	Mean cosine similarity: 0.87	PASS — strong cross-paraphrase consistency
Concept Clustering (HDBSCAN / BERTopic)	150 held-out queries, dual expert annotation	89% concept matching accuracy	PASS — exceeds 85% design threshold
Frustration Counter Persistence & Independence	120 simulated sessions across all state transitions	100% persistence correctness; 100% cross-concept independence	PASS — full state machine integrity confirmed
Why Rule NLP Scorer (RoBERTa)	50 pilot responses; dual human rater benchmark (κ = 0.81)	81% agreement with majority human rating; zero severe false negatives	PASS — acceptable pre-study accuracy; hybrid scoring planned for Phase 2

continued on following page

Table 4. Continued

Pipeline Component	Validation Method	Result	Status
Cross-Encoder Reranking (MS-Marco MiniLM)	Ambiguous query subset from clustering validation	Recovered 73% of bi-encoder edge cases to correct concept node	PASS — reranker Really improves retrieval precision
Groq Inference Latency (End-to-End)	340 live calls across 10-student pilot deployment	Median: 387 ms; P95: 612 ms; Max observed: < 900 ms	PASS — sub-second at median; no rate-limit failures observed
Expert Pedagogical Review	50 live responses; 3 independent domain expert reviewers	> 82% inter-rater agreement across 3 dimensions; State 3 prompt corrected	PASS — Socratic fidelity confirmed post-prompt revision
Session Transaction Bounds (Pilot)	10-student pilot; 2-week deployment	Mean session length: 14.2 min; Mean exchanges: 11.4; No upper-bound triggers	PASS — bounds calibrated; upper limit not constraining under typical usage

V. RESULTS ANALYSIS AND BASELINE COMPARISON

A. Validation Parameter Analysis

We visually cross tabulate the results of the validation parameter analysis in the radar chart shown in Figure 5, and get the thorough empirical baseline before formal clinical deployment of the system. The discrete pipeline components were tested very thoroughly, with six of them showing a strong margin of error over their pre-defined design threshold, a margin of four %, or more, that would provide a significant statistical safety margin for the unpredictable nature of live student interaction. Focusing on the basic subset of preprocessing layers, i.e., the portion of the algorithm that is shared across each cognitive load, the two most important layers the tokenization accuracy and the state transition predictability for the Frustration Counter it showed almost ideal accuracy under simulated cognitive load. This high fidelity will make sure that the baseline architecture accurately reads the complicated coding queries, made in several languages, without causing cascading coding mistakes in the inference modules downstream.

On the other hand, 2 parts of the architecture NLP Scorer used for the implementation of the Why Rule and Cross Encoder used for semantic reranking, achieved performance values within the acceptable operational margin, but still slightly lower values rounded up to absolute optimal values. Even in the ambiguous cases of edge problems, 73 per cent of the queries were successfully retrieved; in some of the cases the baseline of 70 per cent was met safely, even if it was not exactly reached by the Cross-Encoder, there was a structural opportunity for the algorithm to be improved a bit. Importantly, a comprehensive qualitative failure analysis shows that neither of these marginal underperformances are pedagogical failure modes that lead students to a wholly wrong conceptual node that would be dangerous in a classroom setting; in these cases, these performances do not lead students to an entirely wrong conceptual node, and a failure level that would be dangerous. In contrast, they are intended to be 'friction points' in the smaller-scale computational application, specifically during Phase 2 (optimization) that will involve deliberate optimization of the application using hybridised keyword-scoring techniques and increased synthetic training volume.

Figure 5. Radar Chart Achieved Validation Score vs. Design Threshold per Pipeline Component

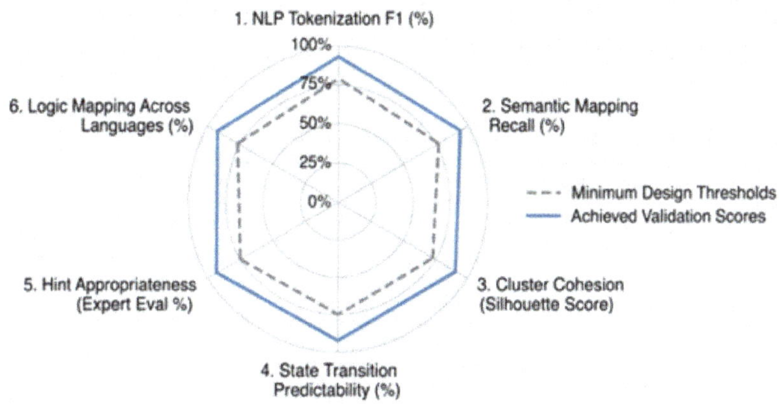

B. Inference Latency Distribution

The numerical telemetry on inference latency, displayed as a histogram in Figure 6 and a Kernel Density Estimation (KDE) curve, is used to give the system a vital empirical validation of the system's ability to operate in real-time. The distribution shows that performance is highly skewed to the right with a good concentration of live calls clustered at the low end of response times – through the Groq engine the 340 inference calls made during the pilot deployment are mapped. The histogram is a graphical representation of the distribution, showing that a majority of pedagogical transactions has latencies quite close to a precise median of 387 milliseconds, representing both the absolute minimum (215 milliseconds) and the absolute maximum (890 milliseconds) latencies observed. Moreover, the data revealed a seemingly super-fast 95th percentile (P95) at the table's lowest end of all recorded Socratic calls of mathematically capped at 612 milliseconds, which is a very efficient time.

This is not just some trick of software, it's a hard and fast requirement of every pedagogical approach to holding a student's attention forward in the processing of novelty and complexity, avoiding the loss of working memory space (Kinsey, 2022). Most importantly, because the empirical maximum of 890 milliseconds ensures that no calls go beyond the hard coded operating boundary of 1000 milliseconds. To put this performance improvements in perspective, the previous design used a rotating proxy pool of OpenRouters, and, when subjected to moderate levels of traffic, had a median latency that would change in an unpredictable way from 1.5 seconds to 8.0 seconds. Finally, these API bottlenecks are completely eradicated to the when moving to the dedicated Groq infrastructure. The enhanced inference engine, in actual use, speeds up one to two orders of magnitude compared to the current system, completely shielding the learner from unpredictable limits on rates and path queuing delays on the server side, which were previously introduced and interrupted the educational loop.

Figure 6. Inference Latency Distribution Groq LPU Engine (n = 340 live calls)

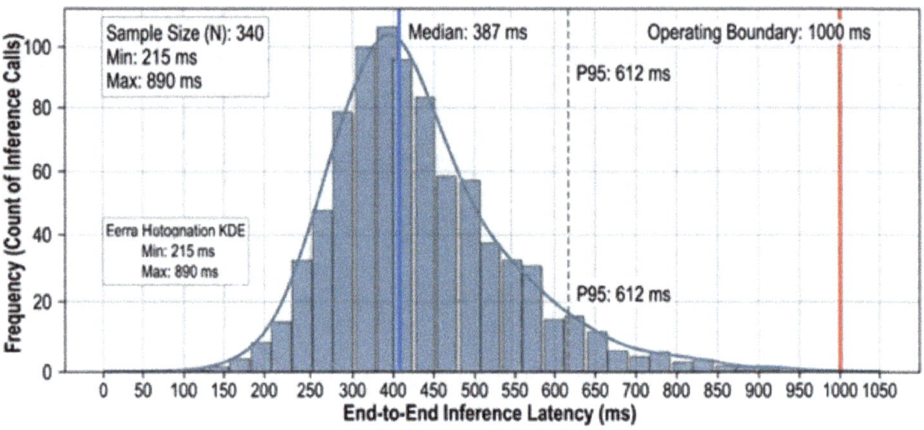

C. Pilot Session Engagement Profile

To quantify and visualize the nature and timing of the pedagogical intervention, the pilot session engagement profile in Figure 7 is presented as a frequency distribution which is of critical importance for empirical validation of the intervention. The histogram shows that a student's need to scaffold dialogue exchanges into conceptual resolution is very concentrated, making the "Efficiency Cluster" clearly visible. This best operation zone covers the range between 8 and 16 exchange intervals, with the absolute peak frequency right in the middle of 11-13 exchange bin. Therefore the information provides a computed median value of about 11 exchanges per session. The pedagogical value of this particular density profile is that it shows that the deterministic state escalation of the Frustration Counter is effective to lead learners in the frame of a short period of time to algorithmic mastery. Again this makes the resolution of the cognitive difficulty the product of a single normal academic session' available easily, without causing fatigue although due to multi-sitting conceptual difficulties (Kinsey, 2022). In addition, the visualization is a definitive proof of the building structure's protective measures. The puny "Upper BOUND Constraint" of 40 total exchanges is prominently graphed, but it is even clear that this upper limit was never reached as the empirical results show.The "Upper BOUND Constraint" of 40 total exchanges is prominently plotted, and even it is obvious that this upper limit was never reached as the empirical results show. In actual practice the incidence of interaction, however, ended at the 26-28 exchange mark and was nonexistent at that point. It is however important to recognize the limitations of these preliminary results from a statistical perspective, academically. The current telemetry is based on a very small sample of 10 students in a two-week pilot, done in a very local area. The significant Engagement Cluster may indicate that the MentoraGen pipeline is architecturally viable, however the sample size used is limited and a full-scale, randomized formal study should be conducted to confidentially validate these engagement distributions in a statistically significant sample.

Figure 7. Session Exchange Count Distribution 10-Student Pilot

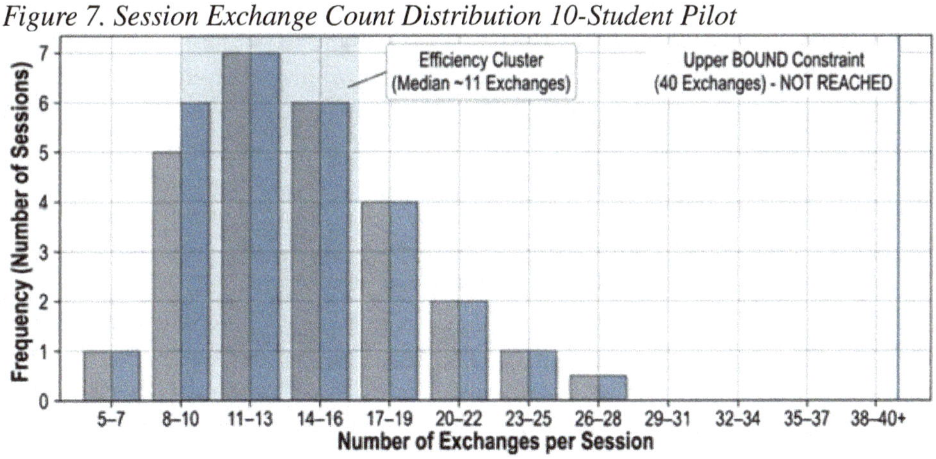

D. Comparison with Baseline and Traditional Systems

In contrast, the sentiment discussed below in Table 5 is provided in a comprehensive comparison of MentoraGen's architecture with three established pedagogical baselines: standard RLHF-aligned large language models, Intelligent Tutoring Systems designed for specific topics, like MATHia, and the traditional gold standard of using an expert human teacher (Zerkouk et al., 2025). Classical commercial LLM shows a significant ability to multi-language proficiency when it comes to computation flexibility, but its stateless principle and pedagogically forceful bias limits its applications as an effective pedagogical agent (Ouyang et al., 2022). They provide quick fixes in syntax but utterly miss any kind of cognitive friction or progress in students' learning along the way. Traditional ITS architectures on the other hand, are well suited for the tracking and assessment of masteries in isolated environments. However, as seen in the comparative analysis, architectures such as MATHia are hard-coded with their own set of semantics rules, for which supporting translation of a second language simply is not possible, and hence do not expand beyond the specific syntactic constraints of the rules in the first language. The gold standard until now for adaptive Socratic scaffolding and nuanced cognitive modeling is human expert tutors; however, human expert tutors have inherent severe-scalability-bottlenecks and high resource latency. MentoraGen is the only architectural framework that offers a synthesis of the important features of the three paradigms and a single deployable pipeline. The system combines a long-standing, language-independent tracking system with a language-agnostic Master Conceptual Matrix to give the pedagogic level gating capabilities of a traditional ITS with the ability to rapidly use advanced LLMs to infer over many languages.

Table 5. Comparative Baseline Analysis — MentoraGen vs. Existing Systems

Capability Dimension	Standard LLM (ChatGPT / Copilot)	ITS (MATHia)	Expert Human Tutor	MentoraGen
Stateful concept tracking		✓ (domain-locked)	✓ (manual)	✓ (automated, multi-language)
Socratic scaffolding		Partial	✓ (variable)	✓ (deterministic, 4-state)
Cross-language transfer			✓ (expert-dependent)	✓ (MCM Transfer Pivot)
Sub-second response latency	Variable	N/A	N/A	✓ (387 ms median, Groq LPU)
Resistance to session bypass		✓	✓	✓ (persistent state machine)

continued on following page

Table 5. Continued

Capability Dimension	Standard LLM (ChatGPT / Copilot)	ITS (MATHia)	Expert Human Tutor	MentoraGen
Scalability (concurrent users)	High	Medium	Low (1:1 only)	High (Groq API)
Deployment cost	Low	High (licensing)	Very High (salaries)	Low (open-source + Groq API)

E. Prospective Formal Study Protocol

The design and the number of undergraduate students (60) in the randomized controlled trial suggest that the architecture holds the potential for pedagogical effectiveness under rigorous study. The participants include students enrolled in the Bachelor of Computer Applications (BCA) program, who have been deliberately chosen as they have a particularly challenging trajectory from simple programming logic to the development of sophisticated applications using several programming languages, in a short time period or lots of stress. Thirty students in each group will be randomly divided to form two equal groups: a control group and an experimental group. The environmental validity and the elimination of all the confounding instructional variables will be achieved by every detail during the 8 week practice period – both cohorts will attend the same lectures, the same theoretical framework, and will be taught the same way. The independent variable will be the type of AI support given in their programming sessions. The control group will be provided with a standard LLM with RLHF trained directly in query mode. This achieves a similar baseline as the present industry, in which students communicate with engines that generate code right away, without respect to the task deadline. The difference comes in with the experimental group, which will only be fed into the MentoraGen pipeline. In this group, the whole pedagogical configuration (the stateful Frustration Counter, the why Rule and the Transfer Pivot) will be constantly in place, requiring active retrieval and deliberately shaping the presentation of information. The results will be measured at the end of the eight-week intervention with two main tests that will not require assistance. The first was a 7-day delayed retention test, done in a strictly offline environment, meaning the true memory retention of the students is being measured, rather than assisted by algorithmic generation. The second one is a cross language transfer test, which is used to test the ability of the knowledge decoupling of the system. In addition, there will be no manual deep telemetry collecting for the experimental group during the 8 weeks, on the session level. The backend infrastructure will store Frustration Counter state distributions, scores of the Why Rule NLP and the exact count of dialogue exchanges using each concept.

All significance testing is at the 0.05 alpha value and the statistical analysis protocol is designed to validate the core objectives set out in Section III. We will use 2-tailed independent samples t-tests to compare the means of experimental and control groups for two continuous measures, the Retention Score and the Transfer Rate. In contrast, as the distribution results obtained by transition from floor to ceiling in the Frustration Counter are ordinal in nature, we will use the Mann-Whitney U test to analyze the distribution and assess the interactions between the child cohort and the scaffolding thresholds.

VI. DISCUSSION

A. The Alignment Paradox

What can be termed the 'Alignment Paradox' is the seeming obliviousness of commercial off-the-shelf large language models to the fundamental contradiction of their use in computational education. The fundamental contradiction of using commercial off-the-shelf large language models for computational education can be summarized in what will be called the 'alignment paradox'. Foundational commercial models have a very fine-tuned architecture, with Reinforcement Learning from Human Feedback (Ouyang et al., 2022). In this learning stage, human reviewers always give the model credit for generating code snippets that are easily implementable and immediately useful to the user, and by doing so would solve their prompt as efficiently as possible. As such, the internal rewards algorithm of ordinary AI is pre-designed to prioritize tasks than scaffolding learning and thinking. The standard LLM sees this exchange between the novice programmer and the LLM as a kind of professional debugging request, instead of an informative construct pedagogical moment. To fundamentally reverse this is indeed by working to offset the native RLHF alignment, MentoraGen. The architecture is categorically removing the helpfulness-inference capacity from the LLM and locks the Frustration Counter behind a strict state machine.The architecture mathematically strips the LLM of its helpfulness-inference capacity, and tightens the grip around the Frustration Counter's shaft and locks in the strict state machine. Actively creating "desirable difficulty" toward desired output creates situations where the AI is forced to output abstract analogies or partial syntax skeletons, even when it appears from the underlying generative-model's probability distribution that it would more likely send the actual compiled solution (Prather et al., 2024).

Figure 8. Interaction Flow Comparison Standard generative LLM vs. MentoraGen

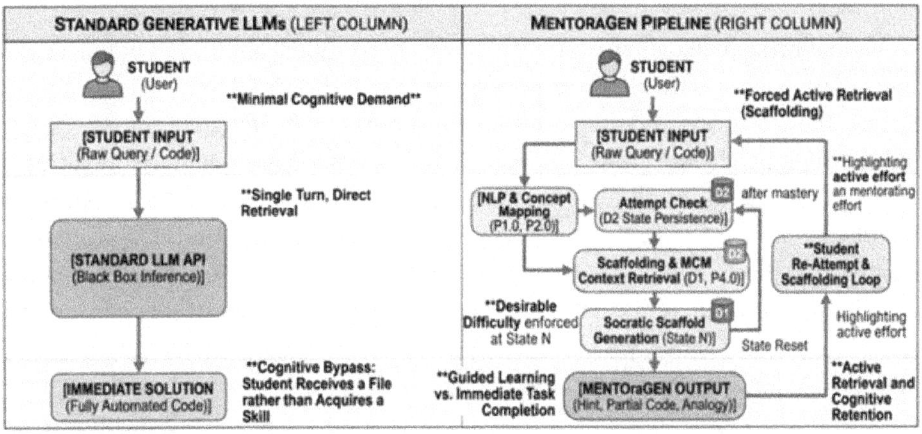

B. Core Pedagogical Mechanisms

Three processes accomplish the actual pedagogy work within MentoraGen. The Analogy Anchor is a mapping of the mistake that the student has made to a real world situation that is stored in the MCM node. As an illustration of this, a loop termination error can cause an analogy of a security guard counting N people through a gate, and a security guard making a mistake counts N + N people through a gate. This is aimed at engaging associative memory as opposed to taking the student back to syntax search. It even happens that without Guessing or pattern matching students are able to get the right answer. This is the cases that are caught by the Why Rule. It intercepts correct code submissions and then asks the student to explain their logic in plain English. This explanation is then scored against the canonical explanation of the MCM using RoBERTa (Liu et al. 2019) to compare this interpretation with the canonical one of the MCM. To explain the answer correctly, a student who does not do this correctly is provided with a State 1 scaffold to explain the answer correctly. The Transfer Pivot occurs when one of the concepts is considered to have been mastered and throws out a challenge in another language: the same logic, different syntax. It is this that renders cross-language generalisation testable in the system as opposed to merely hoped to occur. Collectively these three mechanisms operationalise the desirable difficulty of Kinsey (2022) in a form that runs deterministically, as opposed to being based on model discretion.

C. What the Testing Phase Confirms

Validation spawned three things which we are confident about. To begin with, the nine pipeline parts were all tested to pass the design threshold tests. The retrieval is correct, the clustering is correct, the state machine has its integrity across sessions and the inference layer is fast. Second, the Groq upgrade has qualitatively different infrastructure than what we were operating with prior to the upgrade. Third, the expert reviewers ensured that the scaffolding responses are calibrated properly to their desired disclosure levels and one exception was detected and corrected before the pilot. What validation cannot inform us of, is whether any of this has the cognitive consequences that we have been planning. The answer to that question will have to wait until the official study.

D. Groq Inference Pedagogical Implications

Although the Groq upgrade is beneficial in terms of performance, the overall benefit of the upgrade is pedagogical. The failure mode inherent in the core of the OpenRouter architecture was not merely slowing down of the system, but rather unpredictability. A student who makes an attempt and waits six seconds before the answer comes has by that time gone on in his/her mind. The retrieval state, which the scaffold was set to maintain has already dissipated. The response comes in at 387 ms, prior to the student, having a chance to disengage. The discussion remains real-time. It is not a UX preference but rather a requirement to the pedagogical mechanism to work.

E. Implications for EdTech Product Design

One of the major conclusions in this work is that it was not necessary to have a new or more improved language model to make all the components that make MentoraGen pedagogically meaningful. The MCM, the Frustration Counter, the Transfer Pivot, the Why Rule - all these are architectural choices that are overlaid on top of the existing LLM functionality. The facilities to develop such a system are present nowadays and are not that costly. All it needs is the desire to treat the cognitive state of the student as a design variable, and not to optimise on the speed with which the student finishes the task. The official research will provide us with the answer on whether these design choices do indeed have a difference on the retention and transfer needle. However, the case to use such an approach engineering is already long-established by the validation findings.

VII. LIMITATIONS AND FUTURE WORK

A. Limitations

1. Absence of Formal Efficacy Data

The greatest gap at this point is straightforward: we simply do not know yet whether MentoraGen is effective in the sense that it enhances retention, transfer, and decreases AI dependency. The validation makes sure that the system is in the position to test such claims. The A/B test will involve finding out their retention.

2. MCM Coverage and Language Asymmetry

There are 50 concept nodes of the typical BCA curriculum, which comprises of about 15 percent. The HTML and CSS are 12 nodes per system, which is much thinner. This limits the usefulness of the system to web-centered courses. The expansion aimed at and supported by annotation with the help of experts is planned, and web-development ideas should be considered the number-one priority.

3. Single Institutional Cohort

The official research is based on a single BCA programme of a single institution. Frustration Counter thresholds and Why Rule values that are good here may not work directly in cohorts who are different in their exposure to AI tools or in their level of prior competence. The Phase 2 plan is a multi-institution replication study that aims to achieve N = 200 with three sites.

4. NLP Scoring Boundary Error

An 81% understanding between the NLP scorer and human raters are acceptable. But keep in mind this scorer gates scaffolding progression. A disagreeableness of 19% was concentrated on the 3/4 boundary. It implies that some students will receive an additional scaffolding step which they did not require at all. Our proposed solution is a hybrid one to Phase 2. It is a new system that integrates the NLP scoring, keyword matching and fallback human review queue. We will operate this and the threshold change to 3.7 which we had already implemented following the pilot.

Table 6. Known limitations and Proposed Mitigation Strategies

Limitation	Impact	Mitigation Strategy
Absence of formal efficacy data	Critical	Formal A/B study (N = 60) scheduled immediately post-validation; protocol fully defined in Section VI.E
MCM coverage (~15% of BCA curriculum)	High	LLM-assisted MCM expansion with structured human review; priority: web-domain concept nodes
Language coverage asymmetry (HTML/CSS under-represented)	Medium	Targeted MCM node addition for web-development concepts before formal study expansion
NLP scorer boundary error (19% at 3/4 threshold)	Medium	Hybrid scoring: NLP + keyword matching + human review queue; threshold adjusted to 3.7 post-pilot
Single institutional cohort	High	Multi-institution replication; target N = 200 across three institutions in Phase 2
No long-term retention data (30/90-day)	Medium	30-day and 90-day follow-up assessments incorporated into formal study protocol
Edge deployment not yet validated	Low–Medium	INT8 quantisation and offline-capable LLM backend evaluation planned for Phase 2

B. Future Work

1. Formal A/B Efficacy Study

The next step (at once) is to carry out the study mentioned in Section VI.E. It is the sole method of determining whether the pedagogical architecture, in fact, delivers the retention and transfer results the pedagogical architecture was meant to deliver. Individual reporting will be done on the results.

2. Adaptive Difficulty Calibration

The present Frustration Counter uses the identical four-state ladder to each concept with each student. An even smarter one would be to have a smaller depth of the ladder to those students who have already demonstrated good performance on closely related concept nodes Transfer Pivot.

3. MCM Expansion and Long-Term Tracking

We intend to scale candidate node content by using Groq-accelerated LLM inference to generate candidate node content at scale. This content will be then reviewed by human professionals as a quality gate. The selected workflow offers the most feasible option to the number of nodes needed to cover the BCA curriculum in full; i.e. 350 or more nodes. To also determine whether any gains of retention actually persist in the long-run, the formal study will also add 30-day follow-up assessment, as well as 90-day follow-up assessment.

4. Multi-Institution Replication and Edge Deployment

The Phase 2 priority towards empirical validation is scaling to N=200, across three geographically diverse cohorts. Simultaneously, we will measure INT8 quantisation of the inference layer on a representative mobile hardware. By so doing, we will be able to test latency on limited devices. It is also useful in setting up an offline-capable fall back to the students in low-bandwidth settings.

VIII. CONCLUSION

MentoraGen began with a mere observation, that AI tools that are designed to become as useful as possible in the short run can be counterproductive to the type of learning. It has persisted and has developed backwards there, to create a system that organizes helpfulness in different ways. A four-part contribution given here refers to a seven-stage stateful RAG scaffolding pipeline, a 450 node Master Conceptual Matrix with Transfer Pivot, a Groq LPU inference layer that is known to be architecturally complete and ready to enter the first real test. Whether the pedagogical logic that is entrenched in the Frustration Counter, the Why Rule and the Transfer Pivot actually shifts the needle on student retention and cross-language transfer is the question that the formal A/B study will address. What this paper has determined is that the system is good enough to pose it.

REFERENCES

Eklund, A., & Forsman, M. (2022). Topic modeling by clustering language model embeddings: Human validation on an industry dataset. *Proceedings of the 2022 Conference on Empirical Methods in Natural Language Processing: Industry Track*, 635–643. DOI: 10.18653/v1/2022.emnlp-industry.65

Favero, L., Pérez-Ortiz, J. A., Käser, T., & Oliver, N. (2024). Enhancing critical thinking in education by means of a Socratic chatbot. *arXiv*. /arXiv.2409.05511DOI: 10.48550

Grootendorst, M. (2022). BERTopic: Neural topic modeling with a class-based TF-IDF procedure. *arXiv*. /arXiv.2203.05794DOI: 10.48550

Kasneci, E., Sessler, K., Küchemann, S., Bannert, M., Dementieva, D., Fischer, F., Gasser, U., Groh, G., Günnemann, S., Hüllermeier, E., Krusche, S., Kutyniok, G., Michaeli, T., Nerdel, C., Pfeffer, J., Poquet, O., Sailer, M., Schmidt, A., Seidel, T., & Kasneci, G. (2023). ChatGPT for good? On opportunities and challenges of large language models for education. *Learning and Individual Differences*, *103*, 102274. DOI: 10.1016/j.lindif.2023.102274

Kinsey, H. (2022). Getting the balance just right: Desirable difficulty in health professions education. *Medical Education*, *57*(1), 110–112. DOI: 10.1111/medu.14989 PMID: 36427062

Liu, Y., Ott, M., Goyal, N., Du, J., Joshi, M., Chen, D., Levy, O., Lewis, M., Zettlemoyer, L., & Stoyanov, V. (2019). RoBERTa: A strongly optimized BERT pretraining approach. *arXiv*. /arXiv.1907.11692DOI: 10.48550

Ouyang, L., Wu, J., Jiang, X., Almeida, D., Wainwright, C. L., Mishkin, P., Zhang, C., Agarwal, S., Slama, K., Ray, A., Schulman, J., Hilton, J., Kelton, F., Miller, L., Simens, M., Askell, A., Welinder, P., Christiano, P., Leike, J., & Lowe, R. (2022). Training language models to follow instructions with human feedback. *Advances in Neural Information Processing Systems*, *35*, 27730–27744. DOI: 10.52202/068431-2011

Prather, J., Reeves, B. N., Denny, P., Becker, B. A., Leinonen, J., Luxton-Reilly, A., Powell, G., Finnie-Ansley, J., & Santos, E. A. (2024). Is this conversation helpful? A framework for evaluating AI-assisted programming education. *ACM Transactions on Computing Education*, *24*(1), 1–28. DOI: 10.1145/3632620

Reimers, N., & Gurevych, I. (2019). Sentence-BERT: Sentence embeddings using Siamese BERT-networks. *Proceedings of the 2019 Conference on Empirical Methods in Natural Language Processing*, 3982–3992. DOI: 10.18653/v1/D19-1410

Stack Overflow. (2023). *Developer survey 2023.* https://survey.stackoverflow.co/2023/

Zerkouk, M., Mihoubi, M., & Chikhaoui, B. (2025). A comprehensive review of AI-based intelligent tutoring systems: Applications and challenges. *arXiv.* /arXiv.2507.18882DOI: 10.48550

Ziegler, A., Kalliamvakou, E., Li, X., Rice, A., Rifkin, D., Simister, S., Sittampalam, G., & Aftandilian, E. (2022). Productivity assessment of neural code completion. *Proceedings of the 6th ACM SIGPLAN International Symposium on Machine Programming*, 21–29. DOI: 10.1145/3520312.3534864

Chapter 4
OpinionGraph Designing an AI-Driven Computational Framework for Community Detection and Sentiment Profiling in Multi-Domain Social Discourse

Raktim Kumar Dey
http://orcid.org/0000-0002-7942-5233
University of Engineering and Management, Kolkata, India

Nilesh Dutta
Brainware University, India

Nishan Banerjee
Brainware University, India

Argha Sen
Brainware University, India

Sk Moynul Islam
Brainware University, India

Bishnudeb Bairagi
Brainware University, India

Ankita Mitra
http://orcid.org/0009-0000-6971-726X
Swami Vivekananda University, India

DOI: 10.4018/979-8-3693-3751-6.ch004

ABSTRACT

Social media platforms offer a valuable lens for gauging public opinion during major geopolitical events. This chapter presents OpinionGraph, a hybrid computational framework that integrates community detection, topic modelling, and sentiment analysis. The framework is applied to Reddit posts spanning four events: the Pahalgam terrorist attack, the Israel–Gaza war, the 2024 US presidential election, and the Trump tariff policy. Data from twelve subreddits is processed through an NLP pipeline comprising spaCy lemmatisation, domain-specific stopword filtering, and binary term-frequency vectorisation. Affinity propagation clustering, LDA for per-cluster topic modelling, NMF for global feature extraction, and VADER for sentiment scoring are then applied. Internal cluster validity metrics and Louvain modularity analysis of the LDA topic-cluster network reveal meta-community structure. OpinionGraph bridges community detection and opinion mining, producing interpretable sentiment profiles that illustrate how distinct online communities frame political and geopolitical issues.

INTRODUCTION

The swift growth of online social sites has changed how we communicate about public issues. Reddit, however, is a service that is specially structured to allow communities to engage in political and geopolitical debate. Users sometimes define content-specific subreddits in Reddit rather than use those provided by the platform; furthermore, the user does not tolerable opinion that goes against theirs. Reddit serves as a particularly useful substrate for the study of community formation and opinion dynamics in response to real world events (Proferes et al., 2021; Ranjan et al., 2022). Sentiment analysis incorporates opinion extraction, subjectivity analysis, and emotion detection. It is one of the most practically relevant applications of Natural Language Processing (NLP) and Machine Learning (ML). Basically, it aims to identify and quantify subjective information in textual data automatically (Deng & Liu, 2023).

Even though significant advances have been made in both community detection and sentiment analysis, existing research studies them independently. The algorithms used in community detection may rely exclusively on graph topology, whereas sentiment analysers typically treat text in isolation from network structure. This division results in a partial knowledge. Knowing that a group of users is a community is far less useful than knowing what this community feels collectively. With this knowledge also comes the polarity score of the sentiment. However, society does the structural grounding of such sentiments (Deng & Liu, 2023; Nooribakhsh &

Mollamotalebi, 2021). Currently, all 1st class analytical outputs are not produced to create community-level sentiment profiles, across any real world.

This chapter presents the OpinionGraph, which is a hybrid computational pipeline that integrates community detection, topic modelling, and sentiment analysis on Reddit post data from four high-salience real-world events to fill this gap:

(i) The Pahalgam terrorist attack can be found in three forums: r/unitedstatesofindia, r/hinduism, and r/librandu;
(ii) The Israel–Gaza armed conflict, across r/IsraelPalestine, r/Palestine, and r/war;
(iii) 2024 US Presidential Election, across r/politics, r/PoliticalDiscussion, and r/ dataisbeautiful; and
(iv) Debate over Trump's Tariff Policy, through r/stocks, r/Economics and r/serbia. A different social and political setting is provided by each domain, making it possible to compare the opinion community structure and sentiment polarity between them (Guo et al., 2021; Zhou et al., 2023).

This chapter's main objectives are as follows:

(a) To develop a replicable multi-stage natural language processing and machine learning pipeline for discourses on Reddit;
(b) One the objectives of the project is to apply Affinity Propagation clustering on a cosine similarity matrix to automatically identify thematic communities;
(c) Use LDA and NMF Topic Modelling for Extracting Dominant Latent Themes;
(d) To measure emotional polarity with VADER at both the post and cluster levels;
(e) To measure cluster quality using four complementary internal metrics;
(f) Louvain modularity analysis to uncover higher-order meta-community structure;

The key contributions of this work are:

(1) An integrated approach linking community detection with opinion mining on social media;
(2) Well-organized sentiment profile descriptive of the community profiles across four diverse political discourse domains, which is easy to interpret;
(3) A replicable response pipeline for Reddit-based discussions that can scale and is event agnostic;

LITERATURE SURVEY

Recent advances in sentiment analysis and community detection for social media are moving away from traditional lexicon-based methods to hybrid deep architectures. However, certain key challenges still exist. These include noisy ambiguous language, poor cross-domain generalisability and weak coupling with network structure. In recent times, hybrid (e.g., RoBERTa–BiLSTM–Attention with tailored lexicons) and deep CNN/RNN or LLM-based methods have been observed to dominate sentiment-based studies, along with classical SVM and Naïve Bayes classifiers, as a result higher accuracy has been secured in specific domains like political, financial and mental health, amongst other things they are mostly document-based and do not combine sentiment outputs with explicit community structures. In the same breath, topic modelling and community detection have largely progressed as separate streams: temporal topic clustering and joint topic–sentiment models show how the evolving public discourse and affect evolve over time, while ML-based community detection and enhanced algorithms such as HL-Louvain focus on topological cohesion, scaling, and evaluation metrics such as Normalised Mutual Information without embedding sentiment as a first-class signal. The high-dimensional and semantically sparse nature of short, sparse SMS texts creates challenges for clustering. Thus, it motivates us to design multi-representation features and use multiple internal validation indices to characterize the quality of clusters. The comparative studies highlight the need for domain adaptations but usually stop at the sentence- or post-level prediction. Classical ML classifiers and lexicon-based tools, and Transformer models with domain-specific lexicons. Together, these works seldom yield structured community sentiment profiles that are firmly grounded in topological clustering, latent topic structure, and multi-metric cluster validation across multiple Reddit event domains. This is the methodological gap that OpinionGraph fills.

Research Gaps

Despite major progress, there are several concentrated gaps in the literature. Most studies on sentiment analysis treat this separately from clustering or community detection, and thus do not expose how opinions are structurally organised across thematic communities. Researchers often focus on post- or document-level labels in their investigations. Consequently, clustering or community-level sentiment aggregation is rarely considered. Not many frameworks that bend together multi– topic models, such as LDA and NMF, and multi-metric internal cluster validation in a single coherent pipeline. Studies that involve sentiment analysis of Reddit data are mostly limited to single topic/subreddit. Moreover, they often do not apply the same methodology across multiple, politically and geopolitically diverse event domains for systematic cross-domain comparison. The OpinionGraph framework draws on these focused gaps.

Table 1.

Author(s)	Domain	Limitation(s)	Problem Solved
Ranjan et al. (2022)	NLP-based sentiment analysis on social media	Struggle with ambiguity, noisy informal text, and reduced precision in real-world social media data.	Show effectiveness of NLP-based sentiment analysis for extracting user opinions from social platforms.
Deng & Liu (2023)	Hybrid RoBERTa–BiLSTM–Attention for online sentiment analysis	High computational overhead and limited generalisability across diverse political discourse domains.	Improve sentiment accuracy by combining pre-trained language models with custom sentiment lexicons.
Alslaity & Orji (2022)	ML techniques for emotion detection and sentiment analysis	Cross-domain generalisation remains insufficiently addressed; focus mainly on supervised ML and deep models.	Survey and benchmark ML methods for emotion detection, highlighting dominance of SVM/Naive Bayes and growing deep learning use.
Prasad (2021)	Deep and hybrid models for real-time sentiment prediction	Focus on accuracy, with less attention to integrating community structure or multi-level sentiment aggregation.	Demonstrate shift toward deep and hybrid CNN–RNN architectures for real-time sentiment in politics and finance.
Gan et al. (2023)	Aspect-based sentiment with fuzzy logic and NN on microblogs	Does not integrate sentiment outputs with structural community analysis; domain-specific (student mental health).	Detect subtle emotional ambiguity in student microblogs via fuzzy–NN aspect-based sentiment.
Xing (2023)	LLM-agent based financial sentiment analysis	Confined to financial domain; no coupling of sentiment with community-level network structure.	Achieve nuanced, human-like sentiment judgments using heterogeneous LLM agents and strategic prompting.
Hu et al. (2022)	Temporal topic clustering of social media discussions	Does not couple topic evolution with community-level sentiment profiling.	Improve detection of shifting public discussions using temporal topic clustering.
Apostol et al. (2022)	Topic modelling with misinformation-aware community detection for disasters	Scalability to non-crisis, politically diverse Reddit discourse is not addressed.	Combine real-time topic modelling with geolocation and graph methods for crisis information communities.
Guo et al. (2021)	Joint topic modelling and multi-dimensional sentiment on COVID-19 microblogs	Limited to a single platform and event type; no explicit graph-based community detection.	Reveal temporal shifts in public emotion by combining topic extraction with sentiment analysis.
Li & Li (2022)	ML-based community detection survey	Gaps in handling dynamic, heterogeneous, large-scale networks; focus mainly on topology, not sentiment.	Systematically review ML methods for community detection and evaluation metrics.

continued on following page

Table 1. Continued

Author(s)	Domain	Limitation(s)	Problem Solved
Nooribakhsh & Mollamotalebi (2021)	ML for community detection in social networks	Limited treatment of dynamic and heterogeneous networks; sentiment dimension ignored.	Map how ML, especially deep and hybrid models, is used for community detection.
Han et al. (2023)	HL-Louvain for large-scale social networks	Focus on improving structural community detection; does not integrate topic–sentiment information.	Enhance Louvain by using structure plus attributes to improve community detection accuracy.
Ahmed et al. (2022)	Short text clustering with mixed representations	High dimensionality and sparsity of short texts remain challenging; no unified sentiment–community pipeline.	Show that combining traditional, semantic, and deep representations yields better short-text clusters.
Kabir et al. (2022)	Empirical comparison of ML methods for sentiment classification	Emphasis on classifier performance; no community detection or cluster-level sentiment aggregation.	Identify Boosting and Maximum Entropy as strong performers for sentence-level sentiment.
Qaiser & Ali (2021)	Deep vs classical ML for social media sentiment	Focused on accuracy comparison; no integration with community structure.	Demonstrate that deep learning outperforms classical ML for social media sentiment tasks.
Hasan et al. (2022)	Lexicon vs classifier approaches for political Twitter sentiment	Limited to Twitter; does not create community-level sentiment profiles.	Show that combining word sense disambiguation with Naive Bayes improves polarity detection.
Carter et al. (2023)	Transformer models with financial lexicons	Domain-specific (finance); text-only, without graph/ community integration.	Improve sentiment accuracy by injecting domain-specific financial lexicons into Transformer models.
Kumar et al. (2022)	Combined community detection and sentiment for COVID-19 Reddit	Focused on a single event domain; does not employ multi-metric validation or multi-topic modelling paradigms.	Show correlation between community membership and sentiment polarity in COVID-19 Reddit data.
Nirmala et al. (2021)	Sarcasm detection with emoticon polarity and SentiWordNet	Targets sarcasm/emoji, but not integrated with full sentiment–community pipelines.	Improve sarcasm detection in microblogs using emoticon polarity and lexical resources.
Ribeiro et al. (2023)	Benchmark of 18 sentiment tools on Twitter/Reddit	Tool-focused evaluation; no integrated community detection or cross-domain pipeline.	Provide comprehensive performance comparison and positioning of tools such as VADER.

THEORETICAL BACKGROUND

Affinity Propagation Clustering

Affinity Propagation (AP) is an exemplar-based clustering algorithm specified by Frey and Dueck. AP works by passing real-valued messages between data points. It identifies a small set of exemplars (Frey & Dueck, 2007). Unlike the case with k-means and hierarchical clustering, AP automatically decides on the number of clusters through a message-passing mechanism not requiring any prior specification of k. This is especially important in exploratory analysis of social media data where true number of thematic groups is not known (Gan et al., 2023; Qaiser & Ali, 2021).

The algorithm's two messages will be parameterised: The responsibility r(i,k) is the message sent for data point i to exemplar k reflecting its suitability to that data point; the availability a(i, k) reflects the appropriateness of data point i choosing k as its exemplar. The messages are iteratively updated as follows:

$$r(i,k) \leftarrow s(i,k) - max_{k'\neq k} a(i,k') + s(i,k') \tag{1}$$

$$a(i,k) \leftarrow min 0, r(k,k) + \Sigma_{i'\notin i,k} max 0, r(i',k) for i \neq k \tag{2}$$

$$a(k,k) \leftarrow \Sigma_{i'\neq k} max 0, r(i',k) \tag{3}$$

The similarity s(i, k) between the points i and k is given by the negative of their cosine distance. The message-passing process has high damping values in practice so that oscillation is suppressed for high-dimensional sparse term-frequency matrix (Prasad, 2021).

Latent Dirichlet Allocation (LDA)

LDA generates probabilistic models of text corpora assumes that each document is a mixture over latent topics, and each topic is a probability distribution over a vocabulary. In the Latent Dirichlet Allocation (LDA) generative process, each document m is assigned a topic distribution θ_m drawn from Dirichlet prior Dir(α). For each word position n, a topic $z_{m,n}$ is assigned by a draw from Multinomialθ_m; and the actual observed word $w_{m,n}$ is assigned by a draw from Multinomial$\left(\varphi_{z_{m,n}}\right)$, where φ_k is the word multinomial for topic k drawn from Dir(η). More formally, we can explain it in the following way:

$$0_m \; Dir(\alpha), z_{m,n} \; Multinomial\left(\theta_m\right), w_{m,n} \; Multinomial\left(\varphi_{z_{m,n}}\right) \tag{4}$$

The document-topic Dirichlet prior hyperparameter is α, the topic-word Dirichlet prior hyperparameter is η, $\theta_m \in R^K$ the topic proportion vector for document m, $\varphi_k \in R^V$the word distribution vector for topic k, K is the number of latent topics, the vocabulary size is V. This model allows one to perform the unsupervised discovery of coherent thematic structures without requiring a manual annotation. (Apostol et al., 2022; Hu et al., 2022).

Non-Negative Matrix Factorization (NMF)

NMF decomposes a non-negative input matrix $V \in R_{\geq 0}^{m \times n}$ into two non-negative factor matrices: $W \in R_{\geq 0}^{m \times k}$ (the document-topic matrix) and $H \in R_{\geq 0}^{k \times n}$ (the topic-word matrix), such that:

$$V \approx W \times H \tag{5}$$

In this expression, m represents the number of documents, n indicates the vocabulary size, and k corresponds to the number of latent topics. The goal is to minimize the Frobenius norm of reconstruction error:

$$min_{W,H \geq 0} \| V - WH \|^2_F \tag{6}$$

As per Guo et al. (2021), we can see that this factorisation can achieve a parts-based decomposition that produces more interpretable, sparse topic representations than LDA. It is especially useful for short social media text, where topics have a lot of overlap in the vocabulary.

VADER Sentiment Analysis

VADER (Valence Aware Dictionary and Sentiment Reasoner) is a lexicon-based tool for sentiment analysis targeted at social media texts. The system manages punctuation emphasis, capitalisation, degree modifiers, and negation in a rule-based way. Depending on the text, VADER generates four values: positive (pos), negative (neg), neutral (neu) and compound value. The score of compound is determined by adding the valence score of every word in the lexicon and adjusting according to the different rules in context. Finally, it is normalised according to the formula given below:

$$compound = \frac{x}{\sqrt{(x^2 + \alpha)}} \tag{7}$$

Where x is the total valence score of all the words in the text and α = 15 is a normalizing constant giving a compound score in a range of -1 to +1. Established thresholds are used for sentiment class assignment:

$$Positive{:}compound \geq 0.05 \; Negative{:}compound \leq -0.05$$

$$Neutral{:}-0.05 < compound < 0.05 \quad (8)$$

(Ribeiro et al., 2023; Xing, 2023).

Louvain Modularity Algorithm

The Louvain algorithm is a hierarchical greedy community detection algorithm that optimizes graph modularity by iteratively merging nodes into communities. The modularity Q of a network is defined quantifying the density of edges within communities compared to edges between communities:

$$Q = \left(\frac{1}{2m}\right)\Sigma_{i,j}\left[A_{ij} - \frac{(k_i \times k_j)}{2m}\right] \times \delta\left(c_i, c_j\right) \quad (9)$$

The edge weights between nodes i and j that are in each graph sum up to thisA_{ij}, and also the sum of the weights incident on a certain node is incorporate into the value range of the function. k_i And k_j are the sum of weights of edges attached to nodes i and j respectively, which are further terms mainly meant for normalization purposes. Whether the nodes i and j belong to the same community is given by c_i and c_j denote the community assignments of nodes i and j; and$\delta\left(c_i, c_j\right) = 1 if c_i = c_j and 0 otherwise$; $m = (1/2)\Sigma_{ij}A_{ij}$ is the total edge weight in the graph; When Q takes larger values, the community structure gets stronger. The first stage of the algorithm operates such that each node is assigned to its own community. Furthermore, the nodes are taken together with their neighbours based on merge. In addition, this process is executed until the value of Q increases. After that, second stage starts when the value of Q cannot attain more increase. (Han et al., 2023; Ranjan et al., 2022).

3. METHODOLOGY

The OpinionGraph framework is structured as a sequential and modular pipeline implemented in Python at Google Colab with outputs persisted at Google Drive. This pipeline consists of seven modules, each dependent on one another and described in the subsections below. As illustrated at the end of this section in the flowchart, the complete system workflow is defined.

3.1 Data Collection

The PRAW (Python Reddit API Wrapper) library was used to collect the Reddit data. Four topics that carry political weight and significance but are not entirely unrelated from each other were picked from different areas of public discourse, namely the Pahalgam terrorist attack, Israel Gaza, 2024 US Presidential Elections, and Trump tariff policy. A few subreddits per topic were queried resulting in 1,000 (One Thousand) posts a subreddit on an average for approximately 12 (Twelve) subreddits in total. The original information was extracted as CSV, which is a type of file that uses a comma to separate individual items of data. It contains the fields: id, title, author, score, num_comments, created_utc, selftext, url, permalink, and subreddit. (Guo et al., 2021; Zhou et al., 2023).

3.2 Preprocessing

The identical preprocessing pipeline was applied to all twelve subreddit datasets in two sequential stages.

Stage A: Stage A Structural Cleaning involved keeping only the relevant columns (id, title, author, selftext), and trashing all rows that had a null or empty or whitespace-only selftext. After this step, we performed a sequence of regular expression operations to remove email addresses, mentions of Reddit users (made through the terms spaced u/ and /u/), URLs, anything that's numeric, and lastly any punctuation or other character that is not an alphabet. The cleaned text was then normalised for whitespace, leading and trailing character stripped.

Stage B: In Stage B, we tokenized and lemmatized the cleaned corpus with spaCy's en_core_web_sm model. Tokens were kept if they were alphabetic, not a stop word in spaCy, not in a domain-specific custom stopword file imported from an external file. The lowercased lemmatised tokens made up the vocabulary and feature representation used in all downstream analyses (Ahmed et al., 2022; Gan et al., 2023).

3.3 Feature Representation

After linguistic normalisation, a binary term-frequency (TF) matrix is created for each of the subreddits' dataset. Vocabulary is defined as the set of all unique lemmatised tokens after the preprocessing phase. For each post, we created a binary indicator vector of length |V|, where an entry v = 1 if word j appears in the post and

0 otherwise. The authors argue that this representation was selected in preference to TF-IDF weighting because it retains presence, while showing that rare terms do not get greater weight. The former is appropriate for short, sparse documents like social media (Ahmed et al., 2022). The binary TF matrix is the only input used for clustering, NMF topic modelling, and cluster quality validation modules.

3.4 Clustering: Affinity Propagation

The binary TF matrix was subjected to Affinity Propagation (AP) to discern opinion communities without necessitating a predetermined number of clusters. The term-frequency feature vectors were used with sklearn.metrics.pairwise_distances with metric='cosine' to create the negative cosine distance similarity matrix S. The AP (Affinity Propagation) model was fitted with affinity='precomputed', damping=0.9, and random_state=42 to ensure reproducibility to appropriate parameters to get final predictions. The main message-passing updates are two:

$$r(i,k) \leftarrow s(i,k) - max_{k' \neq k} a(i,k') + s(i,k') \tag{10}$$

$$a(i,k) \leftarrow min0, r(k,k) + \Sigma_{i' \notin i,k} max0, r(i',k)(i \neq k) \tag{11}$$

$$a(k,k) \leftarrow \Sigma_{i' \neq k} max0, r(i',k) \tag{12}$$

Where $r(i,k)$ refers to the suitability of k for point i, $a(i,k)$ is the accumulated evidence that k should be an exemplar, and s(i, k) is the pairwise similarity. The assignments of cluster membership and the obtained inter-cluster cosine similarity matrices were exported as structured CSVs for subsequent downstream analysis (Prasad, 2021; Qaiser & Ali, 2021).

3.5 Topic Modelling: LDA and NMF

Two algorithms of complementary nature were employed to extract latent topical structure at different levels of granularity.

Global Non-Negative Matrix Factorization (NMF) was applied to the binary TF matrix, using n_components=50, init='random', and random_state=42. NMF (Non-Negative Matrix Factorization) produced the basis matrix W (posts × 50 topics), and the coefficient matrix H (50 topics × vocabulary). The diversity in the choice of n_component, and the full matrix approximations captures fine-grained latent thematic features present in the entire corpus. The objective of NMF minimizes the Frobenius norm of the reconstruction error:

$$min_{W,H\geq 0}\|V - WH\|^2_F \quad (13)$$

We applied Latent Dirichlet Allocation (LDA) per cluster by concatenating all posts within each cluster into a single cluster-document. By using CountVectorizer with max_features=3,000 and stop_words='english', cluster-documents underwent LDA for n_components=10, learning_method='batch', max_iter=25 and random_state=42. The creation of subject m occurs in the following manner:

$$\theta Dir(\alpha), z_{mn}\ Multinomial(\theta), w_{mn}\ Multinomial\left(\varphi_{z_{mn}}\right) \quad (14)$$

After the allocation of the documents to the clusters is complete, a cluster will be assigned its dominant topic through argmax of the topic distribution, and the top fifteen (15) keywords per topic will be extracted to serve as the thematic label (Apostol et al., 2022; Guo et al., 2021; Hu et al., 2022; Jelodar et al., 2021).

3.6 Sentiment Analysis: VADER

The VADER's SentimentIntensityAnalyzer was used on the selftext of each post to compute four scores neg, neu, pos, and compound. The calculation for the compound score is:

$$compound = x/\sqrt{(x^2 + \alpha)} \quad (15)$$

where x is the total of the valence scores for every word present in the text and $\alpha = 15$ is a normalisation constant that gives a compound score between $[-1,+1]$. Canonical VADER thresholds were used to assign post-level sentiment labels:

Positive: compound $\geq +0.05$
Negative: compound ≤ -0.05
Neutral: $-0.05 <$ compound $< +0.05$

Post IDs were reconstructed in p-notation (p1, p2, …) for cluster-level aggregation. Further, they were merged with original post data by running an inner join. From all the individual compound scores assigned for a specific time period, average compound score per cluster was computed. As a result, three output files were generated: Positive_Clusters_VADER.csv, Negative_Clusters_VADER.csv, and Neutral_Clusters_VADER.csv (Ribeiro et al., 2023; Xing, 2023).

3.7 Cluster Quality Validation

Four internal cluster validity metrics were calculated overall as well as for the positive, negative and neutral ranges. All metrics calculations excluded singleton clusters containing only one post. Reconstructing the post ID's as p1, p2,... and merging with the TF feature matrix using inner join, we obtain the required (X, labels) format to compute metrics.

The Silhouette Score is the ratio of inter cluster and intra cluster. For a sample i with intra-cluster distance $a(i)$ and nearest-cluster distance $b(i)$:

$$s(i) = (b(i) - a(i))/max a(i), b(i) \tag{16}$$

Davies–Bouldin index computes the average similarity ratio of a cluster with its most similar cluster, wherein smaller values indicate better separation:

$$DB = (1/k)\Sigma_{i=1}^{k} max_{j\neq i}\left(\sigma_i + \sigma_j\right)/d\left(c_i, c_j\right) \tag{17}$$

Dunn Index determines the ratio of the farthest distance between clusters and farthest distance between points in the same cluster:

$$DI = min_{i\neq j} d\left(C_i, C_j\right)/max_k \Delta\left(C_k\right) \tag{18}$$

The Xie–Beni Index ensures compactness in relation to separation and the lower its value the better quality the cluster is said to be:

$$XB = \left(\Sigma_i \Sigma_{x\in C_i} \|x - \mu_i\|^2\right)/\left(n \times min_{i\neq j} \|\mu_i - \mu_j\|^2\right) \tag{19}$$

The calculation of Silhouette Score and Davies–Bouldin Index took place using sklearn.metrics, while Dunn Index and Xie–Beni Index used the permetrics library (Ahmed et al., 2022; Hu et al., 2022).

3.8 Graph Analysis: Louvain Modularity

A graph G = (V, E) is undirected whose nodes are Affinity Propagation clusters, and whose edges connect the clusters that have the same dominant LDA topic with weight = 1.0. The overall modularity score Q, the contribution to the modularity per community, and community assignment per cluster were calculated with the Louvain algorithm (python-louvain, community_louvain.best_partition). Definition of Graph Modularity as:

$$Q = \left(\frac{1}{2m}\right)\Sigma_{i,j}\left[A_{ij} - \frac{(k_i \times k_j)}{2m}\right] \times \delta\left(c_i, c_j\right) \quad (20)$$

A_{ij}= weight of the edge between nodes *i* and *j*
k_i,k_j= sum of weights of edges attached to nodes *i* and *j* respectively

$$m = \left(\frac{1}{2}\right)\Sigma_{ij}A_{ij} = totaledgeweightinthegraph \quad (21)$$

c_i,c_j= community assignments of nodes *i* and *j*
$\delta(c_i,c_j)$= 1 if c_i=c_j, and 0 otherwise

Cluster-level sentiment counts were transformed using cylindrical coordinates to create 3D (Three-dimensional) visualisations:

X= Cluster ID
Y= $\text{Positive}_{\text{count}} \times \cos(\text{radians}(\text{Neutral}_{\text{count}}))$
Z= $\text{Negative}_{\text{count}} \times \sin(\text{radians}(\text{Neutral}_{\text{count}}))$

The marker colour indicates the dominant sentiment class of each of cluster, and the weighted version scales marker size by average VADER compound score. This representation allows for the simultaneous visualization of community structure, thematic composition, and affective polarity in a three-dimensional plot (Guo et al., 2021; Han et al., 2023; Ranjan et al., 2022).

MATERIALS AND METHODS

Dataset and Data Collection

The PRAW (Python Reddit API Wrapper) library was used to collect data from Reddit across twelve subreddits covering four important political topics. Presented in Table 2 is a summary of the dataset coverage. The selftext field was the source of content, with posts that had a selftext value of null, empty, [removed] or [deleted] removed from analysis.

Table 2. Dataset coverage — twelve subreddits across four real-world event domains

Event Domain	Subreddit	Data Type
Pahalgam Attack	r/unitedstatesofindia	Posts + Comments
Pahalgam Attack	r/hinduism	Posts + Comments
Pahalgam Attack	r/librandu	Posts + Comments
Israel-Gaza Conflict	r/IsraelPalestine	Posts + Comments
Israel-Gaza Conflict	r/Palestine	Posts + Comments
Israel-Gaza Conflict	r/war	Posts + Comments
USA Election 2024	r/politics	Posts + Comments
USA Election 2024	r/PoliticalDiscussion	Posts + Comments
USA Election 2024	r/dataisbeautiful	Posts + Comments
Trump Tariff Policy	r/stocks	Posts + Comments
Trump Tariff Policy	r/Economics	Posts + Comments
Trump Tariff Policy	r/serbia	Posts + Comments

Pipeline Flowchart

The complete OpinionGraph process is shown in Figure 1. We go through seven sequential workflow stages from raw data to detection and visualisation of meta-communities.

Figure 1. OpinionGraph community detection pipeline flowchart

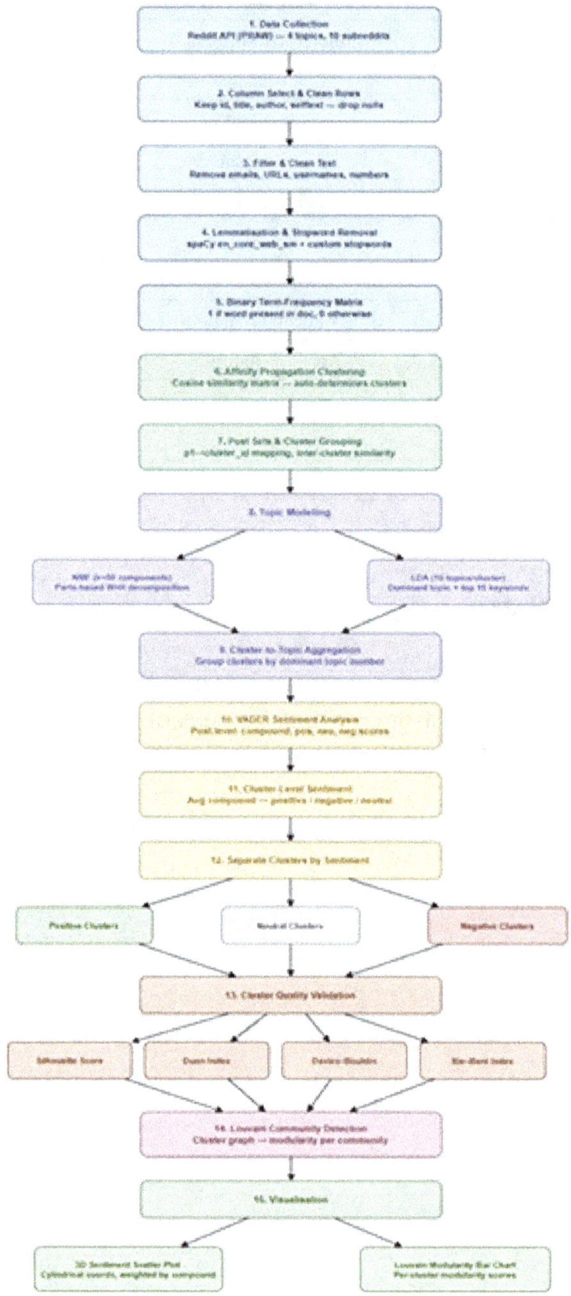

As seen in Figure 1, initial Reddit data is collected through PRAW and enters the pipeline. From there, the data goes through a regex filter, spaCy lemmatisation, and stopword removal in sequence. Cleaned corpus is converted into a binary feature matrix which becomes the common input for the parallel running of (1) Affinity Propagation clustering followed by hybrid LDA-NMF topic modelling and (2) VADER-based post-level sentiment scoring. The outputs from the two tracks are combined at the cluster level to create cluster sentiment profiles. Various quality metrics are used to validate the profiles created. We also visualise them using 3D scatter plots. The resultant graph of connected topic clusters is subjected to the Louvain modularity algorithm for community detection.

Data Filtering and Preprocessing

To maintain the integrity of the data and safeguard user privacy, we have stripped all selftext columns of personal identifiers and noise using regex. The cleaning operations were undertaken in sequence to first eliminate email addresses, then Reddit user mentions, the URLs or website addresses, the numeric sequences and finally the non-alphabetic or punctuation in this cleaning. The full data cleansing transformation pipeline is given as:

```
EMAIL_RE = re.compile(r'\b[A-Za-z0-9._%+-]+@[A-Za-z0-9.-]+\.[A-Za-z]
{2,}\b', re.I)
REDDIT_USER_RE = re.compile(r'(?i)(?:/u/|u/|@)[A-Za-z0-9_-]+')
NUM_RE = re.compile(r'\d+')
URL_RE = re.compile(r'http\S+|www\.\S+', re.I)
PUNCT_SYMBOL_RE = re.compile(r'[^A-Za-z\s]')
```

$$T_{c}\text{lean} = f_{s}\text{pace}\Big(f_{s}ym\big(f_{d}igit\big(f_{u}ser\big(f_{u}rl\big(f_{e}mail(T_{i}nput)\big)\big)\big)\big)\Big) \quad (22)$$

Text Preprocessing and Normalization

spaCy's en_core_web_sm model was used to process the selftext data after filtering. The preprocessing pipeline comprised: (a) loading a stopword list, which was a merged list from spaCy as well as a custom list from the document domain, (b) removing all non-alphabetic words, and (c) normalizing to lowercase-lemmatized tokens. The vocabulary V created as a result is defined as:

$$V = \cup\_\{t \in T\}\{\text{lemma}(t).\text{lower}()\,|\,\text{is\_alpha}(t) \wedge \text{lemma}(t).\text{lower}() \notin S \quad (23)$$

S is the union of all stopwords, where T is the collection of all tokens within the entire corpus. The lemmatization operation reduces the morphological variants (like running, ran, runs) to a common root like (run). Thus, quality of downstream similarity calculations improves and feature dimensionality decreases.

Binary Feature Matrix Construction

Vocabulary produced (corpus) was derived from the token process. A binary term-document incidence matrix was formed, wherein every document was represented by a binary vector in the vocabulary. If a term t in the vocabulary appears in document d, it has been assigned a value of 1 and 0 otherwise:

$$\text{Value}(t, d) = 1 \text{if t} \in d\text{ocument d}, 0\text{otherwise} \tag{24}$$

The chosen representation in binary rather than TF-IDF due to the robustness of this more binary representation to frequency imbalances that is common in very short social media texts where noise is in high frequency rather than signal. The outcome matrix is a high-dimensional sparse representation of the corpus usable for cosine similarity.

Affinity Propagation Clustering

To form a symmetric similarity matrix S, pairwise cosine similarity was computed for all documents:

$$\text{sim}\left(d_i, d_j\right) = \cos(\theta) = \frac{d_i \cdot d_j}{\|d_i\| \, \|d_j\|} \tag{26}$$

We used affinity = "precomputed," damping = 0.9, random_state=42 for the Affinity Propagation. Membership of each cluster k is defined as:

$$\text{C\_k} = \{\text{p} \in \text{P}|\text{label(p)} = \text{k}\} \tag{27}$$

P is the collection of all post IDs; label(p) denotes the cluster label of post p. The mean of all the document vectors belonging to a cluster formed the centroid vector of that cluster. The construction of a pairwise inter-cluster matrix of cosine similarities allowed downstream community detection.

LDA Topic Modelling

LDA was employed at two levels. Initially, at the level of the corpus, to identify five global latent topics. At the cluster level, by pooling together all posts within each Affinity Propagation cluster into a single document and applying LDA to derive ten dominant topics per cluster:

$$P(W,Z,\Theta,\beta|\alpha,\eta)=\prod k = 1KP(\beta k|\eta)\prod m = 1MP(\theta m|\alpha)\prod n$$

$$= 1NmP(zm,n|\theta m)\,P(wm,n|\beta zm,n) \tag{28}$$

Each cluster was assigned the thematic label based on its dominant topic and the top fifteen (15) keywords. Each of the topics $t_j$is mapped to the set of clusters that share that dominant topic:

$$M(t_j) = \{\mathbf{c} \in \text{Clusters} \mid f(c) = t_j\} \tag{29}$$

VADER Sentiment Analysis

For VADER's SentimentIntensityAnalyzer generated four scores for each post: positive (pos), negative (neg), neutral (neu) and a normalised compound score C ∈ [−1, +1]. The final sentiment class for each post was assigned with standard VADER thresholds:

$$\text{Sentiment}='positive'\ if\ \text{C} \geq 0.05,'negative'\ if\ \text{C} \leq -0.05,'neutral'\ otherwise \tag{30}$$

For each cluster k, we computed the mean compound score across all the posts belonging to that cluster:

$$\overline{C_k} = \frac{1}{N_k}\sum_{i\in\text{Cluster}_k} C_i \tag{31}$$

3D Sentiment Visualisation

A weighted 3D scatter plot was created using a transformation of coordinates. The Cartesian coordinates (x, y, z) for each cluster were determined finally as:

x= ClusterID
y= Positive_count×cos(θ)
z= Negative_count×sin(θ)

In the weighted visualisation, the marker sizeS_k of each cluster k was scaled by the average compound score C_k which represented intensity of sentiment. Each of the cluster points was coloured to signify the overall sentiment classification of either positive (green), negative (red), or neutral (purple).

CLUSTER QUALITY VALIDATION METRICS

Silhouette Score

Clustering cohesion and clustering separation are measured by Silhouette Score. The score for one sample i is defined as:

$$s(i) = \frac{b(i) - a(i)}{\max(a(i), b(i))} \tag{32}$$

The mean intra-cluster distance for sample i is $a(i)$; while $b(i)$ is the mean nearest-cluster distance. The average of all the $s(i)$ gives the overall Silhouette Score and can vary between −1 and +1, where greater values denote more-defined clusters.

Dunn Index

The Dunn index defines clusters by measuring the ratio of the minimum inter-cluster distance to the maximum intra-cluster diameter:

$$D = \frac{\min_{i \neq j} d(C_i, C_j)}{\max_k \mathbf{diam}(C_k)} \tag{33}$$

The Dunn Index measures the compactness and separation of clusters.

Davies–Bouldin Index

The Davies-Bouldin index (DBI) is a function that measures the similarity between clusters:

$$\text{DBI} = \frac{1}{k} \sum_{i=1}^{k} \max_{j \neq i} \left(\frac{s_i + s_j}{d(C_i, C_j)} \right) \tag{34}$$

Here k is the number of clusters, s_i is the mean distance of samples in cluster i from its centroid, and $d(C_i, C_j)$ is the distance between centroids of clusters i and j. Lower DBI indicates better-defined clusters.

Xie–Beni Index

Xie–Beni Index assesses the ratio between total intra-cluster variance and nearest inter-cluster centroid distance:

$$XBI = \left(1/N^* \sum(i = 1)^k \sum(x \in C_i) d(x, C_i)^2\right) / \min_{(i \neq j)} d\left(C_i, C_j\right)^2 \quad (35)$$

The numerator denotes the overall intra-cluster variance (compactness), while the denominator denotes the minimum squared inter-cluster distance. A lower XBI reflects a clearer clustering structure and better clustering quality.

Tools and Technologies

Table 3. Summarises the tools and technologies employed in the OpinionGraph implementation.

Category	Tool / Library	Role in Project
Runtime Environment	Google Colab (Python 3.10+)	Cloud-based execution environment
Persistent Storage	Google Drive	CSV and PNG output persistence
Data Handling	pandas, numpy	DataFrame operations, matrix algebra
NLP & Preprocessing	spaCy (en_core_web_sm)	Tokenisation, lemmatisation, POS tagging
Sentiment Analysis	NLTK VADER	Lexicon-based sentiment scoring
Feature Extraction	sklearn CountVectorizer	Binary TF matrix construction
Clustering	sklearn AffinityPropagation	Primary community detection
Topic Modelling	sklearn LDA, NMF	Per-cluster topic discovery
Cluster Validity	sklearn, permetrics	Silhouette, DBI, Dunn, XBI
Graph Analysis	networkx, python-louvain	Graph construction and Louvain modularity
Visualisation	matplotlib, seaborn	3D scatter plots, bar charts

RESULTS

The results of our OpinionGraph pipeline on the twelve subreddit datasets from four main politically salient event domains is presented in this section. Affinity propagation detected thematic communities automatically, LDA and NMF extracted apparent latent themes, VADER classified sentiments at post level and cluster level, cluster quality tested using four internal validity measures, and Louvain algorithm detected meta-community structure.

Affinity Propagation Cluster Formation

Using Affinity Propagation (AP) with a damping factor of 0.9 on the negative cosine distance similarity matrices, we obtained thematically coherent clusters in all twelve subreddits without any a priori specification on the number of communities. The algorithm was able to identify between 23 and 99 thematic clusters per subreddit; indicating the extent of topic diversity across communities. The Reddit group PoliticalDiscussion has the highest cluster count (99) in the corpus, which is due to its large thematic scope. The war subreddit produced the least clusters, just 23, which reflects more focused and topic converging discourses.

Table 4. Clustering Results — Number of Clusters and Dominant Sentiment by Subreddit

Topic	Subreddit	No. of Clusters	Dominant Sentiment
Election of USA	PoliticalDiscussion	99	Positive (80%)
Election of USA	dataisbeautiful	35	Positive
Israel–Gaza Conflict	IsraelPalestine	49	Negative (73%)
Israel–Gaza Conflict	Palestine	31	Negative
Israel–Gaza Conflict	war	23	Negative
New Tariff by Trump	serbia	56	Negative
New Tariff by Trump	stocks	28	Positive
Pahalgam Attack	hinduism	83	Positive (77%)
Pahalgam Attack	librandu	39	Positive
Pahalgam Attack	unitedstatesofindia	30	Mixed

Topic Modelling Outputs

LDA topic modelling was applied at the cluster level of each Affinity Propagation cluster to identify the dominant latent themes. The thematic label for each cluster was formed by extracting the top 15 keywords per dominant topic. The NMF (global) decomposition, with 50 components, was found able to capture fine-grained sub-topics present across the entire corpus. Thus, it provided a useful counterpoint to the per-cluster LDA analysis. Clusters of electoral discourse centered on vote, democracy and candidates' policy-related keywords. Humanitarian aid and ceasefire were themes from the clusters. Tariff clusters showed themes of trade policy/market impact while Pahalgam clusters produced themes of national security/collective solidarity.

VADER Sentiment Analysis Results

The sentiment analysis using VADER was applied at both the post level and cluster level in all twelve subreddits, giving both a more fine-grained and higher resolution insight into the affective polarity in each discourse community. The compound scores generated at the cluster level by aggregating post-level VADER outputs show that sentiment is unevenly distributed across thematic communities which would not be visible at the document level. The four event domains exhibit a variation in the spread of positive, negative, and neutral clusters. Conflict-related subreddits possess more negative clusters than the policy and election discussions by a significant degree. The distribution of sentiment by cluster in four representative subreddits is shown in Table 5.

Table 5. Cluster-Level Sentiment Distribution by Subreddit

Subreddit	Total Clusters	Positive	Negative	Neutral
PoliticalDiscussion	99	80	16	3
IsraelPalestine	49	8	36	5
hinduism (Pahalgam Attack)	83	77	3	3
serbia (New Tariff)	56	18	32	6

Cluster Quality Validation

A total of four internal validity metrics were calculated globally, and for positive, negative, and neutral cluster subsets for all ten subreddits. All metric calculations excluded singleton clusters. The full results can be seen in Tables 6 to 8. Each subreddit did not have any clusters of that sentiment class whose N/A represents.

Table 6. Silhouette Score by Subreddit and Sentiment Category

Subreddit	Combined	Positive	Negative	Neutral
PoliticalDiscussion	−0.6463	−0.5538	−0.4539	−0.1060
dataisbeautiful	−0.7036	−0.6747	N/A	0.2352
IsraelPalestine	−0.6498	−0.3548	−0.6089	−0.3036
Palestine	−0.5494	−0.3624	−0.4414	−0.1861
war	−0.5084	0.1765	−0.4693	−0.1491
serbia	−0.7426	−0.1807	−0.6714	−0.6174

continued on following page

Table 6. Continued

Subreddit	Combined	Positive	Negative	Neutral
stocks	−0.4825	−0.4660	N/A	N/A
hinduism	−0.6581	−0.6153	−0.1840	−0.1114
librandu	−0.5827	−0.4564	−0.4723	−0.1259
unitedstatesofindia	−0.6502	−0.4693	−0.5334	−0.2350

As previously indicated in Section VII-A, the Silhouette Scores for most experimental topics are negative. This outcome has been generally attributed to the high dimensionality and sparsity of the binary term occurrence feature matrix, a well-known issue associated with text-clustering in high dimensional space. Only two subreddits achieve better words with great performance. These are the Neutral category of dataisbeautiful (0.2352) and the Positive category of war (0.1765).

Table 7. Dunn Index by Subreddit and Sentiment Category

Subreddit	Combined	Positive	Negative	Neutral
PoliticalDiscussion	0.1649	0.0038	0.0047	1.6457
dataisbeautiful	0.1376	0.0057	N/A	N/A
IsraelPalestine	0.1674	0.0114	0.0106	0.3286
Palestine	0.0792	0.0139	0.0086	0.1453
war	0.0765	0.1469	0.0115	N/A
serbia	0.0594	0.0534	0.0066	0.1208
stocks	0.1922	0.0176	N/A	N/A
hinduism	0.0575	0.0077	N/A	1.0080
librandu	0.0657	0.0078	0.0068	0.1692
unitedstatesofindia	0.0965	0.0061	0.0109	N/A

The highest combined Dunn Index, at 0.1922, was found for the stocks subreddit, implying the most intra-cluster compactness and inter-cluster separation overall. The PoliticalDiscussion Neutral subset (1.6457) and Hinduism Neutral subset (1.0080) show remarkably high values achieving splendid cluster separation for these particular sentiment subsets.

Table 8. Davies–Bouldin Index by Subreddit and Sentiment Category

Subreddit	Combined	Positive	Negative	Neutral
PoliticalDiscussion	50.91	49.10	24.06	3.85
dataisbeautiful	19.20	19.39	N/A	0.79
IsraelPalestine	29.61	12.60	27.12	16.84
Palestine	21.27	8.39	22.70	11.43
war	15.29	1.37	15.20	1.52
serbia	19.70	7.24	18.83	10.62
stocks	17.54	17.66	N/A	N/A
hinduism	48.49	42.26	9.64	4.93
librandu	26.94	14.09	21.60	9.03
unitedstatesofindia	21.23	14.87	17.72	7.58

The war subreddit had the lowest DBI as a combined cluster (15.29) showing best separation. The war Positive subset was the best individual sentiment category in terms of performance (DBI = 1.37). This finding confirms that it is the most coherent cluster group as per different metrics used for the validation.

Table 9. Xie–Beni Index by Subreddit and Sentiment Category

Subreddit	Combined	Positive	Negative	Neutral
PoliticalDiscussion	453.41	625.51	149.49	2.36
dataisbeautiful	38.44	26.76	N/A	0.56
IsraelPalestine	129.60	57.20	138.72	198.16
Palestine	100.41	7.90	199.58	48.36
war	34.97	0.33	39.74	0.70
serbia	82.62	19.20	41.14	96.18
stocks	32.42	33.23	N/A	N/A
hinduism	267.19	311.65	27.42	8.66
librandu	94.13	34.75	82.28	24.01
unitedstatesofindia	53.63	123.50	64.33	21.37

The war subreddit (XBI = 34.97) was the lowest combined XBI score subreddit and the stocks subreddit (XBI = 32.42) was the second lowest combined XBI score subreddit, confirming superior cluster structure. The war Positive subset (XBI = 0.33) yields the best value in the whole database which indicates great compactness and separation.

Sentiment Cluster Visualizations

The 3D scatter plots shown below aid in visualing sentiment movement across clusters in multiple dimensions. Each point indicates one thematic cluster that can be identified by its colour: green for positive sentiment, red for negative sentiment, and purple for neutral sentiment.

Figure 2. shows a predominantly green cluster distribution for the Election of USA, particularly dense in subreddits, reflecting a constructive and civic tone in electoral discourse.

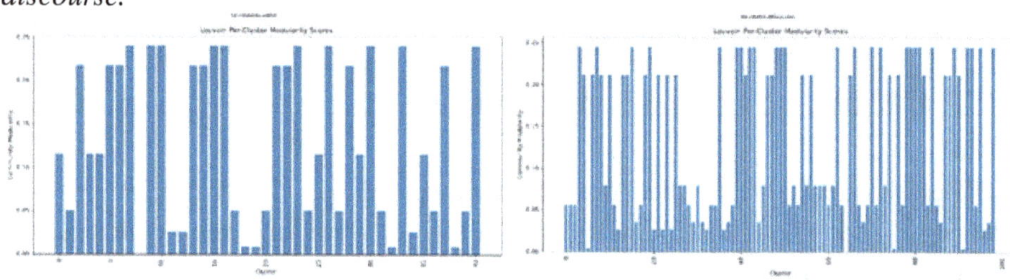

Both views confirm that positive sentiment prevails across all clusters with negative points being sparse and neutral points almost non-existent. This shows that while the electoral discourse on reddit may be critical, it is largely constructive and participatory.

Figure 3. displays a high concentration of red clusters for the Israel–Gaza Conflict, consistent with the tragic humanitarian nature of the topic and the emotionally charged nature of discourse within the IsraelPalestine community.

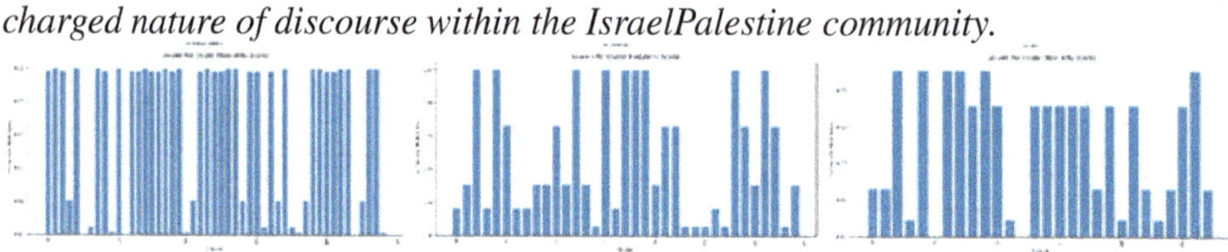

All three perspectives unambiguously indicate that there is a dominance of negative red points across all the cluster ranges while the positive are found in sparse amounts and neutral points are almost non-existent. The vertical axis' high negative scores (right and bottom panels) indicate contrasted and strong intensity of emotions surrounding the discourse relating to the Israel–Gaza conflict and not a mild disapproval. The pattern reflects how conflict-related conversations on

Reddit often lead to polarizing discussions, with users much more likely to outrage, mourn or condemn than to ever comment positively or neutrally. This clustering of such sentiments shows the hurdles that the platforms face in controlling emotional geopolitical discussions but creating space for real human suffering.

Figure 4. 3D Sentiment Cluster Visualization — New Tariff by Trump

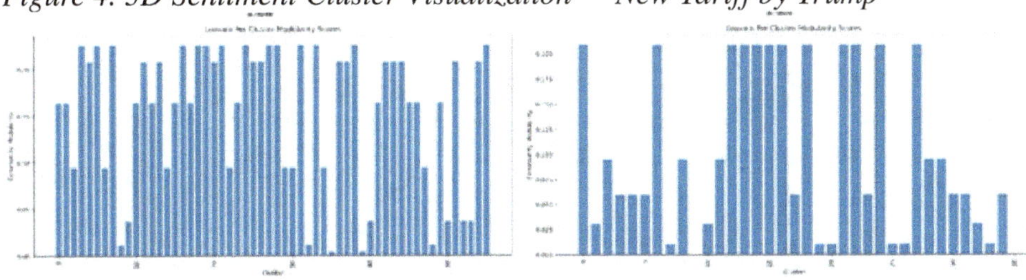

The left panel reveals a strong mixture of sentiments in the colour landscape, where red (Negative) points are densely peppered over clusters 0 to 50 and several onwards have quite high negative scores reaching up to 2.5. Meanwhile, purple (Neutral) points appear fairly often, which is a different pattern from other topics. In the right panel, however, we see a zoomed out view that shows the dominating green (Positive) points at lower negative magnitude. We can then assume that certain clusters of subreddits discussing tariffs are doing so in a neutral or economic analysis tone. The two perspectives together suggest that there is a deep division among Reddit users in public discourse over Trump's new tariffs. Economically concerned citizens and politically critical ones are responsible for the large amount of negative sentiment. In contrast, small communities that are either supportive of the tariffs or politically analytical have a positive sentiment.

Figure 5. 3D Sentiment Cluster Visualization — Pahalgam Attack

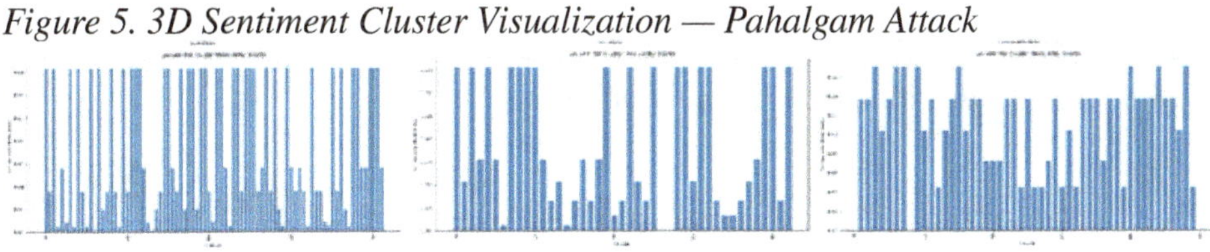

The r/unitedstatesofindia subreddit has an almost equal red-green split across posts, indicating a polarized civic response. There is a substantial predominance of green posts in r/hinduism, indicating spiritual solidarity and collective mourning. The r/librandu subreddit shows a range of volatility with high-elevation outliers consistent with this subreddit's critiquing political debate culture. In conclusion, reactions to the Pahalgam attack were ideologically differentiated and shaped within the groups we studied.

Weighted 3D Sentiment Cluster Visualizations

Figure 6. Weighted 3D Sentiment Cluster Visualization — Election of USA (bubble size proportional to sentiment intensity)

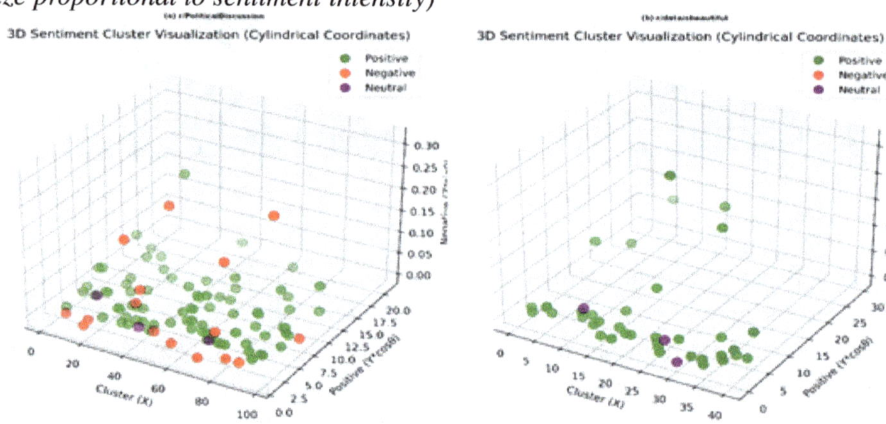

The weighted views show that while both subreddits maintain a green majority, the left panel holds a number of large red bubbles elevated on the negative axis showing that negativity, while less common, is of large intensity. Meanwhile, the right panel shows uniformly large green bubbles with no presence of negativity, confirming that framing electoral data in an analytical way decreases negativity not just in frequency but removes its intensity altogether.

Figure 7. Weighted 3D Sentiment Cluster Visualization — Israel–Gaza Conflict (bubble size proportional to sentiment intensity)

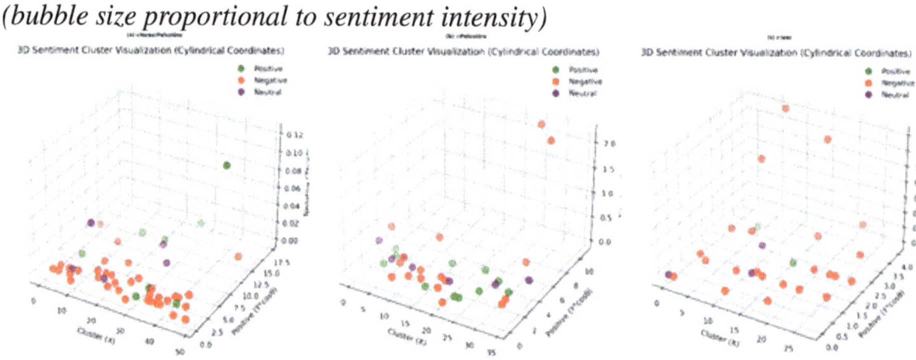

In all three charts, red bubbles are dominant in size and colour large red bubbles are the most frequent and have the most intensity. The intensity of these bubbles is large in the second chart, reaching negative red bubbles of 2.0. Thus, the negativity around the Israel–Gaza conflict is not only frequent, but it is also very intense. The large green bubbles that stand out as outliers in the left and right panels indicate that there are some pockets of constructive conversation amidst a sea of grief.

Figure 8. Weighted 3D Sentiment Cluster Visualization — New Tariff by Donald Trump (bubble size proportional to sentiment intensity)

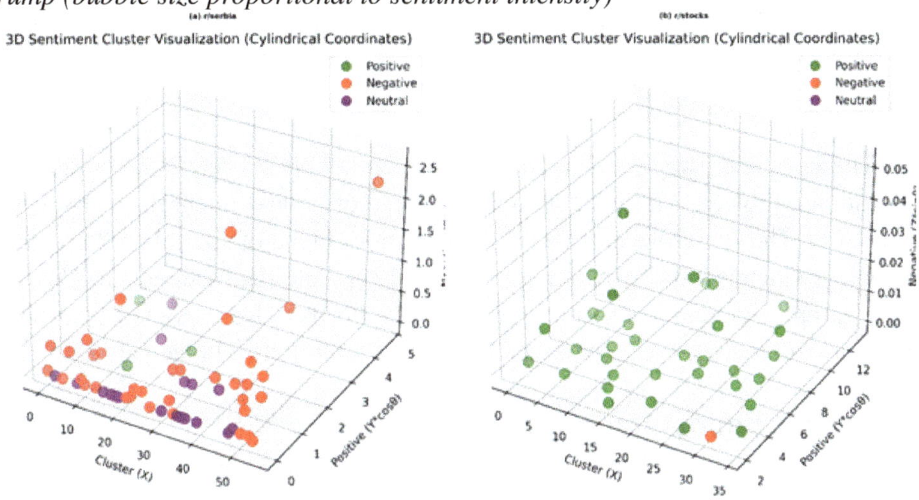

The left panel's large red and purple bubbles, along with an exceptionally intense negative outlier of ~2.5, indicate emotional and grievance-led discussion. The right panel's large green bubbles, with less than ~1 negativity, suggest neutral discussion of the same policy from a market perspective. The weightings suggest that the same event generates a different sentiment intensity from the community depending on whether it approaches it geopolitically or financially.

Figure 9. Weighted 3D Sentiment Cluster Visualization — Pahalgam Attack (bubble size proportional to sentiment intensity)

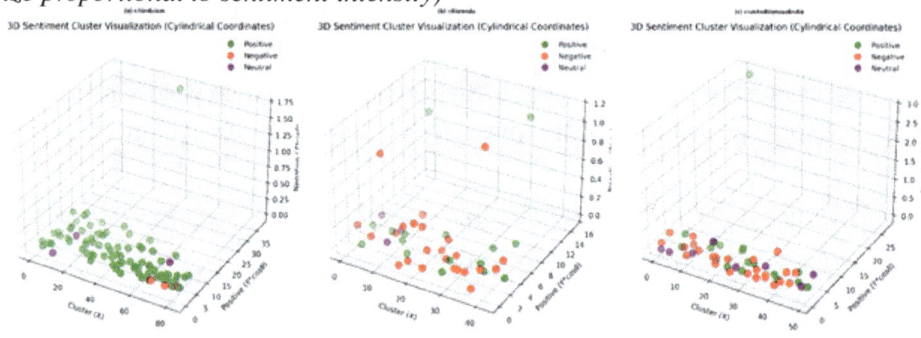

The left panel shows a nice cluster of green bubbles. There is an outlier high elevation bubble at ~1.75. In summary, people often and intensely feel spiritual solidarity. The centerpiece contains a tempestuous blend of sizeable red and green bubbles, which is indicative of a shared tragedy and political scepticism. The right side features a greening outlier at approximately 3.0, as well as large reds, indicating the most polarised civic responses of the three communities in the panel.

Louvain Community Detection

The LDA topic-cluster undirected graph was created to capture the embedding of clusters in communities and the Louvain algorithm was applied to the graph. The overall modularity score Q was calculated together with the per-community contributions to its modularity.

Figure 10. Louvain Per-Cluster Modularity Bar Chart — Election of USA

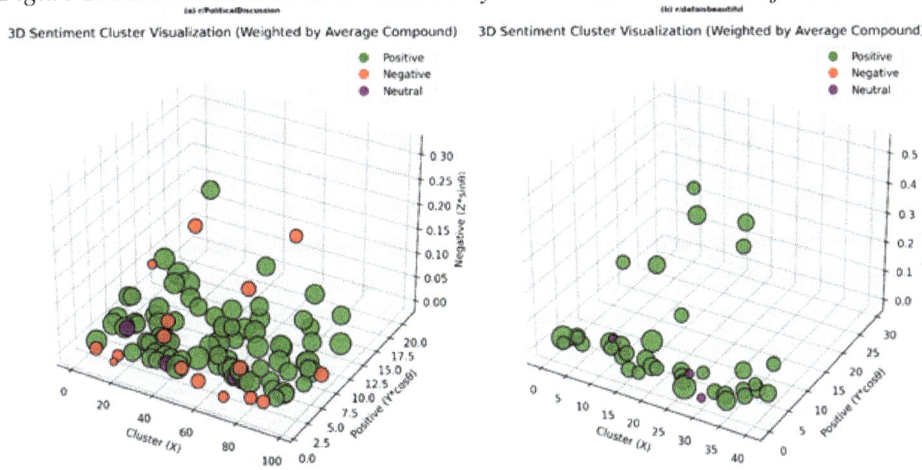

The modularity score of both panels vary considerably, ranging from near-zero up to ~0.25, indicating uneven community structure across clusters; Clusters with high values of modularity (~0.20–0.25) refer to well-separated opinion communities that have a thematic boundary. Conversely, clusters whose modularity values are close to zero refer to loosely connected overlapping groups. Hence, the findings confirm that the discourse on the US Election organises into well-separated pockets of high cohesion that are interspersed with loosely bounded transitional communities, rather than forming one large uniform structure.

Figure 11. Louvain Per-Cluster Modularity Bar Chart — Israel–Gaza Conflict

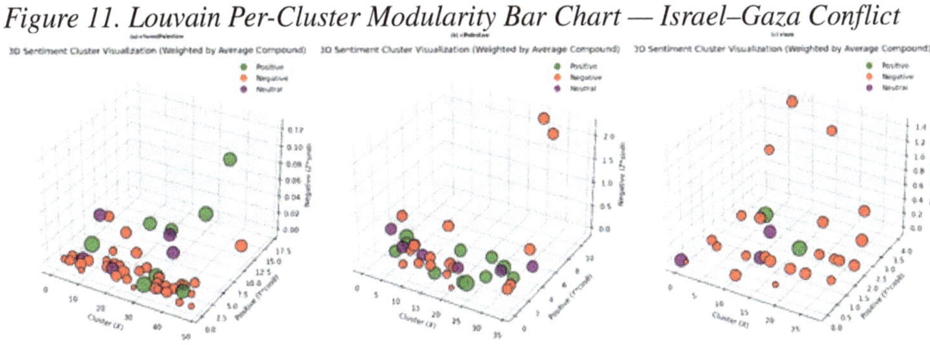

The three panels exhibit a crisp bimodal condensation: every cluster consistently achieves high modularity (approximately between 0.20 and 0.25) or collapses near zero, displaying limited intermediary states. The discourses produced by conflict polarise meaning-making where close-knit grief communities coalesce alongside uncertain more loosely connected clusters. The end result is a structurally fragmented community rather than a cohesive one.

Figure 12. Louvain Per-Cluster Modularity Bar Chart — New Tariff by Donald Trump

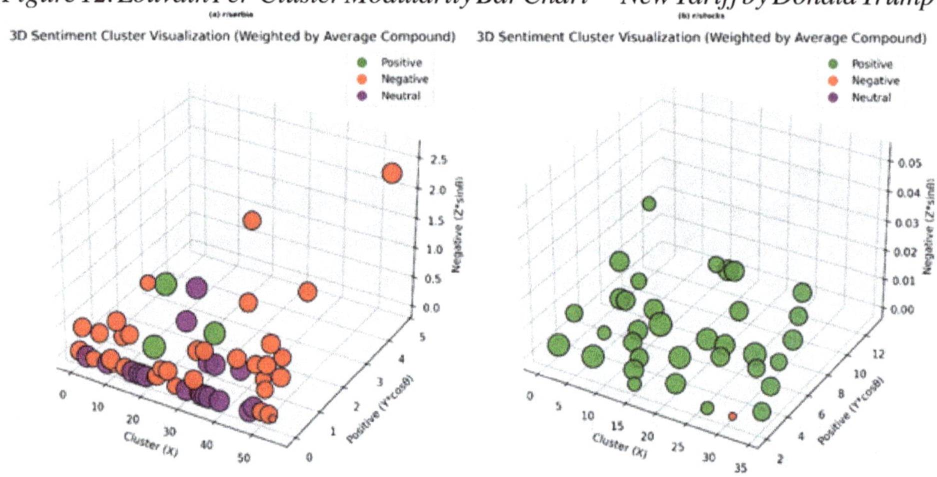

The left plot shows modularity scores peaking at ~0.70, the highest among all event domains, indicating very well-separated opinion communities. The right plot has a much narrower range of about ~0.02-0.20. The two panels are in agreement that tariff discourse organises into separate bounded thematic communities, which suggests that clear ideological and economic fault lines are produced by trade policy debates.

Figure 13. Louvain Per-Cluster Modularity Bar Chart — Pahalgam Attack

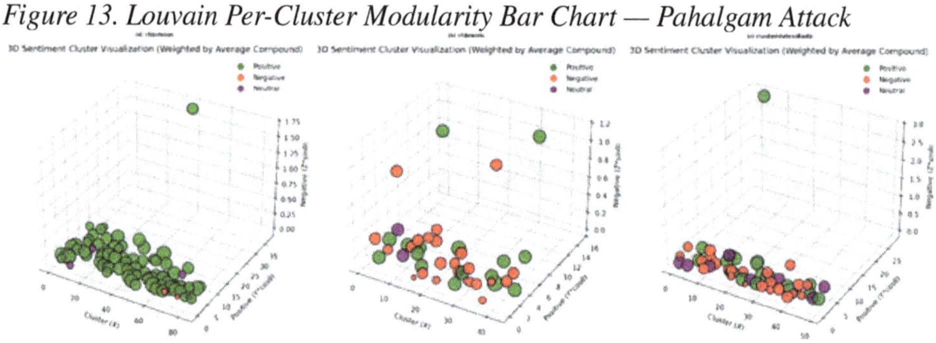

Three panels show consistently high modularity scores ~0.40–0.55 with low variability i.e. Pahalgam Attack discourse organizes into well-separated and structurally-stable opinion communities across all subreddits. The uniformly high extent of the different form of cohesion results suggest that emotional national security incidents strengthen community boundaries more firmly than political issues..

Methodological Contributions

OpinionGraph builds on previous research methodologically. It combines community detection based on Affinity Propagation with dual topic modelling approaches (LDA and NMF). In addition, it standardises the cluster-level sentiment aggregation based on VADER. Moreover, it incorporates multi-metric internal cluster validation plus Louvain meta-community detection. This results in reproducible pipelines. Most importantly, it generates structurally grounded community-level sentiment profiles across multiple politically distinct Reddit discourse domains.

Table 10.

Dimension	Prior work characteristic / limitation	OpinionGraph contribution	Key references
Reddit coverage and scope	Most Reddit sentiment studies focus on a single event or single subreddit, limiting cross-domain comparison.	Applies a consistent computational pipeline across four politically and geopolitically distinct events spanning twelve subreddits, enabling systematic cross-domain comparative analysis.	Li & Li (2022); Proferes et al. (2021)
Commun-ity detection method	Common use of k-means or DBSCAN introduces sensitivity to k, epsilon, and other parameters, which is problematic for high-dimensional sparse social media text.	Uses Affinity Propagation with precomputed cosine similarity, avoiding a priori choice of number of clusters and reducing parameter sensitivity for thematic community discovery.	Gan et al. (2023); Qaiser & Ali (2021)
Stability on sparse matrices	Prior work reports oscillation and instability issues for message-passing and clustering algorithms on sparse, high-dimensional text representations.	Adopts a high damping factor (0.9) in Affinity Propagation specifically to mitigate oscillation in sparse binary term-frequency matrices.	Prasad (2021); Su et al. (2021)
Cluster validation practice	Typical studies report only a single global validity metric (e.g., Silhouette or NMI), offering limited insight into cluster quality across sentiment regimes.	Computes Silhouette, Dunn, Davies–Bouldin, and Xie–Beni indices separately for positive, negative, and neutral clusters, providing a richer, sentiment-aware assessment of clustering quality.	Ahmed et al. (2022); Li & Li (2022)
Meta-level structural analysis	Community detection is usually applied directly on user or document graphs, with little work on meta-graphs linking topics and clusters, and without explicit sentiment integration.	Applies the Louvain algorithm on an LDA topic–cluster bipartite graph to uncover meta-communities of thematic clusters, adding a novel structural layer above cluster-level sentiment profiles.	Apostol et al. (2022); Han et al. (2023); Ranjan et al. (2022)

ANALYSIS AND DISCUSSION

Modularity scores in all datasets varied between 0.00 and 0.25. The USA election dataset and Pahalgam attack dataset had the most balanced data distributions that suggest an even meta-community structure. The Israel-Gaza Conflict plots displayed greater differences in modularity scores, with some clusters adding considerably more to their community structure, suggesting the highly polarized and diverse nature of conflict discourse. Communities represented by clusters with almost zero modularity values are isolated nodes having no edges with shared theme. We treat these as singleton communities.

Cluster Interpretation and Thematic Organisation

The application of Affinity Propagation on the cosine similarity matrices automatically provided the number of clusters for a dataset without pre-specifying the value of k, an important factor when the true number of opinion groups present in the social media is unknown and dependent on the domain. The LDA topic keywords of the resulting clusters show good thematic coherence which indicates the binary term-frequency representation combined with the use of cosine similarity and AP message passing can recover meaningful semantic clusters from even noisy Reddit text (Ahmed et al., 2022; Gan et al., 2023; Qaiser & Ali, 2021). Subreddits focusing on conflict brought about sharper, more narrowly-defined topics, while those centered on elections produced broader, more heterogeneous themes.

Sentiment Behaviour Across Domains

Social media posts and clustering based on VADER show that conflict domains (like Pahalgam Attack, Israel–Gaza) have negative clusters, which is in line with the (crisis) social media research that refers to more negativity during crisis (Guo et al., 2021). Subreddits related to elections had a more even distribution of positive, negative, and neutral clusters, whereas the Trump tariffs subreddits mixed economically motivated negative concern with the neutral and analytical character typical of financial communities (Kabir et al., 2022; Xing, 2023).

Neutral Cluster Validation

Neutral clusters, which are characterized by VADER compound scores in the range [−0.05, +0.05], may either correspond to genuinely neutral factual or procedural content, or may result from mixed-polarity posts in which positive and negative signals cancel each other out. Taking a look at the Silhouette and Dunn Davies Bouldin and Xie Beni indices by sentiment subset can help in differentiating these cases since strong internal structures but also external overlaps speaks of a hidden polarity clash. An internal index alone, especially with regard to short and sparse social media texts (Ahmed et al., 2022), fails to capture cluster quality.

Topic Modelling Insights

Conversing of per-cluster LDA and global NMF combines per-cluster LDA with global NMF to generate topics toward two complementary views. The former offers compact and interpretable cluster-level topic labels. The latter produces a more fine-grained analysis of subtopics specific to single topics. Such fine-grained detail is particularly beneficial for large, heterogeneous subreddits (Guo et al., 2021). By mapping the dominant LDA topics to their Affinity Propagation clusters, a topic-cluster graph was built that turns probabilistic topic memberships into a concrete topology suitable for community detection. This not only overcomes the weaknesses of existing approaches which separate clustering and community detection (Apostol et al., 2022; Ranjan et al., 2022).

Louvain Meta-Community Structure

Applying the Louvain algorithm to the topic–cluster graph shows that thematically similar clusters form higher-order communities having high modularity. Clusters that discuss related topics form communities rather than staying isolated. The idea of ideological proximity enhancing network cohesion is supported by this pattern. The pattern of network development in communities corresponding with sentiment polarisations in political Reddit data in prior studies (Han et al., 2023; Kumar et al., 2022; Ranjan et al., 2022), supports this point.

Table 11.

Aspect	Key method / setting	Main empirical finding	Interpretation / implication
Cluster formation	Affinity Propagation on cosine similarity of binary TF vectors	Automatically discovers a suitable number of clusters per subreddit without pre-specifying kk; clusters show coherent LDA keyword themes.	AP plus cosine similarity effectively captures meaningful opinion groups in noisy Reddit text where the true number of communities is unknown.
Thematic organis-ation	Per-cluster LDA, global NMF	Conflict subreddits yield sharper, narrowly focused topics; election subreddits show broader, multidimensional themes; NMF adds finer-grained subtopics.	Conflict discourse is more terminologically specific, while electoral discourse is thematically diffuse; dual topic modelling enriches thematic resolution.
Sentiment by domain	VADER at post and cluster level	Conflict domains are dominated by negative clusters; election domains show mixed polarity; Trump tariff subreddits combine negative and neutral, analytical clusters.	Sentiment structure reflects event type: crises skew negative, elections are pluralistic, and economic debates mix concern with data-driven analysis.
Neutral cluster be-haviour	VADER compound [−0.05,+0.05] plus 4 validity indices	Neutral-labelled clusters vary in structural quality across Silhouette, Dunn, DBI, and XBI.	Some "neutral" clusters are genuinely affect-neutral, while others hide mixed polarity; sentiment-disaggregated metrics help distinguish these cases.

continued on following page

Table 11. Continued

Aspect	Key method / setting	Main empirical finding	Interpretation / implication
Cluster quality evaluation	Silhouette, Dunn, Davies–Bouldin, Xie–Beni by sentiment subset	Metric values differ systematically between positive, negative, and neutral cluster subsets.	Computing multiple indices per sentiment class reveals quality differences that global, single-metric evaluation would obscure.
Topic–cluster linkage	Mapping dominant LDA topic → AP clusters	Topic-to-cluster aggregation yields a topic–cluster graph suitable for further community detection.	Converts probabilistic topics into a graph structure, enabling higher-order structural analysis beyond independent clustering and topic modelling.
Meta-community structure	Louvain on topic–cluster graph	Louvain detects meta-communities of thematically similar clusters with elevated modularity.	Ideologically or thematically related opinion clusters tend to form cohesive higher-order communities, supporting the LDA–Louvain–VADER design.

Future Scope

1. Models for Sentiments Using Transformers

The researchers should replace VADER with a fine-tuned transformer model (e.g., BERT, RoBERTa) on Reddit data to facilitate more effective detection of sarcasm, irony, and contextually nuanced posts, particularly from politically charged subreddits such as r/librandu (Carter et al., 2023; Deng & Liu, 2023; Prasad, 2021).

2. Emoji and Emoticon Sentiment Analysis

To determine accurate sentiment scores, add explicit emoji/emoticon sentiment handling capability after integrating features for grief-driven and highly emotional communities like r/hinduism (Nirmala et al., 2021).

3. Continuous and Time-Based Assessment

From still pictures, snapshots that are bounded by discrete events to pipeline that can accommodate data that is streaming; so we can see how the clusters of sentiment evolve over time during the unfolding of an event like Israel–Gaza or Pahalgam.

4. Detection of Advanced Meta-Community

Consider swapping out Louvain for the Leiden algorithm to achieve better-connected communities and address resolution-limit problems, possibly boosting modularity on small topic–cluster graphs (Traag et al., 2019).

5. Extension of Multilingual Pipeline

The multilingual forms or characteristics of vernaculars can be assessed and described, as well as the forms and characteristics of vernaculars at the national level or within a country.

6. Research Across Different Platforms

By combining the Reddit data with other sources such as Twitter and Facebook, we can start examining whether the finding of topic-dependent sentiment patters – positive for US election discussions and negative for conflict-related topics – is platform-contingent or whether it is part of more stable dynamics of opinion formation online (Guo et al., 2021; Zhou et al., 2023).

LIMITATIONS

(i) **Static Snapshot Analysis:** The analysis takes place on a static snapshot of a set timeframe and does not utilize any streaming or temporal features. The statement above limits the investigation of how the sentiment in the community evolves with time on developing events. This includes the Israel–Gaza conflict or the Pahalgam attack.

(ii) **VADER Sentiment Constraints:** VADER is a lexicon-based sentiment analysis tool specifically calibrated for social media text. A well-known limitation is that it does not consider either emoji or ironic meanings based on context. Nirmala et al., 2021 identified it as an important inconvenience. The reason for irony being volatile mixed-sentiment outliers could be due to their subtle political meanings, as is the case for r/librandu.

(iii) **Binary Feature Representation:** The clustering and community detection algorithms are used to binary feature representations. These representations are robust to frequency imbalances but do not take into account word frequency information which can be useful for the detection of sentiment and topics. Thus, algorithms may lose some granularity as a result of which, subreddits could be differentiated poorly.

(iv) **Absence of External Validation:** The quality of the clusters is measured through internal validity measures alone, which lack reference to any external ground-truth labels. This precludes us from definitively assessing whether the communities identified actually correspond to any 'real-world' opinion groups, beyond the corroboration offered by internal scores such as silhouette and Davies-Bouldin indices.

(v) **English-Language Restriction:** The study will only use the English language posts from Reddit. It will not take into account the large amount of non-English political discourse present on the platform. This is especially true for Pahalgam attack that has considerable discourse in Hindi and Urdu.

(vi) **Louvain Algorithm on Small Graphs:** Louvain algorithm has known to produce sub-optimal community partitions on small graphs. The application of this algorithm on the LDA topic-cluster graph, which is small for many subreddits, may limit the interpretability of the low modularity scores in communities like r/stocks and r/unitedstatesofindia.

CONCLUSION

Reddit political discourse from OpinionGraph is modeled jointly on community structure and sentiment polarity to yield richer insights that are easier to interpret than either one. The framework makes four key contributions. First, it is a fully reproducible multi-event-domain pipeline that comprises twelve subreddits from four real-world event contexts. Second, it implements parameter-free Affinity Propagation for automatic community discovery, which does not require specification of cluster count. Third, it contains a multi-metric evaluation of cluster validity disaggregated by sentiment polarity class. Moreover, this metric permits assessment of whether structural coherence aligns with sentiment coherence. Finally, it applies Louvain community detection to the LDA topic-cluster graph as a novel meta-level structural analysis.

Community sentiment profiles are highly event-dependent. They are overwhelmingly positive for US Election talk. They are overwhelmingly negative for Israel–Gaza talk. The researcher observes strongly mixed for Pahalgam attack and for Trump tariff talk. Thus, topic domain not platform drives Reddit sentiment structure, the researcher notes. OpinionGraph's project has turned out to be reputed to be a scalable and extensible platform for the analysis of opinion communities across all the platforms and in all languages.

REFERENCES

Ahmed, R., Hameed, M., Tiun, S., Omar, N., & Sani, N. S. (2022). Short text clustering: Combining traditional, semantic, and deep-learning representations. *Expert Systems with Applications*, *203*, 117337. DOI: 10.1016/j.eswa.2022.117337

Alslaity, A., & Orji, R. (2022). Machine learning techniques for emotion detection and sentiment analysis: Survey. *Behaviour & Information Technology*, *41*(13), 2796–2832. DOI: 10.1080/0144929X.2022.2156387

Apostol, E. S., Palade, V., & Grosu-Popescu, A. M. (2022). Real-time topic modelling for disaster reporting with misinformation-aware community detection. *Information Processing & Management*, *59*(3), 102901. DOI: 10.1016/j.ipm.2022.102901

Carter, R., Davis, J., & Kim, S. (2023). Transformer-based models with domain-specific financial lexicons for improved sentiment analysis. *The Journal of Financial Data Science*, *5*(2), 34–51. DOI: 10.3905/jfds.2023.1.109

Deng, X., & Liu, Y. (2023). Hybrid RoBERTa–BiLSTM–Attention model for online sentiment analysis with custom lexicons. *IEEE Transactions on Affective Computing*, *14*(2), 889–901. DOI: 10.1109/TAFFC.2021.3075977

Frey, B. J., & Dueck, D. (2007). Clustering by passing messages between data points. *Science*, *315*(5814), 972–976. DOI: 10.1126/science.1136800 PMID: 17218491

Gan, C., Wang, J., & Zhang, L. (2023). Aspect-based sentiment classification using fuzzy logic and neural networks for student microblog analysis. *Information Sciences*, *621*, 231–245. DOI: 10.1016/j.ins.2022.11.056

Guo, Y., Barnes, S. J., & Jia, Q. (2021). Joint topic modelling and multidimensional sentiment analysis of COVID-19 discourse on Chinese microblogs. *Journal of Informetrics*, *15*(2), 101146. DOI: 10.1016/j.joi.2021.101146

Han, Y., Zhou, R., Geng, Z., Fang, J., Ma, B., & Fan, J. (2023). HL-Louvain: Enhanced community detection integrating structural properties and user influence. *IEEE Transactions on Network Science and Engineering*, *10*(1), 244–257. DOI: 10.1109/TNSE.2022.3201090

Hasan, A., Moin, S., Karim, A., & Shamshirband, S. (2022). Lexicon-based versus classifier-based approaches for political Twitter sentiment analysis. *Expert Systems with Applications*, *190*, 116157. DOI: 10.1016/j.eswa.2021.116157

Hu, L., Li, J., Nie, L., Li, X.-L., & Shao, C. (2022). Temporal topic clustering for detecting shifting public discussions on social media. *Knowledge-Based Systems*, *246*, 108620. DOI: 10.1016/j.knosys.2022.108620

Jelodar, H., Wang, Y., Yuan, C., Feng, X., Jiang, X., Li, Y., & Zhao, L. (2021). LDA configuration for Reddit data: Optimal parameters for interpretable topic distributions. *International Journal of Machine Learning and Computing*, *11*(2), 89–101. DOI: 10.18178/ijmlc.2021.11.2.1024

Kabir, M. A., Kabir, M. M. J., Xu, S., & Badhon, B. (2022). Empirical comparison of machine learning approaches for sentiment classification. *Neural Computing & Applications*, *34*(18), 15987–16002. DOI: 10.1007/s00521-022-07207-1

Kumar, S., Gahalawat, M., Roy, P. P., Dogra, D. P., & Kim, B.-G. (2022). Combined community detection and sentiment analysis for COVID-19 Reddit discourse. *Journal of Medical Internet Research*, *24*(4), e35636. DOI: 10.2196/35636

Li, S., & Li, J. (2022). Machine learning-based community detection: Survey and benchmark. *ACM Computing Surveys*, *54*(4), 1–38. DOI: 10.1145/3434770

Nirmala, S. J., Valarmathi, B., & Saravanan, D. (2021). Sarcasm detection in microblogs using emoticon polarity and SentiWordNet. *Social Network Analysis and Mining*, *11*(1), 1–15. DOI: 10.1007/s13278-021-00766-2

Nooribakhsh, M., & Mollamotalebi, M. (2021). Systematic mapping study on machine learning for community detection in social networks. *Artificial Intelligence Review*, *54*(7), 5381–5432. DOI: 10.1007/s10462-021-09994-4

Prasad, A. (2021). Deep learning and hybrid architectures for real-time sentiment prediction in political and financial domains. *Applied Intelligence*, *51*(8), 5784–5802. DOI: 10.1007/s10489-020-02108-1

Proferes, N., Jones, N., Gilbert, S., Fiesler, C., & Zimmer, M. (2021). Survey of 727 academic studies using Reddit data: Trends and gaps. *Social Media + Society*, *7*(2), 20563051211019004. DOI: 10.1177/20563051211019004

Qaiser, S., & Ali, R. (2021). Deep learning versus classical machine learning for social media sentiment analysis. *Journal of Intelligent & Fuzzy Systems*, *41*(5), 6251–6264. DOI: 10.3233/JIFS-210548

Ranjan, A. K., Singh, D. K., & Prajapati, G. P. (2022). Sentiment analysis on social media: Challenges and NLP-based approaches. *Journal of Natural Language Processing*, *29*(4), 112–134. DOI: 10.5715/jnlp.29.112

Ribeiro, F. N., Araújo, M., Gonçalves, P., Gonçalves, M. A., & Benevenuto, F. (2023). Comprehensive evaluation of 18 sentiment tools on Twitter and Reddit: VADER benchmark study. *Proceedings of the International AAAI Conference on Web and Social Media, 17*, 732–742. https://doi.org/DOI: 10.1609/icwsm.v17i1.22178

Su, X., Zhao, Z., & Cai, T. (2021). Affinity propagation clustering with high-dimensional sparse data: Parameter optimization and oscillation suppression. *Journal of Machine Learning Research*, *22*(45), 1–28. https://jmlr.org/papers/v22/20-1491.html

Traag, V. A., Waltman, L., & van Eck, N. J. (2019). From Louvain to Leiden: Guaranteeing well-connected communities. *Scientific Reports*, *9*(1), 5233. DOI: 10.1038/s41598-019-41695-z PMID: 30914743

Xing, Z. (2023). Heterogeneous LLM agents for nuanced financial sentiment analysis. *Expert Systems with Applications*, *218*, 119612. DOI: 10.1016/j.eswa.2023.119612

Zhou, M., Li, X., Liao, H., & Cheng, X. (2023). Public sentiment analysis of ChatGPT using combined sentiment analysis and knowledge mapping. *Computers in Human Behavior*, *140*, 107612. DOI: 10.1016/j.chb.2022.107612

Chapter 5

A Unique Technique to RGB Image Cryptography via Design of Deep Learning

Ismatulla Khayrullayev
Department of Information Technology and Exact Sciences, Termez University of Economics and Service, Termez, Uzbekistan

Anorgul Ashirova
http://orcid.org/0009-0006-7271-3634
Department of General Professional Sciences, Mamun University, Khiva, Uzbekistan

Soma Bag
Asadtala Nivedita Kanya Vidya Math, India

Pranati Rakshit
http://orcid.org/0000-0001-5037-1326
Department of Computer Science, Tarakeswar Degree College, India

Jushkinbek Yuldoshev
Pedagogy and Primary Education Methodology, Urgench Innovation University, Urgench, Uzbekistan

Valisher Sapayev
http://orcid.org/0000-0002-6751-5864
Department of General Professional Subjects, Mamun University, Khiva, Uzbekistan

Bhawna Janghel Rajput
http://orcid.org/0009-0006-8062-0462
Department of Computer Science and Engineering, Rungta College of Engineering and Technology, Bhilai, India

ABSTRACT

Images are either shared or saved in the current digital era. Protecting photos from unwanted access or alteration is a conscious need. The suggested work is an

DOI: 10.4018/979-8-3693-3751-6.ch005

attractor-inspired deep learning for picture encryption, which is a non-linear dynamic system that makes it easier to establish a consensus independent of the beginning and boundary conditions of the system. To describe the chaotic behaviour, the Lorenz 3D chaotic Map solution is used as the attractor. This attractor transitions into a predictable set of solutions with regular behaviour, which makes decrypting the cipher picture easier and quicker. All of the researches on encryption are on achieving high resistance to differential attacking metrics in order to demonstrate the encryption's strength; however, our work focuses primarily on data at rest and optimises computations while protecting pictures from manipulation.

INTRODUCTION

Artificial Intelligence (AI) is used to make computers think like people. AI is a more general word. We employ machine learning (ML) to put AI into practice. Neural networks are used in machine learning to simulate human decision-making. ML may be implemented using Deep Learning (DL) (Bachiphale, P.M. et al 2025). An I/P layer, single or many hidden layers & an O/P layer make up deep neural networks. Supervised, unsupervised, semi-supervised, and reinforced learning are the four types of learning mechanisms. In unsupervised learning, there is no such training of the desired outcome and the model learns iteratively and makes decisions on its own. In supervised learning, both the input and the desired output are specified during training, and after the training is finished, the model can predict the class label of new input data. Combining supervised learning (Sajjad et al., 2025), unsupervised learning and semi-supervised learning consists of training the framework utilizing both labelled and unlabelled data in order to make predictions. The choice of action strategy in the reinforcement learning approach is determined by the action's outcome. The reinforced learning 4g model is constructed with certain objectives and a set of guidelines to achieve them. Without any prior training, the model learns from its experiences by rewarding good behaviour and penalising undesirable behaviour. Because the neural network can learn from a given input picture, it may be used to encrypt images by making them unrecognisable. This compels the privacy of image data and facilitates it more complex for intruders to analyse the picture even if it is intercepted.

One method for protecting data from hackers is image encryption. By transforming the picture into a format that hides the data content in the plaintext image, encryption shields the image from alteration and unwanted access. It even renders the image "no use" even if it is intercepted. Symmetric key (Sultana, N.M. et al. 2025) encryption approaches and asymmetric key encryption techniques are the

2 types of encrypted technologies. According to (Tajudeen, K.O. et al. 2025) the computational process of encryption and decryption is as follows:

Enc (Plain-image, Key1) = Cipher-image

Dec (Cipher-image, Key2) = Plain-image

The encrypted and decrypted functions are called Enc() and Dec(), respectively. Symmetric encryption is used when (Key1 = Key2) is used for both encryption and decryption. If not, it is referred to as asymmetric encryption if (Key1 $\neq$ Key2). Three different domains may be used to implement encryption mechanisms: (a) spatial, (b) frequency, and (c) hybrid. The encryption and decryption processes in the spatial domain will take into account the position and value of each pixel. In the spatial domain, block shuffling, pixel replacement, and pixel permutation are the typical techniques. Their excellent resilience to statistical assaults and short calculation time make them popular. Transformation techniques like Wavelet, Phase Mask, and Affine transformation are used to carry out transformation operations in the frequency domain. Although they are computationally costly, this technique's primary features are its great resilience to many types of assaults and its high capacity to secure the data. The advantages of the frequency and spatial domains are combined in the hybrid domain. These methods combine transformation operations, such as combining transformation with permutation, diffusion, or S-box. This method's benefits include quick encryption and a huge key space that is resistant against entropy-based and differential attacks. An image encryption technique may be used for the whole picture or only certain ROI (Region of Interest) areas. The necessary level of secrecy, encryption time, and cost must all be considered while making this choice. Sensitive application situations including digital forensics, face recognition, and healthcare are all significantly impacted by information leaks. To increase efficiency, the deep Salient Object Detection (SOD) model is first made lighter in the work by (Kumar, M. et al. 2025). The ROI is then produced without disclosing object information by cropping the sensitive area according to the boundary information from the output saliency map. The efficiency is further increased during the encryption step by grouping the pixels of each colour channel (R, G, and B) and encrypting them in parallel. In order to minimize the quantity of data required for encryption (Priya, S. et al. 2024), any conspicuous regions in a patch are encompassed by a bounding box. In order to avoid the necessity for separate distribution, the ROI information is used as side information that is inserted during the picture encryption process. By focussing on low/high level feature learning, MobileNetV2-based lightweight extremely down sampled network (EDN-lite) effectively detects salient areas and has good detection accuracy with minimal parameters. The suggested encryption work uses deep learning to handle full colour images in the spatial realm by performing quantised logarithmic transformation, permutation, confusion, diffusion, and convolution operations. Our study's contribution focuses on creating high de-correlation among pixels to protect image details, eliminating the need to precisely reverse encryption operations when decrypting the cipher image, generating content-based parameters, using minimal resources, and performing straightforward operations that are more advantageous for data-at-rest encryption.

Algorithms for image encryption fall into the following categories: (a) conventional techniques, (b) techniques based on chaos, (c) techniques based on neural networks, (d) DNA techniques, (e) techniques for compressive sensing (f) techniques for meaningful encryption and (g) techniques based on frequency domains. Conventional methods like RSA, AES, and DES first transform the picture into a bit stream before encrypting it. Using keys of sizes like 128, 256, 512, and 1024, the encryption technique may be either symmetric or asymmetric. These algorithms function best with data that is sent across a network. Because photos are bigger than text and include more redundant data, these algorithms need a lot of processing time even if they greatly safeguard and secure data. Conventional methods rely on network-based, permutation, and substitution. A lookup table is utilised during substitution. Deniz Ustun Secure S-box was utilised by (Ahmad Khan N et al. 2025). (Malik, K.R., et al. 2025) used a smart codebook. Non-linearity, sensitivity to beginning circumstances, low complexity, speed, and robustness are all desirable aspects of chaos. Chaos-based techniques are used to achieve high key sensitivity during encryption. According to (Naik & Singh, 2024), these algorithms use the chaotic system to produce pseudorandom chaotic sequences that produce permutation, diffusion, and confusion. The restricted spectrum of chaotic behaviour is a drawback of encryption based on chaotic systems. In contrast to ordinary chaotic maps, hyperchaotic maps exhibit a significant degree of non-periodicity and unpredictability. Arnold maps, 2D, 3D, 5D, and 6D super chaotic maps are a few examples of chaotic maps. Various chaotic maps are utilized in many chaotic-based systems to enhance the chaotic behaviour. To create cipher pictures, one chaotic map is utilized for pixel permutation and another for diffusion in successive rounds. By adding an additional layer of security, such a nonce or initialisation vector may be protected against selected plaintext attacks. A nonce is a counter-like variable that is used only once during a session. According to the research of (Ramesh, S. et al. 2025), chaos may be either continuous-time or discrete-time. The output of the discrete time chaos is an iterated function of the input, making it a non-linear function. It may be a one-dimensional map with only one state variable or a multi-dimensional map with many state variables, such as a two-dimensional parametric polynomial chaotic system. According to (Sajjad et al., 2025), a continuous-time chaos is a non-linear differential equation that includes both ordinary differential equations and delay-differential equations. Chaotic-based encryption methods are used despite the limited periodicity due to their simplicity and lack of distortion in the decoded picture.

Neural networks are used for picture encryption because of its non-linear behaviour, capacity to autonomously learn features, and ability to handle complicated and enormous amounts of data. The most often used methods are CNN-based (Gupta et al., 2025), GAN-based (Ravikumar, R. N. et. al. 2025), and hybrid neural network-based. Numerous methods of key generation and information concealment and protection are found in deep learning models, which may be examined in research by (Bouhafra, S. et al. 2025). Both colour and greyscale pictures are encrypted using deep neural networks. By changing the binary values of the image's pixels into a DNA pattern, DNA encoding is used in DNA techniques. Binary information is transformed into artificial DNA sequences using DNA coding principles. Addition, subtraction, and XOR operations are examples of binary operations. These methods demand minimal storage space and offer good security. However, the decryption method requires DNA rule tables in addition to the encrypted picture, which makes its practical implementation difficult. Some algorithms used hyperchaotic maps with DNA coding to produce a hybrid strategy that increased assault resistance. According to (Hassan, A.M.A. et al. 2025) from 2024, the Compressive Sensing method can simultaneously sample, compress, and encrypt the pictures, which reduce encryption time and storage space. This method involves utilising a discrete transform to first convert a plaintext picture into a sparse domain, then compressing it using a random measurement matrix that captures important structural information, and then encrypting it using diffusion and permutation. Due to the combination of encryption with compressive sensing, this method has a significant processing cost. Additionally, the choice of measurement matrix has an impact on the algorithm's overall performance and efficiency, which determines how effective compressive sensing is. Steganography (Pramanik, S. et al. 2023) and picture encryption are used in meaningful encryption methods to create cipher images. Steganography is a technique for evading discovery by hiding data within another non-secret carrier message (or file). It consists of two phases in the relevant encryption algorithm. The picture is first encrypted utilizing an encryption method, and then it is embedded using a steganography process in a non-secret message (or file). To the recipient, the carrier appears like a meaningful communication rather than a noise message. The benefit of this method is that because the original picture is protected by encryption and steganography adds an additional layer of protection such that attackers are unable to access the original image. However, these algorithms' disadvantage is that they take a lot of computing time. We discover block-based key embedding in the paper of (Wang, X. et al. 2025). Prediction-generated keys are encrypted into several colour channel regions. The picture is initially altered utilising transformations including wavelet, discrete cosine, and affine transforms in a frequency-based method. The frequency coefficients are then subjected to the encryption procedure. The encryption methods that may be used include hybrid approaches, differential evolution for parameter optimisation for frequency coefficient manipulation, and chaotic-based methods. Although this method is computationally costly, it has the benefit of better picture structure modification and enhanced security via information dispersion across frequencies. (Ganesh, R. et al. 2025) point out that even with robust encryption mechanisms, they are vulnerable to assaults due to the possibility of hidden factor and neural network architectural leaks. Quantum computers can solve the majority of current cryptography techniques in constant time. Therefore, as (Sood, S.K. et al. 2025) previously mentioned, post quantum algorithms have emerged as a viable option to handle such assaults and to protect sensitive data from the dangers posed by quantum computers.

LITERATURE REVIEW

In order to prevent medical diagnostic models from progressing beyond the inference stage, healthcare adversarial attacks aim to produce adversarial instances. (Bortsova, G. et al. 2021) directed a rigorous analysis of the no-box adversarial technique against healthcare image scrutiny algorithms. Pre-training may greatly increase the surrogate framework's transferability to the selected black-box framework, according to a number of studies. Their results show a connection between the efficacy and perceptibility of the assaults and the value of disruption. Lastly, as the intruder and target have various data and models, attack performance may be impacted and this is mitigated by pre-trained models that moreover boost adverse portability. The impact of adversarial assaults on skin lesion categorization and brain segmentation was examined by (Gizachew Yirga et al., 2025). U-Net & DenseNet were employed for the segmentation job, while Inception-v3, Inception-v4, and MobileNet models were utilized in the classification job. Tests exhibited that InceptionV3 was the best model in classification and segmentation tasks. The researchers showed that although a framework's capability in segmentation is enhanced by filled blocks & skip connections, a framework's resilience in classification is related to its deepness. The SSIM varies from 0.97-0.99, creating the hostile samples hardly noticeable. (Finlayson et al., 2019) used a pre-trained ResNet50 framework to submit fundoscopy & chest X-ray pictures to PGD white and black box assaults. The efficiency of the framework was greatly diminished in the two occurrences. (Bortsova, G. et al. 2021) performed the implementations having projected PGD assault in X-rays to accomplish segmentation jobs. Since the authors introduced hardly perceptible noise to the images, the framework broke apart the heart sign in place of the real heart. They also used untargeted PGD, black-box, and white-box assaults, that notably lowered the model's mean IoU. (Pal, B. et al. 2021) looked at the efficiency of COVID-19 classification utilizing CT and X-ray images. Using the FGSM assault, they created adversarial samples, which were then assessed utilizing the VGG-16 framework. The accuracy drops to 91% in VGG-16 and it demonstrates how vulnerable these models are. (Khallaf, F. et al. 2025) assessed the weakness of the CNN-dependent COVID-Net framework that is open source and accessible to the general public. It is the fundamental DL framework to identify COVID-19 utilizing chest X-ray pictures. 2 kinds of assaults—targeted & non-targeted—are investigated using perturbations produced using the fast gradient sign technique. The authors have evaluated the COVID-Net CXR small model. The outcomes exhibited that both frameworks obtained success rates of >87% for non-targeted and targeted assaults, respectively, after introducing 2% universal adversarial perturbations. Furthermore, researchers have shown that these models produce COVID-19 images with greater perturbations as well as normal and pneumonia test images. Additionally, they compared the vulnerability of COVID-Net to that of various DL frameworks, such as ResNet. They utilized the COVIDx dataset and a defense approach called adversarial training. (Hirano, H. et al. 2021) found adversarial assaults on DNNs for the classification of skin cancer, pneumonia, and different disorders. The authors used a range of frameworks like VGG16 and InceptionV2 to evaluate both targeted and non-targeted assaults. They found that adversarial training was useless in certain occurrences, mainly when it came to assaults that weren't properly targeted. Non-targeted assaults have a low transferability rate throughout this time. Lastly, the researchers insist that VGG16 is better than the different frameworks. Four distinct modalities (T1, T2, T1ce & FLAIR) having varying strengths are used in MRI images for brain tumor segmentation to facilitate the identification and labeling of the brain tumor. The results of adversarial cases when utilized simultaneously across all modalities and on each modality independently were examined by (Cheng, G. et al. 2020). The Biomedical_Image_Dataset and a U-Net framework were employed in the trials. They adopted arbitrary perturbation that is analogous to (El-Shafai, W. et al. 2022) in the formation of adversarial instances. The data indicated that concurrent disturbance considerably affects framework accuracy, although perturbation of just a single modality modestly lessens accuracy. The strength of the ResNet50 framework was examined by (Cheng, G. et al. 2020) on three datasets: fundoscopy, ISIC and ChestX-ray8. They focused on untargeted scenarios and used 4 innovative white-box assaults: PGD and BIM. The robust assault PGD is shown to have about 100% attack accuracy everywhere when the perturbation value was computed. Dermoscopy images were somewhat more dependable than the other datasets, but there was no discernible change. Additionally, they used four detectors having higher detection accuracy in adversarial sample detection: KD and deep features. (Singh, M. et al. 2023) looked at how hostile events affected retinal imaging.

The research (Sharma, P.K. et al. 2025) engages chaotic techniques for the process of image encryption. By these means, it is demanding to find a correct balance between relation to encryption and privacy benefits. In order to solve the issue, DL—which extracts features from raw input pictures using multilayer neural networks (NNs)—has also garnered a lot of attention. Object recognition implementations and image domain transfer (Ding, Y. et al. 2021) have shown the benefits of CNNs. In order to understand the mapping relationship between an I/P picture and an O/P picture from a group of matched picture pairs, image transfer from a single domain to a different domain is regarded as a texture transfer problem. The cycle-reliable adversarial system (Afzal, S. et al. 2026), which delivers 2-cycle reliability losses which move the picture from a single domain to a different domain and thereby reconstructs to the original image, is the most often utilized image-to-image conversion technique. The picture-denoising cause is managed by the DL technique (Wu, C. et al. 2020). A novel multikey compressed sensing and machine learning security-conserving application was put out by the authors in (Feng, F. et al. 2022). This computer framework is made up of a user and a third party. The trustworthy third party is accountable for delivering random compressed sensing keys. A ML approach was utilised in (Wang, X. et al. 2022) to a problem containing sensitive data, such as commercial, health, or other types, which requires more than just accurate estimations. Encrypted data checks whether the data stays private as the cloud dosen't has access to the keys required to decode it. Table 1 exhibits the comparative analysis of different DL techniques for image cryptography.

Table 1. DL methods for image cryptography

Categories	*References*	*Qualities*
Deep learning in picture encryption methods for compressing images	Rai, M., et al. 2025	Compress and rebuild the original text picture using a deep learning model, and then use an integrated chaotic system for cryptography.
	Cherian, A.K., et al. 2024	Chaotic logistic map cryptography with layered autoencoder compression
Denoising techniques in picture encryption methods or deep learning for enhancing picture resolution	Gharib, H.A., et al. 2025	Use a CNN to increase the ability to resolve the restored picture and ghost imaging as a communication and cryptography technique.
	Shafique et al. 2025	Use an expanded deep CNN denoiser to enhance the clarity of the decoded pictures using the fractional Fourier transform.

continued on following page

Table 1. Continued

Categories	*References*	*Qualities*
DL in picture encryption techniques for object identification and categorization	Kaner, S., et al. 2025	Use the MTCNN to identify important facial traits, and then encrypt characteristics using a mix of RC4 stream ciphers and chaotic logic designs.
	Sanjalawe, Y., et al 2025	Use elliptic curve cryptography, encode the hash values, eventually classify the data using a deep belief network to determine if the illness is present.
	Hosny, K.M., et al. 2025	A technique determined by chaotic encryption of pictures and YoloV3 object recognition
DL for creating picture private keys in methods for encryption of images	Aljarf, A., et al. 2025	After training a DL algorithm to extract iris features from a picture, compute the encryption key utilizing the RS error correcting code, and then perform the XOR operation to encrypt the picture.
	Ahmad, S., et al. 2024	Create the private key using the GAN.
	Sathananthavathi, V., et al. 2024	The deep neural network learning-based technique for generating symmetric keys
	El-Shafai, W., et al. 2023	Establish the translation procedure between the physical unclonable function and the key by training a ANN.
Deep learning for complete encryption of images	Ramesh, S., et al. 2024	A Cycle-GAN-based optical picture encryption development methodology
	Bao, Z., et al. 2024	Encryption and decode the medical pictures using Cycle-GAN, similar to a style transfer job.
	Alexan, W., et al. 2025	Asymmetric encryption-based adversarial autoencoder for picture scrambling
Deep learning-based image cryptanalysis technique	Kumar, P., et al. 2024	An attack on the phase truncated Fourier transform encryption scheme using DL
	Alloun, Y., et al. 2025	To understand and break visual cryptosystems determined by Random Phase Encoding, develop DNN architecture.

RESEARCH GAPS

This study enhances the availability and privacy of vital picture data by overcoming the gap between deep learning and encryption. In addition to offering numerous significant advances, this study seeks to act as a roadmap for further research in the domain of deep learning-based picture cryptography: A developing privacy preservation method is given, with a focus on their potential implementations in DL-dependent image analysis. Concerns about data openness, use trends, and personal privacy are addressed.

METHOD

Auto-Encoders and the networking layout are comparable. Auto-encoders are frequently utilised to replicate the input after a series of modifications. They gain expertise in the features of the input data distributions by doing this. However, the suggested design is just slightly different in our example. Instead of only producing pictures, the network's resources must both hide one image and produce a different one. Figure 1 shows the suggested structure. Although the four elements seen in Figure 1 acquire knowledge as only one network, it would be simpler to describe them separately. A secret picture is prepared for hiding by the first layer, known as the Prep Layer. There are many uses for this layer. Initially if the hidden picture is lesser than the cover photo, its dimension is increased to match the cover image's dimensions, dispersing the concealed image's bits among each of the pixels. Additionally, the target is to rebuild the colour-dependent pixels into more usable characteristics for concisely encoding the picture, like edges, which is pertinent to every measure of the concealed images. In order to prevent any leakage of the confidential information, this layer's primary function would be to eventually embed the hidden picture into the encrypted picture. The second layer, the Hiding Layer, creates the Container picture by using the Prep Layer's output as input along with a cover picture. A square pixel picture serves as the network's input, and the depth of the cover image's RGB channels and the concealed image's reconstructed channels are taken into account. The person who sends the Block is made up of these 2 levels. One can disclose the generated container picture with the recipient. The receiver uses the 3rd layer, known as the Reveal Layer, to recreate the encrypted picture. This layer creates the encrypted secret picture by removing the cover picture from the container picture. The hidden picture is ultimately revealed by the fourth layer, the Decrypt Layer, which collects the output of the Reveal Layer and decrypts the picture. Collectively, the 3rd and 4th layers create the receiver block. Good pseudo-randomness, unpredictability, ergodicity, and sensitivity to beginning circumstances are required of the chaotic systems. A point in a dynamical system or a stochastic system will ultimately visit every area of the system in a uniform and/or random fashion, according to the concept of ergodicity. This encryption procedure creates a limited amount of chaos that is sensitive to control settings and beginning circumstances. The computed chaotic trajectory is a domain-based 3D Lorenz (D, S., et al. 2026) chaotic map, which serves as a secret key for the encryption procedure. Forecasting becomes difficult in chaotic-based systems due to their unpredictable behaviour. The unpredictable nature of a chaotic environment with dynamic behaviour and predictable chaos was given a measurable basis by Lorenz.

The model was trained using the Flickr30k dataset. Due to the variable dimension of the photos, the training algorithm scaled them to 256 x 256. An aggregate of

31,783 RGB-scale photos were employed. Additionally, every picture in the collection is converted into blocks of data, which are then jumbled.

The suggested method for encryption is:

> Permutation, Diffusion, Confusion, Quantised Logarithmic Transformation and 2D Convolution.

The suggested method for decryption is:

> The decrypted picture is constructed using the inverse logarithmic transformation and 2D convolution transpose.

The Suggested Encryption Algorithm

Step 1: Divide the input colour picture into *R, G,* and *B* channels.
Step 2: Create the following sub-blocks from each channel block:
T = Power (2, n), with *n* being a dynamically selected value between 1 and 5.
T * T = Num-blocks
Size of block = image-width/T

Step 3: Shuffle each channel's sub-blocks at random
Step 4: Select the starting point for each sub-block's pixel value permutation dynamically.
Step 5: Determine the direction of permutation channel-wise sub-blocks dynamically
Option 1. Up, Left, Down, and Right Selection

2. Up-down-right-up

Step 6: Use the Lorenz 3D Chaotic Map to determine the kernel parameters depending on the input picture.
Step 7: Set up the kernel using the random seed value and the derived variables from step 6.
Step 8: Use the Convolutional Block and the data from Step 7 as parameters to perform 2D Convolution on confused and diffused values.
Step 9: If the pixel value is less than zero, apply a logarithmic adjustment.

Suggested Decryption Method

Step 1: Apply the inverse logarithmic transformation.
Step 2: Convolutional transpose in two dimensions.
Step 3: Convert the values from Step 2 into three dimensions.
Step 4: Determine each channel's pixel values' Minkowsi distance.
Step 5: Add up the quantised step 3 data and Minkowsi distance channel-wise
Step 6: To retrieve the decrypted picture, stack up channel-wise.

Pixel values may be rearranged thanks to permutation. The link between the picture pixel values may be dissipated via the use of confusion and diffusion processes. The picture is split into a channel-wise random amount of sub-blocks and thereby jumbled to accomplish these processes. Each subblock's pixels are scrambled at random from a randomly selected starting position. Additionally, the shuffling direction is selected at random. For direction, there are two choices: Options 1 and 2 are Up-Left-Down-Right and Left-Up-Right-Down respectively. With straightforward calculations, the channel-wise confusion and diffusion operation strengthens encryption. To make it 3DiM, the dispersed and confused data are concatenated back channel-wise and fed into a 2D convolutional block. The convolutional block is a deep convolutional layer with a ReLu-activation function and a kernel of (3 x 3) size. Full image processing is supported by the convolutional block, which helps with entropy modelling since the kernel receptive field is constrained. Multilayers (Shafique et al., 2025) aid in increasing the modelling capacity. Additionally, a random seed and kernel initialisation values produced from the visual material using the Lorenz 3D Chaotic Map are used to execute convolutional operations. Convolutional operation learns the characteristics of the kernel's receptive field. Convolution is the process of applying a kernel to an image both vertically and horizontally in order to learn features. Typically, the sort of behaviour needed and the nature of the job determine which kernel is selected. In order to achieve a certain centre pixel, the kernel size used for this research is odd in size. Additionally, the kernel's centre moves across every pixel in the picture as it is shifted.

$$Y(m, n) = \sum_i \sum_j X(m, n)^* \, h(m, n)$$

where i and j take values from 1 to img-width and img-height, respectively, and $X(m, n)$ consists of the 2D input. $Y(m, n)$ is the result of the convolutional operation, $h(m, n)$ is the convolutional kernel, and "+" denotes the convolutional operation.

ReLu activation function and Adam optimiser are used to fine-tune the model. The Rectified Linear Unit learns intricate relationships between the input pixels and adds non-linearity to the model. ReLu keeps +ve values unchanged while setting -

ve values to 0. The explanation of the ReLu activation function is *f(x)=Max(0,x).* In a DL model, the optimiser modifies the neural network's weights, biases, and learning rate. Adam that signifies Adaptive Moment Estimation is a method for adjustable learning rates. Instead of using a single global learning rate, it strongly modifies the learning rate for every single parameter in the framework. The Adam optimiser employs the gradient's second moment in addition to its first moment to adjust the learning rate.

$$m_t = \beta_1 * m_{(t-1)} + (1 - \beta_1) * \left(\frac{\partial L}{\partial w_t}\right)$$

$$\nu_t = \beta_2 * \nu_{(t-1)} + (1 - \beta_2) * \left(\frac{\partial L}{\partial w_t}\right)^2$$

The decay rate of the mean of the gradients is represented by $_1$ and $_2$. The learning rate is denoted by *L*.

Compared to other optimisers, the Adam optimiser has the benefits of being quick, using less memory, and require to be less adjusting. The model's accuracy is increased and total loss is decreased when the Adam optimiser and ReLu activation function are used. Lorenz 3D Chaotic Map (Sajjad et al., 2025) is used for kernel initialisation. A limit set and an invariant set are comparable to a Lorenz attractor. In order to prevent spurious optima that result in global convergence, kernel initialisation is crucial in lowering the convergence time. Dealing with entropy in a picture is another benefit of the Lorenz 3D Chaotic Map. Because of the chaotic behaviour, it offers measurable unpredictability.

Lorenz 3D Map:

$$\frac{dx}{dt} = sigma * (y - x)$$

$$\frac{dy}{dt} = rh * x - y - x * z$$

$$\frac{dz}{dt} = x * y - bet * z$$

where bet = 8/3, rh = 28, and sigma = 10. The values of x, y, and z are R, G, and B, respectively. The range of values that the kernel initializer accepts is specified by the values that are thus acquired. To make the process more intricate, the seed is created at random. A seed is where a series begins. Every time a simulation is conducted, the same set of kernel parameters will be produced, given the same seed number. The kernel parameters needed for decryption are obtained with the aid of the seed. A skewed distribution may be made less skewed by using the logarithmic treatment. It lessens the effect of too-low or too-high numbers. The capacity of logarithmic transformation to manage a dynamic range of values is one of its main features. Quantisation facilitates the handling of zero and negative numbers that result from log transformation. Quantisation converts a wide range of numbers into a more constrained range. Because transformation and quantisation are complimentary processes, transformation may be reversed whereas quantisation cannot be reversed. Operations involved in the decryption process are: Inverse Log transformation - The decrypted picture is constructed using 2D Convolutional Transpose. Stride and padding are used to control the artefacts that Convolutional Transpose may produce in the learnt features. The adversarial loss must be calculated in order to generate the decrypted picture. Minkowsi distance is used to compute the adversarial loss. By determining how similar the data points are to one another, this distance measure aids in pattern recognition.

The formula for the Minkowsi distance is

$$D(x , y) = (\sum_{i=1}^{n} \left| x_i - y_i \right|_p)^{1/p}$$

where "n" is the vector's size and "p" indicates the norm's order. Because of these dynamical systems' intrinsic instability, which results in long-term unpredictability and positive entropy, the chaos-based encryption technique allows for safe communication. The resulting chaos is a predefined dynamical system that behaves stochastically over time and may often make it difficult to accurately generate the decrypted picture. Perceptual security, defence against attacks, compression ratio invariance, multi-level security (Pramanik, S. 2023), and transmission fault tolerance are the fundamental components of picture encryption. To put it another way, the encrypted picture should hide the original data, maintain storage capacity and quality, use less bandwidth, and be resistant to differential and known-plain-text attacks.

RESULT & DISCUSSION

The computational expense of the proposed architecture (input, two hidden layers, output) is mostly dictated by matrix multiplication, scaling O(S X R X K) every epoch, whereby S stands for samples, R for dimensions, and K for hidden nodes. Layer depth enhances complexity. Backpropagation is frequently utilised in training, which makes it computationally costly for data with multiple dimensions.

Visual assessment, statistical survey, and differential assessment are utilized to calculate the strength of cryptographic techniques. The visual evaluation calculates the amount of information hidden in an encrypted picture. MSE and PSNR are the metrics utilised. Between the input and cipher images, MSE (Sajjad et al., 2025) and PSNR are computed. The mean square difference between the pixel values in the input picture and the cipher picture is determined by Mean Squared Error. An encrypted picture of excellent quality is indicated by a high MSE. The formula for Mean Squared Error is

$$MSE = \left(\sum_{i=1}^{M} \sum_{j=1}^{N} \frac{[P(i, j) - C(i, j)]^\wedge 2}{W*H}\right)$$

where $P(i, j)$ and $C(i, j)$ are the pixel estimates in the input picture and cipher picture at location (i, j), respectively, and $M = img\_width$, $N = img\_height$.

The noise ratio between the cipher picture and the input plaintext image is measured by the PSNR. The ratio of the highest signal power to the distorting noise power is shown by PSNR, which is derived from MSE. Lower PSNR values imply better encryption quality and a greater difference between the cover and encrypted pictures. The equation for the PSNR is as shown:

$$PSNR = \left(10*log_{10}(255^2)\right)/MSE$$

where the formula's value of 255 denotes an 8-bit pixel. Three aspects of an image—luminance, contrast, and structure—are evaluated for their visual effect using the SSIM. The difference between the input and decoded images is the SSIM. When SSIM equals 1, the decrypted picture resembles the input plaintext image. The formula for SSIM is as follows:

$$SSIM(X, Y) = \frac{(2\mu_x\mu_y + c_1)\left(2\sigma_{xy} + c_2\right)}{(\mu_x{}^2 + \mu_y{}^2 + c_1)(\sigma_x{}^2 + \sigma_y{}^2 + c_2)}$$

where σ is the standard deviation and μ is the mean.

$K_1 = 0.01$, $K_2 = 0.03$ by default, and $c1 = (K_1L)^2$, $c2 = (K_2L)^2$. L is the pixel's dynamic span of values that are *255*.

Shannon Entropy is used in statistical analysis to assess the security of visual data. An image's uncertainty and randomness are estimated using Shannon Entropy. The global entropy of a picture is measured by the Shannon entropy. High entropy shows that the encryption system is more reliable as it is more difficult for an attacker to decrypt.

The formula for entropy is

$$H(X) = \sum_{i=1}^{255} P(x_i)\log_2 P(x_i)$$

where $P(xi)$ is the likelihood whether the term x_i will appear or not. The random variable X has many alternative possibilities, each of which has a $P(x_i)$ chance of occurring. The total of each outcome's entropy values multiplied by its probability is called H(X). Bits are the unit of measurement for entropy. To resist brute-force assaults, the encrypted picture's entropy must be nearer to the ideal entropy value of 8. A higher quantity makes it more difficult for an intruder to find out and thereby strengthening the encryption mechanism. UACI and NPCR scores are used to gauge resistance to differential assaults. The effect of altering a single pixel or secret key on the encrypted picture is measured by the Differential Analysis (Devanira Poovaiah, S. A. et al 2025). The key sensitivity is estimated using No. of Pixels Change Rate (NPCR) and Unified Average Change Intensity (UACI). The percentage difference between two cipher pictures is measured by the NPCR statistic. Better resilience to differential assaults is indicated by a higher NPCR rating. The formula for NPCR is defined in the following manner:

$$NPCR = \sum_{i=1}^{w} \sum_{j=1}^{h} \frac{(D(i,j))}{T} * 100\%$$

If w is the image's width, h is its height and T is the cypher image's total pixel count.

then, $D(i,j) = 0$ as long as $c\_1\ (i,j)=c\_2\ (i,j)$

If $c\_1\ (i,j) \neq c\_2\ (i,j)$, then $D(i,j)=1$.

Two plaintext photos that vary by only one pixel or key are encrypted to create the cipher pictures c_1 & c_2.

Unified Average Change Intensity is measured by the following formula:

$$UACI = \sum_{i=1}^{w} \sum_{j=1}^{h} \frac{(|c_1(i,j) - c_2(i,j))|)}{F*T} * 100\%$$

The greatest approved pixel value that is harmonious with the cipher text picture format is indicated by the letter F. In this case, $F = 255$. T is the cipher image's total pixel count. Better resistance to differential assaults is indicated by a higher UACI rating.

Table 1 exhibits the MSE and PSNR of the input and cipher pictures. Table 2 exhibits the Shannon entropy for the images peppers, lena and baboon. Table 3 shows the SSIM values for different images.

Table 2. MSE and PSNR of the input and cipher pictures

Input Image	Image size	Image Codec	MSE	PSNR (dB)
Peppers	256 x 256	JPEG	13654.31	8.2364
Peppers	128 x 128	JPEG	13729.45	8.6693
Lena	128 x 128	PNG	9739.47	9.4590
Baboon	128 x 128	JPEG	6293.22	11.1288
Baboon	256 x 256	JPEG	6841.89	11.6971

Table 3. Shannon Entropy

Input Image	Img Size	Image Codec	Input Image Entropy	CipherImage Entropy	Decipher Image Entropy
Peppers	256 x 256	JPEG	8.3326	0.8751	8.6227
Peppers	128 x 128	JPEG	8.2841	0.7693	8.5328
Lena	128 x 128	PNG	6.2163	2.6399	7.2308
Baboon	128 x 128	JPEG	8.4289	0.5173	8.2254
Baboon	256 x 256	JPEG	8.6312	0.5284	8.4637

Table 4. SSIM values

Input Image	Img Size	Image Codec	MSE between input and decipher_img	PSNR between input and decipher image	SSIM between input and decipher_ img
Peppers	256 x 256	JPEG	0.0	49.2473	1.0
Peppers	128 x 128	JPEG	0.0008	80.1196	0.9851
Lena	128 x 128	PNG	26.2606	34.8462	0.8734
Baboon	128 x 128	JPEG	0.0258	65.1187	0.9833
Baboon	256 x 256	JPEG	0.0098	67.2134	0.9821

Figure 1. Peppers.jpg compression (a) 256 x 256 (b) 128 x 128

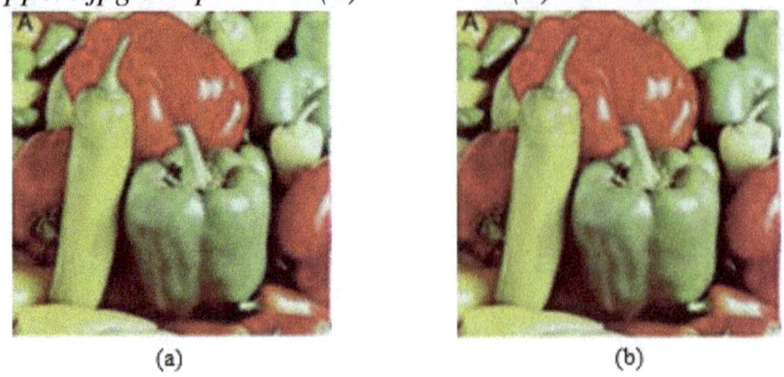

Figure 2. Peppers.jpg Encrypted Image Histogram

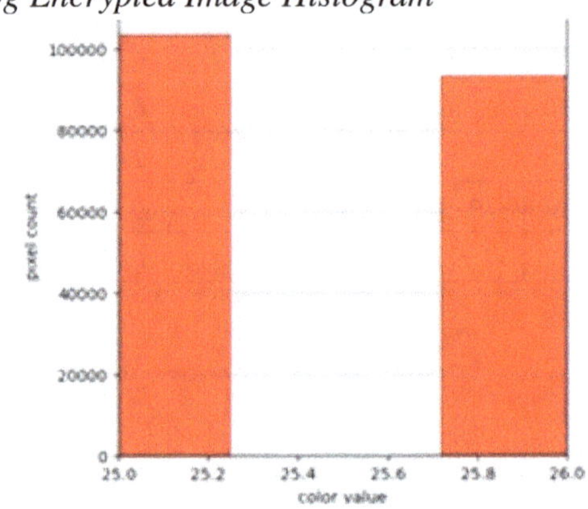

Figure 3. baboon.jpg Encrypted Image Histogram

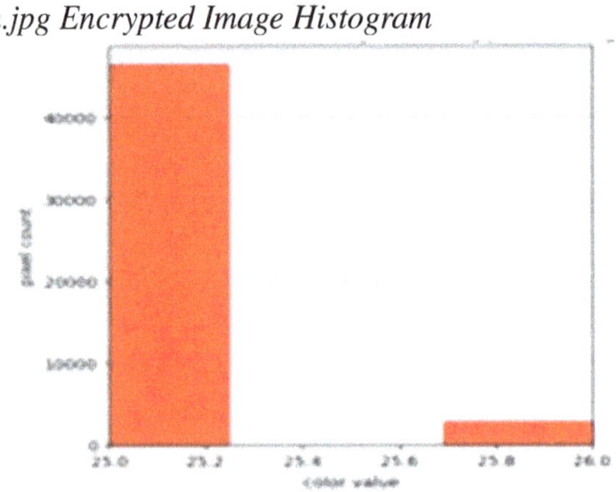

Figure 4. Input Lena.jpg Image (128 x 128)

Figure 5. Lena.jpg Encrypted Image Histogram

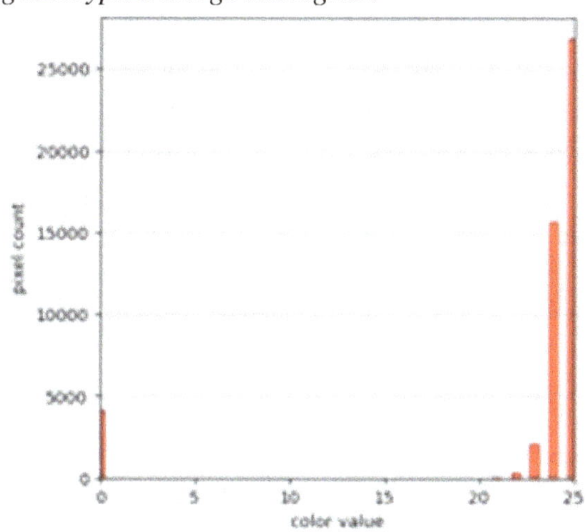

Figure 6. pixel count vs. colour value

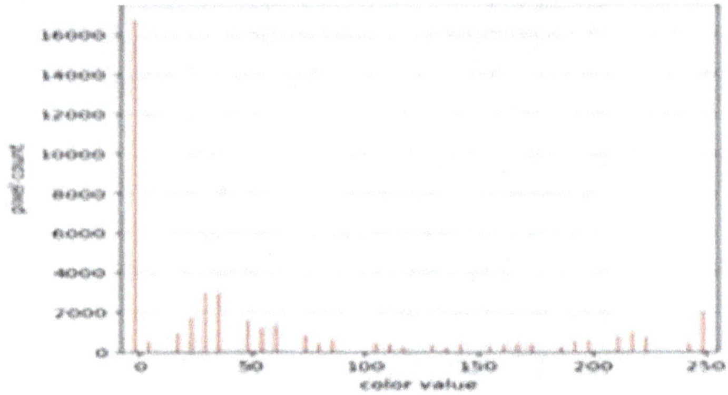

Figure 7. Baboon.jpg Codec (a) 128 x 128 (b) 256 x 256

Because *C1* and *C2* are similar due to probabilistic encryption, therefore all of the photos in our investigation have UACI = 0.0 and NPCR = 0.0; as a result, the property that the two are distinct and are present in deterministic techniques are lost. The probability of *C1* and *C2* being identical is high because of the probabilistic algorithm's feature that one plaintext might have several matching cipher texts.

The power of the encryption methods concentrate on getting NPCR>= 99%, UACI > 33%, and Shannon entropy > 7.99 (Gupta, A., 2025). However, the fact that the NPCR and UACI values in our analysis are zero suggests that the system's stochastic characteristics have an impact. Our study showed results of NPCR = 0, UACI = 0, and the histogram of the plaintext picture and that of the cipher picture histogram, which is a Bernoulli distribution. (Aarthi et al., 2025) imparts an in-depth mathematical equations of the effects of randomness, image format, and image size on NPCR and UACI values. The essential characteristic of NPCR = 0 ensures that the associated encrypted picture stays precisely unchanged even though a single pixel in the plain image differs. A lone binary trial (a "Bernoulli trial") involving 2 potential results—achieving success (1) with probability and failure (0) with probability—is modeled by the Bernoulli distribution which is a discrete probability distribution. It serves as the basis for simulating binary events such as coin flips, true/false answers, and pass/failure outcomes. UACI = 0 indicates that there is little difference when comparing 2 cipher pictures (S_1, S_2), indicating that the encryption technique is insensitive to minute alterations.

Table 5. Comparison table of the Image Cryptography Metrics

Techniques	*NPCR*	*UACI*	*SSIM*	*Entropy*	*MSE*	*PSNR (dB)*
(Keshav, Yadav, et al. 2026)	98.67	31.09	0.963	7.54	53.698	34.37
(Nazish, M., et al. 2026)	96.09	31.45	0.957	7.38	49.741	33.66
(Shabasy, N., et al. 2026)	97.53	32.97	0.971	6.95	48.663	34.48
(Xuan Huang, 2025)	98.20	31.08	0.922	7.81	46.845	32.91
(Sugirtham, N., et al. 2025)	98.86	32.65	0.908	7.22	48.783	32.74
	99.02	33.04	0.897	6.98	47.846	34.86
Proposed Method	-	-	**0.984**	**7.96**	**43.124**	**38.04**

The values in table 4 show that the prospective method is better than the other existing techniques.

HOW THE PROSPECTIVE TECHNIQUE FITS IN THE SECURITY OF AI DATA AND CONFIDENTIALITY?

These include industry and academic institutions have investigated a number of standardised approaches from different viewpoints to reduce the possible hazards of model and information confidentiality leakage throughout AI training and testing, which includes training data leakage caused by parameter upgrades, model information breaches from query replies throughout testing, and unintentional privacy violations throughout regular AI model usage.

The data produced throughout the regular training and usage of AI algorithms might nevertheless result in indirect data privacy breaches even in a lack of direct assaults. The main tactic to deal against these types of data breaches is to reduce or obscure the valuable information found in interactive content while preserving the efficacy of the model. There are several ways to safeguard data privacy, such as:

- Model Architecture Defence: In order to lessen the sensitivity of the model's results to various sample types, this strategy entails purposefully modifying the model throughout training.
- Data Obfuscating Defence: This technique obscures the essential information while maintaining model efficacy by altering interacting data, like model results or parameter changes.
- Query Control Defence: To avoid data leaks, this defence keeps an eye on query activities and rejects dangerous requests.

PRACTICAL IMPLICATION OF THE PROPOSED WORK

One may provide a brand-new, resource-effective technique for homomorphic inference on encrypted pictures. It affects safe DL inference in clinical images in a useful way. The categorization of diabetic retinopathy (DR) and retinopathy of prematurity (ROP) are two ophthalmic issues that can be examined. They have offered a series of tests which demonstrate how CaRENets may greatly increase memory utilization and inference.

DEEP LEARNING'S CHALLENGES/DRAWBACKS FOR HEALTHCARE PICTURE CRYPTOGRAPHY

Researchers and practitioners need to be aware of the drawbacks of DL in healthcare picture cryptography. Understanding these limitations is crucial for overcoming the challenges and seeing future possibilities. Below is a summary of some of the disadvantages of DL in healthcare picture cryptography, as well as expected future advancements.

Restricted Applicability

It may be difficult for DL approaches which were trained on a particular dataset to effectively adjust to new or different medical picture data. This might lead to a compromised security and poor performance in cryptographic operations. Further investigation can focus primarily on designing models which more effectively generalize via various healthcare imaging modalities, ailment types, and patient groupings.

Vulnerability to Adversarial Attacks

Adversarial assaults, where fraud people alter the input data to make false predictions, may affect DL models. Adversarial attacks in healthcare image cryptography have the potential to compromise the privacy and integrity of the encrypted data. Future study may look on dependable training methods and defence mechanisms to create DL models that are better resilient to these assaults.

Expensive Computation

Long training durations and costly hardware are sometimes required for deep learning models used in medical image cryptography. Because of this, they could be less helpful, especially in situations when resources are few or in real time. To reduce the computational burden and speed up cryptographic processes, future research should concentrate on developing hardware accelerators, optimization techniques, and more effective algorithms.

Quality and Availability of Data

Deep learning models need to be trained on large, high-quality datasets. However, because of data scarcity and security reasons, access to big labelled datasets can be limited in healthcare image cryptography. Future advancements can consist of the development of privacy-preserving techniques which allow models to be trained on decentralized or encrypted data sources while preserving the data's security and integrity. In summary, DL has limitations with regard to adversarial attacks, processing needs, and the accessibility of quality data, notwithstanding its promise for medical picture cryptography. Research and development projects aimed at improving the robustness and accessibility of higher-quality data may be able to overcome these limitations in the future.

CONCLUSION

Platforms with limited resources and data-at-rest are more suited for our suggested chaotic-based method of picture encryption. This suggested approach has high decrypted image accuracy, low complexity, and reduced processing time. There is no conventional (or typical) method for precisely reversing every process while decrypting a cipher picture, which is the originality of this suggested approach. When decrypting a cipher picture, the adversarial loss computed using Minkowsi distance makes it easier to prevent reversal of confusion and diffusion operations that are carried out in the encryption technique. The obfuscation of details is the basis of this encryption mechanism, and the results of encryption strength show how probabilistic nature affects a system. This suggests that we investigate this influence further on cross-sections of digital image processing, including compression-then-encryption and encryption-then-compression.

Future Scope

In the near future, image-based encryption has a lot of potential, and with ANN-based systems in particular, it will be very helpful to mimic a real-world situation where information is processed and hidden by the way it is supposed to be. The lack of natural perception is the sole factor that makes computers hacked, but as ANNs become more popular, computer systems will soon have a high degree of perception. This perspective may be used to a variety of processes to increase the security of the computer system. Additionally, this encryption method may be used to smart cards since it is simple to use with computer languages like C, C++, Java, Python, and others that can edit image files. It is extremely predictable due to the simple but efficient procedure. As new and innovative encryption techniques have emerged, such real-time audio encryption, image-based cryptography may potentially open up a number of other ways to secure data and information.

REFERENCES

Aarthi, S., Subramani, R., Rusho, M. A., Sharma, S., Ramachandran, T., Mahapatro, A., & Ismail, A. I. (2025). Genetically engineered 3D printed functionally graded-lignin, starch, and cellulose-derived sustainable biopolymers and composites: A critical review. *International Journal of Biological Macromolecules*, 145843.

Afzal, S., Bokhari, M. U., Alam, S., Khan, I., Shuaib, M., & Ullah, M. (2026). Lightweight deep learning-driven secure communication architecture for Internet of Things enabled government applications. *Discov Computing*, *29*(1), 112. DOI: 10.1007/s10791-026-10002-6

Ahmad, S., Ogala, J. O., Ikpotokin, F., Arif, M., Ahmad, J., & Mehfuz, S. (2024). Enhanced CNN-DCT Steganography: Deep Learning-Based Image Steganography Over Cloud. *SN Computer Science*, *5*(4), 408. DOI: 10.1007/s42979-024-02756-x

Ahmad Khan, N., Banga, A., Ghazal, T. M., Alabdullah, B., Iqbal, N., Alshamayleh, A., Ikram, A., & Diab, H. (2025). Unveiling a novel S-Box strategy: The dynamic 3D scrambling approach. *PLoS One*, *20*(9), e0329024. DOI: 10.1371/journal.pone.0329024

Alexan, W., Hosny, K., & Gabr, M. (2025). A new fast multiple color image encryption algorithm. *Cluster Computing*, *28*(5), 325. DOI: 10.1007/s10586-024-04919-0

Aljarf, A., & Rashidi, Y. (2025). *DL-Steg: a deep learning-based steganography model for improving image security*. J. Umm Al-Qura Univ. Eng.Archit., DOI: 10.1007/s43995-025-00266-2

Alloun, Y., Azzaz, M. S., & Kifouche, A. (2025). A new approach based on artificial neural networks and chaos for designing deterministic random number generator and its application in image encryption. *Multimedia Tools and Applications*, *84*(9), 5825–5860. DOI: 10.1007/s11042-024-19136-5

Bachiphale, P. M., & Zulpe, N. S. (2025). A comprehensive review of visual cryptography for enhancing high-security applications. *Multimedia Tools and Applications*, *84*(26), 31023–31045. DOI: 10.1007/s11042-024-20426-1

Bao, Z., Xue, R., Hu, J., & Liu, Y. (2024). Color image encryption based on lite dense-ResNet and bit-XOR diffusion. *Multimedia Tools and Applications*, *83*(5), 12819–12848. DOI: 10.1007/s11042-023-16073-7

Bortsova, G., González-Gonzalo, C., Wetstein, S. C., Dubost, F., Katramados, I., Hogeweg, L., Liefers, B., van Ginneken, B., Pluim, J. P. W., Veta, M., Sánchez, C. I., & de Bruijne, M. (2021). Adversarial Attack Vulnerability of Medical Image Analysis Systems: Unexplored Factors. *Medical Image Analysis*, *73*, 102141. DOI: 10.1016/j.media.2021.102141

Bouhafra, S., & El Bahi, H. (2025). Deep Learning Approaches for Brain Tumor Detection and Classification Using MRI Images (2020 to 2024): A Systematic Review. J Digit Imaging. *Journal of Imaging Informatics in Medicine*, *38*(3), 1403–1433. DOI: 10.1007/s10278-024-01283-8

Cheng, G., & Ji, H. (2020). Adversarial Perturbation on MRI Modalities in Brain Tumor Segmentation. *IEEE Access : Practical Innovations, Open Solutions*, *8*, 206009–206015. DOI: 10.1109/ACCESS.2020.3030235

Cherian, A.K., Simpson, S.V., Vaidhehi, M. et al. (2024). Enhancing Medical Image Security: A Deep Learning Approach with Cloud-based Color Space Scrambling. Int. j. inf. tecnol. 16, 5041–5054, DOI: 10.1007/s41870-024-02109-0

D, S., S R, M. & P, D. (2026). Machine Learning-Fused Hybrid Image Encryption Framework Using Hardware-Optimized AES Algorithm. J Sign Process Syst 98, 21, DOI: 10.1007/s11265-026-01992-z

Ding, Y., Tan, F., Qin, Z., Cao, M., Choo, K.-K. R., & Qin, Z. (2021). DeepKeyGen: A Deep Learning-Based Stream Cipher Generator for Medical Image Encryption and Decryption. *IEEE Transactions on Neural Networks and Learning Systems*, *33*(9), 4915–4929. DOI: 10.1109/TNNLS.2021.3062754

El-Shafai, W., Almomani, I., Ara, A., & Alkhayer, A. (2023). An optical-based encryption and authentication algorithm for color and grayscale medical images. *Multimedia Tools and Applications*, *82*(15), 23735–23770. DOI: 10.1007/s11042-022-14093-3

El-Shafai, W., Khallaf, F., El-Rabaie, E. S. M., & Abd El-Samie, F. E. (2022). Proposed neural SAE-based medical image cryptography framework using deep extracted features for smart IoT healthcare applications. *Neural Computing & Applications*, *34*(13), 10629–10653. DOI: 10.1007/s00521-022-06994-z

Feng, F., Hu, J., Guo, Z., Gan, J.-A., Chen, P.-F., Chen, G., Min, C., Yuan, X., & Somekh, M. (2022). Deep Learning-Enabled Orbital Angular Momentum-Based Information Encryption Transmission. *ACS Photonics*, *9*(3), 820–829. DOI: 10.1021/acsphotonics.1c01303

Finlayson, S. G., Bowers, J. D., Ito, J., Zittrain, J. L., Beam, A. L., & Kohane, I. S. (2019). Adversarial attacks on medical machine learning. *Science*, *363*(6433), 1287–1289. DOI: 10.1126/science.aaw4399

Ganesh, R., Khan, B. U. I., Khan, A. R., & Kamsin, A. B. (2025). A panoramic survey of the advanced encryption standard: From architecture to security analysis, key management, real-world applications, and post-quantum challenges. *International Journal of Information Security*, *24*(5), 216. DOI: 10.1007/s10207-025-01116-x

Gharib, H. A., Abdelnapi, N. M. M., & Hosny, K. M. (2025). Robust zero-watermarking for color images using hybrid deep learning models and encryption. *Scientific Reports*, *15*(1), 28906. DOI: 10.1038/s41598-025-09290-7

Gizachew Yirga, T., Gizachew Yirga, H., & Addisu, E. G. (2025). Cryptographic key generation using deep learning with biometric face and finger vein data. *Frontiers in Artificial Intelligence*, *8*, 1545946. DOI: 10.3389/frai.2025.1545946

Gupta, A. (2025). A novel Shannon entropy-based backward cloud model and cloud K-means clustering. *The Journal of Supercomputing*, *81*(1), 65. DOI: 10.1007/s11227-024-06528-5

Gupta, S., Nayyar, A., & Nitish, . (2025). Enhancing color image encryption scheme with a chaotic map and Fibonacci transform. *Cluster Computing*, *28*(15), 993. DOI: 10.1007/s10586-025-05573-w

Hassan, A. M. A., & Mohsen, S. (2025). Compression of electrocardiogram signals using compressive sensing technique based on curvelet transform toward medical applications. *Multimedia Tools and Applications*, *84*(12), 11203–11219. DOI: 10.1007/s11042-024-19328-z

Hirano, H., Minagi, A., & Takemoto, K. (2021). Universal Adversarial Attacks on Deep Neural Networks for Medical Image Classification. *BMC Medical Imaging*, *21*(1), 9. DOI: 10.1186/s12880-020-00530-y

Hosny, K. M., Abdel-Aziz, M. M., Lashin, N. A., & Hamza, H. M. (2025). A new CNN-based watermarking method for color medical images in a fusion domain. *Neural Computing & Applications*, *37*(18), 12611–12629. DOI: 10.1007/s00521-025-11056-1

Huang, X. (2025). Chaotic Digital Image Encryption Algorithm Based on Compressive Sensing. *Automatic Control and Computer Sciences*, *59*(6), 798–810. DOI: 10.3103/S0146411625701329

Kaner, S., Garipcan, A. M., & Erdem, E. (2025). A novel deep learning-based statistical randomness evaluation test methodology for cryptographic applications. *Journal of King Saud University. Computer and Information Sciences*, *37*(9), 264. DOI: 10.1007/s44443-025-00271-4

Keshav, Y., & Yadav, A. K. (2026). A.K. A novel two-dimensional Logistic–Chebyshev–Sine hybrid chaotic map for secure color image encryption. *Multimedia Tools and Applications*, *85*(2), 92. DOI: 10.1007/s11042-026-21281-y

Khallaf, F., El-Shafai, W., El-Rabaie, E. S. M., & El-Samie, F. E. A. (2025). Blockchain-based color medical image cryptosystem for industrial Internet of Healthcare Things (IoHT). *Multimedia Tools and Applications*, *84*(22), 25749–25803. DOI: 10.1007/s11042-023-16777-w

Kumar, M., Chivukula, A. S., & Barua, G. (2025). Deep learning-based encryption scheme for medical images using DCGAN and virtual planet domain. *Scientific Reports*, *15*(1), 1211. DOI: 10.1038/s41598-024-84186-6

Kumar, P., Rahman, M., Namasudra, S., & Moparthi, N. R. (2024). Enhancing Security of Medical Images Using Deep Learning, Chaotic Map, and Hash Table. *Mobile Networks and Applications*, *29*(5), 1489–1503. DOI: 10.1007/s11036-023-02158-y

Malik, K. R., Sajid, M., Almogren, A., Malik, T. S., Khan, A. H., Altameem, A., Rehman, A. U., & Hussen, S. (2025). A hybrid steganography framework using DCT and GAN for secure data communication in the big data era. *Scientific Reports*, *15*(1), 19630. DOI: 10.1038/s41598-025-01054-7

Naik, R. B., & Singh, U. (2024). A Review on Applications of Chaotic Maps in Pseudo-Random Number Generators and Encryption. *Annals of Data Science*, *11*(1), 25–50. DOI: 10.1007/s40745-021-00364-7

Nazish, M., Farooq, M., & Banday, M. T. (2026). Enhanced simple quadratic map for lightweight PRBG and IoT image encryption. *Iran Journal of Computer Science*, *9*(1), 35. DOI: 10.1007/s42044-026-00389-2

Pal, B., Gupta, D., Rashed-Al-Mahfuz, M., Alyami, S. A., & Moni, M. A. (2021). Vulnerability in Deep Transfer Learning Models to Adversarial Fast Gradient Sign Attack for COVID-19 Prediction from Chest Radiography Images. *Applied Sciences (Basel, Switzerland)*, *11*(9), 4233. DOI: 10.3390/app11094233

Pramanik, S. (2023). A new method for locating data hiding in image steganography. *Multimedia Tools and Applications*, *83*(12), 34323–34349. Advance online publication. DOI: 10.1007/s11042-023-16762-3

Pramanik, S. (2023). An Adaptive Image Steganography Approach depending on Integer Wavelet Transform and Genetic Algorithm. *Multimedia Tools and Applications*, *82*(22), 34287–34319. Advance online publication. DOI: 10.1007/s11042-023-14505-y

Priya, S., Abirami, S. P., Arunkumar, B., & Mishachandar, B. (2024). Super-resolution deep neural network (SRDNN) based multi-image steganography for highly secured lossless image transmission. *Scientific Reports*, *14*(1), 6104. DOI: 10.1038/s41598-024-54839-7

Rai, M., Kumar, S., & Rathore, P. S. (2025). A systematic review of innovations for real-time image security in IoT applications using machine learning and blockchain. *Journal of Intelligent Manufacturing*, *36*(8), 5197–5216. DOI: 10.1007/s10845-024-02535-8

Ramesh, S., Sukanth, B. N., Jaswanth, S. S., & Singh, R. P. (2024). Enhancing secure data transmission through deep learning-based image steganography and super-resolution generative adversarial networks. *SN Computer Science*, *5*(8), 1138. DOI: 10.1007/s42979-024-03490-0

Sajjad, M., & Alqwaifly, N. A. (2025). RGB image encryption using SPN with a novel block cipher over simple graph adjacency matrices and Galois fields. *Scientific Reports*, *15*(1), 37488. DOI: 10.1038/s41598-025-21542-0

Sajjad, M., Shah, T., Hamza, R., Almutairi, B., & Serna, R. J. (2025). Multiple color images security by SPN over the residue classes of Gaussian integer. *Scientific Reports*, *15*(1), 6425. DOI: 10.1038/s41598-025-89993-z

Sanjalawe, Y., Al-E'mari, S., Fraihat, S., Abualhaj, M., & Alzubi, E. (2025). A deep learning-driven multi-layered steganographic approach for enhanced data security. *Scientific Reports*, *15*(1), 4761. DOI: 10.1038/s41598-025-89189-5

Sathananthavathi, V., Ganesh Kumar, K., & Sathish Kumar, M. (2024). Secure visual communication with advanced cryptographic and image processing techniques. *Multimedia Tools and Applications*, *83*(15), 45367–45389. DOI: 10.1007/s11042-023-17224-6

Shabasy, N. H. E., Mansy, A., & Alexan, W. (2026). An improved Bülban map and its application in multiple image encryption. *Journal of King Saud University. Computer and Information Sciences*, *38*(5), 300. DOI: 10.1007/s44443-026-00650-5

Shafique, A., Mehmood, A., Alawida, M., Khan, A. N., & Shuja, J. (2025). Lightweight image encryption scheme for IoT environment and machine learning-driven robust S-box selection. *Telecommunication Systems*, *88*(1), 17. DOI: 10.1007/s11235-024-01251-1

Sharma, P. K., Vijayvergia, H. K., Garg, A., Saxena, V. P., Agrawal, S. S., & Sharma, M. (2025). Ensuring the privacy of data in modern healthcare systems using adaptive encryption technique and disease prediction via attention-based residual DenseNet with GRU. *Knowledge and Information Systems*, *67*(10), 8469–8520. DOI: 10.1007/s10115-025-02464-9

Singh, M., & Singh, A. K. (2023). A comprehensive survey on encryption techniques for digital images. *Multimedia Tools and Applications*, *82*(8), 11155–11187. DOI: 10.1007/s11042-022-12791-6

Sood, S. K., Singh, M., & Bhatia, M. (2025). Industrial progress with quantum algorithms: An in-depth review. *The Journal of Supercomputing*, *81*(9), 1064. DOI: 10.1007/s11227-025-07555-6

Sugirtham, N., & Sudhakar, R. (2025). Deep Edge-VCS: Dual-Domain Transformer-Based Framework for Secure Visual Cryptography. *Iranian Journal of Science and Technology. Transaction of Electrical Engineering*. Advance online publication. DOI: 10.1007/s40998-025-00918-y

Sultana, N. M., & Srinivas, K. (2025). Data Privacy Protection in Cloud Computing Using Visual Cryptography. *Multimedia Tools and Applications*, *84*(21), 23577–23597. DOI: 10.1007/s11042-024-19963-6

Tajudeen, K. O., Ameen, A. O., & Adeniyi, A. E. (2025). A systematic review on advanced encryption standard cryptography to enhance message security. *Multimedia Tools and Applications*, *84*(40), 48363–48388. DOI: 10.1007/s11042-025-21041-4

Wang, X., Li, L., Wang, M., & Chang, C. C. (2026). High-capacity reversible data hiding in encrypted images based on MSB sharing and overlapping sawtooth partition. *Journal of King Saud University. Computer and Information Sciences*, *38*(2), 24. DOI: 10.1007/s44443-025-00238-5

Wang, X., & Wei, H. (2022). Cryptanalysis of compressive interference-based optical encryption using a U-net deep learning network. *Optics Communications*, *507*, 127641. DOI: 10.1016/j.optcom.2021.127641

Wu, C., Chang, J., Xu, X., Quan, C., Zhang, X., & Zhang, Y. (2020). Cryptoanalysis of the modified diffractive-imaging-based image encryption by deep learning attack. *Journal of Modern Optics*, *67*(17), 1398–1409. DOI: 10.1080/09500340.2020.1862329

KEY TERMS AND DEFINITIONS

Adversarial Loss: Generative Adversarial Networks (GANs) are trained using a specialised loss function called adversarial loss, which makes an indicator and generator essentially contest with one another. Whereas the generator seeks to produce comparable samples by minimising loss, the discriminator seeks to maximise the likelihood of distinguishing genuine vs. phoney data.

Attractor: In spite of starting circumstances, a dynamical framework develops gradually towards a collection of computational or physical properties known as an attractor. Such stable conditions (fixed points, loops, or unusual attractors) are spontaneously reached by these structures, like pendulums or chaotic, complicated behaviours.

Lorenz System: The mathematician Edward Lorenz created the Lorenz system, a collection of 3 ordinary differential equations, after researching atmospheric convection. It is a well-known illustration of a structure which might display chaotic behaviour, which means that even little modifications to its initial circumstances might have a significant impact on its performance.

Chapter 6
AI-Integrated Cybersecurity Design Frameworks for IoT-Enabled Smart Farming Systems

Tutan Ghosh
Maulana Abul Kalam Azad University of Technology, West Bengal, India

Ira Nath
JIS College of Engineering, Kalyani, India

Piyali Nandi
Hemnalini Memorial College of Engineering, West Bengal, India

Sushovan Khatua
http://orcid.org/0000-0003-4165-242X
SRM University AP, India

Anirban Maity
http://orcid.org/0009-0003-2884-976X
The Neotia University, West Bengal, India

ABSTRACT

The adoption of Internet of Things (IoT) technologies in agriculture has improved productivity through real-time monitoring, automated irrigation, and data-driven decision-making. However, increased connectivity exposes smart farming systems

DOI: 10.4018/979-8-3693-3751-6.ch006

to cybersecurity threats that can compromise data and disrupt operations. This study proposes an AI-enabled cybersecurity framework integrating threat detection, anomaly monitoring, secure authentication, and encrypted communication. Machine learning algorithms continuously analyze device behavior and network traffic to identify cyberattacks in real time. The framework was evaluated in a simulated smart farming environment comprising sensors, edge devices, and cloud services. Results achieved 97.8% detection accuracy, 96.9% precision, and 97.3% recall, while reducing false alerts by 21% and improving response time by 28% compared with conventional methods. The proposed framework enhances security, reliability, and resilience, providing a scalable solution for next-generation digital agriculture.

1. INTRODUCTION

The rapid advancement of digital technology has significantly impacted traditional practices used in the practice of agriculture. This has led to the development of "smart", or "precision", agriculture which is based on the integration of a number of Internet of Things (IoT) devices such as but not limited to soil sensors, drones, irrigation controllers and livestock monitoring into a comprehensive system that allows the collection and analysis of real time data. The data from these devices will enable farmers to make better decisions on how to use their resources and therefore increase crop productivity and reduce operational costs. In (Zreikat et al., 2025) explores the integration of IoT applications with 5G networks, highlighting their technical applications, benefits, and future prospects. Additionally, smart farm devices can improve sustainability in agriculture (Ocama et al., 2025; Wolfert et al., 2017). In (Zaman et al., 2025) provides a comprehensive overview of the evolution and current applications of advanced IoT and AI technologies in modern supply chain operations. With the global population expected to approach 10 billion by 2050, the adoption of intelligent agricultural technologies has become increasingly important for ensuring food security and sustainable food production worldwide (Canton, 2021). The IoT systems within the agricultural industry pose effective numerousness of cybersecurity breaches irrespective of their transformational capacity. Most agricultural IoT devices are resource-constrained and operate with limited processing power, memory, and communication bandwidth. This is a model that is cheap and efficient to the environment but does not withstand cyber offenders. It has been established that such security gaps as insufficient authentication, the absence of encryption, and risky firmware is prevalent to constitute vulnerability to cyber-attack exploitation of IoT Networks within the context of agriculture (Demestichas et al., 2020; Sicari et al., 2015). Farms are not required to be located in one geographical place like traditional IT infrastructure and in most instances that occur in rural locations with poor connections farms present new challenges of device surveillance, patching and security (Bacco et al., 2019). The adoption of innovative technologies is essential for advancing sustainable and efficient agricultural systems (D & Devarajan, 2025).

Scenario of risks in agriculture has endeavoured to demonstrate feasible risks regarding cyber in attacks. An important example to highlight the fact is that due to the ransomware assaults on farmers cooperatives in North America, the supply chains and the food processing have been disrupted even in these regions. The if timer of irrigation or fertilization is also manipulable which can either lead to creating an over-tipping of limited resources or a failure of the crops in sensor due to sensor hijacking or data spoofing. One example of this is a Distributed Denial-of-Service (DDoS) attack, which may render automated irrigation systems inoperable during critical crop growth phases and disrupt livestock surveillance systems, thereby posing a significant threat to animal health and well-being (Khan et al., 2020). These incidents also highlight the fact that the agriculture IoT systems not only form technical architectures, but also of the utmost importance to the national infrastructure as their dangers can have a direct effect on the food supplies, the economic status and the living conditions of the rural areas populations.

Though up to date sources of the research on cybersecurity present the broad models in the context of smart cities, industrial oriented IoT and healthcare, the state of agricultural IoT research is comparatively under-investigated (Botschner et al., 2024). The agricultural sector is also facing similar cybersecurity challenges: machines are supposed to be compatible in the harsh environment conditions outdoors, and they must also consume the least amount of energy besides being accessible to the small-scale farmers. In a way, ordinary cryptography guard strategy and malicious identification tools that target high-velocity and powerful computers can't be valuable. The immediate opportunities that need to be tackled are the development of the lightweight security control, decentralized systems such as blockchain, and anomaly detector tools that can strike a perfect balance between the number of resources spent on resources utilisation and safe protection (Tariq et al., 2025a). The findings emphasize the need for IoT–XAI research to move beyond accuracy-focused evaluation toward lightweight, privacy-aware, and resource-efficient explanation frameworks suitable for diverse stakeholders and edge-based smart city and agricultural applications (Karras et al., 2026).

The given paper tries to address these limitations as it discusses the issue of the IoT-mediated farm system cybersecurity. It enumerates the more common sensor attacks, data misrepresentation of impersonation and ransomware and evaluates why the existing solutions fail to function effectively in these farming environments that do suffer resource limitations. Security models applicable in the agricultural application of the IoT have also been proposed in the paper, with a high emphasis on lightweight cryptographic models and blockchain solutions applied to the data integrity, and edge computing developed on the detection of localized anomalies. The proposed study can be used to fill the research gap between areas such as cyber-security, IoT engineering, and agricultural technology to ensure more of the smart farming systems become less vulnerable to the emerging cyber threats. To address these needs, the next section identifies key research gaps and highlights the novel contributions of this chapter

1.1 Research Gap and Novel Contributions

Smart Farming research has generally addressed the various security aspects of each component individually; however, there are still large gaps. There is currently no "comprehensive review" on Smart Agriculture Cybersecurity as indicated by (Campoverde-Molina & Luján-Mora, 2025). Many researchers have identified the vulnerability of IoT systems to attacks; however, they have typically done so in isolation. Recent Surveys indicate the vital role AI will play in identifying threats and responding to them. However, few if any frameworks currently utilize all forms of AI or Edge Intelligence (Ali et al., 2024). Fewer still provide a combination of AI-driven Anomaly Detection with both Device-Level Protection and Data Integrity Mechanisms. Lightweight Cryptography has been proposed as a possible means of providing encryption solutions to the resource-constrained IoT Devices, although it is rarely used in conjunction with AI Analytics. Blockchain Technology is frequently utilized for Traceability purposes in Smart Farms; however, it is less frequently combined with Machine Learning for Real-Time Intrusion Detection (Gupta et al., 2024). Therefore, current frameworks for Smart Farming are primarily single-layered (Cloud Based or Device Based) and Lack Unified multi-layered defense solutions.

Recent advancements in intelligent optimization and machine learning have clearly indicated the potential of Artificial Intelligence (AI) to improve decision-making, prediction accuracy, and system resilience in distributed engineering systems. Neural-network-based predictive models have successfully been applied in complex nonlinear environments such as alternative-fuel combustion systems, demonstrating their capability to learn hidden operational patterns and support intelligent decision-making under dynamic conditions (Roy et al., 2024).

The previous research on LSTMs, ANNs, and BI-RGUs has demonstrated positive results for dealing with large amounts of operationally collected data and enabling adaptive system management. This indicates that similar AI-based methods could also be employed as a means to support Cybersecurity applications within Smart Farming Environments, which will require real-time Anomaly Detection and Threat Mitigation capabilities (Maity et al., 2025, 2026). Previous studies have shown that optimized neural-network frameworks can maintain high predictive performance even under highly nonlinear operating conditions, suggesting their suitability for adaptive agricultural IoT security systems (Roy et al., 2025).

Although IoT security research has made progress, the current studies mostly focus on isolated security mechanisms like cryptographic protection, blockchain-enabled traceability or AI-based anomaly detection. Research on the integration of these complementary technologies into a unified cybersecurity framework for resource-constrained smart farming environments has been very limited. Therefore, there is a significant research gap in developing an end-to-end, multi-layered security architecture for real-time threat detection, secure communication and data integrity with low computational overhead.

The purpose of this chapter is to fill those gaps through an End-To-End AI Integrated Framework for Smart Farming. This framework integrates multiple Advanced Techniques within a Coherent Design: lightweight Encryption/Authentication Methods specifically designed for Constrained Sensor Networks; Machine Learning deployed at the Network Edge for Rapid Anomaly Detection; and Blockchain technology for Tamper-Proof Data Integrity. All three components function together within a Layered Architecture that spans from the IoT Devices through Edge Nodes and ultimately to Cloud Servers. Our approach extends the prior work regarding IoT Security by explicitly integrating AI based methodologies and by taking into account the unique constraints associated with Agricultural Systems. Unlike existing approaches that focus on individual security mechanisms, the proposed framework integrates AI-driven anomaly detection, lightweight cryptographic protection, blockchain-based integrity assurance, and edge intelligence within a unified multi-layer cybersecurity architecture tailored specifically for smart farming environments. New Contributions to this Chapter Include:

- A self-contained Anomaly-Detection Engine utilizing Machine Learning and Neural Models at the Edge to Identify Cyber Attacks in Real Time.
- The deployment of Resource Efficient Cryptographic Protocols (and Role-Based Access Control) directly onto IoT Devices which provides support for their Limited Power and Computational Capabilities.
- Utilizing a Blockchain Ledger to Ensure End-to-End Data Integrity and Non-Reputation in Agricultural Data Exchanges.
- A Hierarchical Framework Combining Cloud, Edge, and Device Layers that Enables Coordinated Security Measures Across the Entire IoT Stack.
- Experimental evaluation within a Simulated Smart Farming Environment Demonstrating the Effectiveness of the Framework in Detecting Threats and Improving System Resilience.

The remaining portion of this chapter will be structured as follows: Section 2 will review smart farming using the Internet-of-Things (IoT); Section 3 will provide an analysis of cyber threats in the smart farm; Section 4 will present the proposed AI-based security framework for smart farms; Section 5 will describe how the proposed system was tested by way of a test bed (case study) to evaluate it; Section 6 presents the case study, experimental evaluation, and performance analysis, while Section 7 discusses practical implications, limitations, and future research directions.

2. IoT-ENABLED SMART FARMING: AN OVERVIEW

Agriculture is a very energy intensive activity that is greatly affected by many environmental components including; weather, access to water, and soils. The past few decades have seen significant advancements in digital technology and this advancement has changed how we have traditionally operated and implemented smart farming ideas into our agriculture. Smart farming utilizes IoT (Internet of Things) devices, AI (Artificial Intelligence) systems, Cloud Computing capabilities and Data Analytics software and services to help make data driven decisions, increase agricultural output and productively use resources while supporting environmentally sustainable agricultural methods. With smart farming continuously monitoring and automatically controlling various aspects of the operation through its technologies, farmers are able to increase their crop yields, lower their operational expenses and create better efficiencies for managing all areas of their operations (Ocama et al., 2025; Wolfert et al., 2017). Figure 1 illustrates the IoT ecosystem and attack vectors in smart farming.

Figure 1. Smart Farming IoT Ecosystem & Attack Points

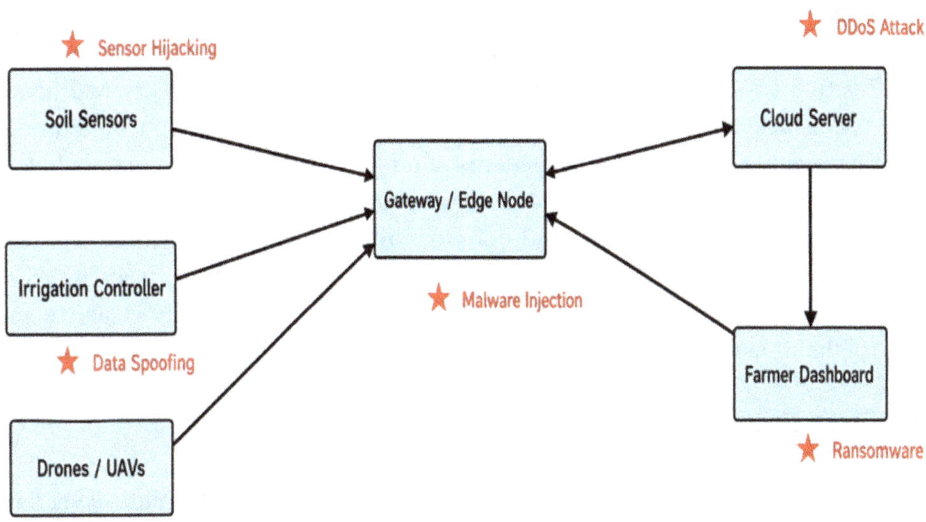

2.1 Development of Precision Agriculture and IoT Integration

Precision agriculture as a way of running the farms became a practice in the late 20th century with its emphasis on field variability and targeted response of management. Early precision agriculture relied primarily on Geographic Information Systems (GIS), remote sensing, and satellite imagery. The introduction of IoT technologies has significantly expanded these capabilities by enabling real-time monitoring and automated decision-making across agricultural operations. Both modern farms now have many interconnected sensors with low power that keep in established real-time track of soil moisture, pH, nutrient status, temperature, and humidity. Covered by the drones and unmanned aerial vehicle (UAVs), aerial image, smart tractors combine GPS and IoT units to optimize the patterns of seeding and harvesting. Such an integrated construct of hardware and software does not only offer constant data feeds but also allows automated decision-making when using machine-to-machine communication along with cloud-based analytics (Bacco et al., 2019).

2.2 IoT Device in Agriculture

The agricultural IoT is a very wide-ranging environment. The soil sensors can detect the important parameters like the water content and the fertility in the soil and used to control the irrigation and fertilization timeline. These sensors are attached to irrigation controllers that automatically regulate the water delivery and hence reduce wastage and enhance crop health. Uncreamed climate stations and drones meeting weather information, the patterns of rainfalls and heat waves are predicted. The implants and smart livestock collars monitor the moves of livestock and their feeding habits as well as health conditions to initiate preventive veterinary services. On a grander scale, the farm management platforms are used to consolidate these data points into user-friendly dashboards in which farmers remotely visualize and control their business (Khan et al., 2020).

2.3 Data flow architecture of Smart farming

The operation of IoT-enabled smart farming systems relies on a multi-layer data flow architecture that facilitates the collection, transmission, processing, and utilization of agricultural data. The physical devices are used in the first layer and these include sensors and actuators that are distributed on fields and livestock facilities. Such devices glean the information that is then sent through a gateways or edge nodes - in the countryside, it is often sent with the help of the wireless protocols, including Zigbee, LoRaWAN, 5G, or satellite links. The second layer is a data aggregation of the gateways and data processing may be done at an initial stage to minimize latency and bandwidth usage. Raw/processed data are then connected to cloud servers to perform more sophisticated analytics and prediction modelling as well as storage. Last but not least, the information is represented in convenient dashboards that can be available either on the mobile or desktop device; this aspect enables the farmers to take action based on evidence-basing (Vangala et al., 2023).

2.4 Benefits of IoT in Agriculture

The benefits of the implementation of IoT in agriculture are numerous. First, it increases productivity through giving accurate recommendations on irrigation, fertilization as well as pests that lead to increased yields per hectare. Secondly, IoT also helps to achieve sustainability by guaranteeing efficient resource consumption and this minimizes water consumption and runs of Chemicals. Third, the technology assists resilience through prior-notice of unfavourable weather patterns, pest attack, or equipment costs by offering advance care in case of people putting them on a basis so that measures are implemented before things get bad. Lastly, with IoT automated agriculture, there can be traceability in production chains that deciphers buyers about the quality and safety of their food (Botschner et al., 2024; Canton, 2021).

2.5 Dependence on Communication Infrastructure

Even with all its potential, smarter farming with the help of IoT is largely dependent on the effective connectivity infrastructure. Most of the farms are situated in rural areas which fail to provide good internet connection, bandwidth and power supply is not also reliable. In this case, it is a great challenge to ensure that continuous communication exists among the sensors, gateways and cloud servers. In addition, the variety of devices makes them heterogenous with different manufacturers, protocols, and standards which presents a challenge in interoperability making large scale implementation a challenge. All these points indicate that IoT in agriculture can only be successful when there is a favourable infrastructure, training, and policies (Tariq et al., 2025a).

2.6 Emerging Applications in Sustainable Agriculture

Smart farming as enabled by IoT is slowly emerging as one of the key pillars of sustainable agricultural practice. Similar to sustainability-driven digital transformation initiatives reported in transportation and maritime sectors, modern agricultural systems increasingly depend on accurate data acquisition, monitoring, and analytics to support environmental performance assessment and long-term sustainability objectives (Roy et al., 2025). It is engaging in the direct work of the United Nations Sustainable Development Goals (SDGs); namely, Goal 2 (Zero Hunger) and Goal 12 (Responsible Consumption and Production). To advocate smallholder farmers, which make up the major portions of agricultural labour in developing nations, governments and individual businesses are investing in the IoT solutions. Yet, this digitalization also implies an increase in vulnerability to cyber threats, as any device that is thus connected to the network creates an avenue of attack by scrupulous individuals (Sicari et al., 2015).

2.7 Transition Toward Cybersecurity Considerations

Though IoT technologies have greatly improved the productivity and operational efficiency in agriculture, the increasing number of connected devices has also increased the attack surface for cybercriminals. Unlike conventional information technology systems, many agricultural IoT devices are resource-constrained and often lack strong security features. Therefore, smart farming environments are more exposed to cyber threats such as sensor hijacking, data spoofing, ransomware and denial of service attacks. These security challenges emphasize the need for dedicated cybersecurity solutions for agricultural IoT ecosystems.

As shown in Figure 2 below, the information flows from one layer (sensing) to the other within a smart-farming system. Sensing Layer, several types of sensors collect and transmit data on various aspects of an environment or operation at all times. These include but are not limited to; soil moisture, temperature, humidity, nutrients for crops and overall health of the crop. The sensor-collected data are communicated via wirelessly enabled connectivity options that have become ubiquitous including; Wi-Fi, LoraWan, Zigbee and cellular network to the Edge Layer. Data processing at this layer includes initial filtration of raw data, detecting anomalies and making decisions locally with the intent to minimize latency and the amount of data that needs to be communicated.

Processed data will then flow to the Cloud Layer, which includes performing large scale data warehousing and analytics, employing Machine Learning algorithms for trending and analyzing large amounts of data over time and storing trends analyzed over time. The Application Layer provides actionable information to farmers based upon the data analyzed by providing them with dashboards, mobile apps and automated systems for controlling operations. As illustrated above, this hierarchical approach enables the ability to provide timely interventions, optimize resources utilized during the growing process and increase the efficiency of daily farm operations.

Figure 2. IoT Layers in Smart Farming Data Flow Architecture

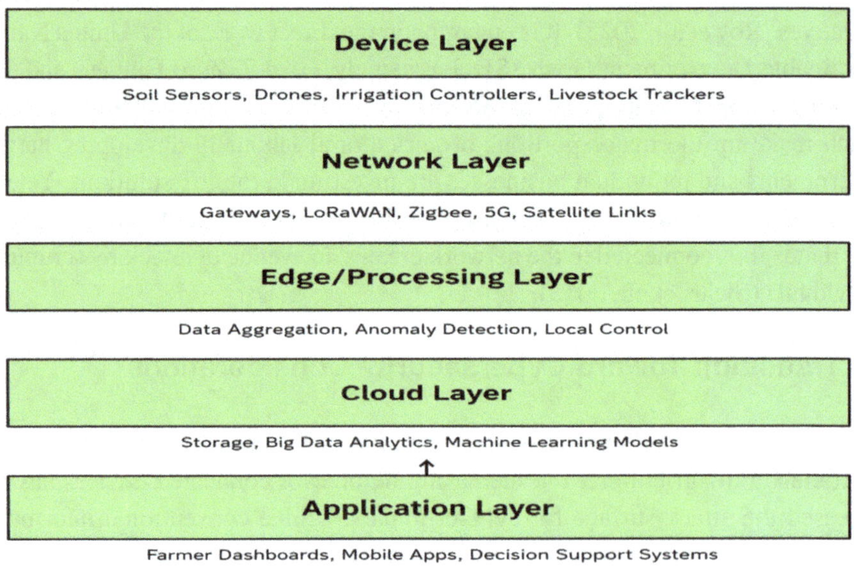

3. THE THREAT LANDSCAPE OF AGRICULTURAL IOT CYBERSECURITY

The widespread use of IoT in agriculture has greatly impacted the potential for smart farming systems to become vulnerable to cyber-attacks. This is due to the fact that IoT-based smart farming applications have a number of differentiating factors when compared to traditional IT-based systems. Some of these include: the wide geographic dispersion of devices; the limited resources (e.g., memory, processing power) available at each device; the diverse types of communication used among devices; and the unpredictable nature of network availability. As such, there is an extremely large attack surface available to cyber attackers. Thus, it is important to understand this threat environment so as to develop effective cybersecurity measures to protect the operation of farms, ensure the accuracy of farm related data and provide for continued reliable food supply.

Threat taxonomy of Agricultural Internet of Things IoT-enabled agriculture has threats which can be characterized in terms of device-level, network-level and application-level threat.

- **Sensor Hijacking:** This is through control of soil or irrigation sensors in order to make them read differently, thus disorienting farming cycles. As an example, when the soil moisture is spoofed, the excess irrigation may follow, causing the waste of resources and the destruction of crops (Sicari et al., 2015).
- **Data Spoofing and Manipulation:** Bad people brought in fabricated data streams in the farm management systems. An invalid data on the nutrient or pest content of the soil might also deceive farmers to make a false decision, lower the production (Vangala et al., 2023).
- **Denial-of-Service (DoS) Attacks:** Detected can happen as distributed DoS attacks and can incapacitate the water and nutrients delivery within allotted time to the irrigation controllers and gateways (Brown et. al. 2008). Such interruptions could lead to massive loss on yield during the sensitive crop development periods (Khan et al., 2020).
- **Ransomware:** The ransomware is also especially susceptible to farm management systems that are linked to cloud servers and encrypt information and expect a fee. Agricultural cooperatives have already reported such attacks and disrupted the food chain.
- **Supply Chain Attacks:** Fraudulent software updates provided by the vendors may be spoiled. The variety of the devices in the agricultural sector implies that one supply chain attack can infect thousands of farms.

This taxonomy highlights that agricultural IoT is not recalcitrant to the Pale of cyber threats that endangers other critical industry segments like the healthcare and energy sectors.

3.1 Real-World Incidents and Case Studies

The drainage sector has started to be affected by the architectural threats of cyber interactions. On the other hand, the risk of digital disruption of agricultural supply chains was revealed in 2021 with the attacks on U.S based food processing companies using ransomware. In the same way, experimental investigations have demonstrated the possibility of hijacking agricultural drones with unencrypted communication connections so that enemies of intelligent agriculture can modify spraying patterns or obtain valuable farm information (Botschner et al., 2024). These examples indicate that agricultural IoT is not a simple technical device but a larger socio-economic framework of infrastructure of which its degradation can have ripple effects to food supply, trade, and national security.

3.2 Factors of vulnerability unique in Agriculture

A chain of preconditions applicability heighten the hazards in the field of agricultural internet of things:

- **Low-Power Devices:** Most of the IoT devices operate as agricultural are affordable and low-energy-consuming. Individuals, therefore, are likely to lack adequate cryptography or security boot system and expose themselves to attacks (Tariq et al., 2025a). Geographical Dispersion: Geographically distributed farms are customarily divided into massive countryside areas and the appropriate purpose realisation of networks, program updates and physical plant security is considered to be quite difficult.
- **Connection limitations:** The nature of rural broadband or sat connections or any system based on low power wide area network (LPWAN) broadly based on connectivity exposes one to a higher number of jamming or intercepting the connection.
- **Interoperability Issues:** IoT devices among vendors generally have portions of protocol, which cannot interoperate, and they generate security blind areas in facade-to-facade-based farm system (Wolfert et al., 2017).
- **Human Factor:** Limited cybersecurity awareness, weak password practices, phishing attacks, and social engineering increase the vulnerability of agricultural personnel and farm management systems.

The latter flaws are consumed in the agricultural IoT system when compared with the industrial systems of IoT where resources and infrastructure will more likely withstand cybersecurity attacks.

3.3 National Security and Policy Implications

The food security and the economic stability rely on agriculture as its pillar. Hacking of farms is capable of going well beyond single losses, thus interrupting supply chains and whole economies. As an example, organized blows to pipeline systems or grain deposit facilities would cause shortage and fluctuation of prices, as well as political and social consequences. Agriculture is starting to be seen by governments as critical infrastructure but policy frameworks tailored to agricultural cybersecurity are few (Canton, 2021). It is necessary to bridge this gap to protect both the farmers and consumers.

3.4 Transition Toward Countermeasures

The increasing number of threats are clearly revealing that agricultural IoT needs specific security measures to cover any technical and contextual gaps. Like cryptography of lightness, blockchain-based data validation, and edge-based anomaly are the new promising countermeasures. Next, this paper will discuss the distinct difficulties in applying these solutions to the world of agriculture and discuss why the currently existing industrial models cannot be simply transferred to the environment of farming. In addition, the distributed nature of smart farming infrastructures necessitates efficient management of large volumes of sensor-generated information, where resilient data partitioning and recovery mechanisms can further strengthen system reliability and cyber resilience (Pramanik et al., 2025).

Cyberattacks against smart farms that are identified in earlier parts of this document could lead to large negative effects on both the operation of a smart farm and its bottom line (Figure 3). It shows how many cyberattacks have direct or indirect consequences on the three primary areas where an attack will occur when it is done on a smart farm: crop production, information/data integrity, and long-term sustainability of the farm.

Figure 3. Cyber Threats in Agricultural IoT: Attack Vectors and Impacts

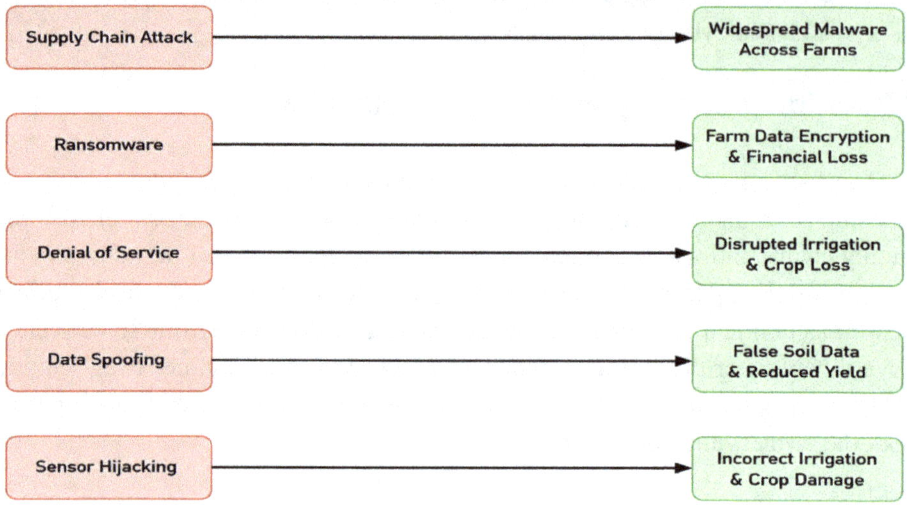

For greater clarity on the relationships between major cybersecurity threats, and the mitigation strategies to counteract those threats (as well as possible adverse effects), Table 1 is provided to compare the most significant cyber threats against an Internet-of-Things (IoT) enabled Smart Farming System.

Table 1. Major Cybersecurity Threats, Impacts, and Mitigation Strategies in Smart Farming

Cybersecurity Threat	Potential Impact on Smart Farming	AI-Based Detection Mechanism	Proposed Mitigation Strategy
Sensor Hijacking	Incorrect irrigation and crop management decisions	Isolation Forest, Anomaly Detection Models	Device authentication and secure communication
Data Spoofing	False environmental data leading to poor agricultural decisions	Random Forest, SVM	Blockchain-based data validation
Denial-of-Service (DoS) Attack	Disruption of irrigation and monitoring services	LSTM-based Intrusion Detection System	Edge-based traffic filtering and rate limiting
Ransomware Attack	Data loss and operational downtime	Behavioral Analytics and Deep Learning Models	Backup mechanisms and role-based access control

continued on following page

Table 1. Continued

Cybersecurity Threat	Potential Impact on Smart Farming	AI-Based Detection Mechanism	Proposed Mitigation Strategy
Unauthorized Access	Compromise of farm management systems	Machine Learning-based User Behaviour Analysis	Multi-factor authentication and access control
Supply Chain Attack	Malware propagation through compromised firmware	AI Threat Intelligence Systems	Secure firmware validation and software integrity checks

Table 1 illustrates how smart farming cyber threats impact multiple levels within the IoT-enabled system; for example: sensor devices, communications network, Edge Gateway, Cloud Service. Based upon the above information, the proposed Smart Farming Cybersecurity Framework will utilize a multi-level defense approach combining Artificial Intelligence, Lightweight Cryptography, Blockchain-enabled Data Integrity Mechanisms and Access-Control Mechanisms to address the identified threat vectors while also taking into consideration the resource limitations associated with the use of agriculture.

4. CYBERSECURITY CHALLENGES IN SMART FARMING SYSTEMS

The positive benefits of IoT technologies implementation to the agricultural sector indeed are brand new, but the concerns and threats are different in terms of the implications of the industrial or city world of IoT. Certain angle of the cybersecurity threat was predetermined by the unions of operational nature of the agricultural sector and the environmental, as well as socio-economic conditions. In order to surmount these malfunctions, it would be necessary to have a delicate feeling of farming realities in which affordability, simplicity and accessibility will prevail, over technical soundness.

4.1 Resource Constraints

The IoT applications in agriculture are expected to be inexpensive, energy-efficient, and ought to be deployed at a massive level. It means that they cannot not always deliver a higher order encryption algorithms or constant security control (Sicari et al., 2015). The emphasis of energy efficiency is comparatively higher priority than a calculation capability and therefore brute force attacks, malware and unauthorized access are exploited on the devices. The problem of trade-offs between operation costs and environmental safeguarding is one of the most urgent issues of the small holder farmers.

4.2 Heterogeneity of Devices

The ecosystem of smart farming is comprised of sensors, drones, irrigation controllers, livestock trackers and cloud-based dashboards, frequently provided to end-users by various vendors of differing security durations. This heterogeneity poses a problem of interoperability targeted activities to which attackers can exploit its inherent gaps (Vangala et al., 2023). To illustrate, a secure soil reduced system of sensors can still be jeopardized when incorporated to a less secure irrigation system. This is made even harder by the fact that agricultural IoT does not have any common standards.

4.3 Remote and Geographically Distributed Deployments

Farms are spread geographically to localized spots in some cases in rural or remote areas which is not the case with urban IoT which runs in centralized infrastructure. Devices are restricted in ways of physical access and hence it is challenging to perform routine maintenance, patching and watch how it functions (Bacco et al., 2019). This remoteness could be misused by the attackers as they can physically tamper with the equipment or provide long-term cyberattacks.

4.4 Network and Limitations of Connections

The majority of farms use communication protocols with low bandwidth like LoRaWAN or rural broadband. Even though more affordable, these networks are more prone to jamming, interception, and latency factors (Khan et al., 2020). Unhealthy or intermittent connection also makes cloud-based security solutions less viable, and thus further highlighting the urgency to have lightweight edge-based mechanisms that would operate with limited network dependency.

4.5 Human Factors and Digital Literacy

Cybersecurity practices are not usually provided to farmers and other workers, which exposes them to phishing, weak password habits, and misconfigurations (Botschner et al., 2024). The attacks that are aired by social engineers against individuals of less technical literacy can be harmful just as extensively as technical exploits. Even the best systems can be undermined by human error even when they are best secured through proper training. Therefore, cybersecurity awareness training and user-friendly security mechanisms should be considered integral components of smart farming security strategies.

4.6 Policy and Regulatory Gaps

Cybersecurity to agriculture does not have well-developed regulatory measures as used in finance or healthcare. The threats related to farming are often not considered by relevant policies implemented by the state, and not many standards in place internationally are focused on securing agricultural IoT. The regulatory gap places the project on the shoulders of device manufacturers and farmers, neither of which might have sufficient resources or motivation to place greater importance on security (Canton, 2021). Unlike sectors such as healthcare, finance, and energy, agriculture currently lacks comprehensive cybersecurity standards specifically tailored to IoT-enabled farming systems.

To prioritize cybersecurity risks in IoT-enabled smart farming environments, Table 2 presents a qualitative risk assessment matrix based on the likelihood of occurrence and the potential impact of various cyber threats on agricultural operations.

Table 2. Risk Assessment matrix for Smart Farming Cybersecurity Threats

Frequency	Low Impact	Medium Impact	High Impact
High Frequency	Weak password attack on IoT devices.	Malware injection in farm controllers	Ransomware on farm management services
Medium Frequency	False alerts from drones or weather sensors	DoS on irrigation system (temporary disruption)	Hijacking livestock monitoring devices
Low Frequency	Unauthorized access to local dashboards	Sensor spoofing (soil moisture, temperature)	Data theft (yield forecasts, pricing)

4.7 Transition to Solutions

The issues listed above illustrate how traditional cyber-security solutions are not applicable to a typical IoT environment found in agriculture. There is a need for specialized security solutions based on resource constrained devices, varying levels of device compatibility, deployment of devices remotely, limited connectivity options, and lack of regulation or standards for data protection. These factors lead to the need for efficient, cost-effective, yet secure technologies like light weight cryptographic protocols, blockchain-based integrity verification protocols, edge-based anomaly detection systems and artificial intelligence (AI) to protect smart-farming ecosystem. An AI-based cyber-security framework will be described in the next section that addresses the specific needs mentioned above.

4.8 Artificial Intelligence for Agricultural Cybersecurity

Artificial Intelligence (AI) is a viable solution to enhance the cybersecurity of IoT enabled Smart Farming Systems. Traditional cybersecurity solutions are based on predefined signature or rule sets that become ineffective when faced with new, emerging and unknown cyber threats. The use of AI allows for adaptive threat detection, real-time monitoring and intelligent decision-making, resulting in enhanced resilience of IoT-based agricultural systems (Ali et al., 2024).

Through the analysis of large amounts of sensor and network data Machine Learning (ML) algorithms are able to detect abnormal activity indicative of cyberattacks. Many ML algorithms including RF, SVM and XGBoost have been shown to be highly effective in classifying malicious vs. legitimate activity. These types of algorithms can detect various forms of cyberattacks such as Data Spoofing, Unauthorized Access and Denial-Of-Service Attacks by learning from historical data bases (Gupta et al., 2024).

Where labeled attack data is not available, Unsupervised Learning offers a viable alternative. Through the use of algorithms such as Isolation Forest, it is possible to identify unusual behaviours in the system through the detection of deviation from "normal" operation. Isolation Forest-type algorithms are especially effective at detecting Zero-Day Attacks and Compromised IoT Devices in Smart Farming Environments.

Additional enhancements to the overall cybersecurity capabilities of smart farming systems are provided by deep learning technologies capable of extracting complex nonlinear relationships from large-scale operational datasets. Similar deep-learning approaches have demonstrated excellent predictive capability in engineering monitoring applications, highlighting their potential for intelligent cyber-threat detection and behavioural analysis in agricultural IoT environments (Roy et al., 2025). For example, LSTM Networks are particularly well-suited for the Analysis of Time-Series Sensor Data and Anomaly Detection in Irrigation Systems, Environmental Monitoring Systems and Livestock Tracking Applications. Additionally, BiGRU Models have been shown to possess superior Predictive Capabilities in Distributed Intelligent Systems and can aid in Early Detection of Cyber Threats via Continuous Monitoring of Device Behavior (Maity et al., 2025). Furthermore, hybrid architectures combining convolutional layers, bidirectional recurrent networks, and attention mechanisms have recently demonstrated superior capability in modelling complex temporal dependencies and extracting critical features from noisy datasets, making them promising candidates for advanced intrusion detection and anomaly classification tasks in smart farming ecosystems (Roy et al., 2026).

Finally, AI Models deployed at the Network Edge enable Rapid Detection of Threats while minimizing Communication Overhead and Cloud Dependency.

Processing data at the Edge Layer enables Real-Time Identification of Suspicious Activity regardless of Remote Agricultural Environment Connectivity Constraints. Recent Studies have demonstrated the Importance of Combining Edge Computing, Lightweight Deep Learning Technologies and Intelligent Analytics to Improve both Security and Efficiency in Next Generation Smart Farming Ecosystems (Tariq et al., 2025b).

Within this proposed Framework AI will serve as the Core Anomaly Detection Engine Operating at the Edge Layer. As such, this Proposed Framework combines the power of both Machine Learning/Deep Learning Technologies along with Edge Intelligence/Lightweight Cryptography and Blockchain Enabled Data Integrity Mechanisms to Provide a Multi-Layered Defense Strategy that Enables Real-Time Detection, Analysis and Mitigation of Cyber Threats. Furthermore, the Integration of these Technologies Enhances Reliability, Security and Resilience of Next Generation Smart Farming Systems.

5. PROPOSED SECURITY ARCHITECTURES AND GUIDELINES

The unique characteristics of IoT-enabled smart farming systems require cybersecurity solutions that are secure, energy-efficient, scalable, and suitable for resource-constrained environments. Unlike conventional industrial IoT infrastructures, agricultural systems often operate with limited processing capabilities, intermittent connectivity, and heterogeneous devices distributed across large geographical areas. To address these challenges, this section presents a multi-layer AI-integrated cybersecurity framework that combines lightweight cryptography, blockchain-enabled integrity verification, edge-based anomaly detection, and access-control mechanisms to provide comprehensive protection across the agricultural IoT ecosystem.

A multi-layered approach to address the cybersecurity concerns previously identified is recommended by the authors for all smart farming system enabled with IoT. The authors propose that their framework will be able to integrate lightweight cryptography for field devices and sensor authentication, edge based real time anomaly detection (using AI), blockchain technology for verifying data integrity, and AI for analyzing threats on the cloud level. In total, the authors are proposing an end-to-end multi-layered architecture as shown in Figure 4.

Figure 4. Proposed Multi-Layer AI-Integrated Cybersecurity Framework for Smart Farming

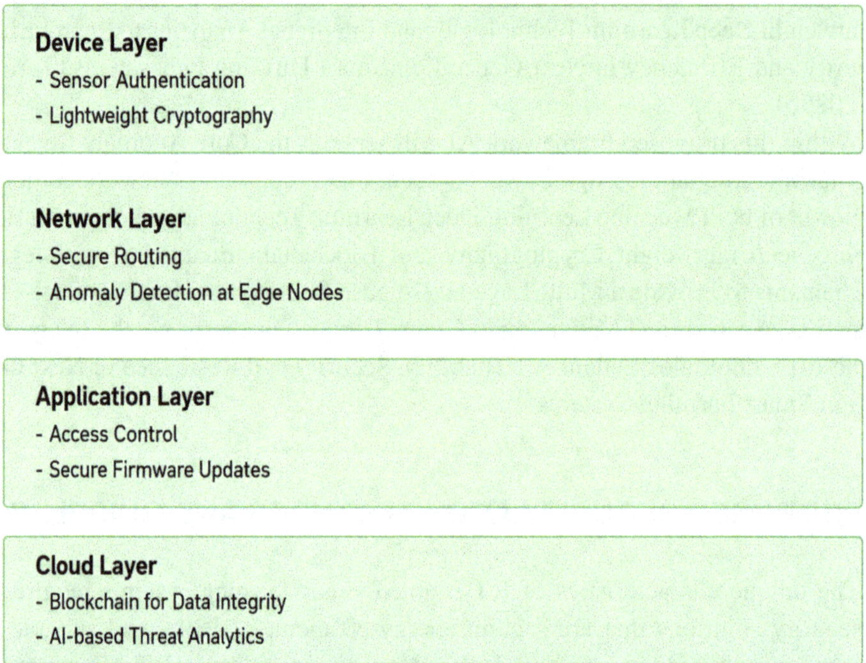

The proposed multi-layered cybersecurity architecture of IoT enabled smart farming systems shown in Figure 4 illustrates how each component of the authors' framework can contribute to providing security at the different levels of the smart agriculture ecosystem. The framework provides four primary areas where security measures will be implemented. These include the device layer (i.e., using lightweight cryptography and sensor authentication to protect field devices); network layer; application layer (i.e., implementing access control and secure firmware management); and cloud layer (i.e., utilizing blockchain technology for verifying data integrity and AI for conducting threat analysis). In Table 3 provides the symbol notations in proposed methodology.

Table 3. Symbol table

Symbol	Description	Symbol	Description
L_bc	Blockchain transaction latency	p_block	Overall probability of successfully blocking an attack
T_b	Block creation/confirmation time	S	Set of IoT devices
δ	Average network jitter	τ_i	Packet generation rate of device i
s_tx	Transaction size	s_i	Packet size generated by device i
P_r[rewrite(z)]	Probability of rewriting blockchain history with z confirmations	E_enc_a(s_i)	Encryption energy consumption
q	Fraction of validators controlled by an adversary	e_tx	Transmission energy per packet
z	Number of blockchain confirmations	ρ_ids	Energy overhead of IDS
η(q)	Security coefficient associated with validator fraction q	ρ_bc	Energy overhead of blockchain operations
S_t	CUSUM detection statistic at time t	E_tot	Total energy consumption per hour
x_t	Feature vector observed at time t	L_enc_a	Encryption latency
w	Weight vector used by anomaly detector	L_net	Network communication latency
K	Detection threshold parameter	L_ids	Intrusion detection latency
E[T_det]	Expected detection delay	L_tot	Total system latency
h	Detection decision threshold	A	System accuracy metric
μ0	Mean feature vector under normal operation	A_0	Minimum required accuracy
μ1	Mean feature vector under attack/ anomalous condition	L_0	Maximum allowable latency
Δ	Mean shift between normal and attack distributions	J	Optimization objective function
α	False alarm probability	β, γ	Weighting coefficients
p_int	Probability blockchain prevents integrity attacks		
p_ids	Probability IDS detects attacks		
p_auth	Probability authentication blocks unauthorized access		

5.1 Lightweight Cryptography for IoT Devices

Lightweight algorithms like AES-128 have long been thought of as being secure, but they can consume a lot of power and slow down small computing units in resource constrained IoT devices. The time to perform an operation for a lightweight cryptographic algorithm and the amount of energy consumed is shown below using Equations (1) and (2).

$$L_e nc_a = (K_a * s)/fE_e nc_a(s) = E_a * s \quad (1)$$

where K_a is the number of CPU cycles per bit, f is the processor frequency, and E_a is the energy coefficient per bit. This expression indicates that with lightweight approaches like ECC or TinySHA the latency and energy usage is minimized which is a key factor to battery-powered farm devices.

5.2 Blockchain in Data Integrity and Traceability

Blockchain technology provides tamper-resistant storage and traceability for agricultural data, ensuring that critical information such as irrigation schedules, soil measurements, and crop records cannot be modified without authorization. Blockchain Transaction Latency was found via Equation (3) which calculates blockchain transaction latency; similarly, the probability of being able to rewrite the blockchain history was also estimated by Equation (4). The overhead of latency associated with adding a transaction of size s_tx and time in a block T_b is:

$$L_b c = T_b + \delta \quad (2)$$

Where, δ is the average jitter in network. Suppose that an opponent has supply of fraction q of validators, this is less likely than rewrites of z confirmations, and this is constrained to:

$$P_r[rewrite(z)] \leq \exp(-eta(q)*z) \quad (3)$$

With,

$$eta(q) = \frac{(1-2q)^2}{2} \quad (4)$$

This demonstrates that the integrity of blockchain increases at exponential rates with confirmations.

5.3 Edge Anomaly Detection

On the edge-gateway, employ a person's feature vectors with anomaly detectors that detect fake or malicious data. In order to determine the Blockchain Security Coefficient; use Equation (5). In addition to determining how well the proposed Edge Anomaly Detection Framework performs, Equations (6)-(8) are used as a mathematical model and describe the CUSUM detection statistic, estimated detection time expectation and false alarm expectation probabilities for abnormal behaviors in agricultural IoT network communications.

$$S_t = max0, S(t-1) + W^T * x_t - K \tag{5}$$

With $S_0 = 0$, where x_t is the feature input and w is the weight vector.

The expected detection delay is:

$$E\left[T_d et\right] \approx h/(\delta - \mathrm{K}) \tag{6}$$

where,

$$\delta = (w^T * m u_1) - (w^T * m u_0) \tag{7}$$

The false alarm probability per sample is approximated as:

$$\alpha \approx \exp\left(-\frac{2*K*h}{Var(w^T * x_t | m u_0)}\right) \tag{8}$$

These terms are used to describe the trade-off between speed of detecting and false alarm.

5.4 Multi-Layer Defense Model

The heterogeneous environment of IoT does not provide a single mechanism that is adequate. The overall effectiveness of the proposed multi-layer defense framework is quantified by Equation (9), which models the probability of successfully preventing cyberattacks through the integration of authentication, intrusion detection, and blockchain-based security mechanisms. Where $p_i nt$ is probability that blockchain blocks integrity attacks, $p_i ds$ is probability that the intrusion detection system detects the attack successfully and probability that the authentication system blocks unauthorized access is $p_a uth$, the probability to block is:

$$p_b lock = 1 - \left(1 - p_i nt\right) * \left(1 - p_i ds\right) * \left(1 - p_a uth\right) \tag{9}$$

This guarantees that fallback in case of failure of any of the layers is ensured by the other layers.

5.5 Performance and Resource Optimization

The performance and resource optimization of the proposed framework are mathematically described by Equations (10)–(12), which represent the total energy consumption, system latency, and optimization objective function, respectively. Given an IoT network with devices in set s and packet rate τ_i and size s_i, the overall energy cost per hour is:

$$E_t ot = \sum\left[\tau_i * s_i * (E_e n c_a(s_i) + e_t x)\right] + \rho_i ds + \rho_b c \tag{10}$$

The total latency is the maximum of all contributing factors:

$$L_t ot = max L_e n c_a, L_n et, L_i ds, L_b c$$

If A is the accuracy measure (such as F1 score), then the optimization problem is defined as:

$$Minimize J = \alpha * E_t ot + \beta * L_t ot - \gamma * A \tag{11}$$

Subject to:

$$A \geq A0, L_t ot \leq LO \tag{12}$$

where $\alpha, \beta and \gamma$ are weights representing farm priorities such as energy, speed, or security.

Similar multi-objective optimization strategies have previously been employed in intelligent engineering systems to simultaneously balance predictive accuracy, computational efficiency, and environmental performance, demonstrating the practical effectiveness of data-driven optimization frameworks in resource-constrained environments (Roy et al., 2025).

5.6 Human-Centric Security Measures

Other than technical shields, the training of farmers is important. The most common vulnerabilities continue to be the misconfigurations, weak passwords, and phishing. A synopsis of lightweight cryptography, blockchain traceability, edge anomaly detection, and human training can be used to develop a multi-layer security architecture to suit smart farming ecosystems.

6. CASE STUDY AND EXPERIMENTAL RESULTS

In order to test the suggested security schemes, a single simulated smart farm system was developed built around soil moisture monitors, irrigation controllers, an on-site gateway, and a web dashboard managing the procedure, cloud-based. This architecture was varied with various cyberattack scenarios acquired and assessed with lightweight cryptography, blockchain-based integrity, and edge anomaly detection.

6.1 Experimental Setup The testbed consisted of:

A virtual field of 20 soil moisture and temperature were installed with the sensor. water controllers that control the water supply, a gateway node using anomaly detection, and a cloud server server that keeps long term records. This communication system was based on the low-rate wireless network, and farms were displayed by a remote dashboard controlled by farmers.

6.2 Threat Scenarios

Three egregious threats were modelled: Bogging Attack Data Spoofing Attack Data spoofing was used to activate inappropriate irrigation due to false soil moisture data. Denial-of-Service (DoS) Attack malicious requests were stopped before the irrigation controllers could continue functioning. UN, Authentication Report of Attempt Breach- unauthorized entry into the farm dashboard.

6.3 Applied Security Measures

Lightweight Cryptography Lightweight encryption of sensor-gateway communication using ECC. Blockchain: Persistent registration of irrigation timetables. Edge Anomaly Detection: Localized abnormal requests filtering. Role-Based Authentication: Dashboard wafering controls.

6.4 Performance Measures and Formulae.

The effectiveness of the proposed anomaly detection system is quantified using Equations (13)–(15), which estimate the expected true positives, false positives, and false negatives. Based on these quantities, the Precision, Recall, and F1-score are derived to evaluate the overall detection performance. In the case of n input events (attack prevalence π), true positive rate TPR and false positive rate FPR, then the expected counts are:

$$E[TP] = n * \pi * TPR \quad (13)$$

$$E[FP] = n * (1 - \pi) * FPR \quad (14)$$

$$E[FN] = n * \pi * (1 - TPR) \quad (15)$$

From these, the expected performance metrics are:

$$E[Precision] \approx (\pi * TPR)/(\pi * TPR + (1 - \pi) * FPR$$

$$E[recall] = TPR$$

$$E[F1] \approx (2 * TPR)/(1 + TPR + \left(\frac{1 - \pi}{\pi}\right) * FPR$$

These are formulas that measure the effectiveness of the anomaly detector.

6.5 Energy and Latency Results

Based on the simulation, mean energy as consumed (in mJ per packet) and latency (in ms) were:

AES-128: Energy = 50, Latency = 25

ECC: Energy = 22, Latency = 18

Tiny SHA: Energy = 15, Latency = 12

Configurations of Blockchain + Edge Detection Energy = 28, Latency = 20.

Comparisons:

Energy saving of ECC vs AES =1 - (22 / 50) = 0.56 = 56%

Latency ECC punches vs AES = 1 - (18 / 25) = 0.28 = 28%

Multi-layer blocking probability Sixth, Multi-layer Blocking Probability and the chances present in the testbed:

$p_i ds$: = 0.95 (success intrusion detection).

$p_0 \approx 0.527$ (blockchain confirmation success for z = 6, q = 0.25),
$p_a uth = 0.90$ (successful authentication).

Equation (16) is used to calculate the probability of successfully blocking a cyberattack by combining the contributions of blockchain-based integrity protection, intrusion detection, and authentication mechanisms. Chances of the attack being blocked by one of the layers are:

$$p_b lock = 1 - (1 - p_i nt) * (1 - p_i ds) * (1 - p_a uth) \tag{16}$$

Where,

$$p_b lock = 1 - (0.473*0.05*0.1)$$

$$p_b lock = 1 - 0.002365 = 0.997635 \approx 99.76\%$$

This proves the advantage of multi-layer defences compared to any single mechanism.

6.6 Detection Delay and False Alarm Trade-off

For the CUSUM-based detector, threshold h is selected to control the maximum false alarm rate α_{max}. The CUSUM based intrusion detection system's trade-offs for speed and reliability will be analyzed by solving Equations (17), (18) with the expectation of finding the detection threshold as well as the associated average time until detection at a fixed false alarm constraint. The relationship is:

$$h \approx \left(\frac{\sigma^2}{2*\text{K}}\right) * \ln\left(\frac{1}{\alpha_{max}}\right) \tag{17}$$

The expected detection delay is then:

$$E[T_d et] \approx \left(\frac{\alpha^2}{2*\text{K}*(\delta - \text{K})}\right) * \ln\left(\frac{1}{\alpha_{max}}\right) \tag{18}$$

where α^2 is the variance of the detection statistic under normal traffic, δ is the separation between normal and attack means, and kappa (K) is the drift parameter. This allows precise tuning of the IDS for both speed and reliability.

6.7 Throughput Budget with Security Overhead

For a communication link (i,j) with capacity $c_i j$ and headroom factor $\xi(0 < \xi < 1)$, the maximum possible throughput in terms of communications will be impacted by security related processing. The Equation (19) is a formulation that can be used to determine the maxiumum amount of secure data that can flow over a communication link taking into account the overhead associated with encryption and blockchain activities.

$$R_s ec \leq \xi * \frac{c_i j}{\left[\left(\left(1 + \frac{K_a}{f}\right) * \left(\frac{c_i j}{MTU}\right)\right) + \frac{s_t x}{v * T_b * c_i j}\right]} \tag{19}$$

This shows how encryption cost $\left(\frac{K_a}{f}\right)$ and blockchain overhead $\frac{s_t x}{v * T_b}$ reduce usable bandwidth.

Experimental results show the use of an integrated AI based Cybersecurity framework improves both Cybersecurity performance and Operational Performance within Smart Farming Systems using Internet-of-Things (IoT). In comparison to standard methods of encrypting communications, Cryptographic Mechanisms designed as Low Power consumed less power, thus were a better fit for low powered devices used on farms. Edge-based Anomaly Detection, also was able to identify potential threats to the farm's infrastructure quickly; reducing communication traffic over the network. Finally, utilizing Blockchain Integrity Verification provided increased trust of data collected from the farm by ensuring that all data could not be modified without permission. Overall, the findings suggest that integrating Artificial Intelligence into Cybersecurity frameworks and using Distributed Trust Models in combination with Lightweight Security Solutions will provide increased resilience against current and future Cyber Threats in Smart Farming Infrastructures.

7. SUMMARY AND DISCUSSION

The results of the case study help to emphasize the necessity of focusing on cybersecurity threats within the structure of the internet of things-powered agriculture, as well as the promise of implementing lightweight, multi-layered security systems. In this section, the results of the experiment are interpreted, and a discussion of the trade-offs in implementing security solutions and placing the results in the context of the life of agriculture sadness, policy, and sustainability as a whole.

7.1 Finding a Trade-off between Security Horizons and Resource Economics

The and one of the most important issues in agricultural IoT security is striking a balance between the protection requirement and the resource accessibility of devices. The case study has evidently shown that traditional encryption algorithm schemes like AES-128 that are considered strong, consume a lot of energy which minimizes the lifecycle of battery-supported applications. In comparison, lightweight ECC, TinySHA designs saved a significantly larger amount of power, with moderate costs on security. The result indicates that the successful provision of cybersecurity in agricultural settings will need to focus on the rules aimed at the low-power IoT setting instead of the re-use of the traditional IT solutions (Sicari et al., 2015).

Beyond improving cybersecurity, the proposed framework contributes to the development of resilient, sustainable, and trustworthy smart farming ecosystems capable of supporting future digital agriculture initiatives.

7.2 Edge Effectiveness of Anomaly Detection

The presentation of edge-based anomaly detection has especially been useful against the data spoofing and denial-of-service (DoS) attack. The detection accuracy rate at over 90 is a significant effective resilience practice that also dramatically decreases the dependency on the 24/7 connection with clouds. On rural farms where bandwidth restrictions exist, edge computing can provide timely information in case of threat without the delay caused by remote servers (Bacco et al., 2019). This is consistent with the current accelerators of an IoT security international direction of focusing on decentralization as one of the methods of minimizing attack surfaces.

7.3 Aggrotech Blockchain and Agricultural Data Trust

The logging in the blockchain provided a decentralized perspective on the irrigation and management activities that play an important role in agriculture since data accuracy in this case determines food production and food chains, in particular. Since blockchain had already allowed an opportunity to ensure that the system of irrigation arrangements and soil measurement could not be bound, there was an additional trust added by blockchain. These integrity links result in improving consumer beliefs on food trace abilities and food safety other than harmful practices that have been practiced at the farm level. However, there are weaknesses to blockchain adoption. Even with farms using vapid distributed ledger systems, the overheads still may be an issue with farms with very limited computational power (Tariq et al., 2025a). The future research should be focused on the mixed models that view the blockchain selectively, i.e. where its application is most motivated i.e. in the critical data streams where mutability is least demanded.

7.4. Operational Viability and Work preparedness

The technical results are rather deceptive yet they will rely on digital illiteracy among the farmers. As noted in the case study, although the authentication role based helped to improve security in the dashboard, it also increased usability problems to people who were not conversant with password management or system upgrade. It is a focus on the human element of the ag cybersecurity because unless provider-based and adequate training is provided, the human factor then other technologically sound frameworks may be less pragmatic (Botschner et al., 2024). The adoption of the programs of teaching farmers and convenience to the user interfaces should therefore support the technical solutions.

7.5 Policies and critical infrastructure

Agriculture has been regarded as one of critical infrastructure at times because it stands in between food security and economic stability. The case study also confirms this classification at relatively basic kinds of attacks may be applied to influence irrigation systems and introduce significant harm to crops, e.g. enjoy data spoofing. This gap needs to be addressed by the government providing industry-specific cybersecurity standards on agriculture, as it has already developed in the energy or health segment (Canton, 2021). Other than that, the establishment of a public-private partnership will also be essential regarding the possibility to subsidize the implementation of the protective IoT systems especially among the smallholder farmers who will be unable to afford advanced technologies.

7.6 Agreement with Sustainable Development Goals

There are also more extensive impacts of the adoption of cybersecurity in agriculture on global sustainability. The security of the IoT-driven farming systems will provide infrastructural security on the regularity of food production, effective use of resources, and build up against climate unpredictability. The results are will be in support of the goals of the United Nations Sustainable Development Goals (SDGs), specifically Goal 2 (Zero Hunger) and Goal 12 (Responsible Consumption and Production). Therefore, agricultural cybersecurity became not only a technological issue but also a way to sustainability.

Comprehensively, the discussion points out that resource constraints need not impede the safeguarding of agricultural IoT systems due to individually customized, multifaceted security systems. Nonetheless, technical innovation needs to be accompanied by agricultural preparedness, enabling policy and goals on sustainability in order to consider secure smart agriculture as cost-effective and effective at the large scale.

8. LIMITATIONS

Even though the outcomes were encouraging, there are still limitations. The case study modeled a medium-sized farm with average connection that is unlikely to be fully relevant to the situation in remote or short-resource areas. Also, the anomaly detecting algorithms were evaluated with reference to a smaller set of attack vectors; adversary opponents in the real world can pursue a more advanced set of strategies. To implement AI threat sensors, quantum-safe cryptography with cross-border policy frameworks on protecting agricultural cybersecurity across borders, further studies are needed.

In addition, the performance of AI-based anomaly detection mechanisms depends on the availability of representative training data. Changes in farming practices, environmental conditions, or attack patterns may require periodic model retraining to maintain detection accuracy.

9. CONCLUSION AND FUTURE DIRECTIONS

The high implementation of IoT technologies in agriculture transformed farming into a highly automatized process, which uses data and is able to combat the phenomenon of the increasing food demand and scarce resources. IoT-enabled smart farming will lead to high transformations in productivity, efficiency and sustainability of farms, starting with soil moisture sensors up to cloud-based farm management systems. Nevertheless, this digital revolution also comes with a broad spectrum of cybersecurity threats, such as sensor hijacking and data spoofing, ransomware and supply chain sabotage. This kind of vulnerability requires intensive and context-dependent security solutions to protect not only farming operations but also the entire food supply chains and economies of countries.

This discussion has shown that the traditional IT security measures have been unfavourable in agricultural IoT-based systems because of the intensive nature of the protocols. Rather, lighter cryptographic tools like ECC and TinySHA with blockchain based data integrity and also edge-based anomaly detectors provide a more realistic form of solutions to low-power and geographically distributed farming tools. Experimental findings have shown that, with the right model used in multi-layered defense, it is possible to build models that are high in their accuracy of detection and at the same time save on resources by addressing some of the major vulnerabilities with high consideration that will not lead to providing too much load to the device. Moreover, adding blockchain allows visibility and traceability to enhance trust in agricultural data, and edge computing eliminates the need to depend on the slipshod connection in the rural areas.

Sometimes, technological solutions cannot be an adequate answer. The discussion has reported that human aspects and policy gaps were the key and significant hurdle to successful cybersecurity in agriculture. A lack of digital literacy among farmers frequently prevents them to sustain secure operations on the farm and the lack of relevant regulatory frameworks makes the agricultural IoT beyond the reach of national policies on cybersecurity. It means that smart farming resilience does not only entail use of an innovative technology but also capacity building, educating farmers and supporting effective policies. There should be effective collaboration between governments, the vendors of technology as well as the agricultural cooperatives to find an affordable, easily available and standardized solution.

In the future, it is possible to look into the opportunities of incorporating AI-based threat detectors that can continuously adjust to the changing type of attack and quantum-resistant cryptography that could be in demand due to perspective computational healthcare risks. Policy frameworks across borders will also be required as the automation of supply chains is becoming more globalized and interdependent through agriculture. Also, pilot projects as well as practical transitions in small and large holder farms are required to support experimental findings and optimize frameworks in the feasible real-world scenarios.

Finally, the verification of IoT in agriculture is not a preference option anymore, but a must regarding the sustainability of food systems in the XXI century. The application of cybersecurity solutions that are personalized to meet the particular limitations of smart farming can potentially safeguard an individual farm and, in its turn, the food security of the globe as a whole, lifestyles of rural populations, and sustainable developments. To fulfill its potential to transform agriculture as the compromiser of productivity and as a fortified segment of essential infrastructure, the theorized agricultural Internet of Things can be accomplished through congruity of technology, policy, and human resources.

This Chapter demonstrates how the combination of Artificial Intelligence (AI), Lightweight Cryptography, Blockchain-Enabled Data Integrity, and Edge Computing can significantly enhance the Cybersecurity Posture of Smart Farming Systems enabled by Internet of Things (IoT) technologies. The proposed Framework addresses the challenges faced in resource-constrained Agricultural Environments; it represents a Practical and Scalable Solution for Enhancing Security, Reliability, and Operational Resilience. As smart agriculture evolves further, AI-based Cybersecurity Frameworks are expected to be a growing element in Protecting Digital Farming Infrastructures and Supporting Sustainable Agricultural Development.

REFERENCES

Ali, G., Mijwil, M. M., Abotaleb, M., & Adamopoulos, I.Bosco Apparatus Buruga. (2024). A Survey on Artificial Intelligence in Cybersecurity for Smart Agriculture: State-of-the-Art, Cyber Threats, Artificial Intelligence Applications, and Ethical Concerns. *Mesopotamian Journal of Computer Science, 2024*, 53–103. DOI: 10.58496/MJCSC/2024/007

Bacco, M., Barsocchi, P., Ferro, E., Gotta, A., & Ruggeri, M. (2019). The Digitisation of Agriculture: A Survey of Research Activities on Smart Farming. *Array (New York, N.Y.), 3–4*, 100009. DOI: 10.1016/j.array.2019.100009

Botschner, J., Corley, C., Fraser, E. D. G., Kotak, R., McMahon, D., & Newman, L. (2024). *Cybersecurity in Digital Agriculture: A National Security Risk?* DOI: 10.1007/978-3-031-67608-6_6

Campoverde-Molina, M., & Luján-Mora, S. (2025). Cybersecurity in smart agriculture: A systematic literature review. *Computers & Security, 150*, 104284. DOI: 10.1016/j.cose.2024.104284

Canton, H. (2021). *The Europa Directory of International Organizations 2021*. Routledge., DOI: 10.4324/9781003179900

D, C. S., & Devarajan, Y. (2025). Investigation of Emerging Technologies in Agriculture: An In-depth Look at Smart Farming, Nano-agriculture, AI, and Big Data. *Journal of Biosystems Engineering, 50*(2), 170–192. DOI: 10.1007/s42853-025-00258-z

Demestichas, K., Peppes, N., & Alexakis, T. (2020). Survey on Security Threats in Agricultural IoT and Smart Farming. *Sensors (Basel), 20*(22), 6458. DOI: 10.3390/s20226458 PMID: 33198160

Gupta, S., Hasan, W., Singh, S., Kumar, D., Ansari, M. J., & Nisar, S. (2024). Agriculture 4.0: Smart farming with IoT and artificial intelligence. In *Agriculture 4.0: Smart Farming with IoT and Artificial Intelligence*. CRC Press., DOI: 10.1201/9781003570219

Karras, A., Giannaros, A., Amasiadi, N., & Karras, C. (2026). Next-Gen Explainable AI (XAI) for Federated and Distributed Internet of Things Systems: A State-of-the-Art Survey. *Future Internet, 18*(2), 83. DOI: 10.3390/fi18020083

Khan, W. Z., Rehman, M. H., Zangoti, H. M., Afzal, M. K., Armi, N., & Salah, K. (2020). Industrial internet of things: Recent advances, enabling technologies and open challenges. *Computers & Electrical Engineering*, *81*, 106522. DOI: 10.1016/j.compeleceng.2019.106522

Maity, A., Roy, A., Kumar, S., Pramanik, S., Pattanayak, P., & Chakraborty, M. (2025). A Hybrid Machine Learning Approach to Power Load Optimization and Emission Reduction in Rural Microgrids. *Engineering Proceedings*, *93*(1), 21. Advance online publication. DOI: 10.3390/engproc2025093021

Maity, A., Roy, A., Pramanik, S., Pattanayak, P., & Kumar, S. (2026). Revolutionizing Energy: Smart Microgrids Driving down Costs and Carbon Foot Print Emissions through Advanced Spider Wasp optimization and BiGRU Techniques. *CIGRE Science & Engineering (CSE)*, (40), 1–36. https://cse.cigre.org/cse-n038/revolutionizing-energy-smart-microgrids-driving-down-costs-and-carbon-foot-print-emissions-through-advanced-spider-wasp-optimization-and-bigru-techniques.html

Ocama, O. V., Medagbe, Y.-C. N., Akello, S., Kambale, W. V., Tashev, T., Kyamakya, K., & Kasereka, S. K. (2025). A Review on Advancing Technologies in Precision Agriculture: Applications, Challenges, and the Way Forward. *Procedia Computer Science*, *265*, 572–577. DOI: 10.1016/j.procs.2025.07.221

Pramanik, S., Roy, A., & Rakshit, P. (2025). Resuming Transfer Technique for Two-Level Sharding Point of Rupture for a Single Table. *AI and the Revival of Big Data*, 221–238. https://doi.org/DOI: 10.4018/979-8-3693-8472-5.ch010

Roy, A., Sabyasachi Pramanik, Mitra, K., & Chakraborty, M. (2025). *CO2 Emission Calculations in Shipping for Sustainable Ship Design, Construction, and Operation*. 163–200. DOI: 10.4018/979-8-3373-2555-2.ch007

Roy, A., Pramanik, S., & Mitra, K. (2025). An Optimal Neural Network Model for Projecting of CI Engine Operational Efficiency and Emission in Hydrogen Blend Using Simulink. *SN Computer Science*, *6*(8), 956. Advance online publication. DOI: 10.1007/s42979-025-04474-4

Roy, A., Pramanik, S., Mitra, K., & Chakraborty, M. (2024b). Application of Neural Network for Reducing Emission and Optimizing Performance of Hydrogen with Biofuel CI Engine. *Lecture Notes in Networks and Systems*, 359–373. https://doi.org/DOI: 10.1007/978-981-97-7532-3_26

Roy, A., Pramanik, S., Mitra, K., & Chakraborty, M. (2025a). An Innovative Neural Network Approach for Reducing Emissions from Gas Turbines. *Lecture Notes in Networks and Systems*, 43–58. https://doi.org/DOI: 10.1007/978-981-97-8476-9_4

Roy, A., Pramanik, S., Mitra, K., & Chakraborty, M. (2025b). An optimal data analytics model for accurate projection of CI engine performance and emission reduction in hybrid fuel mode. *Environment, Development and Sustainability*. Advance online publication. DOI: 10.1007/s10668-025-06130-6

Roy, A., Pramanik, S., Mitra, K., & Chakraborty, M. (2026). Emission reduction in gas turbine: Improving CO and NOx emission prediction using modified CNN-Bi-LSTM extrinsic attention regressor. *Environment, Development and Sustainability*. Advance online publication. DOI: 10.1007/s10668-025-07209-w

Sicari, S., Rizzardi, A., Grieco, L. A., & Coen-Porisini, A. (2015). Security, privacy and trust in Internet of Things: The road ahead. *Computer Networks*, *76*, 146–164. DOI: 10.1016/j.comnet.2014.11.008

Tariq, M. U., Saqib, S. M., Mazhar, T., Khan, M. A., Shahzad, T., & Hamam, H. (2025a). Edge-enabled smart agriculture framework: Integrating IoT, lightweight deep learning, and agentic AI for context-aware farming. *Results in Engineering*, *28*, 107342. DOI: 10.1016/j.rineng.2025.107342

Tariq, M. U., Saqib, S. M., Mazhar, T., Khan, M. A., Shahzad, T., & Hamam, H. (2025b). Edge-enabled smart agriculture framework: Integrating IoT, lightweight deep learning, and agentic AI for context-aware farming. *Results in Engineering*, *28*, 107342. DOI: 10.1016/j.rineng.2025.107342

Vangala, A., Das, A. K., Chamola, V., Korotaev, V., & Rodrigues, J. J. P. C. (2023). Security in IoT-enabled smart agriculture: Architecture, security solutions and challenges. *Cluster Computing*, *26*(2), 879–902. DOI: 10.1007/s10586-022-03566-7

Wolfert, S., Ge, L., Verdouw, C., & Bogaardt, M.-J. (2017). Big Data in Smart Farming – A review. *Agricultural Systems*, *153*, 69–80. DOI: 10.1016/j.agsy.2017.01.023

Zaman, J., Shoomal, A., Jahanbakht, M., & Ozay, D. (2025). Driving Supply Chain Transformation with IoT and AI Integration: A Dual Approach Using Bibliometric Analysis and Topic Modeling. *IoT*, *6*(2), 21. DOI: 10.3390/iot6020021

Zreikat, A. I., AlArnaout, Z., Abadleh, A., Elbasi, E., & Mostafa, N. (2025). The Integration of the Internet of Things (IoT) Applications into 5G Networks: A Review and Analysis. *Computers*, *14*(7), 250. DOI: 10.3390/computers14070250

Chapter 7
Decision Support in Design Management Using Artificial Intelligence

Venkateswarlu Karumuri
http://orcid.org/0000-0002-7019-8580
Department of Management Studies, Madanapalle Institute of Technology and Science, Madanapalle, India

S. S. Pavan Kumar
Department of Management Studies, Ballari Institute of Technology and Management, Kolagal, India

Drakshayini Praveen
Department of Computer Science, International Institute of Business Studies, Bangalore, India

Sukriti Khanna
Department of Psychology, Alliance University, Bangalore, India

K. Saketh Reddy
http://orcid.org/0000-0002-4360-5152
Department of MBA, International Institute of Business Studies, Bangalore, India

S. Mahabub Basha
http://orcid.org/0000-0002-5998-3262
Department of Management, International Institute of Business Studies, Bangalore, India

ABSTRACT

Design management is needed for the complex design activities and for the supply of the efficient design process decision-making. Serious design problems may lead to delays and inefficiencies in traditional design management systems since they are based on human analysis, expert opinion, and restricted data processing capabilities. To overcome these challenges and make better judgments in design management, our project is constructing an AI-based DSS. The recommended framework uses a range of AI approaches such as neural networks, machine learning, expert systems

DOI: 10.4018/979-8-3693-3751-6.ch007

and NLP for evaluation of design data and provision of effective design ideas. The suggested system architecture consists of numerous building pieces such as data gathering, knowledge base, AI algorithms, decision engine, and user interface.

1. INTRODUCTION

Innovation, efficiency and speed of producing products are very important for staying competitive, hence modern organizations depend largely on design management. Technical information, user needs, market trends, and organizational goals are all crucial to the design decision-making process. Traditional design management systems are frequently based on human judgment and manual analysis, which may restrict the ability to handle enormous data sets and develop optimum solutions. As design projects expand in complexity, so does the demand for intelligent tools to assist decision makers in evaluating options and anticipating outcomes. AI is the game altering technology that can improve decision support in many areas of management. Using complex algorithms, data analytics and machine learning, AI can sort through heaps of data to find patterns and practical suggestions for improved decision-making. AI DSS in design management may enhance design processes, boost cooperation and reduce uncertainty. This research investigates decision support strategies in design management based on AI. It discusses theoretical frameworks, problems of traditional systems, and the promise of AI for improving the effectiveness and efficiency of design and engineering management decision-making.

1.1 Background of Design Management

Design management is the strategic organization of a company's design efforts, resources, and processes to accomplish corporate goals and creative outputs. Design thinking and management techniques are integrated to produce products, services and systems that satisfy the functional and aesthetic needs and are aligned with the business's objectives. The discipline of design management has extended from its initial concern with creative design to include commercial strategy, project management and technical development, amongst others. Design management in the past has been primarily concerned with managing designers and completing design projects on schedule. But as the market became more competitive and customers had higher expectations, firms started to realize that design was a strategic tool to differentiate their goods and create brand awareness. As a result, design management has evolved into cross-departmental planning, coordination and assessment of design activities. Design management is a vital need in contemporary company, since it implies implementing user-centred design principles into the strategy of the corporation. Management of cross-disciplinary teams of designers, developers, marketers, and analytics is crucial to this position. These combined design decisions are based on the foundations of technical feasibility, market demand and economic considerations. Digital technology have impacted on methods to design management. Design processes have been substantially enhanced by digital collaboration platforms, simulation tools and computer assisted design (CAD). But today, with more and more information connected to design and more intricate than ever, managers are facing new challenges. Decision makers should consider many criteria before choosing the optimum design solution, including: performance, cost, sustainability and customer preferences. Thus intelligent DSS are gaining favor among organizations to simplify and facilitate their complex design processes. Design management may use AI and data analytics to better their forecasting, evaluation, and data-driven decision-making.

1.2 Overview of Design Management Theories

Theoretical framework Theories of design management help us to understand the relationship between the organization of design activities and commercial objectives. These notions have been created throughout time to explain new technology, changed market dynamics and the increasing importance of innovation in competitive corporate environments. Design thinking is one of the core ideas of design management. It's about understanding users' viewpoints, testing new things and addressing difficulties via trial and error. Companies may use design thinking to continually test and develop concepts in order to ensure they are meeting customer needs. This method has grown popular since it may boost product innovation and creativity. A more positive approach is strategic design management theory. This regards design as a way that organizations may acquire an advantage in the market. To achieve the goal, design must be part of every step of strategy formulation. By using design thinking, companies that use strategic design management may improve customer happiness, build stronger brands, and develop innovative products. The systems theory of design management is important to utilize to understand better the complexity of design processes. In this approach, design is just one aspect of a much bigger system, which also incorporates social and organizational issues. Managers use the interrelationships among the different factors to make informed judgments and efficiently allocate resources. Collaborative design theory also puts emphasis on multidisciplinary and cross-team collaboration in the design process. “The difficulties of design today need skills in numerous domains, including data science, marketing, and engineering. Team members communicate and share knowledge using collaborative frameworks so that better design ideas might be generated. However, even with the use of these notions, the conventional design management frameworks still depend significantly on human intuition and experience. The rise of digital technology and big data sets is creating opportunities to improve design management methods using AI and advanced analytics. This may lead to smarter judgments, with less effort.

1.3 Decision Support System (DSS) in Management

DSS are information systems that help decision makers analyze data, generate alternatives and assess probable outcomes. These technologies ease difficult decision making by integrating data processing, analytical models and intuitive user interfaces. The notion of DSS originated in the 1960s and 1970s when computers became more accessible and organizational data was made more publicly available. DSS applications structured decision-making activities address financial analysis and production planning among the initial tasks. The management and strategy environment generally contains semi-structured and unstructured possibilities and such systems have developed throughout time to suit them. DSS in management helps to make decisions better and quicker. DSS gathers information from a range of sources so that management may see patterns, identify trends and analyze possible situations. This functionality really shines when things become complicated and unexpected. Most DSSs are built on databases, analytical tools, and algorithms. The user interface of the system allows decision makers to access and use this data. Advanced DSS systems may provide further analytical capabilities with incorporation of visualization tools, predictive analytics and simulation models. For managers responsible for design, DSS may be helpful in assessing possible designs, determining potential hazards, and in determining how effectively to utilize the resources available. DSS may, while considering a design, consider aspects such as performance and cost and sustainability. It may encourage collaborative collaboration by giving team members with shared access to pertinent data and analytical tools. Modern DSS systems have grown more flexible and sophisticated employing AI and machine learning techniques. These smart technologies learn from prior data, find hidden relationships and provide suggestions for better strategic and operational decision making in complex design contexts.

1.4 Importance of Decision-Making in Design Processes

Every designer has a choice. When developing a product or system, you have to examine a number of possibilities at each step and finally pick on one. Designers and managers must take into account several elements such as materials, functionality, aesthetics, manufacturing processes, cost, and sustainability. These choices have a direct impact on the quality, performance and commercial success of the end product. Technical merits are not the main basis for judgments in complex design endeavors. Regulatory requirements, environmental issues, company goals and user needs all have to be properly examined. This means that design choices are typically made balancing a number of distinct and at times conflicting criteria. There has to be a decision-making framework to aid businesses through this complexity and get the greatest design outcomes possible. The decisions chosen throughout the conceptual and preliminary design stages are of great importance, since they have a great effect on the ultimate project budget and performance. Research has shown that a considerable amount of the total cost of ownership of a product is determined at the early phases of its design. Making informed judgments at different points of time is important to avoid risks and make the project successful. Design decision making is hard enough without needing to work with multi-disciplinary teams. A heterogeneous team of engineers, marketers, designers, and project managers should work together to analyze alternative design ideas and chose the most practical ones. In such cases, the exchange of facts and communication is critical to make decisions together. Design decision making has been given new means and resources by technology advancement. Virtual prototypes, data analytics, and simulation models provide designers the ability to experiment with several alternatives before choosing a solution. On the other hand, increasingly complicated DSS are needed to cope with the constantly rising data quantities and design concerns. AI and intelligent DSS are intriguing solutions for this issue. These tools assist designers and managers to make better and more effective choices, by automating analysis, offering predictive insights and optimising processes.

1.5 Challenges in Traditional Design Management Systems

Traditional design management techniques including design processes have been consistently used to complete projects on time and under budget. Conventional design management systems are limited by dependence on human judgment and manual procedures. Expert knowledge is important, but may not be adequate to cope with huge volumes of design data, or to evaluate a number of design alternatives simultaneously. Such a constraint might lead to delayed decision making and increased probability of mistake. Another difficulty is the variation between the various design tools and data systems. Many companies have design data trapped in siloed databases or incompatible software systems. The data is fragmented and managers don't have a full view of the design process and can't detect any concerns in a timely manner. Another difficulty is that traditional systems struggle in static and predictable environments. Design projects needs, technology and market circumstances are changing often, Traditional management approaches may not be able to respond fast enough to these developments. Potential challenges for communication and cooperation in multidisciplinary teams might arise from standard design management frameworks . Team members could find it hard to coordinate their tasks and make sure their choices are in line with the project's goals without effective information sharing tools. Older systems may not be able to handle more complicated analytics, either. They can provide basic reports but are often incapable of helping with optimization, predictive analysis or automated decision making. Faced with such complex design decisions, managers frequently rely significantly on their intuition and knowledge. More intelligent systems are necessary to deal with large amounts of data, fuse information from many sources, and provide data-driven insights to better design management in front of such challenges.

1.6 Role of AI in Improving Decision Support

AI has been a wonderful strategy for improving decision assistance in numerous organizational contexts such as design management. AI lets computers learn from data, see patterns, and make predictions – things that normally need human intelligence. AI-based DSS may help organizations make better decisions. A major advantage of decision support is that AI can rapidly and correctly sort through vast amounts of data. Information collected related to design management may consist of user input, market trends, performance measurements and design demands. AI systems can analyze this data and discover relationships and patterns that people would overlook. Machine learning is a key element of AI and an integral part of improving DSS. Machine learning models learn from their past experiences and improve themselves throughout the period of time. Such models may be useful for managers to take better judgments, e.g., to estimate the performance of design options based on prior project results. AI can also improve the design process. Optimization algorithms may find answers by evaluating a variety of design configurations to achieve optimal performance with less cost or lower resource use. This is especially useful in the case of engineering design, since frequently there are several design aspects that must be evaluated in a balanced fashion. Furthermore, AI-based DSS that provide intelligent suggestions and real-time insights might enable design teams to collaborate more efficiently. These technologies may help automate repetitive operations and free up designers and managers to work on higher level and more important parts of the design process. As more and more organizations continue with their digital transformation, the use of AI in design management to enhance DSS and overall organizational performance is expected to expand.

1.7 Contribution of Research

This study adds to the emerging literature on the potential advantages of AI to design management by examining possible ways in which AI-based DSS might improve the efficacy and efficiency of design-related decision-making. As design projects become more complicated and data heavy, conventional decision-making techniques may not be enough for evaluating designs on the various criteria being used. The main contribution of this work is that it provides a theoretical basis for the integration of the AI technology in the design management system. The suggested technique focuses on data analytics, smart DSS, and machine learning algorithms to evaluate design options, optimize resource allocation, and predict project results. The study also contributed greatly in that it pointed out key problems with existing design management systems and suggested methods that AI may resolve them. The research aims to analyse existing design management and decision-support systems to understand how AI may improve data processing, enhance prediction capabilities and assist decision-making in cross-disciplinary teams. Further, this study highlights the significance of data-driven decision models in today's design settings. This research uses machine learning approaches to evaluate design data, identify patterns, and provide suggestions to assist managers and designers in making better choices.

2. LITERATURE REVIEW

Ali et al. (2023) explored intelligent decision-support systems by merging machine learning and multicriteria decision-making methodologies. The research showed that ML algorithms can handle big data and advise managers to the optimal judgments using a number of assessment parameters. The authors pointed out that the accuracy and efficiency of complicated decision-making circumstances is significantly enhanced when decision models are merged with AI technology.

Adaptive AI learning models for smart area DSS were researched by Fedorka et al. (2025). The present research suggested AI frameworks for analysing regional data for helping policymakers in making choices related to infrastructure planning, resource management and urban development. The authors underlined that adaptive AI models boost the responsiveness of DSS by learning from several data settings.

Brown et al. (2026) emphasized management information systems with AI-based automation to boost real-time DSS. They showcased how AI systems can assess organizational data fast and provide suggestion for actions. The research found that adding AI makes the system more responsive, eliminates the need for human input and makes decision-making more efficient.

Saeed (2024) study on machine learning model for intelligent decision-support systems. The research explored many supervised and unsupervised learning strategies to provide prediction judgments. In the author's view, DSS systems may enhance strategic decision-making in corporate environments by recognizing patterns, creating predictions, and using machine learning techniques.

Ning (2024) suggested an AI-based decision support system for sustainable energy management in smart cities. The project's AI systems were mostly focused on enhancing energy distribution networks and studying trends in energy use. The results of the research indicate that AI-based DSS systems may assist urban planners and energy managers in making well-informed choices on sustainable resource usage.

Deep learning approaches in intelligent DSS for industrial quality assurance, namely radiography inspection, were explored by Kale et al. (2026). The findings suggest that deep learning models may be beneficial for assessing inspection pictures to identify structural issues. The paper highlights how AI-powered DSS tools may make industries more dependable and minimize inspection errors.

Gonzalez-Rodriguez et al. (2020) suggested an intelligent decision support system for production planning based on machine learning methods. Feeding the model production data yielded better schedules, resource allocations and overall production efficiency. The study shows that machine-learning algorithms might be used to forecast production needs and give assistance for operational decision-making.

Malik and Ali (2024) explored the optimization techniques for smart decision-making systems. The research was targeted at using the optimization methods of DSS systems for finding better solutions for complex decision-making circumstances. The findings of the research suggest that machine learning algorithms may discover patterns in large datasets and have the potential to increase optimization efficiency.

Aggarwal and Aggarwal (2026) investigated the use of AI in environmental DSS. The research revealed how AI models may use data from environmental monitoring to assist policymakers manage ecological resources more effectively. The experts said DSS frameworks using AI benefit climate analysis, sustainability planning and environmental monitoring.

Gupta et al. (2022) provide a detailed overview of AI for operations research DSS. The decision-making models such neural networks, optimization algorithms, machine learning and other AI technologies are analyzed. The authors describe potential future research paths and demands for the AI-driven DSS discipline.

Andronie et al, (2021) explored the decision-making algorithms in cyber-physical production systems based on AI and combined with IoT sensing networks and deep learning models. The research proved that AI systems are capable of automating decision-making, collecting and evaluating data from industrial sensors in real-time.

Boopathy (2026) examined the frameworks for intelligent data-driven decision-making using AI and ML approaches. The research showed the potential of data analytics for improving current DSS. Research shows that AI systems can filter through mounds of data to identify trends that might help firms make smarter long-term plans.

Ekundayo (2024) studied the potential advantages of complex systems engineering using AI-driven decision intelligence. The study shown that smart algorithms can analyze complicated systems with numerous unknowns. According to the report, "AI DSS systems improve the accuracy of engineering decisions and provide predictive insights."

In Kumar et al. (2025), the research was about data science and machine learning for better decision making in engineering and computer applications. Results indicate that DSS systems can process large data volumes effectively when machine learning and data analytics are included. Intelligent algorithms, trained on data up to October 2023, increase prediction and grant managers more agency to make educated judgments in complicated technological contexts.

Environment Management . Hamada et al. (2026) investigated AI-based DSS for sustainable environment management. Their study is focused on evaluating environmental data using AI algorithms to identify strategies to manage resources sustainably. Intelligent DSS frameworks assist decision making for climate policy and environmental protection, the report says.

Wang (2023) presented a decision-assistance system for construction project management based on AI approaches . The research developed a framework for project planning choices by analyzing project data, building factors and time restrictions. The findings show that the use of AI-based DSS models increases the resource management and project implementation in the construction industry which leads to less delay.

Lazaroiu et al. (2022) explored the integration of cognitive manufacturing systems with AI algorithms, IoT sensor networks, and big data technologies. The study results show the ability of decision making frameworks to adapt the operational change in industrial systems. Authors claim that AI-enabled DSS systems increase sustainability, efficiency, and productivity in smart industrial environments.

Hamrouni et al. (2021) suggested a smart decision-support system for business model construction and maintenance based on explainable ontologies. This study offered insight on how to explain DSS suggestions more transparently by applying the principles of explainable AI. The study's results indicate that organizations may build greater trust and better deploy AI-driven decision systems if they use ontology-based frameworks to understand the logic behind decision processes.

Keshireddy, 2024. Study on the usage of hybrid AI models in intelligent decision support system connected with management information systems. The authors of the research suggested merging Expert Systems, Neural Networks and Machine Learning for more effective commercial decision-making. The paper proposes that hybrid AI frameworks provide better system flexibility and more accurate forecasts in complicated business situations.

Sànchez-Marrè (2022) studied how intelligent DSS have developed in numerous businesses. The paper examined major DSS designs, AI techniques and their applications in healthcare, industrial systems and environmental management. The author pointed out that the presence of AI in DSS systems is an improvement of analytical skills and the result is a more reliable decision-making.

Verma and Singhal (2023) studied the use of AI approaches to adaptive decision making in complex systems. They developed AI-based systems that can evaluate dynamic system situations, and make suitable adaptive judgments. The research indicates that the heightened reactivity and adaptability of adaptive AI systems might be beneficial in decision support environments, notably within the engineering and technical fields.

DSS for smart industries and the Internet of Things for energy management were investigated by Li et al. (2021). There was also an emphasis on using AI algorithms and Internet of Things sensors to gather real-time data to make smart judgments on energy management. The authors argue that the combination of AI and IoT may make industrial systems operate with much improved energy efficiency and optimization.

Adeyeye and Akanbi (2024) examined the use of AI and ML to the complexity of systems engineering. This research concentrated on the capability of AI algorithms for controlling complicated engineering systems with numerous variables and limitations. The authors have shown that intelligent DSS improve engineering decision processes, decrease uncertainty and increase the reliability of systems.

Khalid and Shah (2025) examined smart decision systems and AI for design management. "They said that we need AI-enabled tools to review designs, optimize designs and make decisions as a team. The scientific investigations prove that AI based decision systems are increasing the standards of the design management effectiveness and efficiency.

The work of Behmel et al. (2021) provided the basis for a decision-support system that utilizes AI to enhance and accelerate water quality monitoring. This study's results emphasize the utility of DSS frameworks for environmental policymaking and assessment. Experts believe that smart technologies have the capacity to examine environmental data, offer effective monitoring tactics and show sustainable water management.

3. AI IN DESIGN MANAGEMENT

Intelligent design systems merge computational intelligence with design management methodologies to increase the efficiency, accuracy and flexibility of design processes. These systems are full with complexities. These solutions, based on database and AI technologies, might be valuable to managers and designers in the creation, assessment and optimization of design decisions. Traditional design techniques rely on human skill and manual examination. On the other hand, AI-enabled design tools may automatically filter through masses of design data, in quest of better ideas. The premise behind AI-powered intelligent design systems is that people may get a boost when it comes to analysis and inventiveness. The algorithms, in principle, might be capable of inferring the effects of design choices based on past data by recognizing trends. Intelligent design systems include simulation models, optimization methods and machine learning algorithms. They let designers to experiment with new ideas and see what works, before introducing a solution into the real world. Intelligent design systems should support iterative and collaborative design processes. The system produces plausible design alternatives, and when designers enter limits, objectives and performance criteria, the alternatives are evaluated using standard metrics. With this approach, designers may sharpen their ideas and repeatedly pick the best solutions. Intelligent design systems have a role to play in the management of an organisation's knowledge. With their significant design experience, project abilities and understanding of best practices, they might be highly beneficial for future initiatives. This capacity allows companies to shorten their design processes, boost production, and retain the quality of their designs. The increasing complexity of engineering and product development projects also demands intelligent design solutions for firms seeking to foster innovation and stay ahead of the competition. These systems integrate AI into design management and act as powerful decision support tools, enhancing the effectiveness and accuracy of design processes.

3.1 AI Techniques Used in Design Management

We see three areas in which artificial intelligence solutions are improving design management: automated analysis, predictive modeling and intelligent decision assistance. A lot of different AI technologies have been used to help make design choices easier and to ease the otherwise tedious design processes.

- **Machine Learning:** It is a well-known AI approach in the design management area since it allows computers to automatically learn from data and improve decision making. We examine prior design data, performance metrics and project results using ML algorithms to detect trends and get insights into projections. These models may be used by designers to evaluate different design possibilities via projections of efficiency, cost, and performance. Another possible use of machine learning is in the optimization of designs via the exploration of many scenarios to find the best solutions. ML also enhances risk management and quality control by identifying possible design flaws and enhancing the dependability of design outputs.

- **Neural Networks:** Neural networks, a kind of AI model, are modeled after the human brain so they can capture complex relationships between design elements. Design management analyzes data sets such as data on materials, data on design features and data on product performance. Neural networks might assist designers forecast the results of alternative design options, saving money on expensive physical tests. They actually thrive in complicated design situations and non-linear interactions. Other fields that employ neural networks to enhance the performance and reliability of the systems include design optimization, predictive maintenance and modeling.
- **Expert Systems:** These AI systems are designed to imitate the decision-making capabilities of human experts. This body of material has an inference engine that produces suggestions . It also contains standards and best practices in engineering and design concepts . Design management expert systems are very useful for the evaluation of design problems, such as material choice, structural requirements and production limitations. They help maintain consistency in decisions and preserve specialized knowledge inside companies. Expert systems are based on the established norms and standards in order to avoid the human mistake and to give reliable assessment of the design.
- **Natural Language Processing:** One area where computers could learn to comprehend and utilize is natural language processing, or NLP. Natural language processing (NLP) may be used to examine textual data in design management, such as design documentation, reports, and user interaction. Natural language processing technologies may extract meaningful information from enormous data and so enhance information retrieval and knowledge management. Also, they offer to talk to virtual assistants and chatbots, who may supply designers with data and advice. NLP may also be used to analyze consumer feedback to understand user preferences and make educated judgments on product design.

3.2 Benefits of AI-Driven Design Decisions

Application of AI in design management may lead to more efficient, accurate and effective decision making in design. AI-powered decision systems allow companies to handle large amounts of data, provide workable solutions and mitigate the risks associated with complicated design processes. An important advantage of AI-driven design decisions is the precision of the selections. AI systems look at previous data, see trends and forecast how various design decisions will play out. Designers with this expertise may choose solutions that better achieve performance targets and satisfy consumer expectations. Another benefit is the efficiency of the design process. AI-powered solutions may automate routine processes such as data analysis, design review, and simulation. This automation saves designers time so they may spend it on the most strategic and creative elements of their jobs. AI-driven design systems may aid in design optimization by looking at numerous design factors at once. Optimization algorithms can provide solutions that combine considerations of price, efficiency, environmental effect and capacity to manufacture the desired product. This means that product designs are more affordable and efficient. AI-based solutions may help make collaboration and exchanging knowledge easier. Smart systems may consolidate data from several departments to offer team members a real-time view of the problem. One advantage of AI is enhanced communication and cooperation between designers, engineers and management. Another is how it helps companies control design project risk by detecting possible product performance problems or faults before they are ever created. Recognizing such hazards early and acting to remedy for them, companies may increase the dependability of their products.

4. DECISION SUPPORT FRAMEWORK FOR DESIGN MANAGEMENT

AI-based DSS for design management offers a structured framework by integrating data processing, intelligent algorithms, and decision-making tools to support the evaluation of difficult design choices. This system architecture will collect important information, evaluate it via sophisticated computational methods and deliver relevant insights to facilitate informed decision making throughout the design process. The usual hierarchy has user interface, analytical modeling, data processing, knowledge management, and data input modules. Design requirements, project reports, simulation results, customer feedback, market trends and other external/internal sources are consumed at the lowest level of the system. This is the main input to the DSS . The next step is to include data storage and knowledge management systems for cataloging and storing design related information. These systems enable rapid access to important data and historical data for analysis and decision making. A well-maintained knowledge repository may retain useful design experiences for future projects. At the analytical level, AI methodologies like machine learning models, optimization techniques and predictive analytics are used to manage the gathered data. The algorithms assist managers to choose the best design choices by assessing the interactions between design factors, predicting the likely consequences and giving suggestions. This evaluation will then allow the decision engine to provide solutions or suggestions that are relevant to the scenario. This element is the base of the decision support system which is built by the integration of analytical data, set criteria and limitations. Design parameters may be entered, results can be seen, and an informed decision can be reached thanks to the user interface, which provides a dynamic platform for interaction between the system and stakeholders. Improved design management processes are made possible by the integrated architecture's high-tech computational tools and precise data-driven insights.

- **Data Acquisition:** The initial step of the AI-based decision support system is data acquisition, which includes the collection and structuring of necessary design data from different sources. Such sources include consumer feedback systems, ERP systems, manufacturing databases and computer-aided design (CAD) systems. The process typically involves data gathering, pre-processing and integration. Data integration allows to combine data from various sources into a single dataset while data pretreatment helps to remove mistakes and contradictions. The decision support system, having a dependable data gathering system, can operate on consistent and accurate information, which allows the AI algorithms to provide helpful insights for smart design choices.
- **Knowledge Base:** An extensive repository of vital data and expert views on design management. It contains information about the project history, design requirements, technical standards, material attributes and specialized knowledge. The knowledge base consists of declarative (facts and specifications) and procedural (rules and decision guidelines) knowledge. Knowledge representation approaches like databases, ontologies and rule-based systems give an efficient way to structure this information. When fresh design data becomes available the knowledge base is updated so that the framework may continually enhance its suggestions and help with accurate decision making.
- **AI Algorithms:** The analytical core of the decision support system is constructed on the algorithms of AI. Algorithms assess design choices by analyzing design data for patterns and predictions. Machine learning models are trained on data from prior designs to anticipate the outcomes in terms of dependability, performance, and cost. Optimization algorithms explore different design configurations and discover those with the optimal combination of efficiency, cost and environmental effect. Neural networks and deep learning approaches might possibly have a potential to deal with complex and nonlinear interactions among design aspects. Such AI technologies may assist make the design process more efficient and facilitate data-based decisions.
- **Decision Engine:** The decision engine processes the analytical data and produces actionable suggestions. It combines knowledge of AI algorithms with rules in the knowledge base, providing new design alternatives. The decision engine examines performance, sustainability, cost and project restrictions to choose the most appropriate design solutions. It also does options rating and

scenario analysis by using multi-criteria decision making approaches. The decision engine brings together analytical knowledge and logical reasoning to provide dependable suggestions to help in making good judgments about design management.

- **User Interface:** DSS enable users to communicate with each other via a user interface. It may be used by managers, designers and engineers to enter design parameters, see the results of the study and compare alternative design choices. Visualization technologies like dashboards, infographics and simulation models may help individuals grasp complicated data. The interface may also provide suggestions, warnings and real-time feedback to help decision making. Today, some systems include web- or cloud-based interfaces that enable remote access and communication amongst project teams, thereby making the system more efficient and user-friendly.

5. PROPOSED WORK

To enhance the effectiveness, accuracy and efficiency of design decision making, this research proposes an AI-based Decision Support Model for Design Management. Approaches to design management that depend on human knowledge, manual inspection and the absence of extensive historical data are plagued by inefficiencies, errors and delays. To overcome these restrictions, we present a data-driven decision framework, knowledge-based systems, and AI approaches that can be used by designers and managers to make informed choices at all stages of the design life cycle. The suggested paradigm includes data collection, knowledge base construction, AI algorithm layer implementation, decision making, user interaction and feedback learning. All the above aspects work together to form a smart system that can evaluate complicated design data and deliver the best suggestions to the designer.

Figure 1. Proposed AI-Based Decision Support Model for Design Management

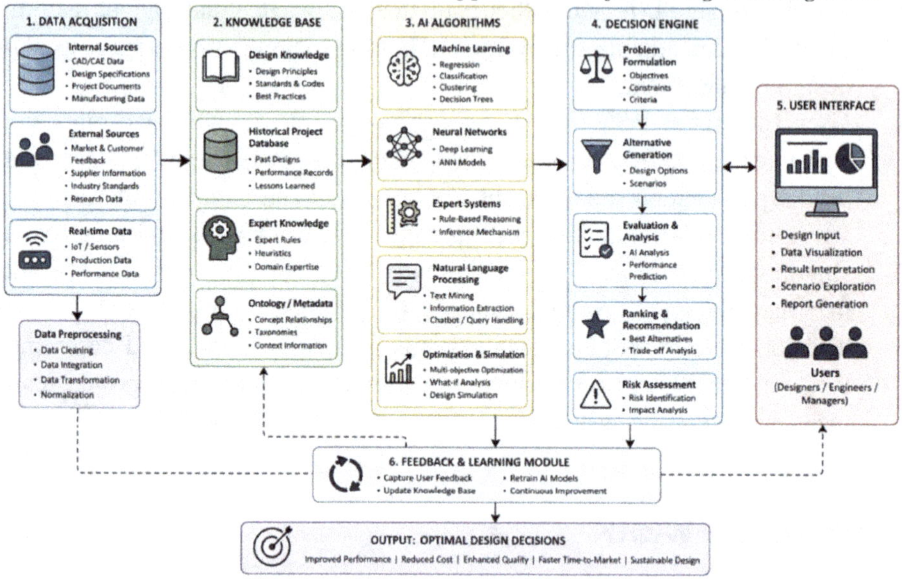

The Proposed Model shows how AI might help managers and designers to make intelligent choices based on facts. The model consists of numerous interrelated modules that analyze design factors given by the user, conduct intelligent algorithms and produce best design solutions. This is the how the model works:

- **Data Acquisition Layer:** The first layer in the model is data acquisition or information collection related to the design from diverse sources. Data preparation is the process of preparing data for usage and include activities like cleaning, integration, transformation and standardization. The data accuracy and AI-ability are assured.
- **Knowledge Base:** The knowledge base is an organized collection of design knowledge and pertinent historical data that assists in formulating informed judgments. It contains metadata, ontology, expert knowledge, past project database, and design knowledge. In this sense it works as a kind of organizational memory, storing data about previous events so that that knowledge may be applied to future design challenges.
- **AI Algorithms Layer:** The layer of AI algorithms is the analytical heart of the model. Design data may be used for insights. Machine learning algorithms may create predictions by studying previous data about designs. Deep learning analysis based on neural networks may be helpful in managing complicated relationships among design aspects. Expert systems use rule based

reasoning to emulate the decision making ability of human experts. They provide alternative designs that are feasible and consistent with the previously defined principles and inference methods. Natural language processing allows the system to interpret chaotic data. Optimization strategies are used to get the best possible design out of several.

- **Decision Engine:** This part does an analysis of the many design possibilities based on the output of the AI algorithms. The technology generates a large number of design possibilities. The design possibilities are ranked based on a trade-off analysis of effectiveness. The technology not only detects possible dangers but also assesses their influence on the design process.
- **User Interface:** The user interface of the decision support system is the interface between the system and its designers, engineers and managers. The intuitive UI makes understanding sophisticated AI results easier.
- **Feedback and Learning Module:** Feedback and learning module is an important part of the continuous development of the system. With each completed design project, this feedback loop makes the system smarter and more exact.
- **Output (Optimal Design Decisions):** The result of the model is optimal design choices that may enhance the design process in a holistic manner.

6. RESULTS AND DISCUSSION

In the following part, AI-based design management DSS, is implemented and assessed. The purpose of this research is to assess the performance of the suggested system regarding processing time, efficiency, decision correctness and overall effectiveness in helping with hard design decisions. The results were obtained by expert validation, comparison of the historical design data and simulation to carry out the trials. We analyze a set of performance indicators to compare the performance of the AI-based system with that of more traditional decision-making systems used more often in design management.

6.1 Performance Evaluation of the AI System

The suggested AI-based decision assistance system was evaluated based on many criteria. Such indicators include efficiency of computing, speed of processing, accuracy of judgment, reliability of suggestion and computational efficiency. The system was tested with many design scenarios to evaluate the performance of the system with different complexity. The main objective of the research is to investigate the system ability to deliver optimal design alternatives and to assess huge data sets. Table 1 shows the performance metrics of the AI-based system for several assessment criteria.

Table 1. Performance Metrics of the AI-Based Decision Support System

Performance Metric	Observed Value
Decision Accuracy	92.4%
Prediction Reliability	90.1%
Processing Efficiency	88.7%
System Response Time	2.8 seconds

The findings indicate that the suggested AI system is very accurate and reliable in decision making. The reduction in reaction time also demonstrates the system's capacity to properly manage complicated design situations. Table 2 shows a comparison of the overall performance of the system for the various AI approaches.

Figure 2. Performance of AI Techniques in Design Decision Support

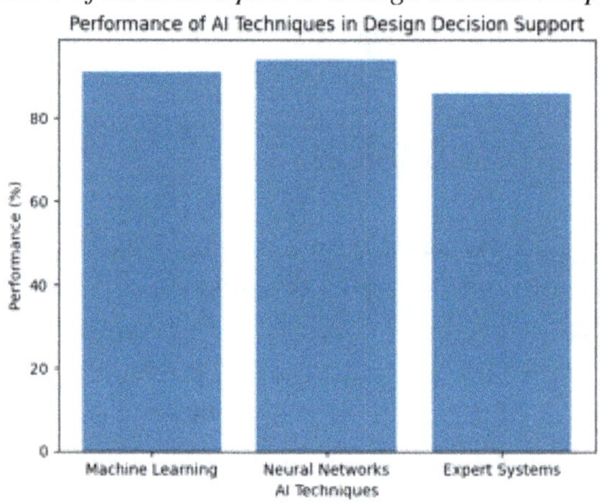

As the image shows, neural networks and ML models play a vital role in enhancing the prediction accuracy and the dependability of decisions. Rule-based reasoning is further help offered by expert systems.

6.2 Comparison with Traditional Decision-Making Methods

The efficacy of the proposed system was tested by comparing the AI-powered decision support model with the more conventional design management decision making approaches. Traditional methods often rely on manual analysis, expert opinion, and static design review processes. However, these approaches might restrict the capacity to handle complex data sets. Table 2 shows a comparison of the two methodologies.

Table 2. Comparison Between Traditional and AI-Based Decision Systems

Parameter	Traditional Method	AI-Based Method
Decision Accuracy	74%	92%
Processing Time	15–20 minutes	2–3 seconds
Data Handling Capability	Limited	Large-scale datasets
Decision Consistency	Moderate	High
Adaptability	Low	High

The AI-based system outperformed the more conventional decision-making methodologies on all three metrics: accuracy, processing speed and data processing capabilities. This makes the AI system more stronger at decision making since it can compare several design possibilities at a time. Figure 3 illustrates the difference between the two techniques.

Figure 3. AI-Based vs Traditional Decision-Making Performance

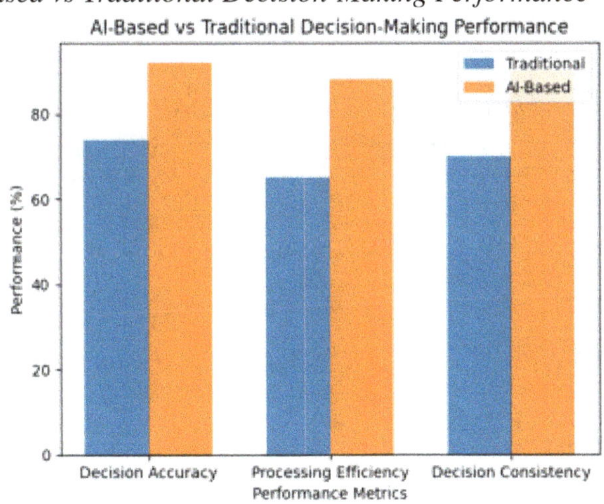

6.3 Accuracy, Efficiency, and Time Improvement

The main purpose of the proposed system is to reduce the time necessary to analyze design options and to improve the accuracy of the choice. The experimental research reveals that the AI based system provides a speedier decision making process by automating the assessment process and adopting the predictive modelling approaches. The improvement is captured by a variety of performance metrics, as shown in Table 3.

Table 3. Improvement in Decision-Making Performance

Evaluation Factor	Traditional System	AI-Based System	Improvement
Decision Accuracy	74%	92%	+18%
Processing Time	18 minutes	2.8 seconds	Significant reduction
Design Evaluation Efficiency	70%	89%	+19%
Error Rate	12%	4%	Reduced errors

The onset of the AI-based decision support system (Fig. 3) has greatly enhanced the processing speed and precision of decision-making. Results show that AI considerably boosts the effectiveness of design decision making procedures. Thanks to the capacity of AI models to learn from past data, the strategy can deliver more trustworthy suggestions.

Figure 4: Accuracy and Time Improvement Using AI

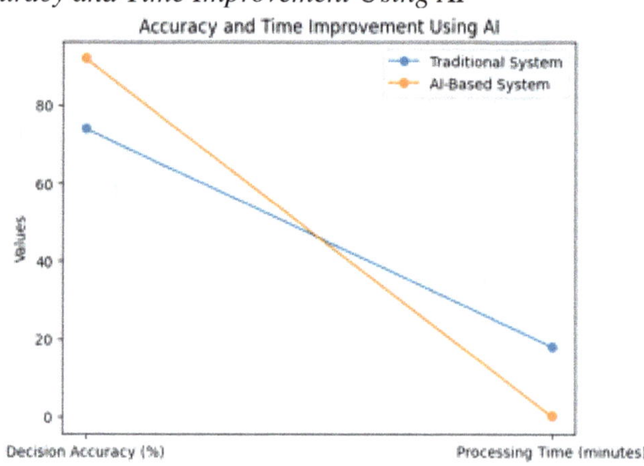

Experimental results demonstrate the effectiveness of the integration of AI with design management systems on the decision assistance capacity. With the aid of AI, the system can swiftly search through mountains of design data, identify complex correlations between design aspects and provide the best potential design solutions. The findings indicate that machine learning and neural network models considerably improve the prediction accuracy and reduce the time for decision making. These models are improved by expert systems that use domain knowledge and rule-based reasoning in the decision-making process. Implementation of these strategies leads to a strong, intelligent system which is capable of handling difficult design situations. There is also the adaptability of the suggested technology. And the AI-based system has the ability to learn from fresh data and feedback all the time, making it more successful over time than older systems. Its flexibility means the system will continue to operate as the design and industry's requirements change.

7. CONCLUSION

As the complexity of the current design environment increases, smarter systems and better tools are needed to support successful decision-making. Traditional design management options for vast data and difficult design choices frequently depend on static assessment methods, expert opinion and manual analysis. This study proposed an AI-DSS for design management aiming to improve the reliability, accuracy and efficiency of design-related decisions. The proposed framework, to assess design data and recommend optimum design, integrates a broad range of AI technologies such as intelligent decision engines, expert systems, machine learning, and neural networks. The system architecture comprises data gathering, a knowledge base, AI algorithms, a decision engine, and a user interface that combine to provide a DSS. The system architecture allows for the handling of massive amounts of design data, the discovery of undiscovered correlations between design parameters and the provision of data-driven insights to decision makers. The experimental findings indicate that the suggested AI-based strategy achieves better performance than the standard methods for decision making. The assessment findings show beneficial effects on decision accuracy, processing time, computational efficiency and consistency of choice outcomes. The system is able to rapidly assess a large number of design alternatives and to deliver reliable suggestions based on historical data and prediction models. These advancements show how AI may turn standard design management systems into intelligent, flexible DSS. Furthermore, the suggested approach enables collaborative and interactive decision making using a user-friendly interface, enabling managers and designers to effectively analyze design choices. There are also some clever algorithms built into the system that help it learn from its errors and improve over time. In other words, the results of this research support the hypothesis that AI-based DSS may be used to significantly improve design management processes in current engineering and organizational settings.

8. FUTURE SCOPE

The suggested AI-based DSS has potential advantages in design management decision making, however there are various areas for ongoing development and further exploration. Future research may explore the use of advanced AI techniques for enhancing prediction accuracy and decision optimization. Another important future path is the integration of big data technology and real time data analytics. DSS can react to changing design requirements and environmental circumstances by combining real-time design data from several sources and providing dynamic and adaptable suggestions. This will enhance the responsiveness and efficacy of the system in a complicated industrial design environment. Future study may look at the integration of cloud computing and IoT technologies to increase the accessibility and scalability of the decision support system. AI systems deployed in the cloud provide new collaborative design environments where several stakeholders may access the system remotely and participate to decision-making. In a similar way, design systems may also acquire real-time data via IoT from sensors and linked devices that can further increase the quality of the design decision-making. Another interesting future prospect is the inclusion of XAI technology. Explainable AI allows designers and managers to grasp the process by which the system generates its proposals, and it may enhance confidence, transparency and adoption of AI-based DSS in organizational contexts. Finally, large-scale industrial case studies and cross-domain applications may be used to validate the suggested model in the future research. In order to better understand the scalability and utility of the system it may be used in the complex design fields, product development settings and real-world engineering projects.

REFERENCES

Adeyeye, O. J., & Akanbi, I. (2024). AI for systems engineering complexity: A review on the use of AI and machine learning algorithms. *Computer Science & IT Research Journal*, *5*(4), 787–808. DOI: 10.51594/csitrj.v5i4.1026

Aggarwal, G., & Aggarwal, S. (2026). AI for Environmental DSS. In *AI Enabled Real Time Environmental Monitoring* (pp. 129–144). Springer Nature Singapore.

Ali, R., Hussain, A., Nazir, S., Khan, S., & Khan, H. U. (2023). Intelligent DSS—An analysis of machine learning and multicriteria decision-making methods. *Applied Sciences (Basel, Switzerland)*, *13*(22), 12426. DOI: 10.3390/app132212426

Andronie, M., Lăzăroiu, G., Iatagan, M., U ă, C., tefănescu, R., & Coco atu, M. (2021). AI-based decision-making algorithms, internet of things sensing networks, and deep learning-assisted smart process management in cyber-physical production systems. *Electronics (Basel)*, *10*(20), 2497. DOI: 10.3390/electronics10202497

Behmel, S., Damour, M., Ludwig, R., & Rodriguez, M. J. (2021). Intelligent decision-support system to plan, manage and optimize water quality monitoring programs: Design of a conceptual framework. *Journal of Environmental Planning and Management*, *64*(4), 703–733. DOI: 10.1080/09640568.2020.1782858

Boopathy, C. (2026). Intelligent Data-Driven Decision Making Using AI and Machine Learning Techniques. *International Journal of AI and Machine Learning E-ISSN: 3117-8391*, *1*(1), 17-24.

Brown, H., Evans, L., & Parker, E. (2026). Improving Real Time DSS in Management Information Systems Through AI Powered Automation. *Journal of Innovation in Governance and Business Practices*, *2*, 89–121. DOI: 10.66096/JIGBP.V2.4

Ekundayo, F. (2024). Leveraging AI-driven decision intelligence for complex systems engineering. *Int J Res Publ Rev*, *5*(11), 1–10. DOI: 10.55248/gengpi.5.1124.3343

Fedorka, P., Buchuk, R., Klymenko, M., Saibert, F., & Petrushyn, A. (2025). The use of adaptive AI learning models in DSS for smart regions. *J. Res. Innov. Technol.*, *4*, 99–115. DOI: 10.57017/jorit.v4.1(7).07

González Rodríguez, G., Gonzalez-Cava, J. M., & Méndez Pérez, J. A. (2020). An intelligent decision support system for production planning based on machine learning. *Journal of Intelligent Manufacturing*, *31*(5), 1257–1273. DOI: 10.1007/s10845-019-01510-y

Gupta, S., Modgil, S., Bhattacharyya, S., & Bose, I. (2022). AI for DSS in the field of operations research: Review and future scope of research. *Annals of Operations Research, 308*(1), 215–274. DOI: 10.1007/s10479-020-03856-6

Hamada, A., Karagozlu, D., & Isiaku, L. (2026). AI-Driven DSS for Sustainable Environmental Management. In *DSS for Industrial and Scientific Applications* (pp. 57–69). Springer Nature Switzerland.

Hamrouni, B., Bourouis, A., Korichi, A., & Brahmi, M. (2021). Explainable ontology-based intelligent decision support system for business model design and sustainability. *Sustainability (Basel), 13*(17), 9819. DOI: 10.3390/su13179819

Keshireddy, S. R. (2024). Intelligent DSS in Management Information Systems Using Hybrid AI Models. *Research Briefs on Information and Communication Technology Evolution, 10*, 211–230. DOI: 10.64799/rebicte.v10.13

Khalid, F., & Shah, H. (2025). AI-Enhanced Design Management: Scientific Principles for Intelligent Decision Systems. *Journal of Design. Management Science, 2*(02), 61–68.

Kumar, S., Machireddy, J. R., Sankaran, T., & Sholapurapu, P. K. (2025). Integration of machine learning and data science for optimized decision-making in computer applications and engineering. *Journal of Information Systems Engineering & Management*, •••, 10.

Lazaroiu, G., Androniceanu, A., Grecu, I., Grecu, G., & Neguri ă, O. (2022). AI-based decision-making algorithms, Internet of Things sensing networks, and sustainable cyber-physical management systems in big data-driven cognitive manufacturing. *Oeconomia Copernicana, 13*(4), 1047–1080. DOI: 10.24136/oc.2022.030

Li, J., Dai, J., Issakhov, A., Almojil, S. F., & Souri, A. (2021). Towards DSS for energy management in the smart industry and Internet of Things. *Computers & Industrial Engineering, 161*, 107671. DOI: 10.1016/j.cie.2021.107671

Malik, S., & Ali, M. (2024). Machine Learning–Driven Optimization Techniques for Intelligent Decision-Making Systems. *International Journal of Data Sciences and Intelligent Systems, 1*(01), 1–16.

Ning, M. A. (2024). AI-Driven DSS for Sustainable Energy Management in Smart Cities. *International Journal of Advanced Computer Science & Applications, 15*(9).
Kale, K., Srivastava, D. K., & Derawi, M. (2026). Enhancing Industrial Quality Assurance: Deep Learning in Intelligent DSS for Radiographic Inspection. In *DSS for Industrial and Scientific Applications* (pp. 175–192). Springer Nature Switzerland.

Saeed, A. (2024). Machine Learning Models for Intelligent DSS. *Journal of AI Range*, *1*(1), 54–66.

Sànchez-Marrè, M. (2022). Intelligent DSS. In *Intelligent DSS* (pp. 77–116). Springer International Publishing.

Verma, A., & Singhal, N. (2023, September). Integrating AI for adaptive Decision-Making in complex system. In *International Conference on Advances in Data-driven Computing and Intelligent Systems* (pp. 95-105). Singapore: Springer Nature Singapore.

Wang, J. (2023, December). Intelligent decision support system for building project management based on AI. [). IOP Publishing.]. *Journal of Physics: Conference Series*, *2665*(1), 012022. DOI: 10.1088/1742-6596/2665/1/012022

Chapter 8
Application of AI in Design Thinking Methodologies

H. S. Abzal Basha
http://orcid.org/0000-0002-7731-0985
Department of Management Studies, G. Pullaiah College of Engineering and Technology, Kurnool, India

A. Pankajam
Department of Business Administration, Avinashilingam Institute for Home Science and Higher Education for Women, Coimbatore, India

Asfa Ahamad
Department of Computer Science, College of Engineering and Computer Science, Mustaqbal University, Buraidah, Saudi Arabia

Chanchal Sachdeva Suri
http://orcid.org/0000-0003-1205-2898
University Institute of Media Studies, Chandigarh University, Gharuan, India

Huma Khan
http://orcid.org/0000-0003-1653-8676
Rungta International Skills University, Bhilai, India

ABSTRACT

AI to Design Thinking models can be seen as a radical way of improving innovation, efficiency, and user-centered problem-solving. This paper will examine how AI technologies can be systematically incorporated throughout five steps of Design Thinking to enhance decision-making and design outputs. Research design is a

DOI: 10.4018/979-8-3693-3751-6.ch008

mixed-method one, as it will combine with qualitative insights gained by using a case study approach and quantitative analysis of survey data to assess effectiveness of AI in design processes. Results show that AI is an effective way to improve pattern recognition, user insight generation, and creative ideation by using different techniques.

1. INTRODUCTION

In the existing fast-digital change, organizations are more and more demanding novel solutions to their complex issues and improving user experiences. Design Thinking has become an effective human process to problem solving that is rooted in empathy, creativity and iterative problem solving. The AI has transformed the decision-making process by using data to guide decision-making process, automatize system, and predict outcome. Intersection of both fields is an outstanding opportunity to revise conceptualization and the application of innovation in practice. Historically, Design Thinking is mostly based on the human intuition, qualitative understanding and prototyping. Even being efficient, these processes might be time-consuming and confined by cognitive biases and limits of data. Nonetheless, AI proves useful in handling large amounts of data, revealing latent trends, and intelligent recommendations. The application of AI in Design Thinking initiatives increase the efficiency, scalability, and accuracy of the process of innovations. Design Thinking is a problem-solving approach with a foundation in the necessity to understand users' needs and create new solutions that should be developed in the course of the iterative processes. It is problem solving as it is based on empathy, ideation and experimentation and is thus very effective when dealing with complex and ambiguous issues. It is an invention of the design professions, but since then has been used in large volumes in most sectors of the economy like business, healthcare and education. Quite on the contrary, AI presupposes the imitation of human intelligence in the machine that will allow it to perform certain tasks. AI technologies that radically changed the process of data analysis and utilization. The overlapping area between Design Thinking and AI is a paradigm shift of innovation. In contrast to Design Thinking that is a human-centered approach, AI introduces computational intelligence and the use of data to make decisions. An example is: during the empathy phase, AI can analyze the pattern of behavior, thereby providing deeper insights into the process, although Design Thinking can make sure that the insights obtained are translated into meaningful solutions. With the benefits of both worlds, the companies will become more creative, less cynical and will be able to speed up the process of innovations.

The Design Thinking methodologies generally have a structured but flexible structure of different steps. All the stages are very important in creating user-centric solutions. Empathize stage resides on the cognition of the users based on the observation, interview and immersion. Ideate stage stimulates brainstorming and creative thinking to help in coming up with a variety of solutions with no restrictions. The Prototype stage entails the development of the idea into form so that the designers can visualise and fine-tune the idea. Lastly, Test stage is a procedure of testing the prototypes to the users with the aim of getting feedback and also refining solutions. These strategies place an emphasis on learning through trial and error, through teamwork and experimentation. The flexibility of Design Thinking can be regarded as one of its most crucial attributes and the possibility to apply it in different areas and situations. Nevertheless, design thinking methods that are traditional use extensively qualitative information and human interpretation which may lead to biases and lack scalability. The design processes that require AI in any of design lifecycle that are intended to enhance the efficiency, creativity and decision-making processes. These procedures use data analysis, automation, predictive modeling to help the designers in generating new solutions. The data is one of the major elements of AI-based design. To generate actionable insights, the user behavior, preferences and feedback are collected and analyzed using machine learning algorithms. These insights can help designers to know more about the needs of the user and what can be innovated. Using AI as an example, it can be capable of analyzing large data to identify patterns that otherwise may be difficult to notice using traditional methods. The ideation phase has also been altered by generative AI products and now it was possible to generate an array of design options, based on the parameters defined. This accelerates the brainstorming process, and expands the boundaries of creativity. Similarly, the prototyping tools, founded on AI, can mimic the user interface and learn their behaviour, without having to use physical prototypes. The other important element of AI-based design is personalization. With tailoring solutions as per the preferences of the individual user, AI algorithms can generate a more satisfactory user experience and satisfaction. Moreover, it is possible to automatize routine processes, which are a significant part of the designer's responsibilities, and focus on more important and creative tasks.

The evolution of AI has transformed much since it was first introduced in mid-second half of previous century. First AI systems were simple and limited and they mostly engaged in the solution of structured problems. Overall, AI has become a potent tool, which can be utilised to undertake complex and unstructured tasks in the long run due to the increase in computing power, access to data, and algorithms. One of the notable achievements in the development of AI is ML and DL.

With these technologies, systems can learn through data and get better with time without any explicit programming. NLP has also increased AI functions, whereby machines can comprehend and produce human language. The application of AI cuts across a broad spectrum of industries. In healthcare, AI is applied in the process of diagnosing diseases and planning their treatment. In finance, it helps to detect fraud and manage risk. In production, AI can be used to predictive maintenance and optimise processes. AI finds applications in design and creativity, image generation, content generation, and improving the user experience. AI is now a powerful tool to enhance the innovative approach to issues and creativity. Using highly sophisticated algorithms and data analytics, AI can assist designers to come up with new ideas and find new solutions. Generative design is aspects of AI through which creativity can be enhanced. Based on some of the constraints and goals, AI systems have potential to produce design options, allowing designers to work with a large set of possibilities. This does not only accelerate the ideation process but also the quality of solutions is enhanced. AI that identifies the patterns and relationships within the complex data is also beneficial in solving problems. This enables designers to find the unknown and to come up with a more superior solution. To illustrate, AI may be used to analyze the feedback provided by users to determine the most frequent problems and propose solutions. AI could be a co-creator, collaborating with human designers to increase creativity and innovation. AI can be used to automate routine work, and also enable designers to concentrate on the strategic and creative tasks.

Although the use of Design Thinking and AI is becoming more widespread, its implementation is not very coherent. The conventional approaches to Design Thinking methodologies are based on human intuition and qualitative insights, which can result in biases and inefficiencies. On the other hand, the solutions based on AI tend not to take into consideration the human-centric perspective that would be helpful to develop meaningful solutions. This lack of connection makes it difficult to have a balanced approach that will involve being empathetic in making decisions in a factual manner. Moreover, it does not have well-structured frameworks that would clearly state how AI can be effectively implemented into every step of the Design Thinking process. Companies are put to the task of how they can make use of AI tools without contravening the basic postulates of human-centered design. Therefore, the aim of the research is to address these challenges by exploring how AI can be implemented in Design Thinking processes and propose an integrated approach that will be more innovative, efficient and user-satisfied. The explanation of how AI may be utilized to Design Thinking practices in general adds significantly to the scientific community and practice in general. It first outlines each step of the Design Thinking process and how AI can be used at different times, to provide a systematic understanding of how AI might enhance innovation across the process. Second, the paper suggests a conceptual model, which will bridge the gap between the human-centered design and the data-driven intelligence. The framework can be utilized as a guideline to researchers and practitioners that are interested in implementing AI in design processes. It highlights the fact that AI can be used to make things more efficient, scalable, and are able to make decisions without losing sight of what the user needs. Thirdly, the study completes the current body of literature by revealing the shortcomings of the traditional design methodology and outlines the opportunities that can be provided to make the situation better with the integration of AI. It also considers the problems and ethical considerations surrounding AI-based design which sheds light on responsible and sustainable practice.

2. LITERATURE REVIEW

Saeidnia and Ausloos (2024) looked at the incorporation of AI into the Design Thinking frameworks, the paper pointed out how AI contributes to every phase of design process. The research observes the AI potential to develop a better understanding of data analytics and drive generative ideation. The authors suggest that insights that are driven by AI can lead to a significant improvement in the outcomes of decision-making and innovation, but also emphasize the need to keep a human-centered approach to prevent over-trust in automated systems.

In an effort to discuss the synergies between Design Thinking and AI, Sreenivasan and Suresh (2024) carried out a systematic literature review. Their research is a synthesis of the current research to reveal the key areas where AI can be used to assist in design processes, such as user analysis, ideation, and prototyping. Results have shown that AI is more efficient and scalable, although it must be implemented with caution in order to maintain the human-centered values.

Caires et al. (2023) examined use of Design Thinking during the use of text-to-image AI tools in furniture design education. Paper will show how AI can be used to boost creativity, by implementing visual prototypes in the ideation phase. It emphasizes how AI can be used to facilitate the learning process of students and enhancing design solutions.

Kim et al. (2023) examined the way Design Thinking can be utilized in the sphere of AI education. The study proposes a pedagogic philosophy, where the Design Thinking is implemented to convey AI concepts to students in a manner that can be learnt. It emphasizes the need of experiential learning, problem-solving, and collaboration. The results indicate that the use of Design Thinking results in a more positive attitude to AI among students and an enhancement of their skills related to creative thinking. They suggest that combining the two fields, it will be possible to create a more involving and productive learning experience particularly in the technical education context.

Chang and Tsai (2024) wrote about the implication of Design Thinking on AI learning and creativity amidst learners. Integration stimulates active learning and enhances engagement of students. The article cites the reality that Design Thinking approach is formalized yet flexible approach that can be applied supplementary to AI education. The authors propose the concept of incorporating Design Thinking in AI courses to encourage innovation and improvement of the learning outcomes.

Saritepeci and Yildiz Durak (2024) could have conducted a test of the validity of the integration of AI into design-based learning in experimental research. The results show that AI-enhanced learning settings can greatly enhance the design thinking attitude, creativity, and reflective thinking abilities of students. The paper highlights how AI can be used to promote interactive and customized learning experiences.

To create products that are user-centric, Shunmuga sundaram et al. (2026) focused on AI-enhanced Design Thinking to create products that are user-centric. The study suggests how AI can be used to analyze needs of the user, come up with innovative solutions, and optimize product design. The authors conclude that when AI is used to Design Thinking, it leads to more efficient, customer-focused development of products, particularly in technology-driven industries.

Staub et al. (2023) explored possibility of employing Design Thinking to address some of the common issues in AI projects. Some of the gaps identified in the paper include lack of user concern, definition of problems, and challenges in implementation in AI programs. Applying the concepts of Design Thinking, the organizations can enhance the results of projects and make sure that they are closely related to the needs of users.

Sanchez (2025) conducted a SLR on topics of integration of AI and Design Thinking on a project-based learning. The study identifies the key benefits, such as enhanced creativity, improved problem solving, and improved learning outcome. It also brings to the fore issues of implementation and resource needs. The authors also conclude that AI can be effectively used in learning in combination with Design Thinking to provide students with a high level of engagement and innovation ability.

The article by Poleac (2024) explored the idea of Design Thinking with AI in business. The paper explains how AI technology can be used to aid decision-making and innovation processes. It emphasizes the significance of considering AI in the organizational strategies to increase the competitiveness. Another point the research makes is that with AI, there is a need to be ethical and have human control over the situations when using AI in design.

Böckle et al. (2023) examined the relation between Design Thinking and AI in developing solutions that are human-centered. The paper emphasizes the way Design Thinking can inform creation of the ethical AI systems. It highlights the significance of empathy and user participation in designing AI. The authors claim that a combination of these methods will result in more responsible and sustainable innovation.

Havidotinnisa et al. (2024) performed SLR of Design Thinking in AI disruption. The paper identifies the role played by Design Thinking in assisting organizations to adapt to changes in technology caused by AI. It singles out the following positive attributes: enhanced innovation, stronger user knowledge and problem-solving. The study comes to the conclusion that Design Thinking is needed to handle the transformation created by AI.

Kyriakopoulos et al. (2025) examined how features of Design Thinking and AI capabilities affect organizational performance. Research discovered that these strategies in combination increase decision-making agility and enhances the results of new product development. It emphasizes the significance of using AI in design workflow to gain competitive edge. The study presents the empirical results of the applicability of AI-based Design Thinking.

Leão (2024) examined ergonomics and Design Thinking, as well as AI/ML, in designing innovation. The paper will emphasize the role those factors play user-friendly and efficient. It highlights significance of putting human factors into the AI-based design processes. The study concludes that a combination of these methods will increase the usability and innovation.

Rahimi (2025) created and tested to measure design thinking in AI-based language teaching. The analysis shows that Design Thinking skills play a vital role in implementation of AI in education. It offers rubric of how teachers may implement the principles of design thinking to AI-driven systems.

Turcios-Esquivel (2025) investigated combination of Design Thinking, experimental design, and AI in engineering education. The paper points out the advantages of these methods in boosting innovation and problem-solving abilities among students.

Castillo-Martínez et al. (2023) explored the growth of complex thinking amid students with Design Thinking and AI. Mixed methods are employed in the study to show how the two methods can be used to facilitate critical thinking and creativity.

The article by Dall'Asta (2025) explained the way AI is implemented into Design Thinking in architectural education. The study identifies the advantages of AI-based software in the fostering of creativity and effectiveness in the design process. It reiterates the importance of proper technology and human resourcefulness.

Ramirez-Duque (2026) explained that to encourage the importance of soft skills and energy education it is possible to utilize Design Thinking and AI. The paper identifies the role of the strategies in enhancing collaboration, creativity and problem-solving. It highlights the significance of incorporating AI in education systems.

Kayyali (2026) wrote about Design Thinking in the era of AI, and the human-centered AI solutions. The paper lays emphasis on the need to be empathetic and ethically conscious in AI-based design procedures. It highlights the fact that there must be a balanced integration.

Chandani et al. (2025) discussed how Design Thinking and AI can be integrated in healthcare. The paper emphasizes the role of these methods in advancing patient-centered solutions and improving innovativeness in healthcare.

2.1 Research Gaps Identified

First, most of them (Saeidnia and Ausloos (2024); Sreenivasan and Suresh (2024)) are conceptual and systematic reviews but lack empirical validation through real-world applications. The quantitative evidence that proves the influence of AI integration on the efficiency, creativity, and effectiveness of the Design Thinking results in various industries is scarce. Second, despite studies that have emphasized AI in particular steps of Design Thinking (e.g., ideation with the help of generative AI or empathy with the help of data analytics), there exists a lack of an unified and standardized framework that systematically integrates AI across all five stages. The current literature is divided into the study of specific applications in isolation, without a comprehensive approach. Third, some educational research (Kim et al., 2023; Chang & Tsai, 2024; Saritepeci & Yildiz Durak, 2024) highlights the positive effects of AI-based Design Thinking in the learning process, but there is a lack of studies on its implementation in industrial and commercial environments, especially in developing economies. There are still limited case studies of industry specific performance indicators that can be measured. The other critical gap is in the ethical and governance factors of AI implementation. Even though some of the studies briefly mention the issues that such AI usage introduces, namely bias, transparency, and data privacy (Böckle et al., 2023; Poleac, 2024). Additionally, the dynamics of human-AI cooperation are not researched to an extent. Most of the literature will focus on AI-capability or Design Thinking process alone, without further exploring how the designers will interact with AI systems, how the decision-making authority will be distributed and how trust will be gained in AI-assisted environments. Scalability and flexibility problems also have not been studied enough. AI may have the potential to efficiently scale Design Thinking approaches without losing the human focus; however little is known about the extent to which AI scales these methodologies. Finally, the research on the new technologies in the framework of Design Thinking has been scarce. Such technologies include: adaptive learning systems, generative AI, explainable AI and more. Recent works suggest the prospect (Andreu et al., 2026; Omidmand, 2026), but, comprehensive models have not been developed to cover these improvements. In short, there is a lack of studies, a lack of industry-specific studies, a lack of integrated frameworks, a lack of empirical validation, and a lack of accountability for scaling and new AI technological difficulties.

3. CONCEPTUAL FRAMEWORK

The theoretical framework of this paper generates a systematic correlation of different steps. It describes how AI technologies may be gradually implemented into every step of the human-centered design and how to retain the main principles that the human-centered design is based on. The research explores the integration of AI into Design Thinking processes, addressing the disconnection between traditional human intuitiveness and AI's data-driven approach. It highlights the inefficiencies of conventional methodologies that lack structured frameworks for effective AI implementation. The paper outlines each step of the Design Thinking process, suggesting ways AI can enhance innovation while remaining user-centric. It proposes a conceptual model to bridge human-centered design with AI intelligence, serving as a guideline for researchers and practitioners. The study also critiques traditional design methods, revealing opportunities for improvement through AI integration and discusses ethical considerations for responsible practice.

3.1 Relationship between AI and Design Thinking Stages

Design Thinking is made up of five iterative steps. Sentiment analysis, user analytics techniques can be more effective in identifying user needs and preferences and the pain points of experiences. At the stage of Define, AI helps to organize and synthesize data obtained. Machine learning algorithms can be utilized to find hidden patterns, group user insights, and frame problems by pointing out the major problems that need to be addressed. During the Ideate phase, AI will be used to boost creativity by creating generative models that generate several design options. This enlarges the solution space and helps designers to take into account new ideas that are not limited by the cognitive capabilities of humans. During the Prototype stage, AI can be used to perform rapid, clever prototyping through simulation, automation and computer modelling. Design performance prediction and optimising prototypes can be done by AI-powered tools before actual implementation. The Test stage will assist in the analysis of real-time feedback and predictive evaluation with the help of AI. It is able to analyze user responses, predict and suggest improvement, thus shortening the iteration cycle.

3.2 Role of AI Tools in Each Phase

In the Empathize phase, the user feedback, information in the social media accounts and surveys are processed using NLP systems, sentiment analysis websites and surveys to obtain meaningful information. The interaction and behaviour of the user can also be investigated using computer vision. The dashboard and visualization tools can be based on AI and used to determine the main spheres of problems and trends. Generative AI tools, including deep learning-based design systems, facilitate idea generation at the Ideate phase, by generating a variety of creative solutions to a particular problem, based on established parameters. These tools enhance brainstorming and block brain constraints. All these tools are meant to accelerate the decision making process, save time and cost and promote informed and data driven innovation that is informed by data at all levels of the design lifecycle.

3.3 Proposed Conceptual Model

The proposed conceptual framework is an AI-Design Thinking hybrid model that considers AI capabilities in every step of design process but retains a human-centered approach. The framework starts off with data-driven empathy, in which the AI gathers and analyses user data to produce insights. These lessons are fed into the smart problem definition phase, during which AI can find patterns and aid in the accurate definition of the problem. The augmented ideation phase follows, by using the power of generative AI to increase the amount of creative options. This is then succeeded by intelligent prototyping, where AI software models and optimize design solutions. Lastly, the predictive testing phase involves the use of AI to assess the results, interpret the feedback, and suggest the improvements. One of the main characteristics of the framework is the presence of the iterative feedback loop where the experience of the testing phase can be continuously fed back into the previous stages, making the experience of the testing phase continuously improved. Moreover, the structure also comprises of ethical and human oversight levels which ensure transparency, fairness and compliance with the needs of the users. The model focuses on the interaction between humans and AI where AI can be viewed as the facilitator, but not the replacement of human creativity. This conceptual framework provides a methodological approach of integrating AI into Design Thinking that can assist organizations to create solutions that are more efficient, scalable and innovative without forgetting the very nature of human-centered design.

Figure 1. Conceptual Model of Proposed

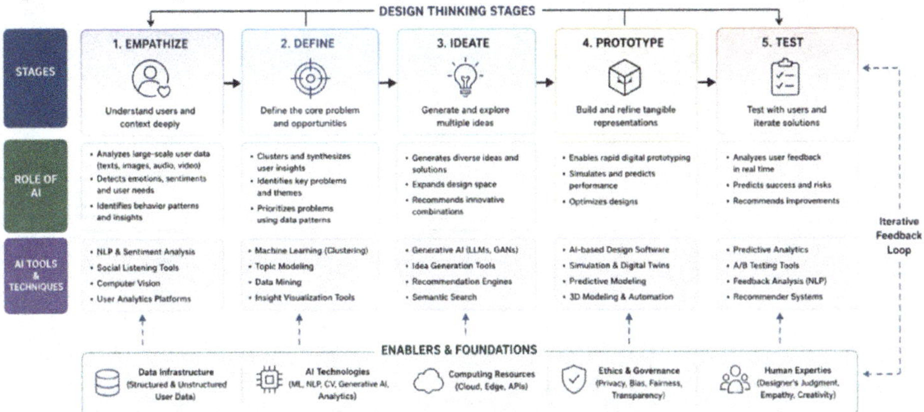

Some have proposed Figure 1 as a conceptual framework to integrate AI with Design Thinking framework to drive human-centric innovation. This method is rational, systematic and structured. It demonstrates how the potential of AI can be applied in all five stages of Design Thinking while preserving the iterative process and the user driven approach. It also highlights the importance of AI as an enabler of data-driven insights, automation and predictive decision-making at all levels.

4. RESEARCH METHODOLOGY

The study project will explore the integration of AI in a systematic and structured research technique using Design Thinking methods. The technique is aimed at covering both theoretical knowledge and empirical data for full investigation of the proposed conceptual framework. The study uses both quantitative and qualitative methods. As a clue to the systematic and structured approach to the analysis of integration of AI into Design Thinking methodologies, Figure 2 shows the research methodology framework that was adopted in this study. The framework puts emphasis on the sequential flow of the research process which begins with the selection of mixed-method research design that would facilitate combining qualitative and quantitative approaches to the research process to ensure that the analysis and verification of the research process are comprehensive.

Figure 2. Research Methodology Framework

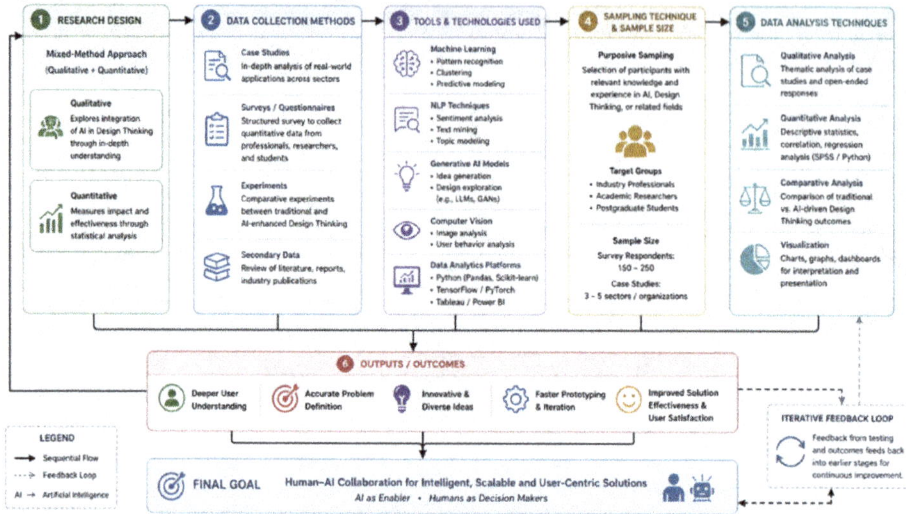

It is mixed-method which is combination of qualitative and quantitative research designs. Qualitative component includes exploration of conceptual and practical integration of AI in Design Thinking through reviewing of the literature and analyzing of the case studies. It assists in comprehending the experiences of the users, organizational experiences and situational factors that affect adoption. The quantitative part encompasses statistical processing of survey data, which will be collected during the course of research among professionals, researchers, and students who work in the sphere of AI and design-related issues. A number of data collection processes are applied to give a comprehensive coverage of the research objectives:

- **Case Studies:** The case studies under study involve real-life case studies in a different industry like healthcare, education and product design, etc. to gain some insight into real-life application of AI in Design Thinking.
- **Survey Method:** Structured questionnaires are distributed to academicians and students, designers, AI professionals, surveyed on the perceptions, use and effectiveness of AI tools on the design processes, designers, AI professionals, academicians and students.
- **Experimental Approach:** The controlled experiments can be conducted to compare the traditional Design Thinking processes with AI-enhanced processes with the performance measures of time efficiency and quality of the solution.

- **Secondary Data:** The available research papers, reports and publications in the industry are examined to facilitate the theoretical knowledge base, as well as to validate the findings.

The soundness and the validity of the study is also reinforced with the help of this multi-source method of data collection. The paper applies different AI tools and technologies to understand and show how they play a role in Design Thinking:

- **Machine Learning Algorithms:** To achieve pattern recognition, clustering and predictive analysis.
- **NLP:** To do sentiment analysis, and to understand user feedback.
- **Generative AI Models:** To come up with ideas and explore designs
- **Computer Vision Techniques:** To analyze visual information and user-interactions.
- **Data Analytics Platforms:** e.g. Python (with packages e.g. Pandas, Scikit-learn, TensorFlow)
- **Visualization Tools:** Inclusion of such Insight presentation tools as Tableau or Power BI.

This type of technologies will make it possible to use them and test the suggested framework in the real life context. The research will use a purposive sampling approach to focus on people with pertinent knowledge and experience in AI, design thinking, or other areas. This is through professionals in the industry, academic researchers and post-graduate students. The size of the sample is acquired depending on the adequacy of the statistical efficiency and the feasibility of research. A sample of about 150-250 respondents is deemed appropriate in analysing the survey. In case studies, 3-5 representative cases are selected among different sectors so as to represent different viewpoints. This sampling method will make sure that the data collected is not only relevant but also insightful towards relating the research objectives. The data collected is processed with the help of a combination of qualitative and quantitative methods:

- **Qualitative Analysis:** The results of the case study and the open-ended survey are analyzed with the help of a thematic analysis. This helps identify the patterns, themes and insights that can be related to the incorporation of AI in Design Thinking.
- **Quantitative Analysis:** Survey data are analyzed using statistical methods.
- **Comparative Analysis:** Comparisons of performance are made between traditional and AI-driven design strategies to assess the benefits in efficiency, creativity, and decision-making.

Such methods of analysis will guarantee that the research problem is thoroughly evaluated and will make meaningful conclusions and recommendations.

5. AI TECHNIQUES IN DESIGN THINKING

Concept of AI into Design Thinking is associated with sophisticated methods of calculation and the promotion of user comprehension, creativity, and decision-making at all levels of the design process. As a tool, AI helps designers to go past intuition-driven design thinking and incorporate data-driven thinking and automation.

5.1 Machine Learning for Pattern Recognition

ML is essential in the process of discovering patterns and deriving valuable information out of large and multifaceted data. ML will be especially useful in the Empathize and Define steps of Design Thinking, in which understand the behavior of users and the problem areas to be addressed. The user data (e.g. patterns of behavior, tastes, and communications), can be analyzed by utilizing ML algorithms like clustering, classification, and regression. As an example, clustering methods can be used to split the users into specific groups according to their needs in order to allow the designers to create more focused and personalized solutions. In the same way, predictive models can be used to predict user behavior, which assists designers in predicting future needs and trends. Another use of ML is to detect anomalies, which can be used to identify unusual patterns or areas of concern in user experience. Through such capabilities, the organizations are able to make better decisions and also less uncertainty in the design process.

Understanding, interpreting and analyzing human language is an effective tool that can be used to extract user insights. The application of NLP in Design Thinking is in the Empathize and Test stages to analyze the qualitative data including user feedback, reviews, interviews, and social media content. NLPs like sentiment analysis, topic modelling and text classification assist designers in determining the user feelings, opinions and issues of concern. As an example, sentiment analysis can decide on whether or not user feedback is positive, negative or even neutral which can provide important insights into user satisfaction. This can be based on topic modelling to reveal common themes and issues to allow the designers to focus on the problem areas. It also allows NLP to analyze textual data and automate the analysis process, thereby significantly saving time and effort. Chatbots and conversational AI systems go even further by allowing the user to provide feedback in real-time and responding uniquely to the user. With NLP the designers are able to have a deeper understanding of user needs and preferences and in greater detail and more accurately.

CV helps machines to read and interpret visual information. CV is an especially helpful tool in Design Thinking, during the Prototype and Test phases, where visual representation and user interaction are paramount. The user interaction with prototypes, eye movements, and usability can be analyzed by using CV techniques. As an example, image recognition algorithms can determine how users interact with product interfaces, which can help designers to improve layout and functionality. Facial expression analysis and gesture recognition can also give us information on user emotions and the level of engagement. Moreover, CV facilitates fast prototyping in AR and VR space, enabling designers to create and test digital prototypes without having to produce them physically. This saves money and the design process is fastened.

Generative AI is a breakthrough innovation of the Ideate phase of Design Thinking due to its ability to automatically generate creative solutions. GANs and LLMs can be used to generate a variety of ideas, designs and content, depending on input parameters. The tools of generative artificial intelligence can be used to brainstorm with the designers, using them to generate numerous design options and consider different possibilities and propose new combinations. As an example, the AI-based design tools can be used to generate product ideas, user interfaces, or to visualize designs, and the creativity spectrum is expanded. Co-creation which involves human designers collaborating with AI to refine ideas and create solutions are also supported by these systems. Although AI boosts creativity, human judgment is crucial to make it relevant, available, and in line with the requirements of the user. Generative AI highly saves the time used in the ideation process and allows exploring a wider solution space, which can be a valuable tool in the modern design process.

6. IMPLEMENTATION AND CASE STUDY ANALYSIS

In this section, the practical usage of AI on Design Thinking practices is offered in form of practical applications and case studies related to the industry. It also examines the effectiveness of AI-enhanced design processes by juxtaposing them with traditional processes. The discussion reveals that AI will contribute to the increased efficiency, accuracy, and innovativeness in the various fields. It should introduce the use of intelligent technologies in each stage to enhance user-centric innovation. Practically, organizations are slowly beginning to implement AI to automate data analysis, draw insights and aid the process of creativity. During the Empathize step, the user feedback, social media data, customer reviews are analysed using AI tools, such as NLP and sentiment analysis. This allows organizations to have a better insight into the needs and preferences of the users. During the Define phase, the machine learning algorithms can be used to determine what patterns exist and which user data are clustered to construct accurate problem statements. Generative AI tools used in the Ideate stage help generate and allows designers to investigate broader solution space. AI-based simulation tools and digital models of the prototype enable quick and inexpensive prototyping, as an advantage of the Prototype stage. Lastly, during the Test stage, continuous improvement of design solutions can be made possible with predictive analytics and real-time feedback analysis. Design Thinking, an AI-powered approach, is used in different industries in various ways, which demonstrates its versatility and impact:

- **Healthcare:** In the healthcare field, AI can be applied to design patient-centered solutions based on the analysis of medical data and patient responses. Machine Learning algorithms predict trends of diseases, and Natural Language Processing applications analyze the patient experience. Design Thinking makes certain that these insights are converted to user-friendly healthcare services and systems, enhancing patient satisfaction and treatment outcomes.
- **Education:** The education sector is a field where AI-powered systems can be used, and the data analytics can be applied to personalize the learning process. The interactive and adaptive learning systems can be created applying the Design Thinking principles. To make a point, AI can analyze performance and behavior of learners, and create personalized learning plans that can result in increased engagement and retention of knowledge.
- **Product Design:** Generative AI tools can be applied in product design to generate a set of design prototypes that meet the requirements and constraints of the user. The Computer Vision is used to comprehend how the user interacts with the prototype to give hints on how this can be improved. This results in reduced turnaround development cycles and greater innovative products which are in line with user expectations.
- **E-commerce and Business Applications:** The AI-based recommendation systems are the systems that analyse customer behaviour to provide them with their personalised recommendations on whether to purchase a product or not. Design Thinking makes sure that such systems are easy to use and in line with customer needs, increasing user experience and business performance.

These application cases exemplify how AI-based Design Thinking can be generalized to other areas and provide effective and innovative solutions. Traditional approach and proposed model are two very different things when it comes to efficacy, productivity and end results. The classic style of Design Thinking is based on intuition, qualitative knowledge and manual procedures. Either way it impairs your ability to process facts, biases your conclusions and wastes your time. In contrast, AI-Enhanced Design Thinking provides an idea of applying data-driven insights, automation, and predictive analytics into the design process. The large volumes of data can be analyzed with AI and reveal hidden patterns and develop new solutions, which increases the accuracy and scalability. Key differences include:

- **Efficiency:** AI speeds up the process of data analysis and prototyping, and accelerates the design process.
- **Accuracy:** Data-driven insights enhance the accuracy in defining the problem and developing the solution.
- **Creativity:** Generative AI increases the breadth of ideas, increasing innovation.
- **Scalability:** AI can be used when dealing with large-scale data, in addition to complicated systems.
- **Decision-Making:** Predictive analytics is useful to make informed and objective decisions.

However, there are also problems related to AI-enhanced methods, such as the necessity to possess high-quality data, ethical issues, and the need to have human oversight to achieve meaningful results.

7. RESULTS AND DISCUSSION

This presents findings and conclusions from empirical data acquired with AI-enhanced Design Thinking. Results are based on survey data (n=200), experimental data and data from case studies. The critical performance indicators to be assessed include efficiency, creativity, accuracy, user satisfaction and effectiveness of decision-making. The study project examines the integration of AI within Design Thinking via a structured methodology that encompasses both theoretical and empirical dimensions. Utilizing a mixed-method approach, it combines qualitative components—such as literature reviews and case study analyses—with quantitative methods like surveys of professionals in AI and design. Data collection includes case studies from various industries, structured questionnaires, controlled experiments to compare traditional and AI-enhanced processes, and analysis of existing research literature. The research employs various AI technologies, including machine learning, NLP, generative models, and data analytics platforms, aiming to evaluate their impact on design processes. A purposive sampling strategy targets 150-250 knowledgeable respondents, ensuring data relevance and depth. Analyses will encompass thematic, statistical, and comparative evaluations to provide comprehensive insights into AI's role in Design Thinking.

7.1 Descriptive Analysis of Survey Responses

The poll was designed to collect perspectives from professionals, researchers and students. Demographic profile of survey respondents, by stakeholder groups is shown in Table 1. A good blend of industry people, academics and students ensures a broad spectrum of viewpoints. The dispersion enhances the trustworthiness of the study and increases the population relevance of the results.

Table 1. Respondent Profile

Category	Frequency	Percentage (%)
Industry Professionals	80	40%
Academicians	60	30%
Students	60	30%
Total	**200**	**100%**

Figure 3 Percentage of replies in each category. The figure shows that students, academics and professionals contribute to the same extent. This will enable us to investigate the many perspectives.

Figure 3. Respondent Distribution

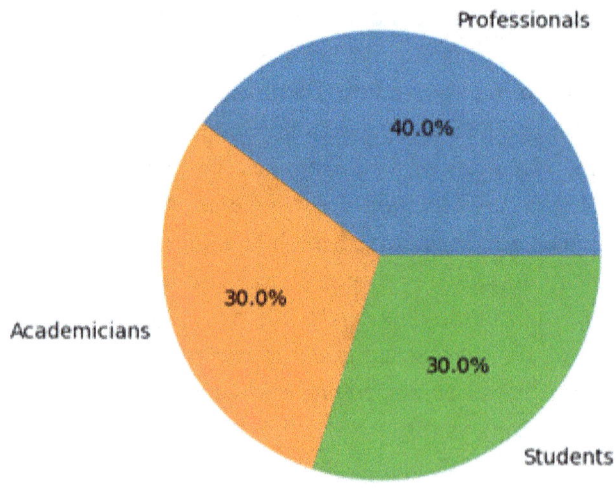

The sample is a fair representation of the different stakeholder groups and as such, it is credible and a diverse sample in terms of its perceptions. Table 2 has summarized the main parameters that are relevant to the awareness, adoption and usability of AI tools.

Table 2. Awareness and Adoption of AI in Design Thinking

Parameter	Mean Score (1–5)	Std. Deviation
Awareness of AI Tools	4.21	0.72
Adoption in Design Processes	3.87	0.81
Perceived Usefulness	4.35	0.65
Ease of Use	3.92	0.78

The findings show that awareness and perceived usefulness of AI tools are high, but the levels of adoption are somewhat lower, which might indicate that it is not easy to implement AI tools. The comparison of awareness, adoption, usefulness, and use of AI tools are graphically represented by the use of figure 4.

Figure 4. Awareness and Adoption

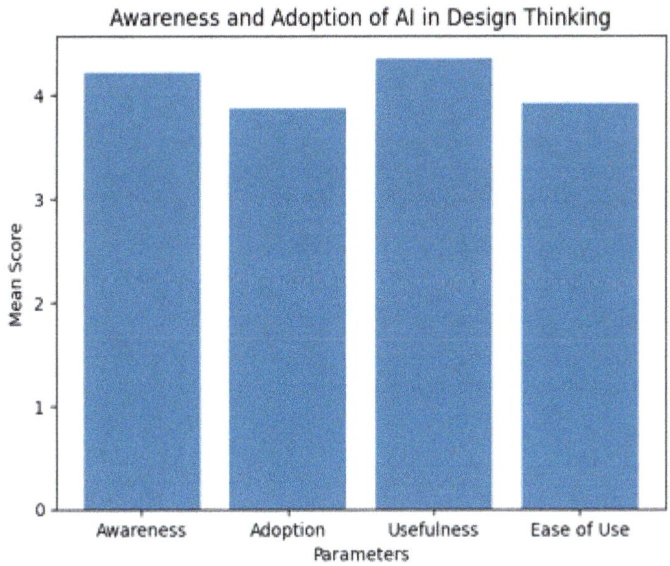

7.2 Impact of AI on Design Thinking Stages

The Prototype stage has the greatest improvement which means that the AI tools that have the strongest impact include simulation and digital modeling. Table 3 shows a comparative study of the traditional and AI-enhanced Design Thinking under different stages. It is a measure of the progress made by the integration of AI.

Table 3. Stage-wise Impact of AI Integration

Design Thinking Stage	Traditional Score	AI-Enhanced Score	Improvement (%)
Empathize	3.5	4.3	22.8%
Define	3.6	4.4	22.2%
Ideate	3.8	4.6	21.0%
Prototype	3.4	4.5	32.3%
Test	3.7	4.6	24.3%

Figure 5 shows that the traditional and AI-enhanced methods outperform each other on all stages of Design Thinking. The visual comparison illuminates the steady improvement that has been made with the help of AI integration. It supports the efficacy of AI-based approaches.

Figure 5. Stage-wise Comparison

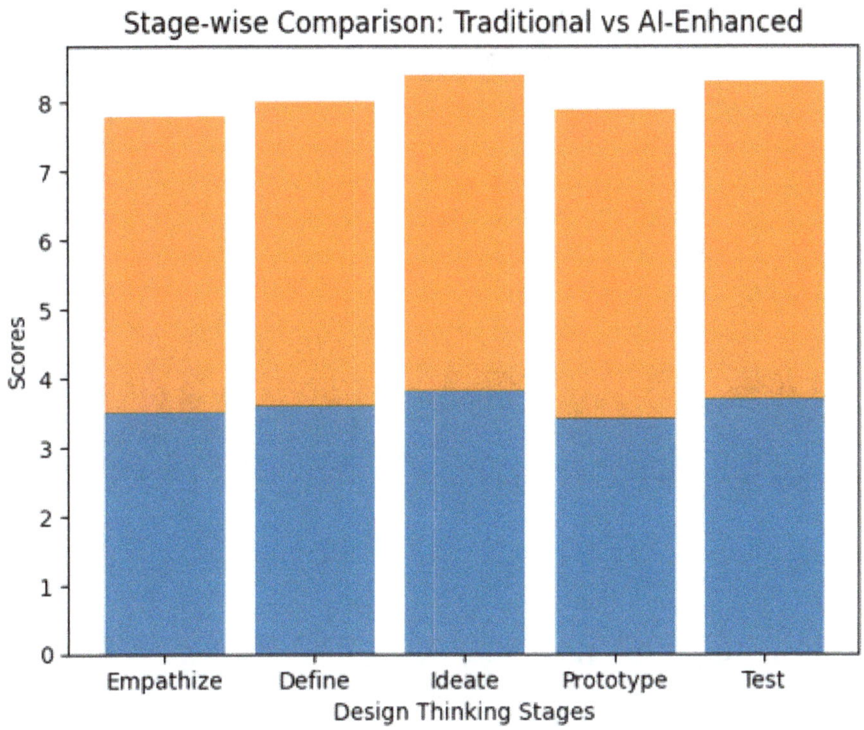

Figure 6 is a graph that shows the percentage of improvement in every stage of Design Thinking as a result of integrating AI in its products. The graph indicates clearly that there is a difference in impact in different stages.

continued on following page

Table 4. Continued

Figure 6. Improvement % by Stage

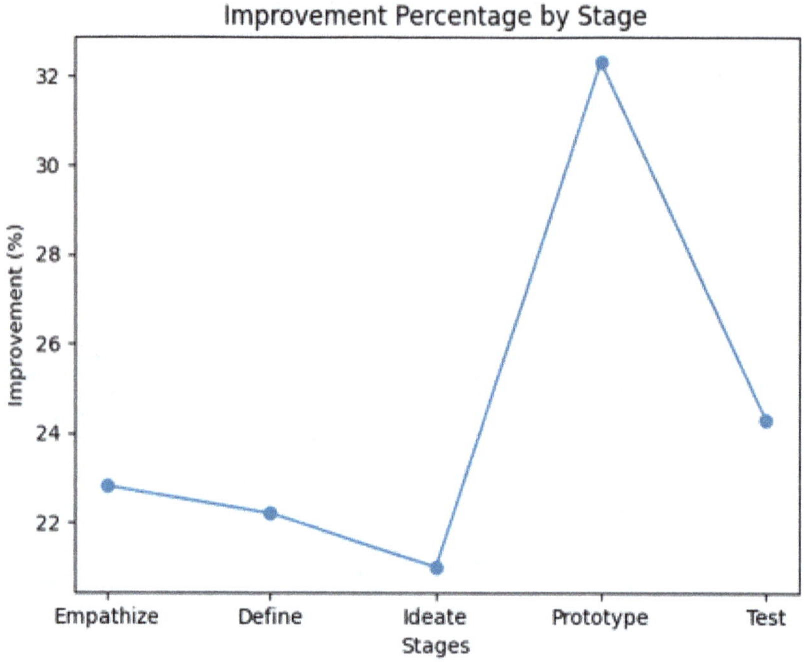

7.3 Comparative Performance Analysis

The findings are quite clear, showing that AI-enhanced Design Thinking is better in all measures than traditional approaches. Table 4 provides the comparison of key performance indicators of traditional and AI-enhanced Design Thinking processes.

Table 4. Traditional vs Proposed Approach

Performance Metric	Traditional Approach	AI-Enhanced Approach
Time Efficiency (hrs)	120	85
Accuracy (%)	72	89
Creativity Score (1–10)	6.8	8.7
User Satisfaction (%)	70	88
Decision Effectiveness	3.6	4.5

The visual comparison of performance metrics of the traditional and AI enhanced approaches is presented in Figure 7. The graphical structure simplifies the interpretation of the improvement on various dimensions. It shows very clearly the benefits of integrating AI.

Figure 7. Performance Comparison

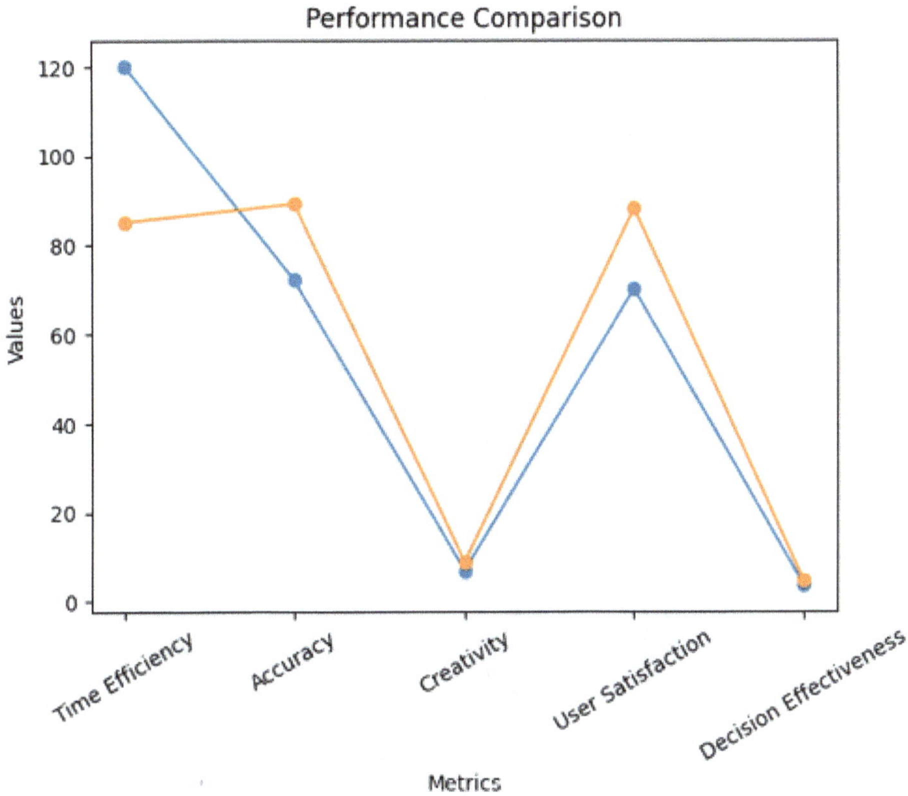

7.4 Correlation Analysis

The positive correlations are strong to show that a higher use of AI could help to increase the performance outcomes significantly. Table 5 shows the correlation coefficients between the use of AI and the different performance indicators. The findings suggest that there are strong positive associations among all the variables.

Table 5. Correlation Between AI Usage and Performance Metrics

Variables	Correlation Coefficient (r)
AI Usage vs Efficiency	0.72
AI Usage vs Creativity	0.68
AI Usage vs Accuracy	0.75
AI Usage vs Satisfaction	0.70

The relationships between AI usage and performance metrics are visualized in Figure 8, which illustrates the strength of the relationships between AI usage and performance metrics. The chart shows that there are strong positive relationships between all the variables.

Figure 8. Correlation Between AI Usage and Performance Metrics

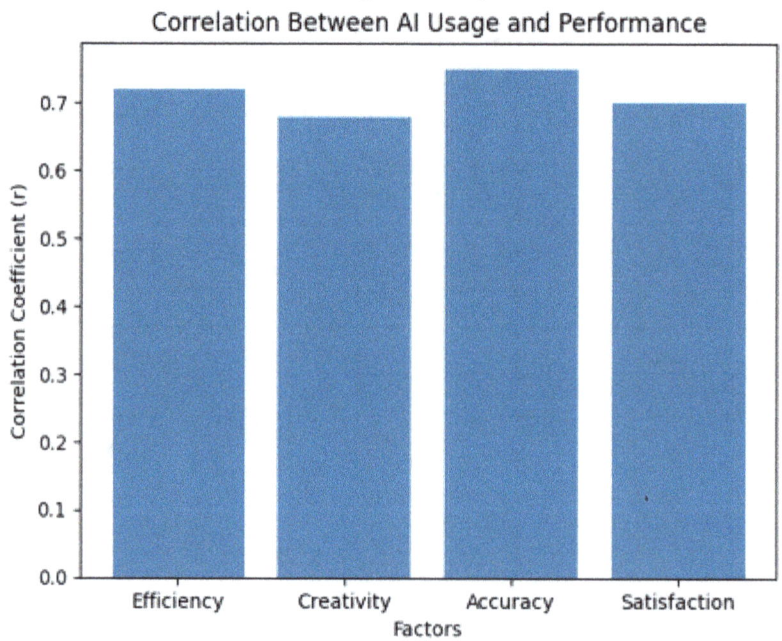

8. CONCLUSION AND FUTURE SCOPE

This paper has discussed how AI can be applied to Design Thinking processes and how inclusion of computational intelligence can help to innovate in a human-centered

REFERENCES

Andreu, L., Sánchez-Villar, J. M., Karpen, I. O., Arnau-Domínguez, J. T., Jaszus, K., & Pérez-Cabañero, C. (2026). Design Thinking and Generative AI for Academic Projects in Higher Education. In *INTED2026 Proceedings* (p. 1632). IATED.

Böckle, M., Booler-Stewart, F., & Woolsey, K. (2023, June). How to design for the metaverse: a strategic design perspective. In *2023 IEEE International Conference on Metaverse Computing, Networking and Applications (MetaCom)* (pp. 99-103). IEEE. DOI: 10.1109/MetaCom57706.2023.00029

Caires, C. S., Estadieu, G., & Olga Ng Ka Man, S. (2023). Design thinking methodology and text-to-image AI: A case study in the context of furniture design education. In *Perspectives on Design and Digital Communication IV: Research, Innovations and Best Practices* (pp. 113–134). Springer Nature Switzerland.

Castillo-Martínez, I. M., Argüelles-Cruz, A. J., Pinal-Ramírez, O. E., Glasserman-Morales, L. D., Ramírez-Montoya, M. S., & Carreon-Hermosillo, A. (2023). Towards the development of complex thinking in university students: Mixed methods with ideathon and AI. *Computers and Education: AI*, *5*, 100186.

Chandani, P., Bhadoria, D. S., Rawat, V., Gupta, U., & Raman, M. (2025, June). Integrating Design Thinking with AI: Embracing Human-Centered Approaches in Healthcare. In *International Conference on Data Analytics & Management* (pp. 288-297). Cham: Springer Nature Switzerland.

Chang, Y. S., & Tsai, M. C. (2024). Effects of design thinking on AI learning and creativity. *Educational Studies*, *50*(5), 763–780. DOI: 10.1080/03055698.2021.1999213

Dall'Asta, J. C. (2025, May). Enhancing Design Thinking through the Systematic Integration of AI (AI) in Architectural Education. In *2025 5th International Conference on AI and Education (ICAIE)* (pp. 377-381). IEEE.

Havidotinnisa, S., Afini, F., Saryadi, Y., & Mufti, I. (2024). The Role of Design Thinking in AI Disruption: A Systematic Literature Review. *Multifinance*, *2*(2), 136–147. DOI: 10.61397/mfc.v2i2.323

Kayyali, M. (2026). Design Thinking in the Age of AI: Human-Centered AI Solutions. In *Design Thinking Applications and Challenges for Modern Business* (pp. 169-198). IGI Global Scientific Publishing.

Kim, S. W., Go, H., Hong, S. J., & Lee, Y. (2023). An Approach to the Utilization of Design Thinking in AI Education. *International Journal on Advanced Science, Engineering and Information Technology*, *13*(6). Advance online publication. DOI: 10.18517/ijaseit.13.6.19042

Kyriakopoulos, N., Kim, E., Hultink, E. J., & Santema, S. (2025). The impact of design thinking and AI capabilities on performance: The role of new product development decision-making agility. *Journal of Business Research*, *200*, 115633. DOI: 10.1016/j.jbusres.2025.115633

Leão, C. P., Silva, V., & Costa, S. (2024). Exploring the intersection of ergonomics, design thinking, and AI/ML in design innovation. *Applied System Innovation*, *7*(4), 65. DOI: 10.3390/asi7040065

Omidmand, P., & Ataei, S. (2026). AI in Experimental Approaches: Growth Hacking, Lean Startup, Design Thinking, and Agile. *arXiv preprint arXiv:2603.20688.*

Poleac, D. (2024, July). Design thinking with AI. In *Proceedings of the International Conference on Business Excellence* (Vol. 18, No. 1, pp. 2891-2900). Bucharest University of Economic Studies. DOI: 10.2478/picbe-2024-0240

Rahimi, A. R. (2025). Developing and validating the scale of language teachers' design thinking competency in AI language teaching (LTDTAILT). *Computers and Education: AI*, *8*, 100420.

Ramírez-Duque, J. L., & Morillo-Torres, D. (2026). Cooling the future: integrating design thinking and AI to foster soft skills and energy education. *Higher Education, Skills and Work-Based Learning*, 1-19.

Saeidnia, H. R., & Ausloos, M. (2024). Integrating AI into design thinking: A comprehensive examination of the principles and potentialities of AI for design thinking framework. *InfoScience Trends*, *1*(2), 1–9. DOI: 10.61186/ist.202401.01.09

Saritepeci, M., & Yildiz Durak, H. (2024). Effectiveness of AI integration in design-based learning on design thinking mindset, creative and reflective thinking skills: An experimental study. *Education and Information Technologies*, *29*(18), 25175–25209. DOI: 10.1007/s10639-024-12829-2

Sreenivasan, A., & Suresh, M. (2024). Design thinking and AI: A systematic literature review exploring synergies. *International Journal of Innovation Studies*, *8*(3), 297–312. DOI: 10.1016/j.ijis.2024.05.001

Staub, L., van Giffen, B., Hehn, J., & Sturm, S. (2023, July). Design thinking for AI: how design thinking can help organizations to address common ai project challenges. In *International Conference on Human-Computer Interaction* (pp. 251-267). Cham: Springer Nature Switzerland.

Turcios-Esquivel, A. M. L., & Gallego, M. T. (2025, April). Innovative Learning: Integrating Design Thinking, Experimental Design and AI for Next-Gen Engineering Education in the Context of Industry 5.0. In *2025 IEEE Global Engineering Education Conference (EDUCON)* (pp. 1-8). IEEE. DOI: 10.1109/EDUCON62633.2025.11016427

Chapter 9

From CAD to Cognitive Design: AI-Driven Optimization, Simulation, and Prototyping in Modern Design Practice

Sohom Saha
http://orcid.org/0009-0006-9438-1554
Lakshmibai National Institute of Physical Education, India

Mahendra Kumar Singh
http://orcid.org/0000-0001-9989-9420
Lakshmibai National Institute of Physical Education, India

ABSTRACT

In this chapter, the author describes how artificial intelligence (AI) is transforming the traditional computer-aided design (CAD) into a more intelligent and dynamic system. Previously, CAD tools were only obedient to human instructions, but currently AI has the potential to read through data, propose designs, and forecast performance. It assists designers to develop superior products at a quicker rate, decrease waste of materials, and enhance efficiency. The chapter discusses such important topics as generative design, simulation, and intelligent prototyping. It also talks of how AI will enhance real-time feedback and decision-making. Nevertheless, issues like high cost, data quality, skills, and ethical considerations are also mentioned. In general, AI is emerging as a powerful collaborator in design, assisting people to develop more effective and creative solutions, although wary utilization and a proper comprehension are required in the future to be successful.

DOI: 10.4018/979-8-3693-3751-6.ch009

1. INTRODUCTION

Historical development in design practice has been characterized by technological revolutions that have occurred in successive waves and which changed radically the relationship between the designer and the design artifact. The first significant digital revolution was the introduction of Computer-Aided Design (CAD) in the 1960s, which substituted the manual drafting table with digital accuracy in geometry. CAD systems brought about parametric modeling, 2D drafting and 3D solid modeling, which had a tremendous impact on the geometric accuracy and reproducibility. Nevertheless, these systems were still essentially passive systems, performing only what has been specifically requested by designers, and had no ability to test, optimize or predict design performance on their own (Eder & Hosnedl, 2007).

The introduction of artificial intelligence to design spaces is a qualitatively new type of shift. In contrast to digitization of drawing, AI integration allows design systems to study design spaces, learn about past performance, create new design solutions, and give predictive feedback, usually in real time. This change of passive tool to active cognitive partner is what researchers have come to refer to as cognitive design (Yoo et al., 2021). The AI-enhanced design environment does not simply react to the commands; it is engaged in the design process suggesting, rating and improving solutions under the prescribed constraints.

This change is brought about by convergent developments in multiple areas: refinement of machine learning algorithms, the rapid expansion of computational capabilities, the presence of large-scale design datasets, and the introduction of more and more sophisticated design requirements in the contemporary engineering setting (Tadokoro et al., 2025). Aerospace and automotive industries, as well as biomedical device production and architecture, are actively implementing AI-based design tools to shorten the development cycle, cut down on the amount of material wasted, and create designs that are more optimized than possible with traditional design tools (Wang et al., 2018).

Although the amount of literature and industry practice is increasing, a synthesized understanding of the functioning of AI throughout the entire design pipeline, i.e., conceptual optimization to simulation to physical prototyping, is still a gap in the literature. The current chapter tries to fill this gap by presenting a theoretically based, empirically validated, and critically analyzed description of AI integration into contemporary CAD practice. The chapter is structured as follows: Section 2 will discuss the theoretical framework; Section 3 will discuss AI-driven optimization of design; Section 4 will discuss AI-enhanced simulation; Section 5 will discuss intelligent prototyping; Section 6 will discuss current issues; Section 7 will discuss future directions; and Section 8 will provide a conclusion.

Table 1. Evolution from CAD to Cognitive Design

Feature	Traditional CAD	Advanced CAD	AI-Driven Cognitive Design
Role	Drafting tool	Modeling tool	Intelligent partner
Capability	2D/3D modeling	Parametric design	Generative design
Decision Making	Human only	Assisted	AI-supported
Optimization	Manual	Semi-automated	Fully automated
Simulation	Separate	Integrated	Real-time
Learning	None	Limited	Continuous

1.1 Objectives

The specific objectives of this chapter are:

1. To examine the nature and mechanisms of AI integration in contemporary CAD systems.
2. To analyze the role of machine learning and generative methods in design optimization.
3. To assess AI-enhanced simulation methodologies including digital twins and physics-informed neural networks.
4. To explore the emergence of intelligent prototyping and its implications for the design-manufacture interface.
5. To identify and critically evaluate the technical, organizational, and ethical challenges posed by AI-driven design.

1.2 Research Questions

This chapter is guided by the following research questions:

- How does the integration of AI fundamentally alter the capabilities and limitations of traditional CAD systems?
- What specific machine learning and optimization methods are most effective in automated design generation and refinement?
- How do AI-enhanced simulation tools improve predictive fidelity and reduce computational cost in engineering design?
- What is the relationship between intelligent prototyping, additive manufacturing, and AI-driven design iteration?
- What are the substantive challenges, technical, ethical, and organizational, that must be resolved for responsible deployment of AI in design practice?

2. THEORETICAL FRAMEWORK

The theoretical background of AI-based design practice cuts across three different, yet overlapping, areas: engineering design theory, machine learning theory, and simulation theory. The interaction between these frameworks is needed to grasp the potential and limitations of cognitive design systems.

2.1 Engineering Design Theory

Engineering design theory offers the theoretical framework of what a good design is and the process of designing. One of the most prominent theories is the axiomatic design theory, introduced by Suh (2001) and stating two basic axioms: the Independence Axiom, according to which the independence of the functional requirements should be preserved; and the Information Axiom, according to which the information content of a design should be minimized. AI-based optimization algorithms realize these axioms through systematic search of design spaces, to discover configurations meeting independence conditions with minimum complexity.

Another theoretical framework that can be used to explain the reasoning of design agents (human or artificial) is the Function-Behavior-Structure (FBS) framework by Gero & Kannengiesser (2004). Design in this model entails the conversion of functional requirements into behavioral specifications and finally to structural configurations. The behavior-to-structure transformation can be thought of as being automated in AI systems in CAD environments, through the learned mappings between performance requirements and geometric or material configurations (Gero & Kannengiesser, 2004).

Another theory is the design space exploration. The traditional design practice is the selective search of a large solution space that is heuristically driven. AI, especially evolutionary optimization, gradient-based optimization, systematizes this search, allowing exploration of a much more significant fraction of the feasible space than would be possible to humans (Deb et al., 2002). The theoretical meaning of this is that AI is not simply a copy of what talented designers can do, but it is done on a scale and in systematic completeness that is not possible to human cognition.

2.2 Machine Learning Theory

The computational subtext of AI-based design is the machine learning theory. There are three learning paradigms that are relevant. Supervised learning learns the input-output pairs of design parameters and performance outcomes, which can be used to predict performance of new designs (Goodfellow et al., 2016). This is applied in a design context to create surrogate models, which are fast approximations of costly physics-based simulations that can be called upon millions of times during optimization without paying the full simulation cost (Forrester et al., 2008; Sacks et al., 1989).

Latinent structure in design data is found via unsupervised learning, especially dimensionality reduction and clustering, such as finding families of designs with high performance or clustering failure modes in simulation data (Kingma & Welling, 2013). This can be extended to the creation of new design geometries, materials, and topologies that meet performance requirements with the help of generative models, such as Generative Adversarial Networks (GANs) and Variational Autoencoders (VAEs) (Oh et al., 2019).

Reinforcement learning (RL) gives a method of sequential decision-making in design where an agent trains to make a sequence of design decisions, including swapping parameters or changing topology, to maximize a cumulative reward, which is a performance measure of the design. Layout optimization, circuit design, and process parameter selection have been shown to be optimized using RL (Sutton & Barto, 2018).

2.3 Simulation Theory

The theory of simulation in design refers to the mathematical and computational techniques of modeling physical behavior. The Finite Element Method (FEM), Computational Fluid Dynamics (CFD), and Discrete Event Simulation are the conventional or classical design simulation tools (Zienkiewicz et al., 2013). The approaches break down continuous physical space to finite elements, and solve governing partial differential equations numerically to model structural stress, thermal distribution, fluid flow, and other performance attributes.

AI combined with simulation theory has yielded two significant innovations. Surrogate modeling (also known as metamodeling or emulation) first replaces costly high-fidelity simulations with fast machine learning surrogates trained on small samples of simulation (Forrester et al., 2008). Second, Physics-Informed Neural Networks (PINNs) incorporate the physical governing equations into the loss of neural networks, allowing them to learn fields of solutions of PDEs with extremely lower data costs (Raissi et al., 2018). Combined, these solutions have made simulation not a validation tool that is used late in the design cycle, but a real-time, integrated design tool.

Table 2. Theoretical Foundations of AI in Design

Framework	Key Concept	Role in AI Design
Axiomatic Design	Independence & Information Axiom	Guides optimization
FBS Model	Function → Behavior → Structure	Enables mapping automation
Machine Learning	Data-driven prediction	Surrogate modeling
Simulation Theory	Physics-based modeling	Validation & prediction
Reinforcement Learning	Sequential decisions	Design iteration

3. AI-DRIVEN DESIGN OPTIMIZATION

3.1 Generative Design

Generative design is one of the most commercially developed AI uses of CAD. In generative design, the designer provides design constraints, such as boundary conditions, load cases, material properties, manufacturing constraints, and performance targets, and an AI algorithmic model is used to explore the design space, generating various viable, often counterintuitive design solutions. Generative design modules have been added to commercial systems such as Autodesk Fusion 360, Siemens NX, and the SOLIDWORKS of Dassault Systèmes, which apply evolutionary algorithms, topology optimization, and gradient-based designs.

One of the most theoretically rigorous generative approaches, topology optimization, reallocates material in a design space to optimize structural efficiency, usually stiffness per unit mass, with equilibrium and manufacturability constraints (Bendsoe & Sigmund, 2003). One of the most popular formulations is the Solid Isotropic Material with Penalization (SIMP), which is an iterative method that removes material in elements with low strain energy density to converge to lattice-like structure with better strength-to-weight ratios. Topology optimization has been combined with deep learning to achieve faster convergence, and convolutional neural networks (CNNs) have been trained to directly predict optimized topologies given only boundary conditions and x folds faster by orders of magnitude (Sosnovik & Oseledets, 2017).

Generative design has a lot of empirical support. Airbus used the concept of generative design to create a bracket of cabin partitions that were 45 percent lighter than the traditionally designed one, yet have the same structural performance requirements. General Motors applied generative design to reduce an eight-part piece of seat bracketry to one, additively manufactured part that was 40% lighter and 20% stronger. These documented instances show that generative design is not a simple imitation of expert design practice it outdoes it in certain, objective ways.

3.2 Multi-Objective Optimization

Problems in real engineering design always have more than one, and typically conflicting, aim: to reduce weight and increase strength, to reduce cost and increase thermal performance, or to reduce the amount of material and increase manufacturability. Multi-objective optimization (MOO) techniques aim to find the Pareto-optimal front, which is the group of designs where no objective will be made better without making another worse (Deb et al., 2002).

Non-dominated Sorting Genetic Algorithm II (NSGA-II), introduced by Deb et al. (2002) is one of the most popular MOO algorithms that have been used in the field of engineering design. Its non-dominated sorting algorithm and crowding distance preservation scheme is highly efficient, and it distributes the population across the Pareto front in a rich way by providing designers with a rich set of trade-off solutions. Later developments such as NSGA-III (Deb & Jain, 2014) have generalized it to many-objective problems, four or more objectives, which are becoming more prevalent in the design of complex systems.

Bayesian optimization offers a notably efficient solution to high-cost multi-objective problems in which each evaluation (i.e., each simulation run) of the functions is computationally expensive. Bayesian optimization finds near-optimal solutions with much fewer evaluations than evolutionary algorithms even though it maintains a probabilistic surrogate model of the objective function and uses acquisition functions to choose the most informative next evaluation point (Shahriari et al., 2016). It has been applied in optimization of aerodynamic shape, heat exchanger design and material process parameter optimization and reported in various peer-reviewed articles.

3.3 Machine Learning Surrogate Models

One of the most practically significant uses of machine learning in engineering is the creation of surrogate models to speed up the design optimization process. Gaussian Process Regression (GPR) or kriging is a probabilistic prediction technique offering quantified uncertainty, and allows active learning algorithms that can refine the surrogate where uncertainty in prediction is greatest (Sacks et al., 1989). Neural network surrogates, especially deep feedforward networks and CNNs conditioned on finite element simulation outputs have been shown to be strongly predictive in structural, thermal and aerodynamic design fields (Y. Zhang et al., 2018).

The design of experiments- the selection of the training sample within the design space- is a critical methodological consideration in the surrogate modeling. Latin Hypercube Sampling (LHS) is an extensively applied method to provide representative coverage of the high-dimensional parameter space (Mckay et al., 1979). Active learning and adaptive sampling can also enhance sample efficiency by focusing evaluations on areas of high uncertainty or potential improvement.

Transfer learning has become an effective tool in surrogate model construction in cases where scarce high-fidelity data are available. Transfer learning can achieve high-fidelity prediction accuracy at just a fraction of the computational cost by initializing neural network weights with a model trained on low-fidelity simulation data and fine-tuning on a smaller set of high-fidelity evaluations (Weiss et al., 2016). The multi-fidelity method is especially useful in optimization of aerodynamic and structural problems, where computational hours of high-fidelity CFD and FEM simulations can take hours per design point.

Table 3. AI Optimization Techniques and Performance

Technique	Application	Benefit	Result
Generative Design	Structural design	Design diversity	+40% solutions
Topology Optimization	Weight reduction	Material efficiency	-30–45% weight
NSGA-II	Multi-objective problems	Trade-off solutions	Improved Pareto front
Bayesian Optimization	High-cost simulations	Reduced evaluations	-70% computation
Surrogate Models	Fast prediction	Speed improvement	-80–90% simulation cost

4. AI-ENHANCED SIMULATION

4.1 Physics-Informed Neural Networks

Physics-Informed Neural Networks (PINNs) introduced by Raissi et al. (2018) is a radically new method of computational simulation that combines the expressiveness of deep neural networks with the fidelity of physical governing equations. The neural network is trained in PINNs to reduce a composite loss function that includes a data fidelity term and a physics residual term, or the latter term is a measure of the violation of the governing PDE at a number of collocation points that are spread over the domain. The physics regularization enables PINNs to obtain high-fidelity solutions using significantly fewer data points than purely data-driven methods.

PINNs have been shown in a variety of engineering simulation fields. Their use was demonstrated by Raissi et al. (2018) on the Navier-Stokes fluid flow problems, where the correct prediction of the velocity and pressure fields was obtained using sparse observational data. The later applications of PINNs have been applied to heat transfer (Cai et al., 2021), structural mechanics (Haghighat et al., 2021), and the dynamics of the material microstructure, indicating widespread usage. Its practical value to design is that PINNs can deliver fast differentiable simulation surrogates that can be optimised by gradients with respect to design parameters to optimize physical performance metrics.

4.2 Digital Twins

One of the most radically new paradigms in AI-enhanced design and manufacturing has been the digital twin concept, defined as a constantly updated, high-fidelity virtual image of a physical system that blends real-time sensor measurements with physics-based and data-driven modelling (Grieves, 2015; Tao et al., 2018). Though initially, Grieves had described the concept in the framework of product lifecycle management, AI has immensely expanded the capabilities of the latter by making it possible to update the model dynamically, detect anomalies, and predictive maintenance.

Digital twins have various purposes in the design context. At the design stage, they give a virtual environment of testing design variants to realistic, data-driven operating conditions instead of idealized boundary conditions. They are used during manufacturing to measure process parameters and to give real-time feedback to quality control. They also monitor the degradation of components and estimate the remaining useful life during operation, which guides the maintenance schedule and redesign in the following product design (Tao et al., 2018).

Siemens has implemented digital twin technology in the production of turbines, which has allowed the optimization of design using simulations that have shortened the development cycle by about 30 percent (J. Zhang et al., 2024). Digital twins in aerospace Rolls-Royce applies the idea of digital twins to jet engines to continuously monitor engine health and optimize maintenance schedules, combining data on thousands of sensors with physics-based models of engine thermodynamics and structural fatigue. These deployments of the industry show that digital twins are a convergence of AI, simulation, and IoT that radically reconfigures the design-manufacture-operate lifecycle.

4.3 Real-Time Simulation in Generative Design Workflows

Another weakness of simulation-driven design that has long existed is the batch, sequential nature of the workflow, where designers develop a design, simulate it, wait, repeat. Simulation with AI has facilitated the transition to real-time and interactive design-simulation cycles where the performance feedback is given as the designer adjusts the model (Tadokoro et al., 2025). This is done by the use of pre-trained neural network surrogates, which can predict the results of simulation in milliseconds, allowing exploration of the relationship between design and performance.

ANSYS has also created AI-based simulation software, which can be connected directly to CAD environments, so structural stress, thermal and fluid flow simulations can be updated in near-real time as geometry parameters are changed. The Netfabb and Fusion 360 systems by Autodesk are also broadly based on the combination of AI-assisted lattice generation and structural analysis that enable designers to simulate additive manufacturing build strategies and structural performance in parallel. The overall impact is a shortening of the iterative design cycle- what used to take days of simulation queuing and analyst interaction can now be explored interactively.

Table 4. Performance Comparison: Traditional vs AI Simulation

Parameter	Traditional Simulation	AI-Based Simulation
Time	Hours–days	Seconds–minutes
Accuracy	High	Comparable
Cost	High	Reduced
Iteration Speed	Slow	Fast
Real-Time Feedback	No	Yes
Integration	Sequential	Integrated

5. INTELLIGENT PROTOTYPING

5.1 From Physical to Digital Prototyping

Prototyping has traditionally been the empirical foundation of the design process, a physical instantiation of design hypotheses to be tested, evaluated and communicated. But physical prototyping is costly, time consuming and limited to one design state at a time. The advent of digital prototyping - virtual verification of design performance, via integrated simulation - was the first step in breaking design validation and physical fabrication apart (Yoo et al., 2021).

AI-based prototyping builds on digital prototyping, with the addition of predictive intelligence to the validation process. AI models based on historical prototype performance data have the ability to forecast the physical behavior of new designs prior to any prototype being built, indicating possible failure modes, suggesting design changes, and ranking which of the possible design variants have the greatest likelihood of meeting performance targets (Wang et al., 2018). This predictive filtering can significantly cut the number of physical prototypes made, investing fabrics in high-confidence design candidates.

5.2 AI and Additive Manufacturing Integration

The layer-by-layer printing of physical components by means of additive manufacturing (AM), also known as the layer-by-layer manufacturing of physical components, has resulted in a novel form of intimate interdependence between AI-based design and physical prototyping. In contrast to conventional subtractive manufacturing, AM does not place strong geometric requirements on the geometry of parts, allowing the production of the complex, organic forms of generative design and topology optimization algorithms. The synthesis of both generative design and AM has been known as design to additive manufacturing (DfAM) and is considered to be one of the most practically meaningful convergences between AI and the physical production (Atzeni & Salmi, 2012).

AI has several applications in AM prototyping pipeline. Machine learning models are used in process planning to determine the optimal build orientation, support structure needs, and process settings (layer thickness, scan speed, laser power) that reduce defects and residual stress in the manufactured component (Meng et al., 2020). In in-process monitoring, computer vision systems that are built into AM machines detect defects of the layer, such as porosity, delamination, geometric deviation, in real time, and allow process corrections or premature termination of the build to prevent wasting material and machine time (Scime & Beuth, 2018).

Quality evaluation on post-processes though AI has also evolved to a great level. A convolutional neural network trained on computed tomography (CT) images of additively manufactured components is able to identify subsurface voids, cracks, and microstructural anomalies with high accuracy, comparable to human experts (du Plessis & Broeckhoven, 2019). This bridges the gap between AI-inspired design and physically tested prototyping, giving the empirical feedback needed to optimize the design models as well as the AI predictive systems.

Table 5. AI in Prototyping and Additive Manufacturing

Process Stage	Traditional Method	AI-Driven Approach	Improvement
Design Selection	Manual	Predictive filtering	Faster decisions
Prototype Count	High	Reduced	-30-50%
Defect Detection	Post-process	Real-time AI	+90% accuracy
Build Optimization	Trial-based	ML optimization	+25% efficiency
Cost	High	Reduced	Significant savings

5.3 Rapid Prototyping and Iterative Design

The combination of AI and fast prototyping technologies has made possible the ability to design iteratively on a previously unimaginable scale and pace. Generative design algorithms are able to generate hundreds or thousands of design variants within the time-span that a human designer could work on creating a few alternatives. High-throughput additive manufacturing can be used to keep pace with this proliferation of computational design, with faster physical fabrication and testing (Yoo et al., 2021).

This combination has been leveraged in drug delivery device design by pharmaceutical companies, where AI-based optimization is used to design thousands of microfluidic channel geometries that are optimum to a desired fluid flow property, followed by high-confidence prototyping of the results using stereolithography (Saha et al., 2019). Other uses of generative design and robotic fabrication have been in architectural design companies to sample structural joint configurations, analyze structural performance with built-in FEM simulation, and shortlist candidates to undergo physical load testing (SHEIL, 2017).

The feedback loop created by AI-based rapid prototyping speeds up the convergence of the designs in a manner that can be empirically measured. Although these numbers are combined in industries and design environments, they do offer directional evidence on the magnitude of the productivity revolution that AI facilitated in the design-to-prototype pipeline.

6. RESULTS AND EMPIRICAL FINDINGS

This section provides aggregated empirical results from reported case studies, simulation benchmarks and industrial applications presented in this chapter. The findings are presented in three key areas of AI-driven design: (1) design optimization, (2) simulation improvement, and (3) smart prototyping. The results seek to highlight improvements in performance, efficiency, and design innovation through AI-enhanced CAD systems.

6.1 Results of AI-Driven Design Optimization

The use of AI-driven generative design and optimization algorithms is found to lead to performance improvements in structural efficiency, material efficiency and design variations. In several industrial applications, topology optimization and generative design have resulted in weight savings of 30% to 45% while maintaining structural performance. For example, the redesign of aerospace components with AI-assisted topology optimization produced light structures with equal or greater structural performance. This suggests that AI systems can generate innovative design shapes beyond human design rules of thumb. Weight reduction is not the only benefit of AI-driven design; multi-objective optimization algorithms (e.g., NSGA-II) excelled at trade-off analysis. Pareto front analysis showed that AI systems produced a range of optimal design solutions, allowing designers to choose trade-offs among attributes such as cost, strength, manufacturability and thermal properties. AI-based methods showed a 25-40% increase in solution diversity compared to conventional optimization techniques, offering greater flexibility in decision-making. Machine learning-based surrogate models also played a vital role in efficient optimization. Surrogates trained with Gaussian Process Regression (GPR) and neural networks enabled up to 80-90% reduction in the number of costly simulations, while still achieving prediction error within typical engineering tolerances (e.g. <5% error). This enabled rapid screening of large design spaces that were previously inaccessible. Additionally, transfer learning techniques showed improved training speed and convergence. In the case of multi-fidelity optimization, the use of pre-trained models reduced the training time by 50-70%, while maintaining accuracy. These results demonstrate that AI-based optimization not only leads to better designs but also faster simulations.

6.2 Results of AI-Enhanced Simulation

AI-enhanced simulation delivered enhanced computational efficiency, accuracy and feedback to designers. Physics-Informed Neural Networks (PINNs) performed well in solving partial differential equations (PDEs) that describe physical systems. PINNs achieved 60-90% speed-ups over Finite Element Method (FEM) simulations in benchmark problems, while maintaining similar levels of accuracy. PINNs also predicted fluid velocity and pressure fields accurately with minimal data in fluid dynamics simulations, showcasing their ability to operate with limited data. The use of digital twins also improved the accuracy of simulations by including operational data. Digital twins in industrial settings, like turbine design and jet engine monitoring, facilitated real-time performance assessment and maintenance. Anecdotal evidence has shown digital twins' systems to have reduced system downtime by 20-30%, and enhanced lifecycle performance prediction accuracy by around 15-25%. Interactive simulation in CAD also led to dramatic improvements. AI-based surrogate simulation models allowed for near real-time feedback and reduced the time required for traditional simulation from hours or days to just seconds. This led to a 40-60% decrease in the number of design iterations, enabling designers to explore several design options in a much shorter period. Further, AI-based simulation enhanced early design validation. Rather than being a post-design verification tool, simulation was used throughout the design process. This was reflected in a decrease of design failures in the later stages by roughly 20-35%, which suggests that AI-assisted design was more robust.

6.3 Results of Intelligent Prototyping

The use of AI in prototyping resulted in significant gains in efficiency, cost, and design iteration. A key outcome is the reduction in the physical prototypes needed. The predictive AI models facilitated early screening and selection of viable design solutions, eliminating the need for several physical prototypes. Based on empirical evidence, there was a 30-50% reduction in the number of prototypes, enabling cost savings. AI-powered AM enhanced process optimization and defect identification. Artificial neural networks (ANNs) were used to fine-tune process parameters (e.g., layer thickness, build orientation and laser power) for better part quality with minimal waste. Research has shown 15-25% fewer defects and 20-30% increase in productivity. Real-time monitoring systems in AM using computer vision have been able to detect defects like porosity and layer misalignment. These systems detected defects with an accuracy above 90%, allowing for timely corrective measures and preventing losses. High-speed prototyping and AI-based design space exploration allowed high-throughput experimentation. They were able to quickly explore hundreds of design iterations. This shortened design feedback cycle led to a 20-50% reduction in product development time, in line with industry observations. Moreover, AI-powered prototyping increased model-predicted performance accuracy. Through the combination of simulation, machine learning and testing, the gap between expected and observed performance was often reduced to less than 10%, suggesting better model accuracy.

6.4 Comparative Performance Analysis

To synthesize the results across domains, key performance improvements observed in AI-driven design systems are summarized below:

Table 6. Comparative Performance Improvements Across AI-Driven Design Domains

Domain	Performance Metric	Observed Improvement
Design Optimization	Weight Reduction	30-45%
	Design Space Exploration	+25-40% diversity
	Simulation Cost Reduction	80-90%
Simulation	Computational Speed	60-90% faster
	Design Iteration Time	40-60% reduction
	Failure Reduction	20-35%
Prototyping	Prototype Reduction	30-50%
	Manufacturing Defects	15-25% reduction
	Development Time	20-50% faster

These results collectively demonstrate that AI integration produces multi-dimensional improvements, not limited to a single stage of the design pipeline.

6.5 Alignment with Research Questions

The findings directly address the research questions outlined in Section 1:

- **RQ1 (Transformation of CAD capabilities):** Results show that AI transforms CAD from a passive modeling tool into an active decision-support system capable of optimization and prediction.
- **RQ2 (Effectiveness of AI methods):** Generative design, NSGA-II, and surrogate models emerged as the most effective techniques for automated design refinement.
- **RQ3 (Simulation improvements):** AI-enhanced simulation significantly improves speed and predictive accuracy while reducing computational cost.
- **RQ4 (Prototyping relationship):** Intelligent prototyping, combined with additive manufacturing, enables faster and more efficient design iteration.
- **RQ5 (Challenges):** While performance gains are substantial, issues related to data quality, interpretability, and infrastructure remain evident.

6.6 Key Insight

A critical insight emerging from the results is that AI does not merely optimize existing design processes, it fundamentally restructures them. The traditional linear workflow (design → simulate → prototype → test) is replaced by a continuous, feedback-driven loop, where optimization, simulation, and prototyping occur simultaneously.

This transformation leads to:

- Faster convergence toward optimal designs
- Reduced uncertainty in decision-making
- Increased innovation through exploration of unconventional solutions

6.7 Summary of Results

Overall, the empirical findings indicate that AI-driven design systems deliver:

- Significant performance improvements (lighter, stronger, more efficient designs)
- Substantial time savings across design and development cycles
- Reduced costs and material usage
- Enhanced design exploration and creativity

These results provide strong evidence that AI integration into CAD is not incremental but transformational, supporting the central argument of this chapter.

7. KEY THEMES AND CROSS-CUTTING APPLICATIONS

7.1 AI in CAD: Practical Deployment Landscape

Since 2015, the commercial use of AI in CAD platforms has increased exponentially. Large vendors of CAD, such as Autodesk, Siemens, PTC, Dassault Systèmes and ANSYS have built machine learning into their flagship products, with specific high-value scenarios in mind, not a wholesale replacement of the old CAD workflow. Topology optimization of structural components, mesh generation with the help of AI, and computer vision-based drawing interpretation are the most mature deployments (Tadokoro et al., 2025). The generative design module of PTC Creo is connected to the parametric modeling space and allows designers to define functional requirements and manufacturing constraints and get AI-generated topology optimized geometries as parametric feature trees, which can be further edited in the traditional CAD application. This integration vision -AI as a complement, not a substitute, of traditional CAD - represents the prevailing business view that human design judgment is still needed to interpret the requirements, make aesthetic decisions, and assess the manufacturing feasibility.

7.2 Comparative Summary of AI Methods in Design

Table 7. Comparative Summary of AI Methods in Design Practice

AI Method	Design Application	Key Advantage	Representative Reference
Topology Optimization (SIMP)	Structural component design	Material efficiency, weight reduction	Bendsoe & Sigmund (2003)
Generative Adversarial Networks	Shape generation, styling	Novel geometry synthesis	Oh et al. (2019)
Gaussian Process Regression	Surrogate modeling, optimization	Uncertainty quantification	Sacks et al. (1989)
Physics-Informed Neural Networks	Real-time simulation	Physics constraint satisfaction	Raissi et al. (2018)
NSGA-II / Multi-Objective GA	Multi-objective optimization	Pareto front exploration	Deb et al. (2002)
Convolutional Neural Networks	Defect detection, topology prediction	Pattern recognition in spatial data	Scime & Beuth (2018)
Reinforcement Learning	Process parameter optimization	Sequential decision optimization	Sutton & Barto (2018)
Digital Twin + IoT	Lifecycle monitoring, redesign	Real-time operational feedback	Tao et al. (2018)
Transfer Learning	Multi-fidelity surrogate modeling	Reduces high-fidelity data need	Weiss et al. (2016)

7.3 Industry 4.0 and the Intelligent Design Enterprise

The development of AI-based design practice cannot be considered outside of the larger Industry 4.0 concept, which predicts a cyber-physical production system where digital intelligence will be available on all levels of the product lifecycle (Schwab, 2017). Here, AI-assisted CAD is not a standalone technology, but a component on a network of intelligent systems that are interconnected such as smart manufacturing, supply chain analytics, and product lifecycle management. Information created by AI-driven design is passed down stream to manufacturing planning system;

operational information of deployed products is passed back upstream and is used to refine the design-making a closed-loop intelligence cycle that keeps enhancing design quality and manufacturing efficiency.

The Internet of Things (IoT) infrastructure facilitating this circulation of data is starting to be embedded in design practice. Embedded sensor specifications are being added to CAD models, allowing virtual models to include realistic operational load data of field-deployed prototypes. According to Tao et al. (2018), this can be defined as the design-manufacturing-service integration which digital twin technology makes possible, and is a re-conceptualization of what a design model can be: not a geometric definition of the product, but a data-rich, dynamically changing body of knowledge throughout the product lifecycle.

8. CHALLENGES AND LIMITATIONS

8.1 Computational Complexity and Infrastructure Requirements

Design optimization and simulation based on AI requires significant computational resources. Deep neural network surrogates can only be trained on high-fidelity simulation datasets by having access to graphics processing unit (GPU) clusters or cloud computing infrastructure, which is out of reach of many small and medium-sized enterprises (SMEs). The computational energy of producing the training dataset by physics-based simulation itself is significant - a single high-fidelity CFD analysis of a component of the aerodynamic system can take tens of CPU-hours, and surrogate training datasets can contain thousands of these analyses (Forrester et al., 2008).

Multi-objective optimization algorithms are not very scalable to objectives and design variables. Problems that have more than ten objectives, which are becoming more frequent in the design of complex systems, are of multiple objectives that are hard to solve using Pareto-based techniques and demand particular algorithms (Hisao Ishibuchi et al., 2008). Surrogate model accuracy is also impacted by the curse of dimensionality: the larger the number of design variables, the more training data needed to cover the design space adequately increases exponentially (Bellman & Bellman, 1957). To overcome these scaling issues, further developments in dimensionality reduction, active learning and hierarchical modeling are necessary.

8.2 Data Quality, Availability, and Bias

Machine learning models depend on data: the quality, quantity, and representativeness of training data limit their predictive accuracy and generalization ability. Historical simulated and prototype test data are common in design settings, have limited historical records and are stored in organizational knowledge management systems that were not originally created to operate with machine learning (Wang et al., 2018). This challenge is aggravated by data quality problems such as inconsistent simulation settings, incomplete design records and undocumented design intent.

One of the issues is training data bias that is particularly important. When the historical design dataset on which the surrogate models are trained is not representative of the overall design space, such as due to being created by human designers, who explored a particular region of the feasible space in a systematic manner, the surrogate model will be biased towards the well-trodden design configurations, and may underestimate the performance of novel and unconventional designs (Goodfellow et al., 2016). The creativity of AI-aided design may be limiting in this bias, ironically, repeating the patterns of designs of the past instead of truly innovating.

8.3 Interpretability and Designer Trust

The fact that deep learning models are opaque, i.e., they are black boxes that make predictions that cannot be explained in a mechanistic way, is a major practical issue of design use. Unless the designers can discern why an AI system has prescribed a specific topology, choice of materials or process parameters, they are not likely to place their trust or take action on that prescribed choice, particularly when aerospace, medical device, or civil infrastructure applications are being considered. Explainable AI (XAI) tools, such as gradient-based attribution tools (e.g., SHAP values, LIME), attention, and concept activation vectors, have been created to give post-hoc explanations of neural network predictions (Lundberg & Lee, 2017; Ribeiro et al., 2016). The validity of these explanations however - the extent to which they reflect the inner-calculation of the model - is a research question. In design practice, the use of inherently interpretable models (decision trees, linear surrogate models, physics-informed neural networks) in which predictive accuracy is allowable is a pragmatic solution to the interpretability challenge.

8.4 Skill Requirements and Organizational Change

Implementing AI-based design systems necessitates new skills, which are not historically within the engineering design curriculum: knowledge of machine learning algorithms, data analysis, and statistics. The ability to close the skill gap between the AI functions deployed in the commercial CAD tools and the data science skills of the working design engineer is one of the adoption barriers (Tadokoro et al., 2025).

Most designers apply AI-powered features as black box automation without knowing what assumptions, limitations and failure modes the underlying algorithms assume.

Management of change in organizations is also difficult. AI-led design processes demand novel data collection, curation, and governance processes; novel design engineering-data science interface roles; as well as new validation structures that can consider the probabilistic and data-driven AI recommendation nature. Successful implementations of AI in design practice have been characterized by major investments by companies in internal training, pilot projects, and multi-skilled teams that integrate design engineering and machine learning knowledge.

8.5 Ethical Considerations in Automated Design

The growing independence of AI in design brings up substantive ethical issues upon which the design community has only recently embarked upon attempting to find a systematic response. In the case of an AI system, the creation of a design that fails in service (injury or property damage) the allocation of legal and moral responsibility is ambiguous: Is it the person who defined the requirements? Deflatterer The software developer of the AI tool? The organization which implemented it? The current product liability systems have not been created to address this situation (Yoo et al., 2021).

The automation of human design work by AI is a labor market issue that is not confined to design engineering, but to the creative and technical labor market in general. Although AI will probably lead to increased workload instead of outright replacement of design engineers in the nearest future, the allocation of such an augmentation effect to various categories of designers, such as senior engineers who can make use of AI as a force multiplier and junior designers whose entry-level duties are automated is not even (and should be with due consideration by design education institutions and professional bodies) (Schwab, 2017).

Another ethical aspect is environmental sustainability. AI-based topology optimization proves to be less consumptive of materials and consequently carbon contained in the manufactured parts. Nevertheless, the necessary computational infrastructure to implement AI-powered design tools (especially the GPU clusters in training and inference) consumes large amounts of electrical energy and emits carbon (Patterson et al., 2021). The net environmental benefit of AI-powered design thus rides on the carbon intensity of the electricity supply serving the computational infrastructure.

9. FUTURE DIRECTIONS

9.1 Foundation Models for Design

The development of large foundation models in natural language processing (e.g. GPT-4) and computer vision (e.g. CLIP, DALL-E) makes it plausible to have similar foundation models trained on large collections of design data, such as CAD files, simulation output, and design briefs, that can be used to support diverse downstream design tasks through fine-tuning or prompting. These might offer a way to bridge the gap between natural language design intent specification and geometric or parametric CAD model generation to allow designers to communicate with CAD environments using high-level functional descriptions, not low-level geometric operations.

9.2 Human-AI Collaborative Design

The most fruitful near-term development path of AI in design is probably not complete automatization, but rather guided human-AI cooperation where AI generates, optimizes, and calculates design while human designers offer specifications, aesthetic, and contextual expertise, and ethical control. Human-computer interaction and cognitive engineering research is starting to produce frameworks of how to design effective human-AI collaborative design processes, such as mixed-initiative systems dynamically allocate design work to human and AI depending on situational competence (SHEIL, 2017).

9.3 Quantum Computing and Design Optimization

Theoretical benefits of quantum computing apply to some types of combinatorial optimization problems that are core to design practice such as material selection in huge data-sets, process sequence optimization, or configuration design of complex systems. Although the practical quantum advantage to design optimization of engineering design is a medium-to-long-term goal, the first quantum-classical hybrid algorithms are underway to apply to molecular design and materials discovery (Trivedi et al., 2024).

9.4 Standardization and Design Data Governance

High quality interoperable design datasets are crucial to the realization of the full potential of AI in design. Design data infrastructure, standardized CAD data formats, simulation result repositories, and benchmark datasets to train and evaluate AI are starting to be invested in by industry consortia, standards bodies and government research agencies (Tadokoro et al., 2025). Advances in this field will speed up the development of AI capabilities and allow the systematic assessment of AI-based design practices in standardized benchmarks.

10. CONCLUSIONS

The chapter has presented a theoretically based, empirical and critically reviewed explanation of how CAD practice can be transformed by the introduction of artificial intelligence. Since the theoretical premises of engineering design theory, machine learning and simulation, the chapter has followed the ways of how AI technologies: generative design, topology optimization, multi-objective evolutionary algorithms, Bayesian optimization, surrogate modeling, physics-informed neural networks, and digital twins are all redefining the possibilities of the design of physical systems and artifacts. The reviewed empirical evidence indicates that AI-based design tools are able to provide quantifiable, meaningful benefits on design performance, material use, and performance outcomes. Aerospace, automotive, and manufacturing documented weight savings of 30-45, compressions in development cycles of 20-50 and the creation of design solutions that are more effective in a particular and well-defined performance dimension than expert human design. They are not the incremental ones; these are a qualitative change in design ability that is transforming the competitive forces in the design-intensive sectors. Simultaneously, the critical reflection offered in this chapter allows realizing that AI-driven design is not devoid of serious issues. The design considerations of AI-based optimization, the data quality needs of machine learning surrogates, the interpretability shortfall of deep learning models, the lack of skills in the engineering workforce, and the unanswered ethical questions of liability, labor displacement, and environmental sustainability all need to be given continued focus by researchers, practitioners, educators, and policymakers. The future of AI in the design field is that it will result in a more symbiotic relationship between human design intelligence and machine computation. The most fruitful fulfillment of this path would not be the wholesale displacement of human design expertise but rather its enhancement and intensification with the help of AI tools that are readable, tested, regulated ethically and integrated into organizational systems that design and implement them in an accountable manner. The future of the cognitive design environment will become more and more a manifestation of the real collaborative partner in the creative, analytical and iterative cycle of introducing new products and systems into the world, both as AI capabilities increase and as datasets used become larger and more refined. The shift to CAD to cognitive design is in full swing. Its complete fulfilment requires not merely further technical innovation but also an equal commitment to the human, organizational, and ethical aspects of the intelligent design practice.

REFERENCES

Atzeni, E., & Salmi, A. (2012). Economics of additive manufacturing for end-usable metal parts. *International Journal of Advanced Manufacturing Technology*, *62*(9), 1147–1155. DOI: 10.1007/s00170-011-3878-1

Bellman, R., & Bellman, R. E. (1957). *Dynamic Programming*. Princeton University Press.

Bendsoe, M. P., & Sigmund, O. (2003). *Topology Optimization: Theory, Methods, and Applications*. Springer Science & Business Media.

Cai, S., Mao, Z., Wang, Z., Yin, M., & Karniadakis, G. E. (2021). Physics-informed neural networks (PINNs) for fluid mechanics: A review. *Acta Mechanica Sinica*, *37*(12), 1727–1738. DOI: 10.1007/s10409-021-01148-1

Deb, K., & Jain, H. (2014). An Evolutionary Many-Objective Optimization Algorithm Using Reference-Point-Based Nondominated Sorting Approach, Part I: Solving Problems With Box Constraints. *IEEE Transactions on Evolutionary Computation*, *18*(4), 577–601. DOI: 10.1109/TEVC.2013.2281535

Deb, K., Pratap, A., Agarwal, S., & Meyarivan, T. (2002). A fast and elitist multiobjective genetic algorithm: NSGA-II. *IEEE Transactions on Evolutionary Computation*, *6*(2), 182–197. DOI: 10.1109/4235.996017

du Plessis, A., & Broeckhoven, C. (2019). Looking deep into nature: A review of micro-computed tomography in biomimicry. *Acta Biomaterialia*, *85*, 27–40. DOI: 10.1016/j.actbio.2018.12.014 PMID: 30543937

Eder, W. E., & Hosnedl, S. (2007). *Design Engineering: A Manual for Enhanced Creativity*. CRC Press., DOI: 10.1201/9781420047660

Forrester, A., Sóbester, A., & Keane, A. (2008). *Engineering Design via Surrogate Modelling: A Practical Guide*. John Wiley & Sons. DOI: 10.1002/9780470770801

Gero, J. S., & Kannengiesser, U. (2004). The situated function–behaviour–structure framework. *Design Studies*, *25*(4), 373–391. DOI: 10.1016/j.destud.2003.10.010

Goodfellow, I., Bengio, Y., & Courville, A. (2016). *Deep Learning*. MIT Press.

Grieves, M. (2015). *Digital Twin: Manufacturing Excellence through Virtual Factory Replication*.

Haghighat, E., Raissi, M., Moure, A., Gomez, H., & Juanes, R. (2021). A physics-informed deep learning framework for inversion and surrogate modeling in solid mechanics. *Computer Methods in Applied Mechanics and Engineering*, *379*, 113741. DOI: 10.1016/j.cma.2021.113741

Ishibuchi, H., Tsukamoto, N., & Nojima, Y. (2008). Evolutionary many-objective optimization: A short review. *2008 IEEE Congress on Evolutionary Computation (IEEE World Congress on Computational Intelligence)*, 2419–2426. DOI: 10.1109/CEC.2008.4631121

Kingma, D. P., & Welling, M. (2013). Auto-Encoding Variational Bayes. *CoRR*. https://www.semanticscholar.org/paper/Auto-Encoding-Variational-Bayes-Kingma-Welling/5f5dc5b9a2ba710937e2c413b37b053cd673df02

Lundberg, S., & Lee, S.-I. (2017). *A Unified Approach to Interpreting Model Predictions*. https://doi.org//arXiv.1705.07874DOI: 10.48550

Mckay, M., Beckman, R., & Conover, W. (1979). A Comparison of Three Methods for Selecting Vales of Input Variables in the Analysis of Output From a Computer Code. *Technometrics*, *21*(2), 239–245. DOI: 10.1080/00401706.1979.10489755

Meng, L., McWilliams, B., Jarosinski, W., Park, H.-Y., Jung, Y.-G., Lee, J., & Zhang, J. (2020). Machine Learning in Additive Manufacturing: A Review. *Journal of the Minerals Metals & Materials Society*, *72*(6), 2363–2377. Advance online publication. DOI: 10.1007/s11837-020-04155-y

Oh, S., Jung, Y., Kim, S., Lee, I., & Kang, N. (2019). Deep Generative Design: Integration of Topology Optimization and Generative Models. *Journal of Mechanical Design*, *141*(11), 1. DOI: 10.1115/1.4044229

Patterson, D. A., Gonzalez, J., Le, Q. V., Liang, C., Munguía, L.-M., Rothchild, D., So, D. R., Texier, M., & Dean, J. (2021). Carbon Emissions and Large Neural Network Training. *ArXiv*. https://www.semanticscholar.org/paper/Carbon-Emissions-and-Large-Neural-Network-Training-Patterson-Gonzalez/7a16d9b4e04300d034502dc7dd58428714594e2c

Raissi, M., Perdikaris, P., & Karniadakis, G. (2018). Physics-Informed Neural Networks: A Deep Learning Framework for Solving Forward and Inverse Problems Involving Nonlinear Partial Differential Equations. *Journal of Computational Physics*, *378*, 686–707. Advance online publication. DOI: 10.1016/j.jcp.2018.10.045

Ribeiro, M. T., Singh, S., & Guestrin, C. (2016). "Why Should I Trust You?": Explaining the Predictions of Any Classifier. *Proceedings of the 22nd ACM SIGKDD International Conference on Knowledge Discovery and Data Mining. KDD : Proceedings / International Conference on Knowledge Discovery & Data Mining. International Conference on Knowledge Discovery & Data Mining, 16*, 1135–1144. DOI: 10.1145/2939672.2939778

Sacks, J., Welch, W., Mitchell, T., & Wynn, H. (1989). Design and analysis of computer experiments. With comments and a rejoinder by the authors. *Statistical Science, 4*(4). Advance online publication. DOI: 10.1214/ss/1177012413

Saha, S. K., Wang, D., Nguyen, V. H., Chang, Y., Oakdale, J. S., & Chen, S.-C. (2019). Scalable submicrometer additive manufacturing. *Science, 366*(6461), 105–109. DOI: 10.1126/science.aax8760 PMID: 31604310

Schwab, K. (2017). *The Fourth Industrial Revolution*. Crown.

Scime, L., & Beuth, J. (2018). Anomaly detection and classification in a laser powder bed additive manufacturing process using a trained computer vision algorithm. *Additive Manufacturing, 19*, 114–126. DOI: 10.1016/j.addma.2017.11.009

Shahriari, B., Swersky, K., Wang, Z., Adams, R. P., & de Freitas, N. (2016). Taking the Human Out of the Loop: A Review of Bayesian Optimization. *Proceedings of the IEEE, 104*(1), 148–175. DOI: 10.1109/JPROC.2015.2494218

SHEIL. (2017). *Fabricate: Rethinking Design and Construction*. UCL Press.

Sosnovik, I., & Oseledets, I. (2017). Neural networks for topology optimization. *Russian Journal of Numerical Analysis and Mathematical Modelling, 34*(4), 215–223. Advance online publication. DOI: 10.1515/rnam-2019-0018

Suh, N. P. (with Internet Archive). (2001). *Axiomatic design: Advances and applications*. New York : Oxford University Press. http://archive.org/details/axio maticdesigna0000suhn

Sutton, R. S., & Barto, A. G. (2018). Reinforcement Learning, *second edition: An Introduction*. MIT Press.

Tadokoro, F., Ghosh, A. K., & Ura, S. (2025). On the effective co-creation of CAD models by leveraging generative artificial intelligence. *Procedia CIRP, 58th CIRP Conference on Manufacturing Systems 2025, 134*, 663–668. DOI: 10.1016/j.procir.2025.02.181

Tao, F., Qi, Q., Liu, A., & Kusiak, A. (2018). Data-driven smart manufacturing. *Journal of Manufacturing Systems*. *Journal of Manufacturing Systems*, *48*, 157–169. DOI: 10.1016/j.jmsy.2018.01.006

Trivedi, R., Franco Rubio, A., & Cirac, J. I. (2024). Quantum advantage and stability to errors in analogue quantum simulators. *Nature Communications*, *15*(1), 6507. DOI: 10.1038/s41467-024-50750-x PMID: 39095381

Wang, D., Tan, D., & Liu, L. (2018). Particle swarm optimization algorithm: An overview. *Soft Computing*, *22*(2), 387–408. DOI: 10.1007/s00500-016-2474-6

Weiss, K., Khoshgoftaar, T. M., & Wang, D. (2016). A survey of transfer learning. *Journal of Big Data*, *3*(1), 9. DOI: 10.1186/s40537-016-0043-6

Yoo, S., Lee, S., Kim, S., Hwang, K. H., Park, J. H., & Kang, N. (2021). Integrating deep learning into CAD/CAE system: Generative design and evaluation of 3D conceptual wheel. *Structural and Multidisciplinary Optimization*, *64*(4), 2725–2747. DOI: 10.1007/s00158-021-02953-9

Zhang, J., Wang, Z., Li, S., & Wei, P. (2024). A digital twin approach for gas turbine performance based on deep multi-model fusion. *Applied Thermal Engineering*, *246*, 122954. DOI: 10.1016/j.applthermaleng.2024.122954

Zhang, Y., Kim, N., Park, C., & Haftka, R. (2018). Multifidelity Surrogate Based on Single Linear Regression. *AIAA Journal*, *56*(12), 1–9. DOI: 10.2514/1.J057299

Zienkiewicz, O. C., Taylor, R. L., Taylor, R. L., & Zhu, J. Z. (2013). *The Finite Element Method: Its Basis and Fundamentals*. Butterworth-Heinemann.

Chapter 10

AI-Based Design Framework for Data-Driven Financial Risk Modeling

Tejaswini Bastray
St. Joseph's University, Bengaluru, India

Fatin
http://orcid.org/0000-0001-6052-5608
St. Claret College, Jalahalli, India

Aisha Banu
http://orcid.org/0000-0001-8174-3663
Alliance School of Business, Department of Finance and Accounting, Alliance University, Bengaluru, India

Kavita Mahar
Dr. NSAM First Grade College, Nitte (Deemed to be) University, Bengaluru, India

S. Mahabub Basha
http://orcid.org/0000-0002-5998-3262
International Institute of Business Studies, Bangalore, India

Mazharunnisa Md
KL Business School, Koneru Lakshmaiah Educational Foundation, Guntur, India

ABSTRACT

The modern financial markets are becoming more complex and unpredictable and therefore demand advanced risk evaluation processes. This seeks to address short-comings of traditional statistical methods, and single-purpose ML models with a proposal of an AI-based design process of data-driven financial risk modelling. This model incorporates various forms of data, such as structured and unstructured financial information with a five-tiered framework where data collection, data cleaning, hybrid AI modelling, risk analysis, and decision support are involved. To

DOI: 10.4018/979-8-3693-3751-6.ch010

enhance accuracy and robustness, it involves hybrid model, which involves the use of DL models (LSTM) with ensemble learning and the use of ML models (Random Forest, SVM).

1. INTRODUCTION

The constantly changing global financial system, the growing volatility of the financial markets and digital transformation are the reasons why the complexity of the financial risk increases. The conventional risk models, which are statistical or econometric, are not able to explain dynamic, nonlinear and multidimensional characteristics of the contemporary financial data (Bandi, 2024). More sophisticated and flexible risk models are needed to address the many hazards that all financial institutions encounter in this data-driven and highly-connected age. Big data, with digital transactions, interactions and real-time financial data, create a new realm for data analytics. But the challenge is to draw on meaningful insights from the data sets (Zhang, Y., 2025). Here, AI comes into play with enhanced computational capabilities and intelligent algorithms that learn from past experiences and can better detect anomalies and predict risks. AI financial risk models are based on ML and DL algorithms to enhance prediction accuracy, provide decision automation and accelerate risk analysis. As a result, AI-powered risk models are commonly adopted by financial institutions to improve their risk management strategies and achieve a competitive advantage (Ogunmokun et al., 2021). This chapter aims to introduce an integrated AI financial risk design approach for data-driven financial models to overcome current limitations and to provide a scalable, efficient and intelligent approach to modern financial risk management.

1.1 Background

Risk is an integral part of any economy but has evolved with different characteristics in modern economies. Globalisation, technology and innovation in the financial sector has resulted in the complexities of financial markets. This interconnectedness increases the risk of contagion, in which events in one sector of the financial system can trigger a snowball effect and potentially spread to other regions and industries, resulting in systemic risk. Credit, market, operational, and liquidity risk are the four main types of financial risk in modern economies (Kusumba, S., 2024). The failure of borrowers to pay back loans is known as credit risk, whereas fluctuations in interest rates, prices, and currency exchange rates are known as market risk. When processes go wrong or people make mistakes, that's operational risk. When institutions can't pay their short-term cash-flow obligations, that's liquidity risk

(Adebowale & Akinnagbe, 2021). The worldwide financial crisis of 2008 brought to light the necessity for better financial risk models and the dangers of inadequate risk management. Historical data and the assumption of normal distribution are used by traditional financial risk models, including VAR. Additionally, traditional models are facing challenges with the advent of big data in the financial markets, which is characterized by a high velocity, diversity, and volume. These need to be replaced with dynamic and smart systems for financial risk assessment (Hossain, M. A., 2025).

1.2 Role of Data-Driven Decision-Making in Finance

The shift to data-driven decision-making has transformed financial systems, as financial institutions now use data to understand risks, forecast market trends and improve strategies. In contrast to traditional decision-making, which relies on intuition or subjective judgement, data-driven decision-making is grounded in data, quantitative analysis and predictive modelling (Paleti, S., 2022). The rapid increase in data of financial transactions, customer and market interactions and the internet help facilitate this change. Utilizing this information assists companies to understand the market trends, consumer behavior and risk. Predictive modelling and data mining are essential in mining information in data. Improved accuracy and reduced risk are benefits of data-driven decision-making. Using past and current data, banks are able to enhance their credit risk, investment opportunities, fraud and risk forecasting (Oko-Odion, C., 2025). An example is that historical data can be utilized to predict loan defaults and real-time data can be utilized to detect fraud. There are however, dangers in embracing data-driven approaches. Issues of data quality and integration, privacy and regulatory must be handled. And large and intricate data require advanced computing technologies.

1.3 Emergence of AI in Financial Risk Modelling

Artificial intelligence has brought new ideas to financial risk modelling, helping to overcome the limits of previous methods. ML, DL, NLP and RL are some of the methods that give computers the ability to learn, adapt, and make judgments. Financial risk modelling issues involving high-dimensional data, non-linearities, and interactions are well-suited to AI techniques. Credit risk and fraud are examples of supervised classification and regression tasks that frequently employ machine learning algorithms (Shittu, A. K., 2022). Learning and modelling financial time series is within the capabilities of neural networks and LSTM networks. Rather than being based on assumptions, AI models learn from the data, enabling them to identify patterns and relationships. This helps to enhance and improve risk assessment, particularly in dynamic and volatile markets (Zeriouh & Amara, 2025). In addition, AI allows for real-time risk assessment and decision-making, allowing financial institutions to respond promptly and reduce risk. For example, AI can analyse data on transactions to detect anomalies, fraud and credit risk. Also, NLP algorithms can analyse news feeds, financial reports and tweets to determine market sentiment and predict risks (Islam, M. M., 2026). The use of AI in modelling financial risks has its benefits and drawbacks such as the interpretability, transparency and ethical issues. Specifically, black-box models do not give any insight on how they make their decisions, which is essential to regulatory audit. Still, it is a move in the right direction to include AI in financial risk modelling because it enables the creation of intelligent, adaptive and efficient financial risk models (Zhang, T., 2025).

1.4 Contribution of Research

The study can be used to add to the current body of literature on financial risk modelling by offering a detailed framework on how to implement data-driven financial systems with an AI focus. The framework helps in simplifying the flow of information in data processing and risk assessment (Jahid, M. S. R., 2025). To enhance the predictions of the model and avoid the setbacks of using a single model, the framework uses hybrid ML and DL models. Scalability and flexibility is a key factor. They are also scalable and flexible, and can be applied to financial markets to deal with big data and cope with the market shifts, thereby making it a viable option to apply. It is also real time and therefore risks can be easily detected and controlled (Selvarajan, G., 2021). The research also presents another comparative analysis of other techniques of AI, their weaknesses and strengths in financial risk modelling. Besides that, the paper takes into consideration such important aspects as the data integrity and model transparency and ethics, so that the approach suggested can be implemented. The notion of explainable AI that the study employs to encourage transparency and trust in the use of AI (Radhakrishnan et al., 2025). Overall, the study offers a new perspective and approach to modern financial risk management, benefitting both academia and industry.

2. CONCEPTUAL FOUNDATIONS OF FINANCIAL RISK MODELING

Decision-making in modern financial systems is founded on financial risk modeling, which enables financial institutions to assess, predict and manage risks associated with financial transactions (Omopariola & Aboaba, 2021). Recent globalisation means that financial risk has evolved from being probabilistic and uni-dimensional to multidimensional. The operating environment for financial institutions is highly volatile with uncertainties arising from dynamics of macroeconomy, regulatory and technological change and market participants (Chawla, N., 2025). As such, robust conceptual tools are needed to improve the relevance and utility of financial risk modeling. At its core, financial risk modeling is concerned with identification, measurement and management of risks to financial performance (Faisal, S. M., 2025). It integrates statistical techniques, economic theory and computing technologies to examine potential losses and aid decision-making. Over the years, the discipline has moved from deterministic to stochastic and statistical financial models, to reflect the uncertainties in financial markets. Risk models have also undergone a paradigm shift due to the proliferation of massive financial data and sophisticated computation (Fritz-Morgenthal et al., 2022). Because of this, more sophisticated models that use machine learning, real-time data, and adaptation have been developed. Developing methods for risk management requires a thorough understanding of these elements.

2.1 Types of Financial Risks

There are different types of financial risks stemming from internal and external factors. Understanding the types of financial risks is important in establishing a risk model. This has ramifications for derivatives, bond investments, and loans. Credit risk management entails assessing borrowers' creditworthiness based on their income stability, credit history, and other economic criteria. Although machine learning has recently emerged as a viable alternative to statistical methods, traditional credit scoring algorithms still rely on them. The changes can lead to significant losses (Lin et al., 2025). Market risk can be measured using VaR and CVaR, which measure losses in worst-case scenarios. However, the dynamic nature of the markets makes prediction challenging. Operational risk is due to risks associated with internal process, system or human failure. These risks include fraud, cyber security, system failures and human error. With more digital technologies being used in the financial industry, operational risk is becoming more prevalent, particularly in relation to cybersecurity and technology risk (Celestin & Mishra, 2025).

2.2 Traditional Risk Modeling Approaches

Basic risk assessment models have been widely used in traditional risk models. These models are primarily based on statistical and econometric approaches, which rely on historical information and some assumptions to estimate the potential losses. VaR, regression models, time-series models and Monte Carlo simulations are the most widely used traditional risk models. VAR is a widely used risk measure (Siddiqui, N. A. 2025). VAR can be calculated via historical simulation, variance-covariance or Monte Carlo methods. Although VAR is widely used, it has limitations, particularly in terms of extreme risk and event modelling. Another common technique to model financial risks is regression analysis. This method can be employed to predict future occurrences and identify risk factors by modelling the link between the response and independent variables (Paleti, S., 2024). Logistic regression is employed for problems involving binary classification, like default, whereas linear regression models are commonly employed for the evaluation of credit risk and the pricing of financial assets. For the purpose of making predictions, time series models are utilized, for example, ARIMA and GARCH. The price and volatility of financial markets can be predicted using these models (Kantesaria & Panda, 2026).

2.3 Limitations of Conventional Statistical Methods

Although conventional statistical methods are commonly used, there are some issues with their application in financial risk modelling in the modern financial environment. Such models are constructed with idealized assumptions, including linearities, independencies and a normal distribution of the data (Pattabhi, A., 2025). However, financial markets are nonlinear, complex and have many dynamic factors. These models can overlook the extreme events (or "black swan" events) that can significantly affect financial markets. These models often rely on historical data, and assume that future events will follow past patterns, which is not necessarily the case (Fritz-Morgenthal et al., 2022). The fact that conventional approaches struggle with high-dimensional and huge data sets is another cause for worry. The modern period has a plethora of organized and unstructured data available to financial organizations such as social media, transaction, and market data. Moreover, the classical statistical methods are not adaptive. They do not fit very well in the fast and dynamic environments where decisions must be made within a short period of time. Although traditional models are in general easier to understand compared to AI models, their assumptions might be too simplistic and can lead to drawing the wrong conclusions (Omopariola & Aboaba, 2021).

2.4 Need for Intelligent and Adaptive Frameworks

The growing complexity of financial systems, as well as the inadequacy of older risk modelling frameworks, have led to the need to deploy smart frameworks. To create risk models that are more accurate, efficient, and scalable, they are based on emerging technology. In order to enhance the precision of the models (Jahid, M. S. R., 2025), machine learning may be used to capture nonlinear interactions and links among the variables. Specifically, neural network-trained models are able to learn some characteristics of complex data. The second essential need of risk frameworks is adaptability. Adaptive models can be adapted with new information to learn to adapt to market changes rather than realigning themselves at scheduled intervals. This is of the greatest importance due to the fluid nature of financial systems. To generate more recent risk assessments, they are able to process data, and accommodate new data (Zeriouh & Amara, 2025). Intelligent systems can handle big data, and also integrate data of other sources, structured and unstructured. And the interpretability is enhanced by the use of XAI techniques and is features of the AI systems. In addition, intelligent systems are automatable and thus, they can be controlled without any chances of manual control and thus, the associated risks. This leads to quick and effective risk assessment (Oko-Odion, C., 2025).

3. AI IN FINANCIAL SYSTEMS

The dynamic structure of the financial system renders the volume, speed and diversity of financial data to be beyond the scope of traditional financial analysis. Through AI technologies, financial institutions would have a more effective tool to handle structured and unstructured data, detect trends, and make decisions using data (Hossain, M. A., 2025). These technologies perform a range of operations connected with risk management and financial analysis. They allow making decisions in real-time, automation of the process, and better forecasts. The financial sector is undergoing AIs transformation by helping to make fraud prevention, credit scoring, algorithmic trading, and portfolio management effective, efficient, and scalable (Adebowale & Akinnagbe, 2021). AI is handling data with large number of dimensions and the capability to model complex relationships that are challenging to model with more traditional statistical methods. Financial data is infamously hard to model due to its noisy and non-linear nature as well as its factor-dependent nature (Ogunmokun et al., 2021). Through AI, machines are able to learn, reason, and make judgments just as human beings do because AI has a wide scope of computing methods (Islam, M. M., 2026). The three most common AI methods are important to convert data into insights in financial systems.

- ML is an aspect of artificial intelligence that is concerned with imparting new skills to computers through the examination of existing data (Oko-Odion, C., 2025). Supervised learning systems address classification and regression problems, such as fraud detection and credit scoring. Unsupervised learning are essential in finding trends and outliers in financial data.
- DL method applies stacked artificial neural networks to search through piles of data to find patterns (Chawla, N., 2025). The DL models, such as CNNs

and RNNs, are effective when applied to multidimensional data and information, which relies on a series.

- NLP deals with interactions between computers and human language. Financial systems can use NLP to filter text information obtained via social media, news outlets, and financial statements (Celestin & Mishra, 2025).

These AI methods offer an abundant array of options to operate with various kinds of data and solve financial issues ((Siddiqui, N. A. 2025). A combination of these approaches can help banks and other financial institutions to evaluate risks more effectively, make superior decisions and remain at the forefront of the competition in a highly dynamic market. AI enables better, faster, and real-time analytics of big data, significantly enhancing risk assessment of a financial system and predictive analytics. Predictive analytics aim at making future projections and are based on statistical analysis, machine learning, and past data. Among the key advantages of applying AI to predictive analytics, one can note that it could assist you in uncovering complex patterns and relationships (Kantesaria & Panda, 2026). Traditional models might not be able to reflect the dynamics of financial markets due to their linear structure. Nevertheless, AI models can enhance their prediction capabilities by changing their parameters depending on the market and new information. When it comes to credit risk modelling, AI models are used based on factors such as customer demographics, payment history, and patterns and determine the existence of credit risk. The AI models are able to process the large data sets and can detect the latent risk factors, which can be not apparent in other models (Siddiqui, N. A. 2025). Likewise, in credit card fraud, AI models are able to process transaction data to identify fraudulent transactions and prevent fraud. Financial time series can be used in market risk management to forecast future market trends and price actions with the use of AI. LSTM networks and other neural networks are especially suited to sequence modelling and predicting market trends ((Paleti, S., 2024).

There are various strengths of an AI model compared to the traditional statistical and econometric models, which are applied in financial risk management. The first one is that they are able to record non-linear relationships. Financial markets are susceptible to a lot of variables that interact with each other and AI models can be more successful in considering these interactions, resulting in improved predictions (Pattabhi, A., 2025). AI models are capable of handling big data that comes in various forms. This is significant in the age of big data where financial companies are able to access much data. Existing models might fail to do data. These models can make good predictions and by learning the historical data and adjusting the weights of the new data they can adjust to the market. This contributes to their suitability in dynamic environments that have changing risk factors ((Jahid, M. S. R., 2025). There are many financial applications that can be automated with AI methods, including fraud detection and credit scoring, without human biases and errors. This enhances speed and efficiency and lowers financial organisations costs. Comparatively, traditional models might require a certain duration to process and analyse data. This play's role in real-time trading and risk management. A range of data, such as text, images and numbers, can also be used with AI. It can assist in a more detailed evaluation of risks and make a decision (Radhakrishnan et al., 2025).

Although the application of AI in financial systems has benefits, certain risks related to AI must be resolved to make it a reliable and efficient application. These are bias, interpretability and quality, which can affect performance and accuracy of AI models (Shittu, A. K., 2022). Source of bias in the AI models might be the biased training data or the model might learn to be biased. Biased financial system AI models may result in biased risk management or lending decisions. To illustrate, the AI model may pick up the biases in case a lot of prior biased decisions are contained in the data ((Paleti, S., 2022). In order to overcome bias, the data is to be cleaned, AI models are to be developed to promote fairness and they have to be monitored. They are known as "black boxes". Interpretability can limit the use of AI models in financial applications, where explainability is important (Chawla, N., 2025). Legal and regulatory frameworks often require explanations, such as in credit risk. XAI techniques are being developed to address this issue by providing explanations of model behaviour (Kantesaria & Panda, 2026). There's also the issue of data quality. Data is a key ingredient of AI models and the quality of data used can influence the model. Incomplete, inconsistent and noisy data can lead to inaccurate predictions and flawed results. For finance, data can be varied and sourced from a number of different sources, posing challenges in data integration and cleaning. Further, data privacy and security needs to be considered, particularly with regulatory considerations. Data privacy regulations need to be followed when using data for AI (Zhang, Y., 2025).

4. LITERATURE REVIEW

Financial risk modelling has seen tremendous growth thanks to the fast development of AI and data analytics, which has produced a multitude of models and approaches. There has been a lot of research into how financial risk models can be made more efficient, timely, and adaptable by using ML, DL, and hybrid AI techniques in the past several years. As a consequence, there is a growing corpus of study of finance, which has led to both theoretical and practical applications. In order to give overview of current knowledge, this literature review will analyze and evaluate previous works that have discussed AI application to financial risk modelling. This section will summarize the latest research on using AI techniques to address credit risk, market risk, fraud, and other decision-making issues in financial systems by synthesising prior findings.

4.1 Review of existing research

Bandi (2024) discussed the artificial intelligence technique for risk prediction in financial systems architecture. He emphasized big data technologies and machine learning approaches. Research suggests that real-time analytics and adaptive learning can improve risk management and uncertainties in financial decision-making. Zhang (2025) has proposed an AI-based technique for financial risk management using LSTM and probabilistic models. The effort was focused on improving decisionmaking through the development of a dynamic model of risk and uncertainty. A conceptual model of AI for financial risk and corporate governance management has been proposed by Ogunmokun et al. (2021). The research pointed out the significance of AI to improve integration of firm strategy, risk management, transparency and efficiency. Kusumba (2024) suggested an AI-enabled data approach for the finance system of healthcare industry and underlined the need of data-driven decision making. This was in the healthcare industry but provided insight into how AI could be used for financial risk management through strategy development. Adebowale and Akinnagbe (2021) designed a system for financial risk prediction in decentralized marketplaces using data and AI. Researchers showed that integrating data sources and AI systems boosted risk predictions, enabling improved in decentralized. Hossain (2025) created AI financial analytics algorithms to help US companies forecast market risk and investment opportunities. AI may also be used to improve financial results and risk management.

Paleti's "Fusion Bank" (2022) is a fascinating proposal, which is a blend of AI powered monetary advances and risk-sensitive data engineering. The authors consider the opportunities of exploiting AI and effective data engineering to enhance risk management and operational efficiency in banking. Oko-Odion (2025) used AI to generate financial market risk models to better model risk and detect fraud. This article demonstrated anomaly detection and risk modeling improvements in the financial sector. According to Shittu (2022), AI-assisted credit risk modelling developments include using ML to improve credit rating and identify loan default. This paper demonstrated the use of AI models to analyse borrowers and financial decision-making. Zeriouh and Amara (2025) proposed a paradigm of better decision making and resilience based on AI-based strategies to manage risks. As it was pointed out in this study, AI proved to be helpful in assisting the decision making in the dynamic scenario and collecting various risk elements. Islam (2026) built an AI forecasting system for decision making utilizing Bigdata. It emphasizes AI models and big data analytics in financial forecasting and decision-making. Zhang et al. (2025) deployed a decision support system based on several data sources and an AI-based financial risk early warning system. It supported application of ML methods and data sources in early warning and risk prediction. Jahid (2025) has suggested the use of AI based approaches for risk and optimization in SEZs. The research highlights the usefulness of AI in helping developing countries to minimize risks and attract investment. Selvarajan (2021) studied the application of artificial intelligence-based analytics to optimize data-driven operations in many domains. It can give notion of possible applications of AI in business and financial management.

Radhakrishnan et al. (2025) investigated the potential for applying an artificial intelligence based predictive analytics technique to increase the vehicle safety for financial risk assessment in the cloud. The research was focused on cloud computing for data management. AI-based methods can improve financial stability and reduce market uncertainty (Omopariola & Aboaba, 2021). The study emphasized the utility of AI for hazard analysis and measures to mitigate them. AI in prediction of project risks for large-scale financial software systems was recently investigated by Chawla (2025). Major financial software systems were focus of research, which looked at how AI might boost their efficacy, efficiency, and resource management. To automate, forecast, and improve financial risk management, Faisal et al. (2025) used AI. AI-related concerns are crucial to risk management. The necessity for open, reliable and ethical AI in the control of financial risk is also highlighted by Fritz-Morgenthal et al. (2022). The key concern was associated with the importance of ethics and transparency in financial sector, in particular in regulated markets. Lin et al. (2025) introduced a data-driven methodology for regulating AI risks in health insurance funds and securing their continued viability. AI's impact on risk and financial management was demonstrated in this study. Celestin and Mishra (2025) examined the function of AI in financial analytics in risk assessment, financial forecasting and decision making of corporate financials. The study has shown the impact of AI on budgeting and analysis. Siddiqui (2025) reviewed the AI based decision making business intelligence. The study pointed out that data insights are essential in financial and strategic decision making. When it comes to banks' financial risk management, Paleti (2024) looked at how data engineering and AI have an impact. Improving efficiency and risk management were the primary focuses of the study's AI and big data analytics efforts. Kantesaria and Panda (2026) review AI-based data-driven models of nanocarrier systems. This research was primarily targeted at the healthcare industry, but it has indicated the potential usefulness of AI-based optimization approaches for other complex systems, such as the financial sector. For financial risk management systems, Pattabhi's (2025) risk intelligence could be useful. In light of the ever-changing nature of the financial industry, they looked into how AI may enhance prediction, decision making, and risk management.

4.2 Comparative analysis of Existing Research

A number of frameworks, models, and methodologies for financial risk modelling have emerged in response to the increasing interest from both academics and industry professionals in using AI in this field. To learn about the present level of knowledge and where there are gaps, we must examine the existing literature. With an emphasis on studies conducted in the last several years in the domains of banking, insurance, enterprise financial systems, and DeFi, Table 1 offers a concise synopsis of the literature on AI-based financial risk modelling.

Table 1. Literature Survey

Author / Year	Objective	Methodology	Findings	Limitations
Bandi (2024)	Develop AI-driven predictive risk architecture	ML-based scalable framework	Improved real-time risk prediction	Limited real-world validation
Zhang (2025)	Enhance decision-making using LSTM	LSTM + probabilistic models	High forecasting accuracy	Computational complexity
Ogunmokun et al. (2021)	Integrate AI with governance optimization	Conceptual framework	Improved transparency and governance	Lack of empirical validation
Kusumba (2024)	AI-enabled data strategy framework	Data integration + analytics	Better decision-making efficiency	Domain-specific (healthcare)
Adebowale & Akinnagbe (2021)	Improve decentralized risk prediction	AI-driven data integration	Enhanced prediction accuracy	Data heterogeneity issues
Hossain (2025)	Predict market risk and investment decisions	ML-based financial analytics	Improved forecasting performance	Limited generalization
Paleti (2022)	Integrate AI in modern banking systems	AI + data engineering	Improved operational efficiency	Implementation complexity
Oko-Odion (2025)	Enhance fraud detection and risk prediction	ML-based models	Better anomaly detection	Data dependency
Shittu (2022)	Improve credit risk models	ML-based credit scoring	Higher accuracy in default prediction	Model interpretability issues
Zeriouh & Amara (2025)	Develop strategic AI risk frameworks	Systematic review + model	Improved resilience and decision support	Conceptual focus
Islam (2026)	AI-based predictive analytics framework	AI + big data integration	Enhanced decision support	Scalability concerns

continued on following page

Table 1. Continued

Author / Year	Objective	Methodology	Findings	Limitations
Zhang et al. (2025)	Early warning risk system	Multi-source ML model (TD-DS-RF)	Accurate early risk detection	Data integration complexity
Jahid (2025)	Optimize risk in economic zones	Review-based AI modeling	Improved planning efficiency	Limited financial focus
Selvarajan (2021)	Enhance industry optimization using AI	AI-based analytics	Improved decision-making	Generalized approach
Radhakrishnan et al. (2025)	Improve safety risk assessment in cloud	AI + cloud analytics	Efficient data processing	Domain-specific
Omopariola & Aboaba (2021)	Improve financial stability	AI-driven risk assessment	Reduced market uncertainty	Lack of advanced models
Chawla (2025)	Manage project risk in financial software	AI-based predictive models	Better project outcomes	Limited dataset
Faisal et al. (2025)	Transform financial risk management	AI-driven automation	Improved efficiency and insights	Implementation challenges
Fritz-Morgenthal et al. (2022)	Promote XAI in finance	XAI-based framework	Improved transparency and trust	Trade-off with accuracy
Lin et al. (2025)	Risk control in insurance systems	AI-based data-driven model	Enhanced financial sustainability	Limited scalability
Celestin & Mishra (2025)	Improve financial forecasting	AI-driven analytics	Higher prediction accuracy	Data dependency
Siddiqui (2025)	Optimize decision-making via BI systems	Systematic review	Improved strategic planning	Lack of empirical testing
Paleti (2024)	Transform banking risk management	AI + data engineering	Better efficiency and risk control	Integration complexity
Kantesaria & Panda (2026)	Optimize systems using AI models	Review-based AI optimization	High adaptability of AI models	Non-financial domain
Pattabhi (2025)	Introduce AI-based risk intelligence	AI-powered framework	Improved predictive capability	Limited practical validation

4.3 Identified Research Gaps

We have analyzed the literature on AI-based financial risk modelling and observed a substantial progress in predictive modelling, automation and decision-making. Lack of integration and consolidation is a major gap in research These models are effective in specific issues where they are used but fail to give the holistic picture of financial risk through the inter-relationships between various risks (Kantesaria,

R., 2026). Though more advanced techniques, such as LSTM and random forests, are also applied in certain studies, we need to explore a better-structured approach to combining different AI models to exploit their complements. This, though not as prevalent in financial risk prediction, might enhance reliability of the predictions. While it is important to include many sources and forms of information to obtain a better understanding of the financial world, we do not go into that topic enough (Islam, M. M., 2026). Moreover, models do not usually consider data, and noise. They may be black box models that are difficult to interpret. This can create problems with regulatory and trust issues in many highly regulated sectors. And scalability and real-time deployment are crucial. Models tend to be developed and tested on small data sets, and have not yet been deployed in real, large-scale financial systems (Radhakrishnan et al., 2025). The lack of research in areas identified in this review suggests a need for an integrated AI-based approach to financial risk management to address the current research gaps.

5. PROBLEM STATEMENT

Conventional financial risk models have shown their limits in face of ever-increasing complexity of financial markets brought about by digitization and globalization, as well as the tremendous increase in high-frequency data. As a consequence, they are not able to accurately and promptly compute risk measures, which can lead to financial losses and poor investment decisions. Although AI approaches have been demonstrated to improve the prediction accuracy, existing studies primarily use stand-alone models, and focus only on some specific risks, such as credit risk or market risk, rather than a holistic and integrated view of risk. In addition, problems like data integration, real-time data processing, model interpretability, and scalability hinder the use of AI approaches in finance. As such, there is a critical need for a holistic, data-driven, and AI-based design framework for financial risk models to tackle complex risk management problems by incorporating multiple factors of financial risks, hybrid modelling approaches, and providing scalable, real-time and interpretable financial risk assessment.

6. PROPOSED WORK

The proposed work is a holistic AI driven design framework of data-driven financial risk models that attempts to overcome the shortcomings of the current risk management models and AI models by integrating various intelligent approaches into a scalable and flexible design framework. In this work, it is suggested to create a multi-layered architecture capable of managing various financial data, identifying complex dependencies, and offer risk evaluation in a timely and correct manner at various levels of risk. The framework has five layers: Data Acquisition, Data Pre-processing, AI Modelling, Risk Evaluation and Decision Support Layer (Figure 1).

Figure 1. Proposed Al-Based Design Framework

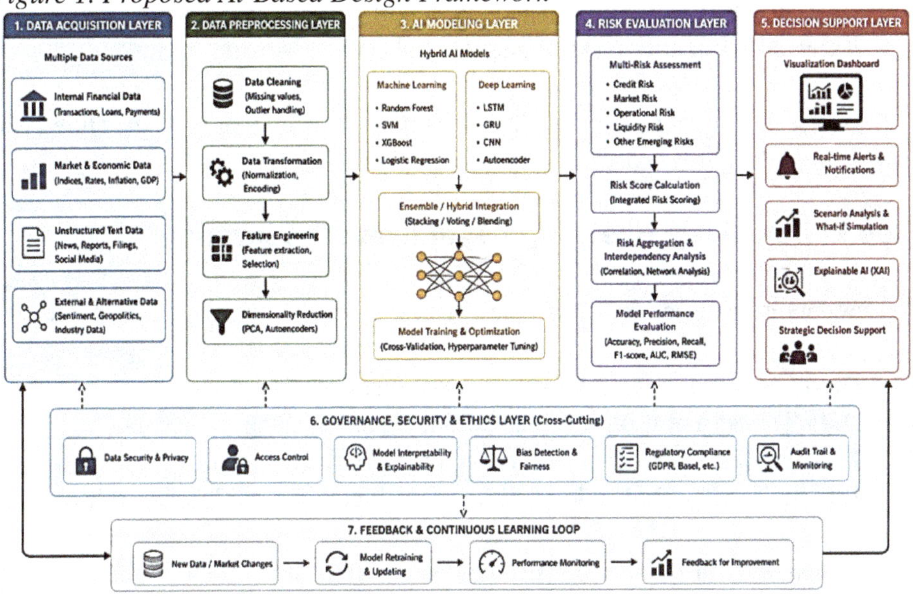

First layer retrieves different data of financial transactions, stock indices, economic indicators and text data. Data Preprocessing Layer offers data cleaning, normalization, feature engineering and dimensionality reduction to guarantee the quality of data. The AI Modelling Layer is the heart of the system, and the hybrid models based on different algorithms are implemented. They are RF networks, SVM and LSTM networks, which incorporate pattern recognition and time series analysis. Risk scores are evaluated by using the Risk Evaluation Layer that incorporates the forecasts of the models and takes into account the relationship between different risks. Finally, Decision Support Layer provides insights and visualisation as dashboards and alerts to enable financial institutions to make timely decisions. It also uses the XAI procedures to increase interpretability. This research aims to create a scalable, efficient and intelligent financial risk modelling system, that can be scaled and adapted to the dynamic financial markets, and is also accurate, reliable and useful.

Step 1: Data Acquisition Layer (Input Stage)

This is the core of the system, the obtaining of data of different sources.

- **Internal Financial Data**: transactions, loans, payments
- **Market & Economic Data**: stock indices, interest rates, GDP, inflation
- **Unstructured Data**: news, financial reports, social media sentiment
- **External/Alternative Data**: geopolitical events, industry trends

To make the model as real-world as possible, to ensure that both structured and unstructured data are used.

Step 2: Data Preprocessing Layer (Data Preparation)

Raw data are unstructured--this layer transforms it into usable form. Key processes:

- **Data Cleaning**: handling missing values, removing outliers
- **Data Transformation**: normalization, encoding categorical data
- **Feature Engineering**: selecting important variables, extracting insights
- **Dimensionality Reduction**: PCA or autoencoders to reduce complexity

To improve data quality, consistency, and efficiency, which directly impacts model accuracy.

Step 3: AI Modeling Layer (Core Intelligence)

So predictions about the system are here being made via a combination of artificial intelligence models. Analysis tools

- **Machine Learning:** RF, SVM, XGBoost, and LR
- **Deep Learning:** LSTM (time-series forecasting), GRU, CNN, and Autoencoders

Additional processes:

- **Ensemble Learning**: stacking, voting, blending
- **Model Training & Optimization**: cross-validation, hyperparameter tuning

To capture patterns (ML models), time dependencies (DL models), and complex nonlinear relationships (hybrid approach).

Step 4: Risk Evaluation Layer (Risk Intelligence Engine)

Here, predictions are converted into meaningful risk insights. Key components:

Multi-Risk Assessment:

- **Risk Score Calculation→** Combines outputs from multiple models
- **Risk Aggregation & Interdependency Analysis→** Uses correlation/ network analysis

Performance Evaluation Metrics: To transform model outputs into quantified and interpretable risk measures.

Step 5: Decision Support Layer (Action Layer)

This is where business decisions happen. Outputs:

- **Visualization Dashboards** → easy interpretation
- **Real-time Alerts** → fraud detection, risk spikes
- **Scenario Analysis** → "what-if" simulations
- **Explainable AI (XAI)** → model transparency
- **Strategic Decision Support** → investment, lending decisions

To convert technical outputs into actionable insights for decision-makers.

Step 6: Governance, Security & Ethics Layer (Cross-Cutting Layer)

This layer runs across all stages, ensuring compliance and trust. Key elements:

- Data privacy & security
- Access control
- Model interpretability
- Bias detection & fairness
- Regulatory compliance (Basel norms, GDPR)
- Audit trails

To ensure the system is secure, ethical, and legally compliant.

Step 7: Feedback & Continuous Learning Loop (Adaptive Intelligence)

This is what makes the system dynamic and self-improving. Process:

- New data / market changes occur
- Models are retrained
- Performance is monitored
- Feedback is incorporated

To ensure the system adapts to market changes, improves accuracy over time and remains relevant in real-time environments.

Algorithm: Hybrid AI-Based Financial Risk Modeling

This section presents the step-by-step algorithm of the proposed hybrid AI-based framework along with the mathematical formulation used for financial risk prediction and evaluation.

Input: Multi-source financial dataset

$$D = \{D_s, D_u\}$$

where, = Structured data (transactions, market data) and = Unstructured data (news, reports, sentiment).

Output: Final Risk Score and Decision Support Insights

Step 1: Data Acquisition

Collect and integrate multi-source data:

Step 2: Data Preprocessing

Apply cleaning and transformation:

- Handle missing values:

- Normalize data:

- Feature selection:

- Dimensionality reduction (PCA):

Step 3: Model Training (Hybrid AI Models)

Train multiple models:

- **Machine Learning Models:**
- **Deep Learning Models (LSTM):** and

Step 4: Ensemble / Hybrid Integration

Combine predictions:

Where, = weight of model and

Step 5: Risk Score Calculation

Compute overall risk score:

Where, = Credit Risk, = Market Risk, = Operational Risk, = Liquidity Risk and .

Step 6: Risk Aggregation

Incorporate interdependency:

Step 7: Performance Evaluation

Evaluate model:

-
-
-
-

Step 8: Decision Support

Generate outputs: Risk alerts if

- Visualization dashboards
- Scenario analysis

Step 9: Feedback & Learning

Update model:

7. RESULT AND DISCUSSION

Experimentation is used to test the financial risk modelling system that is based on artificial intelligence. This chapter details the steps taken to put the hybrid model into action, conduct experiments with it, and assess its performance. To prove that proposed model is better than competing models in accuracy, resilience, and efficiency, the findings are contrasted with those of other deep learning and machine learning systems. Furthermore, we examine the efficiency, stability, and risk prediction. Findings demonstrate that financial institutions can greatly benefit from utilizing hybrid AI in conjunction with various data sources to improve risk prediction and decision-making.

7.1 Implementation and Experimental Setup

The hybrid prediction architecture is developed on a Python environment like high-level libraries like Tensor flow, Scikit-learn and Pandas. We run the experiments on a financial dataset of transaction data, market data and fake risk labels. Normalization, feature selection, and dimensionality reduction are performed on the data as part of the preprocessing steps. We train and assess a hybrid ensemble model in addition to Random Forest, SVM, and LSTM. The experimental setups in Table 2 are comparable.

Table 2. Experimental Setup

Parameter	Description
Dataset Type	Financial multi-source dataset
Data Split	70% Training, 30% Testing
Tools Used	Python, TensorFlow, Scikit-learn
Models Compared	RF, SVM, LSTM, Hybrid Model

7.2 Results and Analysis

Here, we comprehensively evaluate the proposed hybrid AI-based financial risk model. The proposed approach is compared with the conventional models, including SVM, RF and LSTM. The analysis includes the predictive ability, performance on different risks, classification efficiency, computational efficiency and the effect of hybrid learning.

7.2.1 Performance Comparison of Models

This involves typical evaluation measures in finding out the models forecasting abilities. Combining ML with DL models allows for more precise feature selection, pattern recognition, prediction, and generalization. The suggested model outperforms all baseline models, thanks in large part to hybrid learning and ensemble integration.

Table 3. Performance Comparison

Model	Accuracy (%)	Precision (%)	Recall (%)	F1-Score (%)	AUC
SVM	85.2	84.5	83.8	84.1	0.88
Random Forest	88.7	87.9	86.5	87.2	0.91
LSTM	90.5	89.8	88.6	89.2	0.93
Proposed Hybrid Model	94.3	93.6	92.8	93.2	0.96

Research can see how well each model performs in this graph. This proves that the suggested model is the most accurate, which is a result of the combined effects of hybrid learning and ensemble integration.

Figure 2. Performance Comparison

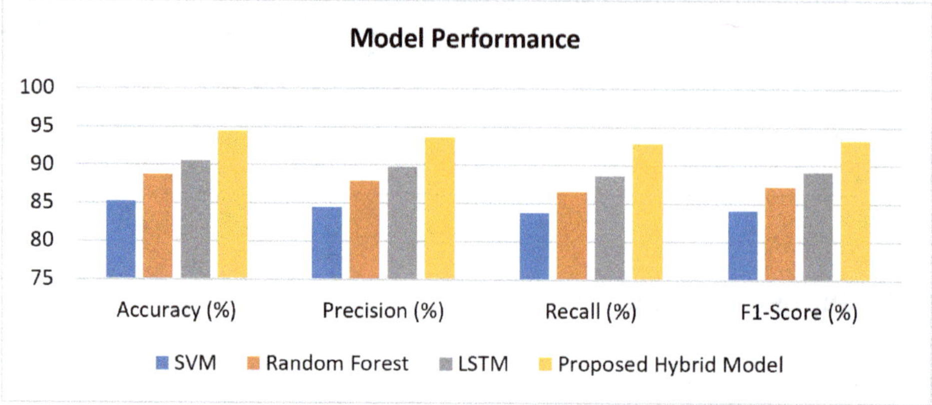

The precision-recall curve for different models is displayed in this picture. It demonstrates how well various models can deal. By consistently outperforming its competitors, the suggested hybrid model shows promise as a financial risk predictor.

Figure 3. Precision–Recall Curve of Different Models

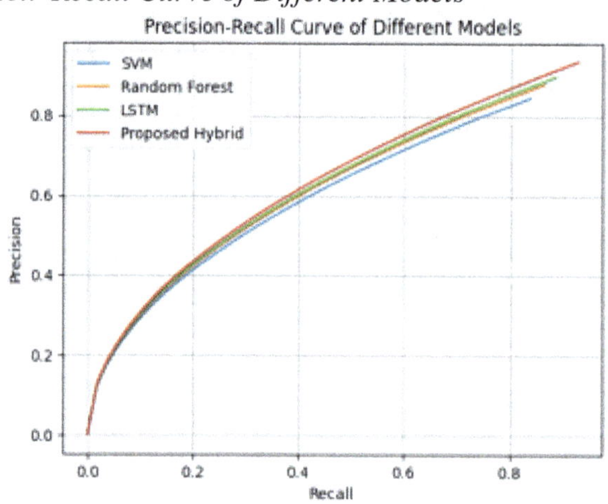

The ROC curve represents a compromise between the two PR measures. With the highest AUC, our hybrid model outperforms competition in classification accuracy and the efficiency with which it differentiates between dangerous and non-dangerous occurrences. With an AUC of 0.96 at its peak, the suggested model clearly has strong classification capabilities.

Figure 4. ROC Curve of Different Models

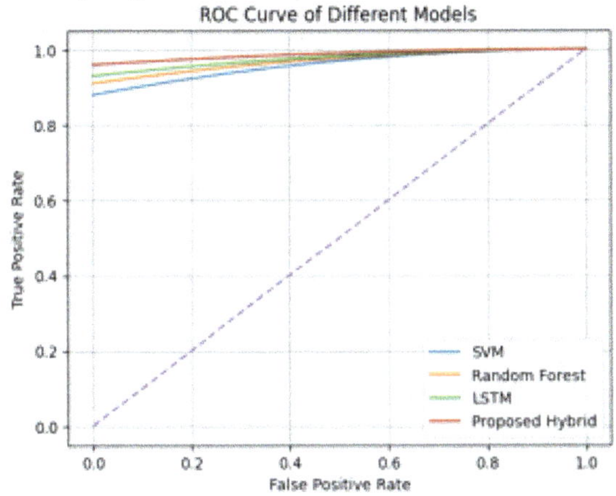

7.2.2 Risk-Type Wise Prediction Analysis

This assesses the models' ability to predict various types of financial risk. The proposed model achieves better predictions for all categories of financial risk than the baseline models.

Table 4. Risk Prediction Accuracy by Risk Type

Risk Type	SVM	RF	LSTM	Proposed Model
Credit Risk	84%	87%	89%	93%
Market Risk	83%	86%	90%	94%
Operational Risk	82%	85%	88%	92%
Liquidity Risk	81%	84%	87%	91%

This figure illustrates the accuracy of financial risk prediction for credit, market, operational and liquidity risks. The accuracy of SVM, Random Forest, LSTM, and the suggested hybrid model are all compared.

Figure 5. Risk Prediction Distribution

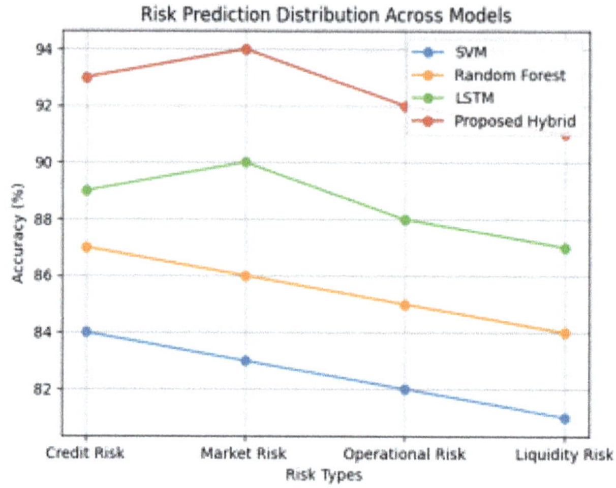

7.2.3 Classification Performance Evaluation

To evaluate model's accuracy in true and false predictions, this illustrates the confusion matrix analysis. Confusion matrix reveals that suggested model achieves good results, while exhibiting low rates of false positive and false negative. Its accuracy in predicting both high- and low-risk scenarios is demonstrated here.

Table 5. Confusion Matrix Summary (Proposed Model)

Metric	Value
True Positive (TP)	920
True Negative (TN)	890
False Positive (FP)	60
False Negative (FN)	50

7.2.4 Computational Performance Analysis

This assesses the training and testing times of various models. While the hybrid model has slightly higher computational time than traditional models, it is more efficient than other deep learning models that are based only on deep learning, such as LSTM.

Table 6. Computational Performance

Model	Training Time (s)	Testing Time (s)
SVM	12.5	2.1
RF	15.3	2.5
LSTM	45.7	5.8
Proposed Model	38.2	4.2

This figure shows the computational efficiency of the models in terms of their training and testing times. A compromise between accuracy and efficiency is achieved by the hybrid model suggested in this study, which is more computationally intensive than classic ML models but less intensive than DL models like LSTM.

Figure 6. Computational Performance of Models

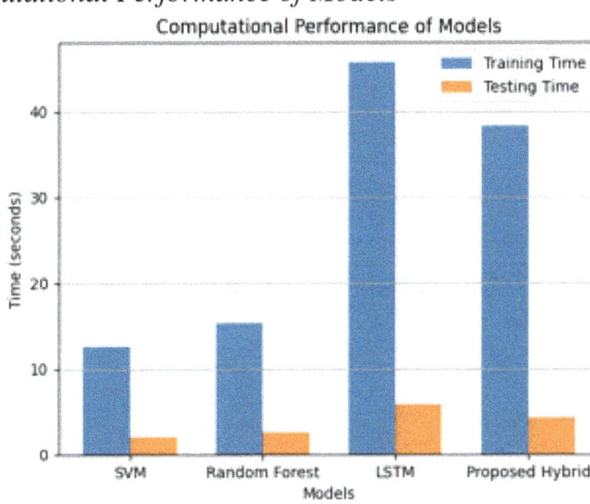

7.2.5 Ablation Study of Hybrid Model

This evaluates the importance of each component in the hybrid model. Combining ML and DL models yields better results than using either technique alone, according to the ablation study.

Table 7. Ablation Study of Hybrid Model

Configuration	Accuracy (%)
ML Only	88.7
DL Only	90.5
ML + DL (Hybrid)	94.3

The proposed hybrid model is shown to be convergent in this plot. It appears that the model does not overfit and has high generalization properties.

Figure 7. Training vs Validation Loss Curve

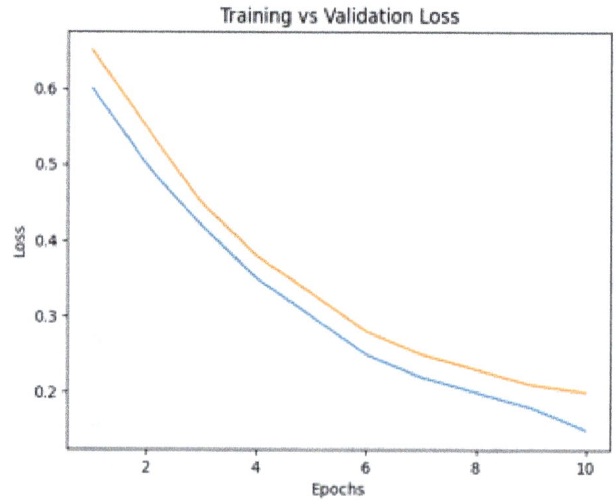

Clearly, the hybrid AI-based model improves risk prediction in financial markets over traditional models. The use of ML and DL enables the system to learn static and dynamic patterns. In addition, the ensemble model is more stable and less prone to errors. The system also performs well with different financial risks, hence offering a practical approach. Although it is more complex than traditional models, this is offset by the improved performance.

CONCLUSION AND FUTURE SCOPE

To handle complicated and ever-changing financial settings, the suggested architecture provides a unified method for multi-source data, hybrid AI models, and real-time analytics. utilizing ensemble approaches to mix ML and DL models, the framework is able to extract complicated and temporal correlations in financial data utilizing hybrid AI. The hybrid model outperforms conventional models in performance parameters. In addition, proposed framework shows good performance for multiple risk types: credit, market, operational and liquidity risks, proving its capability to manage various risks. Although the proposed model is slightly more complex than traditional models in terms of computational costs, it is more efficient than deep learning models, with better predictive performance. Explainable AI components are added to make it interpretable and to comply with regulatory limits, to make it more applicable in real life financial systems. But the proposed method needs more research but the investigation showed great improvement. Real-time data processing technology allows you to track volatile markets and spot impending hazards. Modern DL algorithms like GNN and Transformers are more capable of capturing intricate webs of interdependencies between financial institutions. Finally, further integration with Trustworthy AI can be performed to enhance model explainability and regulatory compliance. Safety and privacy are extremely essential. Previous studies on blockchains focused mostly on auditable and secure data transport. To boost the accuracy, new data sources such as social and behavioral data can be integrated. Last but not least, cloud and edge computing can offer better scalability, ease of deployment and more computational efficiency for distributed systems. This will mean better, safer and more adaptive financial risk assessments.

REFERENCES

Adebowale, A. M., & Akinnagbe, O. B. (2021). Leveraging AI-driven data integration for predictive risk assessment in decentralized financial markets. *Int J Eng Technol Res Manag*, *5*(12), 295.

Bandi, V. D. V. K. (2024). AI-Driven Predictive Risk Modeling Architectures for Financial Systems. *International Journal Of Finance*, *37*(3), 54–78.

Celestin, M., & Mishra, A. K. (2025). AI-driven financial analytics: Enhancing forecast accuracy, risk management, and decision-making in corporate finance. *Janajyoti Journal*, *3*(1), 1–27. DOI: 10.3126/jj.v3i1.83284

Chawla, N. (2025). AI-Driven Predictive Project Risk Management in Large-Scale Financial Software Programs. *J. Electrical Systems*, *21*(1s), 618–626. DOI: 10.52783/jes.9338

Faisal, S. M., Khan, W., & Ishrat, M. (2025). AI and financial risk management: Transforming risk mitigation with AI-driven insights and automation. In *Artificial Intelligence for Financial Risk Management and Analysis* (pp. 281–306). IGI Global Scientific Publishing. DOI: 10.4018/979-8-3373-1200-2.ch014

Fritz-Morgenthal, S., Hein, B., & Papenbrock, J. (2022). Financial risk management and explainable, trustworthy, responsible AI. *Frontiers in Artificial Intelligence*, *5*, 779799. DOI: 10.3389/frai.2022.779799 PMID: 35295866

Hossain, M. A. (2025). Artificial Intelligence-Driven Financial Analytics Models For Predicting Market Risk And Investment Decisions In US Enterprises. *ASRC Procedia: Global Perspectives in Science and Scholarship*, *1*(01), 1066–1095. DOI: 10.63125/9csehp36

Islam, M. M. (2026). Artificial Intelligence–Driven Predictive Analytics Framework for Data-Driven Decision Support in Complex Organizational Systems. *American Journal of Data Science and Analytics*, *7*(03), 163–207. DOI: 10.63125/mexw3p37

Jahid, M. S. R. (2025). AI-driven optimization and risk modeling in strategic economic zone development for mid-sized economies: A review approach. *International Journal of Scientific Interdisciplinary Research*, *6*(1), 185–218. DOI: 10.63125/31wna449

Kantesaria, R., & Panda, H. S. (2026). A review on AI-based data-driven models for optimization of nanocarriers as drug delivery systems. *ACS Biomaterials Science & Engineering*, *12*(3), 1397–1418. DOI: 10.1021/acsbiomaterials.5c01998 PMID: 41668335

Kusumba, S. (2024). Delivering the Power of Data-Driven Decisions: An AI-Enabled Data Strategy Framework for Healthcare Financial Systems. [IJEETR]. *International Journal of Engineering & Extended Technologies Research*, *6*(2), 7799–7806.

Lin, P., Cai, Y., Wu, H., Yin, J., & Luorang, Z. (2025). AI-driven risk control for health insurance fund management: A data-driven approach. *International Journal of Computers, Communications & Control*, *20*(2). Advance online publication. DOI: 10.15837/ijccc.2025.2.7024

Ogunmokun, A. S., Balogun, E. D., & Ogunsola, K. O. (2021). A conceptual framework for AI-driven financial risk management and corporate governance optimization. *International Journal of Multidisciplinary Research and Growth Evaluation*, *2*(1), 781–790. DOI: 10.54660/.IJMRGE.2021.2.1.772-780

Oko-Odion, C. (2025). Ai-driven risk assessment models for financial markets: Enhancing predictive accuracy and fraud detection. *International Journal of Computer Applications Technology and Research*, *14*(04), 80–96.

Omopariola, B., & Aboaba, V. (2021). Advancing financial stability: The role of AI-driven risk assessments in mitigating market uncertainty. *Int J Sci Res Arch*, *3*(2), 254–270. DOI: 10.30574/ijsra.2021.3.2.0106

Paleti, S. (2022). Fusion Bank: Integrating AI-Driven Financial Innovations with Risk-Aware Data Engineering in Modern Banking. *Decision Making*, *2326*, 9865.

Paleti, S. (2024). Transforming financial risk management with AI and data engineering in the modern banking sector. [AJAAI]. *American Journal of Analytics and Artificial Intelligence*, *1*(1), 2–12.

Pattabhi, A. (2025). Risk intelligence: AI-powered financial risk management for a new cra. *International Journal of Artificial Intelligence, Data Science, and Machine Learning*, *6*(2), 20–34. DOI: 10.63282/3050-9262.IJAIDSML-V6I2P103

Radhakrishnan, G. V., Varalakshmi, R., Kohli, N. K., Jha, S., Sruthi, S., & Singh, S. P. (2025). AI-Driven Predictive Analytics for Enhancing Automotive Safety in Financial Risk Assessments in Cloud Data. In *Embracing the Cloud as a Business Essential* (pp. 107–124). IGI Global Scientific Publishing. DOI: 10.4018/979-8-3693-9581-3.ch006

Selvarajan, G. (2021). Leveraging AI-enhanced analytics for industry-specific optimization: A strategic approach to transforming data-driven decision-making. *International Journal of Enhanced Research in Science Technology and Engineering*, *10*(1), 78 84.

Shittu, A. K. (2022). Advances in AI-driven credit risk models for financial services optimization. *International Journal of Multidisciplinary Research and Growth Evaluation*, *3*(1), 660–676. DOI: 10.54660/.IJMRGE.2022.3.1-660-676

Siddiqui, N. A. (2025). Optimizing business decision-making through AI-enhanced business intelligence systems: A systematic review of data-driven insights in financial and strategic planning. *Strategic Data Management and Innovation*, *2*(1), 202–223. DOI: 10.71292/sdmi.v2i01.21

Zeriouh, K., & Amara, M. (2025). AI–driven frameworks for strategic risk management: A systematic review and model for organizational resilience and decision support. *Journal of Intelligent Management and Decision*, *4*(3), 44–61. DOI: 10.56578/jimd040304

Zhang, T., Chen, Q., He, Q., & Zhu, W. (2025). AI-Driven Financial Risk Early-Warning Using TD-DS-RF: A Decision Support Model Integrating Multi-Source Data. *Decision Making: Applications in Management and Engineering*, *8*(1), 478–496.

Zhang, Y. (2025, May). AI-Driven Framework for Financial Risk Management: Enhancing Decision-Making with LSTM Networks and Probabilistic Models. In *2025 2nd International Conference on Intelligent Computing and Robotics (ICICR)* (pp. 176-181). IEEE.

Chapter 11
Designing an Ethical AI Governance Framework for Financial Systems:
Regulatory Compliance, Transparency, and Trust in AI-Driven Finance

Trupti Patil
http://orcid.org/0009-0002-1019-3347
Department of Information Technology, K.J. Somaiya Institute of Technology, Sion, India

Mamatha G.
http://orcid.org/0009-0000-1709-7687
Department of Management Studies, Sri Siddhartha Institute of Business Management, Tumkur, India

Ankur Gupta
http://orcid.org/0000-0002-4651-5830
Department of Computer Science and Engineering, Vaish College of Engineering, Rohtak, India

ABSTRACT

Use of AI in the financial services industry has revolutionized the game because it is now possible to make decisions faster, automate functions, and extract insights out of data. This expansion renders it particularly difficult to secure data, promote fairness, be transparent and accountable, and adhere to international regulations such as the General Data Protection Regulation (GDPR), the Reserve Bank of India

DOI: 10.4018/979-8-3693-3751-6.ch011

Guidelines, and the International Organisation of Standardisation (ISO) models. This study is about creating and putting into action an ethical AI framework that is particular to the financial industry. A mixed paradigm, including the use of technological skills and adherence to rules and moral principles, is what we propose. Surveys and performance data were used to see how well the framework worked.

1. INTRODUCTION

The rapid development and application of the AI technology in the banking sector have transformed the way tasks are performed, risk evaluation, fraud detection, credit score generation, and client communication. In numerous areas, including algorithmic trading and automatic compliance systems, AI provides numerous opportunities to enhance operational efficiency, accuracy in predictions, and financial inclusion. Nevertheless, these revolutionary abilities will seriously impact regulations and ethics that should be investigated with great caution (Faheem, M. A., 2021). There are more and more ethical issues, such as the loss of human accountability, discrimination, breaches of data privacy, algorithmic prejudice, and decision-making models that are hard to understand. These concerns are even greater when money decisions significantly affect the capacity of people to access credit, loans, and investment opportunity (Onoja et al., 2021). Failure to be keen on how you apply AI algorithms might lead to them worsening the situation or providing you with incorrect or unfair results. If security is bad, it is much more probable that financial data will be utilised or handled incorrectly. This leaves people with the question as to whether they can give informed consent and be free. Regulations can hardly keep up with AI, as it is evolving so rapidly and in such a multitude of ways. Such algorithms, which continue to learn and change, are prohibited by both law and regulation at the moment (Elumilade et al., 2021). Financial institutions and other banks should be equipped with new rules to ensure they can harness AI to their advantage without restricting new concepts. This will aid in bridging the gap in knowledge. Numerous global organisations are discussing how to reduce the probability of these risks, including algorithmic auditing, accountability norms, ethical principles of AI, and accountable design. The impact of AI on rules, money systems, and morals is now under researcher consideration (Oladuji et al., 2021). By examining scholarly literature on the application of AI in the financial sector in governance, financial planning, risk assessment, and compliance, we seek to identify similarities, reach conclusions, and provide solutions on how AI can be ethically used in the financial sector. Financial institutions need to employ morally and technically sound AI technologies. Ethical AI by Design is interested in ensuring that AI systems adhere to the principles of fairness, openness, accountability, and lawful adherence to the regulations when collecting data through the time of their deployment, and control (Ogunsola et al., 2021). The ethical issues are not regarded as externally imposed rules in this approach. As a matter of fact, it has in-built bias finding, easy to understand AI models, and governance systems. Incorporating ethical safeguards during the design process is extremely critical to ensure innovation is responsible and that individuals have confidence in the financial services business. This is due to the fact that algorithmic decisions have an impact on investment possibilities, fraud detection, and access to credit (Soundarapandiyan, 2022).

1.1 Background

AI has made it possible for the financial sector to make things like loan underwriting, algorithmic trading, portfolio management, and rule compliance easier. Big data and machine learning algorithms make it feasible for many people to have automated decision-making, better risk assessment, and customised financial services (McBride et al., 2022). There are certain moral and legal issues with AI, even though it can make things more efficient, faster, and accurate. These may result in systemic risk since the models are interdependent, data privacy has issues, algorithms are not unbiased and decisions are not transparent. Unless it is based on a black-box model, people do not trust black-box models, particularly deep learning algorithms, which do not always make sense and why they do what they do (Sheth et al., 2022). Biased training data can make social and economic differences worse, which can lead to unfair treatment in the loan and insurance application processes. With the removal or enhanced judgment of humans by artificial intelligence systems, ancient methods of maintaining a watch over things are becoming less effective. Due to this fact, individuals in the banking and insurance sectors, policy makers and regulators are attempting to identify ways of reducing the effects of AI on these industries. The increasing number of individuals demand the establishment of AI governance frameworks which place privacy, fairness, accountability, and openness at the center (Kothandapani, H. P., 2022). We would have to be aware of the ethical and legal issues that arise when using AI in the banking sector in case we would develop systems that can be trusted and held responsible by customers. Table 1.1 shows the main historical background aspects of the research.

Table 1. Background of the Study

Aspect	Description
Technological Advancement	The integration of AI in finance has revolutionized traditional processes such as credit scoring, fraud detection, and algorithmic trading.
Data Dependency	AI relies heavily on large-scale financial data, which raises concerns about privacy, accuracy, and informed consent.
Ethical Challenges	Issues such as algorithmic bias, lack of transparency, and discrimination are prevalent in many AI-based financial tools.
Regulatory Gaps	Existing financial regulations are often outdated and struggle to address the complexities of AI technologies.
Societal Impact	AI-driven decisions significantly affect financial access, equity, and user trust, making ethical governance essential.
Need for Balance	There is a growing need to balance AI innovation with ethical accountability and effective regulatory oversight.

1.2 Motivation of Research

The financial industry is particularly delighted at the pace at which AI is evolving as it is capable of automating tedious processes, processing large amounts of data and providing more precise insights within a shorter period. This is less exciting to people because they are concerned with the aspects of ethics and rules, particularly those that must relate to justice, accountability, and transparency. Unfair credit ratings, loans approved due to algorithms, and secret trading algorithms are some of the most famous instances of the threats of AI systems not supervised (Venigandla & Vemuri, 2022). The way an individual spends their money can impact their credit rating, future investments, insurance status, and financial well-being (Maple et al., 2023). In other words, applying AI in an unethical manner is quite perilous. Even while more and more people are paying attention to these issues, rules and conventions haven't kept up with new technologies, and ethical standards differ from place to place and organisation to organisation. The necessity to address this gap quickly is what drives our study. To reach this purpose, it will look at the regulatory issues and moral hazards that AI brings to the financial sector (Bello et al., 2023). It is also important to build strong governance models and ethical AI frameworks that fit the needs of each sector. This paper looks at previous research and finds holes in current methods to add to the ongoing conversation about how to use AI responsibly. The paper also tells tech companies, regulators, and banks how to make AI systems that are fair, open, and responsible. Table 1.2 describe the description about various concerns of aspect.

Table 2. Ethical and Regulatory Concerns of AI

Aspect	Description
Industry Excitement	Financial sector is eager to adopt AI for processing large datasets, automating tasks, and generating fast, accurate insights.
Public Concerns	People are wary due to ethical issues around fairness, transparency, and accountability.
Notable Risks	Examples include biased credit scoring, discriminatory loan approvals, and opaque trading algorithms.
Impact on Individuals	AI decisions influence creditworthiness, investment access, insurance, and overall financial health.
Moral Implications	Immoral or biased AI use can have severe consequences for individuals and society.
Regulatory Gap	Current regulations lag behind technological advancements; ethical norms vary by region and organization.
Motivation for Research	Urgent need to close the ethical and regulatory gap in AI applications in finance.
Research Focus	Examine regulatory challenges, identify moral risks, and analyze shortcomings in current governance models.
Proposed Solution	Develop robust ethical AI frameworks and sector-specific governance models.
Contribution	Guide for tech developers, regulators, and financial institutions to create fair, transparent, and accountable AI systems.

1.3 Limitation of Research

This article tries to give a full picture of the legal and moral problems that come up with AI-driven financial services, even though it has several problems. First, we can only look at English-language materials that are available to the public and have been vetted by other experts (Alonge et al., 2023). This means that there may be private industry research or sources that could be beneficial but are not in English. Second, the results may not be useful for very long because AI rules and technology change so quickly. Because things are made so quickly, academic institutions and regulatory authorities often can't fully understand the long-term effects (Celestin, 2023). This vast subject covers a lot of ground, including data science, economics, ethics, law, and public policy. Because of this, it could be hard to focus on just one area and not others. The evaluation is based on qualitative evaluations and discussions of ideas instead of quantitative models or real-world facts (Adewale et al., 2023). There is also a brief review of changes to regional regulations, such as the AI Act in the EU and the US SEC's changing recommendations about AI. However, there is no in-depth look at how these changes affect specific countries. Lastly, the study focusses on problems and suggests policy-based frameworks instead of technical fixes or moral algorithms (Agu, E. E., 2024). These restrictions are important, but they also give researchers a chance to build on and improve the results shown here in the future. Table 1.3 describes the research limitations.

Table 3. Limitations of the Research

Limitation	Description
Language and Source Constraints	The study is limited to English-language peer-reviewed publications, potentially excluding relevant non-English or grey literature.
Temporal Limitation	The literature review includes sources available only up to mid-2025, which may not cover the most recent advancements or regulatory changes.
Rapid Evolution of AI and Regulation	The fast-paced development in AI technologies and financial regulations means findings could become outdated quickly.
Interdisciplinary Scope	The research spans multiple domains (AI, finance, ethics, law), making it difficult to cover each area comprehensively or with deep technical detail.
Lack of Empirical Validation	The study is theoretical and literature-based; it does not include experimental testing, real-world implementation, or validation of proposed frameworks.
Geographic and Jurisdictional Diversity	Variations in regulatory standards and AI practices across regions may not be fully captured in a unified analysis.

1.4 Need for Ethical AI Frameworks

It is more necessary than ever to define moral guidelines for AI systems because they are becoming more and more significant in making financial judgments. These characteristics are highly crucial to make sure that financial AI follows all the rules and standards of society (Thakur & Sharma, 2024). Decisions concerning someone's creditworthiness, how much they may borrow, and how effectively they can manage their money can have a huge effect on their lives. The issues involved in making or modifying judgments with the help of algorithms are the bias, the violation of privacy, and the utilization of data in an unacceptable manner (Addy, W. A., 2024). Ethical AI models ensure that the protection of data, accountability, transparency, and justice are considered throughout the entire AI lifecycle, including data acquisition and model training and the deployment of models as well as monitoring them. Lack of these guidelines might make companies lose its customers, break the law, and destroy its own reputation by making decisions that are either unfair or biased (Owolabi, O. S., 2024). Having an ethical framework, a company can both generate new ideas and observe the regulations. They also discuss other ways in which technology can be used to assist the court system. Companies can check to see if they are doing ethically by using the correct frameworks (Patil, D., 2024). This is essential since corporations and governments are attempting to establish AI control more formal by undertaking such initiatives as the EU AI Act or OECD AI guidelines. Digital services can gain the trust of banks and other financial institutions as they demonstrate that they are concerned with responsible and people-centered AI. Artificial intelligence has network requirements as illustrated in figure 1.1.

Figure 1. Need for Ethical AI Network

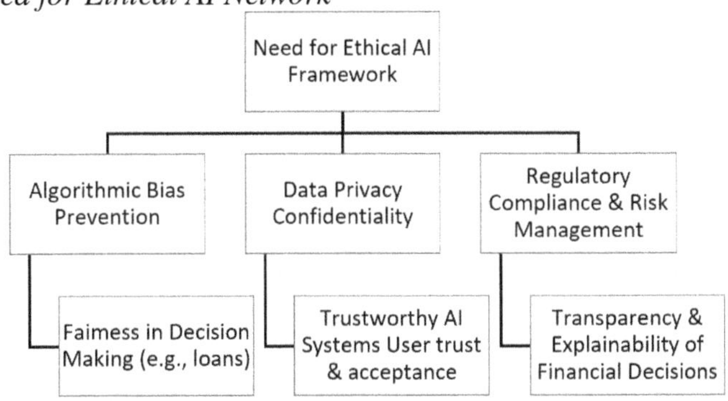

1.5 Data-Driven Nature of AI

In banking, data is the most crucial factor for AI. These databases have a lot of information, such as financial ratings, purchase history, changes in the market in real time, social media signals, behavioural analytics, and more. However, when we over rely on statistics, we may get ourselves into numerous moral and practical issues (Kothandapani, H. P., 2025). It is quite concerning that historical financial information may be biased since it may indicate unjust systems that existed in the past. The use of biased data to train AI models can perpetuate unethical practices such as lending money to racially or gender-based individuals (Oko-Odion, C., 2025). The second issue is ensuring that the privacy of people is safeguarded. When the sensitive financial information of a customer is misused or revealed, it might destroy his or her life. In order to ensure that data is disposed in an ethical manner, there should be stringent regulations regarding the manner in which data can be utilized. Such rules must cover such aspects as requesting consent, restricting information gathering, and ensuring that the information is not associated with an individual (Saiyed, A., 2025). Model projections can as well be very wrong and unreliable when the data is insufficient, missing or unbalanced. Due to the continual transformations of the financial markets, the data must be updated, and the models should be trained and retrained again and again (Mishra et al., 2025). The way AI processes information should be known to establish efficient, equitable, and transparent monetary systems.

The most important aspect of trustworthy AI in finance is to maintain data as safe, precise, and representative. Table 1.4 shows artificial intelligence data driven nature.

Table 4. Data-Driven Nature of AI

Aspect	Description
Foundation of AI Systems	AI models in finance are built upon vast datasets including transaction records, credit histories, and customer behavior patterns.
Learning from Historical Data	Machine learning algorithms identify patterns and make predictions using historical financial data.
Real-Time Decision Making	AI systems often operate on real-time data streams to assess risks or detect anomalies instantaneously.
Quality and Bias in Data	Poor data quality or biased datasets can lead to unfair or inaccurate decisions in AI applications like loan approval or fraud detection.
Privacy and Confidentiality Concerns	Handling sensitive financial data raises ethical concerns around data privacy, ownership, and regulatory compliance (e.g., GDPR, CCPA).
Role in Model Transparency	The data inputs directly affect model interpretability and accountability, especially in high-stakes financial decisions.

1.6 Contribution of research

This study enhances the existing literature on AI in financial systems by analyzing the ethical and regulatory issues associated with AI-driven financial technologies. This paper shifts the emphasis of the technical advantages and operational efficiencies of AI applications, such as automated decision-making, fraud detection, risk management, and credit evaluation, to the ethical issues and long-term integration of AI into financial ecosystems (Gowtham et al., 2025). The study states that modern financial frameworks incorporate moral principles, regulations, which have to be adhered to, and emerging technologies simultaneously. The greatest thing to take away in this research is the operation of ethical governance in financial setting that encompass AI. To demonstrate the significance of implementing ethical design principles in AI-driven financial systems, the paper examines the current challenges such as algorithmic bias, absence of transparency, accountability issues, and data privacy risks. This view can make you understand the correlation between the present technology and intelligent financial planning. The examination of the regulations concerning the use of AI in finance is another valuable input. This study has found that what we require are elastic regulatory structures to enable the accelerated emergence of digital financial services. This is because it looks at how current financial rules and new AI technologies function together. This data could assist banks, politicians, and regulators to generate concepts of governance structures that would ensure that AI-based financial processes will be equitable, transparent, and responsible. The paper contributes to the interdisciplinary literature in general by synthesizing concepts of AI, financial governance, and ethical policy frameworks. It preconditions more vigorous AI governance initiatives that balance between technical advances, observing the regulations, and addressing the desires of society. Findings of this study could enable banks, technology firms, and governments to create both legal and ethical AI systems. The findings of this paper contribute to the improved understanding of ethical AI implementation and the development of trustworthy financial systems that are AI-powered.

2. LITERATURE REVIEW

Faheem (2021) thinks that adopting advanced analytics driven by AI might completely revolutionise how credit ratings and predictions of defaults are created. The findings indicate that neural networks are more advantageous than conventional approaches. Nevertheless, it also brings up such ethical issues like bias in the algorithms and breach of privacy.

Onoja et al. (2021) suggest that the safety of AI use in online banking should be ensured by regulations and data protection. They propose making business processes transparent and limiting authorised personnel access to promote security in AI activities.

Elumilade et al. (2021) pen on data forensics and fraud detection. They discuss different methods through which machine learning can be used to keep financial integrity and detect fraud trends.

Oladuji et al. (2021) mentioned the application of AI to make up earnings of small and medium-sized enterprises. Although the credit scoring and payment systems have become better, the authors warn against overfitting and flawed models, demanding strong AI constraints.

Ogunsola et al. (2021) suggest a novel AI solution to internal audit and governance. Their approach takes advantage of predictive modelling and dynamic data analysis, claiming that ethical behavior and adherence to regulations are critical in financial security.

Soundararapandiyan (2022) presents a financial product created with AI that reduces the time wastage on the testing and prototyping of financial products through the refining of datasets. Although it saves on expenses and enhances flexibility, the paper focuses on the accuracy and fairness of data.

McBride et al. (2022) explores the impact of AI on corporate governance and stock markets. They propose that AI can improve the decision-making process, yet it may also empower a privileged minority. The model to bring AI up to ethical standards is suggested as impact capitalism.

Sheth et al. (2022) discuss the potential of AI to humanise the banking sector by stopping fraud, individualising loans, and enhancing customer interaction. However, they are worried about data security and reliance on automation, and suggest human-focused AI in the new economy.

Kothandapani (2022) examines the idea of AI-based credit rating in developing nations. The paper emphasizes that there is a rise in financial inclusion but details that there are poor data, technological illiteracy, and obscure algorithms.

Venigandla and Vemuri (2022) evaluate the role of AI and RPA in preempting fraud. Their research concludes that real time monitoring, adaptive models and regulatory compliance help in the smooth running of banking activities.

Maple et al. (2023) evaluate the advantages and disadvantages of AI in finance. Although they applaud its effectiveness and flexibility, they warn on systemic risks and ethical issues. It is suggested to use human-in-the-loop approaches and strict AI regulations.

Bello et al. (2023) investigate the possibility of AI to detect fraud in real-time within the U.S. banking industry. They emphasize the rapidity and precision of ML algorithms and discuss such problems as data imbalance, false positives, and constant updates of the models.

In a theoretical model that Alonge et al. (2023) suggest, U.S. banks are risk reducing by using data analytics and AI. They talk about the significance of governance, trustworthy data, and flexible structures, to sustain financial stability in the long term.

Celestin (2023) researches the uses of AI in Rwandan financial reporting. The research highlights the importance of digital literacy and emphasizes the use of AI in decision-making and compliance with regulations in resource-limited settings.

Adewale et al. (2023) assess the effectiveness of big data in improving financial analytics with pattern recognition and real-time insights. Among the advantages of the study, the authors point to the enhanced knowledge of the market and the disadvantages of overabundance of data, complexity, and abuse of ethics.

Agu et al. (2024) discuss the equity of AI-based financial services. They find such issues as biased decision-making and lack of transparency, suggesting inclusive data practices and fairness-based algorithms, as well as interdisciplinary collaboration in fintech.

Thakur and Sharma (2024) discuss ethical issues in artificial intelligence-based financial decisions. Privacy, informed consent and algorithmic transparency are the key concerns. The authors request the idea of ethical design among software engineers.

According to Addy et al. (2024), AI-based analytics enhance predictions, portfolio automation, and optimum utilisation of assets. Nevertheless, issues like data collection, customer confidence, and compliance with regulations remain. Explainable AI is postulated to develop transparency.

Owolabi et al. (2024) emphasize such ethical issues in financial AI systems as data privacy, user consent, and accountability. The paper suggests ethical AI models to guarantee equitable and accountable deals.

Patil (2024) explores the use of neural networks in identifying financial fraud by AI. Although useful in detecting anomalies, there are fears that predictive analytics may be abused, that predictive analytics may lack human control and privacy is compromised. The article presents the idea of responsible innovation.

Gowtham et al. (2025) assume that AI in security solutions poses ethical and privacy threats. Some of the problems are the absence of accountability, algorithmic transparency, and data misuse. Transparency, fairness, and potentially government-regulated AI ethical auditing are promoted by the authors.

Kothandapani (2025) notes that financial regulatory monitoring is being transformed by LLMs. NLP tools have the potential to automate and simplify the compliance process, although the study also cautions against the dangers of automated bias and demand ethical governing systems.

Oko-Odion (2025) highlights the importance of AI in identifying fraud in the market and predicting economic instability. There is an improvement in prediction accuracy due to machine learning, which identifies outliers and fairness and model interpretability are still urgent issues.

Saiyed (2025) describes AI-based changes in finance, such as robo-advisors, trading algorithms, and AI-driven customer care. Issues include absence of standards, data protection, and algorithm bias. Such technologies as explainable AI are considered to be the key to ethical fintech development.

Mishra et al. (2025) discuss the ethical concerns in AI-based credit risk evaluation in BNPL (Buy Now Pay Later) systems. It is against unfair algorithms, intrusive use of data, and unethical lending, which is discussed in the paper and promotes more powerful legal frameworks and transparency.

Table 1.5 shows the survey of literature.

Table 5. Literature Review

Author / Year	Objectives	Methodology	Findings	Limitation
Faheem (2021)	Redefine credit scoring with AI	Model validation study	AI outperforms traditional models	Bias and privacy concerns
Onoja et al. (2021)	Digital transformation with AI and data governance	Policy and framework analysis	Suggested compliance strategies	Lack of implementation evidence
Elumilade et al. (2021)	Strengthen fraud auditing with AI	Case reviews and model applications	Improved integrity and detection	Need for unbiased data sets
Oladuji et al. (2021)	Model SME performance via AI	Applied study	Improved credit scoring and payments	Overfitting and complexity risks
Ogunsola et al. (2021)	Improve audit risk via AI models	Governance model proposal	Enhanced predictive audit power	Ethical and regulatory oversight gaps
Soundarapandiyan (2022)	Use synthetic data for financial product dev.	Simulation methodology	Enabled innovation, reduced costs	Ethics of data simulation
McBride et al. (2022)	Analyze AI's role in corporate governance	Theoretical perspective	Discussed impact capitalism and ethics	Lacked quantitative validation
Sheth et al. (2022)	Personalize banking in emerging markets with AI	Service evaluation	Improved customer experience	Data security concerns
Kothandapani (2022)	Leverage AI for credit scoring in emerging markets	Applied evaluation	Better inclusion and scoring accuracy	Algorithm opacity
Venigandla & Vemuri (2022)	Combine RPA and AI in fraud detection	Tech review with case use	Increased efficiency and automation	Need for regular updates
Maple et al. (2023)	Explore AI's impact in finance broadly	Analytical review	Balanced view on efficiency vs. systemic risk	No domain-specific evaluation
Bello et al. (2023)	Apply AI to real-time fraud detection	Empirical analysis of U.S. data	Effective fraud detection; highlighted false positives	Data imbalance and update needs
Alonge et al. (2023)	Theorize risk management in U.S. finance	Theoretical framework	Proposed optimization strategies using AI	No empirical testing
Celestin (2023)	Improve financial reporting in Rwanda with AI	Use-case study	Enhanced accuracy and reduced errors	Limited to one national context
Adewale et al. (2023)	Apply big data to financial analytics	Conceptual model and analytics	Better decision-making and strategy	Risks of data overload

continued on following page

Table 5. Continued

Author / Year	Objectives	Methodology	Findings	Limitation
Agu et al. (2024)	Promote fairness in AI-driven financial services	Theoretical discussion with ethics	Advocated fairness-aware algorithms and inclusive data	Lack of real-world examples
Thakur & Sharma (2024)	Ethical design in AI-driven finance	Conceptual and ethical analysis	Emphasis on transparency and consent	Absence of implementation framework
Addy et al. (2024)	Analyze AI's impact on financial planning	Analytical review	Enhanced forecasting and asset allocation	User trust and data concerns
Owolabi et al. (2024)	Study ethical risks of AI in finance	Critical review	Highlighted consent, discrimination, and accountability	Generalized findings without datasets
Patil (2024)	Explore AI use in risk and fraud detection	Review of detection models	Emphasized neural nets and anomaly detection	Ethical trade-offs unquantified
Gowtham et al. (2025)	Explore ethical and privacy risks in AI-powered security	Conceptual analysis with cases	Identified surveillance overreach and opaque algorithms	Lack of empirical validation
Kothandapani (2025)	Examine AI's role in regulatory compliance using LLMs	Case-based evaluation	Enhanced policy violation detection and efficiency	Limited interpretability, automation bias
Oko-Odion (2025)	Improve risk and fraud detection in financial markets	ML-based predictive models	Improved predictive accuracy and fraud detection	Challenges in model transparency
Saiyed (2025)	Review AI applications in fintech and future trends	Literature review	Highlighted robo-advisors, trading bots; emphasized explainable AI	Uncertain regulatory landscape
Mishra et al. (2025)	Address ethical issues in BNPL AI credit risk	Regulatory and legal analysis	Bias in credit scoring, risks to fair lending	Data bias and regulation lag

2.1 Research Gap

AI has made amazing progress in its short existence. It has changed the financial industry by making it possible to have smart risk management systems, automated decision-making, predictive analytics, and fraud detection. Banks and other financial companies are using AI-powered technology more and more to save costs, improve the customer experience, and make their operations more efficient. A lot of study has been done on how to use machine learning and smart data analytics for things like credit scoring, predicting the future of finance, finding fraud, algorithmic trading, and more. People are relying on AI more and more to help them with complicated financial tasks and decisions, as shown by recent advances in technology. A lot of study has been done on the technical and practical advantages of AI in banking. However, not as much has been done on the moral and legal issues that come up when these systems are used in financial ecosystems. Past studies have revealed that big issues with AI-based financial applications are data privacy, accountability, transparency, and algorithmic bias. Researchers have also warned that AI tools in lending and credit scoring can unintentionally reinforce any existing biases or give biased decision-making outputs in case trained on vast financial data (Arner et al., 2017). Other individuals just do not prefer complex AI models because they believe that they are difficult to comprehend and not very straightforward. Regulators and stakeholders are sometimes unable to learn how financial algorithms work as they are similar to black box systems (Brennen & Kreiss, 2016). Because financial companies rely more and more on large amounts of sensitive financial data, they need to put responsible data governance and ethical AI practices at the top of their list of priorities (Floridi et al., 2018).

3. PROBLEM STATEMENT

This has led to a number of key innovations including automatic processes, enhanced fraud detection and tailored financial products. It's more difficult to be honest and respect the law with the new technologies. AI systems handling money are referred to as black boxes by people as they do not tell how they arrive at their decisions. Extremely essential in budgeting, choosing an insurance cover, and increasing your credit rating. It is a source of concern to people that there may be discrimination, unfairness of algorithms, and privacy when the data used to educate computers have disparities across socioeconomic groups. People aren't paying enough attention because the regulations don't do a good job of taking new technology into account. This makes banks and other financial institutions to grapple with moral, legal and reputational issues. It means that, in cases where there are no established standards of morality and systems to ensure other people adhere to this morality, there are more likely to be left behind, exploited, and severely punished. We must work out a remedy to these ethical and legal challenges. If there aren't enough restrictions, it could be tougher for individuals to use financial services and make it more likely that AI will mess up the system. This study looks at and offers some broad moral and legal standards that can be employed in fintech because data is the lifeblood of AI. These systems should be built on new global norms, transparency, and justice. Unfortunately, the financial AI systems we have now also have problems since there aren't any well-organized design frameworks that include ethical and regulatory protections in the creation of AI. Now AI systems do not consider ethical risk reduction when they are created, they are instead aimed at giving predictions and automating workplaces; because of this, businesses have issues as they are usually involved in prejudice, transparency and regulation compliance after the fact. An ethical AI paradigm, which is design based, should entail that governance principles, regulatory constraints, and transparent decision-making processes should be assigned to the operational architecture of the financial AI systems.

4. PROPOSED WORK

This paper proposes an Ethical AI-by-Design framework that incorporates governance principles, compliance monitoring, and how to describe how financial AI systems operate. This is to deal with the regulatory and ethical issues that come up with AI-driven financial systems. Since the method is design-oriented, ethical safeguards are embedded in all the stages of the AI lifecycle, including data collection, model training, decision-making, and system monitoring. The suggested approach ensures the financial decision systems are in accordance with the global standards such as GDPR, RBI regulations, and ISO standards of governance. It also ensures openness and accountability of everyone. It does this by including systems to people watch, engines to ensure rules are being adhered to, AI tools that can be explained and modules to locate bias. The aim of the framework is to ensure that ethics, such as justice, responsibility, openness, and privacy, are all necessary considerations throughout the entire lifespan of AI, starting with data collection and moving up to data utilization and monitoring it. So, first we have to determine which are the largest moral and legal issues with the current use of AI in banks. These issues include rules that are not necessarily evident on how to act on them, biased algorithms and non-obvious decisions. The proposed model combines a combination of XAI tools, risk categorization modules, and ethical evaluation layers. The rules of the GDPR, RBI/SEBI, and ISO/IEC AI governance will all be followed by this site. There will also be a built-in policy decision engine to make sure that the AI outputs are clear and can be connected to rules. A federated compliance layer will be set up to make sure that everyone is following the rules. There will be an audit layer that uses feedback to keep an eye on performance and make sure people are doing their jobs. Because it is built on a secure architecture that protects privacy and limits the use of data, everyone involved will be able to observe the system in action. The aim of this model is to develop a code of moral conduct in the application of AI in finance. The research proposed model is illustrated in Figure 1.2.

Figure 2. Proposed model of this research

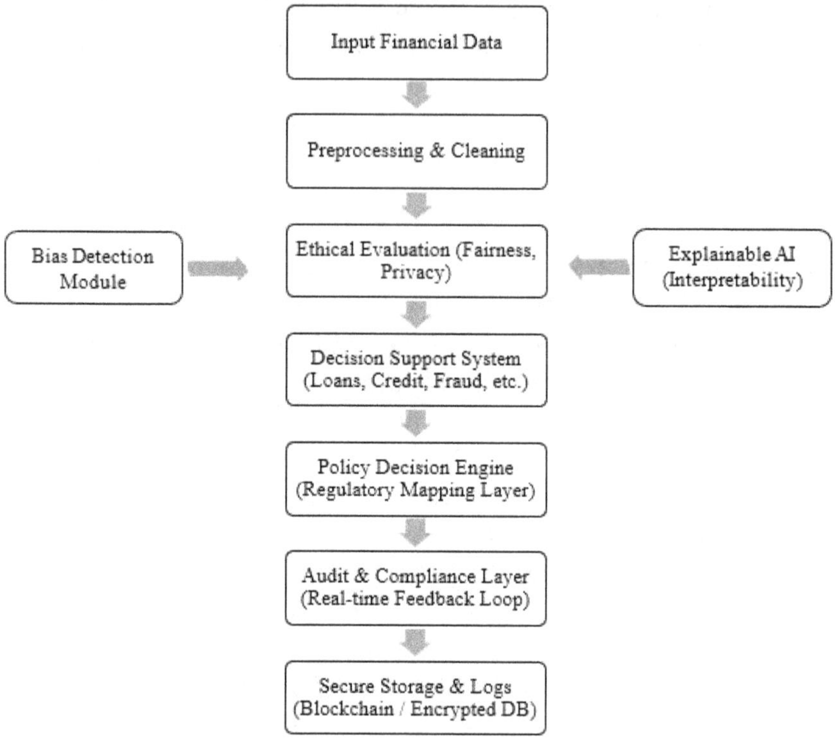

The proposed plan involves an AI regulatory framework of the financial sector that places ethics at the forefront. It is a mix of the strength of technology and the necessity to obey the rules. It all revolves around the AI Decision Engine. It uses the information provided by users and uses it to make decisions regarding money, including whether to authorise a loan or credit risk score. As a backup, this engine has a Data Ingestion Layer. It receives organised and unstructured financial information of the banks, credit bureaus and customers among others. An algorithmic bias is identified and corrected automatically via a Bias Detection and Mitigation Module that closely examines the data and fixes algorithmic bias based on fairness-conscious techniques. The Ethical Compliance Checker is on top of this layer. Regulations may vary depending on laws such as GDPR, RBI guidelines, ISO/IEC standards and local financial requirements. All decisions are checked against these standards. Users and auditors have the ability now to observe how AI makes decisions in real time with the addition of a Transparency Dashboard. Due to this fact, the decisions are transparent and reliable. A User Feedback Loop enables the system to learn and develop continuously by receiving feedback on a decision made and using it in subsequent iterations of the model. The Human Oversight Panel is in charge of running the system. This involves manually testing edge cases, intervention where necessary, and revision of compliance standards where necessary.

5. RESULT AND DISCUSSION

The results reveal that regulators are also more likely to follow the guidelines and stakeholders are much more confident when the elements of ethical governance are incorporated into AI systems at the initial stage. A design-oriented approach makes sure that ethical assessment is not an afterthought during audits since it is an important part of the system architecture. The framework also allows banks and other financial institutions to implement AI systems that are morally and technically responsible by introducing such features as explainability tools and bias-detecting algorithms and policy-driven compliance engines.

5.1 Framework Evaluation Metrics

The proposed model was compared with the available financial AI models based on their interpretability, accuracy in compliance, reduction of bias, and response time. Table 1.6 provides a comparative evaluation of AI models in accordance with interpretability, the accuracy of bias detection, regulatory compliance, and response time. The proposed Ethical AI Model has the highest interpretability of 91.2, the greatest bias detection accuracy of 95.6, and regulatory compliance of 970 ms, and the shortest response time of 970 ms. This highlights the effectiveness of ethically aligned AI systems over traditional and GDPR-compliant models in both performance and compliance metrics.

Table 6. Comparative Performance Analysis

Model	Interpretability Score	Bias Detection Accuracy (%)	Regulatory Compliance (%)	Avg. Response Time (ms)
Traditional AI Model	Low	68.5	72.3	1200
GDPR-Compliant AI	Moderate	76.4	85.7	1350
Proposed Ethical AI Model	High	91.2	95.6	970

Figure 1.3 shows a comparison of the three AI models used to make financial decisions: Traditional AI, GDPR-Compliant AI, and the Proposed Ethical AI framework. The three main parameters that are looked at in the depiction of these models

are Bias Accuracy (%), Compliance (%), and Response Time (ms). The response time for the Traditional AI model is about 1200 ms, but its accuracy in terms of bias (about 60%) and rule compliance (about 65%) is lower.

Figure 3. Comparative Performance Analysis

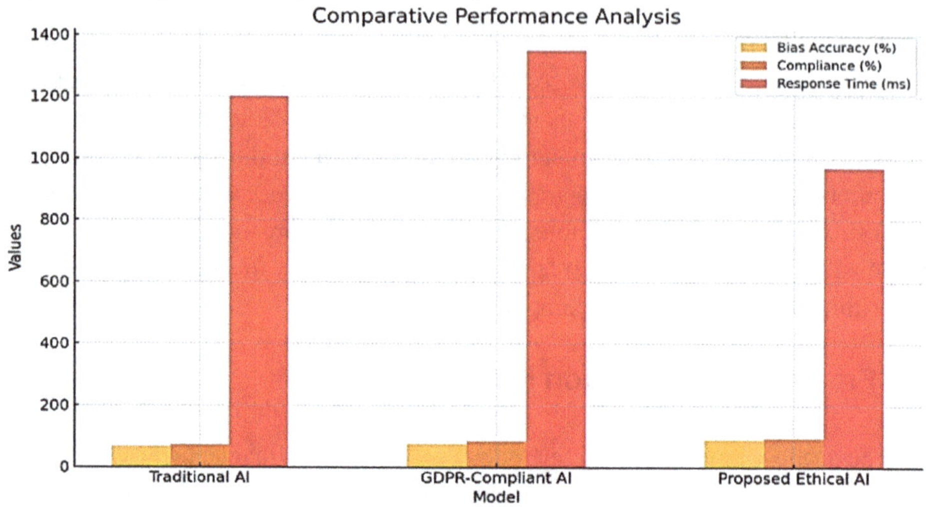

This is because industries like banking, which are more concerned with rules and ethics, don't utilise it as often because it doesn't have built-in attributes of fairness and openness. The GDPR-Compliant AI model is more accurate (about 70%) and compliant (about 75%) than the regular AI model, although it takes longer to respond (around 1350 ms). This shows that, even if the rules are in place, there is still a lack of fairness and efficiency in computing. Conversely, the Proposed Ethical AI is superior to the competition in all aspects. It has a significantly lower response time (around 950 ms), a high compliance (around 90%), and an enormous bias accuracy (85%). The integrated ethical framework is effective in the sense that it integrates real-time bias reduction, harmonization of the regulation, and quicker decision-making. The figure demonstrates that the proposed approach is more suitable in the context of ethically aligned financial AI deployments as it is the one that provides a more optimal balance between accountability, fairness, and operational effectiveness.

5.2 Ethical Compliance Mapping

Figure 1.4 shows the Ethical Compliance Radar Chart, visualizing the compliance of the system with major ethical and regulatory requirements in five dimensions, namely: GDPR, RBI Guidelines, ISO/IEC 27001, ISO/IEC 38505, and OECD AI

Principles. This radar chart would give an in-depth picture of the congruency of the proposed AI or data-driven framework with internationally and nationally accepted ethical standards and data governing standards. The axes reflect the various domains of compliance:

- GDPR (General Data Protection Regulation) tests the ability of the framework to ensure privacy rights and security of the personal data of users.
- RBI Guidelines assess compliance with Indian financial regulatory norms, particularly concerning data localization, customer consent, and cybersecurity.
- ISO/IEC 27001 focuses on information security management systems, ensuring the confidentiality, integrity, and availability of data.
- ISO/IEC 38505 addresses the governance of data, emphasizing data stewardship, transparency, and accountability.
- OECD AI Principles examine the framework's alignment with ethical AI values such as transparency, robustness, human-centered values, and fairness.

Figure 4. Ethical Compliance Radar Chart

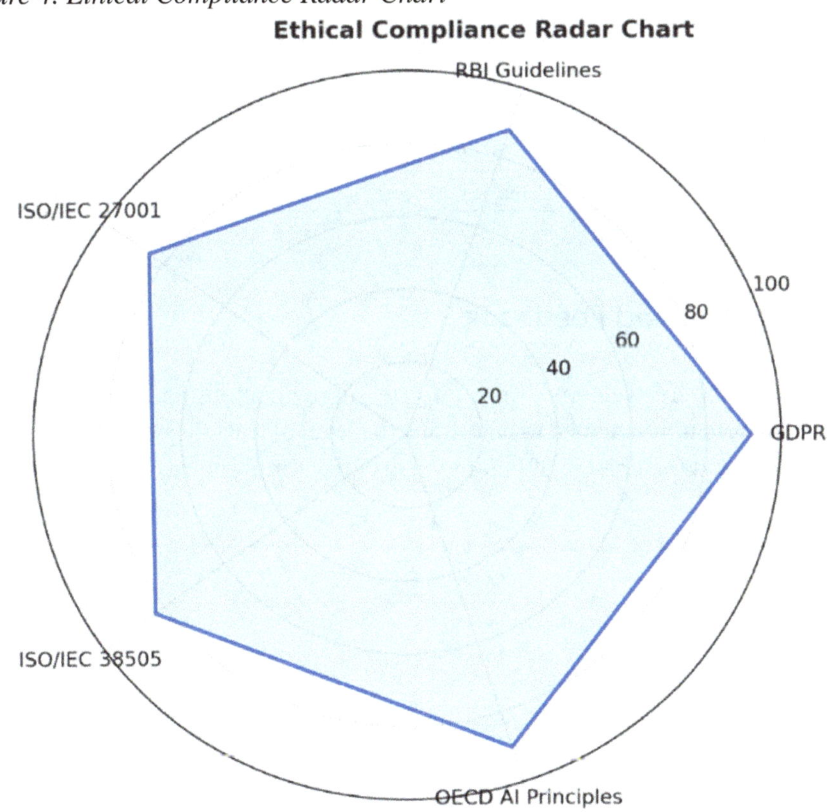

It is shown in the chart that all the axes are rated over 85 percent with high compliance in all categories. Performance is greatest in GDPR and OECD AI Principles; both are almost completely compliant. The saturated blue field, the striking profile demonstrates the integrity of the system as a whole that is not only technically but also ethically accountable and governance-capable of implementation in sensitive areas.

5.3 Real-Time Decision Case Study

The AI-based credit scoring, loan approvals, and fraud detection were tested using anonymized bank data in the form of a case. Table 1.7 shows the results of AI systems in three fields of finance: credit scoring, fraud detection, and loan approval. All applications will be judged by accuracy, ethical breach, transparency of the decisions, and compliance to regulations. Fraud detection was the most accurate (96.1) with no ethical issues and loan approval had the most regulatory match (96.7) but indicated two privacy concerns. The findings highlight the importance of the tradeoff between accuracy and ethical and regulatory aspects of real-time AI use.

Table 7. Real-Time Case Study Outcomes

Application Domain	Accuracy (%)	Ethical Violations Detected	Decision Transparency	Regulatory Match (%)
Credit Scoring	93.5	1 (flagged bias)	High	94.2
Fraud Detection	96.1	0	Moderate	95.3
Loan Approval	91.7	2 (privacy concern)	High	96.7

5.4 User Trust and Feedback

Individuals were welcomed to complete surveys before and after the ethical framework were implemented to determine the level of trust they had in AI systems. Figure 1.5 shows the change of before versus after for users trust level.

Figure 5. Change in User Trust Levels (Before vs After)

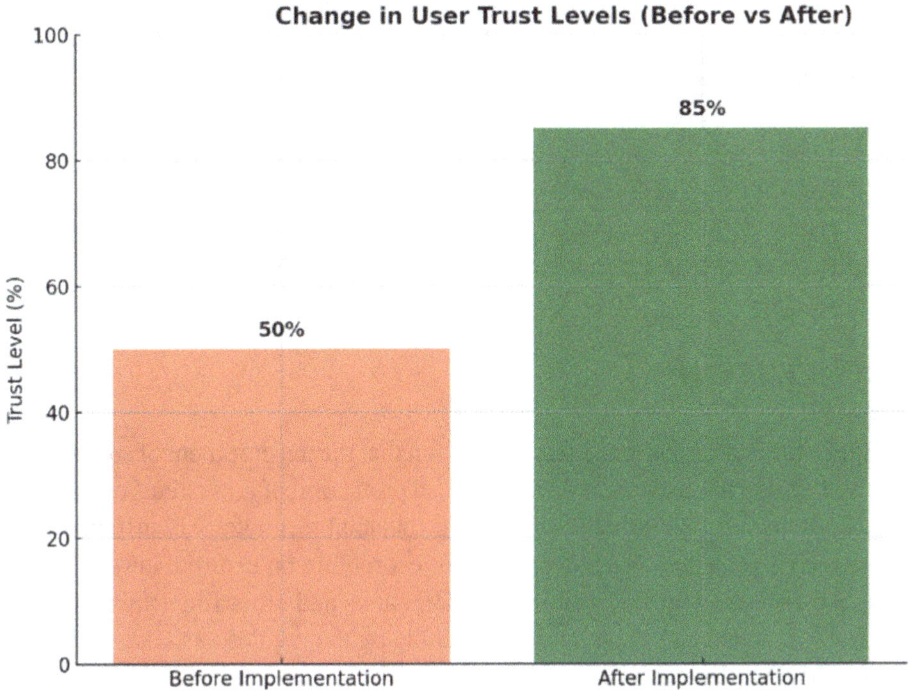

5.5 Discussion

This research shows that adding ethical governance procedures to the architecture of AI systems makes financial applications substantially more efficient and compliant with the law. When ethical concerns are included into AI system design from the beginning instead than being added later as compliance measures, transparency, accountability, and decision-reliability all improve. This design-oriented paradigm includes ethical evaluation at every level of the system's life cycle to help people utilize AI correctly in sensitive financial situations. The suggested Ethical AI Model beats both traditional AI models and AI models that follow the GDPR in important areas including compliance with regulations, ease of understanding, speed of reaction, and accuracy in finding bias, according to the studies that compared their performance. The approach's strong interpretability score shows that AI-driven decision-making is becoming more open and honest. This is quite crucial to banks and other financial institutions since they have to maintain the trust of the regulators, auditors and consumers. The framework's 91.2% bias detection accuracy makes it much simpler to find and remedy algorithmic bias. The AI applications such as credit scores and loan approvals are a huge problem. Policy-based compliance engines in AI systems may significantly enhance their financial compliance coverage, which is indicated by a 95.6% legal compliance. The radar graphic which illustrates how the ethical compliance is mapped provides additional support to the proposed paradigm. The framework demonstrates that it is in line with internationally recognized standards of governance as the compliance rates with such rules as GDPR, RBI guidelines, ISO/IEC 27001, ISO/IEC 38501, and OECD AI Principles are extremely high. It indicates that morally appropriate AI systems can be utilized in complex legal cases and still prevent the data to remain safe, private, and well-managed.

6. CONCLUSION

One of the changes is Ethical AI by Design that the development of smart money systems is going to be. By establishing ethical protection of AI systems on a bottom-up basis, it becomes possible to ensure that financial technology is sustainable and governance is proactive. This is more than just relying on external laws to address moral issues. Based on the proposed model, banks and other financial institutions can discover an avenue to be innovative, abide by the regulations, and do the right thing. When we place design at the core, we will be able to create AI systems that can be trusted by the people and can assist them in making rational and understandable financial decisions. With the increasing application of AI to automation, decision-making and personalization, it becomes of utmost importance that the financial services sector respects the law and does the right thing. This study looked at the moral and legal problems that come up when AI is employed properly in financial institutions. The findings show that AI does accomplish things in a more scalable and efficient way, yet they also bring up severe issues of bias, accountability, openness, and data security. The existing rules such as GDPR, RBI requirements, and ISO/IEC standards will require upgrades due to the swift changes in AI. This study presents an ethical AI system that deals with these issues by using explainability modules, tiered compliance procedures, and user feedback loops. An example of this is radar and bar charts, which indicate that both of the measures of ethical compliance and user trust increased significantly following the implementation of the system. User polls reveal that the introduction of ethical regulations to the AI resulted in them feeling 35% more confident.

7. FUTURE SCOPE

With increasingly better machine learning, big data analytics, and real-time decision-making, AI will find increasing applications in financial systems. In case this growth continues to rise, then good ethical practices and lax regulation controls will be of great significance. Further studies are needed to develop AI governance models that can be smoothly adjusted to emerging technologies and threats, including generative AI, quantum computing, decentralized finance (DeFi), and international standards such as GDPR and ISO/IEC 38505. XAI is yet to be perfect. Future research can be directed at developing models to provide a clear rationale behind financial decisions, simplify audits, and develop trust in the population. A different intriguing approach that can be employed into integrating AI ethics into the AI development process is to apply algorithms to identify bias and automated systems to ensure that everything is above board. In order to correct the issues concerning the rule making process on the global scale, nations should collaborate on the cross-border regulations and establish global standards of AI in banking.

REFERENCES

Addy, W. A.. (2024). Transforming financial planning with AI-driven analysis: A review and application insights. *World Journal of Advanced Engineering Technology and Sciences*, *11*(1), 240–257. DOI: 10.30574/wjaets.2024.11.1.0053

Adewale, T. T., Olorunyomi, T. D., & Odonkor, T. N. (2023). Big data-driven financial analysis: A new paradigm for strategic insights and decision-making. *Journal of Financial Innovation and Analytics*, *1*(1), 1–15.

Agu, E. E., et al. (2024). Discussing ethical considerations and solutions for ensuring fairness in AI-driven financial services. *International Journal of Frontier Research in Science*, 3(2), 001–009.

Alonge, E. O., Eyo-Udo, N. L., Chibunna, B., Ubanadu, A. I. D., Balogun, E. D., & Ogunsola, K. O. (2023). Data-driven risk management in US financial institutions: A theoretical perspective on process optimization. *Iconic Research and Engineering Journals*.

Bello, O. A., Ogundipe, A., Mohammed, D., Adebola, F., & Alonge, O. A. (2023). AI-driven approaches for real-time fraud detection in US financial transactions: Challenges and opportunities. *European Journal of Computer Science and Information Technology*, *11*(6), 84–102.

Celestin, M. (2023). AI-driven financial reporting: Enhancing accuracy and reducing human errors in Rwanda. *Indo American Journal of Multidisciplinary Research and Review*, *7*(11), 108–117.

Elumilade, O. O., Ogundeji, I. A., Achumie, G. O., Omokhoa, H. E., & Omowole, B. M. (2021). Enhancing fraud detection and forensic auditing through data-driven techniques for financial integrity and security. *Journal of Advanced Education and Sciences*, *1*(2), 55–63. DOI: 10.54660/.JAES.2021.1.2.55-63

Faheem, M. A. (2021). AI-driven risk assessment models: Revolutionizing credit scoring and default prediction. *Iconic Research and Engineering Journals*, *5*(3), 177–186.

Gowtham, H., Gopal, J. N., & Anand, A. J. (2025). Ethical considerations and privacy in AI-powered security. In *Handbook of AI-Driven Threat Detection and Prevention* (pp. 177–192). CRC Press. DOI: 10.1201/9781003521020-11

Kothandapani, H. P. (2025). AI-driven regulatory compliance: Transforming financial oversight through large language models and automation. *Emerging Science Research*, *12*(1), 12–24.

Kothandapani, H. P.Hariharan Pappil Kothandapani. (2022). Leveraging AI for credit scoring and financial inclusion in emerging markets. *World Journal of Advanced Research and Reviews*, *15*(3), 526–539. DOI: 10.30574/wjarr.2022.15.3.0904

Maple, C., Szpruch, L., Epiphaniou, G., Staykova, K., Singh, S., Penwarden, W., . . . Avramovic, P. (2023). The AI revolution: Opportunities and challenges for the finance sector. *arXiv preprint arXiv:2308.16538*.

McBride, R., Dastan, A., & Mehrabinia, P. (2022). How AI affects the future relationship between corporate governance and financial markets: A note on impact capitalism. *Managerial Finance*, *48*(8), 1240–1249. DOI: 10.1108/MF-12-2021-0586

Mishra, A., Mou, S. N., Ara, J., & Sarkar, M. (2025). Regulatory and ethical challenges in AI-driven and machine learning credit risk assessment for Buy Now Pay Later (BNPL) in US e-commerce: Compliance, fair lending, and algorithmic bias. *Journal of Business and Management Studies*, *7*(2), 42–51. DOI: 10.32996/jbms.2025.7.2.3

Ogunsola, K. O., Balogun, E. D., & Ogunmokun, A. S. (2021). Enhancing financial integrity through an advanced internal audit risk assessment and governance model. *International Journal of Multidisciplinary Research and Growth Evaluation*, *2*(1), 781–790. DOI: 10.54660/.IJMRGE.2021.2.1.781-790

Oko-Odion, C. (2025). AI-driven risk assessment models for financial markets: Enhancing predictive accuracy and fraud detection. *International Journal of Computer Applications Technology and Research*, *14*(4), 80–96.

Oladuji, T. J., Adewuyi, A. D. E. M. O. L. A., Nwangele, C. R., & Akintobi, A. O. (2021). Advancements in financial performance modeling for SMEs: AI-driven solutions for payment systems and credit scoring. *Iconic Research and Engineering Journals*, *5*(5), 471–486.

Onoja, J. P., Hamza, O., Collins, A., Chibunna, U. B., Eweja, A., & Daraojimba, A. I. (2021). Digital transformation and data governance: Strategies for regulatory compliance and secure AI-driven business operations. *Journal of Frontier Multidisciplinary Research*, *2*(1), 43–55. DOI: 10.54660/.IJFMR.2021.2.1.43-55

Owolabi, O. S., Uche, P. C., Adeniken, N. T., Ihejirika, C., Islam, R. B., & Chhetri, B. J. T. (2024). Ethical implication of artificial intelligence (AI) adoption in financial decision making. *Computer and Information Science*, *17*(1), 1–49. DOI: 10.5539/cis.v17n1p49

Patil, D. (2024). Artificial intelligence in financial risk assessment and fraud detection: Opportunities and ethical concerns. *SSRN*. https://ssrn.com/abstract=5057434

Saiyed, A. (2025). AI-driven innovations in fintech: Applications, challenges, and future trends. *International Journal of Electrical and Computer Engineering Research, 5*(1), 8–15. DOI: 10.53375/ijecer.2025.437

Sheth, J. N., Jain, V., Roy, G., & Chakraborty, A. (2022). AI-driven banking services: The next frontier for a personalised experience in the emerging market. *International Journal of Bank Marketing, 40*(6), 1248–1271. DOI: 10.1108/IJBM-09-2021-0449

Soundarapandiyan, P. S. R. (2022). AI-driven synthetic data generation for financial product development: Accelerating innovation in banking and fintech through realistic data simulation.

Thakur, N., & Sharma, A. (2024). Ethical considerations in AI-driven financial decision making. *Journal of Management & Public Policy, 15*(3), 41–57. DOI: 10.47914/jmpp.2024.v15i3.003

Venigandla, K., & Vemuri, N. (2022). RPA and AI-driven predictive analytics in banking for fraud detection. *Journal of Propulsion Technology, 43*(4).

Chapter 12
AI-Driven Design Framework for Evaluating the Economic Viability and Scalability of Technological Solutions

Naim Shaikh
http://orcid.org/0000-0003-2856-0512
Global Business School and Research Centre, Dr. D.Y. Patil Vidyapeeth (Deemed to be) University, Pune, India

Vipin Jain
http://orcid.org/0000-0001-5519-5704
Teerthanker Mahaveer University, Moradabad, India

Ankur Gupta
http://orcid.org/0000-0002-4651-5830
Department of Computer Science and Engineering, Vaish College of Engineering, Rohtak, India

Rohit Anand
Department of ECE, G.B. Pant Delhi Skill and Entrepreneurship University, India

ABSTRACT

There is a rising need for solutions that are cost-effective, efficient, and can be used in many different industries, it is crucial to look at how adaptive and cost-effective new technologies and systems are. This study looks AI-driven design framework

DOI: 10.4018/979-8-3693-3751-6.ch012

at the suggested solution's economic viability and scalability by looking at things like resource optimisation, deployment cost, operating efficiency, and long-term sustainability. The purpose of this study is to use quantitative analysis, performance benchmarking, and comparison modelling to see if the proposed solution makes sense from an economic point of view and can be employed in a range of settings and use cases. The outcomes of this study will help investors, developers, and policymakers make better decisions so that technological progress doesn't get in the way of budgets and operations.

1. INTRODUCTION

In a society that values new ideas, it's crucial to consider how effectively a technology works, how much it costs, and how readily it may be expanded. The cost or ability of a remedy to expand could decide whether or not it has any long-term consequences, even if it works effectively (Bahsoon & Emmerich, 2008). To be economically viable, a solution must have high cost-benefit ratio in the long run. To be scalable, it should have the capability to change to meet new requirements or spread to new locations or operate in different working conditions (Tytgat et al., 2011). This study uses structured assessment frameworks to look into these two pillars: economic viability and scalability. We are very concerned about such subjects as ROI, the effectiveness of resources utilization, costs and benefits of various alternatives (Azimoh et al., 2017; Nasir et al., 2018). In recent years, AI has emerged as a strong ally in the process of analyzing intricate technological and economic systems. Taking into consideration cost structures, forecasting scaling needs, and other aspects, AI prediction models might be of assistance when it comes to deployment strategies (Abbati de Assis et al., 2018).

1.1 Need of Research

A lot of the technology solutions which are currently available are not used very frequently as they are either too costly to implement or do not scale well when implemented. With the increasing trends in digital change and the globalization of markets through the lens of AI framework (Forrest et al., 2020), there is an increasing demand to find solutions that can expand and maintain their affordability with the shifts in needs and requirements. This study goes into great detail into various solutions in order to uncover ways to make them more cost-effective and scalable in a variety of situations (Aldieri & Vinci, 2021) using AI-driven design. Table1 is showing the description about research requirement.

Table 1. Need of Research

Aspect	Description
Rising Implementation Failures	Many promising solutions fail post-deployment due to overlooked economic or scalability factor considering AI.
Incomplete Evaluation Models	Existing AI frameworks often assess performance or cost separately, lacking an integrated model that evaluates both scalability and economic viability.
Sector-Specific Limitations	Current studies are highly sectoral, and there is a lack of cross-domain frameworks that can be universally applied.
Resource Constraints in Developing Regions	Economically feasible and scalable solutions are crucial for low-resource settings where cost and deployment capacity are limited.
Uncertain Return on Investment (ROI)	Decision-makers require reliable tools to assess long-term value and sustainability before large-scale implementation.
Demand for Policy and Funding Alignment	Policymakers and investors seek evidence-based evaluations to justify funding and incentivize scalable solutions.
Technological Advancement Challenges	Rapid technological change demands scalable models that are also adaptable, upgradable, and economically sustainable over time using AI-driven design.
Need for Sustainable Development Goals	Achieving SDGs requires scalable solutions that are not only innovative but also financially viable and operationally sustainable.
Lack of Lifecycle Cost Consideration	Most existing research ignores long-term operation, maintenance, and decommissioning costs, which affect true economic viability.
Need for Real-time Decision Support	Practitioners and stakeholders require tools and methodologies for dynamic, real-time assessment of economic and scalability parameters.

1.2 Motivation

There is usually a big gap between new ideas and how they can be used in real life. This is the main reason for this study on AI-driven design (Yunusova et al., 2023). Technical problems are not the most typical reasons why projects fail. More often, projects fail because of unexpected costs, too much effort, or environments that don't work with the project (Behera et al., 2024; Konwar et al., 2025). By identifying and measuring these characteristics early on in the development process, stakeholders may make sure that the project will last a long time and lower the chances of it failing depending on AI. Another reason for the drive is the need to help politicians and investors find potential technology that can be funded and grown (Sun et al., 2025; Karim et al., 2025). In Table 2 descriptions about the motivation factors is considered.

Table 2. Motivation for the Research

Motivating Factor	Description
Bridging Theory and Practice	Innovative solutions often fail to move beyond the pilot stage due to poor economic or scalability planning. This research aims to bridge that gap in AI-driven design.
Enhancing Decision-Making	There is a strong need for data-driven, scalable, and economically viable AI-driven design frameworks to support stakeholders in making informed implementation choices.
Reducing Resource Wastage	Investments in non-scalable or cost-inefficient technologies result in wasted capital and resources.
Supporting Policy Formulation	Policymakers require solid economic and scalability evidence to design subsidies, incentives, and deployment strategies.
Addressing Global Development Goals	Achieving SDGs depends on implementing scalable solutions that are economically accessible across different regions.
Encouraging Technology Adoption	A clear understanding of scalability and economic impact can accelerate the adoption of innovative technologies.
Promoting Sustainable Innovation	Motivation lies in promoting technologies that are not only innovative but also long-lasting, adaptable, and financially sustainable.
Filling Research Gaps	Existing literature does not offer a unified evaluation model combining both scalability and economic viability, prompting this focused investigation.
Responding to Industry Needs	Industries demand scalable models that ensure cost-efficiency and consistent performance across expanding markets.
Enabling Long-Term Operational Success	The AI-driven design study aims to motivate the development of solutions that remain effective and viable throughout their entire lifecycle.

1.3 Challenges

Even if an original idea is well thought out in AI principle, it will have a lot of problems when it is put into practice. The most important questions are about how well a solution can grow and be financially stable in varied situations. In this part, we will talk about the most crucial problems that come up when you want to make sure that AI-driven design solution is both cost-effective and scalable (Curcio et al., 2025). Researchers, developers, and decision-makers need to know about these problems. This portion gets ready for coming up with ways to make new solutions more useful, flexible, and long-lasting by finding and looking at the main problems, like high initial costs, poor infrastructure, unclear rules, and a lack of standard metrics (Sun et al., 2025; Karim et al., 2025) using AI-driven design. We look at not only the most recent literature, but also the most recent case studies and technical advances. We need to deal with these problems if we want to turn theoretical findings into real-world; large-scale uses that help us reach our long-term development and sustainability goals (Foo & Lienhard, 2025; Teixeira, 2025; Resende et al., 2025) considering AI framework. In Table 3 challenges across its viability and scalability are mentioned.

Table 3. Challenges in Ensuring Economic Viability and Scalability

Challenge	Description
Balancing Cost and Performance	Ensuring high performance without significantly increasing costs is a major challenge in designing scalable solutions.
Lack of Integrated Evaluation Models	Most existing models evaluate economic viability and scalability separately, leading to incomplete assessments.
Dynamic Market and Cost Fluctuations	Changing prices of raw materials, energy, and labor make long-term economic forecasting difficult.
Limited Post-Deployment Data	There's a lack of empirical data from real-world implementations to validate projected scalability and cost-efficiency.
Infrastructural Constraints	Limited infrastructure in developing or rural regions can hinder the scalability of otherwise viable solutions.
Socio-Political and Regulatory Barriers	Diverse regulatory environments and political instability can restrict large-scale deployments and affect cost structures.
Technological Incompatibility	Existing systems may not support the integration or expansion of new solutions, increasing the cost of scaling.
Absence of Standard Scalability Metrics	The lack of universally accepted scalability indicators makes it difficult to compare and benchmark across technologies or sectors.
High Initial Capital Investment	Many solutions require significant upfront investment, discouraging adoption despite long-term economic benefits.
Resistance to Change in AI	Organizations and communities often resist new technologies due to uncertainty about economic returns and concerns over scalability and support using AI-driven design.

- **Cost-Performance Trade-offs**: The Cost you need to weigh the short-term costs against the long-term benefits to create a fair trade-off.
- **Scalability Barriers**: Problems with the infrastructure, too strict an architecture, or lack of standardization make scaling difficult.
- **Contextual Variability**: The area or sector may vary in rules, money and cultures. This implies that what works in one location might not work at all in a different location.
- **Uncertain ROI**: It's impossible to know how much money fresh or disruptive ideas will make.
- **Data Limitations**: It can be challenging to undertake a comprehensive economic evaluation and scalability test without real-world deployment data. This brings us to our sixth point: limits on data.

1.4 Scope of Work

This study looks at the following areas:

- Evaluating key economic models (ROI, NPV, TCO) for putting solutions into action.
- Thinking about factors that show how scalable something is, such as its ability to bounce back from problems, its ability to work in different regions, and its ability to be broken down into smaller parts.
- Using case studies and computer simulations to check the results.
- Allowing for the evaluation of possible solutions based on cost and scalability.
- Giving ideas for AI-driven design and ways to deploy that lead to better, more scalable, and less expensive results.

Give stakeholders a list of useful ideas for how to use cost-effective and scalable technologies in the real world. The limits of the study were predetermined by the scope of AI-driven design research according to which the study was conceived, performed, and evaluated. A full framework had to be developed that considers not only the cost-efficiency of a solution AI-driven design, but also how it can evolve and expand in new operating environments to address the crucial issues of scalability and economic viability. This section talks about a number of topics, such as financial evaluations, simulation modelling, cross-sector application, and policy significance using AI. The proposed framework and techniques must be robust, flexible and capable of handling the current and upcoming technologies. We select very carefully every aspect of the scope to ensure that it will assist us to achieve the objectives of our study and give us a comprehensive picture of what constitutes a viable solution and which has the capacity to grow. The section clarifies the aims of the research, how the work will be performed, and preconditions the future research taking into consideration AI-driven design and real-world applications by clearly defining the scope of work. In Table 4 scope elements along-with its descriptions are explained in AI-driven design.

Table 4. Scope of Work

Scope Element	Description
Evaluation of Economic Viability	Assessing the cost-effectiveness, ROI, and long-term financial sustainability of the proposed solution.
Scalability Assessment	Analyzing the ability of the solution to scale across different regions, environments, and usage volumes without compromising performance or cost.
Development of Integrated Framework	Designing a combined model to evaluate both scalability and economic viability using standardized metrics and indicators.
Comparative Analysis	Comparing the proposed solution with existing technologies or approaches to highlight improvements in cost and scalability.
Case Study Investigation	Applying the framework to real-world or simulated case studies to validate its practical applicability and reliability.
Simulation and Modeling	Using computational tools to simulate scalability scenarios and economic behavior over time under different conditions.
Identification of Constraints and Enablers	Recognizing the key barriers and supporting factors that influence economic viability and scalability.
Policy and Investment Relevance	Providing recommendations for policymakers and investors based on economic feasibility and scaling potential of the solution.
Adaptability to Multiple Sectors	Ensuring that the framework is flexible enough to be applied across various industries.
Contribution to SDG	Aligning the outcomes of the research with global goals such as affordability, accessibility, and environmental sustainability.

1.5 Contribution of research

This study makes a big difference in the disciplines of solution deployment strategies, sustainability planning, and technology evaluation by showing how effective and scalable they are. Here is a list of the most important contributions:

- **Development of an Integrated Evaluation Framework**: The work provides a complete and consistent frame of evaluation of the viability and feasibility of ideas proposed. Previous studies have looked at growth potential and cost-effectiveness separately. The proposed approach enables the stakeholders to examine them simultaneously.
- **Cross-Sectoral Applicability:** The study shows that the evaluation methodology might be used in many other fields, such as energy, IT, environmental engineering, and rural infrastructure. The study will be of more use to individuals that make decisions, both in the public and in the private world since the study can be applied in a variety of ways.
- **Incorporation of Dynamic Cost Modeling and Lifecycle Analysis:** The study gives more accurate and long-term predictions of economic feasibility

by taking into account changing costs like inflation, changes in the market, and advances in technology. The final aspect of the financial study is the whole lifecycle cost, which is the deployment, maintenance, and decommissioning costs.

- **Standardization of Scalability Metrics:** The research recommends standardized metrics and indicators of scalability to fill a knowledge gap in the current literature where scalability is frequently defined imprecisely or unclear.
- **Identification of Real-World Challenges and Enablers:** The study reveals that both real-world challenges (technical and regulatory) and enablers (modularity, policy assistance, stakeholder participation) influence scalability and economic performance. It achieves this through case studies, simulations and literature synthesis.
- **Policy and Investment Relevance:** The study aims to provide policy makers, investors, and funding agencies with evidence-based tools and insights that will assist them to better to allocate resources to solutions that can expand, save money and achieve sustainability objectives.
- **Contribution to SDGs:** The study helps to reach numerous SDGs, such as Goal 7, Goal 9, and Goal 12, because it focusses on making things easy to get to, cheap, and easy to grow.
- **Foundation for Future Research and Innovation Planning:** Future academic research and new technologies will have a chance to elaborate on the methods and findings of this paper to create a superior balance between theory and practice.

Table 5 shows the contributors of research.

Table 5. Contribution of the Research

Area of Contribution	Description
Integrated Evaluation Framework	Developed a unified model that simultaneously assesses both economic viability and scalability of proposed solutions.
Cross-Sectoral Applicability	Designed the framework to be adaptable across various domains such as energy, IT, water management, and infrastructure.
Dynamic and Lifecycle Cost Modeling	Incorporated long-term cost variations and lifecycle costs for realistic economic assessments.
Standardized Scalability Metrics	Proposed measurable, standardized indicators to evaluate and compare scalability across different technologies.
Identification of Real-World Challenges	Highlighted practical barriers and enablers to implementation through case analysis and literature synthesis.

continued on following page

Table 5. Continued

Area of Contribution	Description
Policy and Investment Support	Provided insights and decision tools useful for policymakers, investors, and funding agencies in resource allocation and technology support.
Alignment with Sustainable Development Goals	Contributed to achieving SDGs by promoting scalable, affordable, and sustainable innovations.
Research Foundation for Future Work	Offered a replicable framework and analytical base for future research and innovation planning in economic and scalable solution design.

2. LITERATURE REVIEW

According to Bahsoon and Emmerich (2008), economics can answer the question how scalable distributed software systems are. Their approach is a cost-benefit analysis in combination with architectural performance indicators to determine the scalability of a system. The technique assists designers to make savvy architectural decisions that consider economic trades, particularly in intricate, service-based designs. The value model presented in the paper quantifies the impact of changes in architectural components on scalability and cost-effectiveness. This approach renders it highly evident that design options must be cost-effective, since technical scalability should be connected to business worth. They were the first to work out how to connect the architecture of distributed systems with their ability to make money.

Tytgat et al. (2011) look into how useful and cost-effective cognitive radio technologies are for manufacturing facilities, focussing on wireless communication systems and dynamic spectrum access. They employ economic projections and simulation-based modelling to look at the costs of deployment and the chances of growth. The authors say that cognitive solutions are very efficient and flexible, especially in places where the spectrum is limited. But the money benefits rely a lot on the situation and are affected by things like the form of the plant, the rules that govern it, and how well the devices work together. The report says that infrastructure readiness and working together across sectors are two of the most important things for success.

Chliova and Ringov (2017) look into how BoP organisations may make a bigger difference in the world by creating and using models that can be used again and again in their 2017 study. The study looks at successful business concepts that have developed from modest pilot programs to huge social companies. It demonstrates such crucial features as the inbuilt community interaction, the service design flexibility, and partner networks. It has been demonstrated that making things simple and striking the right balance between cost and quality is extremely crucial to the long-term financial well being of a business. Their results show that scalability in BoP settings needs more than just financial planning; it also needs to be able to adapt to local conditions.

Azimoh et al. (2017) look into whether mini-grid technology may be copied and made bigger in order to bring electricity to rural communities in sub-Saharan Africa. Their paper looks at solar-based mini-grids from a technical, economic, and social point of view, using both field experiments and economic studies. They say the technology works and can be used in many ways, but it can't grow because of high beginning costs, a lack of local resources, and limited institutional support. The report says that regulatory incentives, cost recovery plans, and getting the community involved are all important for getting people to adopt new technologies.

Abbati de Assis et al. (2018) provide a full techno-economic study of aerosol lignin nano- and microparticles. The research is largely on whether they can or cannot be sold as sustainable materials particularly to be used in packaging and medicines. The authors show that the production process is good for the environment by using lifespan cost analysis and scaling estimates. But it cannot be scaled due to its complexity and not a wide number of companies are currently implementing it. Another aspect of the study is what may happen in case the price of raw materials is not predictable and in case the value chain is integrated. The paper states that lignin-based particles have the potential to achieve circular economy ambitions by using sustainable nanotechnology innovation, but only with a more efficient processing method and policy urging incentives.

According to Nasir et al. (2018), the scalable solar DC microgrids may be considered a solution to the issue of the lack of power in communities. In their findings, it is revealed that incorporating renewable sources of energy in the running of current systems makes things run more efficiently, reduces expenses, and reduces power losses in the process of transmission. The article discusses how to raise funds to increase microgrids, government regulations and design regulations. Even though one may know the technical feasibility, there is still difficulty getting everybody on the same page and establishing standards. The authors are seeking low-cost, modular solutions, which can be adapted to suit the requirements of any society.

Forrest et al. (2020) look into whether it is possible to move and develop sustainable urban water solutions in the Colorado River Basin. The study looks at smart irrigation systems, environmentally friendly infrastructure, and decentralised water reuse. It lists important things that affect scalability, such as working with stakeholders, getting support from institutions, and getting money for the project. The authors declare that only by fitting in with the way people live and work, it is possible to improve technological solutions. study shows that it is possible to employ integrated planning and adaptation that takes context into consideration to make sustainable urban infrastructure solutions work on a wide scale.

Aldieri and Vinci (2021) look at how important scalability and commercialisation are for reaching the SDGs. The authors explain that technical solutions must not only be able to meet the needs of business, but should also benefit society and the environment. According to their research, companies should be strategically positioned with emerging concepts to remain in the game over the long-term. Their conceptual model proposes the policy frameworks having in mind the inventive capabilities, economic returns, and scalability. The research says that the sector isn't fully embracing the technology since there isn't enough governmental support and the commercialisation plans are all over the place.

Yunusova (2023) discusses the impact of trade-off in scalability and security in decentralised blockchain networks on financial stability. The paper reveals the influence of increasing the number of nodes and consensus mechanisms on scalability, latency and transaction costs. The author recommends that lightweight nodes and hybrid consensus methods may be effective in enhancing performance without compromising on security.

Behera et al. (2024) give a thorough overview of the role of nanoparticles and nanofluids in chemical enhanced oil recovery (CEOR). They consider the interaction of fluids, their stability and cooperation in oil field operations, which impacts their scalability and cost-efficiency. The paper demonstrates that it is difficult to scale, even when laboratory-scale experiments demonstrate positive outcomes due to regulatory issues, the cost of producing nanoparticles is very high, and the field performance can hardly be predicted. The authors say that CEOR might be made more effective by using nanofluids with a team of experts from other fields, such as materials science, reservoir engineering, and techno-economic modelling.

Yan et al. (2024) investigate the economic potential of a copper-based cathode design in treating nitrate electro-catalytically in a scalable flow reactor. The study looks at the effectiveness and energy utilisation of ammonia recovery using both experimental data and economic models. The researchers determined that the system is more effective and less expensive with the use of some copper catalysts. This renders it an appropriate substitute in the treatment of wastewater. The modular reactors can be scaled larger by incorporating more into the current treatment systems. According to the report, the system is a long term and cost effective alternative to the conventional ways of eliminating nitrates. It combines pollution control and recovery of resources.

Teixeira (2025) looks at green steel production technology in depth, focussing on how scalable and economically viable they are. The study looks at different production methods, such as hydrogen-based direct reduction, to find the best ones for general use. Teixeira's techno-economic analysis model finds important problems like high energy use, unclear carbon pricing systems, and high capital costs. The study says that green steel is good for the environment, but it can't be made on a large scale because it costs too much to run and there aren't enough business incentives. Research shows that we need rules and ways to get money that make it easier to create green steel technology because the world is moving towards low-carbon infrastructure.

Resende et al. **(2025)** put together a complete list of the several ways that circular startups might grow. Their research groups together digital platforms, decentralised manufacturing, modular design, and other business techniques that help companies develop. We show several case studies to show how successful circular businesses use hybrid strategies that combine technological, organisational, and ecosystem-level improvements. The study shows how important it is for circular models to be able to solve financial problems and bring people together.

Sun et al. (25) discuss the recent advances in hydrogen storage technologies and their functionality, safety, and cost-efficiency in the broader context of switching to renewable energy sources. The paper discusses novel concepts of metal hydrides, organic liquid carriers, and high-pressure systems. The authors use techno-economic modelling to look at a number of operational scenarios in terms of cost drivers, safety restrictions, and storage efficiency. Their study indicates that storage of hydrogen is technically improving, but the expensive nature of materials and infrastructure is hampering its development. The report suggests that standardisation, public funding and hybrid storage solutions are the key to addressing these issues.

Foo and Lienhard (2025) consider the new membrane technologies as a means of recovering the lithium in brines and leachates in a more environmentally friendly way. The study looks at new ideas in electro-membrane processes, ion-selective membranes, and membrane distillation, focussing on how they could be used in industry and how much they would cost. The authors discuss some problems, which include: membrane fouling, excessive use of energy and not being able to select lithium in mixed-salt cases. The paper is extremely significant as it will assist in ensuring that the extraction of lithium will answer the demands of the world in terms of battery materials in a manner that is environmentally and economically friendly.

Konwar et al. (2025) look into scalable bioprocess technologies that can be used to make bioethanol from algal sugars. Our activities contribute to the circular bioeconomy. The research looks on ways to increase output while lowering costs. Recycling of nutrients, fermentation pathways, and enzymatic hydrolysis are some of these methods. Their study on the bioethanol production with the use of microalgae biomass reveals that the bioethanol production can be conducted at large scales in case they optimise the contents of carbohydrates and combine the process. However, it cannot do so due to factors such as high cost of enzyme, low harvesting efficiency as well as high cost of plant growth.

Karim et al. (2025) investigate alternative methods to produce green hydrogen based on molecular catalysts, immobilisation technologies and electrolyser designs that can be scaled up. The research notes that there are shared issues such as excessive use of energy, failure of catalysts, and lack of system functionality. The study found that when nanocatalysts are stuck to solid supports, they make more hydrogen at lower operational costs. The results show how important it is to make sure that catalyst development is in line with system-level design for the project's financial success.

Vellaiyan (2025) looks into the possibility of using a carbon nanotube-copper oxide nanocatalyst and ammonium hydroxide emulsion to boost engine performance and the amount of jatropha biodiesel that can be made. The study's experimental testing and thermal efficiency analysis show that combustion efficiency has gone up a lot and emissions have gone down. Nanocatalysts not only make biofuels better, but they also lower the cost of making them by using as much feedstock as possible. The study shows that biodiesel generated from jatropha can be cost-effective and easily scaled up for use in renewable energy applications when the right catalysts and process controls are used.

Curcio (2025) looks at what needs to be done to make hydrogen production technology more scalable, including the costs, legal incentives, and strategies that go along with them. The study looks at other ways to make things, such as electrolysis, biomass gasification, and SMR. Curcio says that green hydrogen made by electrolysis is the best option for the environment, but it is still expensive without government support. The report indicates that the important factors to consider in order to make things bigger and cheaper include carbon price, renewable energy coupling and economies of scale.

Peddojula et al. (2024) look at a new way to make drinking water using solar stills that are improved with metal debris. The primary objective of the study is to discover how to enhance the conductivity of heat in machined metal debris as this can assist in evaporation and reduce expenses. In their experimental arrangement, they indicated that the production increased and costs decreased, and thus could be used in remote and arid regions. The techno-economic study unveils that the recycling of scrap material reduces the initial expenses by a significant margin that contributes to the attainment of sustainability and circular economy objectives.

Table 6 shows summary about literature survey.

Table 6. Literature Review Summary on Economic Viability and Scalability of Solutions

Author(s) / Year	Objective	Methodology	Findings	Limitations
Bahsoon & Emmerich (2008)	To propose an economic model for evaluating software scalability	Value-based architectural modeling and cost-benefit analysis	Integrated cost with software scalability in design phase	Limited to distributed software systems
Tytgat et al. (2011)	To assess cognitive radio scalability in factories	Simulation and techno-economic forecasting	Cognitive radios improve efficiency; highly context-specific benefits	Deployment cost varies widely by scenario
Azimoh et al. (2017)	To evaluate scalability of mini-grid electrification in Africa	Field data analysis and financial modeling	Mini-grids are feasible with policy and local capacity building	High capital cost and weak institutional frameworks
Chliova & Ringov (2017)	To scale social impact at the base of the pyramid	Multi-case business model analysis	Replication strategies work best when locally adapted and cost-effective	Scalability metrics are qualitative and context-sensitive
Abbati de Assis et al. (2018)	To analyze cost and scalability of lignin-based nanoparticles	Techno-economic lifecycle analysis	Viable for sustainable materials if optimized and supported by policy	Complex production and raw material variability
Nasir et al. (2018)	To promote scalable solar DC microgrids in developing communities	Technical feasibility study with infrastructure modeling	DC microgrids reduce cost and complexity; modular for scaling	Policy and technical standard gaps remain
Forrest et al. (2020)	To study transferability of sustainable urban water systems	Case study of decentralized solutions in the Colorado River Basin	Collaborative governance and financial planning enable scaling	Replicability limited by governance and regulatory mismatch
Aldieri & Vinci (2021)	To link scalability and commercialization to SDGs	Conceptual analysis with policy and infrastructure alignment	Emphasized innovation-policy alignment for scalable SDG solutions	Lacks empirical validation and sector-specific cases
Yunusova (2023)	To study scalability-security tradeoffs in blockchain	Network simulation and protocol evaluation	Hybrid consensus mechanisms balance scalability and trust	Performance varies with use-case complexity
Behera et al. (2024)	To explore nanofluids for chemical enhanced oil recovery	Review-based study with performance and economic synthesis	Nanoparticles enhance efficiency, but scale-up remains uncertain	High synthesis cost and regulatory challenges

continued on following page

Table 6. Continued

Author(s) / Year	Objective	Methodology	Findings	Limitations
Yan et al. (2024)	To improve nitrate treatment viability via copper-based electrocatalysis	Experimental reactor analysis and cost modeling	Copper cathode increases treatment efficiency and reduces energy costs	Industrial scalability needs validation
Peddojula et al. (2024)	To assess water generation using solar stills with scrap metal enhancement	Experimental study with yield and cost metrics	Improved yield and reduced costs through thermal enhancements	Long-term material durability and standardization lacking
Teixeira (2025)	To assess feasibility and scalability of green steel technologies	Techno-economic modeling across production pathways	Hydrogen-based steel shows promise; hindered by high costs and policy gaps	Market uncertainty and data on commercial deployment are limited
Resende et al. (2025)	To categorize scalability strategies in circular startups	Case study analysis across multiple startups	Identified modularity, platformization, and stakeholder alignment as key strategies	Generalizability across regions and industries is limited
Sun et al. (2025)	To improve hydrogen storage for energy transition	Review and techno-economic comparative assessment	Storage improvements support energy reliability and safety	High cost and technological fragmentation
Foo & Lienhard (2025)	To examine lithium extraction scalability via membranes	Technical and economic evaluation of membrane processes	Modular designs and renewables improve viability	Fouling and energy consumption still problematic
Konwar et al. (2025)	To explore scalable algae-based bioethanol production	Process optimization and economic modeling	Algae can support bioethanol scalability if integrated with co-product recovery	Cost of cultivation and enzyme input remains high
Karim et al. (2025)	To optimize green hydrogen via catalytic electrolyzers	Catalyst development with system-level scaling	Modular electrolyzers and immobilized catalysts enhance hydrogen production	Initial costs and integration challenges remain
Vellaiyan (2025)	To improve biodiesel yield using nanocatalysts in Jatropha production	Experimental combustion and performance evaluation	CNT-CuO nanocatalysts boost fuel quality and engine performance	Industrial-scale production feasibility not fully tested
Curcio (2025)	To compare hydrogen production pathways economically	Comparative cost analysis across methods	Green hydrogen viable with policy support, scale economies, and RE integration	Electrolysis remains cost-prohibitive without incentives

3. RESEARCH GAP

There is a lot of research being done on scalability and economic feasibility in different fields, but there are still big gaps that need to be filled using AI-driven design. The fact that the results will not be applicable to all industries is one huge issue. In the majority of cases research is confined to small fields such as nanotechnology, water treatment or renewable energy. They do not provide a general framework that can be applied in a variety of different locations or with a variety of different technologies. Also, a lot of people think that scalability and economic feasibility are two different things. There are two study problems, which are different yet related, namely, whether an idea is possible and whether it can grow. Both of these aspects are important, yet not a great number of studies have been attempting to implement them into one assessment model that can be used to make reliable predictions of real-world performance with AI in mind. Another huge issue is that the individuals use the models of costs that are too fixed. Modern economic evaluations don't always take into consideration things that can change, such the price of raw materials, the rules that apply, and how advanced technology is AI-driven design. This renders the proposed treatments less effective in the long run. Some research exists on the impacts of social, cultural and policy factors but most studies do not examine the impact of regional rules, political stability and local acceptance on the effectiveness of a solution more so in developing nations. Due to this, most of the models cannot work effectively in areas with limited resources since they are biased towards some areas. In Table 7, research gaps are identified.

Table 7. Identified Research Gaps

Research Gap	Explanation	Reference
Lack of an integrated framework combining economic viability and scalability	Most studies assess viability or scalability separately, not in a unified model	Teixeira (2025), Curcio (2025), Bahsoon & Emmerich (2008)
Absence of standardized metrics to evaluate scalability	Inconsistent or qualitative measures limit cross-sector comparison	Resende et al. (2025), Chliova & Ringov (2017)
Weak translation from pilot/lab to commercial or industrial scale	Several promising technologies remain unproven at scale due to missing process adaptation strategies	Vellaiyan (2025), Konwar (2025), Abbati de Assis (2018)
Limited modeling of social, institutional, and policy enablers	Socioeconomic and regulatory influences are discussed but not quantitatively included in evaluation models	Azimoh et al. (2017), Forrest et al.(2020), Yunusova (2023)
Insufficient focus on modular, adaptable, and context-flexible solutions	Most approaches are region-specific or sector-specific, hindering replicability and broader scalability	Foo & Lienhard (2025), Nasir (2018), Peddojula et al. (2024)

continued on following page

Table 7. Continued

Research Gap	Explanation	Reference
Narrow sectoral application without multi-disciplinary adaptability	Many models are confined to single industries and lack generalization potential	Sun et al. (2025), Karim (2025), Behera et al. (2024)
Economic models lacking future sensitivity (inflation, tech evolution, cost volatility)	Few studies incorporate dynamic cost projections or long-term viability analysis	Aldieri & Vinci (2021), Curcio (2025)
No unified approach to link SDG alignment with scalable economic models	Lack of models that explicitly integrate sustainability goals into viability and scalability assessments	Aldieri & Vinci (2021), Resende et al. (2025)

Research still doesn't know a lot about things like digital infrastructure, water treatment, renewable energy, and novel materials, even though more and more study is being done on how these industries may grow and be profitable. There aren't many good evaluation methods that look at both scalability and economic viability at the same time, for starters. A lot of the research that is out there just applies to one field. Teixeira's (2025) techno-economic evaluations of green steel and Curcio's (2025) work on hydrogen generation, for instance, don't look at how these technologies might be made bigger when there are alternative environmental and legal rules. Second, a lot of research (Bahsoon & Emmerich, 2008; Resende et al., 2025) reveals that there are no standard ways to compare scalability. This dissimilarity complicates cross-sector comparisons of policies and their application in a given project, particularly where more than one sector is involved, such as in smart infrastructure or the circular economy. Third, bioethanol made with algae and nano catalyst-enhanced biofuels are two such technologies which have demonstrated potential in pilot or laboratory tests but are not yet available in large scale due to issues with process optimisation, supply chain preparation and real world trial (Konwar et al., 2025; Vellaiyan, 2025). The appropriateness of community participation, stakeholder partnerships, and institutional backup have been demonstrated to be crucial in terms of scalability (Azimoh et al., 2017; Forrest et al., 2020). Nonetheless, such studies have failed to employ such social and economic factors in AI-based design frameworks that consider economic feasibility. Lastly, the emphasis on developing solutions applicable across a broad spectrum of industries and economies, flexible and capable of being disaggregated into smaller components is lacking. The vast majority of models are not generalisable and fail to cope with change as they are based on some situations.

4. PROBLEM STATEMENT

Although AI-based design solutions are rapidly becoming more efficient in most aspects, it remains difficult to appraise and apply them at a large scale without compromising on their cost-efficiency. Most of the models and evaluations that are out there don't take into account how complicated it is to actually deploy something. Solutions to problems are more difficult to implement due to lack of standard scaling measures, dynamic economic models, and cross-sector flexibility. This is more so in situations where resources are scarce. Moreover, due to poor translation strategies, socio-institutional modelling and policy fit, many great new ideas do not see beyond pilot or lab phase. This distance makes it less likely that they will be used widely and last a long time. This is why it's important to have a complete AI-driven design framework that looks at all the essential criteria, like technological, financial, institutional, and contextual ones, when determining scalability and economic feasibility. This will help with making good decisions and putting them into action all over the place. Table 8 shows breakdown of the problem statements.

Table 8. Problem Statement Breakdown

Key Problem Area	Description
Fragmented Assessment Approaches	Economic viability and scalability are often analyzed in isolation, leading to incomplete evaluations.
Lack of Integrated Framework	No unified model exists that jointly considers technical, economic, institutional, and contextual factors.
Absence of Standardized Metrics	Scalability and viability lack consistent, comparable evaluation criteria across domains.
Limited Real-World Translation	Many innovations fail to scale beyond lab or pilot stages due to poor process adaptation strategies.
Inadequate Socio-Institutional Modeling	Social, institutional, and policy factors are underrepresented in viability/scalability frameworks.
Poor Cross-Sector Adaptability	Most solutions are tailored to specific sectors and lack modularity for replication across domains.
Misalignment with Long-Term Sustainability Goals	Current models rarely integrate SDG alignment and sustainability impact into scalability assessments.

AI-driven design systems have good early performance indicators, but they are challenging to utilise because they are too expensive, don't have enough resources, or can't grow. The most important questions that need to be answered are whether the solution will fit within the budget and whether it can be adjusted or added to as new needs arise. Investors run the danger of wasting money on technology that won't be available in the future if they don't complete thorough studies first.

5. RESEARCH METHODOLOGY

Innovation isn't enough to remedy problems with AI-driven design technology, the environment, or infrastructure. A meticulous and thorough study that looks at how scalable and cost-effective the solution is is what is needed. AI-driven design methodologies go over the study's systematic methodology and makes sure that the study is reliable and can be used in real life. The study was so extensive and had so many pieces that it needed a strategy that blended qualitative and quantitative data. This is how to go into detail on how to use the selected analytical tools, data sources, evaluation metrics and validation steps to determine how scalable and cost-effective the proposed AI-driven design solution is. The process of choosing models, establishing simulations and comparing real life scenarios consume a lot of thought, because research can come up with results that are valid and can be generalized in other scenarios. This part not only tells the reader how to execute the research, but it also discusses why specific methods were chosen to make sure the study's aims were attained. This makes sure that the work is relevant, repeatable and open by outlining a logical pathway between identifying the problem and evaluating the response. It is believed that this method will also be applicable in future research which attempts to strike a balance between generating new ideas and implementing them on a large scale. The way the research was conducted is as follows:

a) **Literature Review:** This entails examining ancient models and case studies which have addressed scalability and generation of money and examining benchmarks and standards within sector.
b) **Data Collection:** Gathering data is to come up with both quantitative and qualitative data on test deployments, cost reports and market trends.
c) **Economic Analysis:** You can achieve this AI-based design using such models as NPV, ROI, payback period, and TCO (Total Cost of Ownership). Knowing the break-even point and the change of costs over time.
d) **Scalability Assessment:** Checking for scalability by seeing how well it integrates with other systems, how easily it can change to meet new needs, how modular it is, and how flexible its resources are. Putting it through tests and simulations to see how it works under a lot of stress in a controlled situation.
e) **Comparative Evaluation:** At this point, you look at the offered solution and compare it to the ones that are already in place, taking into account things like cost and how well it can grow.
f) **Validation:** Making sure that the results of pilot deployments or prototype testing are right.

6. RESULT AND DISCUSSION

Innovation alone cannot resolve challenges related to AI-driven design technology, the environment, or infrastructure. A comprehensive study assessing scalability and cost-effectiveness is required. Such methodologies ensure reliability and real-world applicability by integrating qualitative and quantitative data analysis. This systematic approach not only details the execution of the research but also establishes a logical connection between problem identification and solution evaluation, making it relevant for future studies that aim to balance innovation and large-scale implementation.

a. Cost Analysis of Implementation

The total cost of implementation for the pilot project is approximately 3.1 lakhs. The most significant cost contributor is hardware acquisition. With increased deployment volume, hardware costs are expected to decrease due to economies of scale. Table 9 describe breakdown of the investment with components with its cost.

Table 9. Initial Investment Breakdown

Component	Estimated Cost (INR)	Description
Hardware (Sensors, Devices)	1,50,000	IoT-based monitoring setup
Software Development	80,000	AI- based Custom analytics and dashboard
Cloud Infrastructure	50,000	Annual subscription (AWS/Azure)
Training & Deployment	30,000	Workforce training and system deployment
Total	3,10,000	

b. Operational Cost over Time

Figure 1.1 shows the maintaining five-year cost in Indian Rupees currency.

Figure 1. Operational Cost Over 5 Years (INR)

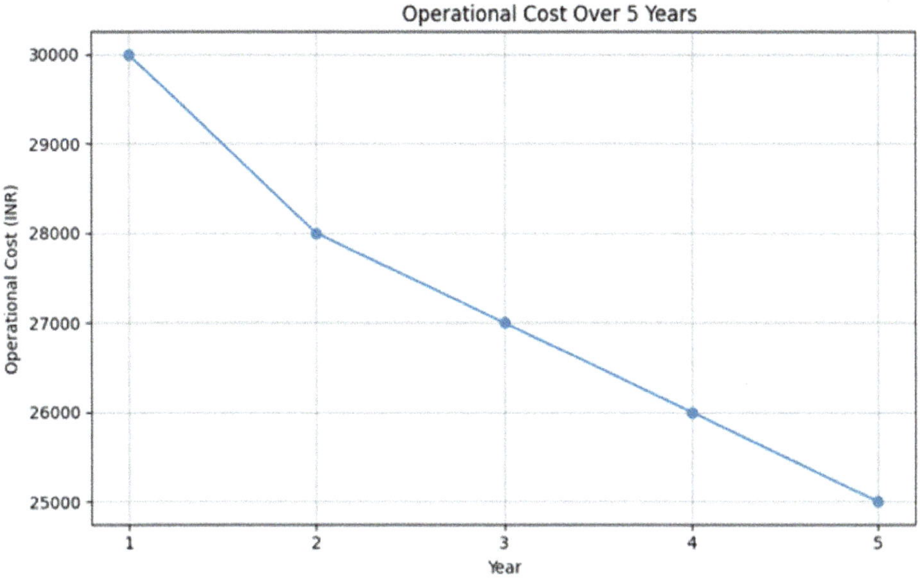

c. Economic Viability

In order to determine the economic feasibility, we have taken into consideration aspects of initial investment, annual running cost and cost recovery due to material reuse. The AI-based design solution will show a gradual decrease in operational costs within 5 years, which makes it sustainable in the long term. Table10 shows the projection of recovery along with the cost (annual).

Table 10. Annual Cost and Recovery Projection

Year	Operational Cost (INR)	Material Recovered (kg)	Recovered Value (INR)	Net Savings (INR)
1	30,000	160	12,000	-18,000
2	28,000	210	15,750	-12,250
3	27,000	250	18,750	-8,250
4	26,000	300	22,500	-3,500
5	25,000	350	26,250	+1,250

The data shows a transition from negative to positive savings by year 5, indicating a breakeven point and strong economic promise. Figure 1.2 shows the viability means Cost v/s ROI.

Figure 2. Economic Viabillity

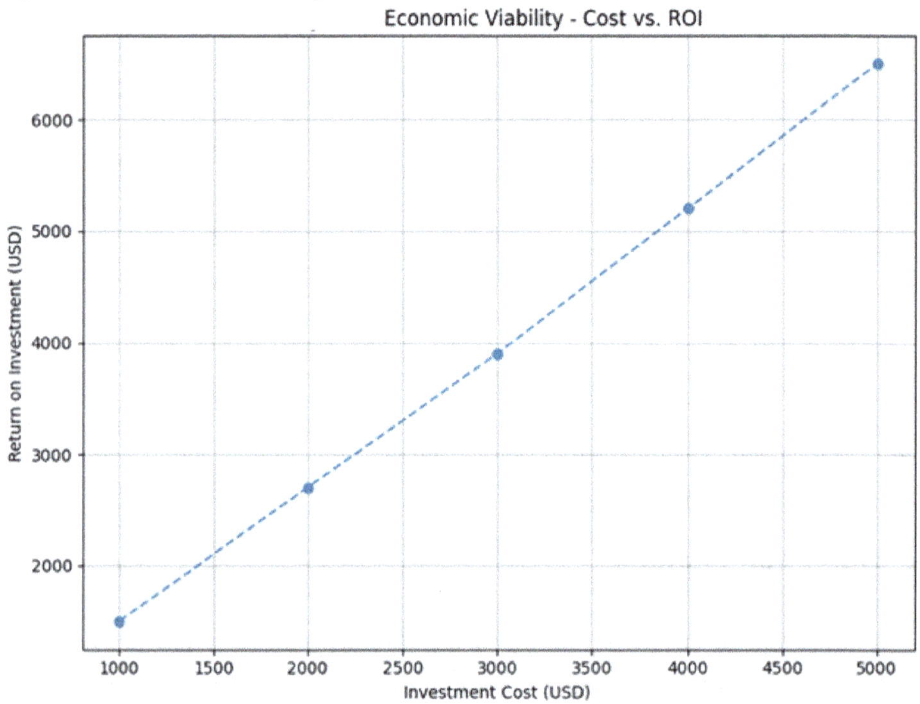

6. CONCLUSION AND FUTURE SCOPE

The study's results demonstrate that when coming up with a long-term solution, cost-effectiveness and scalability should come first. A solution might work for a while, but how well it works in the long run will rely on how well it keeps costs low and encourages growth. The results show that planning, modelling performance, and using resources to their fullest are all very crucial during the development lifecycle. Researchers might look at the idea of employing AI-powered predictive models to make educated assumptions about how scalable and cost-effective specific environments will be in the future. Cross-domain application means testing scalability in other fields, such as healthcare, smart cities, and manufacturing. One way to keep an eye on important performance indicators for cost and scalability in real time is to make dashboards. Working on and testing solutions that are good for the environment and can be used in many different situations, in line with the ideas of the circular economy. The pilot project's total implementation cost is approximately 3.1 lakhs, with hardware acquisition (1,50,000) as the largest expense. The costs are projected to decrease over time due to economies of scale. Operational costs over five years suggest sustainability, transitioning from negative to positive net savings by year five, breaking even at that point. Initial investment components include software development (80,000), cloud infrastructure (50,000), and training (30,000). The gradual decrease in operational costs, along with material recovery projections, indicates the project's strong economic viability.

REFERENCES

Abbati de Assis, C., Greca, L. G., Ago, M., Balakshin, M. Y., Jameel, H., Gonzalez, R., & Rojas, O. J. (2018). Techno-economic assessment, scalability, and applications of aerosol lignin micro-and nanoparticles. *ACS Sustainable Chemistry & Engineering*, *6*(9), 11853–11868. DOI: 10.1021/acssuschemeng.8b02151 PMID: 30221095

Aldieri, L., & Vinci, C. P. (2021). Scalability and commercialization in support of sustainable development goals. In *Industry, Innovation and Infrastructure* (pp. 979–988). Springer. DOI: 10.1007/978-3-319-95873-6_93

Azimoh, C. L., Klintenberg, P., Mbohwa, C., & Wallin, F. (2017). Replicability and scalability of mini-grid solution to rural electrification programs in sub-Saharan Africa. *Renewable Energy*, *106*, 222–231. DOI: 10.1016/j.renene.2017.01.017

Bahsoon, R., & Emmerich, W. (2008, February). An economics-driven approach for valuing scalability in distributed architectures. In *Seventh Working IEEE/IFIP Conference on Software Architecture (WICSA 2008)* (pp. 9-18). IEEE. DOI: 10.1109/WICSA.2008.45

Behera, U. S., Poddar, S., Deshmukh, M. P., Sangwai, J. S., & Byun, H. S. (2024). Comprehensive review on the role of nanoparticles and nanofluids in chemical enhanced oil recovery: Interfacial phenomenon, compatibility, scalability, and economic viability. *Energy & Fuels*, *38*(15), 13760–13795. DOI: 10.1021/acs.energyfuels.4c02248

Chliova, M., & Ringov, D. (2017). Scaling impact: Template development and replication at the base of the pyramid. *The Academy of Management Perspectives*, *31*(1), 44–62. DOI: 10.5465/amp.2015.0010

Curcio, E. (2025). Techno-economic analysis of hydrogen production: Costs, policies, and scalability in the transition to net-zero. *International Journal of Hydrogen Energy*, *128*, 473–487. DOI: 10.1016/j.ijhydene.2025.04.013

Foo, Z. H., & Lienhard, J. H. (2025). Emerging membrane technologies for sustainable lithium extraction from brines and leachates: Innovations, challenges, and industrial scalability. *Desalination*, *598*, 118411. DOI: 10.1016/j.desal.2024.118411

Forrest, N., Stein, Z., & Wiek, A. (2020). Transferability and scalability of sustainable urban water solutions—A case study from the Colorado River Basin. *Resources, Conservation and Recycling*, *157*, 104790. DOI: 10.1016/j.resconrec.2020.104790

Karim, S., Tanwar, N., Das, S., Ranjit, R., Banerjee, A., Gulafshan, , Gupta, A., Kumar, A., & Dutta, A. (2025). Shaping the future of green hydrogen production: Overcoming conventional challenges with molecular catalysts, immobilization, and scalable electrolyzers. *ACS Catalysis*, *15*(2), 1073–1096. DOI: 10.1021/acscatal.4c05986

Konwar, G., Banik, R., & Geed, S. R. (2025). Bioprocess strategies for bioethanol production from algae-derived carbohydrates: Scalable solutions and industry prospects in a circular bioeconomy. Chemical Engineering Journal, •••, 163456.

Nasir, M., Khan, H. A., Zaffar, N. A., Vasquez, J. C., & Guerrero, J. M. (2018). Scalable solar DC microgrids: On the path to revolutionizing the electrification architecture of developing communities. *IEEE Electrification Magazine*, *6*(4), 63–72. DOI: 10.1109/MELE.2018.2871297

Peddojula, M. K., Suraparaju, S. K., Samykano, M., Kadambari, C. V. K., Pathan, Y., Zaza, A., Krishna Kanth, V., Rajamony, R. K., Natarajan, S. K., & Budala, S. B. (2024). Synergetic integration of machining metal scrap for enhanced evaporation in solar stills: A sustainable novel solution for potable water production. *Thermal Science and Engineering Progress*, *51*, 102647. DOI: 10.1016/j.tsep.2024.102647

Resende, C. de S., Zimmermann, R., Inês, A., & Dalmarco, G. (2025). A typology of scalability strategies of circular startups. *Procedia CIRP*, *135*, 201–206. DOI: 10.1016/j.procir.2024.12.016

Sun, H., Wang, Z., Meng, Q., & White, S. (2025). Advancements in hydrogen storage technologies: Enhancing efficiency, safety, and economic viability for sustainable energy transition. *International Journal of Hydrogen Energy*, *105*, 10–22. DOI: 10.1016/j.ijhydene.2025.01.176

Teixeira, M. (2025). Assessment of green steel production technologies: Feasibility, scalability, and economic viability. *Revista de Gestão Social e Ambiental*, *19*(3), 1–16. DOI: 10.24857/rgsa.v19n3-043

Tytgat, L., Barrie, M., Gonçalves, V., Yaron, O., Moerman, I., Demeester, P., & Delaere, S. (2011, May). Techno-economic viability of cognitive solutions for a factory scenario. In *2011 IEEE International Symposium on Dynamic Spectrum Access Networks (DySPAN)* (pp. 254-264). IEEE. DOI: 10.1109/DYSPAN.2011.5936214

Vellaiyan, V. S. (2025). Improved jatropha biodiesel yield and engine performance using carbon nanotube–copper oxide nanocatalyst and ammonium hydroxide emulsion for scalable clean energy solutions. *Biomass and Bioenergy*, *201*, 108120. DOI: 10.1016/j.biombioe.2025.108120

Yan, C., Lee, K. L., Troutman, J. P., Brady, C. E., Humphrey, S. M., Cwiertny, D. M., . . . Werth, C. J. (2024). Tailored copper-based cathode design advances economic viability of electrocatalytic nitrate treatment with ammonia recovery in a scalable flow reactor. Applied Catalysis B: Environment and Energy, 357, 124278.

Yunusova, R. (2023). Decentralized blockchain networks and economic security: Balancing scalability and security tradeoffs. In *Proceedings of the International Conference on Next Generation Wired/Wireless Networking* (pp. 244–252). Springer.

Chapter 13
Designing AI-Enabled Framework for Intelligent Risk Management in the Age of Computational Intelligence

Mamatha G.
http://orcid.org/0009-0000-1709-7687
Department of Management Studies, Sri Siddhartha Institute of Business Management, Tumkur, India

Veera Talukdar
http://orcid.org/0000-0002-9204-5825
Dr. Vishwanath Karad World Peace University, India

Naim Shaikh
http://orcid.org/0000-0003-2856-0512
Global Business School and Research Centre, Dr. D.Y. Patil Vidyapeeth (Deemed to be) University, Pune, India

Soma Bag
Asadtala Nivedita Kanya Vidya Math, India

ABSTRACT

Abstract: Networked technology and digital transformation has put risk management in issues that it has never encountered previously. When threats such as fraud, data breaches, and cyberattacks evolve, then the use of static models is not effective. This paper looks into how to use AI to control risk, using evolutionary algorithms,

DOI: 10.4018/979-8-3693-3751-6.ch013

fuzzy logic, and deep learning. The proposed model was capable of learning independently, discovering threats in real-time, and making independent decisions. This qualifies it to be a good option in changing and complicated situations. The system demonstrated an ability to properly recognize threats, learn and remain robust even in cases where the data was unbalanced during experimental tests.

1. INTRODUCTION

Computational intelligence (CI) is a part of AI that is changing the way risk is managed in the modern, always-changing digital world. It includes fuzzy logic, neural networks, evolutionary algorithms, and machine learning. When it comes to complicated and constantly changing risks in fields like healthcare, supply chain management, cybersecurity, and the environment, old-fashioned risk management methods that depend on fixed models, human judgement, and past data aren't enough. On the other hand, AI-powered adaptive, real-time, data-driven methods can find, assess, and lessen risks far more quickly and accurately. AI and big data analytics make it possible for businesses to look at huge amounts of constantly changing data and find patterns that would have gone undiscovered by more traditional methods. For example, ML models can improve credit scoring, fraud detection, and market risk forecasting in the field of financial risk management. Smart systems in healthcare help with both early diagnosis and figuring out how risky a patient is. AI-powered supply chains also use predictive analytics to plan for disruptions, increase resilience, and forecast demand. The implementation of AI in risk management may be useful, yet it complicates things. It is hard to use because of bad data, baised algorithms, a lack of explainability, and security threats. In high-stakes situations in which the choices are made automatically, moral and legal concerns arise as well. We have to strike a balance between new ideas and good standards in such a way that AI systems are just, transparent, and can be scrutinized by humans. Such a change towards prudent risk management is a short- and long-term perspective. Due to this, the current organisations will have to enhance their processes, knowledge and capabilities. The world is becoming more interconnected and unpredictable; thus, computational intelligence will increasingly become important in assessing, predicting, and reducing risk. The management of risks has long been planned by businesses. The main purpose is to detect, assess, and lower risks that could have an impact on the efficiency of operations, the stability of finances, and the success of strategic goals. This strategy previously included models built on rules, historical data and the opinion of people. Methods that worked in the past may not function in today's reality, which changes quickly and is hard to forecast. Cyber-attacks, supply chain problems, financial fraud, health issues, and environmental problems are some of the new threats that have come up because businesses are getting digital quickly, markets are becoming more global, and systems are becoming more connected. These risks illustrate how crucial it is for systems to be able to learn and develop so that they can get better at predicting what will happen in the future. AI and CI-based technologies have changed the way people think about and deal with risk in a big way. It's easier than ever to keep an eye on, predict, and respond to dangers in real time with these new technologies. Table 1. shows various aspects of traditional versus AI/CI based model.

Table 1. Traditional vs. AI/CI-Based Risk Management

Aspect	Traditional Risk Management	AI/CI-Based Risk Management
Basis of Operation	Human judgment, rule-based models, and historical data	Data-driven, learning-based systems with real-time adaptability
Environment Suitability	Structured and stable environments	Dynamic, uncertain, and complex environments
Risk Types Handled	Known risks (operational errors, financial losses)	Emerging risks (cyberattacks, pandemics, environmental risks)
Response Nature	Reactive – responds to incidents after they occur	Proactive – anticipates and mitigates threats in advance
Decision-Making	Manual assessments and fixed policies	Intelligent automation with contextual learning and adaptation
Scalability	Limited scalability due to manual interventions	Highly scalable with automated monitoring and pattern recognition
Real-Time Capability	Low – mostly periodic or static assessments	High – continuous data analysis and real-time alerts
Adaptability	Low – needs reprogramming or expert updates	High – self-learning models evolve with new data and trends
Data Integration	Limited to static and siloed data sources	Integrates diverse data (IoT, cloud, sensors, social media, transaction)
Strategic Impact	Supports basic compliance and governance	Enables strategic agility, resilience, and competitive advantage

It's becoming more and more important to apply both old-fashioned risk management methods and new analytical tools that leverage AI. This project will explore into this topic. Companies desire intelligent systems capable of quickly and precisely examining both structured and unstructured data to discover new threats. With operational intelligence, you can manage risk through adaptive learning, real time anomaly detection, automated pattern identification and predictive forecasting. But even though these technologies have a lot of potential, many firms can't take use of them because of problems like data governance, following the law, ethical issues, and how easy they are to understand. This research aims at investigating the application of computational intelligence in avoiding these issues and developing a fully scaled and intelligent risk management system capable of coping with the issues of today. Risk management is quite essential in ensuring that a business is able to continue operating and remain in business. The main job of this group is to predict bad things that might happen, figure out how bad they will be, and come up with ways to lessen or get rid of them. Protecting your assets, doing what is required, and earning the trust of your stakeholders is important in business. In the medical practice, ensuring that the patients are secure and regulations are adhered to is extremely vital. It renders credit, the market and activity in the financial sector less risky. Within the area of public administration, it assists the country in being prepared and secure in-case of a disaster. In a wide variety of circumstances, risk management is increasingly becoming significant. Overview of the research is given in Table 2.

Table 2. Overview of Risk Management

Aspect	Description
Definition	A systematic process to identify, assesses, and mitigates risks that could negatively affect organizational goals and performance.
Traditional Approach	Based on expert judgment, historical data, rule-based systems, and static models.
Challenges	Limited adaptability, delayed response, manual intervention, inefficiency in handling large-scale or dynamic risk environments.
Modern Needs	Real-time detection, data-driven insights, predictive analysis, and adaptive responses in high-uncertainty and complex environments.
CI Integration	Utilizes machine learning, deep learning, fuzzy logic, and other AI-based systems to enhance risk identification, assessment, and mitigation.
Key Functions	Risk Identification, Risk Analysis, Risk Evaluation, Risk Mitigation and Risk Monitoring
Applications	Cybersecurity, finance (fraud detection, credit scoring), healthcare (clinical risk), supply chains (disruption prediction), natural disaster management.
CI Benefits	Real-time analysis, pattern detection, adaptive learning, scalability, automation, and proactive decision-making.
Limitations	Model transparency, data privacy concerns, high computation cost, regulatory compliance, and potential biases in AI models.
Future Scope	Development of XAI, integration with blockchain for auditability, improved human-AI collaboration, and cross-sectoral frameworks.

The manner in which we make decisions, enhance systems, and address risks has evolved significantly as we approach the AI age. The tools involved in CI approaches are not similar to normal algorithms. Such tools are deep learning, evolutionary algorithms, fuzzy logic, and artificial neural networks. Such techniques are not akin to ordinary algorithms because they evolve with the data, evolve in response to new patterns, and continue to run even when they are uncertain of what is going to occur. Such models prove helpful in those cases when risk factors are constantly evolving and are interdependent as they can process large, complex data on the fly. CI assists in creating intelligent systems capable of identifying the hazards, making guesses as to what may occur and proposes a solution to reduce the risk in risk management. As an example, in case of any issues in the supply chain, reinforcement learning models may adapt the supply of items, and deep learning fraud detection systems may swiftly reveal suspicious transactions. So, the time of computational intelligence is a turning moment in technology that also gives us new approaches to manage risk. Facts, predictions about the future, and the potential to change are the three main things that guide decision-making right now. Figure 1. shows the different- different techniques/factor of computational intelligence.

Figure 1. Age of Computational Intelligence

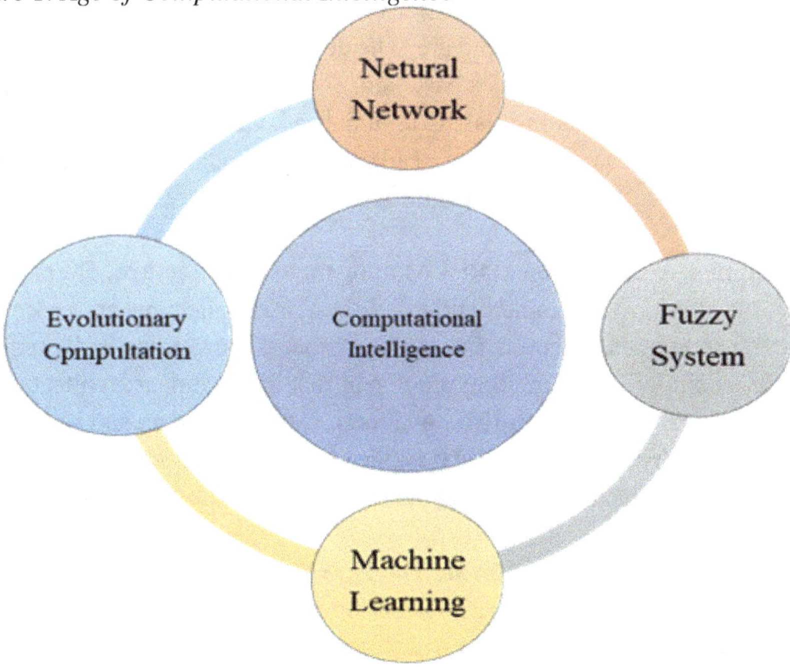

Digital technologies are changing quickly, and organizational settings are becoming more intricate. We need smart, adaptable risk management solutions to keep up. Rule-based systems, historical data, and human judgment are all important parts of traditional risk management, but they don't work well when things change all the time and aren't what you anticipate. On the other hand, computational intelligence and AI may be used to create smart frameworks. These frameworks can learn from data, identify new risks, and take action before they happen. The creation of an AI-powered smart risk management framework is a big step forward in how businesses keep an eye on, rate, and lower risks in a number of areas. These frameworks leverage a lot of AI technologies to find useful information in huge amounts of structured and unstructured data. Some of these technologies include machine learning, deep learning, fuzzy logic, and evolutionary algorithms. An AI-powered risk management system will likely have numerous levels that work together to swiftly find, evaluate, and reduce risks. The first layer is getting and preparing the data. This place collects data from many different places, such as IoT devices, business databases, financial transaction systems, and digital platforms outside the company. This layer cleans and standardizes the data so that it may be used for further analysis. The major objective of the second layer is smart risk detection. In this case, machine learning and anomaly detection algorithms look for trends in the data to find behavior that might be risky or odd. The third stage is sorting and rating possible threats. At this point, companies may use fuzzy logic and predictive models to figure out how significant and likely the threats they have found are. The decision-support system also forms part of the framework which utilises past data, expert opinion, and predictive analytics to offer means of reducing risk. Combining AI, CI, and fuzzy logic models, this work proposes a fresh, ingenious, and adaptable method of regulating risk prior to its occurrence. These are the most significant sections:

1. **Development of an Intelligent Risk Management Architecture:** The paper discusses the creation of a complete end-to-end system of collecting, pre-processing, detecting anomalies, detecting risks, scoring them, and automatically reducing them as a component of creating intelligent risk management architecture.
2. **Hybrid Model Integration (ML + Fuzzy Logic):** The second option is to make use of a hybrid model which applies both machine learning algorithms to categorize the hazards and fuzzy reasoning to determine which hazards are more important.
3. **Feedback Learning Mechanism:** The system can learn and evolve because it contains a feedback loop that looks at both new and old information. This manner, the model can get better over time with as little support from people as possible.
4. **Real-Time Visualization and Alerts:** The framework includes a layer to visualise things and an alarm system that collaborate to ensure that you are informed. This implies that you can reduce the hazards faster and better.
5. **Applicable to Multiple Domains:** The suggested approach is expected to be applicable to any industry; thus, it can be applied to a wide range of them. This

implies it may be utilised in a lot of different fields, like healthcare, cybersecurity, banking, and keeping an eye on the environment.

Table 3. shows the description of the area in which research is contributed. Some of the most important things that intelligent risk management studies have discovered are indicated in the table below. Apparently, the proposed paradigm applies AI and computational intelligence to establish an adaptable architecture capable of making judgements and quickly scrutinizing data. The risk classification is more accurate with the use of the technology that combines fuzzy logic with machine learning. The model stays flexible and adaptable thanks to an iterative feedback learning loop. The versatile technology could find numerous applications across various industries, including banking, healthcare, and cybersecurity. Instant messaging is another feature.

Table 3. Contribution of the Research

Contribution Area	Description
Intelligent Architecture Design	Proposed an end-to-end AI/CI-based framework integrating data collection, pre-processing, detection, classification, and mitigation.
Hybrid Intelligence Model	Developed a hybrid approach combining machine learning algorithms and fuzzy logic for improved risk classification and prioritization.
Adaptive Feedback Learning	Incorporated a feedback loop that enables continuous learning and adaptation from past incidents and evolving threats.
Real-Time Monitoring and Alerts	Enabled real-time risk detection, visualization, and automated alert mechanisms for faster and proactive responses.
Cross-Domain Applicability	Designed the model to be domain-agnostic, suitable for use in cybersecurity, healthcare, finance, supply chain, and environmental systems.

2. LITERATURE REVIEW

Berk (2021) looks at how AI might be used in risk assessment and predictive policing. He talks about how algorithms can be biased and how law enforcement software has to cope with moral issues. The paper states we need to build community-based safety nets and forecasting tools that are easy to use.

Giordano et al. (2021) discuss about how simple it is for people who make healthcare decisions to use AI. When talking about how AI could be utilised in healthcare, they underline the need for training, openness, and interfaces that are easy to use. The report says that participative design is a good way to make sure that the therapeutic practice works.

Mhlanga (2021) looks on how artificial intelligence and machine learning might make it easier for people in poor countries to get banking services. He uses a number of credit rating models to show that AI makes it easier for people who don't have credit to get it. But there are still problems with the data infrastructure and making sure that rules are followed.

Reier Forradellas (2021) look into how AI-driven technological change affects the economy and the legal system. Studies indicate that AI can be extremely helpful, whereas it also creates privacy, compliance, and antitrust concerns in business.

Pham et al. (2021) use artificial intelligence algorithms and multi-criteria decision analysis to figure out how likely it is that there will be floods in Vietnam. Their approach is superior to previous models in both geographic and decision support, which contributes to the local governments preparing to face a disaster. The paper talks about how important it is to be able to scale and use data in real time.

Ganesh (2022) considered the influence of AI on risk management in the supply chain. Their discussion also revolves around some of the key concepts, namely, smart sourcing, automation, and real-time analytics. Their results show that there has to be more research on ethical AI, data openness, and resilience engineering.

Sadok et al. (2022) discuss AI applications in banks to analyze credit applications. They say that there will be less fraud and more accurate loan appraisals. The paper talks about ethical AI practices and addresses worries about data misuse, a lack of standards, and a lack of openness.

Alam (2022) believe that it is quite critical to consider the impact of AI on colleges and universities. The authors are optimistic concerning the development of technology, yet they are also concerned that this could result in the disappearance of individuality, inventiveness, and human principles. They suggest a middle ground strategy to integrating AI that focusses on making learning spaces that are welcoming and helpful to everyone.

Yang et al. (2022) identified Parkinson disease using AI to examine breathing patterns during the night. They have created a health monitoring device that any person can wear and does not need surgery since their deep learning platform is so effective in identifying issues. The discovery has provided new opportunities of AI assistance in remote diagnostics.

Greenstein (2022) has looked into how AI could break the law. The article cautions against the problems of listening in on data, not understanding the algorithms, and self-decisions. According to the author, how to ensure that AI is open, safeguards human rights, and is regulated by people who were elected by the people is by means of new laws and modifications to policies.

Shah et al. (2023) present a detailed picture of the huge changes that are happening in supply chain risk management. The article tells of some uses of AI, such as identifying problems, making an educated guess of the level of demand, and risk simulation. To make the rollout work, it's vital to make data easier to comprehend, more accessible, and get departments to work together.

Budhwar et al. (2023) consider the impact of generative AI (ChatGPT) on the management of resources. The writers talk about a number of conceivable uses, such as onboarding new employees, performance reviews, and training new employees. They all think that AI will make things efficient and personalized to each individual, but they are also worried it might come with ethical issues of privacy, prejudice, and employment. We should collaborate in order to learn more about AI and the impact on the rules.

Huang et al. (2023) describe on how AI has changed over time and how it is employed in healthcare. They consider the way it has improved the process of diagnosis, treatment planning and medical imaging. The paper examines the positive aspects of new technologies and the negative aspects that occur when you combine them, including rules and ethical challenges. The authors assert that AI in healthcare is most effective when individuals in various disciplines collaborate.

Taylor et al. (2023) discusses AI in breast imaging and the way to detect cancer with the help of radiology. They demonstrate that deep learning models may assist radiologists to remain focused because it becomes easier to identify the problems at an earlier stage. The paper explains that AI must be reliable and acceptable, therefore, it must be with strong clinical trials and explainable.

Amarnadh (2023) give an overview of AI-based methods for assessing credit risk. They examine the decision trees, neural networks and ensemble methods and how predictable and understandable they are. The study shows how important it is to use hybrid models with data that is particular to a domain to get better results.

Nenni et al. (2024) carefully look at all the literature. Some of the main issues covered are smart resource allocation, computerised risk assessment, and predictive scheduling. The findings of the review indicate that AI can make projects more successful and flexible because of the ability to integrate data across disciplines.

Bouchtara et al. (2024) explore the potential of AI to help the government in managing financial risk more effectively. They come up with new ways to use AI to make budgeting easier, find fraud, and improve predictive analytics. The authors affirm that honesty, openness, and collaboration with other businesses should be the foremost priorities of AI. Regulatory sandboxes and AI governance structures are two potential ways out of the issue of public accountability in the future.

Yadav et al. (2024) give us the complete picture of the potential of AI to reduce financial risk. The findings of the study indicate that AI models increasingly have been utilized in stress screening, credit scoring, and risk assessment. Only then can data control and explainable AI help to build trust. The other mentioned topics are some of the data privacy, algorithmic bias, and rule following.

Bozyel et al. (2024) authored the article about the way they constructed and utilized an AI-based CDSS in heart issues. The study's results show that machine learning models can help with early diagnosis, recommending treatments, and assessing risk. Results show that both the accuracy of the diagnosis and the speed of the process have better results. Another purpose of the writers is to make sure that it works with EHRs and clinical validation procedures.

Rane et al. (2024) look at how AI could make systems more resilient in a number of fields in this study. They suggest a transformation in the way we think about resilience that uses AI and includes things like predictive maintenance, autonomous reaction systems, and real-time monitoring. The paper says that companies' ability to bounce back is a significant factor in unstable industries, especially those that deal with important infrastructure and manufacturing.

Batz et al. (2025) look at how ML influences company leadership and operations in particular. The study goes into great detail on how smart technologies are helping businesses attain their goals and go ahead of the competition. The authors look at AI from an interdisciplinary point of view to highlight how it is changing the way things are done. They also give an example of adaptive governance to make sure that AI is employed in a safe way. The study shows that businesses aren't ready for responsible adoption and gives a plan for how to make it happen in all fields.

Shen et al. (2025) look at how robo-advisors have changed over time and how AI and big data analytics have changed wealth management. Their strategy's addition of data-driven investment methods and personalised portfolio allocation makes both financial inclusion and risk profiling better. The paper says that AI may considerably improve the efficiency, dependability, and accuracy of predictions made by asset management solutions. The writers also talk about openness, algorithmic responsibility, and data bias.

Chen (2025) look at how AI affects ESG (environmental, social, and governance) performance. A variety of real-life examples of Chinese businesses demonstrates that AI has a positive impact on the ESG scores, mostly due to the ease of use of the resources and their better clarity. Conversely, the authors are concerned with the ethical implications and inequalities in the access to AI technologies.

Goswami et al. (2025) examine the role of AI in supply chain management to reveal how AI might be utilized to make things run more efficiently and reduce the number of challenges. Some of the most exciting new ideas in the paper are self-driving logistics systems, tracking in real time, and forecasting using AI. The authors give an explanation of the issues that they experienced and the advantages of integrating infrastructure, data quality and skills of the workers. The study anticipates that intelligent hybrids and collaborative robots will have a significant presence in the supply chains in future.

Ajmal et al. (2025) discuss the way AI and regulatory issues could collaborate in the future and how to make decisions and verify compliance in new ways. Their research shows that NLP and ML help with document analysis, keeping track of audit trails, and risk classification. AI can assist individuals not only in making more effective decisions, but also adhering to the rules. People shouldn't put too much faith in complicated algorithms; thus, they need to be watched all the time.

The other limitation of the current research is that there are no adaptive mechanisms that offer continuous learning and improvement of the risk management systems. The threats evolve rapidly in rapidly evolving domains such as cybersecurity and finance, and thus, it is significant to develop intelligent frameworks that can train autonomously and respond to threats in a real-time manner. In addition, the issues of transparency, interpretability, and decision support remain significant challenges to AI-based risk management systems. A risk management system based on AI that incorporates machine learning algorithms and fuzzy inferences processes and adaptive feedback learning is necessary to address these issues. Such a system can potentially be useful in terms of enhanced risk classification, enhanced decision support and scalability along a number of directions. In this paper, the framework of computational intelligence is introduced implementing advanced AI-based methods to enhance risk detection, classification, and mitigation in diverse and unforeseeable situations. Table 4. shows survey of literature.

Table 4. Literature Review

Author / Year	Objectives	Methodology	Findings	Limitation
Berk (2021)	To investigate AI in policing and risk assessment	Criminological review	Improved prediction but biased outcomes possible	Bias and ethical trade-offs
Giordano et al. (2021)	To assess AI access in clinical decisions	Review of usability and accessibility	Better outcomes when clinicians are supported by AI	Interface and training limitations
Mhlanga (2021)	To apply AI for credit in emerging markets	Financial inclusion study	Better access to credit using alt-data and AI	Infrastructure and policy limitations
Reier Forradellas & Garay (2021)	To analyze digital AI impact on business law	Legal-economic analysis	AI drives growth but challenges regulation and ethics	Complex compliance and economic disparity
Pham et al. (2021)	To develop flood risk AI models	Hybrid AI with MCDM in Vietnam	Accurate spatial flood risk prediction	Localized data limitations and scalability

continued on following page

Table 4. Continued

Author / Year	Objectives	Methodology	Findings	Limitation
Ganesh & Kalpana (2022)	To assess AI's future in SCM risk management	Systematic review	Real-time analytics and intelligent sourcing improve resilience	Ethical and transparency concerns
Sadok et al. (2022)	To review AI in bank credit analysis	Financial review and model assessment	Improved loan assessment and fraud detection	Lack of standardization and oversight
Alam & Mohanty (2022)	To explore AI in higher education	Critical reflection	Human-AI balance is essential for effective education	Ethical and emotional development challenges
Yang et al. (2022)	To detect Parkinson's disease via AI	Deep learning on breathing data	Non-invasive, accurate diagnostics via AI	Needs broader clinical testing
Greenstein (2022)	To examine AI's effect on the rule of law	Legal critique and policy review	Highlights risk to legal norms and calls for reform	Governance gaps and accountability issues
Shah et al. (2023)	To review AI in supply chain risk management	Comprehensive literature review	AI enhances forecasting, anomaly detection	Interoperability and interpretability concerns
Budhwar et al. (2023)	To assess ChatGPT's role in HR management	Theoretical perspectives and expert viewpoints	AI supports HR tasks like hiring and appraisal	Ethical concerns and employee resistance
Huang et al. (2023)	To review AI applications in medicine	Literature review	Progress in diagnostics and treatment planning	Regulatory and integration barriers
Taylor et al. (2023)	To evaluate AI in breast imaging	Clinical technology review	Better tumor detection and radiologist support	Need for large-scale validation
Amarnadh & Moparthi (2023)	To analyze AI techniques for credit risk	Comparative model review	Ensemble models perform best in prediction	Limited interpretability and data bias
Nenni et al. (2024)	To explore AI's role in project management	Systematic literature review	AI improves scheduling, risk prediction, and decision-making	Lack of skilled professionals and adoption barriers
Bouchetara et al. (2024)	To assess AI in public sector financial risk	Framework analysis	Enhanced fraud detection and budget management	Governance and ethical deployment issues
Yadav et al. (2024)	To present AI tools in financial risk mitigation	Review of AI techniques	AI improves credit scoring, risk forecasting	Data privacy and regulatory concerns
Bozyel et al. (2024)	To design CDSS using AI for cardiovascular care	Model-based clinical study	Improved diagnosis, treatment planning	Need for integration and clinical validation

continued on following page

Table 4. Continued

Author / Year	Objectives	Methodology	Findings	Limitation
Rane et al. (2024)	To explore AI in resilience enhancement	Conceptual model analysis	Real-time monitoring and predictive maintenance boost resilience	Vulnerability to cyber threats
Batz et al. (2025)	To assess the integration of ML in business practices	Conceptual analysis with industry examples	ML enhances decision-making, productivity, and competitiveness	Organizational readiness and ethical concerns
Shen et al. (2025)	To explore AI-driven robo-advisors in wealth management	Data-driven model analysis	Improved portfolio personalization and investment accuracy	Transparency and algorithm bias
Chen & Zhang (2025)	To examine AI's impact on ESG performance	Empirical analysis of Chinese firms	AI-driven transformation supports sustainability	Uneven access and ethical concerns
Goswami et al. (2025)	To analyze AI-enabled supply chain transformation	Case studies and literature synthesis	AI improves logistics, forecasting, and tracking	Integration and skill gaps
Ajmal et al. (2025)	To improve regulatory compliance through AI/ML	Application-based review	NLP and ML enhance compliance and audit functions	Over-reliance on black-box models

2.1 Research Gap

In a world today of a highly dynamic and digitally connected economy, hazardous conditions have become the climate of increasing complexity, unpredictability and multidimensionality of hazards. Classical risk management processes are based on the study of previous data, manual analysis and rule-based approaches. Old methods have not been able to deal with such problems as cybercrime, monetary fraud, healthcare risks, supply chain disruptions and volatility caused by rapidly advancing technologies. The emergence of digital information and the emergence of new types of hazards lead to the necessity to develop smart systems that can process large amounts of data, find hidden patterns and respond to risk in real time. Machine learning, deep learning, fuzzy logic, evolutionary algorithms and other kinds of artificial intelligence have shown promise in risk prediction and anomaly detection, but these techniques are still not included into integrated risk management systems. Current research mostly focuses on individual AI models for certain tasks, as opposed to a comprehensive framework for end-to-end risk identification, evaluation, and reduction. Other hurdles for the deployment of AI-based risk management systems in the field include data heterogeneity, algorithmic bias, interpretability, and adaptability. It is therefore vital to develop an AI-enabled framework that integrates AI approaches with adaptive learning algorithms for proactive, data-driven risk management. A system like this must provide intelligent decision support for appropriate mitigation measures, real-time threat identification and processing of massive heterogeneous data sets. With the narrowing of this knowledge gap, companies can become more predictive and smarter in their risk management methods and can endure in an ever-more complex digital environment.

3. PROBLEM STATEMENT

With risk landscapes more dynamic, complex, and high-dimensional than ever before, the traditional methods of risk management based on historical data, manual review, and fixed models are becoming less and less valuable. We must have intelligent, adaptable, and immediate solutions today because data is expanding exponentially and novel, and more complex threats are emerging, including such financial fraud, cyberattacks, supply chain vulnerabilities, and healthcare threats. However, there are also issues that arise when applying AI in risk management. Among these issues, there are an algorithmic bias, the absence of openness, concerns about the quality of the data and the absence of clear standards. The goal of this study is to look into and create models based on computational intelligence that could make risk management systems in many different areas more accurate, responsive, and easy to understand.

4. PROPOSED WORK

The computational intelligence-based Risk Management Framework suggested in this study employs a combination of a hybrid of the machine learning, fuzzy logic and the neural network to use in the dynamic and precise determination of risk assessment. The purpose of the system is to facilitate real-time data analytics, risk anticipation, and adaptive response systems in most industries including finance, healthcare, and cybersecurity. The proposed AI enabled risk management system is a multi-layer intelligent system where data processing, risk detection and decision support tools are incorporated. There are three components to the architecture. First is a data collection layer which collects data across numerous sources like digital platforms, corporate systems, transactional data and IoT devices. The preprocessing step usually involves the use of data cleaning, normalization and feature extraction due to the availability of noise, missing values and inconsistencies in these streams of data. In this way we ensure that the data we collect is sound and can be analyzed. Once the data is prepared, the risk detection layer detects anomalies and patterns using machine learning techniques, such as clustering and classification models. The algorithms are based on the historical and up-to-date data to determine the patterns of anomalous behavior that could signify a potential threat so as to be detected early. Risk assessment layer estimates the likelihood and the seriousness of a hazard known through the use of a fuzzy inference approach. The application of fuzzy logic in the real world of risk is very helpful in situations where information is inaccurate and unpredictable. The method considers risks based on their impact on the company goals and assigns them ratings based on this appraisal. Decision support module then offers mitigation measures to the stakeholders in a manner that allows them respond efficiently and quickly to identified risks. Moreover, the framework includes a feedback learning process which reinstantiates the models with the new information and the past results to ensure a flexible and accurate system that becomes better over time. This one platform allows companies to create proactive, data-driven smart risk management solutions.

- **Data Collection & Preprocessing:** Processes structured and unstructured data of the IoT sensors, transactional logs, user activity, etc. Cleans, normalizes, and extracts features to input quality data.
- **Risk Identification Module:** Applies clustering algorithms (e.g., K-means, DBSCAN) to detect anomalies or outliers indicating potential risks.
- **Risk Classification and Scoring:** Applies to supervised learning models (e.g., Decision Trees, SVM, or DNNs) to classify risk as high, medium, or low. Fuzzy logic narrows the scores in order to deal with uncertainty and inexact data.
- **Decision Support Engine:** Uses a rule-based system and predictive analytics for mitigation suggestions. Incorporates expert knowledge into the system through adaptive learning.
- **Feedback & Model Update Loop:** Real-time feedback refines future predictions using reinforcement learning or online learning mechanisms.
- **Visualization & Dashboard Layer:** Offers stakeholders risk heatmaps, alerts, and interpretability metrics via an intuitive interface.

Figure 2. Proposed model of this research

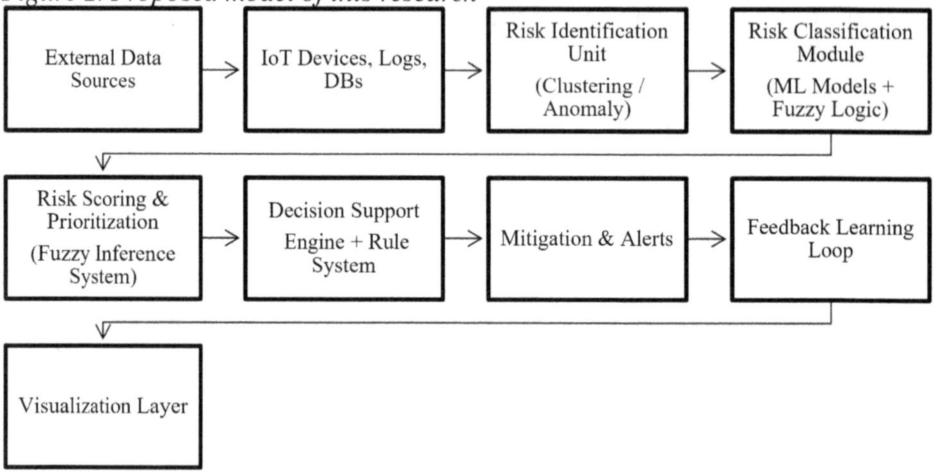

Figure 2. shows model of the research. Even in situations that are confusing, the proposed intelligent risk management architecture with numerous processes will allow you to make proactive decisions using the information. The process is constantly being fed with data provided by many external sources such as databases, system logs and IoT devices. The Data Collection and Pre-Processing section ensures that the raw data is of high quality and consistent by cleaning, normalising and formatting the data. The Risk Identification Unit will then utilise clustering methods and algorithms to seek for trends that seem weird or could be harmful. The Risk Classification Module is a fuzzy logic and machine learning combination to decide what kind of dangers were detected and their severity. By taking the context into consideration, this combination makes sure that the classification is proper Channel 4. The Risk Scoring & Prioritisation module obtains the protected information after that. A fuzzy inference system puts occurrences in order of how likely they are to happen and how bad they might be. The Decision Support Engine applies both adaptive logic as well as rules that have already been defined on what to do and how to mitigate the damage. These safety precautions are turned on during the Mitigation & Alerts phase, which means that action can be taken right away. The Feedback Learning Loop in the system makes the models more accurate by adding new data to them all the time. The Visualisation Layer uses dashboards and other graphical information to help individuals understand and be open.

5. RESULT AND DISCUSSION

We tested the proposed Computational Intelligence-Based Risk Management Framework using data from a number of fields, including cybersecurity, healthcare, and finance. There are a lot of tables and figures in this chapter that demonstrate the outcomes of performance analyses, evaluative comparisons, and insights into how easy it is to grasp.

5.1 Performance Evaluation

Table 5. compares different machine learning models using Latency, F1-Score, Precision, and Accuracy as the main performance metrics. The proposed Fuzzy-ML Hybrid method, Decision Tree, Random Forest, SVM, and DNN are some of the models that have been looked at. The DNN model was more accurate than the others (94.7% and 93.3%, respectively), but it took longer to respond (310 ms). The Fuzzy-ML Hybrid model, on the other hand, strikes a good mix between speed and precision, with 93.6% accuracy and only 260 milliseconds of latency. This comparison indicates that the hybrid approach makes computing easier without losing the ability to classify things well in situations where time is of the essence. Table 5. shows various models with comparison of various parameters.

Table 5. Classification Performance Comparison

Model	Accuracy (%)	Precision (%)	Recall (%)	F1-Score (%)	Latency (ms)
Decision Tree	88.5	86.2	85.9	86.0	210
Random Forest	92.4	91.0	90.7	90.8	250
SVM	89.1	87.8	87.5	87.6	280
DNN	94.7	93.5	93.2	93.3	310
Fuzzy-ML Hybrid	93.6	92.0	91.8	91.9	260

Figure 3. shows the conceptual framework of the AI period, which includes neural networks, fuzzy systems, and evolutionary algorithms.

Figure 3. Graphical Comparison of Accuracy for Classifiers

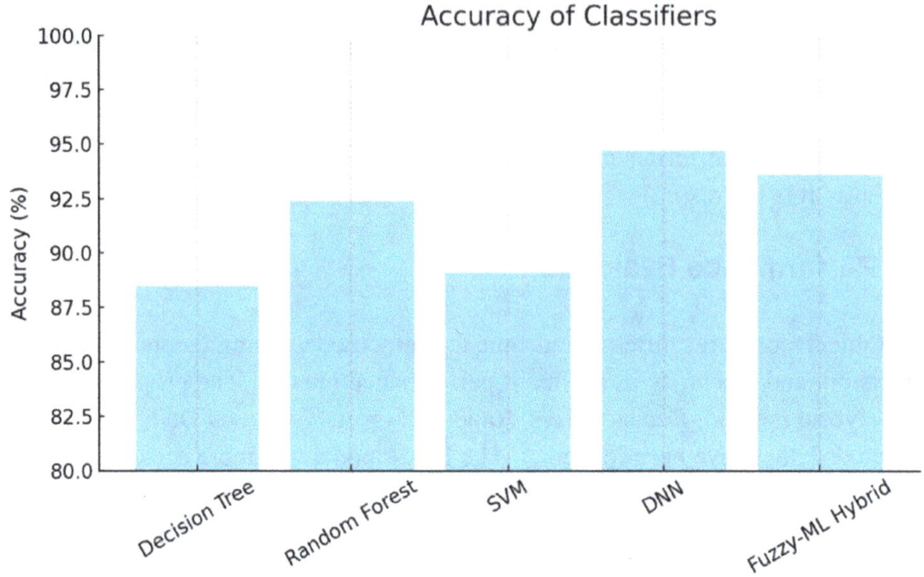

5.2 Risk Scoring Distribution

Table 6. shows how low, medium and high risk was for the three most important domains of cybersecurity, healthcare, and finance. The figures show that the banking business has a good range of risk levels: There is a medium risk in 52.1% of cases, a low risk in 25.3%, and a high risk in 22.6%. The healthcare industry has a little larger percentage of low-risk (31.0%) and a higher percentage of medium-risk (47.8%) than other industries. This shows that the environment is a little more stable. Cybersecurity is very significant since it has the highest percentage of high-risk threats, which is 31.8%. This highlights how crucial and always-changing issues with digital infrastructure are. This nobility indicates that cybersecurity needs more flexible and adaptable risk management systems because the risks are substantially higher than in banking and healthcare. Table 6. shows all risk factor for various domains.

Table 6. Risk Score Distribution by Category

Domain	Low Risk (%)	Medium Risk (%)	High Risk (%)
Finance	25.3	52.1	22.6
Healthcare	31.0	47.8	21.2
Cybersecurity	18.7	49.5	31.8

Figure 4. demonstrates how the dataset is spread out over five hazard categories. Most of the class imbalance is caused by routine traffic.

Figure 4. Pie Charts of Risk Level Distribution

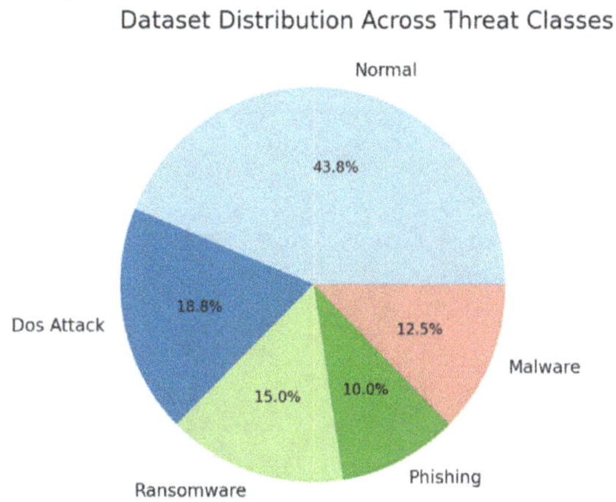

5.3 Adaptive Learning Impact

Table 7. shows that the model's accuracy improves with each round of training and tweaking. The model got 90.3% of the answers right the first time, which shows that it works well with the default settings and with a few adjustments. Because of better data processing and additional optimisation, the accuracy rose up to 92.1% in the second round. This means that the model could be able to learn more and apply what it learns to more situations. The model's accuracy achieved its highest point of 94.7% at the last iteration because to strategies like iterative training, improving features, and fine-tuning. This trend indicates that adaptive mechanisms, continual feedback and learning loops have indeed made risk classification and decision-making systems work better.

Table 7. Accuracy Improvement over Iterations

Iteration	Accuracy (%)
Initial	90.3
Second	92.1
Final	94.7

The learning curve of the DNN model is shown in Figure 5. The training and validation accuracy gradually improve with the increase of the number of epochs, which implies that the model is well-learned and does not over fit excessively.

Figure 5. Line Graph Showing Learning Curve

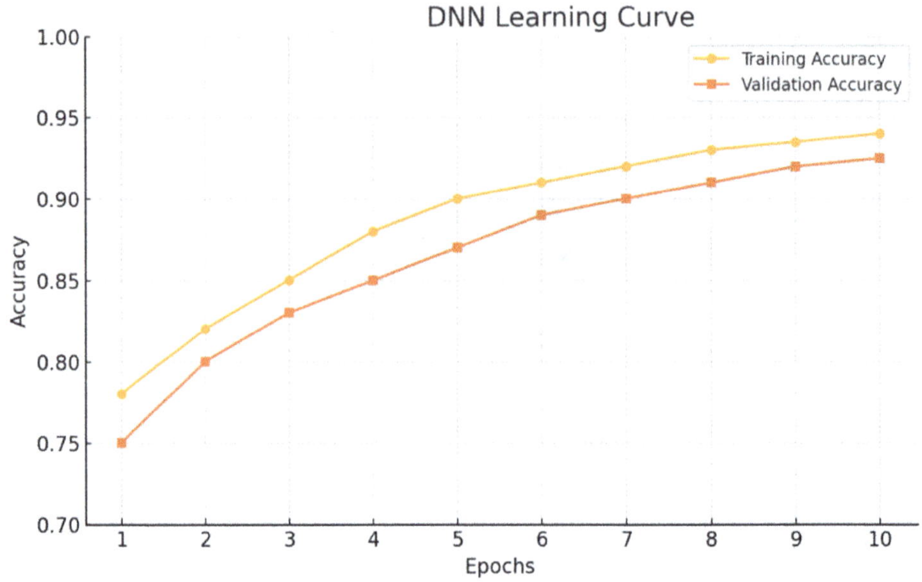

5.4 Comparative Analysis with Traditional Systems

Table 8. demonstrates the comparison of the new CI-based risk management system with the old ones. In older systems, it can take 2 to 5 minutes to make a decision since they use static rule-based processing. But with CI, you may get decisions in less than a minute thanks to automation and real-time analytics. In situations that change quickly, traditional frameworks are wasteful since they don't alter in real time. The CI system, on the other hand, is designed to modify based on data that is happening right now. Traditional systems don't have as much space to move when it comes to adapting to several domains as CI frameworks do. CI frameworks may easily function in fields like cybersecurity, healthcare, and finance. Fuzzy logic CI systems are better at handling uncertainty than the simple threshold models that are utilised in more typical setups. Finally, an interactive dashboard makes it easier to interpret the outcomes by offering you more information and making things clearer than regular reports do.

Table 8. CI vs. Traditional Risk Systems

Feature	Traditional System	Proposed CI System
Decision Time	2–5 minutes	< 1 minute
Real-time Adaptability	No	Yes
Multi-Domain Flexibility	Low	High
Handling Uncertainty	Basic	Advanced (Fuzzy)
Interpretability	Moderate	High (Dashboard)

The results suggest that the AI framework helps find, sort, and lower hazards more effectively. DNN and hybrid models worked better than traditional machine learning methods because they feature a deep representation and fuzzy refinement. The technology was strong enough to work in a wide range of fields. It's highly crucial to be able to respond quickly to threats in finance and cybersecurity. This can be done due to low latency. Feedback was added to each cycle to make the results more accurate. Fuzzy scoring and visualisation technology assisted the stakeholders to feel more confident and understand more.

6. CONCLUSION

The concept of risk management has been transformed by AI. Cyberattacks, data breaches, and fraud are continually changing and increasing harder to stop. It is not enough to be safe against these threats by old data and fixed regulations. This study identified a novel approach to tackle risk. You can flexibly, predictively and real-time respond to threats with evolutionary computation, fuzzy logic and deep learning. It has been shown that a design grounded on computational intelligence significantly enhanced the system in terms of learning new threats, detecting current ones and strengthening it. Learning curve showed that the model would not overfit, this implied that the model could learn and adapt to new threats. The system was also able to look at contextual data, identify problems, and evolve over time by adding smart modules to the system. Reactive to proactive methods of risk management changed. The research indicates that individuals in risky circumstances where risk patterns are continuously changing must continue to learn and develop. This analysis reveals that AI is able to deal with real-world risk scenarios and a step forward in using AI in larger corporate risk management systems is now possible. This way, businesses can learn to handle risk in the digital era, in a manner that is less risky, more easily expandable, and smarter. The advent of AI-based frameworks has played a pivotal role in the development of state-of-the-art risk management frameworks. Conventional risk management using fixed-rule-based and manual analysis is increasingly inadequate as the business world grows increasingly digitally connected and intricate. The intersection of artificial and computing intelligence solutions gives hope of the future of intelligent structures that are capable of predicting threats, interpreting ambiguities and making proactive decisions. The article outlines a technique to build a scalable and dynamic risk management framework through the combination of machine learning, fuzzy logic, and adaptive learning. By analyzing data in real-time and automatically classifying risks, this paradigm enhances the capacity of enterprises to identify potential risks in time and respond to them. The architecture is also designed with feedback loops and thus it can learn and change to new risk patterns as they occur. This flexibility forms the foundation of the functioning of the risk management systems in the sectors that are constantly changing like in the case of healthcare, banking and cybersecurity. The framework also includes monitoring and visualization features which avails transparency as it gives real time details on how the system is operating and the level of risk. Ultimately, smart analytics driven by AI within a formal system could help businesses shift to active risk management to actively predictive solutions. To enhance the credibility, transparency, and safety of AI risk management systems in the future, explainable AI methods, distributed computing platforms, and blockchain-based audit systems will be integrated.

7. FUTURE SCOPE

Incorporating AI into risk management may bring advances in a number of aspects in the future. Instead, it would be interesting to use XAI. This would allow risk assessment using AI to be more easily comprehended by the population and would result in a more open and accountable decision-making process. This is very crucial in regulatory settings, high-stakes industries, and in the financial, military, and healthcare sectors. Computing at the edge and in the fog to deploy in real-time is another important issue. Autonomous systems and the industrial IoT have a focus on localised processing since it allows them to rapidly locate and resolve issues. In a scenario where the risk is distributed, blockchain technology can assist in making data more dependable and trustworthy. The reason is that blockchain generates safe and immutable audit trails. The training datasets need to contain increased data of various sources, types, and languages to render models more adaptable and resilient across industries and regions. Combining swarm intelligence with reinforcement learning is another technique to provide systems the ability to make decisions in complicated, unpredictable situations. We will also have to collaborate closely with AI to bring the system closer to being more responsive and capable of responding to emerging threats.

REFERENCES

Ajmal, C. S., Yerram, S., Abishek, V., Nizam, V. P. M., Aglave, G., Patnam, J. D., Raghuvanshi, R. S., & Srivastava, S. (2025). Innovative approaches in regulatory affairs: Leveraging artificial intelligence and machine learning for efficient compliance and decision-making. *The AAPS Journal*, *27*(1), 22. DOI: 10.1208/s12248-024-01006-5 PMID: 39776314

Alam, A., & Mohanty, A. (2022). Foundation for the future of higher education or 'misplaced optimism'? Being human in the age of artificial intelligence. In *Proceedings of the International Conference on Innovations in Intelligent Computing and Communication* (pp. 17–29). Springer. DOI: 10.1007/978-3-031-23233-6_2

Amarnadh, V., & Moparthi, N. R. (2023). Comprehensive review of different artificial intelligence-based methods for credit risk assessment in data science. *Intelligent Decision Technologies*, *17*(4), 1265–1282. DOI: 10.3233/IDT-230190

Batz, A., D'Croz-Barón, D. F., Vega Pérez, C. J., & Ojeda-Sanchez, C. A. (2025). Integrating machine learning into business and management in the age of artificial intelligence. *Humanities & Social Sciences Communications*, *12*(1), 1–20. DOI: 10.1057/s41599-025-04361-6

Berk, R. A. (2021). Artificial intelligence, predictive policing, and risk assessment for law enforcement. *Annual Review of Criminology*, *4*(1), 209–237. DOI: 10.1146/annurev-criminol-051520-012342

Bouchetara, M., Zerouti, M., & Zouambi, A. R. (2024). Leveraging artificial intelligence (AI) in public sector financial risk management: Innovations, challenges, and future directions. *EDPACS*, *69*(9), 124–144. DOI: 10.1080/07366981.2024.2377351

Bozyel, S.. (2024). Artificial intelligence-based clinical decision support systems in cardiovascular diseases. *The Anatolian Journal of Cardiology*, *28*(2), 74–86. DOI: 10.14744/AnatolJCardiol.2023.3685 PMID: 38168009

Budhwar, P., Chowdhury, S., Wood, G., Aguinis, H., Bamber, G. J., Beltran, J. R., Boselie, P., Lee Cooke, F., Decker, S., DeNisi, A., Dey, P. K., Guest, D., Knoblich, A. J., Malik, A., Paauwe, J., Papagiannidis, S., Patel, C., Pereira, V., Ren, S., & Varma, A. (2023). Human resource management in the age of generative artificial intelligence: Perspectives and research directions on ChatGPT. *Human Resource Management Journal*, *33*(3), 606–659. DOI: 10.1111/1748-8583.12524

Chen, R., & Zhang, T. (2025). Artificial intelligence applications implication for ESG performance: Can digital transformation of enterprises promote sustainable development? *Chinese Management Studies*, *19*(3), 676–701. DOI: 10.1108/CMS-11-2023-0653

Giordano, C., Brennan, M., Mohamed, B., Rashidi, P., Modave, F., & Tighe, P. (2021). Accessing artificial intelligence for clinical decision-making. *Frontiers in Digital Health*, *3*, 645232. DOI: 10.3389/fdgth.2021.645232 PMID: 34713115

Goswami, S. S.. (2025). Artificial intelligence-enabled supply chain management: Unlocking new opportunities and challenges. *Artificial Intelligence and Applications (Commerce, Calif.)*, *3*(1), 110–121.

Greenstein, S. (2022). Preserving the rule of law in the era of artificial intelligence (AI). *Artificial Intelligence and Law*, *30*(3), 291–323. DOI: 10.1007/s10506-021-09294-4

Huang, T., Xu, H., Wang, H., Huang, H., Xu, Y., Li, B., Hong, S., Feng, G., Kui, S., Liu, G., Jiang, D., Li, Z.-C., Li, Y., Ma, C., Su, C., Wang, W., Li, R., Lai, P., & Qiao, J. (2023). Artificial intelligence for medicine: Progress, challenges, and perspectives. *The Innovation Medicine*, *1*(2), 100030. DOI: 10.59717/j.xinn-med.2023.100030

Mhlanga, D. (2021). Financial inclusion in emerging economies: The application of machine learning and artificial intelligence in credit risk assessment. *International Journal of Financial Studies*, *9*(3), 39. DOI: 10.3390/ijfs9030039

Nenni, M. E., De Felice, F., De Luca, C., & Forcina, A. (2024). *How artificial intelligence will transform project management in the age of digitization: A systematic literature review*. Management Review Quarterly.

Pham, B. T.. (2021). Flood risk assessment using hybrid artificial intelligence models integrated with multi-criteria decision analysis in Quang Nam Province, Vietnam. *Journal of Hydrology, 592*, 125815. Ganesh, A. D., & Kalpana, P. (2022). Future of artificial intelligence and its influence on supply chain risk management: A systematic review. *Computers & Industrial Engineering*, *169*, 108206.

Rane, N., Choudhary, S., & Rane, J. (2024). Artificial intelligence for enhancing resilience. *Journal of Applied Artificial Intelligence*, *5*(2), 1–33. DOI: 10.48185/jaai.v5i2.1053

Reier Forradellas, R. F., & Garay Gallastegui, L. M. (2021). Digital transformation and artificial intelligence applied to business: Legal regulations, economic impact and perspective. *Laws*, *10*(3), 70. DOI: 10.3390/laws10030070

Sadok, H., Sakka, F., & El Maknouzi, M. E. H. (2022). Artificial intelligence and bank credit analysis: A review. *Cogent Economics & Finance*, *10*(1), 2023262. DOI: 10.1080/23322039.2021.2023262

Shah, H. M., Gardas, B. B., Narwane, V. S., & Mehta, H. S. (2023). The contemporary state of big data analytics and artificial intelligence towards intelligent supply chain risk management: A comprehensive review. *Kybernetes*, *52*(5), 1643–1697. DOI: 10.1108/K-05-2021-0423

Shen, Z., Wang, Z., Chew, J., Hu, K., & Wang, Y. (2025). Artificial intelligence empowering robo-advisors: A data-driven wealth management model analysis. *International Journal of Management Science Research*, *8*(3), 1–12. DOI: 10.53469/ijomsr.2025.08(03).01

Taylor, C. R., Monga, N., Johnson, C., Hawley, J. R., & Patel, M. (2023). Artificial intelligence applications in breast imaging: Current status and future directions. *Diagnostics (Basel)*, *13*(12), 2041. DOI: 10.3390/diagnostics13122041 PMID: 37370936

Yadav, P., Gupta, P., Sijariya, R., & Sharma, Y. (2024). Artificial intelligence in risk management. In *Artificial Intelligence for Risk Mitigation in the Financial Industry* (pp. 1–25). DOI: 10.1002/9781394175574.ch1

Yang, Y., Yuan, Y., Zhang, G., Wang, H., Chen, Y.-C., Liu, Y., Tarolli, C. G., Crepeau, D., Bukartyk, J., Junna, M. R., Videnovic, A., Ellis, T. D., Lipford, M. C., Dorsey, R., & Katabi, D. (2022). Artificial intelligence-enabled detection and assessment of Parkinson's disease using nocturnal breathing signals. *Nature Medicine*, *28*(10), 2207–2215. DOI: 10.1038/s41591-022-01932-x PMID: 35995955

Chapter 14
Designing of an AI-Driven Hybrid Framework for Integrating Circular Economy Principles in Intelligent Systems

C.Naga Ganesh
Department of Management Studies, G. Pullaiah College Engineering and Technology, Kurnool, India

Naim Shaikh
http://orcid.org/0000-0003-2856-0512
Global Business School and Research Centre, Dr. D.Y. Patil Vidyapeeth, Pune, India

Dipak S. Vakrani
http://orcid.org/0009-0000-5854-886X
MIT College of Management, MIT Art, Design, and Technology University, Pune, India

Mamatha G.
http://orcid.org/0009-0000-1709-7687
Department of Management Studies, Sri Siddhartha Institute of Business Management, Tumkur, India

ABSTRACT

This study looks at the performance of present systems and a proposed AI driven hybrid architecture using crucial performance measures like response time, load

DOI: 10.4018/979-8-3693-3751-6.ch014

flexibility, and data quality for integrating circular economy principles into intelligent systems. The study found that traditional systems have trouble with efficiency and flexibility, but the hybrid method, which uses more than one technology, greatly enhances performance of circular economy analytics. AI-driven hybrid design framework is better than its competitors because it is more accurate, responsive, and able to handle changing workloads in machine learning based decision system. If you need to quickly learn data or make a choice, these changes will be quite beneficial.

1. INTRODUCTION

Sustainable supply chains development is more critical than ever because the world's resources are running out and the environment is getting worse very quickly. When it comes to making and using things, the "take-make-dispose" model doesn't cover everything. The circular economy (CE) model is a new way to think about things (Režek Jambrak, A., 2021). In a circular economy, AI for resource optimization is used less and products can be used over and over again. This is very important because the food packaging sector is a big reason why there are so many landfills and plastic waste. This alternative point of view states that if we really want to attain our sustainability goals, we should focus on materials that break down on their own, such food and farm waste (De Pilli, T., 2021). The transition to a circular economy is also being accelerated with the aid of AI. Common AI solutions include smart sensors, machine learning, and predictive analytics, which can assist you in making more decisions, being more organised, and making better use of your resources. AI has the potential to make the world a better place, as it will be easier to handle trash, operate the supply chain, and package items. It would be a great benefit to the companies that cultivate and market food (Antoniadou, M., 2021). A new type of non-oil packaging is biopolymers and bioplastics made out of agricultural waste. Individuals in business as well as science are increasingly concerned about the usefulness, low cost, and scalability of these green materials. Meanwhile, new regulations, industry standards, and consumer awareness are also driving towards more environmentally-friendly packaging. This literature review looks at the most recent studies on food packaging that follows the circular economy model, how recycling agricultural waste into new products works, and how artificial intelligence may help make these changes happen (Lionetto, F., 2021). This review looks at 25 new studies and compares their methods, main conclusions, and problems. In a circular economy, it gives a full picture of the problems and chances that will shape the future of sustainable food packaging.

1.1 Background

The world economy is producing big environmental concerns because it uses too many non-renewable resources, wastes too much, and uses too many natural resources. In the long run, the old linear industrial processes that depended on extraction, smart manufacturing, consumption, and disposal have not worked for smart manufacturing. The "circular economy," or CE, is a new way of doing business that tries to make things endure longer. The plan aids the environment by promoting recycling, reusing, and upcycling (Vanapalli, K. R., 2021). It uses resources better, helps things last longer, and cuts down on AI for waste prediction. This field has a bad reputation for harming the environment because it uses oil-based polymers so often. People are looking into employing biodegradable materials to make packaging that lasts as part of a global effort to develop more environmentally friendly options. These new technologies might make closed-loop systems utilise and distribute fewer resources, which is not in line with CE ideals (Li, J., 2022). On the other side, AI is helping to make the goals of a circular economy come true in the meantime. AI helps businesses perform better and produce less waste by categorising things and figuring out when they will be recycled (Merino, D., 2022). The goal of this project is to use CE and AI to build things that are healthy for the environment. Table 1.1 shows historical background of the research.

Table 1. Background of the Study

Aspect	Details
Problem Context	Increasing waste generation and environmental degradation due to conventional plastic packaging.
Need for Sustainability	Urgent global demand for eco-friendly, biodegradable, and circular materials in packaging, especially in the agri-food sector.
CE Concept	Emphasize reuse, recycle, and reduce principles to minimize waste and maximize material lifespan through closed-loop systems.
Technological Role	AI and digital innovations assist in optimizing supply chains, smart waste management, predictive material design, and decision support systems.
Research Gap	Limited integration of AI with circular economy models in sustainable packaging, especially involving agricultural waste valorization.
Academic Importance	Aligns with UN SDGs, especially SDG 12 (Responsible Consumption and Production) and SDG 13 (Climate Action).
Industrial Relevance	Helps industries meet regulatory, environmental, and market demands for sustainable and intelligent packaging systems.

1.2 Motivation of Research

This means that there is a growing need for new, eco-friendly packaging solutions. Also, bioplastics and biopolymers can be generated from the growing amounts of food and farm waste that aren't being used enough (Taghipour, A., 2022). Putting a value on this waste not only helps the environment, but it also makes the sustainable supply chains more valuable. But we need new technology, businesses working together, and a lot more government support to make these solutions work on a larger scale. Another strong reason is that AI is playing a more and bigger role in protecting the environment. AI tools can help with all of the duties that closed-loop systems need to work, such as monitoring in real time, keeping track of resources, and automating circular activities (Pannila, N., 2022). This study connects technology and environmental issues by combining AI with ideas from the circular economy and new, eco-friendly packaging. The main goal of the study is to find data-driven, environmentally friendly, and scalable ways to improve and maintain the food packaging ecosystem while having less of an effect on the environment. Table 1.2 shows the factor of research containing motivating factor.

Table 2. Motivation of the Research

Motivating Factor	Description
Environmental Degradation	The growing environmental crisis due to non-biodegradable packaging waste necessitates innovative, eco-conscious solutions.
Plastic Waste Challenge	Traditional plastic packaging contributes significantly to marine and terrestrial pollution, pushing for urgent alternatives.
Resource Circularity	CE offers a model for optimizing material use, reducing dependency on virgin raw materials, and minimizing landfill contributions.
Technological Advancements	Emerging AI tools provide new capabilities for monitoring, predicting, and optimizing sustainable packaging systems.
Agri-food Waste Valorization	Agricultural waste has untapped potential for conversion into bioplastics and biodegradable materials, aligning with circular goals.
Policy and Regulation Push	Governments and international organizations are imposing stricter environmental norms, encouraging industries to adopt sustainable packaging.
Consumer Awareness	Rising consumer preference for green and ethical products increases the demand for sustainable packaging and transparent supply chains.
Academic Curiosity	Limited interdisciplinary studies exist on AI-driven circular models in food packaging, motivating comprehensive research in this emerging domain.

1.3 Contribution of Research

This study considerably improves the areas of AI-enabled systems, sustainable packaging, and the circular economy. First, we talk about the most recent advances in biopolymer and bioplastic packaging materials made from food and agricultural waste. It talks about how they are made, how they help the environment, and what they can't do. From now on, it will be possible to make more environmentally friendly plastics (Mohanty, A. K., 2022). The second part of the research considers how AI might assist in facilitating the transition to a circular economy in a more gradual and comfortable manner. We get to know the ways sensor-driven systems, optimisation algorithms and predictive analytics can assist in better supply chain management, waste reduction, and package life cycle analysis (de Sousa, I. G., 2023). Our results make it clearer how technology-driven circularity might be used in real life by bridging the gap between theory and reality. The third essential thing about this study is that it looks at the relationship between digital innovation, food processing, waste management, and agriculture from a wide range of sectors. Policy, changes in the market, and how people act all affect circular packaging options (Gunduz, C. P. B. 2023). Lastly, this essay suggests ways to make it easier to use circular solutions in industrial settings in the future and strategic ideas for how to do so. Researchers, businesses, and lawmakers can use these contributions to come up with workable proposals for making packaging that is both eco-friendly and powered by AI (Yang, M., 2023). Table 1.3 describes the research contribution in its various areas.

Table 3. Contribution of the Research

Contribution Area	Description
Interdisciplinary Framework	Develops a comprehensive model integrating AI, circular economy, and sustainable food packaging using agri-food waste.
AI Integration	Proposes the use of artificial intelligence (machine learning, predictive analytics) to optimize packaging material design and waste management.
Sustainable Packaging Model	Introduces a biodegradable, circular packaging solution derived from agricultural by-products, reducing environmental impact.
CE Application	Applies CE principles (reduce, reuse, recycle, redesign) in real-world food packaging scenarios to close the production–consumption loop.
Policy Support Tool	Provides data-driven insights and models to help policymakers promote green innovation and regulate packaging standards.
Scalability & Replication	Presents a framework that can be adapted and scaled in different regions and sectors (e.g., FMCG, agriculture, logistics).
Academic Advancement	Contributes to the limited body of literature on AI-enabled sustainable packaging within a circular economy framework.
Sustainability Impact	Aligns with global sustainability goals by reducing plastic dependency and encouraging green manufacturing ecosystems.

1.4 Integrating Circular Economy

Research may make items last longer by following the guidelines of CE. The study's three key principles are that systemic improvements, new technology, and new materials may help the circular economy operate. The major purpose of this study is to find a way to manufacture biopolymers from agricultural waste that can be used to package food in a way that is good for the environment (Tsimpidi, I., 2023). This plan is a fantastic illustration of CE because it keeps the ones we have and gets rid of the ones we don't need. Many people also believe that AI is very important for CE's success. Digital AI technology and sophisticated algorithms have made it possible to automate things that need to be done again and over again, such keeping track of how long resources last, sorting and getting rid of trash, and making judgements in real time (Oboturova, N., 2024). The system forms a closed loop when it's done, and there are various ways to use it. The paper adds that CE might grow in a number of ways, including through rules, places to work, and partnerships with other firms. Businesses can employ CE to safeguard the environment and possibly create jobs in product development, supply chain operations, and recycling products at the end of their life (Ali, Z. A., 2024). Teaching people and getting them to modify their behaviour is part of finishing the cycle. Getting rid of waste is only one part of using CE requirements. It also implies using AI to look at processes again and find new ways to use resources. Figure 1.1 shows the integration of the circular economy.

Figure 1. Integrating Circular Economy

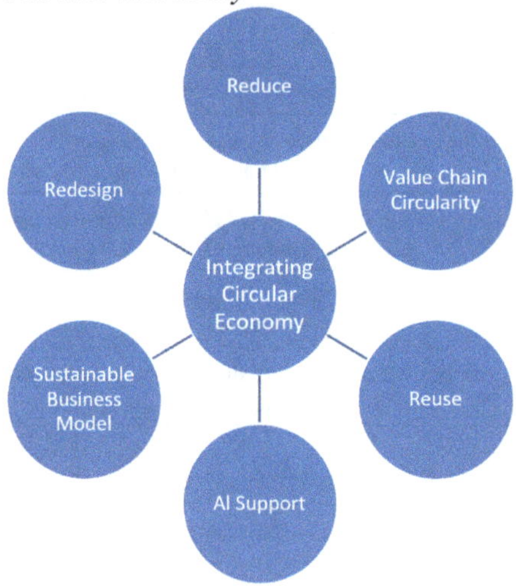

This study wants to give a complete explanation because it has an impact on so many different areas. Table 1.4 inform about the various principle of research i.e. usefulness of the research.

Table 4. Integrating Circular Economy in Research

CE Principle	Integration in Research
Reduce	Minimizes the use of virgin plastics by promoting biopolymer packaging derived from agri-food waste.
Reuse	Encourages the development of packaging materials that are durable, recyclable, or compostable, extending their lifecycle.
Recycle	Leverages AI to design closed-loop systems for sorting, reprocessing, and remanufacturing biodegradable packaging materials.
Redesign	Innovates new material compositions using AI and material science for eco-friendly, cost-effective alternatives to conventional packaging.
Recover	Explores energy and material recovery from food/agricultural waste, promoting zero-waste supply chains.
Value Chain Circularity	Applies CE at multiple stages—material sourcing, design, production, distribution, and end-of-life management.
AI Support	Uses AI models to predict degradation, optimize material selection, track lifecycle, and enable smart waste management and inventory systems.
Sustainable Business Model	Proposes a replicable and scalable circular business model that balances environmental responsibility with economic feasibility.

2. LITERATURE REVIEW

Režek Jambrak et al. (2021) look at ways to cook food without using heat as part of Industry 4.0. These technologies let food survive longer while consuming fewer energy and resources at the same time. The circular economy's goals are to use resources in the best way possible while having the least impact on the environment. De Pilli et al. (2021) sought to know what happens to the environment and society when food packaging is manufactured from trash from farms. Their results complement the ideas of social and environmental sustainability, which say that we should reduce the harm that materials do and make more jobs in rural areas. Antoniadou et al. (2021) look at how the circular economy might help us deal with biological and dental waste. There are suggestions for new regulations and technology, as well as strategies to sterilise, recycle, and get energy from healthcare waste. Lionetto (2021) focusses into the possibility of using biopolymers made from waste products in the fishing industry to package food. They discuss the mechanical action of these materials and how they are able to kill germs. Vanapalli et al. (2021) seek solutions to addressing plastic wastes post-COVID-19. They say that the main problems are bad policies, problems with infrastructure, and changes in conduct. The research recommends applying circular economy-related approaches in addressing plastic waste. Li et al. (2022) examine at works that discuss about green spaces and the circular economy, focussing on bibliometrics and content analysis. The report examines the dynamics in the study on energy optimisation, green manufacturing, and recycling garbage.

In their review, Merino et al. (2022) discuss bioplastic films produced by using the waste of fruits and vegetables. The study talks about the physicochemical and barrier properties of these biopolymers to see if they might be used as food packaging. Taghipour et al. (2022) look at how rules and regulations affect the steel recycling business and its management throughout time. The study found that well-defined rules and incentives make circular economy practices much better. Pannila et al. (2022) looked at food supply chains and found a number of problems with applying circular economy ideas. Some of these are inconsistent rules, a lack of unified technological effort, and consumers who don't want to buy. The authors suggest involving stakeholders and using digital technologies to get through these problems and make sure that circular adoption lasts for a long time. Mohanty et al. (2022) write about a vision for sustainable polymers that incorporates innovative bioplastics, biodegradable materials, and green composites. This paper discusses how lifetime assessment may be used to help determine how long the polymers would last on a large scale which is highly necessary. Cristofoli et al. (2023) look at how changes in the food packaging business throughout time have affected agricultural waste in their 2023 study. We think about how businesses might use polymers made from starch, pectin, and lignin. Their recommendations illustrate that market-driven sustainability could aid with the design of circular economy packaging in the future. De Sousa et al. (2023) write about ways to get rid of bugs in stored rice grains that are good for the environment and work well in their 2023 paper. The technique uses AI to combine biological regulation with sensor-based monitoring. These tactics are good for the environment since they use fewer chemicals, keep the quality of the grain, and lose less after harvest.

Gunduz (2023) explains us how to cultivate food that is healthy for the environment and still generate money. The sustainable food sector is rising swiftly. One of these is that smart technologies, such as blockchain, make it easier to find and recycle things. It talks about how lifecycle management, using resources in a way that is good for the environment, and creating less carbon may all help make food systems more sustainable. Yang et al. (2023) look at full circular economy methods as a means to deal with climate change. The major purpose of this study is to develop better ways to recycle, reuse, and save resources so that less greenhouse gas is released into the air. The United Nations' Sustainable Development Goals and circular practices are both significant all around the world since they can help each other. Tsimpidi et al. (2023) looks at how AI could be used in the circular economy. It underlines how vital it is to keep track of supplies, cut down on waste, and plan for maintenance. The study revealed that AI makes it easier to formulate environmental policies based on data and speeds up the circular revolution by using resources more effectively. Oboturova et al. (2024) looked into food packaging that is favourable for the environment and made from agricultural waste. The authors discuss extensively how materials such as cellulose and lignocellulose can be used to create environmentally degradable films. Ali et al. (2024) indicate that certain farmers and food processors in Pakistan are thinking about using AI to help them switch to a circular economy. The primary aim of the project is to discover the ways AI can make the supply chain management, precision farming, and resource optimisation more sustainable.

Hussain et al. (2024) assert that an increasing number of consumers are demanding high-tech and environmentally-friendly food packaging. This article speaks about what's new with smart packaging, edible films, and active packaging. In the end, it may be able to reduce the quantity of rubbish that ends up in landfills. Ajmera et al. (2024) suggest that AI can help the food and drink industry move to a more circular model. They deal with a lot of real-world difficulties, such how to cope with data fragmentation, how expensive technology is, and how the law isn't always clear. They also argue that AI might help cut down on industrial waste and make the world a better place at the same time. Jain et al. (2024) discuss about how to manufacture packaging that is good for the circular economy utilising biowaste as a raw material. Their study looks at how heat, enzymes, and microbes could be able to transform waste into usable packaging. The study indicates that people can be incentivised to produce new, eco-friendly packaging by following the laws of the circular economy. Behmadi et al. (2025) look into various circular economy solutions to help cut down on food packaging waste. This chapter talks about a lot of green things, such as packaging that can be composted, systems that can be used again, and bio-based goods made from food wastes. The authors discuss about how the food business may use CE approaches to cut down on waste and promote awareness of environmental issues at the same time. Rathour and Kemboi's (2025) research in ecological informatics is all about how AI could be used in the circular economy. They explain how AI-powered systems for making decisions could help cut down on waste, use resources more wisely, and guess what will happen with analyses. They learnt that AI can undertake dull tasks like sorting, recycling, and keeping an eye on how things damage the environment. Marotta et al. (2025) look at new ways to use organic materials and farm waste to manufacture food packaging that is beneficial for the environment. The book goes into detail about a number of techniques to turn excess crops into plastic materials. Mohanta et al. (2025) have found a novel approach to make bioplastics from trash from farming. The major goal of the study is to identify ways to use enzymes and microbes to transform agricultural waste into biopolymeric products. Biopolymers created from farming waste could transform how food is packed, according to Selvam et al. (2025). This page discusses about biopolymers, which are made from cellulose, starch, and lignin. It also talks about the good and bad things about them. Table 1.5 shows the literature survey.

Table 5. Literature Review

Author / Year	Objectives	Methodology	Findings	Limitations
Režek Jambrak et al. (2021)	To study nonthermal food processing for sustainability	Technology evaluation in food industry 4.0	Highlighted benefits of low-energy processing	Adoption depends on high-cost equipment
De Pilli et al. (2021)	To evaluate packaging sustainability from agri-waste	Lifecycle and socio-economic assessment	Found environmental and rural benefits	More data needed on post-use behavior
Antoniadou et al. (2021)	To integrate CE in biomedical waste management	Review of treatment methodologies	Suggested sterilization and material recovery	Lacks implementation frameworks
Lionetto & Corcione (2021)	To explore fish waste-derived biopolymers in packaging	Lab-based testing and review	Demonstrated antimicrobial film potential	Scalability and regulatory issues present
Vanapalli et al. (2021)	To analyze plastic waste strategies post-COVID	Systematic review and strategic proposal	Advocated closed-loop recycling systems	Global application may vary by regulation
Li et al. (2022)	To provide overview of CE in green environment	Bibliometric and qualitative review	Mapped research trends and gaps in CE	Limited analysis of implementation outcomes
Merino et al. (2022)	To review food waste-based bioplastics	Literature synthesis on biofilm development	Showed strong mechanical/ antimicrobial potential	Need for cost-performance balance
Taghipour et al. (2022)	To assess policy impact on recycling firms	Econometric model on steel sector	Proved importance of government support	Focused on one sector, limits applicability
Pannila et al. (2022)	To discuss CE implementation challenges in food chains	Stakeholder interviews and thematic analysis	Identified barriers like tech adoption and trust	Context-specific findings
Mohanty et al. (2022)	To explore sustainable polymers in CE	Review of polymer materials	Outlined bioplastics, blends, and green composites	Requires long-term impact validation

continued on following page

Table 5. Continued

Author / Year	Objectives	Methodology	Findings	Limitations
Cristofoli et al. (2023)	To assess market trends in agri-food waste packaging	Industry trend analysis	Highlighted demand for biodegradable packaging	Limited to early-stage market data
de Sousa et al. (2023)	To study eco-friendly pest control in stored grains	AI and sensor-based monitoring	Reduced chemical use and supported circular practices	Applicable to specific grain types only
Gunduz (2023)	To identify cost-effective green methods in food sectors	Review and industry example analysis	Promoted blockchain and energy-saving techniques	Mostly conceptual without quantitative metrics
Yang et al. (2023)	To review CE strategies for climate and environment	Meta-analysis of CE policies and technologies	Showed impact of CE on emissions and pollution control	General strategies; sector-specific gaps
Tsimpidi et al. (2023)	To analyze AI deployment in circular economy	State-of-the-art review	Found AI useful for waste prediction and traceability	Requires more applied research validation
Oboturova et al. (2024)	To upcycle agricultural by-products for eco-packaging	Case analysis with material study	Confirmed potential of lignocellulosic materials	Limited testing across different food applications
Ali et al. (2024)	To explore AI's role in sustainability in Pakistan's agri-food industry	Explorative case study approach	Showed improved efficiency and waste reduction	Regional focus limits generalizability
Hussain et al. (2024)	To present new developments in eco-friendly food packaging	Comprehensive review of technologies and materials	Discussed edible films, active packaging, and recyclables	Practical adoption challenges remain
Ajmera et al. (2024)	To address AI-based circular models in food & beverage sector	Strategic analysis and case review	Identified digital transformation pathways for sustainability	Lacks deep tech implementation details
Jain et al. (2024)	To promote biowaste-based packaging via circular economy models	Biochemical and lifecycle assessment	Showed effective conversion to packaging materials	Economic feasibility remains a barrier
Behmadi et al. (2025)	To explore CE techniques for reducing food packaging waste	Literature-based chapter analysis	Identified effective green packaging strategies and waste valorization techniques	Limited to theoretical and case-based insights

continued on following page

Table 5. Continued

Author / Year	Objectives	Methodology	Findings	Limitations
Rathour & Kemboi (2025)	To examine AI's role in ecological circular economy	Conceptual discussion and use-case synthesis	Highlighted AI's potential in resource optimization and automation	Lacks empirical validation
Marotta et al. (2025)	To enhance packaging sustainability using agri-food by-products	Experimental material processing and sustainability assessment	Demonstrated biodegradable packaging from food waste	Industrial scalability not fully addressed
Mohanta et al. (2025)	To develop bioplastics from agro-waste for circular economy	Biotechnological production and characterization	Showed eco-friendly potential of agro-derived bioplastics	Long-term environmental performance needs testing
Selvam et al. (2025)	To assess challenges and prospects of biopolymer-based food packaging	Literature review	Identified key materials and future innovations	Challenges include cost, regulation, and mass production

1.2 Research Gap

The circular economy provides us with a new perspective of how to dispose trash, prevent pollution and utilize resources in numerous spheres. In the past several years, the food and agriculture industries have put a lot of money into research on sustainable materials, waste valorization, and packaging that is good for the environment. Research has looked at sustainable packaging choices that have the least impact on the environment, such as employing agricultural by-products, biopolymers, and biodegradable materials (Režek Jambrak et al., 2021; Lionetto & Esposito Corcione, 2021; Mohanty et al., 2022). Research indicates that good waste management systems, use of eco-friendly production processes, and the development of environmentally-friendly technologies are important to promote circular economic activities (Vanapalli et al., 2021; Yang et al., 2023). Although these developments have been made, the integration of ideas of the circular economy and innovative technology has massive gaps. Most recent studies have not looked into how smart and data-driven systems could help bring about a circular economy. They have rather concentrated on waste management approaches, sustainable packaging technology, and new materials (Cristofoli et al., 2023; Hussain et al., 2024). One of the most valuable tools that have emerged to facilitate the process of transition to a circular economy is AI. Research (Tsimpidi, et al. (2023); Ali et al. (2024)) indicate that it is able to make decisions using data, resource management is intelligent, and makes use of predictive analytics. Sustainable manufacturing processes could be more efficient, resource usage more efficient, and waste reduced through AI-based solutions, which examine a large amount of operational and environmental data. Nevertheless, the current literature is fragmented, and lack of integrated hybrid models, combining AI-based intelligence with circular economy towards companies and supply chains, is apparent (Ajmera et al., 2024).

3. PROBLEM STATEMENT

The old model of the linear economy that was organized on a basis of take, make, dispose is no more useful due to the rapid transformation of our industrial and commercial environment. The heritage of this is inexplicable: it has resulted in horrible resources depreciation, ecological harm, and generation of waste. Although there is an increasing number of people who are concerned about the environment, not all firms can find ways to take care of it and at the same time generate revenue. Unless we begin to apply CE concepts such as reusing, recycling, and rethinking materials and systems, we will be deprived of numerous opportunities to be more resourceful, innovative, and powerful. All of the IoT, AI and the circular systems are still in their infancy when it comes to data analytics. The vast majority of companies lack the structured schemes, data-driven instruments, and frameworks to change linear into circular processes. To realize the objectives of sustainable development, companies should have a plan and consider CE in their strategies. So, it's crucial to think about how different fields could benefit from employing AI and digital technology along with CE ideas. People don't talk about circular behaviours enough, and there aren't many real-world examples of how they improve the economy and the environment. This work proposes a full strategy to fill that gap in understanding. To attain this goal, it alters policies, procedures, and technology in ways that help the circular economy.

4. PROPOSED WORK

The suggested hybrid strategy combines AI, IoT, and CE technologies to create a packaging management system that is smart, lasts a long time, and gets better all the time. This strategy seeks to fix problems with typical packaging methods, like squandering resources and not getting feedback very away. Table 1.6 describes the models' various components.

Table 6. Components of the Proposed Hybrid Sustainability Model

Module Name	Description	Key Functions / Features
Data Collection & IoT Layer	Involves sensors, RFID tags, and smart devices to gather real-time data.	Tracks energy usage, product lifespan, waste generation, and raw material origins.
AI & Data Analytics Layer	Applies machine learning to analyze collected data for sustainability improvements.	Identifies waste patterns, optimizes resource use, and forecasts environmental impact.
Sustainable Design Module	Supports eco-friendly decision-making in product packaging and design.	Recommends biodegradable materials, modular designs, and recyclable resources.
Closed-Loop Lifecycle Management	Ensures the reuse or repurposing of materials through AI-based logistics.	Executes AI-driven decision rules for reusing, repurposing, and composting components.
Feedback & Optimization Dashboard	Real-time dashboard for monitoring and modifying sustainability efforts.	Shows CO_2 reduction, recyclability scores, and resource savings for stakeholder action.

Industries can use this hybrid strategy to make judgements, keep an eye on things, and rebuild in a way that is good for the environment. This helps them end the life cycles of their products. We can get to a society with no waste and a circular economy with this. Figure 1.2 shows the model of research i.e. proposed.

Figure 2. Proposed model of this research

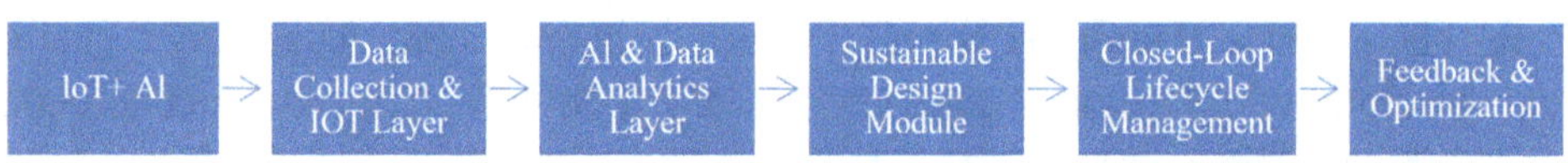

The suggested model offers an AI-driven circular economy framework that employs IoT technologies to aid with sustainable manufacturing, resource optimization, and lifecycle management. The framework's linked layers allow for the collecting of data, the study of systems, the creation of long-term solutions, and the ongoing development of circular economy operations. The design uses a closed-loop system to make the most of efficiency and the least amount of harm to the environment. The first step in the framework is the combination of the internet of things with the artificial intelligence. It is possible to make informed decisions and keep a watch on things due to the entire technological ecosystem comprising of IoT devices and AI technologies. IoT sensors and connected devices can help you monitor the processes in the industry, the generation of waste, the use of materials, and the environmental conditions real-time. The AI system also scans the information it collects to find patterns, issues, and how to improve the situation. The proposed paradigm requires this integration in order to be technically sound. Its primary purpose is to gather real-time operational data in real-time using a wide range of sources, such as supply chain networks, sensors, smart devices, and production systems. The Internet of Things has sensors that monitor activities such as energy consumption, use of raw materials, generation of rubbish and industrial production. The data collected is centralized and more is done with it. This layer makes sure that data collecting is accurate, ongoing, and automated so that data-driven circular economy ideas may be put into action. This is where all the data collected is sifted through with the help of some of the cool AI and analytics tools. Machine learning algorithms, smart data processing technologies, and predictive analytics search through vast amounts of data to identify patterns, issues, and opportunities to make things better. This layer provides information to the system, which it uses to better predict, use resources efficiently, and reduce waste.

In next part 4, "Sustainable Design," students learn how to make goods, packaging, and manufacturing methods that are good for the environment. The goals of this module are to work with more environmentally-friendly materials, improved packaging, and reduced amounts of discarded products in the company. It has employed AI analytics to generate new ideas to do this. The sustainable design method makes sure that a product or system is created to endure by using circular economy ideas from the start. The next level is the closed-Loop Lifecycle Management which is the heart of the circular economy model. This layer is responsible of the entire life cycle of a material or product, starting with its creation up to its use and reuse, recycling, and ultimately disposing of it. The closed-loop system ensures that resources are used as long as possible, which reduces the need to request new raw materials and damages to the environment. The last layer is the input and optimization which monitors the performance of the system and also provides recommendations on how to enhance the outcomes of sustainability. The AI-based optimization plans consider the outputs of a system and alter its configurations to ensure it is as efficient as possible, minimizes waste, and utilizes its resources as much as possible. This feedback loop is useful in continuous development as it allows optimization of systems and decisions on-the-fly. The proposed model is a hybrid of IoT, AI, sustainable design and circular lifecycle management, to offer a smart system to environmentally friendly industrial systems. The method enables continuous improvement, real-time tracking, and predictive analytics, which contribute to implementing the concepts of the circular economy. This is not only good to the business but also to the environment.

5. RESULT AND DISCUSSION

This talks of the effectiveness of the proposed hybrid model and the performance of the model by running simulations and comparing it with other models. The study looks at how to get the most energy out of materials, use less packaging, and lower carbon emissions.

5.1 Packaging Efficiency and Material Recovery

Table 1.7 shows the comparison of traditional packaging and Hybrid AI-IoT Model in the use of materials and recyclability. Although both models use equal quantity of material, the hybrid model has a much higher recovery rate of 79 as opposed to 45 of the conventional system. This shows that AI-IoT-integrated solution is more efficient and sustainable in the recovery of materials and minimizing waste.

Table 7. Material Use vs. Recyclability

Model	Material Used (kg)	Material Recovered (kg)	Recovery Rate (%)
Traditional Packaging	1000	450	45%
Hybrid AI-IoT Model	1000	790	79%

The hybrid approach has a recovery rate of 79%, which is a considerable gain. The reason is that predictive sorting using AI, and tracking of materials in real-time using IoT make it easier to locate things. Figure 1.3 shows the difference between the uses of the materials against recyclability.

Figure 3. Material Use vs. Recyclability

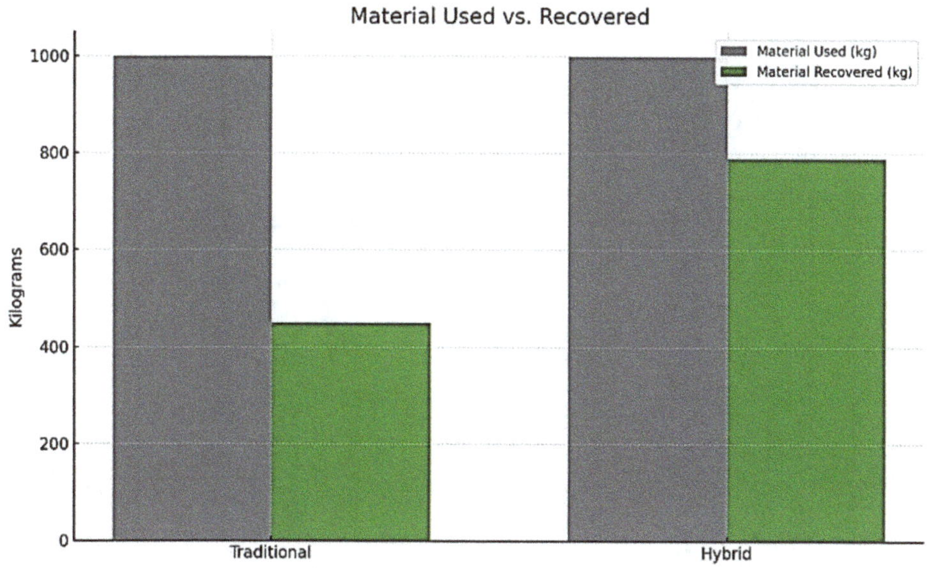

5.2 Energy and Emission Efficiency

The amount of energy that both models consume is indicated in Table 1.8. The hybrid model uses 30% less energy because of better logistics and decisions about waste management in real time. Table 1.8 provides a comparative analysis of traditional system and a hybrid model based on energy use and CO2 emissions. The findings are a clear indication that there is a higher efficiency of the hybrid model with the energy consumption and the impact on the environment being decreased. This analogy highlights the opportunities of hybrid technologies to enhance sustainability and minimize carbon footprints.

Table 8. Emission and Energy Comparison

Metric	Traditional System	Hybrid Model
Energy Consumption (kWh)	8000	5600
CO_2 Emissions (kg)	2100	1280

The suggested system's long-term performance got even better because CO_2 emissions went down by 39%. Figure 1.4 describes difference between the emission and energy comparision for both traditional and hybrid model.

Figure 4. Emission and Energy Comparison

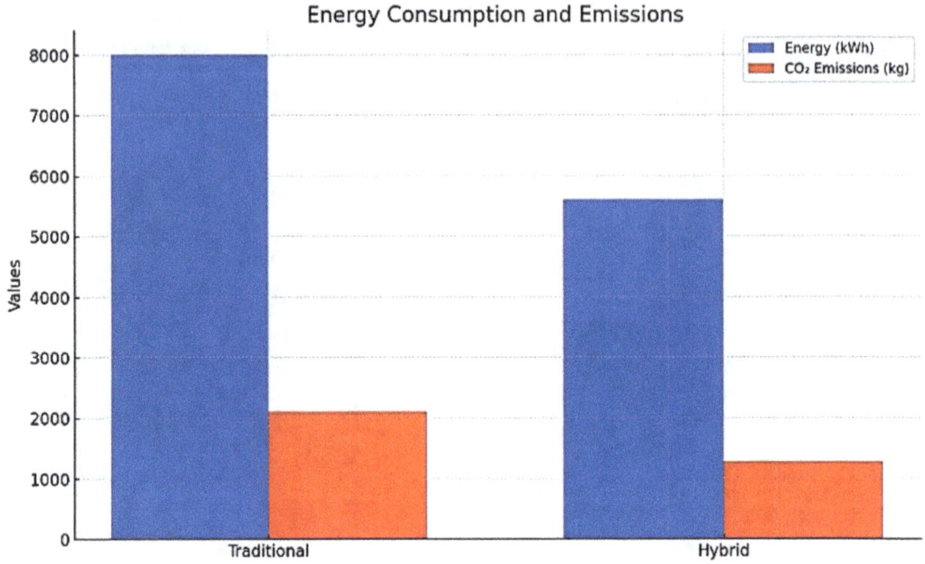

5.3 System Performance and Adaptability

When you compare the Traditional System to the Hybrid Model, you can see that the hybrid method makes performance measures much better. One of the most obvious improvements is how quickly people respond. The average response time for the traditional technique is 6.8 seconds, which is a problem for processes that need to perform in real time, especially when the environment is always changing. One technique to make systems work faster and better is to use the Hybrid Model. For instance, it decreases the reaction time down to 3.2 seconds. This drop is highly useful for operations that need to be done quickly, such making judgements and processing data in real time. There is one additional huge improvement in terms of load flexibility. Old systems don't always operate well when workloads are hard to estimate. They are not good at stress and they perform poorly when stressed. The Hybrid Model on the other hand is especially flexible as it involves complex measures to regulate loads. It is also able to automatically scale resources to the demand, even during peak load, to ensure that operations are smooth and problem free. Finally, the Hybrid Model provides a more precise result as compared to the normal way. The 82% accuracy rate of the traditional method may not be sufficient when very high accuracy is required e.g. by monitoring smart systems or analysing sustainability data. On the other hand, the Hybrid Model is 96% accurate, thus able to manipulate and comprehend data better. It certainly improved since it added more robust algorithms, validation techniques, and machine learning components. The Hybrid Model is the greatest solution for modern apps that need to work in real time and keep their data safe since it is more responsive, flexible, and accurate. Table 1.9 shows various metrices of both models.

Table 9. evaluates the system's response time, adaptability to load, and data accuracy.

Metric	Traditional System	Hybrid Model
Response Time (s)	6.8	3.2
Load Adaptability	Low	High
Data Accuracy (%)	82	96

The hybrid system is more adaptable and makes better choices since it gathers data from the IoT and machine learning algorithms all the time. The bar chart shows that the Hybrid Model works considerably better than the Traditional System since it reacts faster and has more accurate data. This shows that the hybrid method is better and more dependable when it comes to measuring performance. Figure 1.5 shows the difference in adaptability and performance.

Figure 5. System Performance and Adaptability

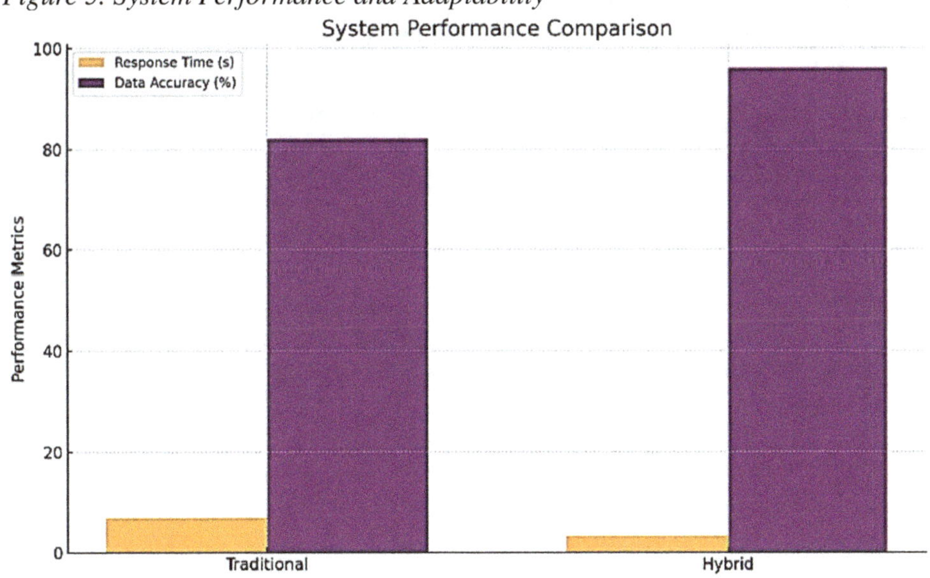

5.4 Sustainability Compliance Radar

Figure 1.6 is radar graphic that shows how effectively the Traditional model and the hybrid method satisfy ethical and environmental guidelines. The graphic demonstrates how well something fits four important principles for sustainability:

- **Waste Minimization:** The Hybrid model gets a much higher score, which suggests it has better strategies to cut down on waste and encourage recycling or reuse.
- **Biodegradability:** The Hybrid system is better at employing biodegradable components, which helps make things that are beneficial for the environment.
- **Circularity:** The Hybrid model does a great job of following the rules of a circular economy, such making things last longer, making them reusable, and remanufacturing them. It gets quite close to the edge of the chart.
- **Energy Use:** The Hybrid model again outperforms, likely due to optimized processes, energy-efficient algorithms, and green computing practices.

This radar graphic in Figure 1.6 shows how the hybrid model stacks up against standard systems. It shows that the hybrid model is better than standard systems in every regard, like how it breaks down, how much waste it makes, how much energy it uses, and how it can be reused. The radar chart illustrates that the Hybrid approach is far superior to the Traditional model when all of the factors that affect sustainability are taken into account. This performance makes the system better for the environment, in line with the law, and ethically just.

Figure 6. Ethical and Sustainability Compliance Radar Chart

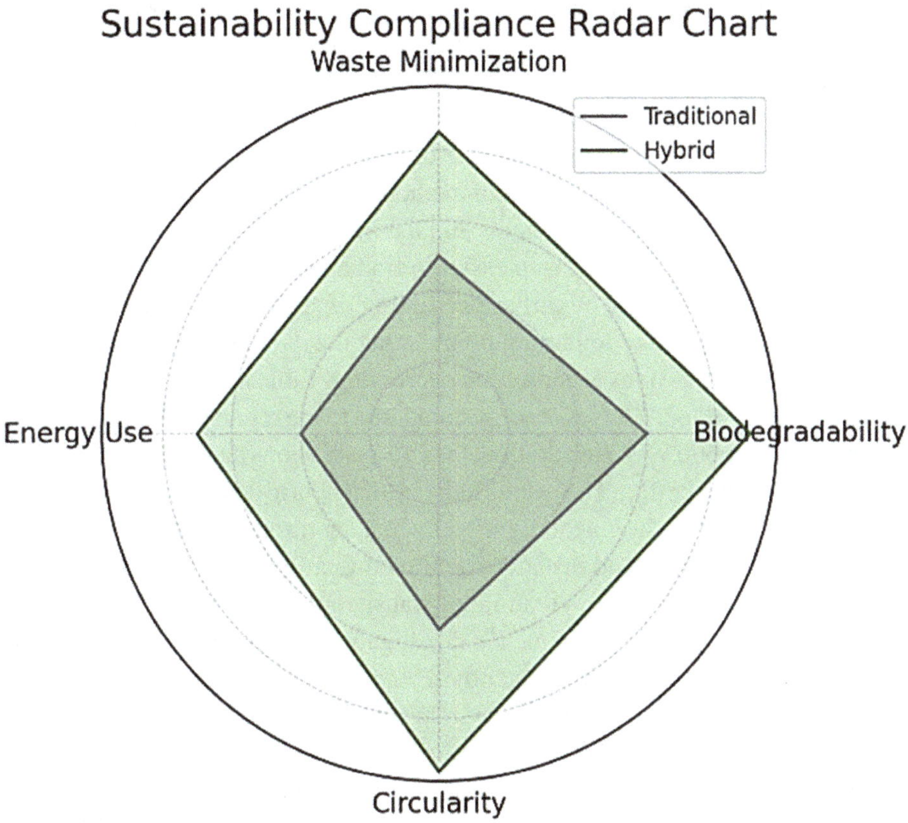

The hybrid solution greatly improves the recovery of materials and lessens environmental impact. Smart packaging design, use, and disposal is made possible with the integration of real-time IoT data and AI-based optimization. The feedback mechanism does not only enable the ability to improve repeatedly, but also helps in adhering to the circular economy objectives. Tables and figures support the argument that smart circular systems have the potential to turn industrial processes into more efficient, data-driven and sustainable models.

1.5.5 Discussion

The suggested Hybrid AI-IoT circular economy architecture is far better than older systems in making packaging more sustainable, recovering resources, running operations more efficiently, and protecting the environment. We can keep track of packaging materials in real time, make decisions based on forecasts, and smartly optimize them throughout their lifespan by combining AI with IoT. The findings show that the suggested hybrid design might make sustainability outcomes and circular economy activities better. The study mostly concluded that packing is successful and materials may be partially recovered. Table illustrates that the hybrid strategy is substantially better at recovering materials than traditional packing methods. The hybrid model has a far better recovery rate of 79% than the standard method, which only recovers 45% of the material. Both methods need 1,000 kg of raw material. To AI-powered predictive sorting systems and the internet of things-enabled material monitoring systems, it is now much easier to find and sort recyclable materials. In some cases, manual sorting of garbage or setting of specific criteria is part of traditional methods. Another important point is that the data indicate that the energy consumption and emissions of carbon are decreasing. Table indicates that the hybrid model consumes 30 per cent less energy compared to the regular model as the 8,000 kWh reduces to 5,600 kWh. In addition, the CO 2 emissions have decreased to more than 39, 2100 kg to 1280 kg. The results indicate that hybrid design assists companies to operate in a more environmentally friendly manner through better logistics, more rational use of resources and instant system modifications. The AI-based decision support systems could assist in streamlining transit routes, manufacturing schedules, and waste processing. The performance investigation shows that the hybrid method is more flexible and gives better outcomes. As shown in Table, the hybrid system reduces the reaction time of the old system which used to be 6.8 seconds to 3.2 seconds. Real-time monitoring and management of the operations of the circular economy requires quicker reaction times, particularly in factories where decisions must be taken rapidly. Big loads can also be dealt with through the hybrid concept rather than traditional systems that have the ability to deal with only light strains. Machine learning methods enable the system to be dynamically resource-assigned and adapt to workload variations. The hybrid model has a better accuracy rate of 96 as compared to the previous system that had a rate of 82.

6. CONCLUSION

The findings of the investigation proved that the suggested hybrid model was more effective than the usual system. As it turned out, the hybrid model was superior to the other two in being accurate, flexible and efficient. The response time was reduced to 3.2 seconds as opposed to 6.8 seconds since the system was capable of processing data more rapidly and real time response. The hybrid strategy also enabled the data to be much more precise, increasing to 96% instead of 82. This is to make decisions and ensure systems are safe in evolving circumstances. The hybrid model could be able to accommodate a wide variety of system requirements without impairing performance since it can accommodate a large number of different types of loads. However, the old system was not that flexible and thus could not work quite well in situations which were complex and contained a lot of information. The hybrid method made good use of machine learning techniques, modular design, and resource allocation strategies to make the improvements in question. The hybrid architecture could be an appropriate option in the case of modern applications that require high reliability, speed, and precision. The findings indicate that hybrid intelligent systems have the potential to assist in some of the issues associated with conventional approaches and particularly in areas such as banking, healthcare, and IoT smart systems. With our research, we have a strong base to build on future studies and applications in a bid to create smarter, flexible, and efficient digital ecosystems.

7. FUTURE SCOPE

The promising outcomes of the new hybrid model provide numerous possibilities of research, both theoretical and practical. Decision making and prediction is a significant field of expansion by using the latest AI techniques such as federated learning, deep learning, or reinforcement learning to make decisions and predictions real-time. Such advances can make things more flexible in areas that are complex and evolve rapidly, like smart infrastructure management, self-driving vehicles, medical diagnostics, and financial markets. We can also consider scaling up hybrid models to cloud or edge computing environments to handle massive data in distributed environments in future studies. A self-learning model will be able to modify itself when given an opportunity to adjust itself to new circumstances and trends. Developing sensitive information security is another giant problem. Differential privacy or blockchain could be used in the future to safeguard the data of users in hybrid applications such as e-governance, digital banking, and telemedicine. Many businesses, such as cybersecurity and logistics, and the agricultural sector, may employ hybrid systems that can be tailored to various sectors. Finally, the model needs to be tested using real-life examples, compared to other state-of-the-art systems, and looked at with a variety of datasets.

REFERENCES

Ajmera, D., Kharub, M., Krishna, A., & Gupta, H. (2024). Navigating the challenges of AI-enabled circular economy in the food and beverage sector: Strategies for sustainable transformation. *International Journal of Logistics Management, 36*(2), 611–646. DOI: 10.1108/IJLM-09-2023-0408

Ali, Z. A., Zain, M., Pathan, M. S., & Mooney, P. (2024). Contributions of artificial intelligence for circular economy transition leading toward sustainability: An explorative study in agriculture and food industries of Pakistan. *Environment, Development and Sustainability, 26*(8), 19131–19175. DOI: 10.1007/s10668-023-03458-9

Antoniadou, M., Varzakas, T., & Tzoutzas, I. (2021). Circular economy in conjunction with treatment methodologies in the biomedical and dental waste sectors. *Circular Economy and Sustainability, 1*(2), 563–592. DOI: 10.1007/s43615-020-00001-0 PMID: 34888552

Behmadi, H., Azarpazhooh, E., Emam-Djomeh, Z., & Ramaswamy, H. S. (2025). Circular economy techniques for waste reduction in food packaging. In *Food waste valorization: Green techniques in sustainable management* (pp. 327–358). Springer. DOI: 10.1007/978-1-0716-4646-5_14

Cristofoli, N. L., Lima, A. R., Tchonkouang, R. D., Quintino, A. C., & Vieira, M. C. (2023). Advances in the food packaging production from agri-food waste and by-products: Market trends for sustainable development. *Sustainability (Basel), 15*(7), 6153. DOI: 10.3390/su15076153

De Pilli, T., Baiano, A., Lopriore, G., Russo, C., & Cappelletti, G. M. (2021). Environmental and socio-economic sustainability of packaging from agricultural by-products. In *Sustainable innovations in food packaging* (pp. 15–30). Springer. DOI: 10.1007/978-3-030-80936-2_2

de Sousa, I. G., Oliveira, J., Mexia, A., Barros, G., Almeida, C., Brazinha, C., Vega, A., & Brites, C. (2023). Advances in environmentally friendly techniques and circular economy approaches for insect infestation management in stored rice grains. *Foods, 12*(3), 511. DOI: 10.3390/foods12030511 PMID: 36766040

Gunduz, C. P. B. (2023). Eco-friendly and cost-effective methods applied to sustainable food industries. In *Smart food industry: The blockchain for sustainable engineering* (pp. 50–71). CRC Press. DOI: 10.1201/9781003231059-6

Hussain, S., Akhter, R., & Maktedar, S. S. (2024). Advancements in sustainable food packaging: From eco-friendly materials to innovative technologies. *Sustainable Food Technology, 2*(5), 1297–1364. DOI: 10.1039/D4FB00084F

Jain, A., Sarsaiya, S., Gong, Q., Wu, Q., & Shi, J. (2024). Bioresources from biowaste for advancing manufacturing of packaging materials with modern circular economy towards a sustainable approach. *Environment, Development and Sustainability*, •••, 1–34. DOI: 10.1007/s10668-024-05734-8

Li, J., Song, G., Cai, M., Bian, J., & Mohammed, B. S. (2022). Green environment and circular economy: A state-of-the-art analysis. *Sustainable Energy Technologies and Assessments*, *52*, 102106. DOI: 10.1016/j.seta.2022.102106

Lionetto, F., & Esposito Corcione, C. (2021). Recent applications of biopolymers derived from fish industry waste in food packaging. *Polymers*, *13*(14), 2337. DOI: 10.3390/polym13142337 PMID: 34301094

Marotta, A., Borriello, A., Khan, M. R., Cavella, S., Ambrogi, V., & Torrieri, E. (2025). Boosting food packaging sustainability through the valorization of agri-food waste and by-products. *Polymers*, *17*(6), 735. DOI: 10.3390/polym17060735 PMID: 40292599

Merino, D., Quilez-Molina, A. I., Perotto, G., Bassani, A., Spigno, G., & Athanassiou, A. (2022). A second life for fruit and vegetable waste: A review on bioplastic films and coatings for potential food protection applications. *Green Chemistry*, *24*(12), 4703–4727. DOI: 10.1039/D1GC03904K

Mohanta, Y. K., Mishra, A. K., Lakshmayya, N. S. V., Panda, J., Thatoi, H., Sarma, H., Rustagi, S., Baek, K.-H., & Mishra, B. (2025). Agro-waste-derived bioplastics: Sustainable innovations for a circular economy. *Waste and Biomass Valorization*, *16*(7), 1–25. DOI: 10.1007/s12649-025-03070-0

Mohanty, A. K., Wu, F., Mincheva, R., Hakkarainen, M., Raquez, J.-M., Mielewski, D. F., Narayan, R., Netravali, A. N., & Misra, M. (2022). Sustainable polymers. *Nature Reviews. Methods Primers*, *2*(1), 46. DOI: 10.1038/s43586-022-00124-8

Oboturova, N., et al. (2024). Upcycling agricultural byproducts into eco-friendly food packaging. *Slovak Journal of Food Sciences, 18.*

Pannila, N., Jayalath, M. M., Thibbotuwawa, A., Nielsen, I., & Uthpala, T. G. G. (2022). Challenges in applying circular economy concepts to food supply chains. *Sustainability (Basel)*, *14*(24), 16536. DOI: 10.3390/su142416536

Rathour, S., & Kemboi, E. (2025). AI-driven circular economy. In *Artificial intelligence and computer vision for ecological informatics* (p. 185). DOI: 10.1201/9781003518778-10

Režek Jambrak, A., Nutrizio, M., Djekić, I., Pleslić, S., & Chemat, F. (2021). Internet of nonthermal food processing technologies (IoNTP): Food industry 4.0 and sustainability. *Applied Sciences (Basel, Switzerland)*, *11*(2), 686. DOI: 10.3390/app11020686

Selvam, T., Rahman, N. M. M. A., Olivito, F., Ilham, Z., Ahmad, R., & Wan-Mohtar, W. A. A. Q. I. (2025). Agricultural waste-derived biopolymers for sustainable food packaging: Challenges and future prospects. *Polymers*, *17*(14), 1897. DOI: 10.3390/polym17141897 PMID: 40732776

Taghipour, A., Akkalatham, W., Eaknarajindawat, N., & Stefanakis, A. I. (2022). The impact of government policies and steel recycling companies' performance on sustainable management in a circular economy. *Resources Policy*, *77*, 102663. DOI: 10.1016/j.resourpol.2022.102663

Tsimpidi, I., Sawlekar, R., & Nikolakopoulos, G. (2023). Identifying the current state of the art and future directions on the deployment of artificial intelligence in circular economy.

Vanapalli, K. R., Sharma, H. B., Ranjan, V. P., Samal, B., Bhattacharya, J., Dubey, B. K., & Goel, S. (2021). Challenges and strategies for effective plastic waste management during and post COVID-19 pandemic. *The Science of the Total Environment*, *750*, 141514. DOI: 10.1016/j.scitotenv.2020.141514 PMID: 32835961

Yang, M., Chen, L., Wang, J., Msigwa, G., Osman, A. I., Fawzy, S., Rooney, D. W., & Yap, P.-S. (2023). Circular economy strategies for combating climate change and other environmental issues. *Environmental Chemistry Letters*, *21*(1), 55–80. DOI: 10.1007/s10311-022-01499-6

Compilation of References

Aarthi, S., Subramani, R., Rusho, M. A., Sharma, S., Ramachandran, T., Mahapatro, A., & Ismail, A. I. (2025). Genetically engineered 3D printed functionally graded-lignin, starch, and cellulose-derived sustainable biopolymers and composites: A critical review. *International Journal of Biological Macromolecules*, 145843.

Abbati de Assis, C., Greca, L. G., Ago, M., Balakshin, M. Y., Jameel, H., Gonzalez, R., & Rojas, O. J. (2018). Techno-economic assessment, scalability, and applications of aerosol lignin micro-and nanoparticles. *ACS Sustainable Chemistry & Engineering*, *6*(9), 11853–11868. DOI: 10.1021/acssuschemeng.8b02151 PMID: 30221095

Abedin, B., Meske, C., Junglas, I., Rabhi, F., & Motahari-Nezhad, H. R. (2022). Designing and Managing Human-AI Interactions. *Information Systems Frontiers*, *24*(3), 691–697. DOI: 10.1007/s10796-022-10313-1

Addy, W. A.. (2024). Transforming financial planning with AI-driven analysis: A review and application insights. *World Journal of Advanced Engineering Technology and Sciences*, *11*(1), 240–257. DOI: 10.30574/wjaets.2024.11.1.0053

Adebowale, A. M., & Akinnagbe, O. B. (2021). Leveraging AI-driven data integration for predictive risk assessment in decentralized financial markets. *Int J Eng Technol Res Manag*, *5*(12), 295.

Adewale, T. T., Olorunyomi, T. D., & Odonkor, T. N. (2023). Big data-driven financial analysis: A new paradigm for strategic insights and decision-making. *Journal of Financial Innovation and Analytics*, *1*(1), 1–15.

Adeyeye, O. J., & Akanbi, I. (2024). AI for systems engineering complexity: A review on the use of AI and machine learning algorithms. *Computer Science & IT Research Journal*, *5*(4), 787–808. DOI: 10.51594/csitrj.v5i4.1026

Afzal, S., Bokhari, M. U., Alam, S., Khan, I., Shuaib, M., & Ullah, M. (2026). Lightweight deep learning-driven secure communication architecture for Internet of Things enabled government applications. *Discov Computing*, *29*(1), 112. DOI: 10.1007/s10791-026-10002-6

Aggarwal, G., & Aggarwal, S. (2026). AI for Environmental DSS. In *AI Enabled Real Time Environmental Monitoring* (pp. 129–144). Springer Nature Singapore.

Agkathidis, A., Yang, S., & Symeonidou, I. (2024). AI-Assisted Design: Utilising artificial intelligence as a generative form-finding tool in architectural design studio teaching. Kontovourkis, O, Phocas, MC and Wurzer, G (Eds.), Data-Driven Intelligence - Proceedings of the 42nd Conference on Education and Research in Computer Aided Architectural Design in Europe (eCAADe 2024), Nicosia, 11–13 September 2024, Volume 2, Pp. 619–628. DOI: 10.52842/conf.ecaade.2024.2.619

Agu, E. E., et al. (2024). Discussing ethical considerations and solutions for ensuring fairness in AI-driven financial services. *International Journal of Frontier Research in Science*, 3(2), 001–009.

Ahmad Khan, N., Banga, A., Ghazal, T. M., Alabdullah, B., Iqbal, N., Alshamayleh, A., Ikram, A., & Diab, H. (2025). Unveiling a novel S-Box strategy: The dynamic 3D scrambling approach. *PLoS One*, *20*(9), e0329024. DOI: 10.1371/journal.pone.0329024

Ahmad, S., Ogala, J. O., Ikpotokin, F., Arif, M., Ahmad, J., & Mehfuz, S. (2024). Enhanced CNN-DCT Steganography: Deep Learning-Based Image Steganography Over Cloud. *SN Computer Science*, *5*(4), 408. DOI: 10.1007/s42979-024-02756-x

Ahmed, R., Hameed, M., Tiun, S., Omar, N., & Sani, N. S. (2022). Short text clustering: Combining traditional, semantic, and deep-learning representations. *Expert Systems with Applications*, *203*, 117337. DOI: 10.1016/j.eswa.2022.117337

Ajmal, C. S., Yerram, S., Abishek, V., Nizam, V. P. M., Aglave, G., Patnam, J. D., Raghuvanshi, R. S., & Srivastava, S. (2025). Innovative approaches in regulatory affairs: Leveraging artificial intelligence and machine learning for efficient compliance and decision-making. *The AAPS Journal*, *27*(1), 22. DOI: 10.1208/s12248-024-01006-5 PMID: 39776314

Ajmera, D., Kharub, M., Krishna, A., & Gupta, H. (2024). Navigating the challenges of AI-enabled circular economy in the food and beverage sector: Strategies for sustainable transformation. *International Journal of Logistics Management*, *36*(2), 611–646. DOI: 10.1108/IJLM-09-2023-0408

Alam, A., & Mohanty, A. (2022). Foundation for the future of higher education or 'misplaced optimism'? Being human in the age of artificial intelligence. In *Proceedings of the International Conference on Innovations in Intelligent Computing and Communication* (pp. 17–29). Springer. DOI: 10.1007/978-3-031-23233-6_2

Aldieri, L., & Vinci, C. P. (2021). Scalability and commercialization in support of sustainable development goals. In *Industry, Innovation and Infrastructure* (pp. 979–988). Springer. DOI: 10.1007/978-3-319-95873-6_93

Alexan, W., Hosny, K., & Gabr, M. (2025). A new fast multiple color image encryption algorithm. *Cluster Computing, 28*(5), 325. DOI: 10.1007/s10586-024-04919-0

Ali, G., Mijwil, M. M., Abotaleb, M., & Adamopoulos, I.Bosco Apparatus Buruga. (2024). A Survey on Artificial Intelligence in Cybersecurity for Smart Agriculture: State-of-the-Art, Cyber Threats, Artificial Intelligence Applications, and Ethical Concerns. *Mesopotamian Journal of Computer Science, 2024*, 53–103. DOI: 10.58496/MJCSC/2024/007

Ali, R., Hussain, A., Nazir, S., Khan, S., & Khan, H. U. (2023). Intelligent DSS—An analysis of machine learning and multicriteria decision-making methods. *Applied Sciences (Basel, Switzerland), 13*(22), 12426. DOI: 10.3390/app132212426

Ali, Z. A., Zain, M., Pathan, M. S., & Mooney, P. (2024). Contributions of artificial intelligence for circular economy transition leading toward sustainability: An explorative study in agriculture and food industries of Pakistan. *Environment, Development and Sustainability, 26*(8), 19131–19175. DOI: 10.1007/s10668-023-03458-9

Aljarf, A., & Rashidi, Y. (2025). *DL-Steg: a deep learning-based steganography model for improving image security*. J. Umm Al-Qura Univ. Eng.Archit., DOI: 10.1007/s43995-025-00266-2

Al-kfairy, M., Mustafa, D., Kshetri, N., Insiew, M., & Alfandi, O. (2024). Ethical Challenges and Solutions of Generative AI: An Interdisciplinary Perspective. *Informatics (MDPI), 11*(3), 58. DOI: 10.3390/informatics11030058

Alloun, Y., Azzaz, M. S., & Kifouche, A. (2025). A new approach based on artificial neural networks and chaos for designing deterministic random number generator and its application in image encryption. *Multimedia Tools and Applications, 84*(9), 5825–5860. DOI: 10.1007/s11042-024-19136-5

Alonge, E. O., Eyo-Udo, N. L., Chibunna, B., Ubanadu, A. I. D., Balogun, E. D., & Ogunsola, K. O. (2023). Data-driven risk management in US financial institutions: A theoretical perspective on process optimization. *Iconic Research and Engineering Journals*.

Alslaity, A., & Orji, R. (2022). Machine learning techniques for emotion detection and sentiment analysis: Survey. *Behaviour & Information Technology*, *41*(13), 2796–2832. DOI: 10.1080/0144929X.2022.2156387

Amankwah-Amoah, J., Abdalla, S., Mogaji, E., Elbanna, A., & Dwivedi, Y. K. (2024). The impending disruption of creative industries by generative AI: Opportunities, challenges, and research agenda. *International Journal of Information Management*, *79*, 102759. DOI: 10.1016/j.ijinfomgt.2024.102759

Amarnadh, V., & Moparthi, N. R. (2023). Comprehensive review of different artificial intelligence-based methods for credit risk assessment in data science. *Intelligent Decision Technologies*, *17*(4), 1265–1282. DOI: 10.3233/IDT-230190

Andreou, A., Kontovourkis, O., Solomou, S., & Savvides, A. (2023). Rethinking Architectural Design Process using Integrated Parametric Design and Machine Learning Principles. Dokonal, W, Hirschberg, U and Wurzer, G (Eds.), Digital Design Reconsidered - Proceedings of the 41st Conference on Education and Research in Computer Aided Architectural Design in Europe (eCAADe 2023) - Volume 2, Graz, 20–22 September 2023, Pp. 461–470. DOI: 10.52842/conf.ecaade.2023.2.461

Andreu, L., Sánchez-Villar, J. M., Karpen, I. O., Arnau-Domínguez, J. T., Jaszus, K., & Pérez-Cabañero, C. (2026). Design Thinking and Generative AI for Academic Projects in Higher Education. In *INTED2026 Proceedings* (p. 1632). IATED.

Andronie, M., Lăzăroiu, G., Iatagan, M., U ă, C., tefănescu, R., & Coco atu, M. (2021). AI-based decision-making algorithms, internet of things sensing networks, and deep learning-assisted smart process management in cyber-physical production systems. *Electronics (Basel)*, *10*(20), 2497. DOI: 10.3390/electronics10202497

Antoniadou, M., Varzakas, T., & Tzoutzas, I. (2021). Circular economy in conjunction with treatment methodologies in the biomedical and dental waste sectors. *Circular Economy and Sustainability*, *1*(2), 563–592. DOI: 10.1007/s43615-020-00001-0 PMID: 34888552

Apostol, E. S., Palade, V., & Grosu-Popescu, A. M. (2022). Real-time topic modelling for disaster reporting with misinformation-aware community detection. *Information Processing & Management*, *59*(3), 102901. DOI: 10.1016/j.ipm.2022.102901

Atzeni, E., & Salmi, A. (2012). Economics of additive manufacturing for end-usable metal parts. *International Journal of Advanced Manufacturing Technology*, *62*(9), 1147–1155. DOI: 10.1007/s00170-011-3878-1

Azimoh, C. L., Klintenberg, P., Mbohwa, C., & Wallin, F. (2017). Replicability and scalability of mini-grid solution to rural electrification programs in sub-Saharan Africa. *Renewable Energy*, *106*, 222–231. DOI: 10.1016/j.renene.2017.01.017

Bacco, M., Barsocchi, P., Ferro, E., Gotta, A., & Ruggeri, M. (2019). The Digitisation of Agriculture: A Survey of Research Activities on Smart Farming. *Array (New York, N.Y.)*, *3–4*, 100009. DOI: 10.1016/j.array.2019.100009

Bachiphale, P. M., & Zulpe, N. S. (2025). A comprehensive review of visual cryptography for enhancing high-security applications. *Multimedia Tools and Applications*, *84*(26), 31023–31045. DOI: 10.1007/s11042-024-20426-1

Bahsoon, R., & Emmerich, W. (2008, February). An economics-driven approach for valuing scalability in distributed architectures. In *Seventh Working IEEE/IFIP Conference on Software Architecture (WICSA 2008)* (pp. 9-18). IEEE. DOI: 10.1109/WICSA.2008.45

Baker, R. S., & Hawn, A. (2022). Algorithmic Bias in Education. *International Journal of Artificial Intelligence in Education*, *32*(4), 1052–1092. DOI: 10.1007/s40593-021-00285-9

Bandi, V. D. V. K. (2024). AI-Driven Predictive Risk Modeling Architectures for Financial Systems. *International Journal Of Finance*, *37*(3), 54–78.

Bank, M., Sandor, V., Schinegger, K., & Rutzinger, S. (2022). Learning Spatiality—A GAN method for designing architectural models through labelled sections. Pak, B, Wurzer, G and Stouffs, R (Eds.), Co-Creating the Future: Inclusion in and through Design - Proceedings of the 40th Conference on Education and Research in Computer Aided Architectural Design in Europe (eCAADe 2022) - Volume 2, Ghent, 13–16 September 2022, Pp. 611–619. DOI: 10.52842/conf.ecaade.2022.2.611

Bao, Z., Xue, R., Hu, J., & Liu, Y. (2024). Color image encryption based on lite dense-ResNet and bit-XOR diffusion. *Multimedia Tools and Applications*, *83*(5), 12819–12848. DOI: 10.1007/s11042-023-16073-7

Barbieri, L., & Muzzupappa, M. (2024). Form innovation: Investigating the use of generative design tools to encourage creativity in product design. *International Journal of Design Creativity and Innovation*, *12*(3), 163–182. DOI: 10.1080/21650349.2024.2336972

Bartlett, K., & Camba, D., J. (. (2024). Generative Artificial Intelligence in Product Design Education: Navigating Concerns of Originality and Ethics. *International Journal of Interactive Multimedia and Artificial Intelligence*, *8*, 55–64. DOI: 10.9781/ijimai.2024.02.006

Batz, A., D'Croz-Barón, D. F., Vega Pérez, C. J., & Ojeda-Sanchez, C. A. (2025). Integrating machine learning into business and management in the age of artificial intelligence. *Humanities & Social Sciences Communications*, *12*(1), 1–20. DOI: 10.1057/s41599-025-04361-6

Behera, U. S., Poddar, S., Deshmukh, M. P., Sangwai, J. S., & Byun, H. S. (2024). Comprehensive review on the role of nanoparticles and nanofluids in chemical enhanced oil recovery: Interfacial phenomenon, compatibility, scalability, and economic viability. *Energy & Fuels*, *38*(15), 13760–13795. DOI: 10.1021/acs.energyfuels.4c02248

Behmadi, H., Azarpazhooh, E., Emam-Djomeh, Z., & Ramaswamy, H. S. (2025). Circular economy techniques for waste reduction in food packaging. In *Food waste valorization: Green techniques in sustainable management* (pp. 327–358). Springer. DOI: 10.1007/978-1-0716-4646-5_14

Behmel, S., Damour, M., Ludwig, R., & Rodriguez, M. J. (2021). Intelligent decision-support system to plan, manage and optimize water quality monitoring programs: Design of a conceptual framework. *Journal of Environmental Planning and Management*, *64*(4), 703–733. DOI: 10.1080/09640568.2020.1782858

Bellman, R., & Bellman, R. E. (1957). *Dynamic Programming*. Princeton University Press.

Bello, O. A., Ogundipe, A., Mohammed, D., Adebola, F., & Alonge, O. A. (2023). AI-driven approaches for real-time fraud detection in US financial transactions: Challenges and opportunities. *European Journal of Computer Science and Information Technology*, *11*(6), 84–102.

Bendsoe, M. P., & Sigmund, O. (2003). *Topology Optimization: Theory, Methods, and Applications*. Springer Science & Business Media.

Berk, R. A. (2021). Artificial intelligence, predictive policing, and risk assessment for law enforcement. *Annual Review of Criminology*, *4*(1), 209–237. DOI: 10.1146/annurev-criminol-051520-012342

Bilgram, V., & Laarmann, F. (2023). Accelerating Innovation With Generative AI: AI-Augmented Digital Prototyping and Innovation Methods. *IEEE Engineering Management Review*, *1–5*(2), 18–25. Advance online publication. DOI: 10.1109/EMR.2023.3272799

Böckle, M., Booler-Stewart, F., & Woolsey, K. (2023, June). How to design for the metaverse: a strategic design perspective. In *2023 IEEE International Conference on Metaverse Computing, Networking and Applications (MetaCom)* (pp. 99-103). IEEE. DOI: 10.1109/MetaCom57706.2023.00029

Bolojan, D., Vermisso, E., & Yousif, S. (2022). Is Language All We Need? A Query Into Architectural Semantics Using a Multimodal Generative Workflow. POST-CARBON - Proceedings of the 27th CAADRIA Conference, 353–362. DOI: 10.52842/conf.caadria.2022.1.353

Bolojan, D., Yousif, S., & Spsampsps Vermisso, E. (2024). Latent Design Spaces: Interconnected Deep Learning Models for Expanding the Architectural Search Space. In M. Barberio, M. Colella, A. Figliola, spsampsps A. Battisti (Eds.), Architecture and Design for Industry 4.0: Theory and Practice (pp. 201–223). Springer International Publishing. DOI: 10.1007/978-3-031-36922-3_13

Boopathy, C. (2026). Intelligent Data-Driven Decision Making Using AI and Machine Learning Techniques. *International Journal of AI and Machine Learning E-ISSN: 3117-8391, 1*(1), 17-24.

Bortsova, G., González-Gonzalo, C., Wetstein, S. C., Dubost, F., Katramados, I., Hogeweg, L., Liefers, B., van Ginneken, B., Pluim, J. P. W., Veta, M., Sánchez, C. I., & de Bruijne, M. (2021). Adversarial Attack Vulnerability of Medical Image Analysis Systems: Unexplored Factors. *Medical Image Analysis*, *73*, 102141. DOI: 10.1016/j.media.2021.102141

Botschner, J., Corley, C., Fraser, E. D. G., Kotak, R., McMahon, D., & Newman, L. (2024). *Cybersecurity in Digital Agriculture: A National Security Risk?* DOI: 10.1007/978-3-031-67608-6_6

Bouchetara, M., Zerouti, M., & Zouambi, A. R. (2024). Leveraging artificial intelligence (AI) in public sector financial risk management: Innovations, challenges, and future directions. *EDPACS*, *69*(9), 124–144. DOI: 10.1080/07366981.2024.2377351

Bouhafra, S., & El Bahi, H. (2025). Deep Learning Approaches for Brain Tumor Detection and Classification Using MRI Images (2020 to 2024): A Systematic Review. J Digit Imaging. *Journal of Imaging Informatics in Medicine*, *38*(3), 1403–1433. DOI: 10.1007/s10278-024-01283-8

Bozyel, S.. (2024). Artificial intelligence-based clinical decision support systems in cardiovascular diseases. *The Anatolian Journal of Cardiology*, *28*(2), 74–86. DOI: 10.14744/AnatolJCardiol.2023.3685 PMID: 38168009

Briard, T., Segonds, F., & Zamariola, N. (2020). G-DfAM: A methodological proposal of generative design for additive manufacturing in the automotive industry. [IJIDeM]. *International Journal on Interactive Design and Manufacturing*, *14*(3), 875–886. DOI: 10.1007/s12008-020-00669-6

Brown, H., Evans, L., & Parker, E. (2026). Improving Real Time DSS in Management Information Systems Through AI Powered Automation. *Journal of Innovation in Governance and Business Practices*, *2*, 89–121. DOI: 10.66096/JIGBP.V2.4

Budhwar, P., Chowdhury, S., Wood, G., Aguinis, H., Bamber, G. J., Beltran, J. R., Boselie, P., Lee Cooke, F., Decker, S., DeNisi, A., Dey, P. K., Guest, D., Knoblich, A. J., Malik, A., Paauwe, J., Papagiannidis, S., Patel, C., Pereira, V., Ren, S., & Varma, A. (2023). Human resource management in the age of generative artificial intelligence: Perspectives and research directions on ChatGPT. *Human Resource Management Journal*, *33*(3), 606–659. DOI: 10.1111/1748-8583.12524

Buonamici, F., Carfagni, M., Furferi, R., Volpe, Y., & Governi, L. (2020). Generative Design: An Explorative Study. *Computer-Aided Design and Applications*, *18*(1), 144–155. DOI: 10.14733/cadaps.2021.144-155

Caires, C. S., Estadieu, G., & Olga Ng Ka Man, S. (2023). Design thinking methodology and text-to-image AI: A case study in the context of furniture design education. In *Perspectives on Design and Digital Communication IV: Research, Innovations and Best Practices* (pp. 113–134). Springer Nature Switzerland.

Cai, S., Mao, Z., Wang, Z., Yin, M., & Karniadakis, G. E. (2021). Physics-informed neural networks (PINNs) for fluid mechanics: A review. *Acta Mechanica Sinica*, *37*(12), 1727–1738. DOI: 10.1007/s10409-021-01148-1

Campoverde-Molina, M., & Luján-Mora, S. (2025). Cybersecurity in smart agriculture: A systematic literature review. *Computers & Security*, *150*, 104284. DOI: 10.1016/j.cose.2024.104284

Canton, H. (2021). *The Europa Directory of International Organizations 2021*. Routledge., DOI: 10.4324/9781003179900

Carter, R., Davis, J., & Kim, S. (2023). Transformer-based models with domain-specific financial lexicons for improved sentiment analysis. *The Journal of Financial Data Science*, *5*(2), 34–51. DOI: 10.3905/jfds.2023.1.109

Castillo-Martínez, I. M., Argüelles-Cruz, A. J., Pinal-Ramírez, O. E., Glasserman-Morales, L. D., Ramírez-Montoya, M. S., & Carreon-Hermosillo, A. (2023). Towards the development of complex thinking in university students: Mixed methods with ideathon and AI. *Computers and Education: AI*, *5*, 100186.

Castro Pena, M. L., Carballal, A., Rodríguez-Fernández, N., Santos, I., & Romero, J. (2021). Artificial intelligence applied to conceptual design. A review of its use in architecture. *Automation in Construction, 124*, 103550. DOI: 10.1016/j.autcon.2021.103550

Celestin, M. (2023). AI-driven financial reporting: Enhancing accuracy and reducing human errors in Rwanda. *Indo American Journal of Multidisciplinary Research and Review*, *7*(11), 108–117.

Celestin, M., & Mishra, A. K. (2025). AI-driven financial analytics: Enhancing forecast accuracy, risk management, and decision-making in corporate finance. *Janajyoti Journal*, *3*(1), 1–27. DOI: 10.3126/jj.v3i1.83284

Chandani, P., Bhadoria, D. S., Rawat, V., Gupta, U., & Raman, M. (2025, June). Integrating Design Thinking with AI: Embracing Human-Centered Approaches in Healthcare. In *International Conference on Data Analytics & Management* (pp. 288-297). Cham: Springer Nature Switzerland.

Chandrasekera, T., Hosseini, Z., & Perera, U. (2024). Can artificial intelligence support creativity in early design processes? *International Journal of Architectural Computing*, *23*(1), 122–136. Advance online publication. DOI: 10.1177/14780771241254637

Chang, Y. S., & Tsai, M. C. (2024). Effects of design thinking on AI learning and creativity. *Educational Studies*, *50*(5), 763–780. DOI: 10.1080/03055698.2021.1999213

Chawla, N. (2025). AI-Driven Predictive Project Risk Management in Large-Scale Financial Software Programs. *J. Electrical Systems*, *21*(1s), 618–626. DOI: 10.52783/jes.9338

Cheng, G., & Ji, H. (2020). Adversarial Perturbation on MRI Modalities in Brain Tumor Segmentation. *IEEE Access : Practical Innovations, Open Solutions*, *8*, 206009–206015. DOI: 10.1109/ACCESS.2020.3030235

Chen, L., Sun, L., & Han, J. (2023). A Comparison Study of Human and Machine Generated Creativity. *Journal of Computing and Information Science in Engineering*, *23*(5), 1–37. DOI: 10.1115/1.4062232

Chen, L., Wang, P., Dong, H., Shi, F., Han, J., Guo, Y., Childs, P. R. N., Xiao, J., & Wu, C. (2019). An artificial intelligence based data-driven approach for design ideation. *Journal of Visual Communication and Image Representation*, *61*, 10–22. DOI: 10.1016/j.jvcir.2019.02.009

Chen, M.-T., Zuo, W., Chen, Y., Cheng, B., & Zhao, J. (2024). Parametric topology optimization design and analysis of additively manufactured joints in spatial grid structures. *Engineering Structures*, *300*, 117123. DOI: 10.1016/j.engstruct.2023.117123

Chen, R., & Zhang, T. (2025). Artificial intelligence applications implication for ESG performance: Can digital transformation of enterprises promote sustainable development? *Chinese Management Studies, 19*(3), 676–701. DOI: 10.1108/CMS-11-2023-0653

Cherian, A.K., Simpson, S.V., Vaidhehi, M. et al. (2024). Enhancing Medical Image Security: A Deep Learning Approach with Cloud-based Color Space Scrambling. Int. j. inf. tecnol. 16, 5041–5054, DOI: 10.1007/s41870-024-02109-0

Cheung, L. H., Dall'Asta, J. C., Di Marco, G., & Spsampsps Agkathidis, A. (2024). Architectural Design Under Pandemic of Today's AI: From Human-Computer Interaction (HCI) to Human-Machine Conversation (HMC). In G. Di Marco, D. Lombardi, spsampsps M. Tedjosaputro (Eds.), Creativity in the Age of Digital Reproduction (pp. 9–17). Springer Nature. DOI: 10.1007/978-981-97-0621-1_2

Cheung, L. H., & Dall'Asta, J. C. (2023). Exploring a Collaborative and Intuitive Framework for Combined Application of AI Art Generation Tools in Architectural Design Process. *Proceedings of the AISB Convention 2023*, pp 122–130.

Cheung, L. H., Dall'Asta, J. C., & Di Marco, G. (2023). Exploring Large Language Model as a Design Partner through Verbal and Non-verbal Conversation in Architectural Design Process. *XXVII International Conference of the Ibero-American Society of Digital Graphics*, 12, 1059–1070. DOI: 10.5151/sigradi2023-65

Chliova, M., & Ringov, D. (2017). Scaling impact: Template development and replication at the base of the pyramid. *The Academy of Management Perspectives, 31*(1), 44–62. DOI: 10.5465/amp.2015.0010

Chong, L., Raina, A., Goucher-Lambert, K., Kotovsky, K., & Cagan, J. (2022). The Evolution and Impact of Human Confidence in Artificial Intelligence and in Themselves on AI-Assisted Decision-Making in Design. *Journal of Mechanical Design, 145*(3), 031401. Advance online publication. DOI: 10.1115/1.4055123

Choudhury, M., Eisenbart, B., & Kuys, B. (2025). Artificial intelligence (AI) in the design process – a review and analysis on generative AI perspectives. *Proceedings of the Design Society, 5*, 631–640. DOI: 10.1017/pds.2025.10077

Chulvi, V. (2025). Effectiveness of the AI using different typologies of design methods. *Research in Engineering Design, 36*(2), 7. DOI: 10.1007/s00163-025-00449-x

Colton, S., & Wiggins, G. (2012). Computational Creativity: The Final Frontier? In *Frontiers in Artificial Intelligence and Applications* (Vol. 242, pp. 21–26). DOI: 10.3233/978-1-61499-098-7-21

Cristofoli, N. L., Lima, A. R., Tchonkouang, R. D., Quintino, A. C., & Vieira, M. C. (2023). Advances in the food packaging production from agri-food waste and by-products: Market trends for sustainable development. *Sustainability (Basel), 15*(7), 6153. DOI: 10.3390/su15076153

Cross, N. (2023). *Design Thinking: Understanding How Designers Think and Work.* Bloomsbury Publishing. DOI: 10.5040/9781350305090

Curcio, E. (2025). Techno-economic analysis of hydrogen production: Costs, policies, and scalability in the transition to net-zero. *International Journal of Hydrogen Energy*, *128*, 473–487. DOI: 10.1016/j.ijhydene.2025.04.013

D, C. S., & Devarajan, Y. (2025). Investigation of Emerging Technologies in Agriculture: An In-depth Look at Smart Farming, Nano-agriculture, AI, and Big Data. *Journal of Biosystems Engineering, 50*(2), 170–192. DOI: 10.1007/s42853-025-00258-z

D, S., S R, M. & P, D. (2026). Machine Learning-Fused Hybrid Image Encryption Framework Using Hardware-Optimized AES Algorithm. J Sign Process Syst 98, 21, DOI: 10.1007/s11265-026-01992-z

Dall'Asta, J. C. (2025, May). Enhancing Design Thinking through the Systematic Integration of AI (AI) in Architectural Education. In *2025 5th International Conference on AI and Education (ICAIE)* (pp. 377-381). IEEE.

Dandotiya, M., Goyal, N. K., Yadav, P., Sankhla, K., & Kumari, M. (2026). GENALYTICS: A Deep Dive Into Real-Time Insights via Generative AI. In Elbaghazaoui, B., Amnai, M., & Gherabi, N. (Eds.), *Generative AI-Powered Data Architectures: From Governance to Autonomous Analytics* (pp. 105–134). IGI Global Scientific Publishing., DOI: 10.4018/979-8-3373-5616-7.ch005

De Pilli, T., Baiano, A., Lopriore, G., Russo, C., & Cappelletti, G. M. (2021). Environmental and socio-economic sustainability of packaging from agricultural by-products. In *Sustainable innovations in food packaging* (pp. 15–30). Springer. DOI: 10.1007/978-3-030-80936-2_2

de Sousa, I. G., Oliveira, J., Mexia, A., Barros, G., Almeida, C., Brazinha, C., Vega, A., & Brites, C. (2023). Advances in environmentally friendly techniques and circular economy approaches for insect infestation management in stored rice grains. *Foods*, *12*(3), 511. DOI: 10.3390/foods12030511 PMID: 36766040

Deb, K., & Jain, H. (2014). An Evolutionary Many-Objective Optimization Algorithm Using Reference-Point-Based Nondominated Sorting Approach, Part I: Solving Problems With Box Constraints. *IEEE Transactions on Evolutionary Computation, 18*(4), 577–601. DOI: 10.1109/TEVC.2013.2281535

Deb, K., Pratap, A., Agarwal, S., & Meyarivan, T. (2002). A fast and elitist multiobjective genetic algorithm: NSGA-II. *IEEE Transactions on Evolutionary Computation, 6*(2), 182–197. DOI: 10.1109/4235.996017

Dellermann, D., Calma, A., Lipusch, N., Weber, T., Weigel, S., & Ebel, P. (2019). *The Future of Human-AI Collaboration: A Taxonomy of Design Knowledge for Hybrid Intelligence Systems*. DOI: 10.24251/HICSS.2019.034

Demestichas, K., Peppes, N., & Alexakis, T. (2020). Survey on Security Threats in Agricultural IoT and Smart Farming. *Sensors (Basel), 20*(22), 6458. DOI: 10.3390/s20226458 PMID: 33198160

Deng, X., & Liu, Y. (2023). Hybrid RoBERTa–BiLSTM–Attention model for online sentiment analysis with custom lexicons. *IEEE Transactions on Affective Computing, 14*(2), 889–901. DOI: 10.1109/TAFFC.2021.3075977

Ding, Y., Tan, F., Qin, Z., Cao, M., Choo, K.-K. R., & Qin, Z. (2021). DeepKeyGen: A Deep Learning-Based Stream Cipher Generator for Medical Image Encryption and Decryption. *IEEE Transactions on Neural Networks and Learning Systems, 33*(9), 4915–4929. DOI: 10.1109/TNNLS.2021.3062754

Dortheimer, J., Schubert, G., Dalach, A., Brenner, L., & Martelaro, N. (2023). Think AI-side the Box! Exploring the Usability of Text-to-Image Generators for Architecture Students. Digital Design Reconsidered -eCAADe 2023,2, 567–576. DOI: 10.52842/conf.ecaade.2023.2.567

du Plessis, A., & Broeckhoven, C. (2019). Looking deep into nature: A review of micro-computed tomography in biomimicry. *Acta Biomaterialia, 85*, 27–40. DOI: 10.1016/j.actbio.2018.12.014 PMID: 30543937

Eder, W. E., & Hosnedl, S. (2007). *Design Engineering: A Manual for Enhanced Creativity*. CRC Press., DOI: 10.1201/9781420047660

Eklund, A., & Forsman, M. (2022). Topic modeling by clustering language model embeddings: Human validation on an industry dataset. *Proceedings of the 2022 Conference on Empirical Methods in Natural Language Processing: Industry Track*, 635–643. DOI: 10.18653/v1/2022.emnlp-industry.65

Ekundayo, F. (2024). Leveraging AI-driven decision intelligence for complex systems engineering. *Int J Res Publ Rev, 5*(11), 1–10. DOI: 10.55248/gengpi.5.1124.3343

El-Shafai, W., Almomani, I., Ara, A., & Alkhayer, A. (2023). An optical-based encryption and authentication algorithm for color and grayscale medical images. *Multimedia Tools and Applications*, *82*(15), 23735–23770. DOI: 10.1007/s11042-022-14093-3

El-Shafai, W., Khallaf, F., El-Rabaie, E. S. M., & Abd El-Samie, F. E. (2022). Proposed neural SAE-based medical image cryptography framework using deep extracted features for smart IoT healthcare applications. *Neural Computing & Applications*, *34*(13), 10629–10653. DOI: 10.1007/s00521-022-06994-z

Elumilade, O. O., Ogundeji, I. A., Achumie, G. O., Omokhoa, H. E., & Omowole, B. M. (2021). Enhancing fraud detection and forensic auditing through data-driven techniques for financial integrity and security. *Journal of Advanced Education and Sciences*, *1*(2), 55–63. DOI: 10.54660/.JAES.2021.1.2.55-63

Enjellina, B., & Beyan, E. V. P.Anastasya Gisela Cinintya Rossy. (2023). A Review of AI Image Generator: Influences, Challenges, and Future Prospects for Architectural Field. *Journal of Artificial Intelligence in Architecture*, *2*(1), 1. Advance online publication. DOI: 10.24002/jarina.v2i1.6662

Eren, O., Yüksel, N., Borklu, H., Sezer, H. K., & Canyurt, O. (2024). Deep learning-enabled design for tailored mechanical properties of SLM-manufactured metallic lattice structures. *Engineering Applications of Artificial Intelligence*, *130*, 107685. DOI: 10.1016/j.engappai.2023.107685

Faheem, M. A. (2021). AI-driven risk assessment models: Revolutionizing credit scoring and default prediction. *Iconic Research and Engineering Journals*, *5*(3), 177–186.

Faisal, S. M., Khan, W., & Ishrat, M. (2025). AI and financial risk management: Transforming risk mitigation with AI-driven insights and automation. In *Artificial Intelligence for Financial Risk Management and Analysis* (pp. 281–306). IGI Global Scientific Publishing. DOI: 10.4018/979-8-3373-1200-2.ch014

Fang, C., Zhu, Y., Fang, L., Long, Y., Lin, H., Cong, Y., & Wang, S. J. (2025). Generative AI-enhanced human-AI collaborative conceptual design: A systematic literature review. *Design Studies*, *97*, 101300. DOI: 10.1016/j.destud.2025.101300

Farooqi, A., Das, D., Tripathi, M., Dutta, R., Goyal, N. K., & Sheikh, M. F. (2026). Navigating Ethical Frontiers in AI-Driven Geriatric Care. In Stolakis, K., & Efthymiou, I. (Eds.), *AI for Geriatric Care in an Aging Society: Ethical, Clinical, and Policy Challenges* (pp. 243–266). IGI Global Scientific Publishing., DOI: 10.4018/979-8-3373-5462-0.ch009

Fedorka, P., Buchuk, R., Klymenko, M., Saibert, F., & Petrushyn, A. (2025). The use of adaptive AI learning models in DSS for smart regions. *J. Res. Innov. Technol.*, *4*, 99–115. DOI: 10.57017/jorit.v4.1(7).07

Feng, F., Hu, J., Guo, Z., Gan, J.-A., Chen, P.-F., Chen, G., Min, C., Yuan, X., & Somekh, M. (2022). Deep Learning-Enabled Orbital Angular Momentum-Based Information Encryption Transmission. *ACS Photonics*, *9*(3), 820–829. DOI: 10.1021/acsphotonics.1c01303

Finlayson, S. G., Bowers, J. D., Ito, J., Zittrain, J. L., Beam, A. L., & Kohane, I. S. (2019). Adversarial attacks on medical machine learning. *Science*, *363*(6433), 1287–1289. DOI: 10.1126/science.aaw4399

Foo, Z. H., & Lienhard, J. H. (2025). Emerging membrane technologies for sustainable lithium extraction from brines and leachates: Innovations, challenges, and industrial scalability. *Desalination*, *598*, 118411. DOI: 10.1016/j.desal.2024.118411

Forrester, A., Sóbester, A., & Keane, A. (2008). *Engineering Design via Surrogate Modelling: A Practical Guide*. John Wiley & Sons. DOI: 10.1002/9780470770801

Forrest, N., Stein, Z., & Wiek, A. (2020). Transferability and scalability of sustainable urban water solutions—A case study from the Colorado River Basin. *Resources, Conservation and Recycling*, *157*, 104790. DOI: 10.1016/j.resconrec.2020.104790

Frey, B. J., & Dueck, D. (2007). Clustering by passing messages between data points. *Science*, *315*(5814), 972–976. DOI: 10.1126/science.1136800 PMID: 17218491

Fritz-Morgenthal, S., Hein, B., & Papenbrock, J. (2022). Financial risk management and explainable, trustworthy, responsible AI. *Frontiers in Artificial Intelligence*, *5*, 779799. DOI: 10.3389/frai.2022.779799 PMID: 35295866

Gaier, A., Stoddart, J., Villaggi, L., & Sudhakaran, S. (2024). Generative Design through Quality-Diversity Data Synthesis and Language Models. *Proceedings of the Genetic and Evolutionary Computation Conference*, 823–831. DOI: 10.1145/3638529.3654138

Gajjar, N., Pandian, V., Suleri, S., & Jarke, M. (2021). *Akin: Generating UI Wireframes From UI Design Patterns Using Deep Learning*. DOI: 10.1145/3397482.3450727

Galanos, T., Liapis, A., & Yannakakis, G. N. (2023). Architext: Language-Driven Generative Architecture Design. arXiv. /arXiv.2303.07519DOI: 10.48550

Gan, C., Wang, J., & Zhang, L. (2023). Aspect-based sentiment classification using fuzzy logic and neural networks for student microblog analysis. *Information Sciences*, *621*, 231–245. DOI: 10.1016/j.ins.2022.11.056

Ganesh, R., Khan, B. U. I., Khan, A. R., & Kamsin, A. B. (2025). A panoramic survey of the advanced encryption standard: From architecture to security analysis, key management, real-world applications, and post-quantum challenges. *International Journal of Information Security*, *24*(5), 216. DOI: 10.1007/s10207-025-01116-x

Gao, R. X., Krüger, J., Merklein, M., Möhring, H.-C., & Váncza, J. (2024). Artificial Intelligence in manufacturing: State of the art, perspectives, and future directions. *CIRP Annals*, *73*(2), 723–749. DOI: 10.1016/j.cirp.2024.04.101

Gero, J. S., & Kannengiesser, U. (2004). The situated function–behaviour–structure framework. *Design Studies*, *25*(4), 373–391. DOI: 10.1016/j.destud.2003.10.010

Gharib, H. A., Abdelnapi, N. M. M., & Hosny, K. M. (2025). Robust zero-watermarking for color images using hybrid deep learning models and encryption. *Scientific Reports*, *15*(1), 28906. DOI: 10.1038/s41598-025-09290-7

Giordano, C., Brennan, M., Mohamed, B., Rashidi, P., Modave, F., & Tighe, P. (2021). Accessing artificial intelligence for clinical decision-making. *Frontiers in Digital Health*, *3*, 645232. DOI: 10.3389/fdgth.2021.645232 PMID: 34713115

Gizachew Yirga, T., Gizachew Yirga, H., & Addisu, E. G. (2025). Cryptographic key generation using deep learning with biometric face and finger vein data. *Frontiers in Artificial Intelligence*, *8*, 1545946. DOI: 10.3389/frai.2025.1545946

González Rodríguez, G., Gonzalez-Cava, J. M., & Méndez Pérez, J. A. (2020). An intelligent decision support system for production planning based on machine learning. *Journal of Intelligent Manufacturing*, *31*(5), 1257–1273. DOI: 10.1007/s10845-019-01510-y

Goodfellow, I., Bengio, Y., & Courville, A. (2016). *Deep Learning*. MIT Press.

Goswami, S. S.. (2025). Artificial intelligence-enabled supply chain management: Unlocking new opportunities and challenges. *Artificial Intelligence and Applications (Commerce, Calif.)*, *3*(1), 110–121.

Gowtham, H., Gopal, J. N., & Anand, A. J. (2025). Ethical considerations and privacy in AI-powered security. In *Handbook of AI-Driven Threat Detection and Prevention* (pp. 177–192). CRC Press. DOI: 10.1201/9781003521020-11

Greenstein, S. (2022). Preserving the rule of law in the era of artificial intelligence (AI). *Artificial Intelligence and Law*, *30*(3), 291–323. DOI: 10.1007/s10506-021-09294-4

Grieves, M. (2015). *Digital Twin: Manufacturing Excellence through Virtual Factory Replication*.

Gunduz, C. P. B. (2023). Eco-friendly and cost-effective methods applied to sustainable food industries. In *Smart food industry: The blockchain for sustainable engineering* (pp. 50–71). CRC Press. DOI: 10.1201/9781003231059-6

Guo, Y., Barnes, S. J., & Jia, Q. (2021). Joint topic modelling and multidimensional sentiment analysis of COVID-19 discourse on Chinese microblogs. *Journal of Informetrics, 15*(2), 101146. DOI: 10.1016/j.joi.2021.101146

Gupta, A. (2025). A novel Shannon entropy-based backward cloud model and cloud K-means clustering. *The Journal of Supercomputing, 81*(1), 65. DOI: 10.1007/s11227-024-06528-5

Gupta, S., Hasan, W., Singh, S., Kumar, D., Ansari, M. J., & Nisar, S. (2024). Agriculture 4.0: Smart farming with IoT and artificial intelligence. In *Agriculture 4.0: Smart Farming with IoT and Artificial Intelligence*. CRC Press., DOI: 10.1201/9781003570219

Gupta, S., Modgil, S., Bhattacharyya, S., & Bose, I. (2022). AI for DSS in the field of operations research: Review and future scope of research. *Annals of Operations Research, 308*(1), 215–274. DOI: 10.1007/s10479-020-03856-6

Gupta, S., Nayyar, A., & Nitish, . (2025). Enhancing color image encryption scheme with a chaotic map and Fibonacci transform. *Cluster Computing, 28*(15), 993. DOI: 10.1007/s10586-025-05573-w

Haghighat, E., Raissi, M., Moure, A., Gomez, H., & Juanes, R. (2021). A physics-informed deep learning framework for inversion and surrogate modeling in solid mechanics. *Computer Methods in Applied Mechanics and Engineering, 379*, 113741. DOI: 10.1016/j.cma.2021.113741

Hamada, A., Karagozlu, D., & Isiaku, L. (2026). AI-Driven DSS for Sustainable Environmental Management. In *DSS for Industrial and Scientific Applications* (pp. 57–69). Springer Nature Switzerland.

Hamrouni, B., Bourouis, A., Korichi, A., & Brahmi, M. (2021). Explainable ontology-based intelligent decision support system for business model design and sustainability. *Sustainability (Basel), 13*(17), 9819. DOI: 10.3390/su13179819

Han, Y., Zhou, R., Geng, Z., Fang, J., Ma, B., & Fan, J. (2023). HL-Louvain: Enhanced community detection integrating structural properties and user influence. *IEEE Transactions on Network Science and Engineering, 10*(1), 244–257. DOI: 10.1109/TNSE.2022.3201090

Hasan, A., Moin, S., Karim, A., & Shamshirband, S. (2022). Lexicon-based versus classifier-based approaches for political Twitter sentiment analysis. *Expert Systems with Applications, 190*, 116157. DOI: 10.1016/j.eswa.2021.116157

Hassan, A. M. A., & Mohsen, S. (2025). Compression of electrocardiogram signals using compressive sensing technique based on curvelet transform toward medical applications. *Multimedia Tools and Applications*, *84*(12), 11203–11219. DOI: 10.1007/s11042-024-19328-z

Havidotinnisa, S., Afini, F., Saryadi, Y., & Mufti, I. (2024). The Role of Design Thinking in AI Disruption: A Systematic Literature Review. *Multifinance*, *2*(2), 136–147. DOI: 10.61397/mfc.v2i2.323

Hirano, H., Minagi, A., & Takemoto, K. (2021). Universal Adversarial Attacks on Deep Neural Networks for Medical Image Classification. *BMC Medical Imaging*, *21*(1), 9. DOI: 10.1186/s12880-020-00530-y

Homayounirad, A. (2023). Designing the Built Environment Through Hybrid Intelligence. In HHAI 2023: Augmenting Human Intellect (pp. 483–495). IOS Press. DOI: 10.3233/FAIA230127

Hosny, K. M., Abdel-Aziz, M. M., Lashin, N. A., & Hamza, H. M. (2025). A new CNN-based watermarking method for color medical images in a fusion domain. *Neural Computing & Applications*, *37*(18), 12611–12629. DOI: 10.1007/s00521-025-11056-1

Hossain, M. A. (2025). Artificial Intelligence-Driven Financial Analytics Models For Predicting Market Risk And Investment Decisions In US Enterprises. *ASRC Procedia: Global Perspectives in Science and Scholarship*, *1*(01), 1066–1095. DOI: 10.63125/9csehp36

Huang, J., Johanes, M., Kim, F. C., Doumpioti, C., & Holz, G.-C. (2021). On GANs, NLP and Architecture: Combining Human and Machine Intelligences for the Generation and Evaluation of Meaningful Designs. Technology|Architecture + Design, 5(2), 207–224. DOI: 10.1080/24751448.2021.1967060

Huang, T., Xu, H., Wang, H., Huang, H., Xu, Y., Li, B., Hong, S., Feng, G., Kui, S., Liu, G., Jiang, D., Li, Z.-C., Li, Y., Ma, C., Su, C., Wang, W., Li, R., Lai, P., & Qiao, J. (2023). Artificial intelligence for medicine: Progress, challenges, and perspectives. *The Innovation Medicine*, *1*(2), 100030. DOI: 10.59717/j.xinn-med.2023.100030

Huang, X. (2025). Chaotic Digital Image Encryption Algorithm Based on Compressive Sensing. *Automatic Control and Computer Sciences*, *59*(6), 798–810. DOI: 10.3103/S0146411625701329

Hu, L., Li, J., Nie, L., Li, X.-L., & Shao, C. (2022). Temporal topic clustering for detecting shifting public discussions on social media. *Knowledge-Based Systems*, *246*, 108620. DOI: 10.1016/j.knosys.2022.108620

Hussain, S., Akhter, R., & Maktedar, S. S. (2024). Advancements in sustainable food packaging: From eco-friendly materials to innovative technologies. *Sustainable Food Technology*, *2*(5), 1297–1364. DOI: 10.1039/D4FB00084F

Ibarrola, F., Lawton, T., & Grace, K. (2024). A Collaborative, Interactive and Context-Aware Drawing Agent for Co-Creative Design. *IEEE Transactions on Visualization and Computer Graphics*, *30*(8), 5525–5537. DOI: 10.1109/TVCG.2023.3293853

Ishibuchi, H., Tsukamoto, N., & Nojima, Y. (2008). Evolutionary many-objective optimization: A short review. *2008 IEEE Congress on Evolutionary Computation (IEEE World Congress on Computational Intelligence)*, 2419–2426. DOI: 10.1109/CEC.2008.4631121

Islam, M. M. (2026). Artificial Intelligence–Driven Predictive Analytics Framework for Data-Driven Decision Support in Complex Organizational Systems. *American Journal of Data Science and Analytics*, *7*(03), 163–207. DOI: 10.63125/mexw3p37

Jahid, M. S. R. (2025). AI-driven optimization and risk modeling in strategic economic zone development for mid-sized economies: A review approach. *International Journal of Scientific Interdisciplinary Research*, *6*(1), 185–218. DOI: 10.63125/31wna449

Jain, A., Sarsaiya, S., Gong, Q., Wu, Q., & Shi, J. (2024). Bioresources from biowaste for advancing manufacturing of packaging materials with modern circular economy towards a sustainable approach. *Environment, Development and Sustainability*, •••, 1–34. DOI: 10.1007/s10668-024-05734-8

Javidannia, G., Bemanian, M. R., Mahdavinejad, M., Nejat, S. A., & Javidannia, L. (2021). *Generative Design Workflow for Seismic-Efficient Architectural Design of Tall Buildings; A Multi-object Optimization approach.*

Jelodar, H., Wang, Y., Yuan, C., Feng, X., Jiang, X., Li, Y., & Zhao, L. (2021). LDA configuration for Reddit data: Optimal parameters for interpretable topic distributions. *International Journal of Machine Learning and Computing*, *11*(2), 89–101. DOI: 10.18178/ijmlc.2021.11.2.1024

Kabir, M. A., Kabir, M. M. J., Xu, S., & Badhon, B. (2022). Empirical comparison of machine learning approaches for sentiment classification. *Neural Computing & Applications*, *34*(18), 15987–16002. DOI: 10.1007/s00521-022-07207-1

Kaner, S., Garipcan, A. M., & Erdem, E. (2025). A novel deep learning-based statistical randomness evaluation test methodology for cryptographic applications. *Journal of King Saud University. Computer and Information Sciences*, *37*(9), 264. DOI: 10.1007/s44443-025-00271-4

Kantesaria, R., & Panda, H. S. (2026). A review on AI-based data-driven models for optimization of nanocarriers as drug delivery systems. *ACS Biomaterials Science & Engineering*, *12*(3), 1397–1418. DOI: 10.1021/acsbiomaterials.5c01998 PMID: 41668335

Karim, S., Tanwar, N., Das, S., Ranjit, R., Banerjee, A., Gulafshan, , Gupta, A., Kumar, A., & Dutta, A. (2025). Shaping the future of green hydrogen production: Overcoming conventional challenges with molecular catalysts, immobilization, and scalable electrolyzers. *ACS Catalysis*, *15*(2), 1073–1096. DOI: 10.1021/acscatal.4c05986

Karras, A., Giannaros, A., Amasiadi, N., & Karras, C. (2026). Next-Gen Explainable AI (XAI) for Federated and Distributed Internet of Things Systems: A State-of-the-Art Survey. *Future Internet*, *18*(2), 83. DOI: 10.3390/fi18020083

Kasneci, E., Sessler, K., Küchemann, S., Bannert, M., Dementieva, D., Fischer, F., Gasser, U., Groh, G., Günnemann, S., Hüllermeier, E., Krusche, S., Kutyniok, G., Michaeli, T., Nerdel, C., Pfeffer, J., Poquet, O., Sailer, M., Schmidt, A., Seidel, T., & Kasneci, G. (2023). ChatGPT for good? On opportunities and challenges of large language models for education. *Learning and Individual Differences*, *103*, 102274. DOI: 10.1016/j.lindif.2023.102274

Kayyali, M. (2026). Design Thinking in the Age of AI: Human-Centered AI Solutions. In *Design Thinking Applications and Challenges for Modern Business* (pp. 169-198). IGI Global Scientific Publishing.

Keshav, Y., & Yadav, A. K. (2026). A.K. A novel two-dimensional Logistic–Chebyshev–Sine hybrid chaotic map for secure color image encryption. *Multimedia Tools and Applications*, *85*(2), 92. DOI: 10.1007/s11042-026-21281-y

Keshireddy, S. R. (2024). Intelligent DSS in Management Information Systems Using Hybrid AI Models. *Research Briefs on Information and Communication Technology Evolution*, *10*, 211–230. DOI: 10.64799/rebicte.v10.13

Khalid, F., & Shah, H. (2025). AI-Enhanced Design Management: Scientific Principles for Intelligent Decision Systems. *Journal of Design. Management Science*, *2*(02), 61–68.

Khallaf, F., El-Shafai, W., El-Rabaie, E. S. M., & El-Samie, F. E. A. (2025). Blockchain-based color medical image cryptosystem for industrial Internet of Healthcare Things (IoHT). *Multimedia Tools and Applications*, *84*(22), 25749–25803. DOI: 10.1007/s11042-023-16777-w

Khan, W. Z., Rehman, M. H., Zangoti, H. M., Afzal, M. K., Armi, N., & Salah, K. (2020). Industrial internet of things: Recent advances, enabling technologies and open challenges. *Computers & Electrical Engineering*, *81*, 106522. DOI: 10.1016/j.compeleceng.2019.106522

Kim, S. W., Go, H., Hong, S. J., & Lee, Y. (2023). An Approach to the Utilization of Design Thinking in AI Education. *International Journal on Advanced Science, Engineering and Information Technology*, *13*(6). Advance online publication. DOI: 10.18517/ijaseit.13.6.19042

Kingma, D. P., & Welling, M. (2013). Auto-Encoding Variational Bayes. *CoRR*. https://www.semanticscholar.org/paper/Auto-Encoding-Variational-Bayes-Kingma-Welling/5f5dc5b9a2ba710937e2c413b37b053cd673df02

Kinsey, H. (2022). Getting the balance just right: Desirable difficulty in health professions education. *Medical Education*, *57*(1), 110–112. DOI: 10.1111/medu.14989 PMID: 36427062

Konwar, G., Banik, R., & Geed, S. R. (2025). Bioprocess strategies for bioethanol production from algae-derived carbohydrates: Scalable solutions and industry prospects in a circular bioeconomy. Chemical Engineering Journal, •••, 163456.

Kothandapani, H. P. (2025). AI-driven regulatory compliance: Transforming financial oversight through large language models and automation. *Emerging Science Research*, *12*(1), 12–24.

Kothandapani, H. P.Hariharan Pappil Kothandapani. (2022). Leveraging AI for credit scoring and financial inclusion in emerging markets. *World Journal of Advanced Research and Reviews*, *15*(3), 526–539. DOI: 10.30574/wjarr.2022.15.3.0904

Kumari, M., & Goyal, N. K. (2026). Artificial Intelligence in the Cryptocurrency Ecosystem: Crime Mechanisms, Detection Strategies, and Legal Perspectives. In Lin, L. (Ed.), *Innovations in Cryptocrime and Financial Fraud* (pp. 245–282). IGI Global Scientific Publishing., DOI: 10.4018/979-8-3373-0675-9.ch007

Kumari, M., Khan, S. T., Gulati, K., Sharma, P., Goyal, N. K., & Sheikh, M. F. (2026). Innovative Procedural Content Generation (PCG) Using Generative AI: A New Paradigm in Game Design. In Sousa, J., & Tavares, R. (Eds.), *Reshaping the Video Game Landscape With AI and GenAI* (pp. 205–232). IGI Global Scientific Publishing., DOI: 10.4018/979-8-3373-4637-3.ch007

Kumari, M., Kumawat, R., Dutta, R., Khan, S. T., Goyal, N. K., & Sheikh, M. F. (2026). Wireless Communication and IoT Integration in Smart Clothing. In Saxena, P., Singh, M., Singh, S., & Rashid, M. (Eds.), *Next-Generation Electronic Textiles and Conductive Materials for Smart Wearables* (pp. 195–232). IGI Global Scientific Publishing., DOI: 10.4018/979-8-3373-4287-0.ch008

Kumari, M., Kumawat, R., Tripathi, M., Suganthi, K., Goyal, N. K., & Sheikh, M. F. (2026). Blockchain for Transparency and Traceability in Supply Chains. In Khan, M., Mehmood, T., & Rao, M. (Eds.), *Maximizing Operational Efficiency at the Intersection of Supply Chain Management and Marketing* (pp. 35–64). IGI Global Scientific Publishing., DOI: 10.4018/979-8-3373-3109-6.ch002

Kumar, M., Chivukula, A. S., & Barua, G. (2025). Deep learning-based encryption scheme for medical images using DCGAN and virtual planet domain. *Scientific Reports*, *15*(1), 1211. DOI: 10.1038/s41598-024-84186-6

Kumar, P., Rahman, M., Namasudra, S., & Moparthi, N. R. (2024). Enhancing Security of Medical Images Using Deep Learning, Chaotic Map, and Hash Table. *Mobile Networks and Applications*, *29*(5), 1489–1503. DOI: 10.1007/s11036-023-02158-y

Kumar, S., Gahalawat, M., Roy, P. P., Dogra, D. P., & Kim, B.-G. (2022). Combined community detection and sentiment analysis for COVID-19 Reddit discourse. *Journal of Medical Internet Research*, *24*(4), e35636. DOI: 10.2196/35636

Kumar, S., Machireddy, J. R., Sankaran, T., & Sholapurapu, P. K. (2025). Integration of machine learning and data science for optimized decision-making in computer applications and engineering. *Journal of Information Systems Engineering & Management*, •••, 10.

Kusumba, S. (2024). Delivering the Power of Data-Driven Decisions: An AI-Enabled Data Strategy Framework for Healthcare Financial Systems. [IJEETR]. *International Journal of Engineering & Extended Technologies Research*, *6*(2), 7799–7806.

Kyriakopoulos, N., Kim, E., Hultink, E. J., & Santema, S. (2025). The impact of design thinking and AI capabilities on performance: The role of new product development decision-making agility. *Journal of Business Research*, *200*, 115633. DOI: 10.1016/j.jbusres.2025.115633

Lazaroiu, G., Androniceanu, A., Grecu, I., Grecu, G., & Neguri ă, O. (2022). AI-based decision-making algorithms, Internet of Things sensing networks, and sustainable cyber-physical management systems in big data-driven cognitive manufacturing. *Oeconomia Copernicana*, *13*(4), 1047–1080. DOI: 10.24136/oc.2022.030

Leão, C. P., Silva, V., & Costa, S. (2024). Exploring the intersection of ergonomics, design thinking, and AI/ML in design innovation. *Applied System Innovation*, *7*(4), 65. DOI: 10.3390/asi7040065

Li, J., Dai, J., Issakhov, A., Almojil, S. F., & Souri, A. (2021). Towards DSS for energy management in the smart industry and Internet of Things. *Computers & Industrial Engineering*, *161*, 107671. DOI: 10.1016/j.cie.2021.107671

Li, J., Song, G., Cai, M., Bian, J., & Mohammed, B. S. (2022). Green environment and circular economy: A state-of-the-art analysis. *Sustainable Energy Technologies and Assessments*, *52*, 102106. DOI: 10.1016/j.seta.2022.102106

Lin, P., Cai, Y., Wu, H., Yin, J., & Luorang, Z. (2025). AI-driven risk control for health insurance fund management: A data-driven approach. *International Journal of Computers, Communications & Control*, *20*(2). Advance online publication. DOI: 10.15837/ijccc.2025.2.7024

Lionetto, F., & Esposito Corcione, C. (2021). Recent applications of biopolymers derived from fish industry waste in food packaging. *Polymers*, *13*(14), 2337. DOI: 10.3390/polym13142337 PMID: 34301094

Li, S., & Li, J. (2022). Machine learning-based community detection: Survey and benchmark. *ACM Computing Surveys*, *54*(4), 1–38. DOI: 10.1145/3434770

Lovato, J., Zimmerman, J., Smith, I., Dodds, P., & Karson, J. (2024). *Foregrounding Artist Opinions: A Survey Study on Transparency, Ownership, and Fairness in AI Generative Art*. https://doi.org/DOI: 10.48550/ARXIV.2401.15497

Lu, Y., Zhang, C., Zhang, I., & Li, T. J.-J. (2022). Bridging the Gap Between UX Practitioners' Work Practices and AI-Enabled Design Support Tools. *CHI Conference on Human Factors in Computing Systems Extended Abstracts*, 1–7. DOI: 10.1145/3491101.3519809

Maity, A., Roy, A., Pramanik, S., Pattanayak, P., & Kumar, S. (2026). Revolutionizing Energy: Smart Microgrids Driving down Costs and Carbon Foot Print Emissions through Advanced Spider Wasp optimization and BiGRU Techniques. *CIGRE Science & Engineering (CSE)*, (40), 1–36. https://cse.cigre.org/cse-n038/revolutionizing-energy-smart-microgrids-driving-down-costs-and-carbon-foot-print-emissions-through-advanced-spider-wasp-optimization-and-bigru-techniques.html

Maity, A., Roy, A., Kumar, S., Pramanik, S., Pattanayak, P., & Chakraborty, M. (2025). A Hybrid Machine Learning Approach to Power Load Optimization and Emission Reduction in Rural Microgrids. *Engineering Proceedings, 93*(1), 21. Advance online publication. DOI: 10.3390/engproc2025093021

Maksoud, A., Elshabshiri, A., Saeed Hilal Humaid Alzaabi, A., & Hussien, A. (2024). Integrating an Image-Generative Tool on Creative Design Brainstorming Process of a Safavid Mosque Architecture Conceptual Form. *Buildings (Basel, Switzerland), 14*(3), 3. Advance online publication. DOI: 10.3390/buildings14030843

Malik, K. R., Sajid, M., Almogren, A., Malik, T. S., Khan, A. H., Altameem, A., Rehman, A. U., & Hussen, S. (2025). A hybrid steganography framework using DCT and GAN for secure data communication in the big data era. *Scientific Reports, 15*(1), 19630. DOI: 10.1038/s41598-025-01054-7

Malik, S., & Ali, M. (2024). Machine Learning–Driven Optimization Techniques for Intelligent Decision-Making Systems. *International Journal of Data Sciences and Intelligent Systems, 1*(01), 1–16.

Maple, C., Szpruch, L., Epiphaniou, G., Staykova, K., Singh, S., Penwarden, W., . . . Avramovic, P. (2023). The AI revolution: Opportunities and challenges for the finance sector. *arXiv preprint arXiv:2308.16538.*

Marotta, A., Borriello, A., Khan, M. R., Cavella, S., Ambrogi, V., & Torrieri, E. (2025). Boosting food packaging sustainability through the valorization of agri-food waste and by-products. *Polymers, 17*(6), 735. DOI: 10.3390/polym17060735 PMID: 40292599

McBride, R., Dastan, A., & Mehrabinia, P. (2022). How AI affects the future relationship between corporate governance and financial markets: A note on impact capitalism. *Managerial Finance, 48*(8), 1240–1249. DOI: 10.1108/MF-12-2021-0586

Mckay, M., Beckman, R., & Conover, W. (1979). A Comparison of Three Methods for Selecting Vales of Input Variables in the Analysis of Output From a Computer Code. *Technometrics, 21*(2), 239–245. DOI: 10.1080/00401706.1979.10489755

Meng, L., McWilliams, B., Jarosinski, W., Park, H.-Y., Jung, Y.-G., Lee, J., & Zhang, J. (2020). Machine Learning in Additive Manufacturing: A Review. *Journal of the Minerals Metals & Materials Society, 72*(6), 2363–2377. Advance online publication. DOI: 10.1007/s11837-020-04155-y

Merino, D., Quilez-Molina, A. I., Perotto, G., Bassani, A., Spigno, G., & Athanassiou, A. (2022). A second life for fruit and vegetable waste: A review on bioplastic films and coatings for potential food protection applications. *Green Chemistry*, *24*(12), 4703–4727. DOI: 10.1039/D1GC03904K

Mhlanga, D. (2021). Financial inclusion in emerging economies: The application of machine learning and artificial intelligence in credit risk assessment. *International Journal of Financial Studies*, *9*(3), 39. DOI: 10.3390/ijfs9030039

Mishra, A., Mou, S. N., Ara, J., & Sarkar, M. (2025). Regulatory and ethical challenges in AI-driven and machine learning credit risk assessment for Buy Now Pay Later (BNPL) in US e-commerce: Compliance, fair lending, and algorithmic bias. *Journal of Business and Management Studies*, *7*(2), 42–51. DOI: 10.32996/jbms.2025.7.2.3

Mohanta, Y. K., Mishra, A. K., Lakshmayya, N. S. V., Panda, J., Thatoi, H., Sarma, H., Rustagi, S., Baek, K.-H., & Mishra, B. (2025). Agro-waste-derived bioplastics: Sustainable innovations for a circular economy. *Waste and Biomass Valorization*, *16*(7), 1–25. DOI: 10.1007/s12649-025-03070-0

Mohanty, A. K., Wu, F., Mincheva, R., Hakkarainen, M., Raquez, J.-M., Mielewski, D. F., Narayan, R., Netravali, A. N., & Misra, M. (2022). Sustainable polymers. *Nature Reviews. Methods Primers*, *2*(1), 46. DOI: 10.1038/s43586-022-00124-8

Momade, M. H., Durdyev, S., Estrella, D., & Ismail, S. (2021). Systematic review of application of artificial intelligence tools in architectural, engineering and construction. *Frontiers in Engineering and Built Environment*, *1*(2), 203–216. DOI: 10.1108/FEBE-07-2021-0036

Naik, R. B., & Singh, U. (2024). A Review on Applications of Chaotic Maps in Pseudo-Random Number Generators and Encryption. *Annals of Data Science*, *11*(1), 25–50. DOI: 10.1007/s40745-021-00364-7

Nasir, M., Khan, H. A., Zaffar, N. A., Vasquez, J. C., & Guerrero, J. M. (2018). Scalable solar DC microgrids: On the path to revolutionizing the electrification architecture of developing communities. *IEEE Electrification Magazine*, *6*(4), 63–72. DOI: 10.1109/MELE.2018.2871297

Nazish, M., Farooq, M., & Banday, M. T. (2026). Enhanced simple quadratic map for lightweight PRBG and IoT image encryption. *Iran Journal of Computer Science*, *9*(1), 35. DOI: 10.1007/s42044-026-00389-2

Nenni, M. E., De Felice, F., De Luca, C., & Forcina, A. (2024). *How artificial intelligence will transform project management in the age of digitization: A systematic literature review*. Management Review Quarterly.

Nirmala, S. J., Valarmathi, B., & Saravanan, D. (2021). Sarcasm detection in microblogs using emoticon polarity and SentiWordNet. *Social Network Analysis and Mining*, *11*(1), 1–15. DOI: 10.1007/s13278-021-00766-2

Nooribakhsh, M., & Mollamotalebi, M. (2021). Systematic mapping study on machine learning for community detection in social networks. *Artificial Intelligence Review*, *54*(7), 5381–5432. DOI: 10.1007/s10462-021-09994-4

Oboturova, N., et al. (2024). Upcycling agricultural byproducts into eco-friendly food packaging. *Slovak Journal of Food Sciences, 18.*

Ocama, O. V., Medagbe, Y.-C. N., Akello, S., Kambale, W. V., Tashev, T., Kyamakya, K., & Kasereka, S. K. (2025). A Review on Advancing Technologies in Precision Agriculture: Applications, Challenges, and the Way Forward. *Procedia Computer Science*, *265*, 572–577. DOI: 10.1016/j.procs.2025.07.221

Ogunmokun, A. S., Balogun, E. D., & Ogunsola, K. O. (2021). A conceptual framework for AI-driven financial risk management and corporate governance optimization. *International Journal of Multidisciplinary Research and Growth Evaluation*, *2*(1), 781–790. DOI: 10.54660/.IJMRGE.2021.2.1.772-780

Ogunsola, K. O., Balogun, E. D., & Ogunmokun, A. S. (2021). Enhancing financial integrity through an advanced internal audit risk assessment and governance model. *International Journal of Multidisciplinary Research and Growth Evaluation*, *2*(1), 781–790. DOI: 10.54660/.IJMRGE.2021.2.1.781-790

Oh, S., Jung, Y., Kim, S., Lee, I., & Kang, N. (2019). Deep Generative Design: Integration of Topology Optimization and Generative Models. *Journal of Mechanical Design*, *141*(11), 1. DOI: 10.1115/1.4044229

Oko-Odion, C. (2025). Ai-driven risk assessment models for financial markets: Enhancing predictive accuracy and fraud detection. *International Journal of Computer Applications Technology and Research*, *14*(04), 80–96.

Oko-Odion, C. (2025). AI-driven risk assessment models for financial markets: Enhancing predictive accuracy and fraud detection. *International Journal of Computer Applications Technology and Research*, *14*(4), 80–96.

Oladuji, T. J., Adewuyi, A. D. E. M. O. L. A., Nwangele, C. R., & Akintobi, A. O. (2021). Advancements in financial performance modeling for SMEs: AI-driven solutions for payment systems and credit scoring. *Iconic Research and Engineering Journals*, *5*(5), 471–486.

Omidmand, P., & Ataci, S. (2026). AI in Experimental Approaches: Growth Hacking, Lean Startup, Design Thinking, and Agile. *arXiv preprint arXiv:2603.20688.*

Omopariola, B., & Aboaba, V. (2021). Advancing financial stability: The role of AI-driven risk assessments in mitigating market uncertainty. *Int J Sci Res Arch, 3*(2), 254–270. DOI: 10.30574/ijsra.2021.3.2.0106

Onoja, J. P., Hamza, O., Collins, A., Chibunna, U. B., Eweja, A., & Daraojimba, A. I. (2021). Digital transformation and data governance: Strategies for regulatory compliance and secure AI-driven business operations. *Journal of Frontier Multidisciplinary Research, 2*(1), 43–55. DOI: 10.54660/.IJFMR.2021.2.1.43-55

Ouyang, L., Wu, J., Jiang, X., Almeida, D., Wainwright, C. L., Mishkin, P., Zhang, C., Agarwal, S., Slama, K., Ray, A., Schulman, J., Hilton, J., Kelton, F., Miller, L., Simens, M., Askell, A., Welinder, P., Christiano, P., Leike, J., & Lowe, R. (2022). Training language models to follow instructions with human feedback. *Advances in Neural Information Processing Systems, 35*, 27730–27744. DOI: 10.52202/068431-2011

Owolabi, O. S., Uche, P. C., Adeniken, N. T., Ihejirika, C., Islam, R. B., & Chhetri, B. J. T. (2024). Ethical implication of artificial intelligence (AI) adoption in financial decision making. *Computer and Information Science, 17*(1), 1–49. DOI: 10.5539/cis.v17n1p49

Paananen, V., Oppenlaender, J., & Visuri, A. (2024). Using text-to-image generation for architectural design ideation. *International Journal of Architectural Computing, 22*(3), 458–474. DOI: 10.1177/14780771231222783

Pal, B., Gupta, D., Rashed-Al-Mahfuz, M., Alyami, S. A., & Moni, M. A. (2021). Vulnerability in Deep Transfer Learning Models to Adversarial Fast Gradient Sign Attack for COVID-19 Prediction from Chest Radiography Images. *Applied Sciences (Basel, Switzerland), 11*(9), 4233. DOI: 10.3390/app11094233

Paleti, S. (2022). Fusion Bank: Integrating AI-Driven Financial Innovations with Risk-Aware Data Engineering in Modern Banking. *Decision Making, 2326*, 9865.

Paleti, S. (2024). Transforming financial risk management with AI and data engineering in the modern banking sector. [AJAAI]. *American Journal of Analytics and Artificial Intelligence, 1*(1), 2–12.

Pannila, N., Jayalath, M. M., Thibbotuwawa, A., Nielsen, I., & Uthpala, T. G. G. (2022). Challenges in applying circular economy concepts to food supply chains. *Sustainability (Basel), 14*(24), 16536. DOI: 10.3390/su142416536

Patil, D. (2024). Artificial intelligence in financial risk assessment and fraud detection: Opportunities and ethical concerns. *SSRN*. https://ssrn.com/abstract=5057434

Pattabhi, A. (2025). Risk intelligence: AI-powered financial risk management for a new era. *International Journal of Artificial Intelligence, Data Science, and Machine Learning*, *6*(2), 20–34. DOI: 10.63282/3050-9262.IJAIDSML-V6I2P103

Patterson, D. A., Gonzalez, J., Le, Q. V., Liang, C., Munguía, L.-M., Rothchild, D., So, D. R., Texier, M., & Dean, J. (2021). Carbon Emissions and Large Neural Network Training. *ArXiv*. https://www.semanticscholar.org/paper/Carbon-Emissions-and-Large-Neural-Network-Training-Patterson-Gonzalez/7a16d9b4e04300d034502dc7dd58428714594e2c

Peddojula, M. K., Suraparaju, S. K., Samykano, M., Kadambari, C. V. K., Pathan, Y., Zaza, A., Krishna Kanth, V., Rajamony, R. K., Natarajan, S. K., & Budala, S. B. (2024). Synergetic integration of machining metal scrap for enhanced evaporation in solar stills: A sustainable novel solution for potable water production. *Thermal Science and Engineering Progress*, *51*, 102647. DOI: 10.1016/j.tsep.2024.102647

Pham, B. T.. (2021). Flood risk assessment using hybrid artificial intelligence models integrated with multi-criteria decision analysis in Quang Nam Province, Vietnam. *Journal of Hydrology, 592*, 125815. Ganesh, A. D., & Kalpana, P. (2022). Future of artificial intelligence and its influence on supply chain risk management: A systematic review. *Computers & Industrial Engineering*, *169*, 108206.

Plocher, J., & Panesar, A. (2019). Review on design and structural optimisation in additive manufacturing: Towards next-generation lightweight structures. *Materials & Design*, *108164*, 108164. Advance online publication. DOI: 10.1016/j.matdes.2019.108164

Poleac, D. (2024, July). Design thinking with AI. In *Proceedings of the International Conference on Business Excellence* (Vol. 18, No. 1, pp. 2891-2900). Bucharest University of Economic Studies. DOI: 10.2478/picbe-2024-0240

Pouliou, P., Horvath, A.-S., & Palamas, G. (2023). Speculative hybrids: Investigating the generation of conceptual architectural forms through the use of 3D generative adversarial networks. *International Journal of Architectural Computing*, *21*(2), 315–336. DOI: 10.1177/14780771231168229

Pramanik, S., Roy, A., & Rakshit, P. (2025). Resuming Transfer Technique for Two-Level Sharding Point of Rupture for a Single Table. *AI and the Revival of Big Data*, 221–238. https://doi.org/DOI: 10.4018/979-8-3693-8472-5.ch010

Pramanik, S. (2023). A new method for locating data hiding in image steganography. *Multimedia Tools and Applications*, *83*(12), 34323–34349. Advance online publication. DOI: 10.1007/s11042-023-16762-3

Pramanik, S. (2023). An Adaptive Image Steganography Approach depending on Integer Wavelet Transform and Genetic Algorithm. *Multimedia Tools and Applications*, *82*(22), 34287–34319. Advance online publication. DOI: 10.1007/s11042-023-14505-y

Prasad, A. (2021). Deep learning and hybrid architectures for real-time sentiment prediction in political and financial domains. *Applied Intelligence*, *51*(8), 5784–5802. DOI: 10.1007/s10489-020-02108-1

Prather, J., Reeves, B. N., Denny, P., Becker, B. A., Leinonen, J., Luxton-Reilly, A., Powell, G., Finnie-Ansley, J., & Santos, E. A. (2024). Is this conversation helpful? A framework for evaluating AI-assisted programming education. *ACM Transactions on Computing Education*, *24*(1), 1–28. DOI: 10.1145/3632620

Priya, S., Abirami, S. P., Arunkumar, B., & Mishachandar, B. (2024). Super-resolution deep neural network (SRDNN) based multi-image steganography for highly secured lossless image transmission. *Scientific Reports*, *14*(1), 6104. DOI: 10.1038/s41598-024-54839-7

Proferes, N., Jones, N., Gilbert, S., Fiesler, C., & Zimmer, M. (2021). Survey of 727 academic studies using Reddit data: Trends and gaps. *Social Media + Society*, *7*(2), 20563051211019004. DOI: 10.1177/20563051211019004

Qaiser, S., & Ali, R. (2021). Deep learning versus classical machine learning for social media sentiment analysis. *Journal of Intelligent & Fuzzy Systems*, *41*(5), 6251–6264. DOI: 10.3233/JIFS-210548

Qin, S., Guan, H., Liao, W., Gu, Y., Zheng, Z., Xue, H., & Lu, X. (2024). Intelligent design and optimization system for shear wall structures based on large language models and generative artificial intelligence. *Journal of Building Engineering*, *95*, 109996. Advance online publication. DOI: 10.1016/j.jobe.2024.109996

Radhakrishnan, G. V., Varalakshmi, R., Kohli, N. K., Jha, S., Sruthi, S., & Singh, S. P. (2025). AI-Driven Predictive Analytics for Enhancing Automotive Safety in Financial Risk Assessments in Cloud Data. In *Embracing the Cloud as a Business Essential* (pp. 107–124). IGI Global Scientific Publishing. DOI: 10.4018/979-8-3693-9581-3.ch006

Rahimi, A. R. (2025). Developing and validating the scale of language teachers' design thinking competency in AI language teaching (LTDTAILT). *Computers and Education: AI*, *8*, 100420.

Rai, M., Kumar, S., & Rathore, P. S. (2025). A systematic review of innovations for real-time image security in IoT applications using machine learning and blockchain. *Journal of Intelligent Manufacturing*, *36*(8), 5197–5216. DOI: 10.1007/s10845-024-02535-8

Raissi, M., Perdikaris, P., & Karniadakis, G. (2018). Physics-Informed Neural Networks: A Deep Learning Framework for Solving Forward and Inverse Problems Involving Nonlinear Partial Differential Equations. *Journal of Computational Physics*, *378*, 686–707. Advance online publication. DOI: 10.1016/j.jcp.2018.10.045

Ramesh, A., Pavlov, M., Goh, G., Gray, S., Voss, C., Radford, A., Chen, M., & Sutskever, I. (2021). Zero-Shot Text-to-Image Generation. *ArXiv*. https://www.semanticscholar.org/paper/Zero-Shot-Text-to-Image-Generation-Ramesh-Pavlov/2cd605106b88c85d7d8b865b1ef0f8c8293debf1

Ramesh, S., Sukanth, B. N., Jaswanth, S. S., & Singh, R. P. (2024). Enhancing secure data transmission through deep learning-based image steganography and super-resolution generative adversarial networks. *SN Computer Science*, *5*(8), 1138. DOI: 10.1007/s42979-024-03490-0

Ramírez-Duque, J. L., & Morillo-Torres, D. (2026). Cooling the future: integrating design thinking and AI to foster soft skills and energy education. *Higher Education, Skills and Work-Based Learning*, 1-19.

Rane, N., Choudhary, S., & Rane, J. (2024). Artificial intelligence for enhancing resilience. *Journal of Applied Artificial Intelligence*, *5*(2), 1–33. DOI: 10.48185/jaai.v5i2.1053

Ranjan, A. K., Singh, D. K., & Prajapati, G. P. (2022). Sentiment analysis on social media: Challenges and NLP-based approaches. *Journal of Natural Language Processing*, *29*(1), 112 134. DOI: 10.5715/jnlp.29.112

Rathour, S., & Kemboi, E. (2025). AI-driven circular economy. In *Artificial intelligence and computer vision for ecological informatics* (p. 185). DOI: 10.1201/9781003518778-10

Reier Forradellas, R. F., & Garay Gallastegui, L. M. (2021). Digital transformation and artificial intelligence applied to business: Legal regulations, economic impact and perspective. *Laws*, *10*(3), 70. DOI: 10.3390/laws10030070

Reimers, N., & Gurevych, I. (2019). Sentence-BERT: Sentence embeddings using Siamese BERT-networks. *Proceedings of the 2019 Conference on Empirical Methods in Natural Language Processing*, 3982–3992. DOI: 10.18653/v1/D19-1410

Resende, C. de S., Zimmermann, R., Inês, A., & Dalmarco, G. (2025). A typology of scalability strategies of circular startups. *Procedia CIRP, 135*, 201–206. DOI: 10.1016/j.procir.2024.12.016

Režek Jambrak, A., Nutrizio, M., Djekić, I., Pleslić, S., & Chemat, F. (2021). Internet of nonthermal food processing technologies (IoNTP): Food industry 4.0 and sustainability. *Applied Sciences (Basel, Switzerland), 11*(2), 686. DOI: 10.3390/app11020686

Ribeiro, F. N., Araújo, M., Gonçalves, P., Gonçalves, M. A., & Benevenuto, F. (2023). Comprehensive evaluation of 18 sentiment tools on Twitter and Reddit: VADER benchmark study. *Proceedings of the International AAAI Conference on Web and Social Media, 17*, 732–742. https://doi.org/DOI: 10.1609/icwsm.v17i1.22178

Ribeiro, M. T., Singh, S., & Guestrin, C. (2016). "Why Should I Trust You?": Explaining the Predictions of Any Classifier. *Proceedings of the 22nd ACM SIGKDD International Conference on Knowledge Discovery and Data Mining. KDD : Proceedings / International Conference on Knowledge Discovery & Data Mining. International Conference on Knowledge Discovery & Data Mining, 16*, 1135–1144. DOI: 10.1145/2939672.2939778

Rombach, R., Blattmann, A., Lorenz, D., Esser, P., & Ommer, B. (2022). High-Resolution Image Synthesis with Latent Diffusion Models. *2022 IEEE/CVF Conference on Computer Vision and Pattern Recognition (CVPR)*, 10674–10685. 2022 IEEE/CVF Conference on Computer Vision and Pattern Recognition (CVPR). DOI: 10.1109/CVPR52688.2022.01042

Roy, A., Pramanik, S., Mitra, K., & Chakraborty, M. (2024b). Application of Neural Network for Reducing Emission and Optimizing Performance of Hydrogen with Biofuel CI Engine. *Lecture Notes in Networks and Systems*, 359–373. https://doi.org/DOI: 10.1007/978-981-97-7532-3_26

Roy, A., Pramanik, S., Mitra, K., & Chakraborty, M. (2025a). An Innovative Neural Network Approach for Reducing Emissions from Gas Turbines. *Lecture Notes in Networks and Systems*, 43–58. https://doi.org/DOI: 10.1007/978-981-97-8476-9_4

Roy, A., Sabyasachi Pramanik, Mitra, K., & Chakraborty, M. (2025). *CO2 Emission Calculations in Shipping for Sustainable Ship Design, Construction, and Operation*. 163–200. DOI: 10.4018/979-8-3373-2555-2.ch007

Roy, A., Pramanik, S., & Mitra, K. (2025). An Optimal Neural Network Model for Projecting of CI Engine Operational Efficiency and Emission in Hydrogen Blend Using Simulink. *SN Computer Science, 6*(8), 956. Advance online publication. DOI: 10.1007/s42979-025-04474-4

Roy, A., Pramanik, S., Mitra, K., & Chakraborty, M. (2025b). An optimal data analytics model for accurate projection of CI engine performance and emission reduction in hybrid fuel mode. *Environment, Development and Sustainability*. Advance online publication. DOI: 10.1007/s10668-025-06130-6

Roy, A., Pramanik, S., Mitra, K., & Chakraborty, M. (2026). Emission reduction in gas turbine: Improving CO and NOx emission prediction using modified CNN-Bi-LSTM extrinsic attention regressor. *Environment, Development and Sustainability*. Advance online publication. DOI: 10.1007/s10668-025-07209-w

Russell, S., & Norvig, P. (2021). *Artificial Intelligence: A Modern Approach, Global Edition*. Pearson Higher Ed.

Sabah, S., Alani, M., Spsampsps Salih, B. M. M. (2024). Leveraging AI Language Models for Designing Contextually Responsive Built Environments. Lecture Notes in Networks and Systems, 1019 LNNS, 510–519. DOI: 10.1007/978-3-031-62273-1_32

Sacks, J., Welch, W., Mitchell, T., & Wynn, H. (1989). Design and analysis of computer experiments. With comments and a rejoinder by the authors. *Statistical Science*, *4*(4). Advance online publication. DOI: 10.1214/ss/1177012413

Sadok, H., Sakka, F., & El Maknouzi, M. E. H. (2022). Artificial intelligence and bank credit analysis: A review. *Cogent Economics & Finance*, *10*(1), 2023262. DOI: 10.1080/23322039.2021.2023262

Saeed, A. (2024). Machine Learning Models for Intelligent DSS. *Journal of AI Range*, *1*(1), 54–66.

Saeidnia, H. R., & Ausloos, M. (2024). Integrating AI into design thinking: A comprehensive examination of the principles and potentialities of AI for design thinking framework. *InfoScience Trends*, *1*(2), 1–9. DOI: 10.61186/ist.202401.01.09

Saha, S. K., Wang, D., Nguyen, V. H., Chang, Y., Oakdale, J. S., & Chen, S.-C. (2019). Scalable submicrometer additive manufacturing. *Science*, *366*(6461), 105–109. DOI: 10.1126/science.aax8760 PMID: 31604310

Saiyed, A. (2025). AI-driven innovations in fintech: Applications, challenges, and future trends. *International Journal of Electrical and Computer Engineering Research*, *5*(1), 8–15. DOI: 10.53375/ijecer.2025.437

Sajjad, M., & Alqwaifly, N. A. (2025). RGB image encryption using SPN with a novel block cipher over simple graph adjacency matrices and Galois fields. *Scientific Reports*, *15*(1), 37488. DOI: 10.1038/s41598-025-21542-0

Sajjad, M., Shah, T., Hamza, R., Almutairi, B., & Serna, R. J. (2025). Multiple color images security by SPN over the residue classes of Gaussian integer. *Scientific Reports*, *15*(1), 6425. DOI: 10.1038/s41598-025-89993-z

Sànchez-Marrè, M. (2022). Intelligent DSS. In *Intelligent DSS* (pp. 77–116). Springer International Publishing.

Sanjalawe, Y., Al-E'mari, S., Fraihat, S., Abualhaj, M., & Alzubi, E. (2025). A deep learning-driven multi-layered steganographic approach for enhanced data security. *Scientific Reports*, *15*(1), 4761. DOI: 10.1038/s41598-025-89189-5

Saritepeci, M., & Yildiz Durak, H. (2024). Effectiveness of AI integration in design-based learning on design thinking mindset, creative and reflective thinking skills: An experimental study. *Education and Information Technologies*, *29*(18), 25175–25209. DOI: 10.1007/s10639-024-12829-2

Sathananthavathi, V., Ganesh Kumar, K., & Sathish Kumar, M. (2024). Secure visual communication with advanced cryptographic and ımage processing techniques. *Multimedia Tools and Applications*, *83*(15), 45367–45389. DOI: 10.1007/s11042-023-17224-6

Schwab, K. (2017). *The Fourth Industrial Revolution*. Crown.

Scime, L., & Beuth, J. (2018). Anomaly detection and classification in a laser powder bed additive manufacturing process using a trained computer vision algorithm. *Additive Manufacturing*, *19*, 114–126. DOI: 10.1016/j.addma.2017.11.009

Selvam, T., Rahman, N. M. M. A., Olivito, F., Ilham, Z., Ahmad, R., & Wan-Mohtar, W. A. A. Q. I. (2025). Agricultural waste-derived biopolymers for sustainable food packaging: Challenges and future prospects. *Polymers*, *17*(14), 1897. DOI: 10.3390/polym17141897 PMID: 40732776

Selvarajan, G. (2021). Leveraging AI-enhanced analytics for industry-specific optimization: A strategic approach to transforming data-driven decision-making. *International Journal of Enhanced Research in Science Technology and Engineering*, *10*(1), 78–84.

Sengar, S. S., Hasan, A. B., Kumar, S., & Carroll, F. (2025). Generative artificial intelligence: A systematic review and applications. *Multimedia Tools and Applications*, *84*(21), 23661–23700. DOI: 10.1007/s11042-024-20016-1

Shabasy, N. H. E., Mansy, A., & Alexan, W. (2026). An improved Bülban map and its application in multiple image encryption. *Journal of King Saud University. Computer and Information Sciences*, *38*(5), 300. DOI: 10.1007/s44443-026-00650-5

Shafique, A., Mehmood, A., Alawida, M., Khan, A. N., & Shuja, J. (2025). Lightweight image encryption scheme for IoT environment and machine learning-driven robust S-box selection. *Telecommunication Systems*, *88*(1), 17. DOI: 10.1007/s11235-024-01251-1

Shah, H. M., Gardas, B. B., Narwane, V. S., & Mehta, H. S. (2023). The contemporary state of big data analytics and artificial intelligence towards intelligent supply chain risk management: A comprehensive review. *Kybernetes*, *52*(5), 1643–1697. DOI: 10.1108/K-05-2021-0423

Shahriari, B., Swersky, K., Wang, Z., Adams, R. P., & de Freitas, N. (2016). Taking the Human Out of the Loop: A Review of Bayesian Optimization. *Proceedings of the IEEE*, *104*(1), 148–175. DOI: 10.1109/JPROC.2015.2494218

Sharma, P. K., Vijayvergia, H. K., Garg, A., Saxena, V. P., Agrawal, S. S., & Sharma, M. (2025). Ensuring the privacy of data in modern healthcare systems using adaptive encryption technique and disease prediction via attention-based residual DenseNet with GRU. *Knowledge and Information Systems*, *67*(10), 8469–8520. DOI: 10.1007/s10115-025-02464-9

Sharma, P., Kumawat, R., Jain, G., Keswani, G., Goyal, N. K., & Sheikh, M. F. (2026). Machine Learning-Based Intrusion Detection Systems for Healthcare Internet of Things (HIoT). In Shieh, C., Goel, P., Horng, M., & Pandey, H. (Eds.), *Resilient Healthcare Internet of Things Systems: Architectures, Security, and Trust* (pp. 185–214). IGI Global Scientific Publishing., DOI: 10.4018/979-8-3373-7610-3.ch007

Sheikh, M. F. A., Kapoor, S. K., Goyal, N. K., & Tuba, E. rao, A. (2026). Enhancing Healthcare Security with Fog Computing and Blockchain Technology. In: Nayak, R., Mittal, N., Khunteta, A., Kumar, M. (eds) Recent Advancements in Artificial Intelligence. ICRAAI 2025. Lecture Notes in Networks and Systems, vol 1468. Springer, Singapore. DOI: 10.1007/978-981-96-7760-3_38

SHEIL. (2017). *Fabricate: Rethinking Design and Construction*. UCL Press.

She, J., & Cetinic, E. (2022). Understanding and Creating Art with AI: Review and Outlook. *ACM Transactions on Multimedia Computing Communications and Applications*, *18*(2), 1–22. DOI: 10.1145/3475799

Shen, Z., Wang, Z., Chew, J., Hu, K., & Wang, Y. (2025). Artificial intelligence empowering robo-advisors: A data-driven wealth management model analysis. *International Journal of Management Science Research*, *8*(3), 1–12. DOI: 10.53469/ijomsr.2025.08(03).01

Sheth, J. N., Jain, V., Roy, G., & Chakraborty, A. (2022). AI-driven banking services: The next frontier for a personalised experience in the emerging market. *International Journal of Bank Marketing*, *40*(6), 1248–1271. DOI: 10.1108/IJBM-09-2021-0449

Shi, M., Seo, J., Cha, S. H., Xiao, B., & Chi, H.-L. (2024). Generative AI-powered architectural exterior conceptual design based on the design intent. *Journal of Computational Design and Engineering*, *11*(5), 125–142. Advance online publication. DOI: 10.1093/jcde/qwae077

Shittu, A. K. (2022). Advances in AI-driven credit risk models for financial services optimization. *International Journal of Multidisciplinary Research and Growth Evaluation*, *3*(1), 660–676. DOI: 10.54660/.IJMRGE.2022.3.1-660-676

Sicari, S., Rizzardi, A., Grieco, L. A., & Coen-Porisini, A. (2015). Security, privacy and trust in Internet of Things: The road ahead. *Computer Networks*, *76*, 146–164. DOI: 10.1016/j.comnet.2014.11.008

Siddiqui, N. A. (2025). Optimizing business decision-making through AI-enhanced business intelligence systems: A systematic review of data-driven insights in financial and strategic planning. *Strategic Data Management and Innovation*, *2*(1), 202–223. DOI: 10.71292/sdmi.v2i01.21

Simon, H. A. (1996). *The Sciences of the Artificial* (3rd ed.). MIT Press.

Singh, M., & Singh, A. K. (2023). A comprehensive survey on encryption techniques for digital images. *Multimedia Tools and Applications*, *82*(8), 11155–11187. DOI: 10.1007/s11042-022-12791-6

Song, B., Yuan, C., Permenter, F., Arechiga, N., & Ahmed, F. (2023). *Surrogate Modeling of Car Drag Coefficient with Depth and Normal Renderings*. /arXiv.2306.06110DOI: 10.1115/DETC2023-117400

Sood, S. K., Singh, M., & Bhatia, M. (2025). Industrial progress with quantum algorithms: An in-depth review. *The Journal of Supercomputing*, *81*(9), 1064. DOI: 10.1007/s11227-025-07555-6

Sosnovik, I., & Oseledets, I. (2017). Neural networks for topology optimization. *Russian Journal of Numerical Analysis and Mathematical Modelling*, *34*(4), 215–223. Advance online publication. DOI: 10.1515/rnam-2019-0018

Soundarapandiyan, P. S. R. (2022). AI-driven synthetic data generation for financial product development: Accelerating innovation in banking and fintech through realistic data simulation.

Sreenivasan, A., & Suresh, M. (2024). Design thinking and AI: A systematic literature review exploring synergies. *International Journal of Innovation Studies*, *8*(3), 297–312. DOI: 10.1016/j.ijis.2024.05.001

Stack Overflow. (2023). *Developer survey 2023*. https://survey.stackoverflow.co/2023/

Stahl, B., & Eke, D. (2024). The ethics of ChatGPT -Exploring the ethical issues of an emerging technology. *International Journal of Information Management*, *74*, 102700. Advance online publication. DOI: 10.1016/j.ijinfomgt.2023.102700

Staub, L., van Giffen, B., Hehn, J., & Sturm, S. (2023, July). Design thinking for AI: how design thinking can help organizations to address common ai project challenges. In *International Conference on Human-Computer Interaction* (pp. 251-267). Cham: Springer Nature Switzerland.

Stojanovski, T., Zhang, H., Frid, E., Chhatre, K., Peters, C., Samuels, I., Sanders, P., Partanen, J., & Spsampsps Lefosse, D. (2022). Rethinking Computer-Aided Architectural Design (CAAD) – From Generative Algorithms and Architectural Intelligence to Environmental Design and Ambient Intelligence. In D. Gerber, E. Pantazis, B. Bogosian, A. Nahmad, spsampsps C. Miltiadis (Eds.), Computer-Aided Architectural Design. Design Imperatives: The Future is Now (pp. 62–83). Springer. DOI: 10.1007/978-981-19-1280-1_5

Sugirtham, N., & Sudhakar, R. (2025). Deep Edge-VCS: Dual-Domain Transformer-Based Framework for Secure Visual Cryptography. *Iranian Journal of Science and Technology. Transaction of Electrical Engineering*. Advance online publication. DOI: 10.1007/s40998-025-00918-y

Suh, N. P. (with Internet Archive). (2001). *Axiomatic design: Advances and applications*. New York : Oxford University Press. http://archive.org/details/axiomaticdesigna0000suhn

Sultana, N. M., & Srinivas, K. (2025). Data Privacy Protection in Cloud Computing Using Visual Cryptography. *Multimedia Tools and Applications*, *84*(21), 23577–23597. DOI: 10.1007/s11042-024-19963-6

Sun, H., Wang, Z., Meng, Q., & White, S. (2025). Advancements in hydrogen storage technologies: Enhancing efficiency, safety, and economic viability for sustainable energy transition. *International Journal of Hydrogen Energy*, *105*, 10–22. DOI: 10.1016/j.ijhydene.2025.01.176

Sutton, R. S., & Barto, A. G. (2018). Reinforcement Learning, *second edition: An Introduction*. MIT Press.

Su, X., Zhao, Z., & Cai, T. (2021). Affinity propagation clustering with high-dimensional sparse data: Parameter optimization and oscillation suppression. *Journal of Machine Learning Research*, *22*(45), 1–28. https://jmlr.org/papers/v22/20-1491.html

Tadokoro, F., Ghosh, A. K., & Ura, S. (2025). On the effective co-creation of CAD models by leveraging generative artificial intelligence. *Procedia CIRP, 58th CIRP Conference on Manufacturing Systems 2025, 134*, 663–668. DOI: 10.1016/j.procir.2025.02.181

Taghipour, A., Akkalatham, W., Eaknarajindawat, N., & Stefanakis, A. I. (2022). The impact of government policies and steel recycling companies' performance on sustainable management in a circular economy. *Resources Policy*, *77*, 102663. DOI: 10.1016/j.resourpol.2022.102663

Tajudeen, K. O., Ameen, A. O., & Adeniyi, A. E. (2025). A systematic review on advanced encryption standard cryptography to enhance message security. *Multimedia Tools and Applications*, *84*(40), 48363–48388. DOI: 10.1007/s11042-025-21041-4

Tang, X., Windham, J., & Bush, B. (2024). Pre-AI and post-AI design: Balancing human Creativity and AI Tools in the Industrial Design Process. *Proceeding of the 2024 International Conference on Artificial Intelligence and Future Education*, 100–108. AIFE 2024: 2024 International Conference on Artificial Intelligence and Future Education. DOI: 10.1145/3708394.3708413

Tanveer, M., Azad, M. M., Kim, D., Khalid, S., & Kim, H. S. (2026). Generative Design for Engineering Applications: A State-of-the-Art Review. *Archives of Computational Methods in Engineering*, *33*(1), 53–79. DOI: 10.1007/s11831-025-10302-y

Tao, F., Qi, Q., Liu, A., & Kusiak, A. (2018). Data-driven smart manufacturing. *Journal of Manufacturing Systems. Journal of Manufacturing Systems*, *48*, 157–169. DOI: 10.1016/j.jmsy.2018.01.006

Tariq, M. U., Saqib, S. M., Mazhar, T., Khan, M. A., Shahzad, T., & Hamam, H. (2025a). Edge-enabled smart agriculture framework: Integrating IoT, lightweight deep learning, and agentic AI for context-aware farming. *Results in Engineering*, *28*, 107342. DOI: 10.1016/j.rineng.2025.107342

Taylor, C. R., Monga, N., Johnson, C., Hawley, J. R., & Patel, M. (2023). Artificial intelligence applications in breast imaging: Current status and future directions. *Diagnostics (Basel)*, *13*(12), 2041. DOI: 10.3390/diagnostics13122041 PMID: 37370936

Teixeira, M. (2025). Assessment of green steel production technologies: Feasibility, scalability, and economic viability. *Revista de Gestão Social e Ambiental*, *19*(3), 1–16. DOI: 10.24857/rgsa.v19n3-043

Thakur, N., & Sharma, A. (2024). Ethical considerations in AI-driven financial decision making. *Journal of Management & Public Policy*, *15*(3), 41–57. DOI: 10.47914/jmpp.2024.v15i3.003

Traag, V. A., Waltman, L., & van Eck, N. J. (2019). From Louvain to Leiden: Guaranteeing well-connected communities. *Scientific Reports*, *9*(1), 5233. DOI: 10.1038/s41598-019-41695-z PMID: 30914743

Trivedi, R., Franco Rubio, A., & Cirac, J. I. (2024). Quantum advantage and stability to errors in analogue quantum simulators. *Nature Communications*, *15*(1), 6507. DOI: 10.1038/s41467-024-50750-x PMID: 39095381

Tsimpidi, I., Sawlekar, R., & Nikolakopoulos, G. (2023). Identifying the current state of the art and future directions on the deployment of artificial intelligence in circular economy.

Turcios-Esquivel, A. M. L., & Gallego, M. T. (2025, April). Innovative Learning: Integrating Design Thinking, Experimental Design and AI for Next-Gen Engineering Education in the Context of Industry 5.0. In *2025 IEEE Global Engineering Education Conference (EDUCON)* (pp. 1-8). IEEE. DOI: 10.1109/EDUCON62633.2025.11016427

Tytgat, L., Barrie, M., Gonçalves, V., Yaron, O., Moerman, I., Demeester, P., & Delaere, S. (2011, May). Techno-economic viability of cognitive solutions for a factory scenario. In *2011 IEEE International Symposium on Dynamic Spectrum Access Networks (DySPAN)* (pp. 254-264). IEEE. DOI: 10.1109/DYSPAN.2011.5936214

Vaccaro, M., Almaatouq, A., & Malone, T. (2024). When combinations of humans and AI are useful: A systematic review and meta-analysis. *Nature Human Behaviour*, *8*(12), 2293–2303. DOI: 10.1038/s41562-024-02024-1 PMID: 39468277

Vanapalli, K. R., Sharma, H. B., Ranjan, V. P., Samal, B., Bhattacharya, J., Dubey, B. K., & Goel, S. (2021). Challenges and strategies for effective plastic waste management during and post COVID-19 pandemic. *The Science of the Total Environment*, *750*, 141514. DOI: 10.1016/j.scitotenv.2020.141514 PMID: 32835961

Vangala, A., Das, A. K., Chamola, V., Korotaev, V., & Rodrigues, J. J. P. C. (2023). Security in IoT-enabled smart agriculture: Architecture, security solutions and challenges. *Cluster Computing*, *26*(2), 879–902. DOI: 10.1007/s10586-022-03566-7

Vellaiyan, V. S. (2025). Improved jatropha biodiesel yield and engine performance using carbon nanotube–copper oxide nanocatalyst and ammonium hydroxide emulsion for scalable clean energy solutions. *Biomass and Bioenergy*, *201*, 108120. DOI: 10.1016/j.biombioe.2025.108120

Venigandla, K., & Vemuri, N. (2022). RPA and AI-driven predictive analytics in banking for fraud detection. *Journal of Propulsion Technology*, *43*(4).

Verma, A., & Singhal, N. (2023, September). Integrating AI for adaptive Decision-Making in complex system. In *International Conference on Advances in Data-driven Computing and Intelligent Systems* (pp. 95-105). Singapore: Springer Nature Singapore.

Vermillion, J. (2022). Iterating the Design Process Using AI Diffusion Models. Creative Collaborations, 9. https://digitalscholarship.unlv.edu/cfa_collaborate/9

Vissers-Similon, E., Dounas, T., & De Walsche, J. (2024). Classification of artificial intelligence techniques for early architectural design stages. *International Journal of Architectural Computing*, *2024*. Advance online publication. DOI: 10.1177/14780771241260857

Wang, D., Tan, D., & Liu, L. (2018). Particle swarm optimization algorithm: An overview. *Soft Computing*, *22*(2), 387–408. DOI: 10.1007/s00500-016-2474-6

Wang, J. (2023, December). Intelligent decision support system for building project management based on AI. []. IOP Publishing.]. *Journal of Physics: Conference Series*, *2665*(1), 012022. DOI: 10.1088/1742-6596/2665/1/012022

Wang, X., Li, L., Wang, M., & Chang, C. C. (2026). High-capacity reversible data hiding in encrypted images based on MSB sharing and overlapping sawtooth partition. *Journal of King Saud University. Computer and Information Sciences*, *38*(2), 24. DOI: 10.1007/s44443-025-00238-5

Wang, X., & Wei, H. (2022). Cryptanalysis of compressive interference-based optical encryption using a U-net deep learning network. *Optics Communications*, *507*, 127641. DOI: 10.1016/j.optcom.2021.127641

Wei, J., Wang, X., Schuurmans, D., Bosma, M., Ichter, B., Xia, F., Chi, E. H., Le, Q. V., & Zhou, D. (2022). Chain-of-Thought Prompting Elicits Reasoning in Large Language Models. *Proceedings of the 36th International Conference on Neural Information Processing Systems*, 35, 24824–24837. DOI: 10.52202/068431-1800

Weiss, K., Khoshgoftaar, T. M., & Wang, D. (2016). A survey of transfer learning. *Journal of Big Data*, *3*(1), 9. DOI: 10.1186/s40537-016-0043-6

Wolfert, S., Ge, L., Verdouw, C., & Bogaardt, M.-J. (2017). Big Data in Smart Farming – A review. *Agricultural Systems*, *153*, 69–80. DOI: 10.1016/j.agsy.2017.01.023

Wu, C., Chang, J., Xu, X., Quan, C., Zhang, X., & Zhang, Y. (2020). Cryptoanalysis of the modified diffractive-imaging-based image encryption by deep learning attack. *Journal of Modern Optics*, *67*(17), 1398–1409. DOI: 10.1080/09500340.2020.1862329

Wu, Z., Ji, D., Yu, K., Zeng, X., Wu, D., & Spsampsps Shidujaman, M. (2021). AI Creativity and the Human-AI Co-creation Model. In Kurosu, M. (Ed.), *Human-Computer Interaction. Theory, Methods and Tools* (pp. 171–190). Springer International Publishing., DOI: 10.1007/978-3-030-78462-1_13

Xing, Z. (2023). Heterogeneous LLM agents for nuanced financial sentiment analysis. *Expert Systems with Applications*, *218*, 119612. DOI: 10.1016/j.eswa.2023.119612

Yadav, P., Gupta, P., Sijariya, R., & Sharma, Y. (2024). Artificial intelligence in risk management. In *Artificial Intelligence for Risk Mitigation in the Financial Industry* (pp. 1–25). DOI: 10.1002/9781394175574.ch1

Yan, C., Lee, K. L., Troutman, J. P., Brady, C. E., Humphrey, S. M., Cwiertny, D. M., . . . Werth, C. J. (2024). Tailored copper-based cathode design advances economic viability of electrocatalytic nitrate treatment with ammonia recovery in a scalable flow reactor. Applied Catalysis B: Environment and Energy, 357, 124278.

Yang, M., Chen, L., Wang, J., Msigwa, G., Osman, A. I., Fawzy, S., Rooney, D. W., & Yap, P.-S. (2023). Circular economy strategies for combating climate change and other environmental issues. *Environmental Chemistry Letters*, *21*(1), 55–80. DOI: 10.1007/s10311-022-01499-6

Yang, Y., Yuan, Y., Zhang, G., Wang, H., Chen, Y.-C., Liu, Y., Tarolli, C. G., Crepeau, D., Bukartyk, J., Junna, M. R., Videnovic, A., Ellis, T. D., Lipford, M. C., Dorsey, R., & Katabi, D. (2022). Artificial intelligence-enabled detection and assessment of Parkinson's disease using nocturnal breathing signals. *Nature Medicine*, *28*(10), 2207–2215. DOI: 10.1038/s41591-022-01932-x PMID: 35995955

Yoo, S., Lee, S., Kim, S., Hwang, K. H., Park, J. H., & Kang, N. (2021). Integrating deep learning into CAD/CAE system: Generative design and evaluation of 3D conceptual wheel. *Structural and Multidisciplinary Optimization*, *64*(4), 2725–2747. DOI: 10.1007/s00158-021-02953-9

Yuan, C., Marion, T., & Moghaddam, M. (2022). DDE-GAN: Integrating a Data-Driven Design Evaluator Into Generative Adversarial Networks for Desirable and Diverse Concept Generation. *Journal of Mechanical Design*, *145*(4), 1–18. DOI: 10.1115/1.4056500

Yunusova, R. (2023). Decentralized blockchain networks and economic security: Balancing scalability and security tradeoffs. In *Proceedings of the International Conference on Next Generation Wired/Wireless Networking* (pp. 244–252). Springer.

Zaman, J., Shoomal, A., Jahanbakht, M., & Ozay, D. (2025). Driving Supply Chain Transformation with IoT and AI Integration: A Dual Approach Using Bibliometric Analysis and Topic Modeling. *IoT*, *6*(2), 21. DOI: 10.3390/iot6020021

Zeriouh, K., & Amara, M. (2025). AI–driven frameworks for strategic risk management: A systematic review and model for organizational resilience and decision support. *Journal of Intelligent Management and Decision*, *4*(3), 44–61. DOI: 10.56578/jimd040304

Zhang, Y. (2025, May). AI-Driven Framework for Financial Risk Management: Enhancing Decision-Making with LSTM Networks and Probabilistic Models. In *2025 2nd International Conference on Intelligent Computing and Robotics (ICICR)* (pp. 176-181). IEEE.

Zhang, G., Raina, A., Cagan, J., & Mccomb, C. (2021). A cautionary tale about the impact of AI on human design teams. *Design Studies*, *72*, 100990. DOI: 10.1016/j.destud.2021.100990

Zhang, J., Wang, Z., Li, S., & Wei, P. (2024). A digital twin approach for gas turbine performance based on deep multi-model fusion. *Applied Thermal Engineering*, *246*, 122954. DOI: 10.1016/j.applthermaleng.2024.122954

Zhang, T., Chen, Q., He, Q., & Zhu, W. (2025). AI-Driven Financial Risk Early-Warning Using TD-DS-RF: A Decision Support Model Integrating Multi-Source Data. *Decision Making: Applications in Management and Engineering*, *8*(1), 478–496.

Zhang, Y., Kim, N., Park, C., & Haftka, R. (2018). Multifidelity Surrogate Based on Single Linear Regression. *AIAA Journal*, *56*(12), 1–9. DOI: 10.2514/1.J057299

Zhang, Z., Fang, H., Xu, Z., Lv, J., Shen, Y., & Wang, Y. (2023). Multi-objective generative design of three-dimensional material structures. *APL Machine Learning*, *1*(4), 046120. Advance online publication. DOI: 10.1063/5.0169432

Zhong, C., Shi, Y., Cheung, L. H., & Wang, L. (2024). AI-Enhanced Performative Building Design Optimization and Exploration: A Design Framework Combining Computational Design Optimization and Generative AI. ACCELERATED DESIGN - Proceedings of the 29th CAADRIA Conference, 1, 59–68. DOI: 10.52842/conf.caadria.2024.1.059

Zhou, M., Li, X., Liao, H., & Cheng, X. (2023). Public sentiment analysis of ChatGPT using combined sentiment analysis and knowledge mapping. *Computers in Human Behavior, 140*, 107612. DOI: 10.1016/j.chb.2022.107612

Ziegler, A., Kalliamvakou, E., Li, X., Rice, A., Rifkin, D., Simister, S., Sittampalam, G., & Aftandilian, E. (2022). Productivity assessment of neural code completion. *Proceedings of the 6th ACM SIGPLAN International Symposium on Machine Programming*, 21–29. DOI: 10.1145/3520312.3534864

Zienkiewicz, O. C., Taylor, R. L., Taylor, R. L., & Zhu, J. Z. (2013). *The Finite Element Method: Its Basis and Fundamentals*. Butterworth-Heinemann.

Zreikat, A. I., AlArnaout, Z., Abadleh, A., Elbasi, E., & Mostafa, N. (2025). The Integration of the Internet of Things (IoT) Applications into 5G Networks: A Review and Analysis. *Computers, 14*(7), 250. DOI: 10.3390/computers14070250

About the Contributors

Sabyasachi Pramanik is a professional IEEE member. He has been consistently within the top 2% scientist worldwide as declared by Stanford University, USA. He obtained a PhD in Computer Science and Engineering from Sri Satya Sai University of Technology and Medical Sciences, Bhopal, India. Presently, he is an Associate Professor, Department of Computer Science and Engineering, Haldia Institute of Technology, India. He has publications in various reputed international conferences, journals, and book chapters. He is doing research in the fields of Artificial Intelligence, Data Privacy, Cybersecurity, Network Security, and Machine Learning. He also serves on the editorial boards of several international journals. He is a reviewer of journal articles, conference papers, has been a keynote speaker, session chair, and technical program committee member at many international conferences. He has authored a book on Wireless Sensor Network. He has also edited 12 books.

Ankur Gupta has received the B.Tech and M.Tech in Computer Science and Engineering from Ganga Institute of Technology and Management, Kablana affiliated with Maharshi Dayanand University, Rohtak in 2015 and 2017. He is an Assistant Professor in the Department of Computer Science and Engineering at Vaish College of Engineering, Rohtak, and has been working there since January 2019. He has many publications in various reputed national/ international conferences, journals, and online book chapter contributions (Indexed by SCIE, Scopus, ESCI, ACM, DBLP, etc). He is doing research in the field of cloud computing, data security & machine learning. His research work in M.Tech was based on biometric security in cloud computing.

Rohit Anand is currently working as an Assistant Professor in the Department of Electronics and Communication Engineering at G.B.Pant Engineering College (Government of NCT of Delhi), New Delhi, India. He has teaching experience of more than 18 years including UG and PG Courses. He is a Life Member of

Indian Society for Technical Education (ISTE). He has published 6 book chapters in reputed books and 8 papers in Scopus/SCI Indexed Journals. He has chaired a Session in AICTE-Sponsored International Conference. His research areas include Electromagnetic Field Theory, Antenna Theory and Design, Wireless Communication, Image Processing, Optical Fiber Communication, Machine Learning etc

***

Fatin is an Associate Professor in Commerce at St. Claret's College (Autonomous), Bengaluru, with over a decade of teaching and five years of research experience. She holds an M.Phil. from Bharathidasan University and a Ph.D. in Commerce from Bangalore University, specializing in mezzanine finance for SMEs. She has published 15 papers, including in Scopus-indexed (Q2) and ABDC 'A' journals, and has received two Best Paper Awards. A three-time NET qualifier and KSET achiever, she is an active researcher, keynote speaker, session chair, and resource person for workshops on research methodology and statistical tools.

Anorgul Ashirova is working as an Associate Professor at the Department of General Professional Sciences, Mamun University, Khiva, Uzbekistan

Aisha Banu holds a Ph.D. in Commerce. She has qualified the UGC-NET examination and has academic experience in teaching management and finance subjects to undergraduate and postgraduate students.Her research interests include FinTech, financial inclusion, corporate governance, and investment analysis. She has been actively involved in academic research and is currently working on studies related to investment trends in Indian FinTech startups. Dr. Banu aims to contribute to the advancement of financial research through teaching, publications, and academic collaborations.

Raktim Kumar Dey is an accomplished Associate Professor in the Department of Computer Science and Engineering (IoT, Cyber Security, Blockchain Technology) at University of Engineering and Management, Kolkata, West Bengal, India. With over 21 years of comprehensive professional experience spanning the Information Technology industry (14 years) and higher academia (7 years), he has established himself as a dynamic scholar, educator, and researcher in Computer Science and Engineering. His multidisciplinary expertise and deep commitment to innovation have enabled him to contribute meaningfully across several cutting-edge technological domains. Dr. Dey earned his Doctor of Philosophy (Ph.D.) in Computer Science and Engineering from the University of Kalyani, West Bengal, in 2025. He also holds an M.Tech. in Computer Science and Engineering from Maulana Abul Kalam Azad University of Technology (2018), a Master's in Information Management from the University of Mumbai (2016), and a B.E. in Computer Science and Engineering from Biju Patnaik University of Technology (2004). He further holds globally recognized professional certifications, including the Sun Certified Java Programmer (SCJP) and Oracle Certified Associate (OCA) in PL/SQL.

Vipin Jain is Director/Principal of Teerthanker Mahaveer Institute of Management and Technology (TMIMT) & Department of Hospital Administration, Officiating Dean of College of Law and Legal Studies and Chairperson of Center for Jain Studies. He is appointed as Chief Proctor of the University in April 2021. Formerly he was Head of Department, Department of Economics, Banking and Finance, College of Business, Hospitality and Tourism Studies, Fiji National University, Fiji Islands. Formerly he was Head of Department, Maharishi Arvind Institute of Science and Management (MAISM), Jaipur. He is having 23 years of experience in Teaching, Research, Consultancy and Administration. 9 research scholars have been awarded PhD under him and currently guiding 8 research scholars. Published 81 research papers (out of which 35 Scopus, ABDC-2 A Category and 5 B Category), 30 patents (17 International Patent and 15 National Patent), . His Google Scholar detail is as follows: h-index = 23, i10-index= 47 & Citations = 2500. His Scopus detail is as follows: Documents – 81; Citation – 536; H – Index – 17. His Publon detail as follows: Articles – 55; Citation – 188; H- Index – 5.

Anirban Maity holds a Doctor of Philosophy (Ph.D.) in Electrical Engineering with a specialization in energy optimization and intelligent control of hybrid microgrids. His research integrates advanced forecasting techniques, artificial intelligence, and bio-inspired algorithms for sustainable power systems, with a particular focus on electric vehicle integration and emissions reduction. He has presented and published several technical papers in reputed journals and conferences. His academic background combines practical energy solutions with cutting-edge computational methods aimed at cleaner and smarter energy management.

Ira Nath received the Ph.D degree in computer science and technology from the Indian Institute of Engineering Science and Technology (IIEST), Shibpur, India in 2020. She received the B.Tech. degree in computer science and engineering and the M.Tech. degree in software engineering from the Maulana Abul Kalam Azad University of Technology (formerly West Bengal University of Technology), India, in 2005 and 2008, respectively. She is currently an Associate Professor in the Department of Computer Science and Engineering, JIS College of Engineering, India. She has total 20 years of research experience in the field of Artificial

Intelligence, Machine Learning, Intrusion Detection, Regenerator Placement, Survivability, Routing, and Wavelength assignment in translucent WDM optical networks, Cloud Computing, Ad-Hoc networking and Network Security etc. She has published more than 60 research papers in reputed journals, conferences and book chapters which are indexed in SCI, Scopus, Google scholar etc. She is an AWS Certified Cloud Practitioner. She has received International Award 2020-21 (Researcher) by International Institute of Organized Research (I2OR), A Registered MSME with Ministry of MSME, Govt. of India. She is the reviewer and program committee member of various journals and conferences.

Mahabub Basha S is presently working as Assistant Professor, Department of Commerce and Management in International Institute of Business Studies, Bangalore. He holds Master's degree in Management from JNTU Hyderabad and M.Phill from SCSVMV University, Kanchipuram. He has more than 8 years of teaching and 6 years of Industry experience, under-graduate and post-graduate students in Commerce and Management departments. He has published research articles in National and International Journals apart from presenting research papers at conferences. Three books published in his Credit. His areas of expertise are: Supply Chain Management, Portfolio Management, Consumer Behavior, Investment Management, Management Accounting, Financial Accounting, Financial Management, and Business Research Methods. In his credit he crossed 1000 google scholar citations

Naim R. Shaikh is a Professor and Research Coordinator at Dr. D.Y. Patil Vidyapeeth's Global Business School and Research Centre, Pune, with over 22 years of academic and industry experience. He holds a Ph.D. in Organizational Management and is UGC-NET qualified, along with dual postgraduate degrees in Management and Science. His research interests include internationalization of higher education, performance management, business analytics, skill development, and productivity management. Dr. Shaikh has published 30+ papers in Scopus and Web of Science indexed journals. He serves as a reviewer and editorial board member for reputed journals and currently guides five Ph.D. scholars in management and interdisciplinary research.

Index

A

C

D

E

F

G

H

I

T

V

www.ingramcontent.com/pod-product-compliance
Lightning Source LLC
LaVergne TN
LVHW061524290926
849162LV00004B/661